The Concise Encyclopedia of Antiques

VOLUME THREE

The Concise Encyclopedia of Antiques

VOLUME THREE

COMPILED BY THE CONNOISSEUR
EDITOR: L. G. G. RAMSEY, F.S.A.

Publishers
HAWTHORN BOOKS, Inc.
New York

 All inquiries should be addressed to Hawthorn Books, Inc., 70 Fifth Avenue, New York City 11. This book was designed and produced for *The Connoisseur* by Rainbird, McLean Ltd, London, and printed in England by Hazell Watson & Viney Ltd, Aylesbury and London. It is published simultaneously in England.

LIBRARY OF CONGRESS CATALOGUE CARD NUMBER 55-5162

THE CONTENTS

FOREWORD

WITH certain obvious exceptions, as for example the individual productions of known Masters, most objects of art which have survived and which are now termed antiques – if, indeed, they are not of international importance – have invariably, however apparently simple in construction, been the joint effort of more than one craftsman. Certainly in medieval England the carpenter, the joiner, the turner and the carver might all be working in the closest harmony upon the construction of one important object; or a series of objects, such as the choir stalls in Westminster Abbey. Each was skilled in his own trade, and in England there has always existed this breaking down of skilled craftsmanship. In due course, with the greater sophistication of the eighteenth-century furniture and the foreign influences imposed upon its design, we duly find such craftsman-specialists as the cabinet- and chair-maker, the gilder, the upholsterer, the japanner, the worker in porcelain, metal-work and glass, and so on. The source of these foreign influences, moreover, on English artistic productions of all types should be studied by all serious collectors: in the same way as it is now increasingly recognized that the arts of a period constitute a unity or synthesis and should be studied together, thus enhancing the understanding and appreciation of each.

The three volumes now published of the *Connoisseur Concise Encyclopaedia of Antiques*, in fact, carry a number of subjects which are precisely illustrative of this very question of *influences*: that is to say of one country's styles upon another and of one particular craftsman's work upon another, and how prevailing domestic habits often influenced the designs of and uses for certain objects in daily use. In the second of these volumes much of the contents clearly showed the origins and influences of France, or of their development by French craftsmen. It showed that today we are in the collecting era of the *bonbonnière* and the *bonheur-du-jour* and that the meaning of these terms, and others like *repoussé* and *cloisonné*, which appear so often in museum and saleroom catalogues today, should no longer have any mystery for us. The second volume also demonstrated that American silver, whilst it showed close connexions with English, yet it was also influenced by Dutch seventeenth-century styles prevailing in New York at the time. We know, too, that the first furniture made in North America was based on the English Jacobean style: and that – in this volume – because the Renaissance saw the introduction of cleaner domestic habits, which in turn called for new tableware, Cellini was able to record a vase as: 'a huge silver piece, used at table by Pope Clement (VII), into which he flung away bits of bone and the rind of divers fruits, while eating; an object of ostentation rather than necessity'.

This third volume, in turn, shows the influence of French designs upon Viennese furniture in the eighteenth century; the relationship of styles between the Continental wood-carvers and those working in England; the inferences to be drawn from the records of England's thriving export trade of alabaster 'images' and altar-pieces from Nottingham in the fifteenth century; that one of the oldest wallpapers to be discovered *in situ* (at Christ's College, Cambridge, in 1911) had a textile pattern indicating that this was strongly influenced by the silk hangings and brocades of the Italian Renaissance; that almost all bird prints come from Germany (and a good many model soldiers, too), France and Great Britain; and how van Meegeren (1889–1947), proud of his skill, eventually obtained virtually the same pigments used by Vermeer by making them out of the chemicals used in the seventeenth century. The list of *influences* is endless.

Finally, just as the study of French furniture formed one of the most enlightening sections to the second volume in this series, so the highly important chapter dealing with English Victorian furniture labels this third volume as one of singular moment. It is said that probably fifty per cent of all the furniture ever made in England was made during the sixty-four years of Victoria's reign, and that even today perhaps twenty per cent of all surviving furniture dates from those years. Yet it has, until now, been almost a closed field to serious scholarship or collecting. Most standard works on the history of furniture stop at 1830. Others have skated their way over the surface of the subject. The same terminal date of 1830 is recognized at the London Antique Dealers' Fair, and a few dealers and collectors have begun tentatively to edge their way, by way of *papier mâché*, into the 1840's. Now, with the aid of Mr Floud's Victorian Furniture chapter in this volume, there will no longer be cause for guesswork in establishing a true Victorian sideboard, settle, chair or cabinet. We need no longer be in doubt as to what was the 'Arts and Crafts Movement'. The designs of A. W. N. Pugin (1812–1852) and William Burges (1827–1881), the first conscious reformers of Victorian furniture design, are now revealed as having radical differences: and there are certain examples of Victorian furniture which even require to be traced and thereafter studied by research worker and collector. It is therefore appropriate that an encyclopaedia such as this, produced by *The Connoisseur*, should be the first to show the way to a proper and lasting appreciation of Victorian furniture.

L. G. G. RAMSEY
Editor: *The Connoisseur*

A CAVEAT TO COLLECTORS

By WOLF MANKOWITZ

THE basic fact of an antique chair is wood. A carpenter took that raw material and, with generations of skill behind him, an age of experience which enabled him to understand it for the living thing it is, fashioned a chair. A machine will make you twenty serviceable chairs in the time he took. These chairs can all be sat on. But nowhere in them will be a trace of those human qualities with which some unknown carpenter worked before the machines came to make it all so simple and inhuman.

By the same argument, a beautiful vase is a handful of mud scooped out of a river-bank somewhere. Everything that happens to it after that is the history of man. In the hands of a master potter this mud has been fashioned painfully and lovingly, taught to become a finer material, performing feats of incredible beauty.

Twenty million plates made cheaply and quickly, gross upon gross of chairs, benefit a lot of people, but once benefited, a minority of these people hanker after a fine vase or a beautifully worked piece of wood. It is a tendency towards this kind of nostalgia which produces a collector.

The essential antique collector is someone with this weakness for objects. Ideally he is very rich and extremely well informed, but here, as elsewhere, reality falls short of the ideal. The average collector has no more to spend on antiques than the average gambler has to lose on horses. It is a hobby (or a bad habit) which has to be contained within a hard-pressed economy. Once it breaks those confines, all pleasure is lost. So that the average antique collector has to be a shrewd and careful buyer, working to a budget and aware of market prices and the danger of too hasty purchase. Knowledge, then, is as essential to the collector as nostalgia. And knowledge of collecting involves not only the study of objects, their origins and distinguishing characteristics – it refers to dealing and auction-buying, too. For though a collector may have the good fortune to possess elderly relatives inclined to make, and then leave to him, valuable collections, by and large the treasures he seeks will be found in shops and auction-rooms.

There is a fascination about auction-rooms which has often enough proved fatal to those innocents who forget that an auction is a place of business. In every business there are rules which even punters must observe. After the rules comes experience – which may be even more expensive to gain. So, the next time the bargain hunt is on just remember that tempting auction-room is full of hunters who know far more about the game than you do. If you must go auction-loafing, rule number one is – leave your enthusiasm at home, and examine the goods well before bidding for them.

Before any auction takes place, a few days are allowed for 'viewing' the numbered lots into which the goods are arranged and catalogued. Your catalogue is a guide to the auction, but it works best on viewing days. Then you will have time to examine piece by piece the bric-à-brac and furniture which takes your eye. You must examine them thoroughly, because if you bid and buy, then – as the conditions of sale by auction put it – 'all lots must be taken away and paid for, whether genuine and authentic or not, with all faults and errors of description, at the Buyer's expense and risk within TWO DAYS from the Sale'.

To translate that into practical terms – if you bid ten pounds for a Louise Quinze chair, you must pay for it and remove it yourself within two days. If you pick up the chair after the auction, and it falls to pieces from wood-worm, you still own the pieces. If it is intact but a fake, the auctioneer is not responsible. He has described it to the best of his ability, and he is not supposed to be infallible. If the chair is perfect, is actually Louis Quinze and is worth a hundred pounds – it is still yours for ten pounds, quite legally, with no grounds for complaint from anyone.

Clearly you have to know something about what you're buying – you must know what faults to look for because when you buy by auction you buy 'with all faults'. It is assumed that you know what you're doing, and if you pay pounds for something which is worth only pence, it is your own look-out.

The basic rule of auction-buying is that 'the highest bidder is the buyer'. Where the bidding stops, there the lot auctioned rests. But auctioneers, eagle-eyed as they are, don't always see you bid. In which case you may point out that you were still bidding when the lot was 'knocked down' – and the lot will be put up for auction again.

Bidding never rises by less than a shilling; above five pounds the minimum bidding units are five shillings, and so on in proportion. But, by and large, the auctioneer establishes the bidding units in relation to what is being sold. Try to make a ten shilling bid for a Rembrandt and you'll be ignored. For a Rembrandt copy even a shilling rise may be too much.

It is in the bidding that most collectors become baffled and sometimes bankrupt. The auctioneer will call out, 'Five I am bid, six, seven, ten'. Unless you are on your toes from the start, you may continue in shillings and find you have spent pounds.

You must be realistic about auction-buying. Remember that today really valuable things are extremely rare – too many dealers are chasing too few goods. The rarities more often than not bring more money than they are worth, because dealers must have things to sell – they fiercely compete with one another – and bidding leaps up. Furthermore, most people who have valuable things put them into auctions in order to realize the highest possible prices. The auctioneer collects his commission on the price realized, and he isn't, if he can help it, going to let something worth a thousand pounds be sold for twenty. He will advise the vendor on the value of the goods he wants to sell, and between them they will agree on a 'reserve' price. That is to say, that in no circumstances can the item be sold for less than that price – and the auctioneer himself is entitled to bid against you until that figure is reached.

If in spite of all these complications you still go to auctions – and if, regardless of fair warning, you do buy something, you must give your name and address to the auctioneer or his clerk, and pay down at least five shillings in the pound deposit. If the goods you have bought are not cleared within two days, your deposit is forfeit and the goods are re-auctioned.

Points to remember then, for would-be auction buyers, are in brief:

1. Examine the goods thoroughly before the auction.
2. Don't rely on your catalogue except as the barest guide.
3. Know what you are looking for.
4. Decide exactly how much any particular thing is worth to you and never get so excited that you pay more.

5. Remember (always remember) that an auction-room is the arena of one of the toughest and most complicated business games ever devised by the tortured ingenuity of man.

Far more tough, complicated, tortured and ingenious than you can possibly imagine when you walk into that quiet gallery where the dusty air is disturbed only by the auctioneer's even voice, the slight swish of the catalogues, and the mutter of a dealer communicating (what?) to another dealer who bids even as he listens.

As to these dealers and dealing with them when they have returned with their quarry to their shops – never resent the profit they must make on the goods they sell. In principle, that profit is the price for a service. Pick out the dealer who, by his knowledge of the goods and the game, his reputation and his connexions, can offer you the best possible service. If you yourself have knowledge and taste, it will be very difficult for the dealer to overcharge you for the service he provides. And if you think he is overcharging, don't be afraid to argue a little. Even the most important collectors bargain slightly with even the most important dealers.

For the study of bargaining no university can offer the facilities of your local junk-shop. The fascination of junk-shops is not less than that of auction-rooms – they are safer, however, because dealing with them is conducted on a much more personal basis. Most junk dealers enjoy a short good-natured tussle over the goods, although there are some who maintain an aloofness more frigid than that of the most expensive West End dealer. By and large, this tussle will be more enjoyable if you and the dealer both know something about the goods you are arguing over; though there is no doubt that much of the fascination of junk-shops is the result of a vain hope on the part of collectors that they will find an invaluable treasure for a few shillings. The hope is vain because goods are becoming scarcer every year and the trade has become more educated, so that nowadays even junk dealers are highly knowledgeable. If they find important goods, they almost certainly recognize them before pricing them up.

Still, you may well buy more cheaply from them than from the West End dealers, for whom they are often an important source of supply. But if you do it is because the overheads of the junk man are very much lower. He normally buys at a less expensively competitive level, and consequently can sell cheaper than the specialist dealer. Furthermore, the small dealer, working on a much smaller capital, needs to turn his goods over considerably faster than his West End *confrère*, who must carry large stocks and capital in order to support his position. A cash offer, then, to a small dealer always has considerable attraction. In fact, so long as he isn't treated as a fool, a curmudgeon or a thief, the local junk-man can be an agent of great value to the small but intelligent collector.

Antique collecting is much subject to snobbism. Buyers are bludgeoned by consideration of fashion. Fearing that they will be thought poorly of, they desert their own taste and judgment and flair for the sake of some interior decorator's successfully promoted chic and chicanery. With antique collecting you must back your own feeling, support it with knowledge, and never desert it because some sedulous ape of fashion baffles you with phoney shop-talk. The fashions pass, the misguided fashionable buyers have to redecorate every season – which costs them a lot of money, and all their personal judgment. You should only collect for yourself the objects that mean something to you; that meaning is worth what money you can afford – no more and no less. Whoever buys in order to impress, shame or beggar his neighbour, shames the objects he mishandles, impresses no real connoisseur and beggars himself.

VICTORIAN FURNITURE

By PETER FLOUD

INTRODUCTION

In the history of the decorative arts Victorian furniture occupies a strange position. Although it is probable that fifty per cent of all the furniture ever made in this country was made during the sixty-four years of Victoria's reign, and that even today perhaps twenty per cent of all surviving furniture dates from those years, it is almost a closed field to serious scholarship or collecting. All standard works on the history of furniture stop at 1830, and the same terminal date is recognized, for example, by the Antique Dealers' Fair. In the last few years some dealers and collectors have begun tentatively to edge their way into the 1840s, usually with a limited interest in one line only (e.g. papier-mâché), and a few books have skated over the surface. The main course of Victorian furniture remains, however, totally uncharted, with the result that whereas there are thousands who can confidently date a fifteenth-century brass-rubbing to within thirty years, there is no one in this country who can be equally certain about a Victorian sideboard.

The normal justification given for this curious position is that after about 1830 there was such a disastrous deterioration in standards of taste and craftsmanship that Victorian furniture does not merit the attention legitimately bestowed on earlier periods, and that in particular the eclectic enthusiasm of Victorian designers for copying the historic styles of the past deprives their productions of that degree of originality which is essential to serious connoisseurship. These arguments are not convincing. Firstly, the deterioration can only be established if the evidence is studied rather than ignored. Secondly, ugliness in the products of earlier periods has never proved a bar to serious research or enthusiasm on the part of either antiquarians or collectors. Thirdly, the accusation of unoriginal eclecticism can equally be brought against the furniture designers of the eighteenth century, and was indeed used by many nineteenth-century writers to dismiss the works of Chippendale and the Adams brothers, for example, as debased rehashes of Chinese, classical and renaissance elements. Finally, it is surely absurd to suppose that the vast amount of earnest and informed effort put into the design of furniture by leading architects and others, especially after 1850, could have produced nothing whatever of interest.

The real explanation for the neglect must be sought elsewhere, namely in the totally different research techniques which are required to investigate Victorian furniture by comparison with that of earlier periods. The difference arises mainly from the change in the nature of the documentary evidence available after about 1840. Research into earlier furniture has always taken actual examples as its starting-point, and has, where possible, worked back from the furniture to surviving documents (family records and the like) as supporting evidence for attributions and dating. For these earlier periods the tangible evidence of the furniture itself far outweighs that of the fragmentary documentary references, and even after the appearance of pattern books in the eighteenth century the majority of surviving examples must be assessed without the aid of any contemporary visual or even verbal sources. After about 1845 the development of illustrated periodicals, trade catalogues and exhibition catalogues rapidly transformed the situation, so that for the Victorian era the bulk of systematic contemporary day-by-day visual evidence far outweighs the quantity of authentic surviving furniture, with the result that research must necessarily take the documents as the starting-point and work from them to the furniture instead of vice versa. This necessarily places collectors at a disadvantage, for it means that those who might hope to pick up interesting Victorian items at country auctions will probably find their time wasted unless they have first spent many tedious hours ploughing through trade periodicals in Shoreditch Public Library.

The clearest proof of the significance of this change in research requirements after about 1840 is the fact that the small amount of systematic research into Victorian furniture that has hitherto been undertaken has appeared in journals such as the *Architectural Review* rather than the *Connoisseur*, and has been the work of experts on twentieth-century taste (who take the bulk of contemporary visual evidence for granted) pushing their researches backwards, rather than of eighteenth-century experts (who are trained in the opposite technique) pushing forwards. It is equally significant that the only substantial collection of Victorian furniture in existence – that of the Victoria & Albert Museum – has been mainly built up as a result of a systematic search for particular pieces, the original existence of which had first been established from a study of contemporary periodicals and catalogues.

It is as well that this watershed which divides pre-1840 from post-1840 research and collecting should be widely recognized as soon as possible, for otherwise there is a serious danger that the established practice of collecting without prior documentation will itself produce a cumulative distortion in the public assessment – even in informed circles – of Victorian design, by fostering a process of 'selective survival'. For example, in the absence of a study of the contemporary records, there is a general but erroneous belief that Early Victorian furniture (in contrast to mid-Victorian) retained some of the lightness and elegance of the Regency. Once such a stereotype is established, collectors tend to be interested only in pieces whose authenticity seems to be attested by their conformity to it, and dealers will come to prefer such pieces and reject others as untypical, until in the long run the only pieces which survive in quantity are those which fit into the mistaken picture, while the examples whose survival would establish its falsity are weeded out. By that time it will be too late to redress the balance and all the really interesting pieces will have disappeared.

However, even after it is recognized that the prior research into and the subsequent collecting of Victorian furniture is a legitimate, indeed a praiseworthy, pastime, there still remains the problem of the type of furniture to be sought, for so much has survived, and there is documentary evidence of so many parallel levels of taste, that some choice is inevitable. The problem is aggravated by the appearance for the first time after 1850 of two separate streams: namely the *avant-garde* (what would today be called the 'contemporary') furniture, consciously produced by designers from outside the ranks of the trade – often inspired by a missionary zeal to reform public taste – and appealing to a very small educated clientele; and the enormously larger bulk of trade productions designed anonymously in the studios of the large manufacturers on conservative and traditionalist lines. At first sight these two streams appear to be not only separate but entirely opposed, each contemptuous of the other; the former believed by the latter to be constantly changing in a feverish search after novelty at the whim of each individual designer, the latter believed by the former to be stolidly unchanging and impervious to any progressive influence. Both pictures are distorted, for the evidence shows that a clear logical development can be traced through the apparently unrelated twists and turns of the *avant-garde* designs, and that this in its turn, and with a long time-lag, is reflected in a modified form by changes in the trade designs. The length of the time-lag naturally varies between London and the provinces and according to such factors as the price of the furniture and the nature of the firm, so that a comparison of trade catalogues demonstrates at any one time the whole gamut between the most advanced and the most conservative in current production side by side. Any systematic charting of the history of Victorian furniture – at least after 1850 – must therefore take constant account of this overlapping of styles, though necessarily giving prior attention to those pioneer, and indeed often rebel, designers upon whose inspiration the entire development ultimately depends. Collectors have the choice of furniture at every level of taste, though for obvious reasons it is usually only the more 'advanced' pieces, in so far as they survive, which can provide the additional interest of exact dating and documentation.

In the absence of an accepted body of doctrine on Victorian furniture, the opinions expressed in the survey which follows are necessarily personal and tentative. Moreover, they are unavoidably based as much on an examination of contemporary documents as of actual surviving furniture. The survey concentrates on cabinet-makers' furniture, and excludes upholstered furniture and those sidelines, such as metal furniture, wicker, cane and bent-wood furniture and garden furniture, which require separate study.

Early Victorian Furniture: 1837-51

The first fifteen years of Victoria's reign mark the lowest ebb ever reached in the whole history of English furniture design. Indeed, the most severe strictures so often applied indiscriminately to Victorian taste as a whole are entirely justified if only directed against the products of this initial period. It would, however, be absurd to suggest that a sudden deterioration set in as soon as the new reign had begun; the most that can be said is that a debasement which was already evident as early as the late 1820s gained steady impetus during the 1830s and 1840s. The Great Exhibition of 1851 is always taken to mark the culmination of this debasement. In a sense this is true; although it is only right to remember that by stimulating competitive ostentation among manufacturers it tended to exaggerate the most vulgar elements in Early Victorian design, while the fact that, for the first time, the various illustrated catalogues of the exhibition provide a permanent record of its horrors, unfairly weighs the evidence against the Early Victorians. Had a similar exhibition been held in 1837 instead of 1851, it would hardly have demonstrated a higher average standard.

As always in such debased periods, it is impossible in retrospect to discern any logical development of design, to distinguish the personal styles and influences of the leading designers and manufacturers or even to specify any criteria enabling one to date a surviving piece in default of documentary evidence. The pattern books of this period, such as those of R. Bridgens, R. Brown, Thomas King and Henry Whitaker, throw no light on the matter, for each exhibits the same tepid eclecticism in which a slavish copying of past styles is accompanied by a straining after novelty in trivial details. Judgment is made more difficult by reason of the fact that no surviving examples have so far been precisely related to these patterns, with the exception of a few commonplace pieces designed by Whitaker for Osborne House in about 1845, and still there.

Two characteristics stand out in the general confusion: an emphasis on rich and elaborate carving, preferably with a narrative or anecdotal interest, and a delight in the numerous new substitute materials which technical progress was making available. Lacking any accepted architectural framework, the shape and outline of such items as cabinets and sideboards was frequently entirely subordinated to an overall covering of carving, often worked not by hand carving but by new methods such as the burning techniques of the Burnwood Carving Company's 'Xylopyrography' and Harrison's Wood Carving Company (Pimlico), or the machine stamping of Jordan's Patent Wood Carving, or even produced from materials such as gutta-percha, Jackson's 'carton-pierre', Bielefeld's 'Patent Siliceous Fibre', White and Parlby's 'furniture composition', or Leake's sculptured leather.

Elaborate carving became so established as the hall-mark of fine furniture during this period that the furniture section of Wornum's Report on the Great Exhibition is actually headed 'Carving and Modelling', and the only artists known to have been commissioned during the years 1837–51 to design funiture from outside the trade (with the exception of Pugin, to be mentioned below) were not architects as one would expect, but sculptors, such as Sir Francis Chantrey (1781–1841), John Thomas (1813–62) and Baron Marochetti (1805–67). Inevitably the most popular examples of English furniture at the Great Exhibition were the elaborately carved cradle presented to Queen Victoria by W. G. Rogers (1792–1875) – known as the 'Victorian Grinling Gibbons'; the monstrous 'Kenilworth' buffet (now at Warwick Castle), the *chef-d'oeuvre* of the Warwick school of wood carvers which flourished throughout the nineteenth century; and Arthur J. Jones's ludicrous patriotic carved furniture in Irish bog-oak.

The only one of the new materials which may be said to have produced something new and attractive was papier-mâché, enriched after 1842 with Jennens's and Bettridge's patent jewelled effects. This plastic material, though suitable for trays, caskets and the like, is, however, basically unsuitable for load-bearing furniture, and has no real place in the development of Victorian furniture. Owing to the natural attraction of the smaller items for collectors, it has, nevertheless, received disproportionate attention, and has helped to spread the myth that Early Victorian furniture is lighter and less clumsy than mid-Victorian. In a few cases, of which the settle illustrated in Plate 1A is a good example, the techniques for decorating papier-mâché (e.g. lacquer painting and encrustation with shell and mother-of-pearl) were applied to a normal wooden framework, thus producing a legitimate piece of furniture; but such examples are rare.

Mid-Victorian Furniture: 1851-67

The furniture of the period 1851 to 1867 differed very markedly from that of the preceding period. In particular the wild eclecticism and confusion of styles was rapidly replaced after 1851 by a surprising uniformity, and a single consistent style soon imposed itself on the great bulk of fashionable productions. Victorians themselves gave no name to this style, but usually described examples of it with generalized phrases such as 'following the purest taste of the Italian Renaissance'. Twentieth-century writers have hitherto ignored its existence, although a careful analysis of, for example, the copious records which have survived from the vast Modern Furniture Court of the 1862 Exhibition makes its existence perfectly clear.

Its main characteristics were the use of solid wood, usually walnut or mahogany, rather than veneers or inlay, a repudiation of baroque or rococo curves in favour of more severe outlines, and a continuing emphasis on carving. The latter, however, was now no longer allowed to sprawl over the whole surface with a profusion of unrelated motifs, as in the 1840s, but was concentrated into carefully disposed and deeply cut masks, swags and trophies (usually of 'appropriate' objects, such as dead game birds on sideboards), and almost invariably incorporated human figures in the form of caryatids or brackets. Indeed, this emphasis on human figures became something of an obsession with designers during this period, so that no fashionable sideboard or cabinet was considered complete without them – as large as possible and preferably free-standing. Equally indispensable was an enormous mirror, backing, and usually dwarfing, the whole piece – a direct consequence of the technical developments in mirror making first displayed in the industrial section of the 1851 Exhibition.

It cannot be doubted that the best examples in this manner – however unacceptable to present-day taste – show a sense of style and consistency that had been completely lost in the 1840s, and certainly justify the enthusiasm with which all writers in the 1860s refer to the great improvement in the stylistic purity of English furniture since the nadir of 1851. The improvement must be mainly attributed to the influx of French designers imported from Paris by all the leading firms after the 1851 Exhibition had so clearly exposed the general superiority of French design. Some, such as Eugène Prignot and Alfred Lormier, who acted as chief designers to Jackson and Graham throughout the 1850s and 1860s, were brought over permanently, while in other cases designs were commissioned from artists in Paris, such as Ernest Vandale and Hugues Protat. In either case, the manufacturers always emphasized that 'the piece has been entirely executed by English workers'.

Although this dominant style was pervasive enough to influence not only the productions of all the leading London houses (i.e. Gillow, Trollope, Howard, Thomas Fox and Johnstone and Jeanes) but also the cheaper mass-production manufacturers such as Lucraft, Smee and Snell, and the leading provincial firms (i.e. Henry Ogden, Henry Lamb and Bird and Hull in Manchester, John Taylor, Whytocks, and Purdie, Bonnar and Carfrae in Edinburgh, and C. and W. Trapnell in Bristol), some furniture was, of course, produced in other manners. Thus, a few firms (Charles Hindley, William Fry of Dublin and J. G. Crace) worked in the 'Gothic taste' (see next section); Wright and Mansfield produced an entirely untypical series of copies of original Adams designs; and Dyer and Watts had considerable success with cheap, stained bedroom furniture, an example of which was even purchased by the Empress Eugénie from the Paris Exhibition of 1867.

This nameless mid-Victorian style must be regarded as the last style to have originated within the trade. Thereafter all further developments took place under the shadow of the individual reformist artist-designers and architect-designers whose appearance on the scene so decisively changed the whole trend of English furniture design.

The Gothic Revival

The first conscious reformers of Victorian furniture design – A. W. N. Pugin (1812–52) and William Burges (1827–81) – cannot be said to have had a direct or decisive influence on the general trend of trade design. Nevertheless, the developments of the late 1860s cannot be explained without a reference to their role. Though they both worked within the orbit of the Gothic Revival, their actual designs differed very radically.

The influence of Pugin on English furniture design has usually been overrated. His general influence as a propagandist, his key position in the mid-century transition from a sentimental to a scientific medievalism and the significance of his teachings on church furnishings have tended to obscure the fact that his own domestic furniture had little influence and that his following among furniture designers was always small. He himself designed a good deal of furniture in an extremely plain and unromantic Gothic style for the numerous houses which he erected in the 1840s, but as this was never published, it had no effect on the trade.

By contrast, the much more ornate and monumental furniture which he designed for the Houses of Parliament, and in particular the elaborate display piece which he designed for J. G. Crace for the Medieval Court of the 1851 Exhibition, and which was purchased by the Museum of Ornamental Art in 1852 (illustrated in Plate 2A), were much publicized and copied. Consequently the trade furniture of the 1850s which was claimed by its manufacturers to be 'in the purest Gothic taste, after recognized authorities', and dismissed by its detractors as 'Puginesque', tended to repeat all those faults of over-elaboration with architectural conceits in the way of finials, crockets and the like, which Pugin himself had so trenchantly attacked in his *Contrasts* and which his own domestic work so skilfully avoided. In fact, this type of architectural Gothic furniture was far too closely associated in the public mind with Pugin's catholicism to have any wide vogue, and soon came to be the exclusive preserve of a number of specialized houses – of which the most prominent were Hardman and Cox – dealing mainly in church fittings, and generally referred to by contemporary writers as the 'Wardour Street ecclesiastical upholsterers'. It is true that in 1862 the young Norman Shaw (1831–1912) designed an elaborate bookcase in this style, which has often been quoted since, merely by virtue of having been illustrated in the official catalogue of the Exhibition, but it typified no general trend and was produced not by a furniture firm but by James Forsyth, a specialist in stone carving.

The Gothic furniture of William Burges occupies a somewhat different position. The main body of his furniture – designed largely for his own use or as part of the huge schemes of interior rebuilding which he undertook for the Marquis of Bute at Cardiff Castle and Castell Coch – involved a far too personal interpretation of thirteenth-century Gothic to have any wide influence (a typical example is illustrated in Plate 5). Its fanciful – even facetious – adaptation of medieval forms to present-day needs, and its garish polychromatic decoration, made its incorporation into a normal domestic interior quite impractical. However, two particular pieces in a rather more restrained style, which were shown in the Medieval Court – not (significantly) in the Modern Furniture Court – of the 1862 Exhibition, received a great deal of favourable attention and publicity and deserve separate consideration. They were a huge bookcase, admittedly castellated but otherwise severely unelaborated, painted by no fewer than eleven leading artists, and now in the possession of the Ashmolean Museum, Oxford, and a celebrated plain rectangular cabinet painted to Burges's specifications by E. J. Poynter (1836–1919) with scenes representing 'the Battle of the Wines and the Beers' (bought for the South Kensington Museum from the Exhibition). The main significance of these pieces is that they are both in the plainest possible shape, entirely unlike the Wardour Street architectural Gothic, and depend entirely for their appeal on the painting of their surfaces. A subsidiary significance lies in the fact that their message to the trade was simultaneously endorsed at the 1862 Medieval Court by the furniture here displayed to the public for the first time by the newly created association of Morris, Marshall, Faulkner and Co.

Morris Furniture

Several pieces exhibited by the Morris firm in the 1862 Court have survived (the least known but most attractive example is illustrated in Plate 3B), and all are similar to Burges's exhibits in being solidly constructed, supposedly Gothic, carcases, used as surfaces for painting. They belong by rights to the history of painting rather than of furniture. However, the Morris firm also produced (though it did not exhibit in 1862) several other types of non-Gothic furniture each of which had an influence on the general trend of furniture design. So many misconceptions are current about Morris furniture that it is necessary to examine these in some detail.

Morris himself (despite frequent statements to the contrary) never designed any furniture, nor do his writings indicate much interest in it. All the furniture produced by the firm was the work of his various collaborators. Four different types were manufactured in these early years. Firstly, Philip Webb (1831–1915), the architect, designed a number of large tables depending for their effect entirely on the use of unstained oak and on the interest of their unconcealed joinery construction, thus marking a conscious revolt against the debasement of mid-Victorian cabinet making. Though they were exaggeratedly massive and monumental (one of the most interesting is illustrated in Plate 1B), their proportions and their simple chamfered decoration reveal the hand of a sensitive architect. Their importance lies not in any immediate influence on the trade but in their delayed influence on the Arts and Crafts furniture designers of the 1890s, and they can be legitimately regarded as the original prototypes of the whole Cotswold school of joinery.

Secondly, Ford Madox Brown designed a set of cheap bedroom furniture, produced by the Morris firm in large quantities, usually in a green-stained version, of which a few examples have survived. These appealed particularly to those mid-Victorians who felt that the introduction of examples of good plain design into servants' bedrooms could not but help raise the taste, and even the morals, of the lower classes. Their success led to plagiarism by many firms in the 1880s.

Thirdly, the firm produced and sold right up to the 1920s a set of cheap rush-bottomed chairs and settle in turned ebonized wood, including seven alternative shapes, which quickly became immensely popular with middle-class families anxious to escape from the general philistinism of contemporary decoration. These also were copied with minor modifications by numerous other firms. This set was not originally designed by the firm, but was adapted from a traditional-type country chair seen by William Morris in Sussex.

Fourthly, the firm produced with equal success a drawing-room easy chair with an adjustable bar at the back, which became so popular that in the United States the type is still known as a 'Morris chair' (one is illustrated in Plate 4B). Though often spoken of as designed by Morris himself, it was in fact copied directly from a chair seen in 1866 by Warington Taylor, the young manager of the firm, at the workshop of a Herstmonceux furniture maker named Ephraim Coleman.

Later in the century the firm evolved several entirely different types of furniture, which are referred to below in connexion with the Arts and Crafts movement.

Bruce J. Talbert and C. L. Eastlake

Although neither the architectural Gothic of Pugin nor the painted-plank Gothic of Burges and the Morris firm had much direct influence on trade design, they were nevertheless responsible for providing the point of departure for the development of what ultimately became the most widespread and original of all Victorian styles – a development that was so rapid that in the decade 1868 to 1878 it transformed the whole course of Victorian furniture design. Two stages – or rather two overlapping strands – can be traced in it: the first associated with Bruce J. Talbert (1838–81) and C. L. Eastlake (1836–1906), the second with T. E. Collcutt (1840–1924). Once again the usual Victorian confusion about labels has served to obscure the significance of these changes and the originality of the furniture which developed from them, for contemporary writers gave the style no name and referred to its products as simply Gothic, Early English, Old English or even Jacobean.

The first stage dates from 1867, when Talbert, a prolific and neglected designer, won a silver medal for Holland and Sons at the Paris Exhibition with a so-called 'Gothic dressoir' and several smaller cabinets. The influence of this success was consolidated by the publication in the same year of Talbert's *Gothic Forms, applied to Furniture, Metalwork, etc. for Interior Purposes*, and in 1868 of Eastlake's *Hints on Household Taste*, a book which exerted an enormous influence in sophisticated middle-class circles – especially in America, where it gave rise to a so-called 'Eastlake style'.

Although Talbert's Paris Exhibition pieces were still in a heavy semi-Gothic style, not so far removed from the 'Puginesque', the more unpretentious examples in both his book and in Eastlake's, which were of course, those which had most influence on trade production, marked a definite step away from the Gothic of both Pugin and Burges towards a style more practical and three-dimensional. Its main characteristics were a rigid avoidance of curves or florid carving, a concentration on straight lines and an elaboration of surface colour and texture (but always in the lowest possible relief) by the use of a great variety of different techniques and materials, including the insertion of painted and stained panels, tiles, stamped leather, embroidery, enamels and chased metal. Talbert produced large quantities of this furniture, not only for Hollands, but also for Gillow, and for Marsh, Jones and Cribb of Leeds. However, only two authenticated examples of his work have so far been traced (both are now in the Victoria & Albert Museum, and one is illustrated in Plate 3A). They are both in this modified Gothic style, and demonstrate the particular flavour of rich sobriety which characterized his work. Other examples must certainly survive, along with pieces by Eastlake himself (he designed for Heaton, Butler and Bayne), and those designers who closely followed this style in the 1870s, such as E. J. Tarver (working for Morant Boyd) and Owen Davis, the eclectic assistant of Sir Matthew Digby Wyatt and author of *Art and Life* (1885) (working for Shoolbred).

Despite the acclaim with which Talbert's book was received and the designs in it copied, he himself quickly abandoned the style, and already in the early 1870s turned towards a dull and unoriginal rehash of

Jacobean motifs, with a tedious elaboration of carved strap-work and a generally baronial air. This change can be clearly traced in the designs which he exhibited at the Royal Academy over these years, and in his second book of designs, *Examples of Ancient and Modern Furniture*, published in 1876. Its influence was slight, for it merely provided additional models for the large firms of traditionalist decorators, such as Gillow and Trollope, who had in any case always found in late Elizabethan and early seventeenth-century oak carving a ready-made source of inspiration for their more pretentious schemes.

T. E. Collcutt

The second stage in these developments, though it stemmed directly from the first and rapidly followed on its heels, was due neither to Talbert nor Eastlake, but to Thomas Edward Collcutt. Though remembered as the architect of the Imperial Institute, his role as a furniture designer has been entirely forgotten. It opens in 1871, when Collcutt exhibited at the South Kensington International Exhibition a cabinet designed for Collinson and Lock (illustrated in Plate 4C), which was bought by the Commissioners of the Great Exhibition and finally found its way into the South Kensington Museum. The publication in 1872 of a large catalogue of designs by Collinson and Lock (mostly the work of Collcutt, although J. Moyr Smith, the author of *Ornamental Interiors* (1887) later claimed some credit for them) gave the style a wide currency in the trade, so that already by the time of the Paris Exhibition of 1878 firms such as Cooper and Holt, and Bell and Roper of London, and Henry Ogden of Manchester were copying it precisely. By 1880 its influence appears in the catalogues of mass-production firms such as Hewetson and Milner, Smee, and Lucraft.

In Collcutt's hands the style, though following Talbert in the emphasis on straight lines and the use of coved cornices and painted panels, was elaborated in a far more fanciful and light-hearted spirit, which marked a further stage in the evolution away from the medieval. A simultaneous emphasis on both verticals and horizontals, and a proliferation of shelves and divisions, diversifies the façade and provides variety by giving space for the display of knick-knacks. As always, the rapid spread of the style was accompanied by an equally rapid debasement, so that by the early 1880s it was responsible for a mass of elaborate but gimcrack cabinets, what-nots, corner-cupboards (a particular favourite) and the like, with spindly supports, a profusion of small pigeon-holes, often divided off by little railings of turned balusters or embroidered curtains, and panels painted with floral sprays or willowy female figures, usually on a gold ground. A persistent cliché which became almost a trade-mark for the style was a double panel in which an inner oblong or hexagon is joined to an outer frame by ties at the four cardinal points.

At its best, the style must be regarded as the Victorian era's most individual contribution in the whole field of furniture design. Quantities of its cheaper manifestations have survived, particularly in country rectories. Overmantels, usually backed with numerous small mirrors, have tended to survive as being fixtures, and examples of a drawing-room version of the style, decorated in black and gold, can also be found. Authentic pieces from the Collinson and Lock 1872 catalogue are, however, very difficult to come by.

The surprisingly rapid spread of Talbert's original style, and Collcutt's later version of it, can only be explained if account is taken of the way in which Eastlake and the many publicists who followed him supported their influence with arguments which seemed to provide would-be connoisseurs and purchasers with certain easily remembered maxims for judging furniture, and which buttressed their own uncertain taste with apparently authoritative criteria. These all derived ultimately from the teachings of Pugin, Owen Jones and Ruskin on 'honesty in design'. The most telling was the proposition that because wood has a straight grain it should always be used in the plank and never debased by being carved or curved into twisted shapes more appropriate to plastic or ductile materials. This argument was strengthened by simultaneous appeal to economic and nationalist considerations, for

(A) Wood settle with painted panels and encrusted decoration, *c.* 1845. *Victoria & Albert Museum.*

(B) Oak table, designed by Philip Webb, 1859. *Dr D. C. Wren, Kelmscott Manor.*

PLATE I

(A) Oak cabinet, designed by A. W. N. Pugin, and made by J. G. Crace, 1851. *Victoria & Albert Museum.*

(B) Satinwood cabinet inlaid with Wedgwood plaques; Wright and Mansfield, 1867. *Victoria & Albert Museum.*

PLATE 2

(A) Oak sideboard decorated with carving and enamel, designed by Bruce Talbert, 1867. *Victoria & Albert Museum.*

(B) 'The Backgammon Players', cabinet, designed by Philip Webb, painted by Edward Burne-Jones, 1862. *Metropolitan Museum of Art, New York.*

(A) Ebonized wood cabinet with metal fittings, designed by E. W. Godwin, made by William Watt, *c.* 1877. *Victoria & Albert Museum.*

(B) Adjustable chair, made by Morris, Marshall, Faulkner and Co., *c.* 1866. *Mrs Tozer.*

(C) Painted and ebonized mahogany cabinet, designed by T. E. Collcutt, made by Collinson and Lock, 1871. *Victoria & Albert Museum.*

Carved and painted wood washstand with marble and silver fittings, designed by William Burges, 1880. *Victoria & Albert Museum.*

PLATE 5

(A) Satinwood cabinet, designed by A. H. Mackmurdo for the Century Guild, made by E. Goodall and Co., Manchester, 1886. *William Morris Gallery, Walthamstow.*

(B) Painted oak cabinet, designed by C. R. Ashbee, 1889. *Abbotsholme School, Rocester, Staffs.*

(C) Escritoire decorated with sycamore marquetry, designed by George Jack for Morris and Co., 1893. *Victoria & Albert Museum.*

(A) Oak dresser inlaid with ebony and bleached mahogany, designed by W. R. Lethaby, 1900. *Victoria & Albert Museum.*

(B) Oak chair, designed by C. F. A. Voysey, made by Story and Co., 1899. *Victoria & Albert Museum.*

(C) Cabinet inlaid with ivory, designed by Ernest Gimson for Kenton and Co., 1890.

(D) Oak chair, designed by Charles Rennie Mackintosh, *c.* 1900. *Glasgow School of Art.*

PLATE 7

Oak wardrobe inlaid with pewter and ebony, designed by Ambrose Heal, made by Heal and Son, 1900.
Lieutenant-Colonel C. G. Price.

PLATE 8

To face page 25

the carving or curving of wood obviously involves the cutting-to-waste of good timber, while 'wanton curves' and 'meaningless scrolls' could be condemned as symbolizing the decadent extravagances which had so recently brought the French Second Empire to the ground.

During this period a parallel movement in favour of straight lines, a lighter and more varied colouring and texture and a shunning of the deep carving of the 1860s can be traced even in the luxury productions of firms such as Jackson and Graham, and Wright and Mansfield. At its best it produced some very handsome pieces, such as the cabinet by Wright and Mansfield illustrated in Plate 2B, which won the highest awards at the Paris Exhibition of 1867 and was purchased for the South Kensington Museum for £800. Judging from contemporary descriptions, the elaborate inlaid furniture produced by Jackson and Graham in the early 1870s for Alfred Morrison's palace at 16, Carlton House Terrace, to the designs of Owen Jones (1809–74), must have reflected the same trend. The 1870s also saw the production of furniture designed by Norman Shaw for Lascelles and Co. Unfortunately, in the absence of surviving photographs or specimens, the wildly conflicting opinions of contemporary critics provide no clear picture of its style.

The Anglo-Japanese Style

Owing to the absence of furniture in the European sense in the traditional Japanese home, the revolutionary influence on Victorian design of the displays of Japanese craftsmanship at the International Exhibitions of 1862 (London) and 1867 (Paris), following the opening-up of Japan by the West, had rather less effect in the field of furniture design than in those, for example, of wallpapers, textiles or book illustration. Nevertheless, the impact of the new culture – providing, as it did, a heaven-sent stimulus to jaded designers in search of some authentic historical style that had not already been copied *ad nauseam* – was sufficient to inspire a vogue for so-called 'Anglo-Japanese' furniture in the 1870s and 1880s.

The first enthusiast was E. W. Godwin (1833–86), the architect and stage designer and associate of Whistler and Ellen Terry. He is said to have decorated his own house in the Japanese manner as early as 1862, and was certainly designing furniture showing a strong Japanese influence by the late 1860s. An illustrated catalogue issued by William Watt in 1877 contained many examples of his work and did much to familiarize the general public and the trade with his particular style. His best pieces, such as two fine cabinets in the Victoria and Albert Museum (one of which is illustrated in Plate 4A) and a collection of furniture belonging to the Bristol Art Gallery, show a remarkable capacity for translating into European terms, and into the scale of full-size furniture, the asymmetrical elegance, the attenuated supports and in particular the subtle three-dimensional interplay of void and solid, which are the main characteristics of the Japanese lacquer boxes and cabinets which were then being imported in large quantities. To these he added certain personal mannerisms of his own, such as the use of elbow-like struts, square in section but rounded at the angle, which serve no function but to span the spaces between the component parts of a cabinet or sideboard and thus draw the whole composition together.

Inevitably the trade version of Godwin's style, worked out in the 1880s by hack designers, produced some deplorable furniture, in which the Japanese inspiration was limited to such obvious tricks as imitation bamboo legs, and asymmetrical fretwork panels. However, a few of the better professional designers managed to design some quite pleasing pieces by grafting certain Japanese motifs on to the Talbert-Collcutt style. The most successful of these was H. W. Batley, who designed some very elaborate furniture for James Shoolbred and for Henry Ogden of Manchester. It is possible, also, that some of the 'Anglo-Japanese' furniture produced by the short-lived 'Art Furnishers' Alliance', founded in 1880 by Christopher Dresser (1834–1904), the indefatigable but eccentric designer and publicist (he was for a time Art Editor of the *Furniture Gazette* in the

1880s), may have been of interest, for Dresser had a real understanding of Japan, which he visited officially in 1876; but the only two surviving examples are too unimportant to justify an opinion.

This Anglo-Japanese vogue was accompanied in the 1880s by a revival of interest in other exotic styles, such as the Indian, Persian and Moorish, as a result of which such features as 'Anglo-Arab lounges' and 'Hindoo smoke-rooms' became popular, particularly in clubs and hotels. However, this fashion was largely met by the importation and adaptation of genuine Oriental examples (Egyptian mushrabiya panels, Chinese embroidered screens, Indian mother-of-pearl and ivory tables and the like) by firms such as Liberty's, rather than by Western manufacturers, and no serious English designers seem to have been influenced by it.

The Arts and Crafts Movement

Late Victorian furniture design – indeed, the Late Victorian decorative arts generally – was dominated by the birth of what has come to be known generically as the 'Arts and Crafts movement' (i.e. the Century Guild, 1882; the Art Workers' Guild, 1883; the Arts and Crafts Exhibition Society, 1888; the Guild of Handicraft, 1888; the Home Arts and Industries Association, 1889; the Wood Handicraft Society, 1892; and many others). In fact, during the last dozen years or so of the Victorian era no furniture of interest was designed outside its orbit.

In these its initial stages the movement gave rise to a bewildering variety of different styles of furniture, and it would be quite wrong to suppose that its productions were in the main limited to that particular type of austere and undecorated cottage-style joinery which, as we have already seen, had been practised by Philip Webb in the 1860s, and which has come to be associated with the Arts and Crafts movement during the twentieth century and particularly with its important Cotswold offshoot. Indeed, two equally strong tendencies were pulling in an exactly contrary direction.

In the first place the movement fostered a revival of interest in the styles and craftsmanship of the eighteenth-century English cabinet makers, partly no doubt as a natural reaction against the disrepute in which they had been held by the medievalists of the 1860s, partly as a corollary to the renewed interest in eighteenth-century architecture stemming from the Queen Anne revival, and partly in continuation of that general movement towards greater lightness and elegance of detail which we have already noted in the work of both Collcutt and Godwin. In the second place, the move away from austere joinery was stimulated by the natural temptation for furniture designers to put into practice the movement's beliefs about the need for greater co-operation between the various crafts, by calling in workers in pewter, ivory, brass, stained glass, leather and so on to adorn the efforts of the carpenter and cabinet-maker.

These contrasting tendencies can be seen very clearly in almost all the furniture shown at the various Arts and Crafts Exhibitions (1888, 1889, 1890, 1893, 1896, 1899). They are certainly evident in the Morris furniture, for though almost all designed by George Jack (1855–1932), Philip Webb's closest pupil, it bore little resemblance to the latter's solid-wood joinery. Most of it consisted of florid and very expensive walnut and mahogany pieces, covered all over with elaborate floral marquetry and inlay. Two particular pieces have survived in several versions, namely a free-standing escritoire (illustrated in Plate 6c) and a handsome glass-fronted bookcase. The latter, as also an elegant circular mahogany tea-table with shaped legs, are entirely urban pieces and as far removed as possible from any Gothic or medieval influence. The same is true of some curious furniture which the firm produced at this date to the designs of W. A. S. Benson (1854–1924), the metalworker, in which he incorporated elaborate metal panel-frames, locks, handles and hinges.

Curiously enough, it remained for Ford Madox Brown (1821–93) – now no longer associated with the Morris firm – to produce the type of furniture which would presumably have accorded better with Morris's philosophical views than did Jack's expensive projects. In 1890 he exhibited a 'Cheap Chest of Drawers for a Workman or Cottager' which created a great deal of interest. Judging from a contemporary photograph, the piece was so far in advance of its times that it could easily have passed for an example of utility design in the Second World War – even to the use of sunk finger-holes instead of drawer handles.

The furniture of the short-lived association of architect-designers known as Kenton and Co. (named after a street near its Bloomsbury workshop), which lasted for eighteen months in 1890–1 and exhibited at the Arts and Crafts Exhibition of 1890, throws these contradictory tendencies within the movement into even sharper relief. Reginald Blomfield (1856–1942) and Mervyn Macartney (1853–1932) used the workshop to produce eclectic walnut and mahogany pieces in adaptations of eighteenth-century styles. (R. S. Lorimer produced some similar designs at the very end of the century.) Ernest Gimson's designs (apart from some turned ash chairs which he made himself by the traditional methods which he had learnt from a Herefordshire chair-turner in 1888, and one or two Windsor-type examples) were entirely original, and clearly adumbrated that combination of angularity and elegance and of austere outlines and elaborate surface decoration which he later developed so successfully in the Cotswolds (one of his Kenton pieces is illustrated in Plate 7C). On the other hand, Sidney Barnsley's solid pieces in unstained oak acknowledge a direct debt to Philip Webb and clearly anticipated the more unsophisticated and rustic side of the Cotswold movement. The same is true of W. R. Lethaby's (1857–1931) essays in the use of a coarse type of floral marquetry using unstained woods (an example dating from a few years later than the Kenton experiment is illustrated in Plate 7A), though, as if to emphasize the confusion of styles, Lethaby was simultaneously designing in 1890 some entirely dissimilar rosewood and mahogany drawing-room furniture in a modified Chippendale manner, executed by Marsh, Jones and Cribb of Leeds.

When we come to consider the furniture designed by other pioneers of the Arts and Crafts movement, the picture is even more complex. On the one hand, each tended to strike out in his own individual direction, uninhibited by the existence of any accepted norms. On the other hand, the very frequency of the Arts and Crafts exhibitions, and in particular the extent to which the illustrated journals immediately published photographs of every interesting piece as it appeared, made it quite impossible to design in isolation. As a result, the years between 1888 and 1901 witnessed a most complicated pooling of ideas and interplay of influence and counter-influence which would require a large volume to unravel. For example, a characteristic square-cut tapering leg with an enlarged foot, first used by Mackmurdo in the 1880s, was taken up and exploited by Voysey in the 1890s; the latter's weakness for fanciful spreading hinges was immediately copied by C. R. Ashbee; Ashbee's use of thonged leather was plagiarized by Baillie Scott and Wickham Jarvis – and so the list could continue. In fact, so interwoven are the various strands that it is difficult to date precisely, and to pin down initial responsibility for, the introduction of even the most emphatic mannerisms of the period, such as the addition of elongated finials to the corners of cupboards and sideboards (probably first used by Walter Cave on a piano exhibited in 1893) or the decoration of chair backs with cut-out heart shapes (almost certainly due to Voysey).

Although a painstaking examination of the huge mass of contemporary periodical literature of these years is an indispensable prerequisite to any definitive unravelling of these developments, the story must equally remain obscure until more of the key-pieces of the period are unearthed. Many have unhappily disappeared for ever, but others undoubtedly survive, as yet unrecognized and awaiting discovery by enterprising collectors. Century Guild furniture, for example, which was designed by A. H. Mackmurdo (1851–1942), is known only by a small group of pieces in the William Morris Gallery at Walthamstow (one of which is illustrated in Plate 6A), and yet much more must surely survive, for a good deal was sold by Wilkinson's of Old Bond Street in the late 1880s. Examples of the work of C. R. Ashbee's (1863–1942) Guild of Handicraft are even scarcer, for only three have so far been traced (one is illustrated in Plate 6B). Contemporary photographs exist, however, of many more examples, and it is inconceivable that they have all disappeared.

C. F. A. Voysey (1857–1941) is rather easier, and a fair amount of his furniture has already been located. It is unlikely that many more of his elaborate – and often eccentric – individual pieces have survived untraced, but many examples of the several styles of chair which he designed for standard production (one of which is illustrated in Plate 7B) must still be in use. Furniture by Charles Rennie Mackintosh (1868–1928), the Glasgow architect, is in a different category, for although considerable quantities of it survive (a typical example is illustrated in Plate 7D), it is almost all concentrated in the hands of the Glasgow School of Art and the Glasgow City Corporation, and therefore unavailable to the private collector. It also differs from all other Victorian furniture in that it has already been fully catalogued and documented.* There should be considerable scope for pioneer collecting in the early furniture of M. H. Baillie Scott (1865–1945), for though a number of his Edwardian pieces have survived, notably in Switzerland, nothing of his work in the Isle of Man (1887–1900) has been traced. Minor figures of the movement, such as Edgar Wood, Charles Spooner, Wickham Jarvis and Walter Cave, all of whom designed interesting if not startlingly original furniture in the last years of the century, await the attention of both research workers and collectors. Many photographs of their work exist in contemporary periodicals, but nothing has so far been traced.

If so many different cross-currents are discernible among the furniture of the leading Late Victorian designers, it is not surprising that the changes of fashion in the run-of-the-mill trade furniture produced during the 1890s should be even more difficult to chart. The days when the trade could afford to ignore the existence of the reformers were now long past, and Arts and Crafts developments were recorded as a matter of course – and usually respectfully – in the various trade periodicals. Indeed, in 1893 the firms of Gillow, Howard and Sons and Collinson and Lock participated in force at the Arts and Crafts Exhibition, though for some reason this experiment was not repeated.

The direct influence of the movement on the trade seems to have operated at two quite different levels. In the first place, a certain number of hack designers simply added to their repertory of styles some of the more obvious mannerisms of the Arts and Crafts designers and evolved from them a bastard concoction which they christened the 'Quaint Style'. This first appeared in 1891, and became more monstrous as the century ended, especially after 1893 when the so easily aped and misunderstood extravagances of Parisian 'Art Nouveau' were added to the mixture. This so-called style is too debased and spurious to merit serious attention, though the student of the bizarre can trace its ramifications week by week by simply following the so-called 'original' designs by A. Jonquet and H. Pringuet published for the use of manufacturers in the *Furniture Gazette* and the *Cabinet-maker* respectively. Its existence need hardly be drawn to the attention of collectors were it not that in the early stages of collecting, before the field has become familiar, there is always a danger that the most extreme and fantastic specimens will be given undue prominence, both because they are the most easily identifiable and because their very extravagance exercises a certain ludicrous charm. It would, however, be a great pity if, for these reasons, the attention of collectors was diverted from the serious work of the real pioneers of the movement to the entirely derivative corner cupboards and ingle-nooks of the 'Quaint Style' with their shoddy stained glass and machine-stamped repoussé tulips.

On an entirely different level was the furniture produced at the very turn of the century by a few firms, such as Heal and

*See Thomas Howarth: *Charles Rennie Mackintosh and the Modern Movement* (London, 1952).

Son, the Bath Cabinet Makers, J. S. Henry, and Wylie and Lockhead, which had taken the trouble to assimilate the basic principles of the Arts and Crafts movement. Though the full fruits of this most important development fall properly outside the Victorian era, some of the exhibits at the Paris Exhibition of 1900 and the Glasgow Exhibition of 1901 (the most striking of which is illustrated in Plate 8) already herald the change.

SMALLER FURNITURE OF ALL PERIODS

By E. T. JOY, M.A.

A FAIRLY wide interpretation has been given here to the term 'small furniture'. It includes, in general, those smaller pieces which were not dealt with in the chapters on furniture in the previous volumes of this series, or which were there given only a passing mention. It has also been assumed that readers will be familiar with the main developments of English furniture styles, to which smaller furniture, as well as the larger, conformed; with the warning that 'country' furniture might continue to be made in a style which had passed out of fashion, perhaps some considerable time previously, in London and the chief provincial towns.

The collection of small pieces of furniture can be a most fascinating pastime, not only for obvious financial reasons but also because they are a constant delight to the eye, and – a point of special weight in these days when living room is not so spacious as in times gone by – because they can be frequently used as their original makers and owners intended.

The study of the evolution of smaller articles of furniture can also be a study of social history; for they portray, as Horace Walpole wrote of the furniture in Hogarth's pictures, 'the history of the manners of the age'. One can see how they came into use as the rooms of houses began to take on their separate character and as new conventions established themselves in society. Note, for example, how, at the end of the seventeenth century, the two new fashions of tea-drinking and displaying china produced a whole range of small pieces among which can be included, on the one hand, tea-boards, kettle-stands and caddies, and, on the other, china-stands, brackets and shelves. With the coming of home manufacture of mirror glass, the development of special processes of decoration such as Tunbridge ware and straw-work and the introduction of new materials like Clay's papier-mâché, many new articles came into production or new forms and modes of decoration were given to older ones. The great diversity of small pieces in Georgian dining-rooms tells its own story of the importance placed by the upper classes in those days on eating and drinking.

With regard to the furniture which is described hereunder, one might be tempted to write, as did Sheraton in his *Cabinet Dictionary*, that 'the reader will find some terms which he will probably judge too simple in their nature to justify their insertion'. One feels, however, that this apology is unnecessary; the simplest articles are often the most useful, and their names, though no doubt very familiar, do not give what is, after all, the intention of this section, viz. their history and development. It might be added, in conclusion, that Sheraton's own period delighted in small furniture which combined, to a greater degree than at any other time, usefulness with extreme delicacy of appearance.

GLOSSARY

Basin-stand: *see* Washing-stand.

Beer-wagon: *see* Coaster.

Book-rest: a stand used in Georgian libraries to support large books, consisting of a square or rectangular framework with cross bars, the upper bar being supported by a strut which was adjusted on a grooved base. This kind of stand was sometimes fitted into the top of a table.

Book-shelf: *see* Shelves.

Box and Casket: boxes were among the most attractive of the smaller pieces of furniture, and were used from medieval times for a multitude of purposes – personal effects, toilet and writing materials, valuables, documents, etc. Tudor and early Stuart boxes were usually square in shape and made of oak, carved, inlaid or painted, and occasionally stood upon stands, few of which have survived. In the later seventeenth century walnut was commonly used (sometimes decorated with marquetry or parquetry), but other materials included parchment, tortoise-shell and stump-work, the latter particularly on the boxes kept by ladies for their cosmetics, etc. The interiors were often ingeniously fitted with compartments and drawers. In the eighteenth century some beautiful mahogany and satinwood boxes were made, until they were gradually replaced by small work-tables, though boxes on stands, conforming to the prevailing decorative fashions, were to be found. Among other examples were Tunbridge ware (q.v.) boxes, and travelling boxes fitted with spaces for writing, working and toilet requisites. About 1800 work and toilet boxes covered with tooled leather were in vogue (Plate 16B).

Bracket: the detachable wall-bracket, as distinct from the fixed architectural feature, appeared towards the end of the seventeenth century, and seems to have been used at first for displaying china. Its prominent position in the room singled it out for special decorative treatment in carving or gilding. In the early Georgian period the bracket was often used to support a bust or vase, and as a result it tended to become larger in size and more heavily ornamented; but with the return of the fashion for displaying china about 1750 and the growing use of the bracket for supporting lights, it became altogether more delicate in appearance, and was adapted to the various styles of the Chippendale and Adam periods. The wall-bracket supporting a clock was a popular form of decoration in the later eighteenth century.

Brazier: a portable metal container used from Tudor times for burning coal or charcoal; with handle and feet, or sometimes mounted on a stand.

Butler's Tray: a tray mounted on legs or on a folding stand, in use throughout the eighteenth century. The X-shaped folding stand was in general use from about 1750, the tray normally being rectangular and fitted with a gallery. Oval trays were sometimes made in the later part of the century.

Candle-box: a cylindrical or square box, of metal or wood, widely used in the Georgian period for storing candles.

Candle-stand: a portable stand (known also as a lamp-stand, guéridon and torchère) for a candlestick, candelabrum or lamp. After 1660 the fashion arose of having two candle-stands flanking a side table with a mirror on the wall above; the stands usually took the form of a baluster or twist-turned shaft, with a circular or octagonal top and a tripod base. At the end of the century more elaborate kinds, copying French stands, became fashionable, with vase-shaped tops and scrolled feet, all carved and gilded. Other examples were of simpler design, but had rich decoration in gesso or marquetry. In the early Georgian period, when gilt stands followed architectural forms, the vase-shaped tops and baluster shafts were larger, and the feet curved outwards, replacing the scrolled French style. About 1750 stands became lighter and more delicate, many of them being enriched with rococo decoration. There was a distinct change in design in the later eighteenth century: the traditional tripod continued, often in mahogany, with turned shaft and a bowl or vase top in the classical taste; but a new type, which was originated by Adam, consisted of three uprights, mounted on feet or a plinth, supporting usually a candelabrum, or with a flat top. Smaller examples of the latter type were made to stand on tables (Plate 9). A much smaller version of candle-stand was also popular after 1750 – with a circular base and top, and sometimes an adjustable shaft.

Kedleston Hall, Derbyshire. The dining-room by Robert Adam, showing candle-stands, sconces, knife-cases and fire-screen.

PLATE 9

To face page 32

(A) Mahogany Canterbury music-stand, *c.* 1810. *Hotspur, Ltd.*

(B) Late eighteenth-century plate-pail with brass handle, and cellaret of octagonal form. *Mallett & Son.*

(C) Mahogany tripod pole screen with needlework panel, *c.* 1750. *Frank Partridge & Sons.*

(D) Late eighteenth-century mahogany tripod basin-stand with shelf and drawer and soap receptacle. *Hotspur, Ltd.*

(B) Mahogany kettle-stand, *c.* 1755, with aperture for kettle spout, and slide; enriched with rococo carving. *Formerly in the F. H. Reed Collection.*

(A) Mahogany tripod kettle-stand, *c.* 1755, with lattice-work gallery, kettle and heater. *Mallett & Son.*

(C) Hepplewhite period mahogany urn-stand with slide. *Frank Partridge & Sons.*

(A) Library steps made to fold into a small table, *c.* 1790. *Hotspur, Ltd.*

(B) Chair and steps combined, *c.* 1810. *Hotspur, Ltd.*

(A) Sconces: Early eighteenth-century, carved and gilt. *Frank Partridge and Sons.*

(B) *c.* 1760, in the Chinese taste, carved and gilt. *Frank Partridge and Sons.*

(C) Late eighteenth-century, in the classical style, with cut-glass ornament. *Frank Partridge and Sons.*

(D) Late eighteenth-century metal lantern with classical ornament. *Mallett & Son.*

(A) Mahogany wine cooler inlaid with satinwood, *c.* 1775. *Mallett & Son.*

(B) Kingwood and satinwood 'French Work-table' with tray, and trestle feet, *c.* 1790. *Frank Partridge and Sons.*

(A) Top of writing-table shown in 15C below.

(B) Gate-leg writing-table with folding top, *c.* 1690. *Private Collection.*

(C) Writing-table with drawer and folding top decorated with floral marquetry, *c.* 1690. *Private Collection.*

(A) Late eighteenth-century mahogany night-table with tray top. *Hotspur Ltd.*

(B) Late seventeenth-century brass-bound casket on a George II period carved mahogany stand. *Private Collection.*

(C) Walnut bureau or secretaire on turned legs with curved stretchers and finial, *c.* 1690. *The Hart Collection.*

PLATE 16

Canterbury: (1) a small music-stand with partitions for music-books, usually mounted on castors, and sometimes with small drawers, much used in the early nineteenth century (Plate 10A); and (2) a plate and cutlery stand particularly designed for supper parties in the later eighteenth century, with divisions for cutlery and a semicircular end, on four turned legs. The name 'Canterbury' arose, wrote Sheraton, 'because the bishop of that See first gave orders for these pieces'.

Cat: a stand used after about 1750 to warm plates in front of the fire; it had three arms and three feet of turned wood (or three legs of cabriole form). The turning was well ringed to provide sockets for plates of various sizes.

Cellaret: the name given generally after 1750 to a case on legs or stand for wine bottles; prior to that date, from the end of the seventeenth century, the same kind of case was called a cellar. In the early eighteenth century cellarets, lined with lead and containing compartments for bottles, stood under side-tables, and they were still made later in the century (Plate 10B) when sideboards, which had drawers fitted up to hold bottles, came into general use. Sheraton classified the cellaret with the wine cistern (q.v.) and sarcophagus, and distinguished them from the bottle-case, which was for square bottles only.

Cheval-glass: a larger type of toilet mirror in a frame with four legs; also known as a horse dressing-glass; dating from the end of the eighteenth century. The rectangular mirror either pivoted on screws set in the uprights or moved up and down by means of a weight within the frame ('the same as a sash-window' – Sheraton). Turned uprights and stretchers were often found on these pieces about 1800.

Cheveret: *see* Secretaire.

Chiffonier: a piece of furniture which has given rise to a certain amount of confusion. The French chiffonier was a tall chest of drawers, but the *chiffonière*, a quite different piece, was a small set of drawers on legs. It was the latter which seems to have been copied in England in the later eighteenth century. Another form of chiffonier was popular in the Regency period – a low cupboard with shelves for books. As this was similar to contemporary commodes, it can be taken that the English version of the *chiffonière* was the only true small piece of furniture.

China-stand: an ornamental stand for displaying china or flowers, introduced at the end of the seventeenth century and at first taking the form of a low pedestal on carved and scrolled feet, or of a vase on a plinth. In the early eighteenth century the form was sometimes that of a stool with cabriole legs, in mahogany. More fanciful designs, in the rococo taste, were evident after 1750, as in the 'Stands for China Jarrs' presented in Chippendale's *Director*. In the Adam period some attractive stands for flower-bowls resembled the contemporary candle-stands with three uprights. Little four-legged stands with shelves were also made at this time for flower-pots.

Coaster: a receptacle which came into use before 1750 for moving wine, beer and food on the dining-table; also variously known as a slider, decanter stand and beer-wagon. For ease of movement, the coaster was normally fitted either with small wheels or with a baize-covered base, and the materials used in good examples included mahogany, papier-mâché and silver. Beer-wagons were sometimes made with special places for the jug and drinking vessels.

Croft: a small filing cabinet of the late eighteenth century (named after its inventor) specially designed to be moved about easily in the library; it had many small drawers and a writing-top.

Cutlery Stand: *see* Canterbury (2).

Daventry: a small chest of drawers with a sloping top for writing; said to be named after a client of the firm of Gillow who claimed to have invented it.

Decanter Stand: *see* Coaster.

Desk: a term of varied meaning, but taken here to refer to two portable pieces. (1) The commonest meaning was that of a box (originating in medieval times) with a sloping top for reading and writing. Early examples in oak in the Tudor and Stuart periods had carving and inlay, and sometimes the owner's initials and date. When bureaux came into use at the end of the seventeenth century these small desks were too useful to discard, and were fitted with drawers and pigeon-holes; many were veneered with walnut, or japanned, and some were mounted on stands. In the Georgian period they became less decorative, and were usually of plain mahogany; few were made after 1800. (2) In the later eighteenth century 'desk' was the current term for what would now be called a music-stand (which was also used for reading); it generally took the form of a tripod base supporting a shaft and a sloping, adjustable top.

Dumb-waiter: a dining-room stand, an English invention of the early eighteenth century, with normally three circular trays, increasing in size towards the bottom, on a shaft with tripod base. This established design gave way to more elaborate versions at the end of the century; four-legged supports and rectangular trays were found; and quite different kinds were square or circular tables with special compartments for bottles, plates, etc.

Fire-screen: an adjustable screen made from the end of the seventeenth century to give protection from the intense heat of large open fires. Two main kinds were used. (1) Pole screen: with the screen on an upright supported on a tripod base; known as a 'screen-stick' in the late seventeenth century; and in very general use in the eighteenth. The screen, often of needlework, was at first rectangular (Plate 10C), but oval and shield shapes were fashionable in the late eighteenth century. In the Regency period the tripod was replaced by a solid base, and the screen was a banner hung from a bar on the upright. (2) Horse or cheval screen – two uprights, each on two legs, enclosing a panel (Plate 9). Elaborate carving and gilding of the crests was often found until the end of the eighteenth century, when lighter and simpler screens were in vogue. Needlework was the popular material for the panel.

Flower-stand: *see* China-stand.

Guéridon: *see* Candle-stand.

Horse-glass and Horse-screen: *see* Cheval-glass and Fire-screen.

Kettle-stand (also **Urn-** and **Teapot-stand**)**:** a special stand which was introduced with tea-drinking in the later seventeenth century, of two main kinds. (1) A small table, tripod or four-legged, with a gallery or raised edge round the top. Slender four-legged tables were common in the later part of the eighteenth century, nearly always with a slide for the teapot. (2) A box-like arrangement set on four legs; the box was usually lined with metal, and had an opening in one side for the kettle spout, as well as a slide for the teapot. Another version of the box type had a three-sided enclosure with a metal-lined drawer. The two main types of stand persisted until the end of the eighteenth century, when they were superseded by occasional tables. (Plate 11A, B, C).

Knife-case: a container for knives (and other cutlery) introduced in the seventeenth century for use in dining-rooms. Two distinct varieties appeared. (1) Until the later eighteenth century the usual shape was a box with a sloping top and convex front (Plate 9); the interior had divisions for the cutlery. Walnut, shagreen (untanned leather with a roughened surface) and later mahogany, sometimes inlaid, were the main materials. (2) This was succeeded by the graceful vase-shaped case the top of which was raised and lowered on a central stem around which the knife partitions were arranged; this type was designed to stand on a pedestal or at each end of the sideboard. Straight-sided cases were favoured in the early nineteenth century.

Lantern: a container for a candle or candles; portable, fixed to the wall or hung from the ceiling; especially useful for lighting the draughty parts of the house. Early lanterns (*c.* 1500–1700) were made of wood, iron, latten (a yellow alloy of copper and zinc) and brass, the most common filling being horn (whence the Shakespearean 'lanthorn'). After 1700, when glass became more plentiful, lanterns were increasingly fashionable, particularly as they prevented candle-grease from falling about, and their frames, of metal, walnut and mahogany, followed the main decorative modes (Plate 13D). In addition to these more elaborate kinds, simpler lanterns of glass shades, in a variety of forms, were in wide use in the eighteenth century.

Library Steps: found in libraries of large houses after about the middle of the eighteenth century, and of two main kinds: (1) the fixed pair of steps, some with hand-rails, and (2) the folding steps, sometimes ingeniously fitted into other pieces of furniture, such as chairs, stools and tables (Plate 12A, B).

Linen-press: a frame with a wooden spiral screw for pressing linen between two boards, dating from the seventeenth century.

Lobby Chest: defined by Sheraton as 'a kind of half chest of drawers, adapted for the use of a small study, lobby, etc'.

Mirror-stand: an adjustable mirror mounted on a shaft and tripod base, resembling a pole-screen; popular at the end of the eighteenth century.

Music-stand: *see* Canterbury (1) and Desk (2).

Night-table: a pot cupboard which replaced the close-stool after 1750; sometimes also fitted as a washing-stand (q.v.). Among the features commonly found on these pieces may be noted a drawer under the cupboard, a tambour front and a tray top (Plate 16A). Some night-tables were given a triangular shape to fit into a corner.

Papier-mâché: moulded paper pulp used for many small articles and particularly suitable for japanning and polishing; the original process came to England via France from the East as early as the seventeenth century. Considerable stimulus was given to this kind of work in 1772, when Henry Clay of Birmingham, and later London, patented a similar material and began manufacturing various pieces among which trays, boxes, tea-caddies and coasters were prominent.

Pipe-rack: a stand for clay pipes. Of the various wooden kinds in use in the eighteenth century one can distinguish (1) the stand of candlestick form with a tiny circular tray on the stem, pierced with holes for holding the pipes, and (2) the wall rack, either an open frame with notched sides so that the pipes could lie across or a board with shelves from which the pipes hung down (cf. spoon-rack). In addition to these, metal pipe-kilns were widely used from the seventeenth century – iron frames on which the pipes rested, deriving their name from the fact that they could be baked in an oven to clean the pipes.

Pipe-tray: a long and narrow wooden tray with partitions for churchwardens, in use throughout the Georgian period.

Plate-pail: a mahogany container with handle for carrying plates from kitchen to dining-room (often a long journey) in large houses in the eighteenth century; of various shapes, generally circular with one section left open for ease of access (Plate 10B).

Pole-screen: *see* Fire-screen (1).

Sconce: a general name for a wall-light consisting of a back-plate and either a tray or branched candle-holders. Metal seems to have been the chief material from later medieval times until the end of the seventeenth century when looking-glass became fashionable for back-plates (and when 'girandole' was another name for these pieces). The use of looking-glass meant that sconces tended to follow the same decorative trends as contemporary mirrors, but metal back-plates continued to be made, and for a period after 1725 there was a preference for carved and gilt wood and gesso-work, often without looking-glass. About 1750 sconces provided some of the freest interpretation of the asymmetrical rococo mode, either with looking-glass in a scrolled frame, or in carved and gilt wood only; Chinese features were often blended with the rococo. In contrast, the sconces of the Adam period had delicate classical ornament in gilt wood or in composition built up round a wire frame. Cut-glass sconces were in vogue at the end of the century (Plate 13A, B, C).

Secretaire (or **Secretary**): the name somewhat loosely applied to different kinds of writing furniture of which two small varieties call for mention here. (1) At the end of the seventeenth century appeared the small bureau mounted on legs or stand, very similar to the contemporary desk on stand (q.v.) (Plate 16c). This kind seems to have been designed for ladies' use, and sometimes had a looking-glass at the top. (2) In the late eighteenth century large numbers of light and graceful secretaires were made, one popular kind taking the form of a small table with tapering legs enclosing a drawer and supporting a little stand with drawers and shelf. The stand, which was used as a small bookshelf, was often provided with a handle so that it could be lifted off. This type of table was also known as a cheveret.

Shelves: taken here to refer to hanging or standing shelves without doors, for books, plate and china. Small oak shelves of the Tudor period were square in shape; while arcaded tops appeared in the early seventeenth century. Carving was the chief decoration, and this became more ornate after 1660. It is probable that many walnut shelves were made, but few of these seem to have survived. It was at this time that shelves were used for displaying china; a fashion which continued into the early eighteenth century, but was then replaced by that of keeping china in cabinets and cupboards. Open shelves, however, returned to favour in the Chippendale period, when they were often decorated in the Chinese taste, and had fretted sides and galleries. Simple, light shelves were generally in vogue in the later eighteenth century (Fig. 1), for books or china; Sheraton emphasized that shelves should be light enough for ladies to move about and to contain their 'books under present reading'.

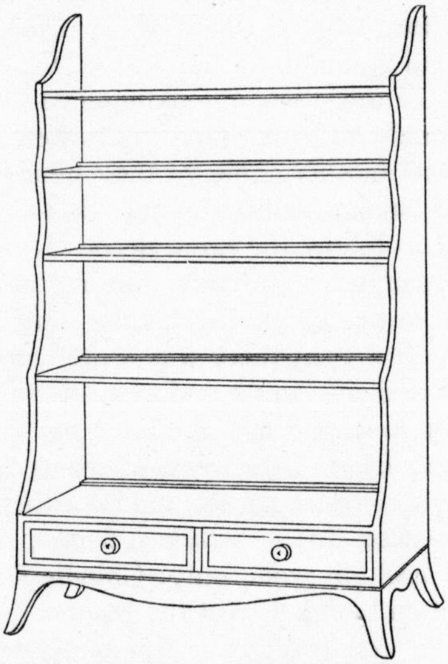

FIG. 1. A set of light SHELVES

Slider: *see* Coaster.

Spoon-rack: a stand for hanging spoons, dating from late Tudor times when metal spoons came into general use. The usual form, until the end of the eighteenth century, resembled a miniature dresser – a wooden board with small slotted shelves for spoons, and, attached to it at the bottom, a box for knives and forks.

Straw-work: a method of decorating furniture, particularly smaller pieces, with tiny strips of bleached and coloured straws to form landscapes, geometrical patterns, etc. This craft came to England from the Continent towards the end of the seventeenth century and was centred at Dunstable. There was a big increase in output during the Napoleonic Wars, when French prisoners, many of whom were craftsmen who had been conscripted into the French Navy, decorated articles in this way during their captivity in England. Among the chief pieces thus decorated were tea-caddies, desks and boxes.

FIG. 2. Rectangular TEA-CADDY

Tea-caddy and Tea-chest: a small box for storing tea. 'Tea-chest' was the common name for this piece from the end of the seventeenth century, when tea-drinking was introduced, until the second half of the eighteenth century, when 'caddy', a corruption of 'kati', a Malay measure of weight of just over one pound, came into general use. The custom of

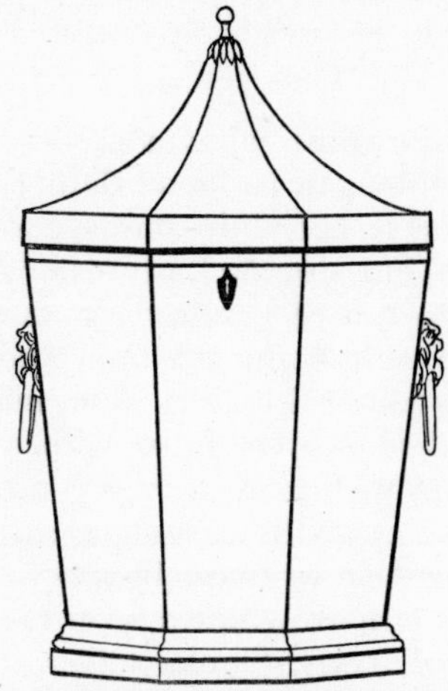

FIG. 3. Octagonal TEA-CADDY

locking up the family's tea in a box continued long after tea had ceased to be an expensive luxury; caddies, therefore, were invariably provided with locks, and were either divided into small compartments or were fitted with canisters (q.v.) for the different kinds of tea. A great variety of materials was used in their construction, including woods of all kinds – carved, inlaid, veneered, painted or decorated with tortoise-shell, ivory, straw-work (q.v.), Tunbridge ware (q.v.), etc – metal (silver in the best examples) and papier-mâché (q.v.). There was also considerable diversity in shape, from rectangular (Fig. 2) to square and octagonal (Fig. 3); while vase and pear (Fig. 4) forms were introduced after 1750.

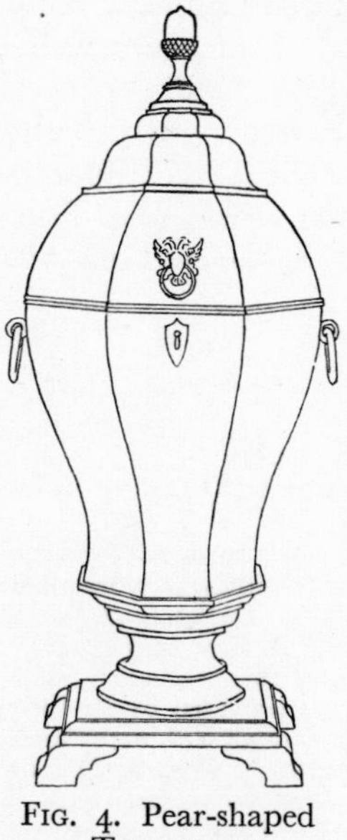

FIG. 4. Pear-shaped TEA-CADDY

Tea-canister: the container for tea in the caddy (if the latter were not already divided into compartments); made of glass, metal or earthenware; usually bottle-shaped until *c.* 1750, and vase-shaped later.

Teapot-stand: *see* Kettle-stand.

Toilet Mirror (or **Dressing-glass**): a small mirror designed to stand on a table or, in early examples, to hang on the wall. This kind of mirror was a luxury in the medieval and Tudor periods, and did not begin to come into wider use until the late seventeenth century. Post-Restoration mirrors were usually square in shape, and frequently had their frames decorated with stump-work; they stood by means of a strut or hung by a ring. By about 1700 oblong mirrors with arched tops, in narrower moulded frames, veneered or japanned, had begun to replace the square shape. In the eighteenth century several changes occurred. Shortly after 1700 appeared the mirror supported by screws in uprights mounted on a box stand; the box was often in the form of a flap or desk above a drawer which contained the many toilet requisites of the time; the mirror had a pronounced arched heading at first, and the front of the box was sometimes serpentine in form. The older type of strut support, without the box stand, continued to be made, however, and occasionally a stand with small trestle feet was found. By 1750 mahogany was in general use for toilet mirrors, though some in the Chinese style were gilt or japanned. Simpler designs were introduced in the neo-classical period; mirror frames, in mahogany or satinwood, were often of oval or shield shape, and the uprights were curved to correspond. The stand was also a simpler arrangement, as toilet articles were now placed in the table on which the mirror stood. At the very end of the century and later, a wide oblong mirror was fashionable, and was usually swung on turned uprights. Mahogany and rosewood, often decorated with stringing, were the chief woods for such mirrors at this time.

Torchère: *see* Candle-stand.

Tray: for food, tea-things, plates, etc; also known as a voider (the medieval term for a tray which was still in use in late Georgian times). Tea-trays (or 'tea-boards') were introduced in the late seventeenth century, and most of them were japanned; none, however, seem to have survived. Japanned trays were still popular in the middle of the eighteenth century, though by then ornamental mahogany trays with fretted borders were being made. Later, oval trays decorated with fine inlay were in vogue. About 1800 there was a considerable production of trays in japanned metal and papier-mâché.

Tunbridge Ware: a special form of inlay which developed at Tunbridge Wells *c.* 1650, employing minute strips of wood, in a great variety of natural colours, to build up geometrical patterns and, later, floral decoration, landscape scenes, etc; used for boxes, trays, desks, tea-caddies, etc.

Urn-stand: *see* Kettle-stand.

Washing-stand (or **Basin-stand**): specially adapted for bedroom use after 1750, and of two main kinds. (1) A tripod stand with three uprights, a circular top fitted with a basin, and a central triangular shelf with a drawer (or drawers) and receptacle for soap (Plate 10D). A four-legged version of this type was also made. (2) A cupboard or chest of drawers on four legs with a basin sunk in the top, the latter covered by a lid or folding flaps.

What-not: a portable stand with four uprights enclosing shelves, in use after about 1800 for books, ornaments, etc.

Wine Cistern (or **Cooler**): a case for wine bottles, very similar to a cellaret (q.v.), but normally larger, without a lid and designed to contain ice or water for cooling the wine. Bowl-shaped wooden cisterns on feet or stand were lined with lead and came into wide use after *c.* 1730 (Plate 14A); stone and metal (especially silver) cisterns were also found. At the end of the century the tub form, with hoops of brass, was general.

Work-table: the name usually applied to the special table made in the second half of the eighteenth century for ladies' needlework, etc. In Sheraton's time these tables were of several kinds; some, mounted on four tapered and reeded legs or on trestle feet, might include, in addition to a drawer, such fittings as a pouch for the work materials, an adjustable fire-screen and a writing-board or slide. Another type, the 'French Work-table', was a tray on trestle feet with a shelf or shelves below (Plate 14B).

Writing-table: many varieties of small writing-tables can be found dating from the end of the seventeenth century, when they were first introduced. Early examples were made with turned baluster legs and folding tops, and were frequently used also as side- and card-tables. Gate-legs were usual (Plate 15B), and some were fitted with a drawer. Decoration with marquetry was often found (Plate 15A, C). In the early eighteenth century small knee-hole writing-tables were popular, with tiers of narrow drawers on each side of the central recess. Similar tables, it may be noted, were also used as dressing-tables, and it is not always possible to determine their exact purpose. After the introduction of mahogany, when the fashion arose for larger pedestal tables in libraries, many versions of the convenient lighter table continued to be made. It was at the end of the century that perhaps the most elegant kinds of these smaller tables were seen, frequently of satinwood. Some closely resembled contemporary secretaires and cheverets; others were fitted with an adjustable board for writing and with a screen.

BOOKS FOR FURTHER READING

The most comprehensive work on small furniture (and for furniture generally), and immensely useful for all students of the subject, is the *Dictionary of English Furniture*, by P. MacQuoid and R. Edwards (3 vols.); revised edition by R. Edwards, 1954.

A good short introduction is provided by R. Fastnedge's *English Furniture Styles* (1955), with many interesting extracts from contemporary sources. For the later period M. Jourdain's *Regency Furniture* (1948) is the chief authority. Country furniture is dealt with in F. G. Roe's *English Cottage Furniture* (1950).

The design books by Chippendale, Hepplewhite and Sheraton make many references to the smaller furniture of their periods, while Sheraton's *Cabinet Dictionary* (1803), from which quotations are made in the above chapter, provides a great deal of useful information.

VIENNESE FURNITURE IN THE EIGHTEENTH CENTURY

By Dr FRANZ WINDISCH-GRAETZ

The photographs accompanying this study show examples of furniture from the reigns of the Emperor Charles VI (1711–40), of the Empress Maria Theresa (1740–80) and of the Emperor Josef II (1780–90).[1]

The cultural life of Vienna in the eighteenth century reached a high degree of brilliance, and its traces still determine the character of the city today. The Court, the Church and the nobility contributed to her restoration and embellishment by their extensive rebuilding activities, in which the gentry joined in increasing numbers during the latter half of the century. Celebrated architects, especially Johann Bernhard Fischer v. Erlach (1656–1723), Johann Lucas v. Hildebrandt (1668–1745) and the former's son, Josef Emanuel Fischer v. Erlach (1693–1742), were destined to carry out the typical work of the period.

Vienna was the Emperor's official residence, and as such was the capital of the Holy Roman Empire as well as the capital of the Habsburg territories, which made her one of the most important political centres of Europe at that time. In addition to these political ties, which bound her to all countries, Vienna was also the focal-point of all-round artistic influences. Among them those of the Italian states and their leading art centres should be particularly mentioned, together with those of France.

As the great architects produced their imperial buildings and palaces for the nobility from a synthesis of ideas on secular monumental architecture, so the cabinet-makers evolved their furniture from a similar synthesis of ideas. Generally speaking, research has failed so far to trace the names of well-known Viennese craftsmen, as is the case in other countries.[2] With the help of illustrations we can now follow up the development of Viennese furniture.

Plate 17A: Writing-table with two Vase Stands (guéridons); Hofburg in Vienna. Height (of back), 116 cm.; width, 110 cm.; depth, 68 cm. Tin, brass, tortoise-shell and ebony; first quarter of the eighteenth century.

The ornamentation of rich foliage, scroll-work and palmettes corresponds to the French style propagated by Jean Bérain (1640–1711). The technique of using tortoise-shell inlay in connexion with metal is a form of decoration developed to perfection by André Charles Boulle (1642–1732), and was therefore named after him.

The style of Bérain also spread to Austria, so much so that his decorative treatment became the characteristic feature of the first four decades of the eighteenth century. This period was ruled entirely by his influence. His ideas were universally adopted for every kind of ornamentation and material, whether stucco or furniture intarsia. But the Boulle technique was restricted to the Court and to the highest circles of the nobility and the Church.

In fact, when it concerned an important order, Vienna so far recognized the artistic superiority and leadership of France as to submit to her influence in that respect. She thus showed her unbiased attitude to art even though the political relationship between the two countries was anything but cordial. The Imperial Court, and above all the Emperor himself, was on bad terms with France, particularly during the reign of Leopold I (1658–1705). The reason for this was the perpetual difficulties which Imperial policy had to meet from that quarter.

Though the décor is French, there is something fundamentally Viennese about the simplicity of construction, wherein all the usual sumptuousness of Paris is eliminated. This will be noticeable again in other examples.

Plate 24A and 24C: Furniture from the Schlosshof. These well-known pieces, of which the majority have remained intact in the Museum für angewandte Kunst and in the government furniture depository in Vienna, form part of the original contents of the hunting-lodge – the Schlosshof – near Vienna. This magnificent castle was designed by the celebrated architect Johann Lucas v. Hildebrandt, who had it built by order of Prince Eugene of Savoy during the years 1725–29. Its contents are probably of the same date or a little later; possibly *c.* 1730.

Armchair with high back (Plate 24A): overall height, 126 cm.; height of seat, 43 cm.; front width, 66 cm.; depth, 56 cm. Walnut. Side-chair (Plate 24C): overall height, 100 cm.; height of seat, 50 cm.; front width, 50 cm.; depth, 47 cm. Walnut. Stool (Plate 24C): height, 47 cm.; width and depth, 44 cm. Walnut, re-covered; *c.* 1730.

These pieces reveal the extensive artistic horizon and extravagant taste of the princely owner of the Schlosshof. His foreign origin, his knowledge of the world and his patronages are reflected in the French (Plate 24A) and Italian (Plate 24C) influence in the form and in the exquisite manner of execution. The ideas are derived from the leading art centres which propagated the style of the period. The richly ornamented armchair (Plate 24A) is somewhat conservative and essentially of the beginning of the century. There are innumerable closely related examples in France. The other two (Plate 24C) have a more modern look about them, and their imaginative construction resembles Italian workmanship. It must be remembered that the contemporary furniture of Italy and France (of the 'Regence') is, on the whole, more pompous, more richly carved and more elaborately adorned with figure motifs, than the native Austrian.

Vienna, as the capital city of the Empire, could afford to allow those foreign ideas expression because her native talent and influence were strong enough to turn them to her own uses as and when she wished. She came to develop her great baroque architecture by the same process.

Plate 18A: Library Table with four Chairs. These are at the Oesterreichisches Museum für angewandte Kunst, Vienna. The four chairs, with their collapsible backs, can be drawn out of the hollow body of the table side. The corresponding parts of the table are attached to the back of each chair. Height, 82 cm.; length, 159 cm.; width, 112 cm. of the table top. Length, 137 cm.; width, 92 cm. of the lower plinth. Predominantly walnut. The lighter inlay of the table top is of maple, showing a checkered pattern and the inscription 'charitas'; date *c.* 1735.

This is part of a particularly beautiful suite of the Baroque period. The table belonged to the library set of the old University in Vienna.[3] The ceiling of the great apartment still shows the old fresco displaying the various branches of science in allegorical representations. It is signed and dated 'Anton Herzog, 1734'. The side walls were covered with bookcases from the ceiling to the floor, and the upper rows were accessible from a richly ornamented gallery.

But the interior architectural composition would not have been complete had only the ceiling and the walls been considered in the scheme. The furniture was to be so constructed as to correspond. It was made massive to match the solemn architecture. The great library table is made to look like an altar and resembles a sarcophagus, as was often the case with Baroque altars.

The idea of constructing such a table is in keeping with the typical Baroque conception of associating the real world with the world of

(A)

(A) Writing-table with two vase stands (guéridons) in the Boulle manner. First quarter of the eighteenth century. *Hofburg, Vienna.*

(B)

(B) Corner cupboard of the Baroque period, walnut and cherry inlay, *c.* 1735–40. *Palais Harrach, Vienna.*

(C)

(C) Small bombé commode, 'Palisander' ormolu mounts, *c.* 1750. *Palais Czernin, Vienna.*

PLATE 17

(A) Library table with four chairs, from the old University Library in Vienna, *c.* 1735. *Oesterreichisches Museum für angewandte Kunst, Vienna.*

(B) Armchair and small table, carved, white-gold mounts, *c.* 1770. *Oesterreichisches Museum für angewandte Kunst, Vienna.*

(A) Dressing-table in cherry, *c.* 1760. *Palais Schwarzenberg, Vienna.*

(B) Commode of the period of Josef II, with Italian style inlay. 'Palisander', *c.* 1780–90. *Palais Schwarzenberg, Vienna.*

(A) Upholstered walnut settee, after 1740. *Palais Schönborn, Vienna.*

(B) Rococo settee in beech, walnut stained, *c.* 1755. *Palais Czernin, Vienna.*

(A) Low armchairs, beech, carved and gilded (re-covered), *c.* 1750. *Palais Harrach, Vienna.*

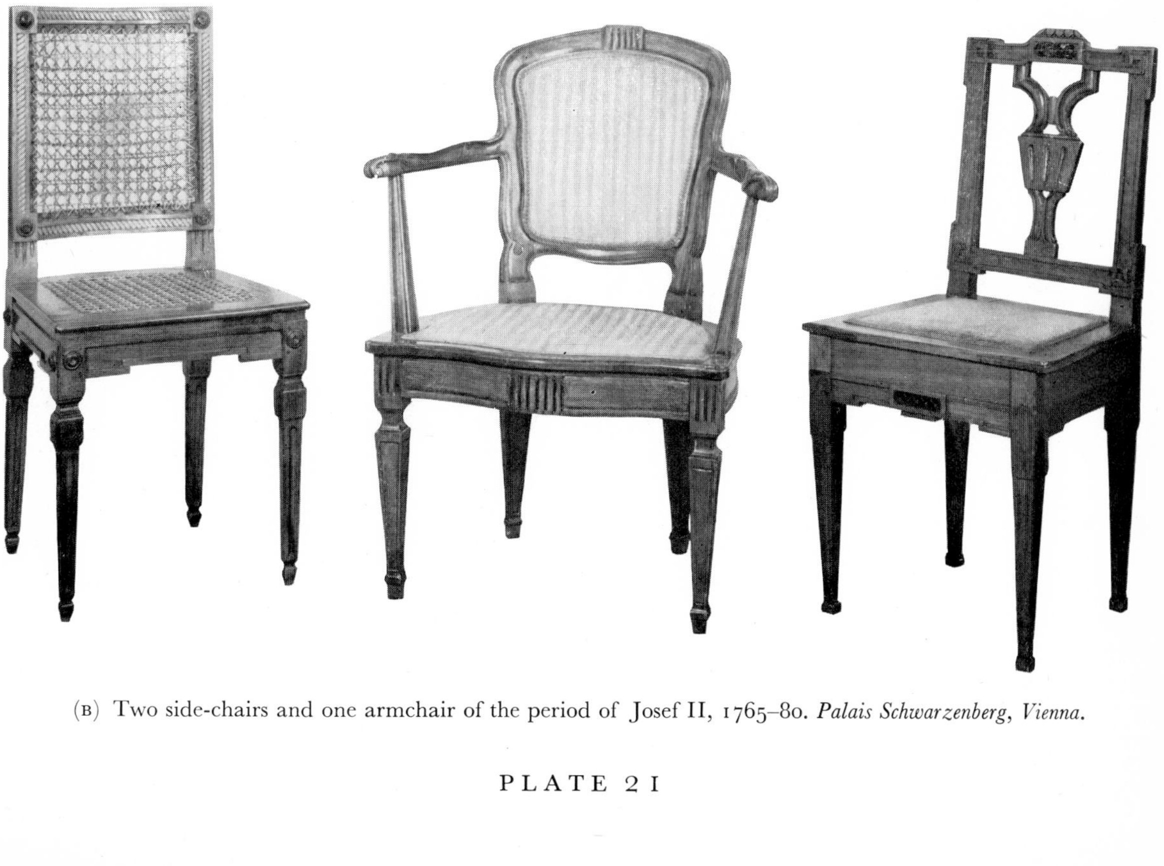

(B) Two side-chairs and one armchair of the period of Josef II, 1765–80. *Palais Schwarzenberg, Vienna.*

PLATE 21

(A) Wardrobe of the latter Baroque period in walnut and maple, 'Palisander', engraved décor, before 1740. *Oesterreichisches Museum für angewandte Kunst, Vienna.*

(B) Secretaire commode with pediment ('tabernacle-cabinet'), walnut inlay, *c.* 1735. *Oesterreichisches Museum für angewandte Kunst, Vienna.*

PLATE 22

(B) Wardrobe of the period of Josef II in oak and cherry, 1770–80. *Palais Schwarzenberg, Vienna.*

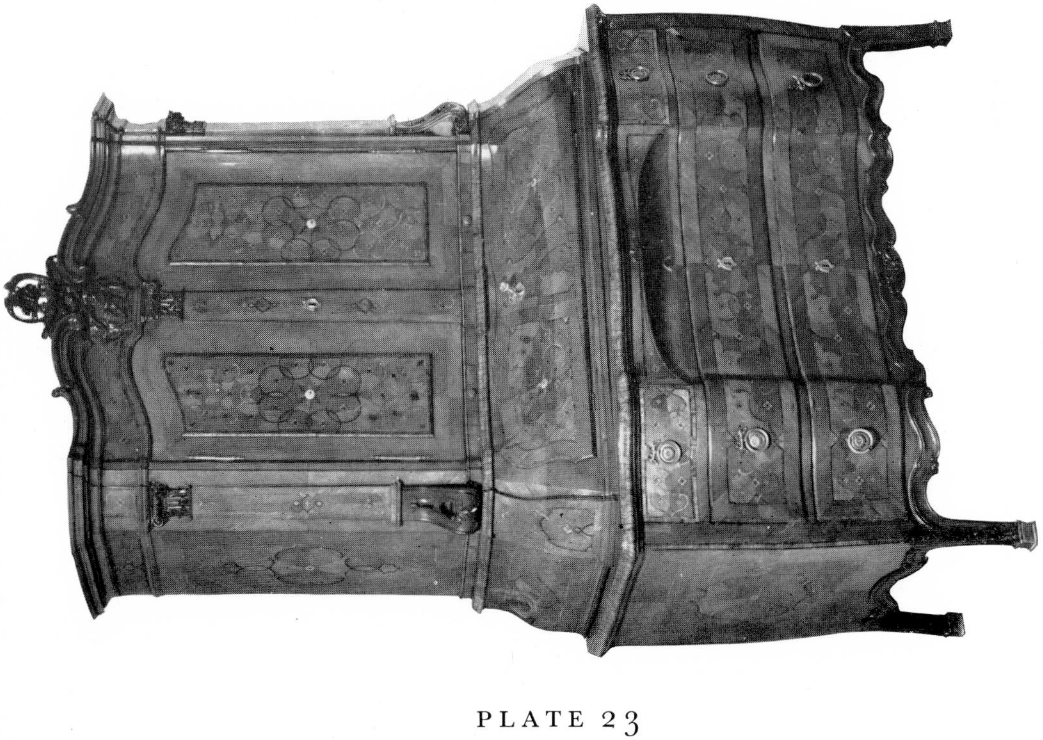

(A) Rococo tall secretaire in alder, with inlay of different kinds of wood, *c.* 1760. *Palais Schwarzenberg, Vienna.*

PLATE 23

(A) Armchair with high back. The property of Prince Eugene of Savoy (from his hunting lodge, the Schlosshof near Vienna), *c.* 1730. Now in the *Oesterreichisches Museum für angewandte Kunst, Vienna.*

(B) Four-post bed. Walnut and maple with engraved decoration, before 1750. *Palais Harrach, Vienna.*

(C) Side-chair and stool, as above (Fig. A).

(D) Side-chair in cherry, gilded ornaments, transition from rococo to the style of Josef II, *c.* 1765. *Palais Czernin, Vienna.*

PLATE 24

ideas. The mythological imagery is so consistently related to real life by the allegorical interpretations in the painted ceiling that the solemn, altar-like shape of the table is inevitably made to blend with their illusionism and theatrical effect. The work which the scholarly artist carries out here under the eyes of his patrons becomes a ritual. It was to heighten the massive effect of the table that the chairs were constructed in such an original fashion. Thus there is nothing at all to disturb the architectural unity of the composition.

In Baroque composition, the nature and peculiarity of the material is of little importance compared to the ingenuity employed to arrive at the desired effect. Everything is entirely subordinated to the artistic and intellectual components of form. Here the wood is cleverly carved to look like the work of a sculptor, an illusion which demands great skill on the part of the cabinet-maker. But when the most ingenious technique is employed at the same time to embellish the surface of the wood in order to show its quality to the best advantage, the idea becomes a contradiction, which is one of the fascinating features of Baroque furniture.

The master craftsman of this table is not known. But since the library belonged to members of a religious order, it is probable that it, like the rest of the furniture in this apartment, was made by lay brothers of the community, as in the majority of similar cases in Austria. Its date of origin probably corresponds to that of the fresco (1734). The structure is in keeping with the architecture of that period, and has all the boldness of form characteristic of the Imperial style of Viennese Baroque introduced by Fischer v. Erlach.

Plate 17B: Corner Cupboard. At the Palais Harrach, Vienna. Height, 275 cm.; overall width, 78 cm.; overall depth, 41 cm. Predominantly walnut, combined with lighter shades of cherry. The lighter inlay, particularly the architectural motifs and the narrow banding on the door of the base section, is of maple; *c.* 1735–40.

This is a particularly original example of the classical style of Viennese Baroque. The composition is based entirely on architectural principles. The components are clearly grouped into sections, which become less heavy towards the top. The plinth is massive and more uniform, the middle section is more broken up by the shape of the recess and the decorative detail of inlaid motifs, which is brought to a head by the mobile design and plasticity of the crowning members.

Observe the varied use of scrolls. In the lowest section they merely serve as a pilaster base, in the main section they become important architectural and decorative components. Yet they are 'edged' and sharp. Only the top section shows the true moulding of a scroll breaking away with a smooth, elegant curve from the massiveness of the rest of the structure. The treatment of the wood is similar to the technique employed in the library table (Plate 18A), especially with regard to the pinnacle. Imaginative ingenuity is of primary importance: the material has to yield to skilful craftsmanship.

The inlay ornaments correspond to essential features of the first third of the century, the fine, clear lines on the door being derived from the banding commonly used. The architectural inlay is also taken from contemporary ideas, and includes the fretted panels of the dome and frieze, lattice-work in the pediment, a silhouetted string of bell-flowers (on the side of the pilasters) and the balustrade design.

Plate 22B: Secretaire Commode with Pediment (tabernacle). In the Oesterreichisches Museum für angewandte Kunst, Vienna. Overall height, 212 cm.; height of commode, 88 cm.; depth of commode (at sides), 59 cm.; depth of pediment (side), 30·5 cm. Walnut; *c.* 1735.

This is in the typical Viennese style of the latter period of Charles VI. The native craftsman uses his discretion when conforming to the general Baroque tendencies of vigorous movement, rich grouping and general usefulness. The last point is particularly well thought out and successfully achieved. This is confirmed by the great popularity of such pieces up to the present day. The bulbous and hollow surface curves are modified, the structure is complete and clearly defined, the inlay motifs are sporadic and full of movement, but not excessively so. This piece of furniture therefore represents a happy medium which distinguishes it as a product of the Imperial capital, where many potentialities and incentives meet and harmonize. With one swing of the pendulum we find influences from the north-east – the Netherlands – showing sometimes greater severity or a heavy, somewhat bombastic unwieldiness. With the other, the more elaborate forms, more costly materials, a profusion of ornaments and a lack of tectonics, often found in Italian and German furniture construction, tend to produce an ostentatious and unbalanced effect. French sumptuousness is also reduced to a happy medium with a certain savour of preciosity.

Plate 22A: Wardrobe of the latter Baroque period. In the Oesterreichisches Museum für angewandte Kunst, Vienna. Height, 226 cm.; width, 182 cm.; depth (side), 63 cm. Walnut and maple with rosewood veneering, graphic decoration; before 1740.

The door-panels are adorned with canopies, foliated scrolls, urns and lambrequins which are typical of the 'Regence'. On closer inspection, however, one notices a curious transformation about them. The foliage is less like a real plant, but more like graphic renderings of carvings. They have lost the realistic style of the beginning of the century. Moreover, there is a new form of moulded bracket (on the pilasters and bottom drawer) that tends to asymmetry. It is one of the first elements of *rocaille* ornamentation that seems to suggest a revival of seventeenth-century ornamentation, but which in fact corresponds to a new sense of movement and spaciousness, with a certain preference for the bizarre. This tendency also becomes apparent in the bulbous and hollow pilasters frequently recurring on very mannered early Baroque wardrobes. The acceptance of these particular decorative effects is a sure sign of a return to Mannerism. And what else, indeed, is the early approach of Rococo, if it is not a mannered, late form of Baroque? There is little change in the general structure of the wardrobe. It still retains all the massiveness, vigorous movement and bold grouping of the Baroque style.

Plate 20A: Upholstered Settee. Palais Schönborn, Vienna. Overall height, 96 cm.; height of seat, 45 cm.; height of arm-support, 79 cm.; length, 203 cm.; depth, 66 cm. Walnut, light gold relief on carvings; after 1740.

Plate 24A and 24C have already shown the extravagant elaboration of the majority of chairs. Their massiveness in particular gave ample scope to the skilled cabinet-maker in exploiting his fancy for a carved, plastic, decorative effect.

In place of earlier forms used by Bérain – palmettes, shells, masks, foliage and bandings – there appears a new motif, resembling shells and breakers, of a whimsical form which is in no way bound to conventions, and can therefore be used in every conceivable combination of ideas. This is the *rocaille* ornament, original and lavish. We now formally approach the Rococo. But the presumptuous appearance of this settee and its dimensions have nothing yet in common with the intimate character of Rococo and still look formal and solemn. In the Palais Harrach there is a wardrobe which is architecturally almost identical with the one shown in Plate 22A. One could well assume that they were both done in the same workshop. The ornaments, too, are engraved in both cases.

Nevertheless, there is the distinct difference that the décor consists of fully developed *rocaille*. At the same time the 'Regence' ornaments in the panels are replaced by figurative details and graceful little scenes adapted from the School of Watteau and his successors. The tester is crowned (Plate 24B) with imaginatively flourished, delicate carvings. All this is typical of Rococo.

There is probably a decade between the two wardrobes. In studying the development of the style of Viennese furniture, it should be observed that the embellishment is in accordance with the principles of the new fashion, whereas the basic structure remains essentially true to Baroque tradition.

Plate 24B: Four-post Bed. Palais Harrach, Vienna. Height of headboards, 202 cm.; width, 157 cm.; height of footboard, 115 cm.; width, 157 cm.; length, 210 cm.; height of canopy (including the 'vase' motif), 263 cm. Predominantly walnut, centre and side panels of maple, bandings of rosewood and maple. All carvings are of lime, walnut stained; posts of walnut, engravings on panels of maple. On the footboard and sides are pastoral scenes of the four seasons – flowers, corn-harvest, fruit and grape gathering, sledging scene. On the headboard is a shepherd and shepherdess representing the Madonna and Child. Its date is *c.* 1750.

This bed is decorated in the same style as the wardrobe in Plate 23B. The two belong together. The engraved ornaments are far more rich, intricate and imaginative than on the older wardrobe (Plate 22A), but not as precise and the figures are more primitive.

Apart from a strong element of rococo in the décor, the whole construction of the bed speaks quite a different language than would have been the fashion during the first four decades of the century. The decisive factor is that the contours have become soft and flowing. It is significant that the shape of the headboard follows the curvilinear movement of the floral design. From now on and during the Rococo period, severe construction gives way to an easy flowing outline which links up the *rocaille* ornamentation with a realistic treatment of floral motifs, and this is the most distinctive feature of the style of Rococo furniture. The turned members of the posts are characteristic of Viennese conservatism, a seventeenth-century motif.

Austrian furniture is rarely found to be so true to the French style of Rococo as to correspond to it both in construction and decorative treatment. As a rule, the French influence is restricted to the ornamentation, but is found there in great measure and a variety of ways. The Rococo period produced some of the finest and most successfully constructed examples of Viennese eighteenth-century furniture, and they still remain popular. The structure has not changed much, but the general appearance is softer and more graceful than it used to be. There is a strong international element about those period pieces that have more in common with the French style. This is only to be expected, as they belonged to a cosmopolitan and cultured section of the society. All the same, they are not excluded from this study.

Plate 21A: Open Armchairs. Palais Harrach, Vienna. (Left to right): Overall height, 87 cm.; height of seat, 42 cm.; front width, 62 cm.; depth, 53 cm. Overall height, 93 cm.; height of seat, 42 cm.; front width, 66 cm.; depth, 54 cm. Overall height, 85 cm.; height of seat, 42 cm.; front width, 60 cm.; depth, 53 cm. Beech, carved and gilded, recovered; date *c.* 1750. Observe the straight back of the centre chair and the curved hollowed one of the two others made to fit the figure of the occupant. The one in the centre therefore looks stiffer and more old fashioned. Another interesting point is the elegant continuity of the design, the *rocaille* ornament and realistic floral décor being in keeping with the whole construction. The latter is more typically Austrian than French in its ponderous and solid style.

Plate 17C: Small Bombé Commode. Palais Czernin, Vienna. Height, 95 cm.; overall width, 67 cm. diminishing to 40 cm. Rosewood of various kinds and colouring. Very fine ormolu mounts; *c.* 1750. Here the French influence is decidedly marked in the quality of the wood, the construction and finish of the mounts and the graceful contours of the body of the furniture. The swelling curve of the outline gives it a realistic, lively and unusual appearance.

Plate 20B: Rococo Settee. Palais Czernin, Vienna. Overall height, 94 cm.; height of seat, 40 cm.; overall width, 144 cm.; depth, 48 cm. Beech, walnut stained, caned seat and back; *c.* 1755. Compared with earlier examples, this piece of furniture is very typically Viennese in its simplicity and unpretentiousness. It is well balanced and elegant. The parallel spacing that runs all along between the edge of the seat and the back, from one arm-support to the other, accentuates the neatness. The moulded arm-support is made to resemble a small cushion and shows great originality.

Lacquer was a painting medium of great popularity in other countries – particularly in Italy where it produced some of the most enchanting results so typical of Venetian Rococo – but apparently found little support in Austria and Vienna. Neither are there many pieces extant which were decorated with lacquered work. There is one example where two table tops of the second quarter of the eighteenth century are decorated with flowers and chinoiserie of painted lacquer. They belong to a set of furniture from the porcelain room in the Palais Dubsky, Brünn.[4, 5] Not only are they carved and gilded, but small porcelain plaques are inserted into the wood. This was another very favourite decorative fancy for furniture at that time. In this case there are floral miniatures made by the Du Paquier porcelain factory in Vienna. The rare and costly material of these delicately coloured insertions raised the price of the furniture much above the usual. (In Venice, the town renowned for the finest glass, cut plate-glass was used to decorate furniture by the same method.) Although the set belonged to Brünn (it is now the property of the Museum für angewandte Kunst, Vienna), it can be assumed with certainty that most of the workmanship is Viennese.

There is another lacquered piece of a later date, in the same museum, which must originally have come from Austria, perhaps Vienna – a secretaire with a small cabinet on top, signed and dated *P. Georgius Henner e S.I. Anno* 1788. It shows very fine paintings of flowers, animals and allegorical figures in gold-framed fields, representing the four continents. The great beauty and originality of this piece makes up for the rare use of this technique in Vienna.[6]

Plate 23A: Rococo Tall Secretaire. Palais Schwarzenberg, Vienna. Overall height, 225 cm.; height of commode, 88 cm.; front width, 135 cm.; depth, 66 cm. Larger areas of alder, dark inlay of 'Palisander', light inlay of rosewood, cornice bordered with olive-wood, mounts of a later date; *c.* 1760.

Here is a curious example, but typically Viennese, where the characteristic style of Rococo and the traditions of Baroque are combined. The first is noticeable in the carvings on the upper section and on the curved apron below. But it is above all marked in the shape and contours of the furniture itself, the kettle-shape of the sides, the serpentine front.

The endeavour to render the piece as generally useful as possible is traditional, in contrast to France where furniture is usually made for a specific purpose. The cabinet is furnished with drawers and compartments of many different sizes. To allow enough room for them, this section was made more massive. This gives it a slightly unbalanced appearance, but it is just that utility of the upper section which renders it so typically Viennese. The pilaster bases of the cabinet are again bulbous and hollow, like those of the Baroque wardrobe (Plate 22A), and this time even pierced. The interlaced rings and quatrefoil design are interesting features. The latter was a favourite French ornament of the style of Louis XVI. Should this and the strictly geometrical circles suggest perhaps the approaching change of style and diversion from the bizarrerie of Rococo? The use of native, less costly woods is another pointer in that direction. The mounts are already typically Josef II.

Plate 19A: Dressing-table. Palais Schwarzenberg, Vienna. Height, 77 cm.; length, 94 cm.; depth, 53 cm. Cherry, cross-banded in plum wood. The centre of the top opens to display a mirror, the side members folding over to the left and right, uncovering two partitions of which one is deeper than the other. Its date is *c.* 1760.

The reigns of Maria Theresa and Josef II are marked by the reforms of both rulers. Josef II could never have become the reformer except for the first and probably decisive impulse given him by his Imperial mother. Both the liberal education he received from her and the example of her initial reforms in particular had a bearing on his later course of action. In fact, just as the reforms of Maria Theresa served to prepare for those of Josef II, so in the sphere of art the one reign led on to the other. The new style, named after the young Emperor, had already been initiated long before his reign, during the lifetime of his mother.

The reforms had a far-reaching effect on class distinction and social developments, including the standard of living and social customs. They are, therefore, found to have left as strong a mark on furniture and domestic arrangements. The appreciation of practical usefulness, simplicity and excellence, together with the tendency to give first consideration and prominence to everything native, is very much in evidence. The example (Plate 19A) shows this so clearly that comment is almost superfluous. The preference given to native products is found in the choice of woods employed. But this dressing-table is still essentially Rococo, and therefore of the period of Maria Theresa. A notable point is that the table edges and the legs appear to be inseparable, in each case one merges into the other. The usual rules of furniture construction normally applicable to these two component parts are here concealed in order to fulfil the aesthetic purpose of an easy flowing outline.

Another similar example is in the government furniture depository, a writing-desk which is said to have been used by the Emperor Josef II. The simplicity of design in combination with the principles of tradition and the use of cherry wood, all confirm what has already been said.[7]

Plate 24D: Side-chair. Palais Czernin, Vienna. Overall height, 98 cm.; height of seat, 50 cm.; width, 47 cm.; depth, 45 cm. Cherry, the carvings gilded; *c.* 1765. The curious thing about this is the combination of two styles in the construction and décor. The shape of the back is Rococo (Venetian influence?), so is the modest *rocaille* ornamentation. Yet the front legs and the decoration generally are typically Josef II.

Plate 18B: Open Armchair and Small Table. Oesterreichisches Museum für angewandte Kunst, Vienna. Overall height, 106 cm.; height of seat, 44 cm.; width, 68 cm.; depth, 58 cm. Height of table, 81 cm.; length, 89 cm.; width, 55 cm.; *c.* 1770. This set belonged to the Schlosshof, which, as has been said, was owned by Prince Eugene of Savoy. In 1775 it was bought by Maria Theresa, and in 1760 was rebuilt, enlarged and partly refurnished for the requirements of the Court.

The century-old differences between the two Courts and governments of Vienna and Paris were brought to an end at the treaty of alliance between Austria and France in 1756. Doubtless this also paved the way for a closer relationship between their culture and art, so that Vienna was much more ready to accept the artistic attitude of Paris from then onwards. This is evident in this set of furniture. The ornamentation is typically Louis XVI. But it must be remembered that Austria's classical tendencies were also to a great extent influenced by Italy, since Italy's ties with Vienna were as strong then as they had been before.

Now and again the habitual over-elaboration of the Baroque and Rococo ornamentation of the Imperial style continues to prevail as it is applied to the new decoration. The varied use of small detail and accumulation of motifs have little in common with the decorative treatment of French furniture. There the ornamentation is more discreet and delicate. These examples therefore mark a stage of transition to the more simple style of Josef II.

Plate 21B: Two Side-chairs and One Armchair. Palais Schwarzenberg, Vienna. (Left to right): Overall height, 91 cm.; height of seat, 46 cm.; front width, 43 cm.; depth, 42 cm. Mainly walnut, the turned members framing the back of lime. Writing armchair: overall height, 88 cm.; height of seat, 41·5 cm.; front width, 60 cm.; depth, 51 cm. Beech, walnut stained. Side-chair: Overall height, 91 cm.; height of seat, 45 cm.; front width, 45 cm.; depth, 41 cm. Cherry. Small carvings in a dark, painted softwood; *c.* 1765–80.

With these chairs we have reached the period of Josef II. The back of the centre chair may still show some form peculiar to Rococo, but the general design has no longer anything in common with the past. One of the most important features of the new style, and one that already determined the form of the two previous examples (Plate 24D and Plate 18B), is the manner in which the seat and legs are conjoined. There is no more of that easy flowing continuation and concealment shown in Plate 19A. The useful purpose of the seat, to carry weight, and its support are well defined in the structural design. The individual components of the piece of furniture are clearly differentiated.

The writing arm-chair in particular shows

that they were no longer interested in a coherent, continuing outline, though all the past had led in that direction. The joint of the arms and seat is obvious enough in the hard effect of the two supports. How different it would have been had it been Rococo!

The chair shown on the right of Plate 21B has a particularly interesting back. Its form shows a strong tendency to imitate the English style of Hepplewhite. But the result is coarser and heavier, in accordance with Viennese-Austrian preference for massiveness, plasticity and volume, though these attributes are by no means to be associated with stockiness or clumsiness, which is important. On the contrary, there is something graceful about it. In those days, English influence won more and more support in every sphere, and is, moreover, also expressed here in the desire to preserve the particular quality and beauty of the wood.

Plate 23B: Wardrobe. Palais Schwarzenberg, Vienna. Height, 208 cm.; width, 163 cm.; depth, 64 cm. Highly polished, solid oak with inlays of cherry and 'Palisander' (instead of ebony) and walnut. Carvings of solid oak; *c.* 1770–80.

There is here still much of the Baroque wardrobe: the pilasters on the corner edges and the centre piece, the solid base and cornice. But details are altered in accordance with the new style. This is particularly obvious in the cornice. The easy flowing composition of the top mouldings of Baroque and Rococo wardrobes is here converted into a straight crown of dentil moulding, which is far removed from the variety of shells and carvings. The panels also are no longer filled with interlaced designs. The main idea is to display the beauty of different kinds of wood in a framed décor. Veneering is so applied as to accentuate the grain of the wood at its best. Light-coloured, native wood is again in evidence.

Plate 19B: Commode. Palais Schwarzenberg, Vienna. Height, 87 cm.; width, 122 cm.; depth, 58 cm. Larger areas in 'Palisander', cross-banded with rose-wood, maple and dark-stained wood inlay; *c.* 1780–90.

The structural element and decorative treatment of this commode display features rarely found in Vienna. It is a pretentious piece of furniture, and the décor is distinctly Italian. There, and particularly in Lombardy, it was a common thing to find such a delicate, extravagant and somewhat sensuous form of classicism. It should be remembered that Lombardy was then a part of Austria and Vienna was always in close contact with her Italian provinces. Therefore the commode is another apt example of the liberal and unbiased attitude of the Habsburg capital in its relationship to all its peoples. Indeed, it was only to be expected that all the different trends which the cultural life of the monarchy had to offer should be reflected in one of the noblest estates of the land.

This survey of Viennese furniture, which concludes with the description of this period piece, was intended to cover the particular era of the eighteenth century which began when the spirit of Baroque and its influence on intellectual and social values was at its highest, and which ended when these were gradually giving way to the new trends of the emancipation and Classical period. The fundamental principles which led to the intellectual and social changes have been traced, and their tendency to move away from the rule of an hierarchical authority in order to make room for a natural, individual common-sense expression.

Just as the simplicity of Viennese furniture strikes us in comparison with the contemporary workmanship of other countries, so the very refusal to submit to an exaggerated pomp and refinement, together with the desire to reproduce the natural beauty of a well-balanced design, contributes most to its particular charm. Surely it is no mere coincidence to find this tendency most marked during the reign of so maternal a ruler as Maria Theresa, when furniture was constructed in a happy, gracious manner to suit the home and family in their intimate surroundings. This has remained a salient feature of Viennese furniture ever since.

NOTES

[1] Since 1765, German Emperor and co-ruler with his mother, Maria Theresa, his influence affected all the

activities of his subjects, and was as strongly felt in the sphere of culture.

[2] The two most important publications on Viennese furniture, though limited to time and subject-matter, are: Eduard Leisching (Vienna), *Theresianischer und Josephinischer Stil, Kunst und Kunsthandwerk*, XV, 1912, pp. 493–563 (Verlag von Artaria, Vienna). Also published in a separate issue (Staatsdruckerei, Vienna, 1912). Marianne Zweig, *Wiener Bürgermöbel aus Theresianischer und Josephinischer Zeit* (1740–90), Kunstverlag Anton Schroll, Vienna, 1921.

[3] Before its new erection on the Ring (1873–83), the University was housed in the extensive buildings of the Jesuit College, and the Jesuits were in charge of it until their religious order was dissolved in 1773. The library of this University was, therefore, also one of the most important of this order in Austria, and in its artistic excellence was clearly meant to compete with other beautiful monastic libraries in the country.

[4] The entire room, including the windows, doors, wainscoting, chimney (of porcelain) and the complete set of furniture were removed and re-installed in the Oesterreichische Museum für angewandte Kunst in Vienna.

[5] Julius Leisching (Brünn), *Das Brünner Porzellanzimmer aus Dubsky'schem Besitze*, Kunst und Kunsthandwerk, XVI, 1913, pp. 281–99 (Verlag von Artaria, Vienna).

[6] Eduard Leisching (Vienna), *Neuerwerbungen des K.K. Oesterreichischen Museums Seit Kriegsbeginn*, Kunst und Kunsthandwerk, XIX, 1916, pp. 185, 210, 215 (Verlag von Artaria, Vienna).

[7] Marianne Zweig, *Wiener Bürgermöbel*, *op. cit.* (note 2) Plate 49, p. 26.

The author wishes to acknowledge the help and assistance of his sister Princess Mathilde Windisch-Graetz in the translation of this article.

GARDEN STATUARY AND FURNITURE

By HUGH HONOUR

CHASTE sphinxes, monitory gods and goddesses, over-indulged putti, coy country maidens and leering satyrs, all delicately mossed and lichened, people our more formal parks and gardens where, like foreign trees, they have been naturalized to the English soil and climate. Pedestalled beneath dripping beeches or niched in obscure yew hedges, the "Apollo Belvedere" and the "Venus de Medici" guard the northern arcadia of which they form so important and so delightful a part. Never so numerous as in Italy, they look perhaps a little lonely for, as Hugh May told Pepys, 'a little mixture of statues and pots which may be handsome' is sufficient to ornament a garden. Too dense a population can only give an impression of vulgarity as at Timon's villa where, according to Pope:

The suffering eye inverted nature sees,
Trees cut as Statues, Statues thick as trees;
With here a fountain never to be played;
And there a Summer-house, that knows no shade;
Here Amphitrite sails thro' myrtle bow'rs;
There Gladiators fight, or die in flow'rs;
Unwater'd see the drooping seahorse mourn,
And swallows roost in Nilus' dusty urn.

The phrase garden statuary is inclined to given an impression of a minor art, practised by masons rather than sculptors. It should, however, be remembered that much sculpture of the highest order was intended to grace the garden. In England, as well as in France, Italy and Germany, the best sculptors of the day were commissioned for such works. Bernini's *Neptune*, in the Victoria & Albert Museum, and Giovanni Bologna's *Samson and the Philistine*, in the same collection, were both designed as the centre-pieces of fountains for private gardens. It was for Fontainebleau that Benvenuto Cellini designed his *Colossus*, and Giovanni Bologna erected his giant *Appenino* in the garden of the Villa Pratolino. Versailles is peopled with figures by Pierre Le Gros, Girardon, G. B. Foggini and Bernini; the walks of Vietshöchheim are lined by the grotesques of Ferdinand Dietz. Any full history of garden sculpture would have to take all these names into account, in addition to treating of the myriad figures produced in every European country by anonymous or forgotten artists. Here we are principally concerned with Britain, where garden sculpture was never as important and rarely as fantastic as it was abroad. We have nothing to parallel the superb group of Diana and Acteon, which stands in the lake at Caserta, acting as the central point of the gardens; we have no vast water-ramps headed with a Parnassus of mythological beings as at Caprarola, nothing to compare with Antonio Bonazza's walks lined with mondaine Venetian actors at Bagnoli di Sopra. There is no British garden like Bomarzo where gigantic elephants, rhinoceroses and nightmarish monsters dwarf the ilexes. 'A little mixture of statues and pots' has generally been preferred.

ENGLISH GARDEN SCULPTURE

Garden statuary first became popular in England in the sixteenth century. When Henry VIII took over Hampton Court in 1526, he set about the transformation of the royal privy garden for which he ordered thirty-eight stone statues of kings and queens, a quantity of dragons, lions, greyhounds, harts and unicorns, sixteen of the 'King's Beasts' and sixteen sundials – all to be crowded into an area of but a few acres, which must, as Mr Dutton remarks, 'have resembled a heraldic zoo'. The fashion for this form of statuary in wood and stone appears to have been current throughout the century and to have diminished only with the introduction of a more classical taste in the Stuart period. Nicholas Stone the elder supplied statues of Cupid, Venus, Ceres, Hercules and Mercury for the Paston family in 1632. But it was not until after the Restoration that the great age of the formal garden, and consequently of garden sculpture, dawned. A neat geometrical lay-out intersected with balustrades provided excellent opportunities for the placing of statues, sundials, urns and fountains, but, as Sir William Temple remarked in his essay *Upon the Gardens of Epicurus* (*c.* 1680), 'good statues are in the reach of few men, and common ones are generally and justly despised and neglected'. As the century drew to its close, these enclosures were superseded by the landscaped parks modelled on Le Nôtre's Versailles, and great urns were much used to terminate the vistas hacked through the woods. Figures were placed on the parterre, and occasionally used to give interest to a general scheme. Elaborate fountains, like that at Blenheim (a small copy of Bernini's *Fontana Navona*), were erected by those rich enough to afford them. As at Versailles, figures and urns were occasionally gilded, but this distasteful ballroom fashion seems to have declined in the late 1720s, for William Kent, and others, had 'leaped over the fence and saw that all nature was a garden'. Kent did not eschew the use of statues, terms and pots, which he used sparsely but effectively, circling the neat exedrae and standing in the glades. But their popularity diminished as 'Capability' Brown transformed the parkland of England, and sculptors who had specialized in supplying lead figures for gardens fell upon hard times in the 1760s. There was, indeed, little room for statuary on Brown's shaven lawns, though figures were still needed to stand in the niches of temples and to flank the doorway to the house. Heraldic beasts, carved in stone or cast in lead, held their appropriate place on the park gates, where they were often joined by the more fashionable sphinxes. When the parterre was politely grassed over, the lead Fames and deities seem to have been banished to the 'wilderness'. The invention of Coade stone brought statues within the reach of modest purses, and they must frequently have found a place in smaller gardens, even if they were little used in the grander lay-outs (Plate 26D). Humphrey Repton seems to have had still less room for them than Brown, but they returned to popularity with the revival of the formal garden in the nineteenth century.

MATERIALS

Various materials have been used for garden sculpture, stone being the most popular as the cheapest of the more durable substances. Wood was used in the sixteenth century and probably in succeeding ages, but naturally no complete statues have survived. Figures in marble appear to have been imported more frequently than carved in England; Sir John Clerk of Penicuik, remarking on the statuary in the garden of Lord Cadogan's house near Reading, says: 'His lordship at vast expense brought several large marble statues from Holland; there are here several Goddesses but of such a clumsy make as one may see that they were made in a country where women are valued by the pound of A——.' Marble was, of course, an expensive substance and weathers badly in the British climate. The most durable of metals, bronze, was also costly, and such statues as were made of it appear to have been imported—like the figures Massimiliano Soldani supplied for Blenheim. On account of its comparative cheapness and immunity to weather, lead was greatly favoured, especially in the early eighteenth century, and most of the best English garden statues and urns have been made of it. In the 1760s it was, however, falling into disrepute, and William Shenstone pleaded for its use in his *Unconnected Thoughts on Gardening* – 'I wonder that lead statues are not more in vogue in our modern gardens. Though they may not express the finer lines of an human body, yet they seem perfectly well calculated, on account of their duration, to embellish landskips, were they some degrees inferior to what we generally behold. A statue in a room challenges examination, and is to be examined critically as a statue. A statue in a garden is to be considered as one part of a scene or landskip. . . .' Though it limits the sculptor by its weight and is not capable of fine effects, lead is one of the most satisfactory substances for garden statuary, and so far from being spoilt by the weather is improved by patination. Its use was greatly revived in the last century when copies of many late seventeenth- and early eighteenth-century statues and pots were put on the market – some carefully patinated. In the late 1760s the invention of Coade stone, a moulded artificial stone impervious to frost but capable of delicate effects, caused a minor revolution in garden sculpture. The Coade factory at Lambeth could supply anything from an Ionic capital (ten shillings) or a frieze of griffins (fifteen shillings a foot) to 'A River God 9 feet high, with an urn through which a stream of water may be carried' (one hundred guineas). Many prominent sculptors were commissioned to design objects in Coade stone, which were produced both individually and in stock patterns. Its fashion lasted until the 1840s, when its place was taken by cheaper and generally less attractive substances.

STATUES

COPIES AFTER THE ANTIQUE

Of all the types of figure used for the decoration of British gardens, copies of the well-known Roman and, as was believed, Greek statues in Italy were most favoured, especially in the eighteenth century. In the Hyde Park Corner yard of JOHN CHEERE (fl. 1739–87), one of the most popular statuaries, stood:

The gods of Athens and of Rome.
Here Squabby Cupids take their places
With Venus and the clumsy Graces.
Apollo there with aim so clever
Stretches his leaden bow for ever. . . .

The Venus de Medici, the clapping Faun, the fighting Gladiator and the dying Gaul were frequently cast in lead or carved in stone for English parks. From a stock list sent by ANDRIES CARPENTIÈRE (167?–1737) to the Earl of Carlisle in 1723, we may judge of the prices paid for such figures in lead: a Narcissus 7½ feet high cost £25; a Venus de Medici 6 feet high, £15; an Antinous of the same height, £18; and a Cleopatra (probably a copy of the Capitoline figure that went under this name) 5 feet high, £8. Such figures were probably copied from plaster casts made in Italy, and some were faithful, if somewhat heavy-handed, versions of the originals. Modifications were occasionally made for convenience or, towards the end of the century, for the sake of modesty; and some figures are derivations from rather than copies after the antique. Michael Rysbrack's celebrated Hercules is, in fact, a combination of the Farnese statue and the best-developed limbs of the more notable London boxers; but it is not, strictly speaking, garden statuary, for it was designed to stand in a temple at Stourhead. The category of figures derived from the antique also includes terms – armless busts on pedestals tapering towards the base – which enjoyed a great vogue in the first half of the eighteenth century (Plate 25D).

COPIES AFTER MODERN STATUES

The sculptor whose works were most frequently copied for eighteenth-century gardens was Giovanni Bologna, the Fleming who worked in Italy from about 1545 until his death in 1608. It may seem strange that a mannerist artist should enjoy so much favour at this time; but he stood supreme among modern sculptors, and the patron who lived in a house based on a design of Palladio and whose gallery was filled with copies of pictures by the Italian painters of the sixteenth and seventeenth centuries would naturally wish to have copies of figures by Giovanni Bologna in his garden. His most popular figure was the Mercury at Florence which, despite the unsuitability of so heavy a metal for the graceful tip-toe poise, was often cast in lead, subsequently acquiring a drunken stagger – there is one by JOHN VAN NOST (fl. 1686–1729) at Melbourne, Derbyshire. His famous groups of the Rape of the Sabines (at Florence) and Samson and the Philistine (formerly at Hovingham and now in the Victoria & Albert Museum) were also popular; there is a copy of the former at Painshill and of the latter at Harrowden. Another Flemish sculptor who worked in Italy and was copied in England was François Duquesnoy, called Il Fiammingo. John van Nost adapted his works on occasion, and was paid ten guineas in 1706 for 'two boys after Flamingo modelled apurpose and cast in a hard metall'. The only other foreign sculptor who appears to have been fashionable in eighteenth-century England was François Girardon (1628–1715), who was responsible for much of the statuary in the gardens of Versailles; copies of his figures of Winter and The Rape of Proserpine by John Cheere are now at Southill. In the early nineteenth century the vogue for Antonio Canova crowded our parks with his coy Graces, in marble and all manner of artificial stone.

ORIGINAL WORKS

Statues of notable people were occasionally set up in gardens, either designed expressly for that purpose or copied from public monuments. There are lead figures of Prince Eugene and the Duke of Marlborough at Glemhall Hall, and at Wrest Park there is a fine statue of William III which bears a suspicious likeness to Grinling Gibbons' bronze of James II. At Hartwell, in Buckinghamshire, there is an equestrian statue of Frederick Prince of Wales also in lead. Lord Burlington commissioned a small population of statues for the gardens of his elegant villa at Chiswick, where a semicircle of sombre Romans stands in the exedra, and Rysbrack's Palladio and Inigo Jones appropriately guard the portal. Busts of Roman and British worthies mounted on pillars also decorated the classical landscaped garden. Other notabilities have found their way into the garden; the equestrian statue of Charles II which Sir Robert Vyner gave to the city of London in 1672 is now in the park at Newby in Yorkshire. When Bird's Queen Anne was taken from its place outside St Paul's Cathedral, Augustus Hare re-erected it in his garden at Holmhurst, near Hastings.

Gods, goddesses and personifications in the classical taste were made for gardens throughout the eighteenth century. PETER SCHEEMAKERS (1691–1781) executed groups of Cain and Abel, Apollo with a Muse and a Satyr for the grounds of Chiswick House. A lead group of Perseus and Andromeda by John van Nost is at Melbourne, Derbyshire; a lively lead Pan is at Glemham; and there are personifications of the arts at Hardwick Hall. In the grotto at Stourhill there is a large River God by Scheemakers. *Amorini* or winged *putti* were also much in demand, the finest being those made for Melbourne, Derbyshire, by John van Nost, some cavorting in pairs and others single – the most endearing shows an inquisitive child who has disturbed a hornets' nest and is suffering the consequences. Other amorini made by Nost or his successor, Cheere, are at Wilton, and a good set from Stowe was, until recently, in the possession of Messrs Crowther (Plate 26A).

J. T. Smith, the biographer of Nollekens, referring to what he termed 'the despicable manufactory' of lead figures, goes on to remark that they 'consisted of Punch, Harlequin, Columbine and other pantomimical characters, mowers whetting their scythes, gamekeepers shooting and Roman soldiers with firelocks; but, above all, an African slave kneeling with a sundial upon his head found the most extensive sale'. All too few figures of this description survive either in lead or stone. Blackamoors appear to have been popular throughout the first half of the century, not only as sundials but also as independent ornaments. At Melbourne, that *locus classicus* for the study of garden sculpture, there is a fine early eighteenth-century pair of kneeling figures, one a blackamoor, the other an Indian, each supporting rather perilously upon his head a tray that carries a small urn. Shepherds and shepherdesses, which were popular after the turn of the eighteenth century, were a speciality of John Cheere, who had taken over Van Nost's yard and effects in about 1739. Normally of lead, they were occasionally painted and are not lacking in rustic elegance (Plate 26B, C). Cheere is also recorded, in the 1770s, as having in his yard 'spruce squires, haymakers with rakes in their hands . . . bagpipes and pipers and fiddlers, Dutch skippers and English sailors enough to supply a first-rate man-of-war'. One can only presume that they found their way into the gardens of the bourgeoisie rather than into the great landscaped parks, where immortals were the rule.

ANIMALS

Animals and birds in lead and stone were not infrequently made for the garden in the eighteenth century. Naturally enough, the Roman boar in the Uffizi was popular, and its progeny are frequently to be seen in English glades. In 1724 Captain Gough is recorded as having bought for Gough Hall two 'estriidges 6 ft. high' and two 'cocketresses' from John van Nost, as well as two boars from another lead statuarist, Manning. Dogs and lions were often made, but a lead cow, reproduced by Weaver (see bibliography on p. 56), must be numbered among the rarities. Throughout the century heraldic beasts

FIG. 1. Mid-eighteenth-century lead SPHINX

held their popularity for the decoration of gates – two of the best being the large wyverns made for the entrance to Glynde Place, Sussex, by John Cheere in 1759, for £48 5*s*. The sphinx appears to have been brought to wide popularity by the neo-classical revival, and it held its place at the gate, the entrance to the house and on the balustrade of the bridge until the Victorian era. John Cheere supplied sphinxes, lions and lionesses for Castle Hill in Devonshire, and he was also responsible for the sphinxes placed on the bridge at Blenheim in 1773. There are many statues of dogs – some derived from the famous dog of Alcibiades at Duncombe Park – but none is more charming than the Coade-stone memorial to Jock, a favourite spaniel, made for Southill in 1806 to the design of GEORGE GARRARD (1760–1826) (Plate 27A).

SUNDIALS

Sundials have held their popularity as garden ornaments from the sixteenth century to the present day. Most are of a fairly simple baluster shape, but more elaborate patterns have occasionally been used. Heraldic beasts were sometimes made to support the dial – a very fine seventeenth-century example at Glamis Castle has four rampant lions each holding a dial in its paws. The kneeling blackamoor was fashionable in the early eighteenth century, but as taste changed more classical figures came into vogue. A sundial in the form of a lead *amorino* who holds the dial above his head was made in the eighteenth century and extensively copied in recent times.

URNS AND VASES

According to William Shenstone, the owner of Leasowes, poet, theorist and practitioner of the eighteenth-century picturesque garden, 'urns are more solemn if large and plain; more beautiful if less and ornamented. Solemnity is perhaps their point, and the situation of them should still co-operate with it'. They have, indeed, been the most popular of all items of garden statuary, and some are among the very finest. In the formal garden they stood at the focal-points of the lay-out; in the early landscaped gardens they were placed at the heads of vistas to act as eye-catchers; in the picturesque garden they found a place beneath the trees, and were often engraved with lines calculated to summon up the sweet tear of Sensibility. Among the best are the magnificent specimens carved in marble by CAIUS

GABRIEL CIBBER (1630–1700) and EDWARD PEARCE (fl. 1658–95) between 1690 and 1700 for Hampton Court (Plate 25A and B). These vast works, seemingly based on French designs, were enriched with carvings of classical subjects around their bodies, and cost more than £400 apiece; they are now at Windsor Castle. Scarcely less fine is John van Nost's richly ornamented lead urn supported on four monkeys and crowned with a fantastic

FIG. 2. Early eighteenth-century lead URN

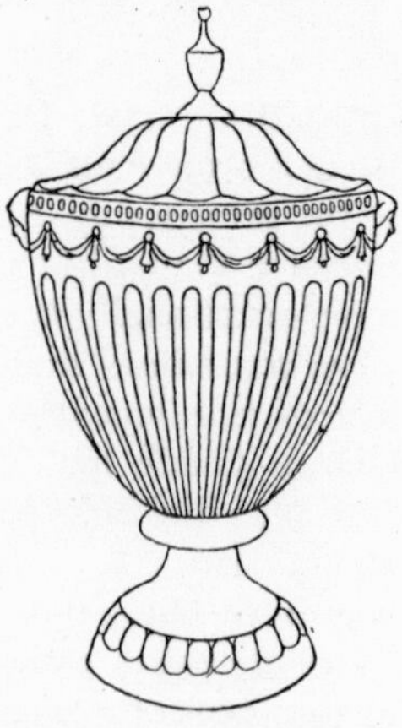

FIG. 3. Late eighteenth-century URN

bouquet of flowers at Melbourne; a similar one with a fox sitting on the top was recently in the possession of Messrs Crowther (Plate 25C). Less grandiose urns made in the early eighteenth century often have a fluted base and cover, a plain body, and are topped with a flame-like motif. Globe-shaped urns enriched with swags of heavy fruits and flowers were also popular at this time. With the change in taste in the middle of the century, simpler patterns became the rule, and in the last three decades the Adamesque type predominated (Fig. 3). In the later part of the century urns were used for the decoration of the balustrades by the house or raised on columns in the park, to commemorate a person or a pet.

Seventeenth-century vases or pots were often in the shape of baroque urns without covers, and were generally provided with two handles of human or animal shape. Lead was much used for making these vessels, which vary in height from one to three feet. In the eighteenth century their decoration varied with the taste of the time, and after the 1760s they were frequently modelled on Greek and Roman vases. Some are, indeed, copies of classical vessels; the famous Vasa

FIG. 4. Early eighteenth-century lead VASE

Medicea in the Uffizi and the great Warwick Vase were particularly popular as models, and are to be found in lead and stone as well as marble. Vases and urns were also made in Coade stone and, in the nineteenth century, in various types of hard earthenware.

CISTERNS

Rainwater cisterns made of lead and decorated in low relief survive in not inconsiderable numbers from the seventeenth and eighteenth centuries. Generally the work of

FIG. 5. Mid-eighteenth-century lead VASE

provincial craftsmen, their decoration is often a little behind the times. The surface was usually divided into sections each of which contained an heraldic device, initial or monogram; many are dated. Occasionally they were decorated with bunches of fruit and flowers or personifications of the seasons. A particularly fine example of 1750 is in the courtyard of Sackville College, East Grinstead; its relief panels are identical with those on one of 1725 in the possession of Bert Crowther Ltd. (Plate 27B).

GARDEN FURNITURE

The earliest garden seat seems to have been made of turf, like that in the arbour which Chaucer describes:

That benched was, and all with turves new
Freshly turved, wherof the grene gras
So small, so thick, so short, so fresh of hew,
That most like to grene wool, wot I, it was.

This type has been revived in recent years in the thyme seat. Benches were also found in the arbour, and in the early seventeenth century Bacon recommended 'seats set in some decent order'. It seems probable that wood was generally used for garden furniture, which has subsequently perished. Stone benches were, however, in use by the end of the seventeenth century, and have held their popularity ever since, more for their looks than comfort. Usually simple, they were occasionally supported on figures of lions or other conveniently shaped animals. Lead might also be used for a small bench – there is a ponderous classical example at Castle Hill in Devonshire. In the eighteenth century the design of garden seats naturally followed that of interior furnishings; a book of designs published in about 1790 illustrates an Adamesque garden bench decorated with swags along its back and a classical urn on each arm. Marble thrones in the Grecian taste were also popular at the end of the century.

It is difficult to determine when the rustic garden seat first appeared; it was probably made of wood. In the late 1740s Gainsborough painted Mrs Andrews sitting upon what appears to be a rococo iron seat designed for the garden, but in Zoffany's picture of the Garrick family taking tea at the river-side, some thirty years later, the chairs look as if they have been brought out from the dining-room. Rustic conversation pieces suggest that boulders and fallen trees were sometimes used by the hardy aristocrat.

As far as may be judged, the great age of garden furniture came only with the increased use of cast-iron in the nineteenth century. In 1818 John Papworth remarked that although 'the present greatly improved and highly esteemed practice of landscape gardening' was beautiful, the result was 'yet perhaps a little "unfurnished", if the term may so be used'. He consequently set about the design of charmingly elegant garden seats, 'claiming a share of novelty' in the Regency taste; one was beneath an umbrella of iron and thin copper plates, the other 'of the marquee character' was covered with cloth upon an iron frame (Fig. 6). Simpler seats of the period were made out of twisted

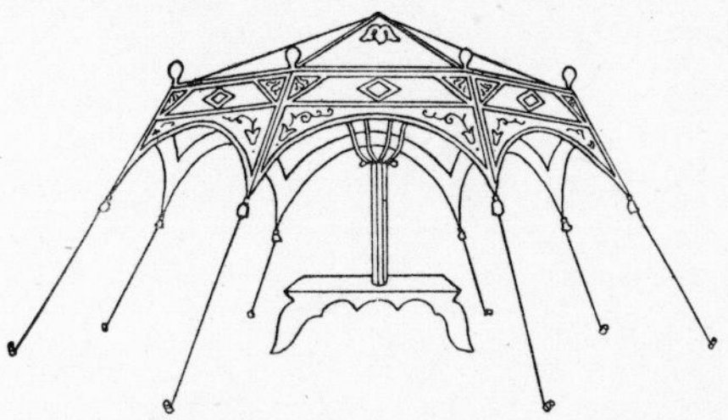

FIG. 6. REGENCY GARDEN SEAT designed by J. B. Papworth

and twirled iron wire (Plate 28A). With the ripening of the nineteenth century, garden furniture naturally became heavier and more elaborate. A good Gothic settee in cast-iron (Plate 28B) illustrates the change in taste.

Rustic seats, made to look as if they had been assembled out of odd fragments of wood, probably originated in the hermitages of the eighteenth-century park, but were never so popular as in the Victorian era. At the Great Exhibition of 1851, J. T. Alexander of Dumfries exhibited an 'ornamental garden chair of roots and branches of the oak'. But wood was not the only material used; the Coalbrookdale Company exhibited a rustic chair in cast-iron, and the Dale Hall Pottery one in earthenware. Slate appears to have been used for whole chairs and the tops of tables. The catalogue of the Great Exhibition also lists a number of more grandiose items of garden furniture, such as vast fountains, coy figures, huge forbidding park gates and an 'ornamental rustic dome, in cast-iron bronzed', an erection of great complexity which sheltered John Bell's heroic statue of the Eagle Slayer. Towards the end of the Victorian period, the interest in formal gardening brought about a revival of seventeenth-century ornaments and discreet stone furniture.

BOOKS FOR FURTHER READING

DUTTON, RALPH: *The English Garden* (1945).
GUNNIS, RUPERT: *A Dictionary of British Sculptors* (1953).
WEAVER, L.: *English Leadwork* (1909).

(A)

(B)

(C)

(D)

(A) Urn made for Hampton Court by Edward Pearce between 1690 and 1700. Now at Windsor Castle. Marble. *By gracious permission of Her Majesty the Queen.*

(B) Urn made for Hampton Court by Caius Gabriel Cibber between 1690 and 1700. Now at Windsor Castle. Marble. *By gracious permission of Her Majesty the Queen.*

(C) Early eighteenth-century lead urn by John van Nost.

(D) Early eighteenth-century stone term figure.

(A) Group of lead *amorini* in the style of John van Nost. Formerly at Stowe.

(B) Lead shepherd in the style of John Cheere.

(C) Shepherdess in the style of John Cheere.

(D) Classical figure in Coade stone, dated 1803.

(A) Monument to Jock, a favourite spaniel, by George Garrard, 1806, in Coade stone. Southill Place. *By courtesy of Major Simon Whitbread, Southill Park.*

(B) Lead rainwater cistern, dated 1725.

(A) Early nineteenth-century table and two chairs in iron wire. *Bert Crowther Ltd.*

(B) Early Victorian Gothic garden-settee in cast-iron. *Bert Crowther Ltd.*

PLATE 28

CONTINENTAL SILVER

By HUGH HONOUR

COLLECTORS of British plate who turn their attention to continental silver may well find themselves a little bewildered. And it must be admitted that the multiplicity of marks and the frequency of genuine but unmarked pieces, together with false but impressively marked objects, make the road to connoisseurship a thorny one. Fakes abound and many have been deceived by them, as were the keepers of the Imperial Treasury of Austria when a Viennese goldsmith named Weininger returned to them a copy of his own manufacture in place of the famous reliquary of the Holy Thorn. (See the excellent brief account of goldsmiths' work in *Fakes*, by Otto Kurz.) Furthermore, the literature on European plate as a whole is poor, and several regions are barely charted at all. Only by a careful study of authentic pieces or by reliance on well-informed opinion can the collector be sure of what he is acquiring. But the unparalleled craftsmanship, the gay fantasy and exquisite beauty of the best continental plate will adequately compensate for the initial difficulties.

The study of plate in all countries is hampered by serious losses and confused by chance survivals. Objects made as an ostentatious store for wealth and valued primarily for their weight were melted either to provide ready money or to conform with changes of fashion. The Thirty Years War in Germany, the Turkish wars in Austria, the French Revolution and the Napoleonic wars all took their toll of silver. It is only by the greatest good fortune that two of the very few surviving pieces of French medieval domestic plate should be such supreme examples of the goldsmith's art as the eagle-shaped ewer in the Louvre and the Royal Gold Cup in the British Museum (see 'The Connoisseur Period Guides': *Tudor* [Plate 33]. Generalizations about the influence of one country upon another, or about the quality of silver at any period, must be based principally on what survives, and must therefore be tentative. But by taking ecclesiastical and domestic plate together, it is possible to sketch out a rough stylistic history of silver in Europe from the eleventh to the nineteenth centuries.

ROMANESQUE (*c.* 700–*c.* 1150)

Too few objects have survived to give us a very clear idea of how the romanesque style was applied by goldsmiths, and the exquisite porphyry-mounted eagle ewer which was made in about 1140 (Plate 29A) probably gives a false impression of the quality of their work. The two main influences on the decoration of silver seem to have been illuminated manuscripts and architecture. A chalice of about 780, at Kremsmünster (Fig. 4), is ornamented with figures in interlaced decoration exactly paralleled by the illumination of a manuscript of the same date in the Stiftsbibliotek at St Gall. The popularity of the semi-barbaric interlaced ornament died out fairly early in the period, to be succeeded by somewhat fussier abstract decorations. Architectural influences are particularly notable in reliquaries, some of which were made in the form of miniature churches guarded by little ivory or silver saints. Many of the surviving objects are encrusted with precious stones, always set *en cabochon.*

GOTHIC (*c.* 1150–*c.* 1500)

In this period church plate achieved an unprecedented magnificence and, some maintain, an unsurpassed beauty. Crocketed, pinnacled, enriched with little statues of saints, enamelled and set about with stones, the gaudy silver and gold chalices, monstrances, censers, reliquaries and pastoral staves often give a clearer impression of the medieval love of magnificence than the churches which have suffered more violent ravages of time and weather. No single object shows this more vividly than the little gold reliquary of the Holy Thorn (British Museum), which is probably French work of the fourteenth century (Plate 29B). Silversmiths were a little slow in accepting the new style, but after the middle of the thirteenth century, Gothic motifs borrowed from architecture dominated the decoration of both ecclesiastical and domestic vessels. Some late medieval cups were, indeed, made in the form of little castles, and even so small an object as a spoon might be provided with a delicately pinnacled handle. Many objects, like mazers and drinking-horns, were simply mounted in silver or copper-gilt, which was less frequently left plain than engraved with leaf ornament or Gothic lettering. Enamelling was much employed especially in France, whence the Royal Gold Cup in the British Museum originates. In this period the spirit of fantasy began to manifest itself in silver, and is well exemplified by a ewer of about 1453 in the museum at Kassel; this curious vessel has a spout fashioned like a swan with a crown round its neck, and rests upon four Gothic turrets with a fifth as a thumbpiece.

RENAISSANCE (*c.* 1450–*c.* 1600)

Ecclesiastical silver was much less strongly affected by the Renaissance than was domestic, particularly in Northern Europe, where the conservatism of the Church authorities dictated a continuance of Gothic motifs and patterns throughout the sixteenth century. A chalice made as late as 1590 at Breslau was decorated with flamboyant Gothic tracery on its base, and a monstrance of about the same date, in the Church of St Amelberga, Zandhoven (Plate 29D), was enriched with Gothic pinnacles and buttresses. Even in Italy, where the influence of the new style was naturally strongest, Gothic and Renaissance motifs were often combined in one object. The superb crucifix, made by Antonio Pollaiuolo for the Baptistery of S. Giovanni in Florence, between 1457 and 1459, has a Gothic style cross above a purely Renaissance *tempietto*; and a silver crozier made for Pope Clement VII some three-quarters of a century later was decorated with Gothic ogee arches. The early Renaissance style in church silver is exemplified by the reliquary of St John the Baptist in Siena Cathedral, which was made in 1465 by Francesco d'Antonio and has four female figures carrying cornucopiae at the corners of a coffer which rests upon claw feet strongly reminiscent of Desiderio da Settignano's *Marsuppini* monument carved a decade earlier. Much of the finest Italian plate of the early Renaissance is marked by the elegant simplicity apparent in the silver-gilt and crystal altar set of a cross and two candlesticks in the Victoria & Albert Museum (Plate 34A). In place of the richly coloured enamels, black and white niello decoration became increasingly popular, especially for crucifixes and paxes. (*Niello* is a black composition used for filling in engraved designs on silver and other metals; the Florentine, Maso Finiguerra, was one of the most notable artists in this medium.)

Unfortunately, too little Italian domestic plate of the Renaissance has survived for us to have a very clear impression of it. Benvenuto Cellini's famous salt-cellar at Vienna ranks as high in the annals of sculpture as in those of goldsmiths' work, and was always regarded as an object of singular magnificence. It is probable that other silversmiths made good use of the human form, as did the maker of the knife, fork and spoon in the Metropolitan Museum, New York (Plate 31B). The period saw the introduction of cleaner eating habits, which demanded new vessels, not only the fork but such a vase as Cellini describes: 'a huge silver piece, used at table by Pope Clement [VII], into which he flung away bits of bone and the rind of divers fruits, while eating; an object of ostentation rather than necessity'.

Towards the end of the fifteenth century the Renaissance styles spread to other countries where the new motifs were happily mixed with the old, as on a German nielloed beaker of about 1480 (in the British Museum) on which Italianate *putti* sport gaily amid the Gothic foliage. But once the Renaissance had been assimilated by the craftsmen of Germany, Holland, France, Spain and Portugal, they used the new motifs – *putti*, urns, satyrs, nymphs and acanthus leaves – with reckless abandon if scant respect. The sixteenth century was the great age of the German silversmiths, especially those of Augsburg and Nuremberg, whose work influenced all Europe. Most of the important pattern books were published in Germany and copied in other countries. It was, moreover, the great age of mounted nautilus shells and hard-stone vessels, of monstrous cups a yard high and gargantuan heavily wrought dishes, all of which reflect a desire for showy magnificence. The Mannerist style of the later sixteenth century also found expression in the decoration of silver in Germany, its most notable exponents being Hans and Wenzel Jamnitzer who worked in Nuremberg.

BAROQUE AND ROCOCO (*c.* 1600–*c.* 1760)

As the baroque style was largely and initially the artistic expression of the Counter-reformation, its influence on the design of ecclesiastical plate was considerable, and continued to be active long after its sway over architecture, painting and sculpture had slackened. Indeed, baroque, and its later manifestation, rococo, became as much the official ecclesiastical style for silver as Gothic had been. The severer neo-classic forms which became apparent in domestic silver after about 1770 are less frequently to be found in Church plate. Silversmiths made full use of the flame-like curve of the baroque on which designs and ornaments were based. Architects of the seventeenth and eighteenth centuries were, moreover, alive to the decorative value of silver, and sometimes designed not only the vast candlesticks and altar frontals but such objects as monstrances (Plate 35B). Even the smallest items, censers and chalices, were made to fit into the general scheme.

In domestic plate the baroque influence is most notable in the grander pieces, such as andirons, and the fantastic designs of Adam van Vianen who founded a school of Dutch silversmiths, working in a sinuous and slithery 'art nouveau' style, which may be illustrated by a dish in the Victoria & Albert Museum (Plate 30A). The seventeenth century was the great age of the Dutch silversmiths, who excelled in embossed work and produced some of the masterpieces of European plate. It may be said that the Dutch influence almost superseded the German in the first half of the seventeenth century, but with the establishment of the Louis XIV style the centre moved to France.

Refined, sensitive, beautifully wrought and exquisitely designed, French plate of the eighteenth century is the triumph of the silversmith's art, but unfortunately all too little survives (the best collections are in Portugal and Russia). As Bouilhet said: 'It is certain that never better than in the XVIIIth century has art lent greater eloquence to silver: never has it been made to express with greater charm and virtuosity the piquancy and relish of its disclosures: never has the *métier* accomplished with such virtuosity and perfect understanding of its limitations, *tours de force* more extraordinary than this silverware, at one and the same time sinuous, caressing, tormented, capricious, and deliciously original'. Not only the great candelabra, the huge centrepieces (Plate 31A), the salts and tureens, by such master craftsmen as the Germains, but even the smaller objects, *écuelles* with artichoke finials, little winetasters and exquisitely engraved knives and forks, were designed and finished with the greatest artistry. The French influence spread throughout Europe, and made itself felt from Russia to Portugal and from England to Italy. Only in the rococo silversmiths of Bavaria (*see* Plates 35A, B) did the French find their near equals.

NEO-CLASSIC (*c.* 1760–1820)

No less elegant than the rococo, but becoming increasingly more chastened and restrained, the neo-classic style first appeared in the 1760s. Wherever French influence predominated, the Louis XVI style was accepted, but English patterns, in the manner of the Adam brothers, were also copied in Scandinavian countries, parts of Germany, Portugal and, to a certain extent, in France itself. Robert Louis Auguste, the silversmith of Louis XVI, did not entirely eschew the sinuous curves of his master, Thomas Germain, but he rarely allowed them full play. By the 1790s the ground was fully prepared for the advent of the Empire style, in which the sparkling curves, playful animals, gay *putti* and seductive females of the rococo finally gave way to the rigid lines, sphinxes, Grecian dames and Egyptian goddesses of the neo-classic. Jean Baptiste Odiot, Napoleon I's goldsmith, was one of the most notable craftsmen to work in the new style, and died in 1850, a year before the Great Exhibition at which silversmiths from all parts of the globe showed objects in which the styles of many centuries were unhappily combined – the great and proud craft of the silversmith had become one of the industrial and decorative arts.

GLOSSARY

The principal types of silver vessels made on the Continent are listed below. Little mention has, however, been made of objects differing but slightly from those referred to in the chapters on British and American plate in Volumes I and II of this series.

Altars: since the early Middle Ages, altar frontals, and sometimes whole altars, have occasionally been made in silver. At Città di Castello, in Umbria, there is a fine twelfth-century frontal which is an important specimen of late romanesque sculpture. One of the best examples of a complete silver altar is that of St James made, between the thirteenth and the fifteenth centuries, for Pistoia Cathedral (cf. *The Connoisseur*, November 1956). Among numerous seventeenth- and eighteenth-century altars that by G. B. Foggini for the Corsini Chapel in the Carmine at Florence, and that of 1730 at Frieburg (near Augsburg), should be mentioned.

Andirons: were frequently made in silver for palaces, but few of these heavy pieces of furniture have survived. In the Victoria & Albert Museum there is a very fine rococo one made by Philip Jacob Drentwitt of Augsburg (1747–79).

Armour: in the sixteenth century it was not uncommon for the pageant armour of great princes to be made either wholly or partly of silver. The Louvre has a magnificent enamelled gold shield and morion made for Charles IX between 1560 and 1574. A great shield of iron, in the British Museum, damascened with gold and plated with silver, was made by Giorgio Ghisi of Mantua in 1554, and is a notable example of Mannerist art.

Aspergill: the orb-ended rod or brush used for sprinkling holy water; the handle is often of silver and made to match a holy-water bucket (q.v.).

Basons: were frequently made in gold, silver or mounted crystal, and the decoration of some is so elaborate that one suspects that they were intended primarily for display on the sideboard. A fairly simple Flemish example, of about 1560, with a raised centre, belongs to the Corporation of Guildford. In the Louvre there is a magnificent bason (with its ewer), made at Antwerp 1558–9, chased with scenes of Charles V's expedition to Tunis in 1535. A large Portuguese bason in the Wallace Collection (*c.* 1565) is richly embossed with symbols of the seasons, the elements and the planets. Basons were used for the essential hand-washing before and during meals, but their popularity as decorative pieces lasted until after the introduction of forks and declined in the early eighteenth century (Plate 32c).

Beakers: stemless drinking cups were popular in various parts of Europe from the fifteenth until the eighteenth century. In the fifteenth century they were especially popular in Germany, where they usually had covers decorated with over-hanging Gothic leaf decoration around the rim. A superb nielloed example of about 1480 is in the British Museum. Some were made in fantastic shapes, like the copper-gilt one in the Victoria & Albert Museum which is very intricately fashioned to resemble a castle. Norwegian beakers of the sixteenth century usually rest on feet in the form of lions or female busts. Simple, uncovered beakers, much like those made in England at the same time, reached the height of their popularity in the sixteenth and seventeenth centuries in Holland (Fig. 1), where they also served as

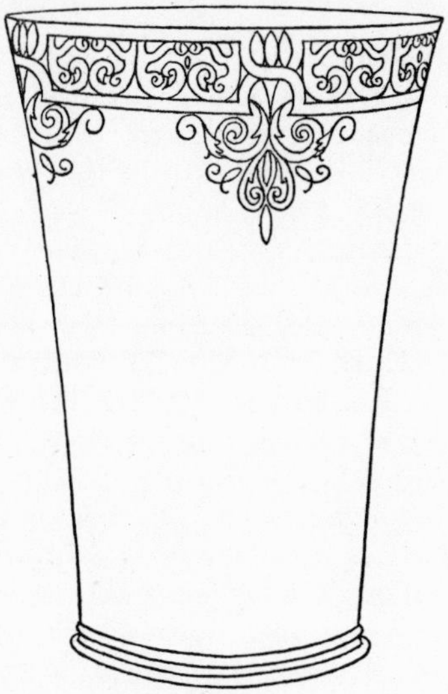

Fig. 1

communion cups in Protestant churches. In Hungary, very tall beakers, decorated in national fashion, were favoured, and in Italy they were occasionally covered with filigree work (Plate 34B).

Bedwarmers: were occasionally made in silver, but few have survived. One by the French craftsman Charles Petit in 1661 was in the Puiforcat Collection.

Bekerschroef: a stand for a wine-glass, shaped like the stem of a large cup. These objects are peculiar to Holland, where they were made in the early seventeenth century.

Bells: table bells of silver have been made since the sixteenth century, varying in style with the taste of the times. A famous bell, decorated with snakes, lizards and insects, made by Hans Jamnitzer at Nuremberg in about 1558, is in the British Museum, and a similar one attributed to the same craftsman, is in the Schatzkammer der Reichen Kapelle at Munich.

Brandewijkom: an oval, two-handled bowl peculiar to Holland, where it was made in the seventeenth and eighteenth centuries. It was used on festive occasions to hold raisins steeped in brandy.

Brandy-bowls: flat, two-handled bowls called *orekovsken* in Denmark, *oreskaal* in Norway and *dopskal* in Sweden, used for serving hot brandy, were popular throughout the Scandinavian countries in the seventeenth century.

Bratina: a globular, covered cup with a contracted lip (usually decorated with a sententious inscription), peculiar to Russia. It was a form of loving-cup, intimately associated with its owner and used at his funeral feast. Sometimes they were richly enamelled and begemmed; a rare example in gold is in the museum at Vienna.

Bridal-crowns: a Swedish peculiarity of the seventeenth and eighteenth centuries, they were frequently made of silver or silver-gilt, and enriched with traditional ornament which was reproduced from generation to generation.

Candelabra: of silver were too heavy to survive in great quantities. In the Portuguese royal collection there is a magnificent rococo one by the French craftsman François Thomas Germain whose pupil, Robert Joseph

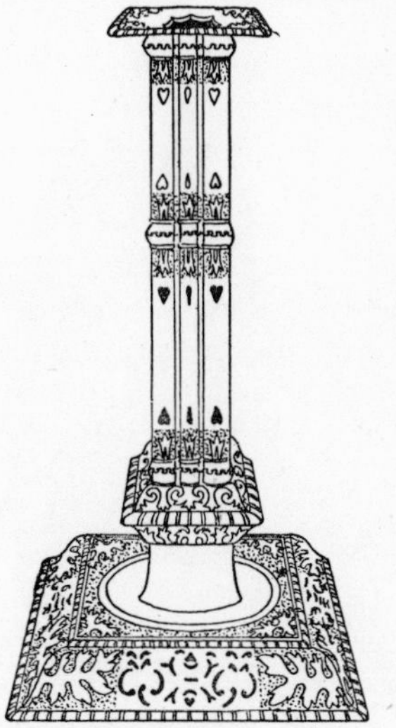

Fig. 2

Auguste, made three great candelabra for the Winter Palace at Petrograd. Silver wall-sconces of the seventeenth and eighteenth centuries are commoner, especially in Holland and Germany. A pair of fine candle-brackets with tulip-shaped holders, made by Nicholas Verhaar at Utrecht, is in the Brum Collection in that city. Single candlesticks of silver have been made since the sixteenth century in all sizes, for use in churches and houses, varying with the stylistic trends of the times. In the seventeenth century domestic candlesticks were normally square and solid, like the Dutch examples in the Victoria & Albert Museum (Fig. 2). They provided great scope for the rococo silversmiths and designers like Meisonnier, who made roses sprout and blossom from the hollows of the contorted pillars.

Caskets: large caskets of silver were made in Germany in the sixteenth century, but elsewhere they were usually of other materials, mounted in silver, like the famous Renaissance *Cassetta Farnese* in the Naples Museum. Small wedding-caskets for jewellery, no more than three inches high and fashioned like miniature chests, were made in Holland in the seventeenth century.

Censer: occasionally called a *thurible*. The vessel in which incense is burnt; it is more frequently of base metal than silver. Gothic examples are usually architectural in form,

Fig. 3

and resemble fantastic spires or octagonal chapter-houses. In Renaissance times a simpler, vase-shaped type came into use, and in subsequent periods its decoration varied with current trends in architectural taste. A very fine silver censer of 1767–79 in the Bayerisches Nationalmuseum, echoes in its broken curves the decoration of the rococo pilgrimage churches of Bavaria (Fig. 3).

Centre-piece: a large and often fantastic object, sometimes called a *surtout de table*, used to decorate the centre of a table; in some ways it took the place of the ceremonial salt. One of the most famous is that made by Wenzel Jamnitzer (1546) in the form of a woman, standing on a mound covered with leafy plants, holding on her head a covered dish crowned by a vase of flowers (Rijksmuseum, Amsterdam). A Swedish example of the late seventeenth century has four candle branches, a dish supported by a five-headed dragon, casters for sugar and shell-shaped dishes for sweetmeats. Rococo silversmiths allowed their ingenuity to run riot when designing such objects, and one of the finest of all was that made in 1730 by Thomas Germain, now in the Museum de Arte Antigua, Lisbon, which stands some three feet in height, bears two three-branch candleholders and is enriched with *putti*, dogs, tortoises and hunting-horns (Plate 31A; *see also The Connoisseur*, December 1954, p. 259).

Chalice: the cup in which wine is consecrated at the Eucharist. When intended for the use of the Roman Catholic Church, it was invariably made of gold, silver or silver-gilt, frequently enriched with enamel and relief decoration and occasionally encrusted with precious stones. The earliest chalices have a hemispherical bowl on a spreading, knopped stem, and some romanesque examples, like that at Kremsmünster, are decorated with Christian symbols amid interlaced decoration (Fig. 4). In the Gothic period the stems were occasionally enriched with buttresses and pinnacles, like the fifteenth-century Venetian one in the Victoria & Albert Museum, but such becrocketed vessels must have been difficult to

FIG. 4

handle, and a simpler, more practical type, in which the decoration was limited to engraving on the bowl with enamelling on the knop and foot, was generally preferred (Fig. 5). In the fourteenth century a deeper form of bowl came into use, and a pattern was established that did not alter radically until the nineteenth century, when the hemispherical bowl was revived; but the decoration of

FIG. 5

both bowl and stem varied considerably with the times. In the seventeenth and eighteenth centuries the lip of the bowl was normally left free from the baroque or rococo decoration, which swirled round the lower part to riot on the stem and foot (Plate 35A). Many chalices of these periods were enamelled and some decorated with stones; one in the Vatican, made in Rome for the Cardinal of York, being studded with diamonds. Rococo craftsmen occasionally made the stem in the form of a standing figure, as in the example of 1707 in the Church of St Paul, Antwerp.

Charka: a small cup with a single handle, peculiar to Russia; it was used for drinking strong liquors. A characteristic, richly enamelled example is in the British Museum.

Ciborium: the receptacle used for the reservation of the Eucharist. It is normally provided with a hinged cover and a lock. Gothic examples usually have a spire-shaped cover above a cylindrical (occasionally polygonal), font-shaped bowl (Fig. 6). Flatter covers, usually crowned by a cross, were introduced at the Renaissance.

FIG. 6

Coffee-pots: and **Chocolate-pots** were first introduced in the seventeenth century, and vary but slightly from one region and date to another. They were normally vase-shaped with a spout, but exotic patterns also occur, like that entwined with snakes and crowned with a toad, which was made at Dresden in about 1700 by J. M. Dinglinger.

Crozier: the head of the crozier, or bishop's pastoral staff, has often been made of silver. Gothic examples usually have a circle of crocketed niches beneath the volute which contains the figure of a saint. The sinuous curve of the crook naturally appealed to eighteenth-century silversmiths; there is a fine rococo example at Eichstätt.

Crucifixes: altar crucifixes and processional crosses (which are decorated on both sides) generally follow, somewhat tardily, the stylistic development of sculpture. The Gothic type of cross, which had arms terminating in trefoils or quatrefoils enclosing symbols of the evangelists or half-figures of saints, persisted into the sixteenth century. Italy is particularly rich in silver crosses some of which were designed by great artists like

Antonio Pollaiuolo, who was responsible for the magnificent altar cross in the Museo dell' Opera del Duomo at Florence. A simpler type, introduced at the Renaissance, has generally persisted ever since.

Cruets: the vessels containing the wine and water for use at the Eucharist. Sometimes wholly of silver, they are frequently of glass with silver mounts, and follow the patterns prevalent in domestic plate. A fourteenth-century Burgundian cruet in the British Museum is quite plain except for the animal head at its spout. There is a curious pair of fifteenth-century workmanship in the Victoria & Albert Museum – one labelled A for *acqua*, the other V for *vinum*.

Cups: silver and gold cups have been made from very early times until the present day, but after the mid-eighteenth century their popularity as drinking vessels declined, and they have since been used mainly for presentation. So great was the diversity of cups in the sixteenth and seventeenth centuries, that no account of all the patterns made can be attempted here, but a list of the principal types would include the following.

ANIMAL CUPS: covered cups fashioned like animals – foxes, hounds, deer, unicorns, dragons, elephants, etc – were made in Germany between the sixteenth and eighteenth centuries, being at the zenith of their popularity from about 1575 to about 1650. Some, made principally at Augsburg, were in the form of groups, St George and the Dragon or Diana riding a Centaur, and a few were fitted with clockwork mechanism so that they could be made to run across a table (Plate 33A).

BIRD CUPS, in the form of owls, larks, griffins, pelicans, etc, enjoyed the same popularity as animal cups, but seem to have been more widely made. A Portuguese owl-cup of the seventeenth century is in the collection of Comandante Ernesto de Vilhena, and at Clare College, Cambridge, there is a falcon cup made at Antwerp in about 1555.

COCONUT CUPS appear to have been made as early as the thirteenth century, but the oldest survivors are those made in Germany in the sixteenth century. Coconuts, polished and occasionally carved, were enclosed in delicate silver mounts and set upon stems (Fig. 7). They appear to have been popular in Holland in the sixteenth century, and to have been introduced into Russia in the seventeenth, shortly before they went out of fashion in Western Europe.

FIG. 7

COLUMBINE CUPS were often, but not invariably, trial pieces made by candidates for admission to the goldsmiths' guilds of Germany. Their complicated form (Plate 32B) tested the skill of the young craftsman without trying his ingenuity. Nuremberg was probably the first town to define the form in the sixteenth century.

CRYSTAL AND HARD-STONE CUPS were mounted in silver and gold from the end of the fifteenth century. In the sixteenth century Prague and Vienna were notable centres for this work, which was also practised in Germany and Italy. Rock-crystal was much favoured as it was believed to act as a poison detector, but all manner of precious and semi-precious stones – emerald, agate, onyx, chalcedony, jasper, etc – were also used. The precious nature of the material which could not be wasted in making regularly shaped vessels determined some of the most bizarre patterns and tested the invention of the craftsmen.

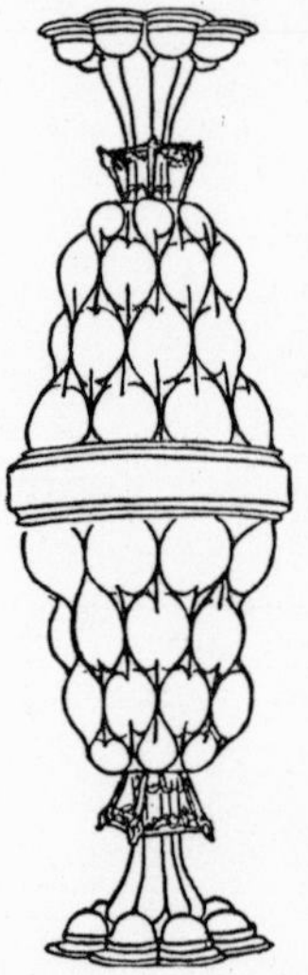

FIG. 8

DOUBLE CUPS are intimately identified with Germany, and became increasingly popular there from the end of the fifteenth century. Formed out of a cup of normal pattern with a cover that could be used as a second one, usually a smaller cup intended for the mistress of the house (Fig. 8), they were occa-

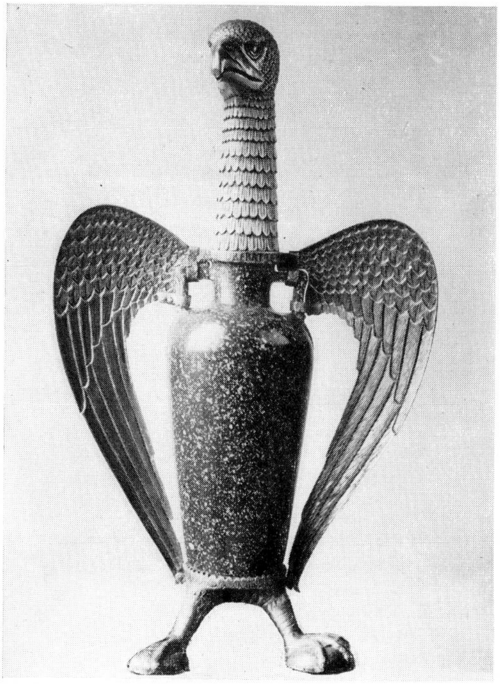

(A) Ewer made in about 1140. Silver-gilt and porphyry. *The Louvre.*

(B) The Reliquary of the Holy Thorn. Gold, enamelled and set with jewels. French work of the late fourteenth century. *British Museum.*

(C) (*Left*) The Belem Monstrance. Gold and enamel. Portuguese work of the early sixteenth century. *Museu de Arte Antigua, Lisbon.*

(D) (*Right*) Monstrance in the Gothic style, late sixteenth century, Dutch. *St Amelberga's Church, Zandhoven.*

PLATE 29

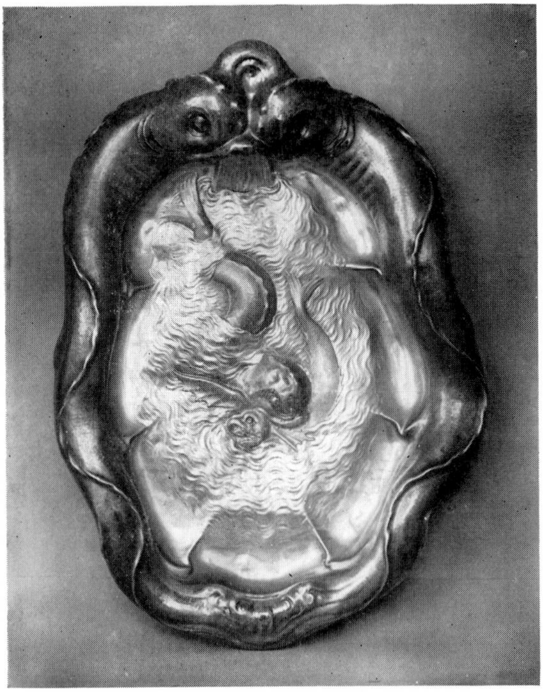

(A) Large dish. Made by Van Vianen in 1635. *Victoria & Albert Museum.*

(B) Tankard. Partly gilt. Made by Albrecht Biller at Augsburg, *c.* 1690. *S. J. Phillips.*

(C) One of a pair of salts in the Van Vianen style. Made at Utrecht, *c.* 1620. *S. J. Phillips.*

(D) One of a pair of candlesticks made by Jacques Nicolas Roettiers at Paris in 1771 and hall-marked at Leningrad in 1784. *S. J. Phillips.*

(A) Centre-piece by Thomas Germain of Paris, 1730–31. *Museu de Arte Antigua, Lisbon.*

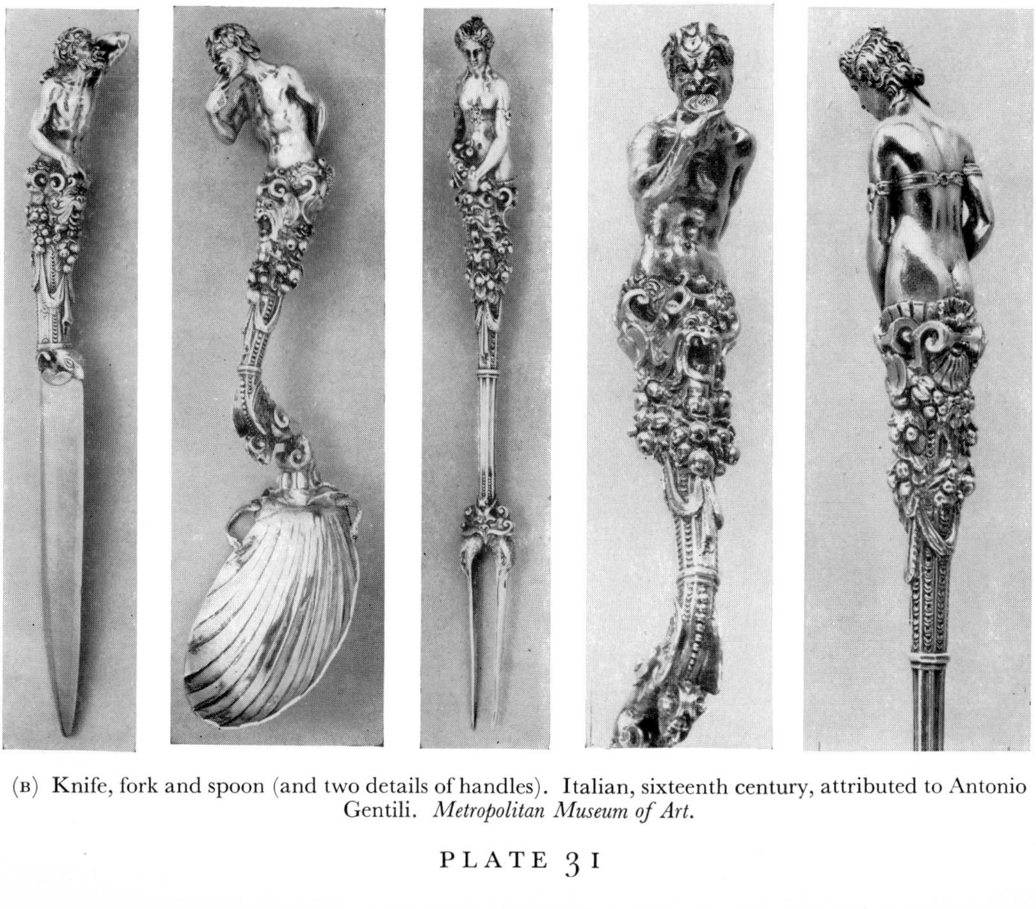

(B) Knife, fork and spoon (and two details of handles). Italian, sixteenth century, attributed to Antonio Gentili. *Metropolitan Museum of Art.*

(A) Salt. Silver-gilt, decorated with Limoges-enamel plaques. French, late sixteenth century. *Wallace Collection.*

(B) Columbine cup made at Nuremberg in about 1572. *Victoria & Albert Museum.*

(C) Bason and ewer. Silver-gilt. Made by the Genoese Franco Lercaro and the Portuguese Antonio de Castro in 1565. *Wallace Collection.*

PLATE 32

(A) Stag cup. Silver-gilt. Made at Augsburg in the late sixteenth century. *British Museum.*

(B) Nef. Silver partly gilt. Made by Esias Zur Linden at Nuremberg, *c.* 1620. *S. J. Phillips.*

(C) Windmill-cup. Made at Enkhuizen in 1621. *S. J. Phillips.*

(D) Nautilus-shell cup. Mounted in silver-gilt. Made by Hans Anthony Lind, Nuremberg, *c.* 1590. *S. J. Phillips.*

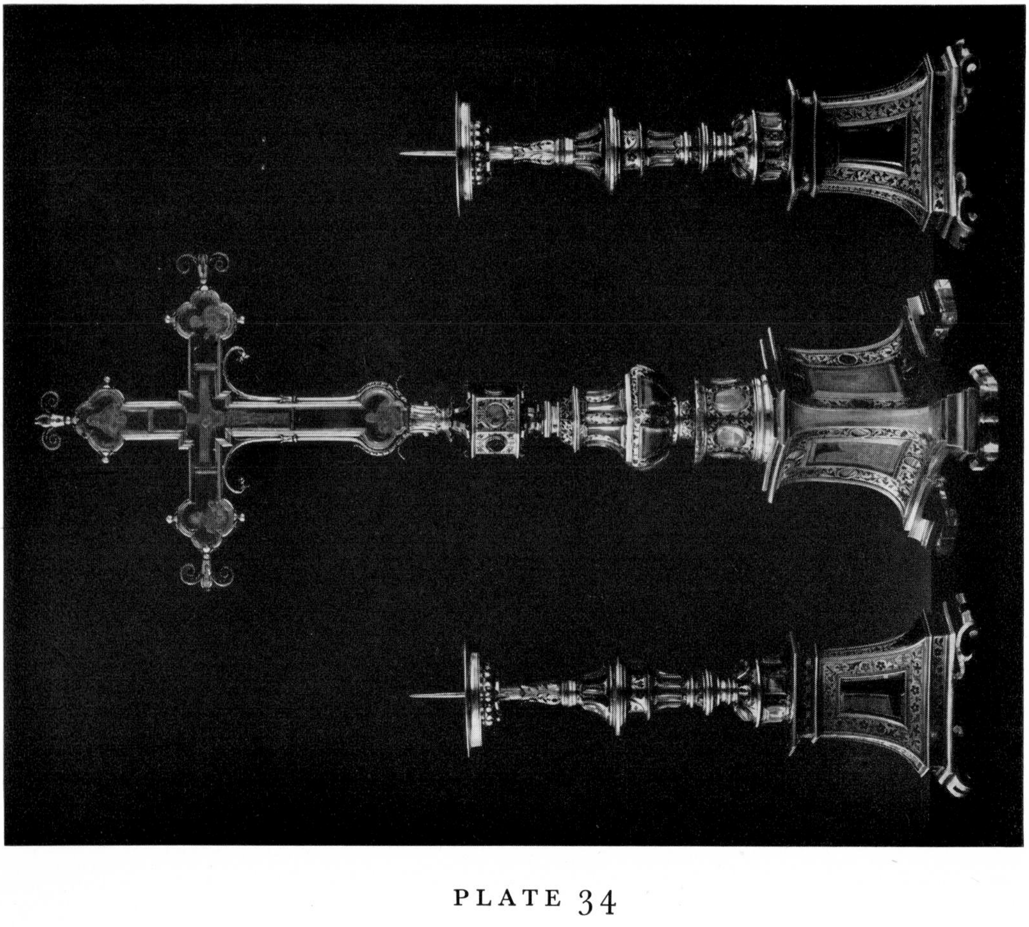

(A) Crucifix and candlesticks. Crystal and silver, gilt and enamelled. North Italian, *c.* 1520. *Victoria & Albert Museum.*

(B) Covered beaker. Silver parcel gilt. German, late fifteenth century. *Victoria & Albert Museum.*

(A) Chalice. Silver-gilt, enamelled and set with precious stones. Made by F. A. Gutwein at Augsburg, 1765–67. *Benediktiner-Abtei, Ottobeuren.*

(B) Monstrance. Silver-gilt, set with precious stones. Made at Munich in about 1740 by J. C. Steinbacher to the design of Aegid Asam. *Johannes Nepomuk-Kirche, Munich.*

(A) Travelling table service made for Cardinal York by L. Valadini at Rome, *c.* 1790. *By gracious permission of Her Majesty the Queen.*

(B) Part of a tea-set. Made at Augsburg, 1771–73. *S. J. Phillips.*

(C) Drinking horn. Mounted in copper-gilt. Danish, fifteenth century. *British Museum.*

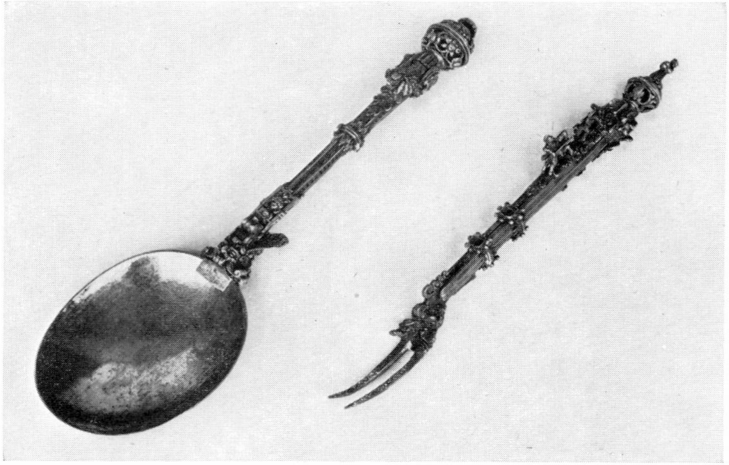

(D) Folding spoon and fork. Silver parcel-gilt. Flemish, sixteenth century. *British Museum.*

PLATE 36

sionally shaped like double mazers. Hans Petzolt, a conspicuous Nuremberg silversmith of the sixteenth century, made several double cups. Such vessels are rarely found to date from after the middle of the seventeenth century.

Globe Cups, in the form of terrestrial globes, usually supported by a human figure, were made in France, Germany and Switzerland in the sixteenth and seventeenth centuries. Abraham Gessner of Zurich appears

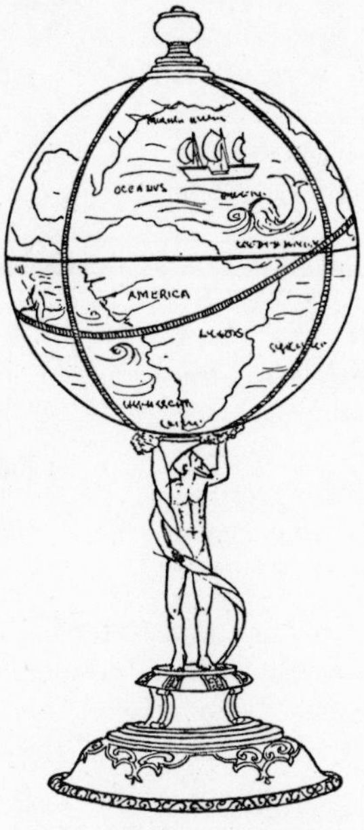

Fig. 9

to have specialized in making these vessels, some of which were as much as 20 inches high (Fig. 9).

Gourd-shaped Cups were made in Germany in the late sixteenth century, inspired by the design of Brossamer and Solis. They frequently stand on twisted tree stems.

Nautilus Shells, elaborately mounted as cups in gold or silver, were very popular in Germany some hundred years after 1550. An unusual example of 1580, in the British Museum, is mounted on a foot fashioned like the claw of a bird, and has a shell which was engraved in China. They were introduced into Holland in the sixteenth century. The greatest ingenuity was used in mounting the shells, which were sometimes made to resemble birds and beasts. It must be assumed that these vessels were intended for display rather than use. On occasions, nautilus shells were also made into flasks or cups (Plate 33D).

Ostrich Eggs, sometimes supposed to be the eggs of griffins or phoenixes, were often mounted as cups (and occasionally made into flasks) in the later Middle Ages. Most surviving specimens are German and date from the sixteenth or early seventeenth centuries. A notable example is mounted as an ostrich, the egg serving as the body.

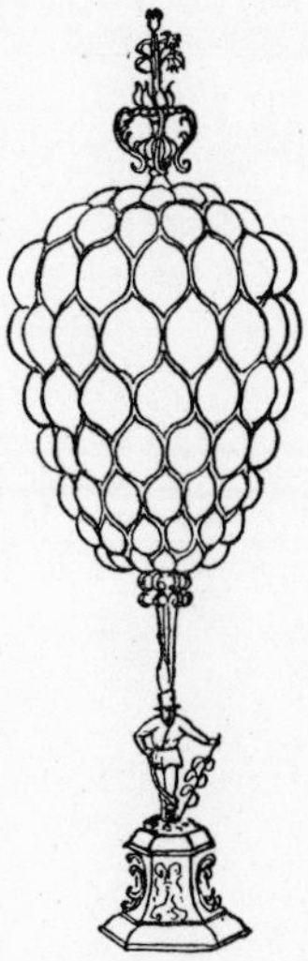

Fig. 10

Pineapple Cups, with covered bowls, in the shape of stylized pineapples, were distinctive products of Germany (called *ananaspokal*), where they were made in the seventeenth century. Some stand as much as 30 inches in height (Fig. 10).

Windmill Wager Cups were shaped like model windmills so that when they were inverted the body of the mill acted as the bowl. They were used for wagers on festive occasions, the drinker having to consume the contents before the sails had stopped revolving (Plate 33C). (*See also Jungfrauenbecher.*)

Miscellaneous: among many other types of cup the following may be mentioned. They were occasionally made in the form of human heads, one, made by Albrecht Biller of Augsburg between 1696 and 1700, being that of a hideous witch. Cups fashioned like peasants carrying barrels, which act as the bowls, are not uncommon. Presentation cups given to distinguished Dutch sailors in the seventeenth century were often enamelled with sea-fights. (For other drinking vessels see: beakers, brandy-bowls, bratina, chalices, charka, goblets, *haufenbecher*, horns, *jungfrauenbecher*, mazer, *prunkgefass*, *riesenpokal*, tankards, tazza, and wine-tasters.)

Dishes: vast dishes, intended for display rather than use, were a speciality of Augsburg in the seventeenth century (of the nineteen gigantic dishes in the Kremlin, fourteen are of Augsburg manufacture). A fine early seventeenth-century Italian example, embossed with the departure of Christopher Columbus, is in the collection of the Marchese Spinola at Genoa. Circular dishes embossed in the centre with flowers or birds, frequently peacocks, were popular in Portugal in the second half of the seventeenth century. A large dish decorated with dolphins by Christopher van Vianen, a member of the famous family of Dutch seventeenth-century silversmiths, is in the Victoria & Albert Museum (Plate 30A).

Écuelle: a shallow, two-handled, covered dish peculiar to France, where it was a favourite piece of plate in the Regence and rococo periods. Late seventeenth-century écuelles usually had flat covers with a handle

FIG. 11

on top, but in the eighteenth century the covers were usually domed and surmounted by finials (Fig. 11). A fine silver-gilt example of 1672 is in the Victoria & Albert Museum. Some were provided with a dish, knife, spoon and fork enclosed in a leather case for travelling. In spite of the strong influence exerted by French silversmiths, écuelles were rarely made in other countries, though a few German and Italian examples are known.

Ewers: large jugs to carry water for the ablutions at meal-times were essential items of plate in the later Middle Ages and the sixteenth century; they were often made of silver and intricately wrought. The most popular type was vase shaped with a grotesque handle, and German examples frequently had disproportionately narrow necks (Fig. 12). A fine German ewer of 1559 in the British Museum has a low relief of the Rape of Helen on its body and a handle fashioned like a satyr leaning backwards. They were usually matched with basons, many of which have since disappeared. Spanish ewers of the late sixteenth and early seventeenth centuries tended to be rather small and to stand on short feet. Like cups and basons, they were frequently made in rock crystal or hard stone. Later French and Spanish examples were helmet shaped, but their popularity declined as a result of the change in eating habits occasioned by the introduction of the fork.

FIG. 12

Flagons: were usually much like those made in England, but fantastic shapes were also used; in about 1610 Melchior Gelb of Augsburg made one in the form of a vine-covered head of Silenus.

Forks: in the later Middle Ages small forks were made in most countries, but they do not appear to have been used for eating meat; it is significant that they were frequently made to match spoons, never knives. Some late fifteenth-century examples are of great delicacy, like that of Flemish workmanship with a rock-crystal handle in the Victoria & Albert Museum. Folding forks were frequently made in conjunction with spoons (q.v.). The use of forks for eating meat seems to have originated in Italy in the sixteenth century, and to have spread through the rest of Europe in the course of the next hundred years. A fine sixteenth-century set, consisting of a fork, knife and spoon, each with a handle in the form of a human figure, attributed to Antonio Gentili, is in the Metropolitan Museum, New York (Plate 31B). The earliest forks were two-pronged, the three-pronged type being introduced in the early eighteenth century. In the eighteenth century the handles of forks, as of spoons and knives, varied slightly with the changes in taste.

Fountains: made to stand in the centre of a table and dispense scented water or wine in the course of a meal, enjoyed some popularity in the richest households of the sixteenth century; but few have survived. In the British Museum there is a German example, dating from about 1580, which is formed out of a Seychelle nut with silver-gilt mounts.

Goblets: silver goblets, closely imitating German glasses with heavy bases and bulbous tops, were popular in Scandinavia in the late sixteenth and early seventeenth centuries. Two Swedish examples in the British Museum have bosses typical of glass decoration (Fig. 13). Imitations of glass in silver do not

FIG. 13

appear to have been usual after the middle of the seventeenth century.

Haufenbecher: alternatively called a *Setzbecher*: literally a piling cup. Beakers that could be fitted into one another, in pairs and in sets of six or twelve, popularized by the designs of Virgil Solis, were made in Germany in the late sixteenth century, but appear to have gone out of fashion before 1650. Each beaker has a band of moulded decoration around its rim, like a modern picnic cup. They were much used for hunting parties.

Holy-water Bucket: the receptacle for the holy water sprinkled in the *asperges* at the beginning of the Mass. Early examples are normally straight sided, polygonal or cylindrical, and occasionally waisted; the bombé-vase shape came into fashion in the seventeenth century. Handles were occasionally terminated with dragon heads. A good Spanish example of about 1500 is in the Victoria & Albert Museum.

Horns: in the *De Bello Gallico*, Caesar observed that the Germans drank from horns tipped with silver, and this practice persisted in Scandinavia, and less extensively in Germany, until the close of the Middle Ages. Originally the normal drinking vessels, they acquired in time an almost ritualistic significance, were carried into the hall for the assembled guests by girls, and used for mead and wine rather than ale. The majority do not seem to have been mounted in silver – eighteen out of the twenty-four horns in the Copenhagen Museum have mounts in copper-gilt. Normally the mounts are simple, but a Norwegian example of 1300 (in the Copenhagen Museum) is decorated with Gothic architectural features, and a Danish one in the British Museum has been made to resemble a bird, mounted on claw feet, the point of the horn fashioned into a tail (Plate 36c).

Incense Boat: the vessel in which the incense is carried before it is placed in the censer to burn. Normally it is a fairly simple boat-shaped vessel, and it was occasionally made to match a censer. Many were of base metals or of other materials mounted in silver; a crystal incense boat mounted in silver-gilt is in the Victoria & Albert Museum.

FIG. 14

Jungfrauenbecher: a wager-cup in the form of a girl with a wide-spreading skirt holding a bowl above her head (Fig. 14). The bowl is pivoted so that when the figure is inverted the skirt forms an upper cup and the bowl a lower one. Such vessels were used specially at wedding feasts when the groom was expected to drink the contents of the larger cup without spilling any of the contents of the smaller, which he passed to his bride. They first appeared in Germany in about 1575, and their fashion continued throughout the seventeenth century, when many were made at Nuremberg. A simpler form, apparently popular in Holland, replaced the head and shoulders of the girl with a mesh ball, which occasionally contained a die.

Kovsh: a boat-shaped vessel with a single handle used for ladling out drinks, such as *kvass* and beer. It is peculiar to Russia, where its popularity lasted until the middle of the eighteenth century. There is a silver example in the Victoria & Albert Museum, and a rare gold one was in the Green Vaults at Dresden.

Lamps: were occasionally made in silver, conforming in design with those made in glass or other materials. A fantastic Genoese example of the eighteenth century, shaped like a pagoda, is in the collection of Dott. F. Fassio at Genoa.

Mazer-bowls: made of spotted maple wood and mounted in silver, silver-gilt or base metals, appear to have originated in Germany, and were popular throughout Northern Europe in the later Middle Ages. Double mazers (Fig. 15) in the form of a large one with a single handle surmounted by a smaller were occasionally made, and this pattern was sometimes copied for double cups. Handles were often richly fashioned; a double mazer in the Wallace Collection has a handle shaped like a Gothic chapel.

FIG. 15

Monstrance (occasionally called an **Ostensory**): the vessel in which the Host is displayed or, less frequently, in which a relic is shown. They vary in size according to whether they were intended primarily to be placed on an altar or carried in procession. Frequently enriched with enamelling and precious stones, they are among the most magnificent pieces of Church plate. Gothic monstrances tended to be of architectural design with a cylindrical container for the Host in the centre. The famous Portuguese Belem monstrance (Plate 29C), of the early sixteenth century, shows little figures of the Apostles kneeling in adoration of the Sacrament. In many countries the Gothic pattern persisted until the end of the sixteenth century, when it was superseded by a baroque pattern in which the Host is placed in a cylinder flanked by angels or framed by a flaming sun the rays of which were often decorated with jewels. A Spanish chalice of about 1600 (in the Victoria & Albert Museum) has a detachable monstrance as a cover; both parts being lavishly decorated with Renaissance motifs. A fine Flemish example of 1670, by Joannes Moermans, is in the Church of Notre Dame at Rupelmonde. One of the most beautiful (Plate 35B) was designed in about 1740 by the great Bavarian architect, Aegid Asam, for the little Church of St Johannes Nepomuk, which he and his brother built in Munich. A diamond-set monstrance made by Johann Baptist Känischbauer von Hohenreid and Mathias Stegner, in 1699, is (or was) in the Church of St Loretto at Prague.

Morse: a clasp for fastening a cope, occasionally made of gold or silver and decorated with jewels. The most famous was that made by Benvenuto Cellini for Pope Clement VII.

Nef: a vessel shaped like a ship and used in the later Middle Ages for the lord's napkin, knife and spoon. In 1392 a nef on wheels was recorded in the Papal collection. In the sixteenth century ornaments, jugs and cups were made in the same form, notably in Germany and Switzerland. Many were very elaborate and accurate models, richly enamelled and peopled with little figures of sailors. A Swiss example is in the British Museum, and a wheeled nef, made at Nuremberg in about 1620 and probably intended as a jug, is in the Rothschild Collection on show at the Victoria & Albert Museum (Plate 33B).

Ostensory: *see* Monstrance.

Paten: the shallow dish on which the bread is 'offered' at the Offertory of the Mass, and on which the consecrated Host is placed after the Fraction. Invariably of gold or silver, it was often made to match a chalice normally circular, with a circular or sexfoil depression in the centre. Patens offered little scope to the silversmith though some have a little engraved decoration and a few are partly enamelled.

Pax: a tablet with a projecting handle behind, used in the Eucharist when it is kissed by the celebrant, the other priests and, very occasionally, the communicants. It is usually decorated on the front with a sacred symbol, a scene from the Gospel (usually the Crucifixion) or the lives of the saints, engraved, nielloed or enamelled. A large silver-gilt Spanish pax of about 1530 in the Victoria & Albert Museum has a low relief of St Idelfonso receiving the chasuble from the Virgin.

Plateau: a shallow dish on a short stem. A type characteristic of Spain and Portugal in the sixteenth century is derived from Valencia pottery.

Prunkgefass: a cup intended for display rather than use. A typical example is the gold cup supported somewhat insecurely on a coral figure, made by Peter Boy in about 1700, in the Schönborn Collection at Pommersfelden.

Przeworsk: a Polish method of decorating belts with chased silver plaques sewn on to the leather.

Pyx: a small vessel, usually a round silver box, in which the sacrament is carried to the sick. They were frequently richly decorated, like the French one of 1562 in the Victoria & Albert Museum, embossed with the Last Supper and other Biblical scenes, and crowned by a standing figure of Christ at the column.

Reliquary: the vessel in which a relic or relics of the saints are kept. Reliquaries have been made in a great variety of patterns, offering the maximum scope for the invention of the goldsmith. Early examples were generally of architectural design, like the reliquary of Pepin d'Acquitain in the treasury of Ste Foy at Conques, which dates from the ninth century and, with its high roof and round-headed niches, resembles a shrine. Some made in the Rhineland in the twelfth century (one is in the Victoria & Albert Museum and another at the Schlossmuseum, Berlin) were made as model romanesque churches. Church-shaped reliquaries followed, a little tardily, the changes in architectural taste, and the shrine of St Elizabeth at Marburg (1236–9) is decorated with a mixture of romanesque and early Gothic ornaments. Reliquaries in the form of limbs and busts were also made as early as the eleventh century, and held their popularity for some five hundred years. They were frequently enriched with precious stones, which have in some instances (the bust of St Agatha at Catania) been so richly augmented by the offerings of the pious that the original work is now practically obscured. The early busts were normally stylized and expressionless, but during the Renaissance period they were treated with greater naturalism. One of the most famous medieval reliquaries is that of the Holy Thorn in the British Museum, which was made of gold richly decorated with enamel and precious stones by a Burgundian craftsman of the fourteenth century (Plate 29B). (This object may also be called an Ostensory, as it is intended for the display of the relic.)

During the Renaissance the architectural type of reliquary developed into the coffer-shaped, of which the best example is that of St John the Baptist in the Cathedral at Siena (see introduction). This type, richly ornamented with reliefs and statuettes, was normal throughout the baroque period. Among the curiosities is the early eighteenth-century reliquary of St Anthony in the Victoria & Albert Museum, which is shaped like a spire.

Riesenpokal: literally a travelling cup. The name is usually given to the vast cups, standing up to 40 inches in height and usually gilt, intended for ostentation rather than use, and made in Germany in the sixteenth century.

Roses: golden roses were sent by the Popes to princes who had rendered signal service to the Roman Church and, later, to important ecclesiastical bodies. Of the many made in the fourteenth and fifteenth centuries few survive; one of the most notable, the gift of Pius II, is at Siena. All were made by goldsmiths working in Rome.

Salts: the ceremonial salt occupied a prominent position on the medieval dining-table, and its importance did not decline until the seventeenth century; but the surviving French and German salts of the sixteenth century look plain and insignificant beside English examples of the same date. Some French salts were of great delicacy enriched with Limoges-enamel plaques, like the one in the Wallace Collection (Plate 32A); and German salts were occasionally fantastic, as may be seen from one in the British Museum which is in the form of a whale supporting a shell on its tail. An exotic pair made at Breslau in about 1600 are fashioned like turkeys with spotted shells for their bodies. The most famous of all salts is, of course, that made in gold by Benvenuto Cellini for Francis I. Dutch silversmiths of the seventeenth century occasionally used human figures or fish for decoration (Plate 30C); a beautiful example of about 1625 by Thomas Bogaert of Utrecht, supported by a kneeling girl, is in the collection of the Duke of Buccleuch. In spite of their diminished importance, French rococo craftsmen saw the decorative value of salts as table ornaments, and one of the finest sets ever made, consisting of four double and three single cellars supported by *putti* with feathered Red Indian head-dresses, by François Thomas Germain, was in the Portuguese Royal Collection. (*See The Connoisseur*, December 1954, p. 264.)

Samovars: or tea-urns, though principally connected with Russia, were also made in other countries. A fine rococo specimen by François Thomas Germain was in the Portuguese Royal Collection.

Shaving-dishes: kidney-shaped bowls, usually accompanied by helmet-shaped ewers,

FIG. 16A

enjoyed great popularity in Spain and Portugal in the eighteenth century (Figs. 16A and 16B).

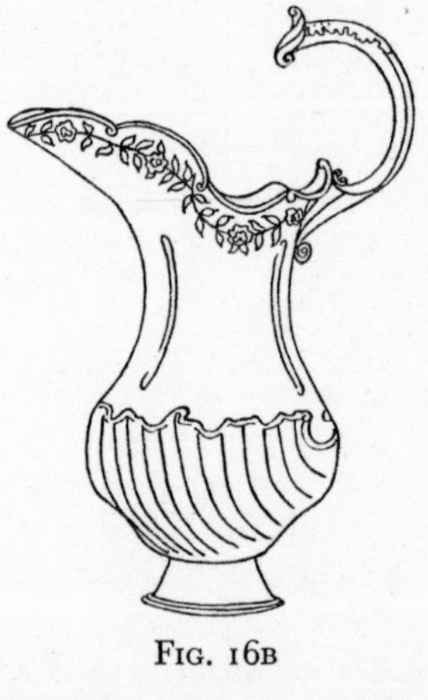

FIG. 16B

Spoons: in medieval times spoons, used for consuming thick, sweet liquids, were usually carried as personal possessions and not provided on the table. Some very elaborate early examples have survived, with bowls of shell, agate or other hard stones, exquisitely mounted in gold or silver. Occasionally they were combined with forks; in the British Museum there is a folding spoon and fork in a Gothic handle which also contains two dice and a pen (Plate 36D). With the general introduction of forks, the variations in pattern became fewer. Generally speaking, the fig-shaped bowl remained normal until the middle of the seventeenth century, when it was superseded by the egg-shaped. Incense spoons, used for placing incense in the censer, usually had spade-shaped bowls.

Standing Dishes: occasionally, and incorrectly, called *tazze*, have shallow bowls on baluster stems, and were used for sweetmeats or fruit. The interior of the bowl is often richly adorned with relief decoration, and some have standing figures in the centre

FIG. 17

(notably those made by Paul Hubner of Augsburg between 1583 and 1614) (Fig. 17). They were popular, especially in Germany and Holland, from the late sixteenth to the early eighteenth centuries. The British Museum possesses an exceptionally fine set of a dozen made at Augsburg, and there is a notable example, made by Adam van Vianen at Utrecht in 1612, in the Victoria & Albert Museum.

Table Decorations: small silver objects, figures, animals, miniature coaches, etc, were occasionally made as table decorations in the eighteenth century; in style they are similar to contemporary porcelain figures. Genoese craftsmen appear to have specialized in these objects, which they decorated with filigree work.

Table Services: complete table services in silver did not come into any general use until the eighteenth century, when those made for princely houses were often of the greatest magnificence. Small travelling table services were occasionally made, the most notable being the Italian one which belonged to Cardinal York and is now at Windsor (Plate 36A).

Tankards: appear to have been among the most popular silver vessels made in Northern Europe, especially Scandinavia, in the seventeenth and eighteenth centuries. The type that first appeared in Germany in the sixteenth century had a small tapering body, but in the next hundred years patterns became larger and more ornate (Plate 30B). In the late seventeenth and early eighteenth centuries, tankards set with coins were in demand. In Scandinavia and the Baltic states tankards with tall cylindrical bodies were favoured in the late sixteenth and early seventeenth centuries. Later Swedish examples tended to have shorter bodies which tapered downwards, lower and broader covers projecting over the lip and larger thumb-pieces. Heavy, squat ones standing on ball feet were usual in the Baltic states in the later seventeenth century; five massive examples of this type being in the collection of the Kompagnie der Schwarsen Haupter at Riga. In Hungary, tall, hexagonal, octagonal or cylindrical tankards narrowed in the middle of the body and sometimes decorated with medallions of Roman heads, were popular during the seventeenth century.

Tazza: the Italian word for a cup, a shallow-bowled drinking vessel on a stem, occasionally confused with the standing dish (q.v.).

Teapots: modelled on those made in ceramics and imported from China, appear to have been made in all countries in the eighteenth century. A very early tea-set of

Augsburg craftsmanship (Plate 36B) shows the application of rococo motifs to a pot and jugs. Towards the end of the century, English patterns were occasionally used on the Continent.

Toilet-sets: of gold or silver were made for the *grandes dames* of the seventeenth and eighteenth centuries. They might contain as many as fifty-three pieces, as did the gold one made for the Empress Maria Theresa by Anton Mathias Domanek in about 1750, and sometimes included, besides pots, brushes and combs, such objects as bodkins, tongue scrapers and combined tooth- and ear-picks.

Tureens: for serving vegetables and soup, came into use early in the eighteenth century. They are usually simple oval vessels with domed lids and finials, but in the hands of a craftsman like François Thomas Germain they might receive the fullest rococo treatment.

Wine-tasters: small vessels, usually two-handled, found in all wine-growing countries, though the Portuguese type with a domed centre, to reflect the colour of the wine, is said to be of English origin.

BOOKS FOR FURTHER READING

JONES, E. A. : *Old Silver of Europe and America* (1928).
LÜER AND CREUTZ: *Geschichte der Metallkunst*, Vol. II (1909).
ROSENBERG, M.: *Der Goldschmiede Merkzeichen* (third edition).

Denmark

BOESEN, G. AND BØJE, C. A.: *Old Danish Silver* (1948).

France

BOUILHET, H.: *L'Orfèvreries Française* (1890–93).
NOCQ, H.: *Orfèvreries Civile Française* (1927).

Germany

LEITERMANN, H.: *Deutsche Goldschmiederkunst* (1954).

Holland

FREDERIKS, J. W.: *Dutch Silver, Embossed Plaquettes, Tazze and Dishes* (1952).

Italy

ACCASCINA, M.: *Orificeria Italiana* (1934).
BUNT, C. G. E.: *The Goldsmiths of Italy* (1926).
MORAZZONI, G.: *Argenterie Genovesi* (1951).

Sweden

UPMARK: *Guld-och Silversmeder i Sverige 1520–1850* (1925).

AMERICAN GLASS

By HELEN McKEARIN

'WE sent home ample proofs of pitch, tar, glass . . .' wrote Captain John Smith in his *Historie of Virginia*. Whatever the forms given to those 1609 proofs of glass, it is certain they were neither omens of a new national style nor of a New World contribution to glass as an art. And they never expanded into profitable production of this indispensable man-made substance. As to the glass blown and the articles fashioned during the abortive struggles of the four or five subsequent seventeenth-century attempts to root glassmaking, they can only be conjectured.

With but few exceptions, all this is true of the ten or eleven eighteenth-century houses in which hopeful colonial business-men sank their capital. One was sufficiently successful making window glass and blowing bottles and jars to operate nearly forty years: Wistar's, whose small glasshouse community, near Salem in southern Jersey, was called Wistarburg (*c.* 1739–75). Similar utility wares, mainly green glass and inevitably counterparts of European prototypes, were made at the New York and New Windsor (*c.* 1752–67) works of the Glass House Company of New York, and at the Germantown works near Boston (1753–68). Bottles and window glass were to be the financial backbone of glassmaking for well over a century.

Only two pre-Revolutionary enterprises (so present evidence indicates) attempted to specialize in tablewares: Henry William Stiegel's second glasshouse (1769–74) at Manheim, Pennsylvania, and the Philadelphia Glass Works at Kensington. But both Stiegel and the proprietors at Kensington produced window glass and bottles also. In fact, these necessities of life were the paying output of Stiegel's Elizabeth Furnace Works (1763) and the principal products of his first at Manheim (1765). However, tableware production was intensive from 1769 into 1774 at Manheim, and from about 1772 into 1777 at Kensington. Each claimed to be the first flint-glass manufacturer in the country, but Stiegel, at least, made non-lead glass as well. Though *flint glass* was the popular name for lead glass, it seems likely that in the eighteenth as well as the nineteenth century non-lead-glass tablewares were often called *flint* because it implied quality.

At Manheim, Continental and English styles met but apparently did not blend. Actually Continental casually and shallowly engraved glass of the type today called *peasant glass* was followed so closely that few students consider physical characteristics alone a safe basis for attribution. The same, unfortunately, is true of English pattern-moulded types. The enamelled tumbler, Plate 37 (*right*) having an English inscription is an exception, but not the tumbler, Plate 37 (*left*), with sunken panels below the typical engraved tulips. The bottle, Plate 41D, is pattern-moulded in the diamond-daisy design, one of the few believed to be a Stiegel original since, as yet, no *exact* foreign counterpart is known. Articles listed in Stiegel's account books and his advertisements indicate that the range of articles was wide and followed imports. In 1771 the American Philosophical Society in Philadelphia pronounced the specimens exhibited to its members 'equal in beauty and quality to the generality of Flint Glass imported from England'. As for Kensington wares, advertisements and owners' nationality indicate they were *English*. They represented the last effort to make fine glassware until after the Revolution.

In the first forty-two years – from 1783 to 1824 – of the United States as a sovereign nation, about ninety-four glasshouses were built in spite of turbulent, unfavourable economic conditions. The depressed state of trade and commerce following the Revolution could not dampen optimism for various domestic manufactures. Shortly before 1800 westward migrations encouraged the establishment of glassmaking in the Midwest, where the Pittsburgh Glass Works erected America's first coal-burning furnace (1797) – right then sealing the doom of many as yet unplanned eastern wood-burning houses and determining the future hub of the glass industry. Optimism ran higher still with President Jefferson's embargo on trade with Britain (1806–7) and the Non-Importation Act (1811). It climbed to greater heights during the war of 1812. With each encouraging event or condition, a graph of glasshouses would rise to ever higher peaks and, between them, their failures drop to greater depths. New houses were built; some old ones were abandoned; others were taken over by new firms. In the whole period at least three times as many firms were formed by an even larger number of glassmen, merchants, brewers and other business-men. The few houses planned for tableware production either failed, or became green-glass houses, or added its production in order to survive. Not until 1824 did Congress pass a tariff ensuring survival with profit of flint-glass manufacturing as well as window glass and bottles. Fought unsuccessfully by importers and independent glass-cutting shops, the 1828 and 1832 tariffs doubled the insurance.

Among the post-Revolutionary tableware houses important from the collector's viewpoint only one was eighteenth century: the New Bremen Glass-manufactory (1785–95) of John Frederick Amelung & Company, near Frederick, Maryland; an over-ambitious project misreading desires of the fashionable and over-estimating demand for domestic glassware, luxury or ordinary. The New Bremen commercial tablewares presumably followed prevailing fashions, especially some of the finer Continental cut and engraved glass, and were non-lead, as are the authenticated pieces which have been tested for lead content. These latter, among them Plate 38B, are mainly so-called 'presentation pieces' or gifts. Their shapes, engraving technique, decoration by individual combinations of mainly Continental motifs and metal are Amelung earmarks. Similarity to their stylistic and physical characteristics has been the basis for attributing other pieces to New Bremen. The decorative techniques practised in addition to engraving were pattern-moulding, applied and tooled decoration and, to a limited degree, enamelling and gilding.

In the early nineteenth century there were several important houses. Bakewells' (1809–80) was prominent in the Pittsburgh area. This first successful flint-glass manufactory in the country (even so green glass was added to the output in 1811) was without effective rival among the few other Midwestern houses before John Robinson's Stourbridge Flint Glass Works (1823–45). By then demand and other favourable conditions were sufficient to support several houses. In the East, flint-glass production was rooted firmly by Thomas Cains, to whom the Boston Glass Company gave permission to erect a small flint-glass furnace in its South Boston works. Briefly (*c.* 1815–22) at Keene, New Hampshire, the Flint Glass Works on Marlboro Street made lead-glass bottles, flasks and tablewares before becoming just a 'bottle' house. At Cambridge, across the Charles River from Boston, the New England Glass Company, for over half a century probably the East's largest producer of fine glasswares (1818–80), took over a post-war casualty, the Boston Porcelain and Glass Company, organized in 1814. In New York, there were the Fisher Brothers' Bloomingdale Flint Glass Works (1822–45) and the Brooklyn Flint Glass Works founded by John L. Gilliland & Company (1823–68, moved to Corning, N.Y.), which won the prize for the best flint-glass metal at the London Crystal Palace, 1851. The Jersey Glass Company (1824–*c.* 1862), one of the improvers of mechanical pressing, built its works on Paulus Hook, across the Hudson from New York. That all, including the Midwestern, had ready access to water carriage is significant. Their production included pattern-moulded and free-blown wares, new commercial types as they evolved and, naturally, cut and engraved like popular imports. Also, by 1823, *export* of American glass, particularly to the West Indies and South America, had started.

Vast reaches of country, continual westward expansion, inadequate and slow transportation – by land or water – were among the factors determining locations and quantities of glasshouses. Scattering was logical if the country was to be independent of imports, as its glassmakers so vainly hoped. The increase, checked briefly by the 1830s depression, continued so that at least ninety new works were erected from 1825 to 1850. More than ever before were dedicated to flint-glasswares. For collectors the foremost among them were the Boston and Sandwich Glass Works, Sandwich, Massachusetts (1825–88), the Union Glass Works, Kensington, Philadelphia (1826–?), the Providence Flint Glass Works, Rhode Island (1831–5) (short-lived but leaving marked pressed salts), the Curlings' Fort Pitt Glass Works, Pittsburgh (1826–*c.* 1900), and the Sweenys' (1831–67) and the Richies' (1829–?) works, Wheeling, West Virginia. However, as always, the majority were bottle and/or window-glass houses. Not all the new houses survived; many old ones drew their fires; the inevitable westward shift accelerated. Most eastern houses, especially in New England and western and northern New York depended upon wood for fuel. For many exhaustion of wood holdings and prohibitive cost of transporting fuel, even if furnaces were converted to coal, meant extinction. Also canals and improved roads, by enabling some houses to transport materials and wares more efficiently and cheaply, contributed to the failure of less fortunately situated works.

During this period glassmaking was ineradicably rooted in the United States. Future pioneering was to be in glass technology and production. Experiments with blowing glass by machine had already begun, and even more immediately fateful to glassblowing as an art, John P. Bakewell of Pittsburgh obtained a patent on machine pressing in 1825. By the mid-century, the machine had made mass-production possible. Experiments in colour and composition bore strange and sometimes lovely fruits, forerunners of the later remarkable *art glasses.* The conscious effort to create the novel, symptomatic of an industrial society, became habit. Then, too, the term *glasshouse,* with its aura of craftsmanship and the art of glass-blowing, no longer fitted most establishments, but rather *factory,* with all its twentieth-century connotations.

In all these years neither social, economic nor psychological conditions were favourable for the emergence of a national style in blown tablewares. Glassmen, manufacturers, merchants and customers were too fixed in their orientation to Europe's fashions and traditions. The glassmen enticed across the Atlantic brought inherited traditions and techniques practised in European houses. Almost without exception they were Continentals until Stiegel persuaded English blowers and decorators to Manheim. Afterwards the numbers from Britain increased, especially for flint-glass manufacture, familiar far longer and to more British glassmen than to Continentals. If they remained in their crafts, their techniques and traditions were taught to native-born boys. Still, since defection to easier occupations or to the land was constant, thinned ranks had to be refilled from Europe. Thus, unless deliberately diverted, the stream of European traditions in glass-blowing and ornamentation – Continental and British – played continuously upon American-made glass.

The men who started the glasshouses were necessarily more concerned with finances than aesthetics. Many were merchants and importers familiar with the glassware demand, and well aware that competition entailed imitating imports of which *English* were considered *best.* Consequently style and design of commercial glasswares were determined mainly by imports. Nevertheless, along with glass cut or engraved to the 'latest London pattern' but within an accepted style, there were inevitable deviations, differing details and features. Though as yet this field of American glass has received limited scrutiny, it seems proved that idiosyncracies and types peculiar to certain houses and areas developed, more Midwestern than Eastern. In houses removed geographically and socially from the more European-style-conscious East conditions were more favourable for the emergence of local features and types. The sugar-bowl, Plate 40A (*centre*), in its combination of shape, engraving, motifs and lacy foot, illustrates one such type.

Actually, if flint-glass makers had depended solely upon the carriage trade – and in a free market – few would have survived. Fortunately a sizable pedestrian trade developed and expanded rapidly. Its needs could be met by new commercial wares such as blown-three-mould, early pressed and lacy glass and a new type of bottle packaging too – historical, pictorial and decorative flasks and bottles. These categories contain distinctive United States designs. While they do not represent *art in glass* many, especially among the flasks, may be called *popular art in glass*. The inexpensive blown-three-mould and early pressed wares enjoyed a comparatively brief reign; the flasks, with their blown-moulded designs, such as portraits of presidential candidates, emblems and slogans, monuments and heroes – even George Washington – were popular for nearly three-quarters of a century. They were a national style in packaging potables.

As a type of tableware, blown-three-mould may have originated in the United States shortly after 1812, perhaps at South Boston under Thomas Cains. It was a sort of poor man's cut-glass created by using a full-size mould having its inner surface the size and shape of an article and with an intaglio pattern. The patterns, an earmark, are classified as *arch*, *baroque* and *geometric* (Plate 40B and Plate 40A (*right*)). Of over 150 recorded, the majority are geometric, inspired by and in some instances identical with cut-glass. Also the majority apparently are peculiar to the United States. British production seems to have been limited to a few articles and a few geometric patterns, composed mainly of ribbings and diamond diapering in bands and blocks. The *arch* and *baroque* patterns have no known foreign counterparts.

The number of different articles in which each pattern appears and the number of moulds bearing each pattern varies widely. In the most common, McK GII-18 – band of diamond diapering between bands of vertical ribbing – over twenty articles have been recorded, over fifty individual moulds determined. While 400 moulds have been determined by analysis of actual pieces, they were for few articles, principally decanters and tumblers of many sizes and several shapes, castor bottles and inkwells. However, these were used to *pattern* gathers of glass to be fashioned, partially or entirely, by blowing and manipulation into other articles. For instance, a pitcher like Plate 40A (*right*) usually was patterned in a decanter mould, the body form was retained but the neck expanded and lipped, and the handle, of course, applied. Bowls like Plate 40B (*centre*), and dishes were fashioned free-hand after the gather was patterned in either a tumbler or a decanter mould.

By 1830 the popular demand for blown-three-mould was shrinking and had focused on the early pressed glasses. From 1825 when Bakewell patented mechanical pressing of knobs, the process developed so rapidly that by 1828 creamers, similar to Plate 42, could be pressed with handles and bodies in one piece. The invention of mechanical pressing and development of this revolutionary production method has been charged to America. Apsley Pellatt's 1831 specifications (British Patent No. 6091) for his press and mould referred to the 'mode' as 'lately introduced from America'. By 1852, to paraphrase Deming Jarvis, founder of the Boston and Sandwich Glass Works, the American invention had so reduced cost of production, thus lowering retail prices of glasswares, that consumption had increased tenfold. It undoubtedly was a factor also in any successful competition with European glass in the export markets.

By then there had been several phases in pressed-glass design. As in the case of blown-three-mould, the earliest patterns were inspired by cut-glass and adopted its motifs, especially the strawberry and fine-cut diamonds and, for rims, the fan escallop. However, about 1828 lacy glass, which was to be typically American for well over a decade, was evolving. With limitless variety made possible by mechanics, decorative design quickly passed beyond the close confines of contemporary cut-glass, with its simple geometric motifs regimented in stiff bands and into both simple and intricate patterns composed from an infinite variety of motifs on a stippled background. The stippling, tiny relief dots, was a glitter-producing device new in glassmaking and the earmark of *lacy*. The patterned surface of the glass was lustreless; the smooth, through which the innumerable facets and angled planes refracted light, brilliant and sparkling.

Lacy designs reveal a catholicity in taste and free use of many sources in the arts and crafts. They adapted motifs and treatments popularized by the classical and Gothic revivals, from architectural ornament, ceramics; turned to conventionalized and naturalistic flowers and leaves; used local and national emblems, symbols, national heroes' portraits; favoured geometric figures; never completely discarded the various diamond motifs. Many designs were well realized, with motifs in sound balance and accent; many were over-elaborate and poorly composed. Some Eastern were closely similar to some foreign lacy, and others counterparts of Meissen porcelain forms and decoration. However, as yet the majority have been found only on American lacy. Plates 42 and 43 show characteristic Midwestern and Eastern lacy design.

During the depression starting in 1837, apparently another design phase appeared. As lacy moulds with stippling and many-planed patterns were expensive, their cost, as well as general economic conditions, doubtless contributed to the decline of lacy production and the rise of a simpler style. The new designs emphasized form and simple geometric motifs, unquestionably influenced by cut-glass of that period. They were ideal for the *pressed-pattern glass*, as the table and bar glass popular from around 1840 were called. In many patterns table sets were quite complete, including, as American lacy did not, various types of drinking glasses. The new style found expression also in innumerable lamps, candlesticks and vases (Plate 39B) produced in all the old and many new tints and tones of greens, blues, amethyst, and yellows, transparent, translucent and opaque. However, in pressed glass, early or late, good or bad designs, American or derivative, *art* had passed to the mould-maker.

But even as the machine was dominating commercial glasswares, wherever there were bottle- and window-glass houses the art of glass-blowing was being practised freely and unhampered by fashion or a designer's specifications. So it always must have been in such glasshouses. In the Midwest until about 1835, and in the East into the late nineteenth century, distinctively American glass was fashioned for local custom in the early years and in isolated communities, always for friend and family. Vessels for use in pantry, kitchen and on the table – they were individual, functional and honestly sturdy, free-blown from window and bottle glass mainly in natural colours. In general, the Midwestern colour range outstripped the Eastern in quality of vibrant brilliance, subtle nuances of colour tone and use of artificial colours. Many were plain or simply ornamented – perhaps a folded rim, threading or a scalloped foot, the last rare in the East. The Midwestern tended to be thinner walled than the Eastern, and in other aspects were quite different, as a comparison of Plates 38A, 39A and 44 illustrates in part.

Major differences lay largely in shape, proportions and decorative techniques. In Midwestern houses, shapes evolved which were peculiar to the region; for instance, the sugar-bowl, Plate 39A (*left*), with its wide galleried rim, high, short, sharply angled shoulder, straight sides sloping abruptly to the base, and the type of double-domed cover. The salt, Plate 39A (*centre*), and pitcher, Plate 39A (*right*), are others. Eastern shapes conformed more closely with commercial wares, and more seldom included an eighteenth-century feature or treatment. For bottles and flasks as well as hollow-ware, the preferred Midwestern decorative technique was pattern-moulding, mainly ribbing, fluting, the broken-swirl and various expanded diamonds. The broken-swirl was tight 'popcorn', as on Plate 39A (*centre*), or widely expanded resembling feathery diamond-on-the-diagonal. Though far from frail in appearance, this Midwestern glass seems to derive lightness and poised strength from its patterned surface and brilliance of metal.

Blowers in New Jersey, New York and New England bottle- and window-glass houses rarely used the pattern-mould: they practised the centuries-old arts of glass-blowing and decorating, applying glass to itself and tooling it into ornamentation. Of many devices, several of them illustrated in Plates 38A and 44, perhaps the favourites were threading, prunts, quilling, crimping, also swagging, gadrooning and (nineteenth century) the so-called lily-pads fashioned from a superimposed layer, and embedded loopings. Though the devices were traditional or variations of ancient devices, it is unlikely the blowers, especially in the nineteenth century, realized their vessels' close kinship with Continental 'forest glass' and more remote ancestors. In fact, many expressions, the lily-pads in particular, probably were independent inventions. As yet neither true Type II as on Plate 44 (*centre*), nor Type III as on Plate 38A (*left*), has been identified with any European glass. All these individual pieces, plain and decorated, are called *South Jersey type*; the first of their kind unquestionably were from Wistar's eighteenth-century glassworks, southern Jersey. They are called *folk art in American glass*, largely because they are individual within a traditional stream and independent of sophisticated commercial style.

Folk art in American glass is a comparatively new term in the American collectors' glossary which, as in trades, professions and other hobbies, contains many words unintelligible to the uninitiated. It is a compilation of the glassman's obsolete and modern technical terms, English and Anglo-Irish glass terms, and terms coined by American collectors and writers to meet descriptive needs and afford identification of forms, types and decoration. Many of those in common usage follow in the glossary.

GLOSSARY

Air-twist: spiral veins of air formed by extension of tears (air bubbles), usually in stems of drinking vessels and shafts of candlesticks; in U.S. found occasionally in individual non-commercial pieces of South Jersey Type.

Applied Decoration, Finial, Foot, Stem: ornament and parts formed from separate gather of metal and tooled into form. *See* Finials, Foot.

Arch Patterns: (1) blown-three-mould patterns classified as *arch*, having an arch, Gothic or Roman, as a predominating or conspicuous motif (Plate 40B (*right*)), (2) pressed-glass patterns also.

Baroque Patterns: blown-three-mould patterns classified as *baroque*, composed of bold motifs in relief; chosen instead of rococo to distinguish typical American designs from contemporary French glass related in design but tighter in composition and lower in relief (Plate 40A (*right*)).

Blown-moulded: glass (1) ornamented by blowing a gather of metal into a mould, either a dip-mould or a part-size piece-mould, to impress a design before fashioning an object by blowing and manipulation; (2) blown in a full-size piece-mould for shape and (Plate 40B (*right*)) shape and decoration. *See* Moulded Glass.

Blown-three-mould Glass: collector's name for a category of inexpensive blown-moulded ware, popular from about 1815 to 1835; blown in full-size piece-moulds for (1) shape and decoration (Plate 40B (*right*)), (2) decoration and partial shape (Plate 40A (*right*)); (3) for decoration only, thus using the full-size mould as a pattern-mould (Plate 40B (*centre*)); transitional between pattern-moulded and fully moulded; characterized by patterns classified in three categories, according to predominating or most conspicuous motifs, *arch*, *baroque* and *geometric* (the last, the earliest and simulating cut-glass); concavo-convex surfaces, an identifying characteristic.

Bottles

(1) **Calabash:** ovoid body tapering into cylindrical neck with collared lip; blown in full-size two-piece mould with intaglio designs falling in the pictorial, decorative and historical categories; *c.* 1850–70 (Fig. 1).

Fig. 1

(2) **Carboy:** large demijohn; usually set in wooden tub; used mainly for corrosive liquids, such as *aqua fortis*.

(3) **Chestnut:** somewhat carelessly free-blown bottles with long neck and fat chestnut-shaped body, frequently full of bubbles and asymmetrical; without uniformity of size, ranging from a few ounces to a gallon or more in capacity; ranging, in natural bottle-glass colours, from ambers through olive-ambers to greens; called also *Ludlow* because of a tradition of having been made in a Ludlow, Massachusetts, glasshouse, and *junk*; made generally, eighteenth–early nineteenth centuries (Fig. 2).

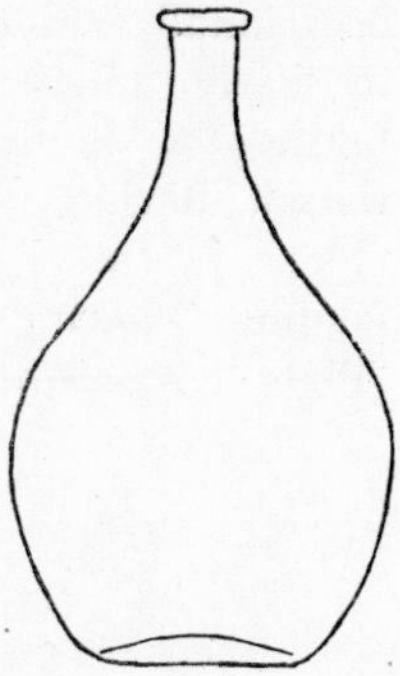

Fig. 2

(4) **Demijohn:** mainly a storage and shipping bottle, often with wicker jacket; free-blown or moulded for symmetrical, globular or oval form, with long neck and lip usually collared; quart to twenty-gallon sizes.

(5) **Nursing (Sucking):** flattened ovoid flask rounded at end, short neck with sheared, sometimes flaring, lip; plain and pattern-moulded in ribs, flutes and diamonds; eighteenth–early nineteenth centuries (Fig. 3).

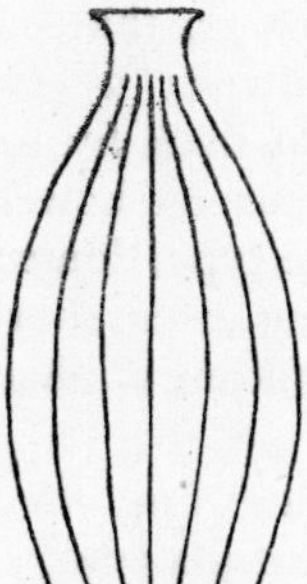

Fig. 3

(6) **Pocket Bottle:** flask of about half-pint to pint capacity. *See* Flasks.

(7) **Stiegel-type Pocket or Perfume:** chunky bulbous form, slightly flattened wide sides; pattern-moulded designs (Plate 41D).

(8) **Swirl:** a Midwestern type, pattern-moulded in vertical ribs or flutes, swirled usually to right, occasionally to left; wide colour range, from aquamarines to deep greens, olive greens, citron, ambers and blues; including two distinctive shapes: (*a*) globular, nearly spherical body, slender neck, slightly tapering or straight, collared lip; (*b*) short cylindrical body, sides often tapering slightly, sloping shoulder, short neck, collared lip; proportions, distinguishing features; some forms also with vertical and broken-swirl ribbing or fluting (Figs. 4A and 4B).

Fig. 4A Fig. 4B

Broken-swirl: pattern-moulded ribbed design obtained by twice moulding a gather in ribbed or fluted dip mould; first impression of vertical ribs, twisted or swirled, gather re-inserted in mould impressing vertical ribs upon the swirled; occurring most frequently on Pitkin bottles, jars and flasks having two-layered body (half-post) and on Midwestern bottles, flasks and hollow-ware blown from single gather (Plate 39A (*centre*)); ribs varying in closeness.

Cased Glass: two or more layers of glass differing in colour; called overlay when designs cut through to body colour.

Castor: (1) bottle form with perforated cap, usually metal; called also shaker;

(2) frame for condiment bottles or containers such as castors (shakers), cruets and mustard-pots.

Castor Bottles: bottles to set in castor or cruet frame – shakers, cruets, mustard-pots.

Chain: applied, tooled decoration; links formed by drawing together at regular intervals two threads of glass laid-on around a parison or body of partially formed object, called also *guilloche*; in England, *trailed circuit* (Fig. 5).

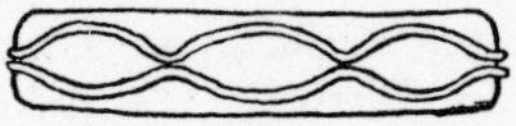

FIG. 5

Checkered Diamond: decorative motif, large diamond enclosing four small ones: (A) pattern-moulded German diaper design; used in the U.S., by Stiegel at Manheim, Pennsylvania (possibly), at the New Bremen Glass-manufactory and in one or more early nineteenth-century Midwestern bottle houses, principally for flasks and salts of type having slender double-ogee bowl and applied circular foot; (B) full-size, piece-moulded, blown-three-mould motif in geometric pattern (McK. GII-29) (Figs. 6A and 6B).

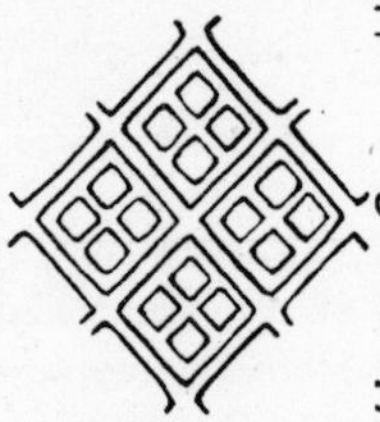

FIG. 6A

FIG. 6B

Chestnut Bottle: *see* Bottles.

Collars: heavy applied thread or ribbon, plain or tooled, laid on around (1) lips of bottles and flasks; (2) necks of decanters: (*a*) plain round, single or double, (*b*) rigaree, single or double, (*c*) triangular, usually single, rarely double, (*d*) triple ring (wide single with medial rib), (*e*) chain, rare; in U.S. infrequently called *neck rings*; (3) around stem or shaft, also part of composite stem or shaft; vermicular (wavy), rare in American glass (Fig. 7).

Collar-rib: moulded rib simulating round plain collar; mainly on blown-three-mould decanters and toilet bottles (Plate 40B (*right*)).

Composite Stem or Shaft: built up of two or more parts welded together; found on drinking vessels, compotes, candlesticks, occasionally on covered sweetmeat dishes, sugar-bowls, pitchers.

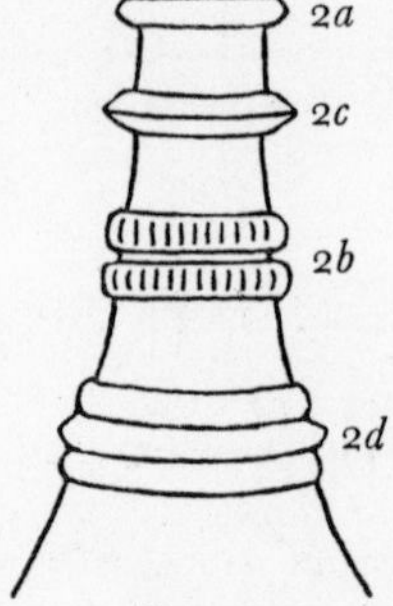

FIG. 7

Compote: bowl on standard (stem and foot); also on domed or pedestal foot.

Corrugated Handle: *see* Handles.

Covers: made principally for compotes and bowls. (1) Domed: (*a*) low flattened usually on eighteenth-century set-in type, occasionally individual pieces blown mainly in early nineteenth-century Mid-western bottle-glass houses (Fig. 8A); low or high round, flaring rim, plain or folded edge (Plate 44 (*centre*)); (*c*) low or high conical (sloping), flaring rim, plain or folded edge (Plate 40A (*centre*)); (*d*) double, proportions of upper and lower dome varying, that on Plate 39A (*left*), peculiar to Midwest; (2) set-in, flanged, with short, straight neck fitting inside bowl's rim so flange rests on bowl's rim (Fig. 8B); (3) set-over, rare type, domed with straight-sided neck fitting over short neck of bowl and resting on moulding applied on bowl (Fig. 8B).

FIG. 8A

FIG. 8B

Crimped Foot: dents or flutes impressed by a tool, usually diagonal (Plate 38A (*right*)).

Cruet: (1) lipped bottle with or without handle; (2) castor bottle.

[*Continued on page 82*

Stiegel-type tumblers, Continental style; colourless glass. (*Left*) Engraved tulips, moulded sunken panels. (*Right*) Enamelled, probably Stiegel, *c.* 1769. *Corning Museum of Glass.*

PLATE 37

To face page 80

(A) South Jersey type, free-blown, bottle-glass individua pieces, ornamented by glass itself applied and tooled, first half nineteenth century. (See page 81 for detailed descriptions.) *George S. McKearin Collection.*

(B) Amelung presentation pieces; colourless glass; engraved decoration characteristic of the New Bremen Glass Manufactory, Md. (See page 81 for detailed descriptions.) (*Left*) *George S. McKearin Collection.* (*Centre and right*) *Corning Museum of Glass.*

PLATE 38

(A) Pattern-moulded individual Midwestern pieces, *c.* 1815. (See page 81 for detailed descriptions.) *George S. McKearin Collection.*

(B) New England canary candlesticks and vases pressed in two parts, joined by a merese, 1830–50. (See page 81 for detailed descriptions.) *George S. McKearin Collection.*

PLATE 39

(A) Colourless flint-glass commercial wares. (See page 81 for detailed descriptions.) *George S. McKearin Collection.*

(B) Blown-three-mould, commercial flint-glassware, colourless, 1820–30. (See page 81 for detailed descriptions.)
George S. McKearin Collection.

PLATE 40

(A)

(B)

(C)

(D)

(A, B, C) Historical and Masonic pint flasks. (D) Diamond-daisy pocket bottle. (See page 81 for detailed descriptions.) *George S. McKearin Collection.*

PLATE 41

Midwestern lacy glass (mechanically pressed), *c.* 1830. (See page 81 for detailed descriptions.) *Corning Museum of Glass.*

PLATE 42

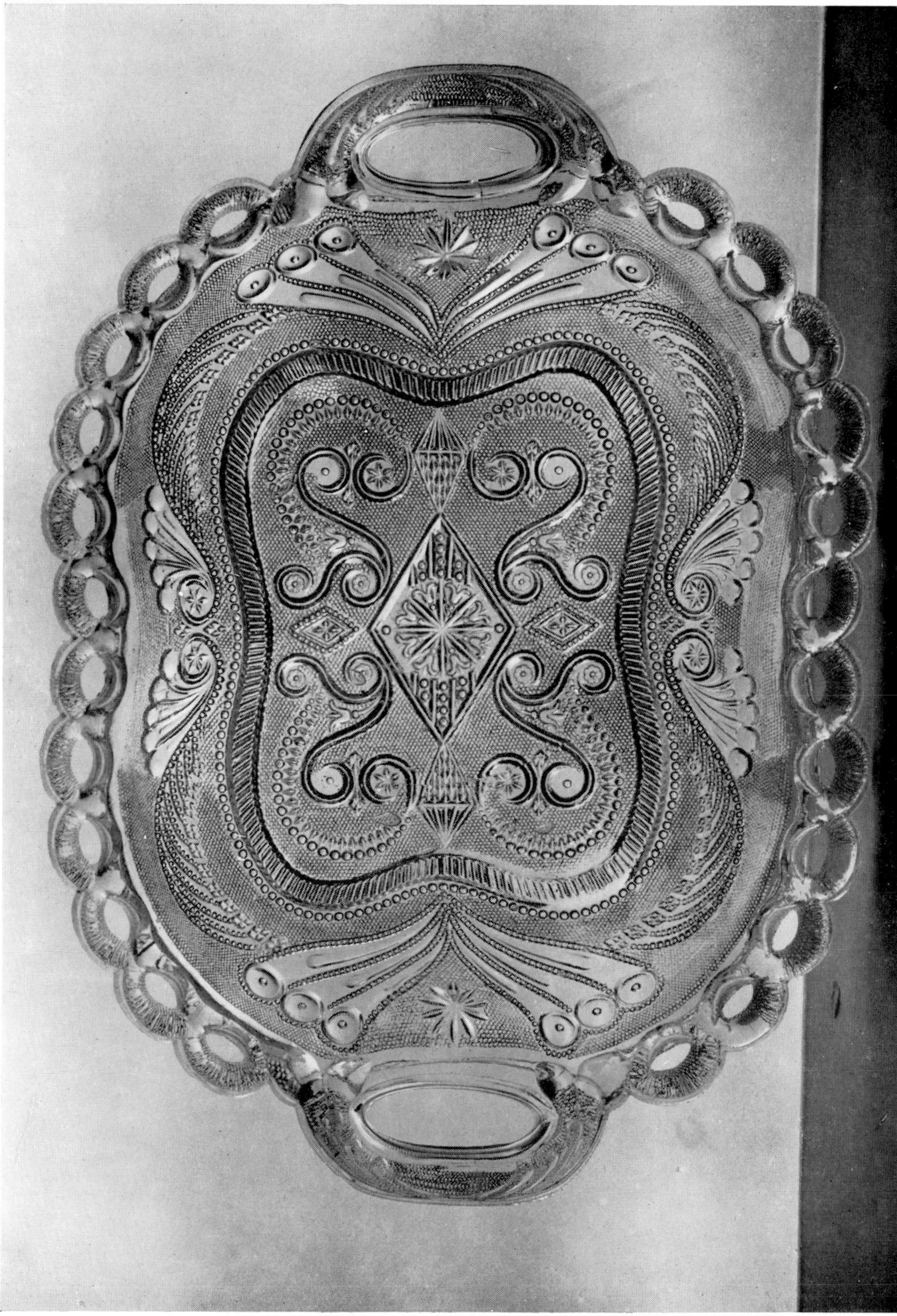

Eastern lacy glass cake tray with pierced border and open handles; typical elaborate design on stippled ground; attributed to the Boston and Sandwich Glass Works, *c.* 1830. Measurements, $11\frac{3}{4}$ in. × $8\frac{1}{4}$ in. *Private collection.*

Individual free-blown bottle-glass pieces. (See page 81 for detailed descriptions.) *Corning Museum of Glass.*

PLATE 44

FURTHER DESCRIPTION OF PLATES

PLATE 38

(A) *Left*: New York State pitcher, clear light green; threaded neck, lily-pad type III on unusual ovoid body; height 6⅛ in. *Centre*: New York State vase, blue aquamarine; threaded neck, girdling ring topping swirled gadroons tooled in second gather on body; height 4½ in. *Right*: South Jersey bowl, pale green; folded rim, lily-pad type I on body, crimped applied foot; height 5⅛ in. (B) *Left*: Covered goblet made for George Jacob Schley, Frederick, Md., *c.* 1790; showing one of the elaborate floral and foliated wreaths; height overall 11⅞ in. *Centre*: Flask showing the simplest of the Amelung wreaths; inscribed on reverse 'F. STENGER' '1792'; height 6⅝ in. *Right*: Tumbler, amethyst cast in thick base; vignette depicting a typical Maryland farmhouse and yard, and, on reverse, elaborate medallion with 'GMR', the initials of George M. Repold, Baltimore merchant and friend of Amelung; height 7⅞ in.

PLATE 39

(A) *Left*: Sugar-bowl, brilliant clear green bottle glass; expanded vertical ribbing; shape and proportions peculiar to Mid-west. *Centre*: Salt, colourless; broken-swirl ribbing, double-ogee bowl of typical Midwestern proportions, ribbed drawn knop, applied foot with twelve irregular petals or scallops; height 3 in. *Right*: Pitcher, 'moonstone' glass; expanded in large diamond or ogival pattern; shape similar to ceramic form, not found in eastern individual pieces; height 4¼ in.
(B) *Left*: Dolphin, petal socket and baluster joined to dolphin on stepped square base; height 10⅜ in. *Centre left*: Vase, three-printie-block bowl with scalloped rim joined to hexagonal standard with large knop above flaring foot; height 9¼ in. *Centre right*: Petal socket and baluster joined to fluted column rising from two round steps on stepped square base; height 9⅛ in. *Right*: Vase, slender loop bowl with scalloped rim and ringed knop joined to standard with hexagonal baluster, circular foot with petal-like panels; height 10¾ in.

PLATE 40

(A) *Left*: Midwestern pitcher, pattern-moulded with eight wide-spaced pillar ribs; parallel incised lines below rim and notching tops of ribs; applied hollow strap handle with leaf end; typical of Pittsburgh area, *c.* 1825–40; height 8 in. *Centre*: Sugar-bowl, characteristic of Pittsburgh area; sloping-domed cover with button knob and folded rim; bowl with galleried rim, shallow engraved decoration, and, at bottom, moulded round-top panels, low-pedestal lacy-glass foot, *c.* 1830; height overall 7 in. *Right*: Blown-three-mould pitcher, patterned in decanter mould in Baroque pattern GV–13, *c.* 1830; height 6¾ in.
(B) *Left*: Tumbler in geometric pattern GIII–16, with bulls'-eye sunburst; patterned in the pint decanter mould identified with the Flint Glass Works, Marlboro Street, Keene, N.H.; height 5⅞ in. *Centre*: Bowl with folded rim; patterned in tumbler or decanter mould in geometric pattern GIII–6 and fashioned by blowing and manipulation; height 3¼ in. *Right*: Labelled pint decanter in Arch pattern GV–7 with snake medallion enclosing 'WHISKEY'; Boston and Sandwich Glass Works, Sandwich, Mass.

PLATE 41

Blown in full-size piece moulds for form and decoration. (A) McKearin's *American Glass*, GII–54: American eagle perched on shield; reverse, U.S. flag and 'FOR OUR COUNTRY'; olive green; Coffin & Hay, Hammonton, N.J., *c.* 1836. (B) McK. GIV–7: Masonic emblems; reverse, American eagle above beaded oval frame enclosing eight-pointed star; yellow-green with amber streaks; Marlboro Street works, Keene, N.H., *c.* 1814–20. (C) GI–40a, Zachary Taylor, Mexican war hero, President of the United States, and 'GEN TAYLOR NEVER SURRENDERS'; reverse, Washington and 'THE FATHER OF HIS COUNTRY'; deep olive-green; Dyottville Glass Works, Kensington, Philadelphia, *c.* 1847–49. (D) Stiegel-type pocket bottle; pattern-moulded, attributed to Stiegel, *c.* 1764–74.

PLATE 42

Left: Creamer with body and handle pressed in one piece; design on stippled ground, including basket of flowers (more lineal in composition than the eastern) and geometric motifs; marked on base 'R. B. CURLING & SONS FORT PITT', Pittsburgh, Pa.; height about 4 in. *Right*: Octagonal plate with American eagle in centre on plain ground, 13 encircled eight-petalled flowers—'stars'— palmette and fleur-de-lys on stippled, bull's-eye serrated rim, Midwestern characteristic; depth 6 in.

PLATE 44

Left: Pale yellow-green; threaded at top, band of gadrooning moulded on cup-like layer on lower bowl, graduated rings at top of applied stem attributed to New Geneva Glass Works, Albert Gallatin & Co., Pennsylvania, *c.* 1798–1810; height 5¾ in. *Centre*: New York State, aquamarine; lily-pad type II on body and dome of cover, chicken finial on hollow ball-knob containing 1829 silver half-dime, and 1835 in hollow ball-stem of bowl, *c.* 1835–50; height overall 11 in. *Right*: South Jersey in amber, opaque white loopings; on body, girdling ring at top of cup-like layer tooled into gadroons, flat foot, applied handle with leaf end; blown by Jackie Getzinger, Bridgeton, N.J., glassworks, *c.* 1836–50; height 7½ in.

Continued from page 80]

Cruet Frame: *see* Castor (2).

Cup Plate: small plate from about $2\frac{5}{8}$ to $4\frac{5}{8}$ inches in diameter; used as saucer for cup; also used when beverage was drunk from saucer, a custom among some groups, not sanctioned by fashionable society; found mainly in inexpensive glasswares such as pressed; nineteenth century, mainly second quarter.

Cut-corners: chamfered; formed by bevelling the corners formed by the meeting of two sides, making eight planes, narrow at corners; term usually applied to *square* and *rectangular* bottles shaped in full-size piece moulds (Fig. 9).

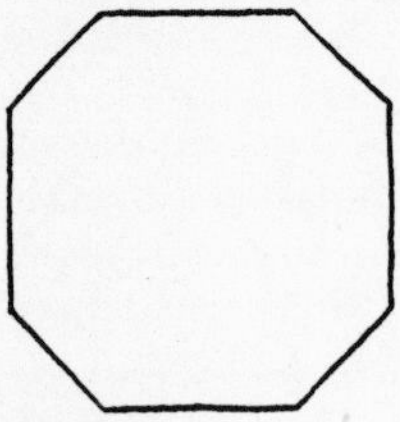

FIG. 9

Cut-glass: glass decorated by grinding designs and motifs by means of abrasive agents and iron, stone and polishing wheels.

Daisy-in-hexagon: daisy-like flower within hexagon, in pattern-moulded diaper design; believed to be a Stiegel original; found mainly on pocket bottles similar to Plate 41D.

Decanter: (1) English terminology generally used for shapes, but *sugar-loaf* synonymous with *mallet* and *semi-barrel* instead of *Prussian* (*see* Hughes, *English Glass*, Concise Encyc. of Antiques, Vol. II); (2) labelled, *c.* 1825–50: (*a*) occasionally engraved *wine* or with name of a spirit; (*b*) blown-three-mould, moulded labels in four geometric patterns and one arch (Plate 40B (*right*)), include WINE, BRANDY, RUM, GIN, H. GIN, CHERRY and WHISKY.

Diamond: (1) diamond diaper, blown-three-mould motif, used in square (Plate 40B (*left*)) or in band; (2) expanded diamond, pattern-moulded and expanded in process of fashioning an unformed but patterned gather into an object; in U.S. three principal varieties: (*a*) diamond diaper (units varying in size and number in different moulds), (*b*) rows of diamonds above flutes. *See also* Checkered Diamond; (*c*) strawberry diamond (cross-hatched relief diamond), pressed and cut-glass motif.

Diamond-daisy: daisy-like flower within square-diamond, in pattern-moulded diaper design; believed to be a Stiegel original; found mainly on pocket or 'perfume' bottles (Plate 41D).

Dip Mould: one-piece open-top fluted or ribbed mould, varying sizes and depths.

Double-ogee Bowl: in U.S., bowls with sides rising in distorted 'S', varying widely in proportions and lengths of curves; Plate 39A (*centre*), like Haynes' pan-topped, others like his cup-topped (*Glass Through the Ages*); in so-called Stegel-type salts, often an attenuated 'S'.

Eagle, American: like or derived from (1) seal of the U.S.; (2) U.S. coins; most common historical motif in pressed lacy glass and historical flasks (Plates 41A and 42), occasionally engraved on blown glass.

Engraved Glass: glass decorated by chasing design or motifs by means of (1) copper wheels of various sizes from about $\frac{1}{8}$ to 2 inches in diameter, occasionally polished, (Plate 40A (*centre*)); (2) by diamond point, rare usage in U.S., mainly for inscriptions and dates.

Etched Glass: glass decorated by *biting* out designs or motifs by means of acid applied to unprotected surfaces.

Eye-and-scale: cut, blown-moulded and pressed motif having round or oval disc or boss, plain or ornamental, at top of relief *scales* in vertical or swirled line, usually forming band; called *horn-of-plenty* in blown-three-mould glass (Fig. 10).

FIG. 10

Finials: (1) cover knob, drawn or applied, usually with short stem: (*a*) ball (Plate 39A (*left*)), (*b*) ball and button (Fig. 11A), (*c*) button (Plate 40A (*centre*)), (*d*) mushroom, (*e*) pointed globular (spire), plain and ribbed; (2) decorative finish of plain cover knob, including (*a*) chicken, nineteenth-century hen-like bird into which the eighteenth-century 'swan' degenerated, used on nineteenth-century pieces of South Jersey Type (Plate 44 (*centre*)); (*b*) swan, unswan-like in having crest, similar to Continental forms, found occasionally on late eighteenth- and early nineteenth-century glass (Fig. 11B);

FIG. 11A

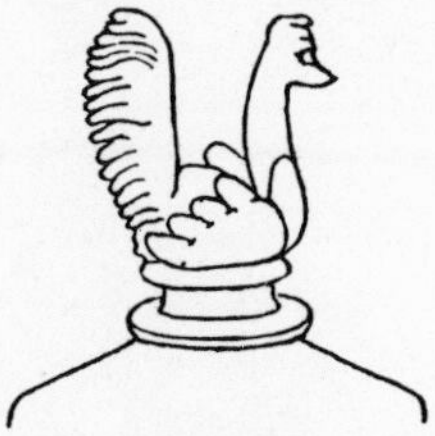

FIG. 11B

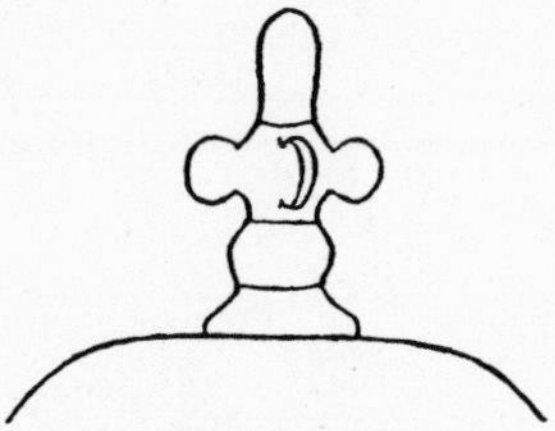

FIG. 11C

(*c*) turned with or without ornamental fins (wings) (Fig. 11C).

Flasks

(1) **Chestnut:** free-blown and pattern-moulded, rarely blown-three-mould, of the timeless and universal shape resembling a slender chestnut; without uniformity of size,

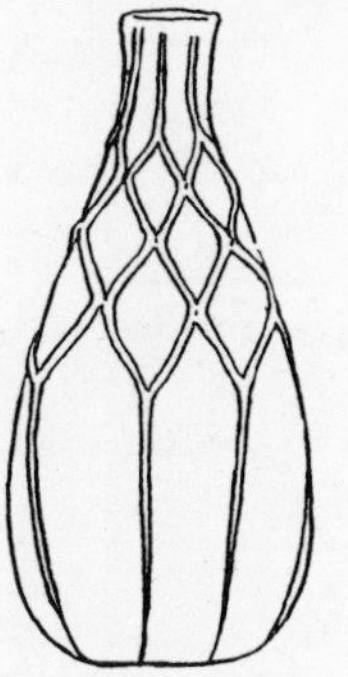

FIG. 12A

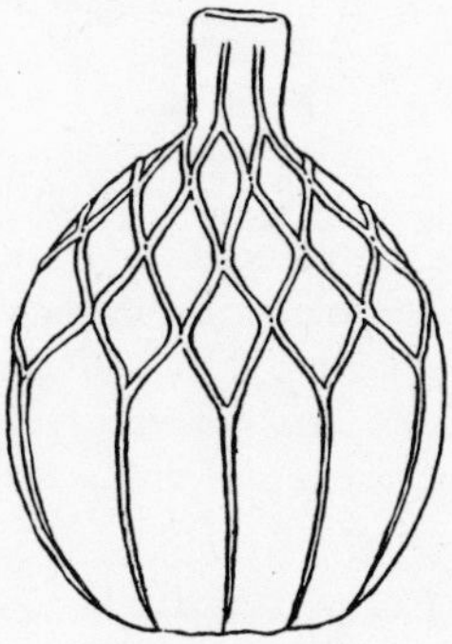

FIG. 12B

ranging from a few ounces to over a quart capacity, majority of pocket-bottle size; mainly late eighteenth, early nineteenth century (Figs. 12A end view, 12B side view).

(2) **Decorative:** blown in full-size two-piece moulds bearing intaglio devices such as

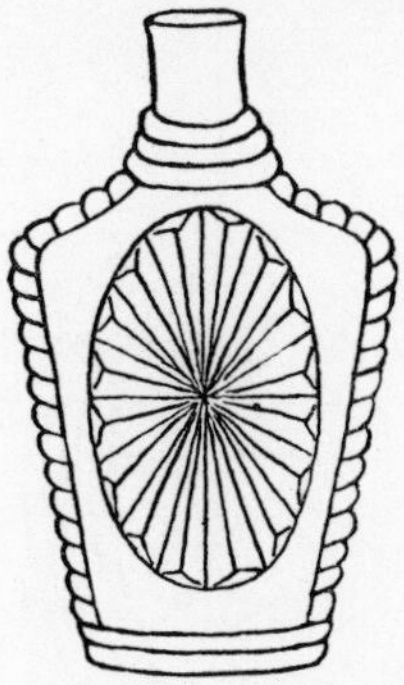

FIG. 13A

FIG. 13B

the sunburst, urn of fruit and cornucopia; mainly half-pint and pint sizes; *c.* 1815–40 (Figs. 13A, 13B and 13C).

(3) **Grandfather:** Midwestern chestnut flask of quart or more capacity; pattern-moulded in ribbed designs.

FIG. 13C

(4) **Historical:** moulded like (2); designs of historical import; commemorative of events and public figures, emblems, slogans, candidates in presidential campaigns; emblems and designs related to economic life; also national and other symbolical emblems; *c.* 1815–late nineteenth century, majority before 1870 (Plates 41A and 41C, Fig. 14).

FIG. 14

(5) **Masonic:** moulded like (2); designs with (*a*) Masonic emblems each side, (*b*) Masonic emblems one side; reverse, different design, American Eagle most common; *c.* 1815–30 (Plate 41B).

(6) **Pictorial:** moulded like (2); designs depicting people and/or flora and fauna; *c.* 1815–70 (Figs. 15A and 15B).

FIG. 15A

FIG. 15B

(7) **Pitkin:** generic term for pocket bottles or flasks, blown by German half-post method and pattern-moulded in ribbed designs – vertical, swirled and broken-swirl; eight-

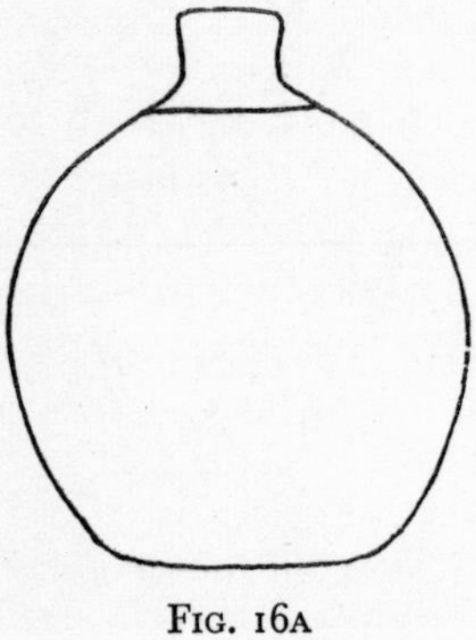

FIG. 16A

FIG. 16B

eenth–early nineteenth century; first identified by tradition with the Pitkins' glassworks, East Hartford, Connecticut, *c.* 1790–1830 (Figs. 16A and 16B).

Flint Glass: (1) literally, glass made with silica of calcined flints; seemingly not used in the U.S.; (2) glass made with lead as a flux, called *lead glass* by collectors; (3) trade name for fine glassware, after 1864 including lime glass of William Leighton, Hobbs, Brockunier & Co., Wheeling, West Virginia.

Flip or **Flip Glass:** collector's term for tumblers, usually of pint or more capacity; *flip* (beverage) probably rarely served in glass vessels.

Fluting: used when wider unit of ridged design is concave; fan-fluting, short tapering flutes or panels, blown-three-mould motif.

Folded Rim: *see* Rims.

Folk Art in American Glass: *see* South Jersey Type (Plates 38A and 44).

Foot: on blown and blown-moulded glass. (1) Applied: occasionally square; mainly circular (*a*) short-stemmed, eighteenth-century type (Fig. 17A); (*b*) flat (Plate 38A

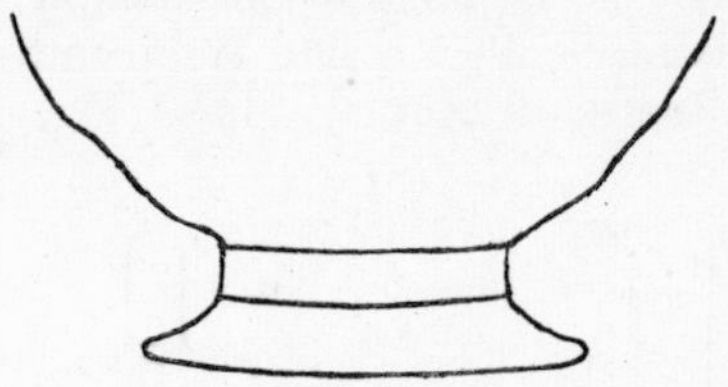

FIG. 17A

(*left*)); (*c*) sloping (Plate 38A (*centre*)); (*d*) petalled (scalloped) (Plate 39A (*centre*)); (*e*) domed, high and hollow, conical (sloping) or round with flaring plain or folded rim, eighteenth–early nineteenth century (Plate 38B (*left*)); (*f*) pedestal, high and hollow,

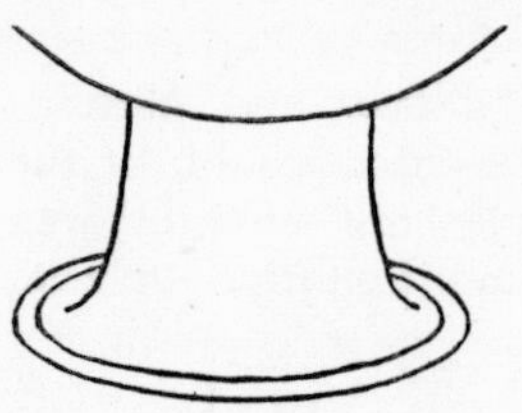

FIG. 17B

FIG. 17C

cylindrical (eighteenth-century type) or truncated cone flaring at rim (late eighteenth and nineteenth centuries) (Figs. 17B and C); (*g*) flaring (low pedestal), found also pressed (Plate 40A (*centre*)). (2) Drawn: drawn from the bottom of vessel's body and fashioned by tooling.

Free-blown: glass formed by blowing and manipulation with hand tools, without aid of moulds; called also *handblown* and *off-hand-blown*.

Full-size Mould: mould composed of two or more hinged pieces (leaves), having inner surface with or without decorative design, and the size and form of an article; glass thus moulded characterized by concavo-convex surfaces.

Gadroon or Gadrooning: heavy rounded ribs or flutes (1) tooled on layer of glass formed from a pearl (round gather of metal) attached to end of parison and pulled up over it (Plate 44 (*right*)); (2) dip-moulded on cup-like layer (Plate 44 (*left*)); (3) full-size moulded convex ribs, high relief, tapering from rounded end, forming band.

Galleried Rim: *see* Rims.

Gather: uninflated and unformed blob of metal taken from the pot on end of blowpipe.

Gauffered Rim: *see* Rims.

Geometric Patterns: (1) category of blown-three-mould patterns composed of motifs such as ribs, flutes, diamonds, sunbursts, circles, ovals (Plate 40B); (2) cut-glass patterns composed of ribs, diamonds and fans on thick blown-moulded glass, called 'imitation cut-glass'; (3) cut-glass motifs, strawberry diamond in particular, on mechanically pressed glass.

Guilloche: *see* Chain.

Half-post: second gather forming two-layered body, giving added strength through double wall and terminating below neck of vessel; the post (first gather) given a half-post (second gather) by redipping in pot of metal; in U.S. associated with Continental and American case bottles and Pitkin flasks and bottles.

Hand-blown: free-blown; used in contradistinction to machine-blown.

Handles: on blown glass, applied. (1) Either round in section or strap (flattened), hollow or solid, ending in (*a*) turned-back tip, (*b*) curled tip, (*c*) crimped end with *a* or *b*, (*d*) leaf (tooled diagonal lines) with *a* or *b*, probably after 1825. Plate 40A (*right*): 1, hollow strap, *d*; Plate 40A (*left*): 1, round hollow, *c*. (2) Principal shapes: (*a*) 'D', rarely found on nineteenth-century glass (Fig. 18A), (*b*) loop (Plate 38A (*left*)), (*c*) semi-ear-shaped (Plate 39A (*right*)), (*d*) swan: long and arching above rim (Fig. 18B). Commonest, *b* and *c*. (3) Principal decoration: (*a*) medial rib: a centre rib, often on round, occasionally on strap, the English *trailed*; (*b*) corrugated, ridged or ribbed strap; (*c*) double; paralleled contiguous sections, occasionally round, usually strap; (*d*) ribbed: hollow handle formed

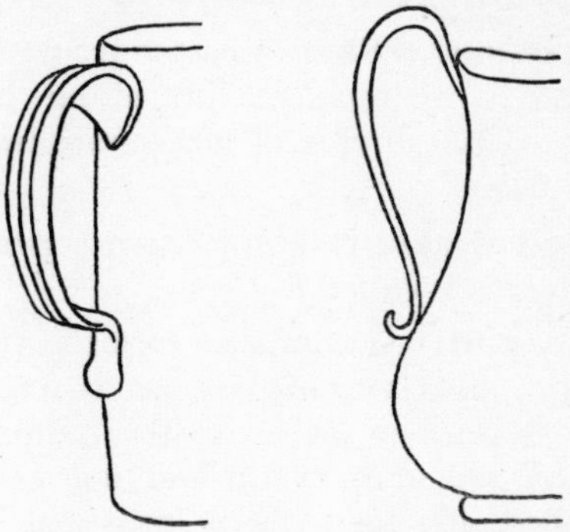

FIG. 18A FIG. 18B

from ribbed or fluted (pattern-moulded) gather, drawn out into a tube, English *incised* and *reeded*.

Historical Glass: glass bearing decoration associated with national or local events, heroes, public figures; agriculture, trade, commerce, transportation, etc; engraved, rare; mainly moulded in flasks and pressed in lacy glass (Plates 41A and 41C, and Plate 42 (*right*)).

Horn-of-Plenty: (1) cornucopia of fruit or produce; common motif on decorative flasks; occasionally in lacy glass; (2) in pressed pattern ware, stylized cornucopia-shaped motif with waffled disc at top, 'horn' with round bosses or vice-versa; similar to the *peacock eye* in lacy glass. *See* Eye-and-scale.

Jug: bottle-like vessel with narrow neck, collared and/or lipped mouth and handle; in U.S., not used synonymously with *pitcher*.

Knob: *see* Finial.

Knop: solid or hollow knob or protuberance in stem or shaft of a vessel; formed by tooling in continuous stem or a separate unit in composite; types designated mainly by Haynes' terms, *Glass Through the Ages*.

Lacy Glass: pressed glassware (*c*. 1828–40). Characterized by intricate relief designs on finely stippled background; matt appearance on pattern side, brilliant sparkling on smooth (Plates 42 and 43).

Lazy-susan Castor: footed castor, usually metal, with shaft terminating in handle and, at top of foot, movable circular frame with rings in which to suspend condiment containers; probably after 1830.

Lazy-susan Shape: castor (cruet) bottle formed with shoulder projecting beyond sides to rest on ring of lazy-susan castor or cruet frame.

Lead Glass: collector's term; glass containing lead; called *flint glass*.

Lily-pad: Decoration formed from a superimposed layer of glass, that is, a rounded gather (pearl) attached to the bottom of a parison, pulled up over it and tooled into the so-called lily-pad; three principal types: Type I – slender stem, beadlike pad (Plate 38A (*right*)). Type II – wider and more valleyed stem, blobbly or small flattened pad (Plate 44 (*centre*)). Type III – long curving stem, flattened ovoid pad, probably type giving rise to the term (Plate 38A (*left*)).

Loopings and Draggings: parallel glass threads, one or more colours contrasting with body colour, laid around parison, then at nearly equidistant points dragged upward by pincers or hooked tool and rolled on marver to embed in parison; decorative device from antiquity, used for commercial wares, also for pieces of South Jersey Type, probably from about 1825 or 1830 in U.S. (Plate 38A (*right*)).

Masonic Flasks: *see* Flasks.

Metal: Glass either in the molten or hardened state.

Merese: Glass wafer or button joining parts of a vessel or units in a stem or shaft.

Midwestern: Collector's term for glass made from about 1790 in glasshouses between the Allegheny Mountains and the Mississippi, principally the Pittsburgh–Monongehela area, Pennsylvania, Ohio, and the Wellsburg–Wheeling area, West Virginia.

Moulded Glass: glass ornamented and/or given partial or final body shape by use of a mould; applicable to pressed glass but reserved generally for blown-moulded.

Mould-blown: English equivalent of blown-moulded.

Neck Rings: collars; infrequently used in the U.S. *See* Collars.

Nursing Bottles: *see* Bottles.

Off-hand-blown: free-blown.

Ogival: Expanded diamond, pattern-moulded diaper in diamond-like formation reminiscent of English *nipt-diamond-waies* formed by tooling applied threads; usually loosely formed diamonds above flutes (Plate 39A (*right*)).

Open-top Mould: *see* Dip Mould.

Overlay: *see* Cased Glass.

Panelling: moulded contiguous round- or oval-topped arches with (1) narrow flattened upright in bold relief, mainly eighteenth century (Plate 37 (*left*)); (2) thread-like upright and arch top, often tapering at bottom (Plate 40A (*left*)), like Haynes' 'moulded wide fluting', late eighteenth–early nineteenth century. Both often called *sunken panel*.

Parison: inflated, unformed gather of metal.

Part-size Mould: small two-piece hinged mould; long handle usually attached to each piece to open and close mould; used to impress design on gather.

Pattern-moulded: term designating glass moulded for decorative pattern or design only, in dip and part-size moulds and expanded; coined to differentiate glass so patterned from that blown in full-size moulds.

Peacock Eye: pressed lacy glass motif similar to stylized horn-of-plenty in pressed pattern-ware (*see* Horn-of-Plenty); *eye* usually

FIG. 20

a large circular dot within beaded ring and 'horn' either stippled or fine-diamonded; called also *peacock feather* (Fig. 20).

Pedestal Foot: *see* Foot (1, *f*).

Petalled Foot: *see* Foot (1, *d*), (Plate 39A (*centre*)).

Picot: tooled decorative device, usually forming crest of wavy decoration or swagging,

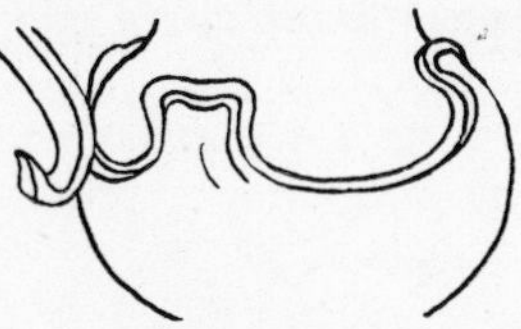

FIG. 19

found mainly on South Jersey Type glass; sometimes called *aborted* or *vestigial* lily-pad (Fig. 19).

Piece Mould: part-size and full-size moulds composed of two or more pieces (leaves); necessary for motifs and designs with crossed lines, such as diamond diapering. *See* Part-size and Full-size.

Pillar Moulded: glass ornamented with pattern-moulded pronounced ribs, vertical or swirled, presumably by the method described in Pellatt's *Curiosities of Glass Making*; in U.S. associated mainly with a Midwestern commercial ware from the Pittsburgh and Wheeling areas, having wide-spaced pillar ribs; *c.* 1825–50 (Plate 40A (*left*)).

Pillar Rib: (1) pronounced relief, pillar moulded, rib (Plate 40A (*left*)); (2) wide, short heavy ribs forming band in a geometric pattern.

Pinched Trailing: English term; *see* Quilling.

Pitkin: *see* Flasks (7).

Pontil Mark: punty mark, scar left on completed article at point where punty rod (pontil), attached during processes of manipulation, was detached; seemingly less frequently ground off and polished on early U.S. ordinary wares than on British.

Portrait Flasks: group of historical flasks bearing portraits of public figures and heroes (Plate 41C).

Pressed Glass: glass pressed in moulds; (1) manually, using die-and-plunger mould; (2) mechanically, machines including mould and lever-operated plunger; method attributed to the U.S.

Pressed Pattern Ware: pressed glass sets for table, bar, etc; articles matching in pattern; earliest, about 1840.

Prunts: applied blobs of glass tooled or moulded into various devices.

Quilling: ribbon of glass laid on and pinched into pleats; *pinched trailing*.

Ribbing: used when ridged design's wider unit is convex; gadroon ribbing. *See* Gadroon (3).

Rims: (1) folded: edge finish of foot or bowl-top, sheared edge folded back forming double wall; called also welted (Plate 38A (*right*)); (2) galleried, nineteenth-century bowl-top finish; flaring rim having short straight-side and flattened plane at right angles to body, thus forming cover support (Plate 39A (*left*)); (3) gauffered, on vases and occasionally pitchers; flaring with wide-scallop edge; called also ruffled; mainly nineteenth century (Plate 39B (*left centre*)); (4) sheared or plain, excess glass cut away evenly and edge smoothed by reheating (Plate 38A (*centre*)).

Scalloped Foot: petalled.

Set-in and Set-over Covers: *see* Covers.

Shaft: usually applied to section between socket or font and base of candlestick or lamp; in blown glass, applied forms similar to stems; in early pressed glass, in two sections – one with base and one with socket, joined by a merese (Plate 39B); in later pressed glass, in one with socket and base.

Shakers: term usually preceded by *salt* or *pepper*; castors.

Sheared Lip: plain; *see* Rims (4).

South Jersey Tradition: tradition of glass blowing and decorating presumed to have had its American beginnings in Wistar's and other South Jersey houses; *see* South Jersey Type.

South Jersey Type: generic term for individual pieces blown from bottle- and window-glass in natural colours, occasionally artificial, fashioned by free-blowing and manipulation, plain and decorated by glass applied to itself and tooled, very rarely pattern-moulded; first associated with the

Wistars' eighteenth-century glassworks, southern Jersey; then later houses in the area; now known to have been blown in most Eastern bottle- and window-glass houses into the late nineteenth century; called folk art in American glass, largely because of individual rendering and centuries-old traditional techniques in blowing and decorating; besides devices shown in Plates 38A and 44, *prunts*, *quilling*, *swagging*, *picots*, *bird finials* occur.

Stems: *see* Applied, Composite, Drawn, Knop, Straw and Stuck Shank.

Stiegel Tradition: tradition of glass blowing and decorating by use of pattern-moulds, presumed to have had its American beginnings in Stiegel's second Manheim glassworks (1769–74). *See* Stiegel Type (3).

Stiegel Type: term applied to main types of ware produced in Stiegel's Manheim glass-houses, *c.* 1765–74. (1) Engraved (shallow copper-wheel) and (2) enamelled glass like common Continental commercial wares of mid-eighteenth–early nineteenth century, today called *peasant glass* in Europe (Plate 37). (3) Pattern-moulded glass, usually flint glass, like the British ware produced *c.* 1750–1800; coloured (mainly blues, greens and amethysts) and colourless. *See also* Diamond-daisy and Daisy-in-hexagon.

Stiegel-type Salt: vessel with deep double-ogee bowl, knop drawn from bottom of bowl, applied circular foot, flat or slightly sloping, occasionally scalloped (petalled); like English *bonnet* or *monteith glass*; uses probably included salt, sweetmeats, beverages (Fig. 21).

Stippling: minute raised dots forming the background in lacy glass, glitter-producing device never used in glassmaking until made possible by mechanical pressing; an ear-mark of lacy glass.

Strap Handle: *see* Handles.

Straw Stem: thin, drawn.

Stuck Shank: applied stem.

Sunken Panel: *see* Panelling.

Superimposed Decoration: any decoration or device fashioned by tooling layer of glass formed from a pearl. *See* Lily-pad.

Swagging: superimposed layer tooled into wavy formation, usually crested by a picot.

Swirled Ribbing: pattern-moulded design formed by twisting vertical ribs impressed in a gather inserted in ribbed or fluted dip mould; English, *wrythen ornamentation.*

Trailed Circuit: *see* Chain.

Twisted Ribbing: swirled ribs or flutes; on solid canes, used as stems, sometimes handles; English, *incised* or *reeded.*

Welted Rim: *see* Rims.

FIG. 21

BOOKS FOR FURTHER READING

LEE, RUTH WEBB: *Early American Pressed Glass.* Enlarged and revised 1946 (Northboro, Mass.).
LEE, RUTH WEBB: *Sandwich Glass.* Revised edition 1947 (Northboro, Mass.).
MCKEARIN, GEORGE S. AND HELEN, *American Glass* (New York, 1941).
MCKEARIN, HELEN AND GEORGE S., *Two Hundred Years of American Blown Glass* (New York, 1950).
MCKEARIN, HELEN: *American Historical Flasks* (Corning, N.Y., 1953).
ROSE, JAMES H.: *The Story of American Pressed Glass of the Lacy Period* (Corning, N.Y., 1954).
WATKINS, LAURA WOODSIDE: *Cambridge Glass* (Boston, 1930).

IRISH GLASS

By G. BERNARD HUGHES

IRELAND's earliest flint-glass house was established in Dublin during the early 1690s by Captain Philip Roche. This was known as the Round Glass House, and under various proprietorships continued operating until 1755. Productions by the mid-century, according to an advertisement in *Faulkner's Dublin Journal* quoted by Westropp, included 'all sorts of the newest fashioned drinking glasses, water bottles, claret and burgundy bottles, decanters, jugs, water glasses with and without feet and saucers, plain, ribbed, and diamond moulded jelly glasses of all sorts and sizes, sillybub glasses, comfit and sweetmeat glasses for desserts, salvers, glass plates for china dishes, toort covers, pine and orange glasses, hall lanthorns for one to four candles, glass branches, cut and plain barrel lanthorns, globe lamps, etc, all in the most elegant and newest fashioned mounting now used in London. . . . All sorts of cut and flowered glasses may be had of any kind to any pattern, viz.: wine glasses with a vine border, toasts, or any flourish whatsoever; beer ditto with the same, salts with and without feet, sweetmeat glasses and stands, cruits for silver and other frames all in squares and diamond cut, tea cannisters, jars and beakers of mock china, mustard pots, crests and coats of arms, sweetmeat bowls and covers'. It is doubtful if any English glasshouse could exceed the scope of productions shown on this list.

The Round House was no doubt a highly flourishing business until the export of glass from Ireland was prohibited under the Excise Act of 1745, which at the same time levied a duty of one penny a pound on English flint-glass. This prohibition was directly responsible for the glasshouse closing down ten years later, and from then until 1764 no fine flint-glass appears to have been made in Ireland. Then an already existing bottle-house at Marlborough Green, Dublin, was enlarged to produce flint-glass. By 1770 this glasshouse was under the control of Richard Williams & Company, who then announced in the *Limerick Chronicle* that their productions included 'all the newest fashioned enamelled, flowered, cut and plain wine, beer and cyder glasses, common wines and drams, rummers, decanters, water-glasses and plates, epergnes and epergne saucers, cruets, casters, cans, jugs, salvers, jellies, sweetmeat glasses, salts, salt linings' in flint-glass. This firm must have operated on a large scale, for in addition to flint-glass and bottles they made and ground looking-glass plates. There is no doubt that Williams made virtually all the flint-glass sold in Ireland during the 1770s.

When in 1780 import restrictions were removed, several well-equipped glasshouses were established in Ireland, notably at Waterford, Belfast, Dublin and Cork. Orders poured into Ireland from the Continent and America, for prices, and quality, were much lower than English flint-glass. In 1785 Lord Sheffield observed that 'nine glasshouses have suddenly arisen in Ireland, and the best drinking glasses are sold at three to four shillings a dozen less than the English'.

Although English executives and leading glassworkers and decorators were employed and much of the material obtained from England, it was long before the industry became self-supporting, although still free from paying *excise duty*. The Dublin Society subsidized several firms: the Williams glasshouse, for instance, received £28,145 from this source between 1784 and 1794.

Irish glass of the 1780s and 1790s for the most part displayed a slightly dusky tint. From about 1800 more efficient furnaces were installed by the larger glasshouses and a clearer metal produced. This glass proved ideal for the *cutting* in deep relief which now became overwhelmingly popular. Every potful of metal produced two qualities – *tale* and fine glass. During this period, too, some glass was issued with a faintly *blue tint*.

The nineteenth century also introduced a new era in *blown-moulded* glass, new techniques producing a wholly new range of designs, shapes and decorations at prices lower than formerly. Moulded glass was produced in a fraction of the time possible with handwork. Blown-moulded table-glass was made in shapes and designs approximating to those of *free-blown* and hand-cut glass.

The decline in the Irish flint-glass trade was brought about first by the imposition of an *excise duty* from 1825, such as had existed in England from 1745, and was hastened from the early 1830s by the introduction in England of glass-pressing machines capable of producing handled hollow-ware at a single operation. Such a machine was first installed by W. Richardson, of Wordsley, who sold pressed glass as intagliated table-ware. Other firms quickly followed, but not a single machine is known to have been acquired by an Irish glasshouse. Because of vastly lowered prices, the Irish hand-blown trade languished, and died soon after removal of the *excise duty* in 1845.

Even the celebrated *Waterford* firm failed to survive English competition at the Great Exhibition, 1851, and closed immediately afterwards. The only Irish-made exhibit in the glass section at the Dublin Industrial Exhibition, 1853, was some 'richly cut flint-glass manufactured by the Dublin Flint Glass Works'. At a further exhibition in 1865, Irish flint-glass was not represented.

GLOSSARY

Attribution: no Irish glass unless marked or pedigreed, or closely resembling a marked example in metal and in design, can be definitely attributed to any one glasshouse. The majority of designs were copied from the cut-glass men of London and Glasgow.

Belfast (Benjamin Edwards): the earliest reference discovered by Westropp was an advertisement dated 1781. The wording suggests that the costly Perrott furnace was in use and 'enamelled, cut and plain wine glasses' made as well as cheaper table-glass. From 1783 Edwards was making all kinds of glass-making machinery and hollow-ware moulds, some fluted, which he sold to the newly established Irish glasshouses. By 1805 Edwards was issuing a wide variety of cut table-glass and blown-moulded *decanters*, as well as lustres and girandoles. The glasshouse continued with varying degrees of prosperity until 1829.

Bloom: an all-over film of opaque dullness occasionally found on the surface of flint-glass, English and Irish alike, although usually associated with Irish. It has been described by Mrs Graydon-Stannus as 'rather like the bloom of grapes and if cleaned off it will return'. This effect is caused by the use of high-sulphur fuels in the lehr. Bands of bloom may be found encircling hollow-ware a little distance below the rim; these are the result of reheating at the furnace mouth. This bloom is not to be confused with the milkiness found inside old decanters.

Blown-moulding: this is a little-known aspect of the Irish glass trade.

1. *Types*

(*a*) One-piece moulds were used during the early period in which inexpensive hollow-ware was blown and shaped. Molten flint-glass solidified quickly on the surface in contact with the mould; a quick-setting flint-glass was therefore evolved, not possessing the high brilliancy of metal used for free-blown glass. A gather of this molten metal was taken and blown into a mould smaller than the finished glass vessel; the semi-molten glass was then expanded by further blowing. Such a mould had always to be made slightly greater in diameter at the top than at the base to permit easy withdrawal. Glass shaped by this process may be recognized by its slightly pebbled appearance caused by contact with the mould. The lower part of the mould interior might be intaglio-cut with a circuit of slender flutes rising vertically from the base. Inflation forced the glass closely against the inner surface forming a clean impression. The quick-setting glass ensured that the section of the metal remained constant so that the flutes on the outer surface appeared as corresponding depressions within.

(*b*) The two-piece open-and-shut mould was invented in 1802 by Charles Chubsee of Stourbridge. Glass blown into such a mould was both shaped and decorated with diamond and other motifs in deep relief. Patterns followed those worked on free-blown glass by the wheel-cutters. From 1825 the long-accepted geometrical designs met active competition in the form of baroque scrolls, fan patterns and arch patterns. The gunmetal mould with an intaglio design sunk into the inner surface was the same size as the finished article which was fully inflated in a single operation.

(*c*) The three-piece mould, with one fixed and two hinged sections each cut with an intaglio pattern, dates from about 1830. When the glass was inflated within the mould the blowing force caused the joints to open infinitesimally, thus producing slight ridges on the surface of the glass or a slight break in the pattern.

2. *Patterns*

These are innumerable, but the majority fall into one of the following four groups.

(*a*) Geometric decoration was most frequently used, and included diamonds; diamond diapering; vertical, horizontal and diagonal flutings; oval and round printies.

(*b*) Baroque decorations dating from the mid-1820s featured such motifs as the guilloche pattern; honeysuckle or anthemion; heart; trefoil; gadrooning around the base.

(*c*) Arch decoration, usually in higher relief than geometric. Gothic arches encircling the body often display a spray of foliage between each pair, or there might be a fern leaf within each arch.

(*d*) Bases were usually plain and showed a punty mark. Others are patterned in any of some three dozen simple designs which have been grouped into six classes: rays; circles; rays and arches; flutes and circles; circles of printies; circles of intaglio petal shapes.

3. *To Distinguish from English Pressed Work*

(*a*) Mould marks are no more than slightly convex swellings on the surface of the glass in no way resembling the hair lines or threads on pressed glass which are so sharply defined that they appear to have been applied. The number of mould marks indicates the number of pieces forming the mould. From 1835 blown-moulded glass was finished by *fire polishing*.

(*b*) The concave-convex relation of inner and outer surfaces of blown-moulded glass increased its refractive properties, thus accounting for its typical brilliance. The inflation of the gather of molten glass within a full-sized mould not only caused the air within the gather to force the glass into the sunk pattern, producing relief ornament on the outer surface, but also made corresponding hollows on the inner surface. A smooth inner surface indicates that the glass has been either free-blown or pressed; a slightly rippled surface proves the glass to have been moulded for pattern only and then expanded.

(*c*) The impression received on the surface of blown-moulded glass differs from that of pressed glass. Decoration motifs of the former appear to merge into each other instead of displaying the sharp, almost photographic, definition of pressed glass.

Blue Glass: the leading Irish glasshouses produced a blue glass resembling the English Bristol blue flint-glass coloured by the addition of smalt. A recipe for such glass was found among the *Waterford* papers dated 1786. The finer quality blue glass was prepared in small covered pots, known as piling pots, placed on the ordinary pots. The quality of the glass was improved by keeping the pot in the furnace long after completion of vitrification, thus making it harder and freer from specks and bubbles. In the early nineteenth century a less gorgeous blue was acquired by using less expensive ultramarine. A wide variety of domestic ware was made. A set of six dark blue wine-glass coolers has been noted marked 'Penrose Waterford'.

Blue Tint: the faint bluish hue present in the texture of some late-Georgian flint-glass. For more than half a century collectors deemed this to be solely a *Waterford* characteristic, and as such was sold at greatly enhanced prices. This claim for Waterford cannot be substantiated. True, such blue-tinted glass was issued by Waterford, for Mrs Graydon-Stannus exhibited marked examples to the Royal Society of Arts in 1925, but it is found in other Irish glass, as well as among the productions of Stourbridge, Birmingham, Bristol, Scotland and elsewhere.

This peculiar depth of tone shows the glass to contain lead oxide prepared from Derbyshire mined lead, preferred at many glasshouses because of the superior manipulative properties it gave to the molten metal. Unfortunately the Derbyshire lead contained an impurity which caused this bluish tint, recognized as a defect by the late-Georgian glassmen and which they endeavoured to eliminate.

The Irish glasshouses for the most part used lead oxide made by Wilson Patten, Bank Quay, Warrington, from Derbyshire lead. Not every consignment contained the blue-tingeing impurity, then known to glassmen as Derby blue. There was, therefore, no consistency in the presence of Derby blue in flint-glass during the period concerned, and depth and tone of tint varied.

In 1810 Blair Stephenson, Tipton, Staffordshire, invented a process by which this tint could be eliminated. By 1816 most English and Irish glasshouses were using Stephenson's purified lead oxide, its manufacture proving a profitable monopoly until his manager joined another firm as a competitor. It is doubtful if the Derby blue tint is to be found in Irish glass made later than 1815.

Recent efforts to reproduce the genuine Derby blue tint have failed, but a bogus 'Waterford Blue' has been in production for more than thirty years.

Cork Glasshouse, later **Cork Glasshouse Company:** established in Hanover Street, 1793, as makers of plain and cut flint-glass and black bottles. The firm specialized in light-weight *blown-moulded hollow-ware.* Although heavily subsidized by the Dublin Society, such as £1,600 in 1787 and £2,304 in 1793, throughout its existence the Cork Glasshouse appears to have laboured under financial instability and ever-changing proprietorship. A newly patented Donaldson furnace was installed under a new proprietorship. This gave to flint-glass a clarity and brilliance never before achieved, and some outstanding hand-cut work was produced. The number of hand-cutters employed was such that they founded the Cork Glass-cutters' Union.

In 1812 the firm, under the proprietorship of William Smith & Company, became the Cork Glasshouse Company. Pieces marked 'Cork Glass Co.' date no earlier than this. In 1817 steam-power was installed in a final effort to survive against competition from the newly established *Waterloo Glasshouse.* A year later, however, the glasshouse was closed.

Cork Terrace Glasshouse: established in 1819 by Edward and Richard Ronayne. Their productive capacity was equal to Waterford, for when the firm closed in 1841 it was announced that they possessed tools and machines for forty glass-cutters. They made all kinds of table-glass as well as lustres and Grecian lamps, and were specialists in cut and engraved dessert services.

Cut Motifs

Diamond Cutting: (*a*) Relief, convex, deep-cut and raised are various terms given to diamonds made by deeply incising V-shaped grooves or mitres crossing each other at right angles and at such a distance apart that they produce a series of four-sided pyramids, each with a sharp apex. These were at first shallow-cut in plain bands, but from the 1790s were usually deep, invariably so after about 1805.

(*b*) Cross-cut diamonds were simple relief diamonds with a tiny four-pointed star cut into the apex of each, the star points bisecting each flat surface. Such cutting was difficult to work and is seldom found on large objects.

(*c*) Strawberry diamonds were simple relief diamonds with flat tops produced by cutting the mitred lines farther apart than in (*a*). Upon each flat apex was cut a small relief diamond. In fine-quality work, the centre of every tiny diamond rises to a sharp point.

(*d*) Hobnail diamonds were flat-topped diamonds cut with a simple cross or star.

(*e*) Checkered diamonds were large, flat-topped diamonds cut with four minor diamonds.

Fan or Escallop Shell Borders: the rim of the glass was cut into a series of deep arcs each following the outline of an escallop shell. A fan was then cut with ten, eleven or twelve flutes radiating to each arc. The extremity of each cut was notched.

Fluting: (*a*) Hollowed or slightly concave is found either above or in association with diamond motifs. The crest might be notched until early in the nineteenth century.

(*b*) Pillared fluting consists of half sections of cylindrical columns used in broad bands. This was a favourite Irish motif, dating from *c.* 1790 until the early 1800s, although costly to work.

(*c*) Comb-fluting consists of thin hollow flutes closely spaced and encircling the base of a decanter, finger-bowl or other hollow-ware.

Herring-bone or Blaze: lightly cut upright or slanting lines in graduated lengths forming alternations of crests and troughs.

Notching: an intermittent series of nicks cut into the sharp crests of flutes.

Printies: circular or oval concavities cut into hollow-ware. These might cover the entire surface; two or three rows encircle the body of a decanter, jug, rummer or bowl; or a single row might encircle a bowl rim.

Prismatic Cutting: horizontal parallel grooves cut in deep, sharp prisms and requiring metal of thick section for its perfect display. Fashionable 1800–20 and revived during the 1830s. Sometimes termed step-cutting.

Slice or Edge-flute: flat cutting carried out by holding the glass at an incline against a rotating mitred wheel and removing a film of glass.

Split: a small angular groove.

Sprig: three angular grooves placed to resemble a conventional arrow-head, usually found at the angles of other motifs. Late sprigs were cut more deeply than early examples.

Stars: the early radiating stars were cut with six or eight points: by the nineteenth century twelve-, sixteen- or twenty-four-pointed stars were becoming fashionable. The Brunswick star had a considerable vogue on expensive glass: this was based on a sixteen-point radiating star with every seventh point joined. To produce this star twenty-four cuts were required; as many as seventy-two have been noted.

Step-cutting: see Prismatic Cutting.

Sunburst: a motif composed of closely spaced cut lines radiating from a *printie* or other plain hollow. Associated chiefly with *Cork* productions.

Vesica: a plain incised oval with pointed ends often containing an eight-pointed star. Where they join, *sprigs* are cut above and below. The vesica is usually cut, but is also found engraved and the oval filled with trellis-work. Associated chiefly with *Cork* productions.

Cutting, Types of: (*a*) flat or panel – cut on the flat edge of a wheel.

(*b*) hollow – cut with a convex-edged wheel, producing shallow concavities in the glass.

(*c*) mitre – cut with a V-edged wheel of about 60 degrees.

All cut motifs were produced by some fifty variants of the above until about 1800, when the double-mitre wheel was introduced.

Decanters: the majority of Irish decanters were blown-moulded, the usual size being a quart. In light-weight metal a dozen might cost as little as nine shillings, but those of average thickness with *neck-rings* were much more costly. The features on some marked examples are as follows:

Collins, Dublin: have bases on which radiate carefully moulded V-shaped flutes extending to the edge. The vertical sides are encircled with narrow flutes extending half-way up the body, and the punty mark is larger than noted on other marked decanters.

Cork Glasshouse Company: Prussian-shaped and mallet-shaped decanters were made by pure blowing and cut with all fashionable motifs of the period. *Blown-moulded* types were also made. Probably because of its bottle-making activities, decanters are characterized by their long slender necks. Neck-rings were mainly of the double-feather type, although plain triple rings, square-cut rings and facet-cut rings were made. Stoppers of the shallow mushroom type pinched with radial gadroons were in the majority, but pinched target stoppers and a conical type encircled with several ridges are found.

Blown-moulded decanters have sides only slightly off-vertical. The flutes start a little above the lower rim and extend about two-thirds up the body. The shoulder is often decorated with the vesica pattern.

Benjamin Edwards, Belfast: pyriform blown-moulded decanters bearing the name of this firm encircling the punty mark, have basal corrugations radiating to the rim, a pair of triangular neck rings, mouth slightly everted and finished with a narrow flat rim. The pinched stoppers are vertical, flat-sided and impressed with trellis-work, or target type cut with a six-pointed star. Engraving encircling the shoulders consists of scrolls, swags and stars, carefully executed. The shoulder from the lower neck ring might be encircled with wide-cut flutes.

Waterford: those by Penrose are usually of squat Prussian shape, with three *neck-rings*, a wide, flat mouth rim, and a mushroom stopper pinched with radial fluting and a knop below raising it above the lip. The *mark* is more neatly moulded than on other decanters.

Waterloo Glasshouse Company: decanter shapes and decorations closely followed those of contemporary Waterford. The majority of marked specimens are perceptibly wider at the shoulder than the base. Flutes are longer than those of the Cork Glasshouse Company. The vesica pattern was frequent: an engraved band of stars between two pairs of feathered lines; ribbon scroll engraving rows of hollow encircling the shoulders. It is thought that engraved circles and loops encircling the body are a characteristic feature. Neck-rings usually consist of three of the plain triple variety. Stoppers were low-domed mushroom-shape pinched with radial gadrooning, often with a ball knop immediately below. Pinched target stoppers were also used.

Dishes: date from early in the nineteenth century, and might be circular, oval or octagonal. Early dishes were cut with shallow patterns in relief and later with deep diamonds. Sections are usually variable; sometimes one edge will be considerably thicker than the other.

Drinking Glasses: Westropp found the following named in the Waterford papers in his possession: 'Regents, Nelsons, Masons, Rummers, Hobnobs, Flutes, Draws, Thumbs and Dandies'. To these may be added Rodneys, Coburgs and Thistles.

Dublin – Chebsy and Company: made fine table-glass, at a glasshouse known as Venice, from 1784 to 1798. Between 1787 and 1793 they sold glass to the value of £37,849, receiving meanwhile premiums from the Dublin Society (Westropp). They made the magnificent lustres for Dublin Castle in 1789.

Excise Duty: when in 1745 an excise duty of one penny a pound was imposed on raw materials used in flint-glass making, this applied to Great Britain only. Ireland was excluded, but more devastatingly the export of glass from Ireland was prohibited. In 1780 when the American War of Independence was harassing the British Government, Ireland asserted herself and was granted free trade: all export restrictions were abolished. Within five years glasshouses were established at Dublin, Belfast, Waterford, Cork and Newry, all operating on a large scale and underselling English flint-glass table-ware upon which excise duty had been doubled in 1777.

Irish glass-making continued as a prosperous industry for forty-five years. Then in 1825, under pressure from English competitors labouring under a heavy excise duty of 10½*d.* a pound, the Government laid the impost on Irish glass too. Each furnace in a glasshouse was also required to be licensed at an annual cost of £20. The duty was reduced in 1835, and finally repealed in 1845. The Irish glass trade had meanwhile rapidly declined, competing unavailingly with the glass *presses* installed by the English glassmen from the mid-1830s.

Finger-bowls: large numbers of *blown-moulded* finger-bowls and two-lipped wine-glass coolers were made. They are usually in clear flint-glass, but examples are found in

Part of a table-service of 95 pieces with bands of strawberry diamonds as the main motif, *c.* 1810. *Delomosne & Son Ltd.*

PLATE 45

To ace page 96

(A) Pair of blown-moulded decanters with three feathered neck-rings, engraved with the vesica pattern, and impressed on base 'CORK GLASS CO'. Early nineteenth century. *Delomosne & Son Ltd.*

(B) A pair of blown-moulded decanters engraved with pendant crescents and stars, marked beneath 'WATERLOO CO CORK' in raised letters, and a blown-moulded jug marked 'CORK GLASS CO'. *Messrs. Delomosne & Son Ltd.*

(A) Finger-bowl cut with deep concave flutes with notched crests, band of diamonds and scalloped rim. George IV. *Corning Museum of Glass.*

(B) George IV moulded pickle jar, flat lid cut with circular prisms, foot radially cut beneath.

(C) Kettle-drum shape fruit bowl with knopped stem and round foot. Early nineteenth century. *Corning Museum of Glass.*

(D) Blown-moulded decanter encircled by the vesica pattern associated with Cork; feathered neck rings; target stopper. Early nineteenth century. *Corning Museum of Glass.*

(E) Sweetmeat glass with ogee bowl, facet-cut knopped stem and rims of foot and bowl edged with scalloping, *c.* 1780. *Corning Museum of Glass.*

(F) Sweetmeat glass with band of large relief diamonds, wide fluting and deeply scalloped rim. Early nineteenth century. *Corning Museum of Glass.*

Wine fountain with shallow-cut flutes, silver tap. Late eighteenth century. *Corning Museum of Glass.*

PLATE 48

Pair of two-light candelabra with deep blue canopies, *c.* 1785. *Corning Museum of Glass.*

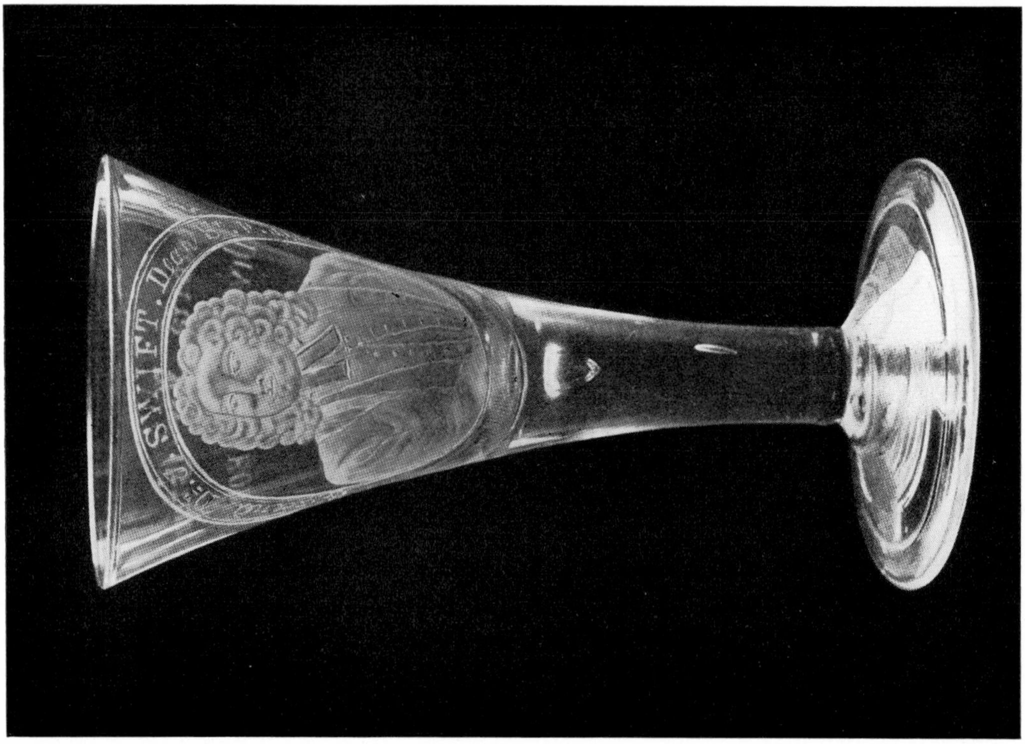

(A) Wine glass with drawn trumpet bowl, tear in stem and engraved with portrait of Dean Swift; dated 1745. *Formerly in the collection of the Earl of Cork and Orrery.*

(B) Toddy rummer with engraved bowl. Its metal displays a faintly blue tint known contemporaneously as Derby blue. Early nineteenth century. *O. T. Norris's Collection.*

(A) Dessert plate with smooth surface, but central crest moulded in relief; rim encircled with diamond cutting and base with narrow and wide flutes, *c.* 1830. *Corning Museum of Glass.*

(B) Butter dish or cooler with horizontal and vertical prismatic cutting. Regency period. *Corning Museum of Glass.*

(C) Fruit bowl with canoe-shaped body cut with large diamonds, a trefoil scalloped rim and moulded foot. Early nineteenth century. *Corning Museum of Glass.*

(D) Bowl cut with alternating eight-pointed stars and single diamonds cut with small diamonds. *Corning Museum of Glass.*

(A) Stemmed sugar bowl with two bands of cross-cut diamonds and shell border to rim, on knopped stem and round foot. *John Bell Collection.*

(B) A lemon holder with shallow-cut body and round convex foot, *c.* 1780. *Corning Museum of Glass.*

(C) Water jug, body cut with large relief diamonds, shoulder with concave flutes, neck with prisms, and notched rim. *Corning Museum of Glass.*

(D) A regency cream jug, body deep-cut with diamonds; shoulder with concave flutes; rim and handle notched.

(E) Bowl cut with strawberry diamonds and engraved with a crowned harp and Irish inscription with a wreath of shamrock. *Howard Phillips.*

PLATE 52

To face page 9

blue, purple, amethyst, red and green. The finest were in heavy cut-glass (Plate 47A).

Fire Polishing: a method of processing *blown-moulded* ware to obliterate tool marks and produce a smooth, even surface. This gave to moulded diamonds, flutes, scrolls, arches and other motifs smoothly defined edges easily mistaken for cut-glass.

Gilding: little Irish glass is known to have been gilded. That such glass was so decorated is shown by the fact that in 1786 the Dublin Society paid John Grahl thirty-five guineas for disclosing glass-gilding secrets, which were then placed at the disposal of the industry. Such gilding appears to have been impermanent, however, and has worn away, leaving the surface beneath pitted and rough. Careful examination of a lavishly cut piece will sometimes reveal traces of gilding.

Jugs: were made in large numbers in the nineteenth century. At first they were tall and narrow on a hollow foot, or, more usually, short and wide, thus giving a more shapely field for cutting in diamonds, flutes, leaf designs, prisms and so on. These at first had the base ground flat; from about 1820 a flanged foot extending outwards was usual. Some jugs were free-blown and engraved.

Marks: a considerable amount of blown-moulded hollow-ware – decanters, finger-bowls, jugs – bears the name of the glasshouse in raised letters on a flat ring encircling the punty mark. Such marks are unknown on English glass. Nine such marks are known: Penrose Waterford; Cork Glass Co; Waterloo C° Cork; B. Edwards Belfast; Francis Collins Dublin; Mary Carter & Son Dublin; Armstrong Ormond Quay; C M C° (Charles Mulvany & Co., Dublin); J. D. Ayckbowm, Dublin. The last five were wholesale glass-sellers whose sales were sufficient to warrant the manufacture of special moulds.

Neck-rings on Decanters: seven types are found: plain round, plain double, plain triple, feathered, triangular, square and diamond-cut. The feathered ring is a double ring impressed with transverse lines. Occasionally the rings – there are usually three – do not match. Neck-rings were applied by rotating the red-hot decanter and dropping a thread of hot glass around the neck. This became welded by contact, and the surplus was tapered and torn suddenly away. The whole was reheated and a tool pressed upon the ring, giving it shape and width. Joints are always faulty, and visible as hair-lines having the appearance of flaws.

Newry Flint-glass Manufactory: a small glasshouse was established in the early 1780s advertising both cut and plain flint-glass, and closed 1801. A new glasshouse was opened in 1824, closing in 1847.

Pressed Glass: (*a*) specialized workers known as 'pinchers' used hand-operated presses for making square feet in a piece with a pedestal or double stem. Target and mushroom decanter stoppers were also made in this way.

(*b*) Mechanical presses for making hollow-ware by a single process were installed in English glasshouses from 1833, but were not used in Ireland.

Quality of Metal: Mrs Delany in 1759 writing from her home in Delville, Ireland, commented, 'I send to England for good glass'. This state of affairs appears to have been fairly general throughout the period of Irish glass, for there are intermittent records that Ireland imported her finest glass from England. The Excise Commission of 1835 recorded that great quantities of English glass entered Ireland, and that all the richly cut decanters and heavy table-ware were English made.

Sugar-bowls: have a boldly concave outline and a flat base, and are for the most part boldly cut with diamond patterns or moulded with thick gadroons.

Tale-glass: a second-quality metal taken from the top of the pot, and sold more cheaply than the lower, finer metal.

Waterford: the earliest record of flint-glass making at Waterford was discovered by Westropp in *The Dublin Journal*, 1729: 'a glasshouse near Waterford now producing all sorts of flint-glass, double and single . . . sold at reasonable rates by Joseph Harris at Waterford, merchant'. This glasshouse was at Gurteens, three miles from the city, and operated until 1739, producing a negligible quantity of glass.

The now celebrated Waterford glasshouse started production in 1784, financed with a capital of £10,000 by George and William Penrose, merchants. The Irish Parliament, however, granted the Penroses a subsidy to cover the expense of building and equipping their glasshouse. As works manager they employed John Hill, member of a family operating the important Coalbournhill Glasshouse near Stourbridge. In evidence given before a committee examining commercial relations between Great Britain and Ireland in 1785, John Blades, a leading cut-glass manufacturer in London, stated that, 'Mr Hill, a great manufacturer of Stourbridge, has lately gone to Waterford, and has taken the best set of Workmen he could get in the County of Worcester'. There is no doubt that the Penroses installed a furnace of the Perrott type costing more than £3,000, such as were already in use at Stourbridge. The Penroses sold flint-glass on a ready-money basis only.

The Penrose glasshouse was bought in 1799 by Ramsay, Gatchell and Barcroft, who built a new factory in Old Tan Yard, advertising the old premises to be let. It is to be assumed that the most modern innovations were included in the new furnace, and that cutting was carried out by means of annealed cast-iron tools, harder and longer wearing than anything formerly available. With these were produced the lavishly decorated cut-glass now inevitably associated with Waterford. Not until 1817 was a steam-driven cutting machine installed.

Gatchell had become sole proprietor by 1811, and with successive partners the firm remained in the family. At an exhibition in Dublin, 1850, George Gatchell displayed table-glass 'all of opaque blue, and white or crystal'. At the Great Exhibition, 1851, he exhibited a magnificent 'etagere or ornamental centre for a banqueting table, consisting of forty pieces of cut-glass, so fitted to each other as to require no connecting sockets of other material; quart and pint decanters cut in hollow prisms. Centre vase or bowl on detached tripod stand. Vases and covers. Designed and executed at the Waterford Glass Works'. This was Gatchell's swansong; his final effort to compete with England was a failure, and he closed the glasshouse later in the same year.

Few collectors realize that Waterford imported glass from England for merchanting purposes; Belfast and Cork were also supplied with Waterford glass.

Waterford Blue: *see* Blue Tint.

Waterloo Glasshouse Company, Cork: established in 1815 by Daniel Foley, a glass and china seller of Hanover Street, who set up as a specialist in extensive table-services in cut-glass for military messes, particularly for regiments occupying France. By the end of 1816 he employed about a hundred men and women, many experienced workers deserting from the Cork Glasshouse Company under the lure of higher wages. On Christmas Eve, 1816, an editorial in the *Cork Overseer* recorded that 'Foley's workmen are well selected, from whose superior skill the most beautiful glass will shortly make its appearance to dazzle the eyes of the public, and to outshine those of any other competitor. He is to treat his men at Christmas with a whole roasted ox and everything adequate. They have a new band of music with glass instruments with bassoon serpents, horns, trumpets, etc, and they have a glass pleasure boat, a cot and a glass set which when seen will astonish the world'. Glass trumpets were made for sale. A steam engine was installed to operate the cutting wheels and other machinery, thus drastically reducing costs.

Geoffrey O'Connell was taken into partnership during 1825, the firm operating as Foley and O'Connell, Waterloo Glass Works Company. They advertised that they had introduced a new annealing process which enabled them to guarantee their flint-glass to withstand hot water without breaking. The excise duty was too heavy a burden, and in mid-1830 the firm ceased operating. Fifteen months or so later it was reopened by O'Connell, who introduced up-to-date methods of blown-moulding and advertised that he had 'restored one hundred families to employment'. An advertisement in the *Cork Comet* four months later announced that the Waterloo Glass Works continued to enjoy military patronage.

The venture could not compete with English prices, however, and in 1835 he was made bankrupt owing to his failure to pay excise duties. The *Cork Constitution* contained an auctioneer's advertisement regarding the sale of plant and stock 'of splendid cut and plain glass at the Waterloo Glass Works until the entire splendid stock is disposed of, consisting of rich cut decanters, jugs, salad bowls, celery and pickle glasses, dessert plates and dishes, tumblers and wine-glasses of every description, hall and staircase globes, side lights, water crafts and tumblers'.

BOOKS FOR FURTHER READING

Dudley Westropp, M. S.: *Irish Glass* (Herbert Jenkins, 1920).

Elville, E. M.: *English and Irish Cut Glass* (Country Life Ltd., 1953).

Hughes, G. Bernard: *English, Irish and Scottish Table Glass* (B. T. Batsford Ltd., 1956).

CARVED WOODEN FIGURES

By HUGH HONOUR

CARVED wooden figures exhibit all the styles employed by sculptors from the twelfth century to the present day. Ranging from the hieratic Madonnas and Christs of the romanesque era to the abstract fancies of Miss Barbara Hepworth, they vary in size from great religious images larger than life to little cabinet ornaments three or four inches high, and include the masterpieces of Donatello and Ignaz Günther and the spare-time achievements of provincial carpenters. But a complete history of sculpture in wood, while including all styles and many important names, would necessarily leave unmentioned the many great sculptors who spurned so tractable, cheap and impermanent a substance. For the worst defect of wood is its liability to damage, not only from fire and water, but also from insects.

Although it must have been the earliest of media employed by sculptors (an ancient Egyptian figure in wood is in the Gizeh Museum at Cairo), we cannot speak with any authority of wood-carving before the twelfth century, and much of the sculpture of that age has been well nigh ruined. Tractable as the substance is, it enforces its own limitations on the carver who has always been most successful when, like Ignaz Günther, he has respected its structure and fully recognized its potentialities.

Naturally enough, the art of wood-carving has flourished where timber is most easily available and, more notably, where other materials are scarce, as in Bavaria. But the availability and tractability of wood have not been its sole advantages; its lightness has recommended it for figures that must be moved about and permitted effects that may hardly be achieved in stone.

MATERIALS

Nearly every type of wood has been employed by carvers. Oak, because of its hardness and durability, has been much used for large figures in Northern Europe, but in the south, where it is scarce, carvers have worked in walnut, cedar, cypress and pine. In Germany lime, which permits an exquisite finish and presents a good surface for paint, has been extensively used. For small figures hard, close-grained box-wood and pear-wood, unobtainable in large pieces, have usually been preferred. Generally speaking, these little statuettes were polished to resemble bronze and occasionally gilt, while large figures were nearly always painted. Unfortunately the painting of many figures, especially those carried in processions, has been their undoing, for they have often been so thickly repainted that the delicacy of the original carving is now obscured and garish colours distract the eye.

Although the collector of wooden figures is unlikely to find outstanding examples of the work of the greatest artists mentioned below, he may frequently be able to acquire beautiful statues by minor artists, most of whom are likely to remain anonymous. Fine Flemish and German carvings of the sixteenth century are occasionally available; baroque angels and *putti* are often to be met with, but fakes abound. As Professor Kurz has pointed out, the forger of wooden figures 'encounters few technical difficulties. A block of wood, a knife and the will to cheat are all that is needed. And the two latter elements are sufficient if an old piece of wood carving has the bad luck to fall into the forger's hands'. Many a genuine but uninteresting early carving has been ruined by the faker's desire to make it conform with some trend of modern taste in art. GIOVANNI BASTIANINI (1830–68) and ALCEO DOSSENA (1878–1937) were among the more gifted forgers of wooden sculpture, and their works were until recently (to be studied as originals) in several notable public collections. (A brief chapter in *Fakes*, by Otto Kurz, should be sufficient to put the collector on his guard.)

THE ROMANESQUE PERIOD

The earliest considerable groups of woodcarvings date from the twelfth century, and were executed in Spain, France, Southern Germany and Italy. As far as may be judged, they were limited almost exclusively to figures of the Virgin and Christ, many of which have been treasured as images and copied throughout subsequent ages. Some were as large as, or larger than, life, but the clean, unbroken lines give the smallest figures of the Virgin a grand statuesque appearance. The Virgin is normally enthroned holding the Child on her knee, the figures being painted and, occasionally, enriched with precious stones. A rare dated example of 1199, formerly at Borgo San Sepolcro and now in the Kaiser Friedrich Museum, Berlin, shows a strong Byzantine influence. Another Italian example of about twenty years later is in the Museo di Palazzo Venezia, Rome. Both are the work of a school of woodcarvers who flourished in Tuscany, Umbria and Lazio from the middle of the twelfth to the end of the thirteenth century. The late twelfth century Deposition group at Tivoli, one of the masterpieces of Italian sculpture, shows the great ability of these anonymous artists, who interpreted the revolutionary style of the Emilian BENEDETTO ANTELAMI in wood. Stiff and unbending, the tall, slender figures assist at the removal of Christ from the Cross, showing in their sombre ineloquent faces a depth of compassion rarely met with in the art of any other period. A similar but later group is in the cathedral at Volterra. The type was apparently popular in Spain at the same period; one formerly at Tahull is now in the Plandiura Collection at Barcelona, and another, dated 1251, is at San Juan de las Abadesas (Gerona).

Several large, carved-wood crucifixes of the twelfth century have survived, invariably showing the living Christ with open eyes. German examples dating from about 1180 are in the Bayerisches Nationalmuseum at Munich. In Spain and in Italy, the *Volto Santo* type, supposedly derived from the crucifix carved by Nicodemus and probably originating in the eastern Mediterranean, showing Christ in majesty dressed in the long *colobium* or seamless garment, enjoyed great popularity in the late twelfth century. The most famous of these, the *Volto Santo* at Lucca (Plate 53A), is, however of a slightly later date, and was probably made to replace one of great antiquity. (*See The Connoisseur*, November 1955, pp. 151–4.) This most beautiful of all carved crucifixes is imbued with a new sense of naturalism, which endows the figure of Christ with a suggestion of His earthly nature, as well as giving the hieratic impression which was one of the great achievements of romanesque sculpture.

THE GOTHIC PERIOD

From the greater quantity that survives, it is possible to obtain a wider impression of Gothic than of romanesque wood carvings. Large figures naturally follow the general current of sculptural taste from the early thirteenth to the late fifteenth centuries, but small groups, like those made in the Low Countries and Germany, demonstrate the medieval love of realistic incident applied to religious scenes which reflect the common life of the period. French figures of the Virgin show the same smiling face and meticulously creased drapery as the stone carvings, and also the small ivories from which the Gothic bend, or backward stoop, is said to have been derived. The beautifully coiffed head, delicately fragile wings and slightly affected gesture of an angel in the Victoria & Albert Museum exemplify the style of the French school towards the end of the fifteenth century. It should be compared with the etiolated and supremely elegant figure of an angel (in the same collection) by a Pisan artist of the mid-fourteenth century – one of many figures which express the high achievement of Italian Gothic sculpture (Plate 53C). Such figures, deriving from the school of NINO PISANO, are well represented in the Museo Civico at Pisa. An interesting school of wood sculptors flourished at Siena in the late fourteenth and early fifteenth centuries, its most notable member being DOMENICO DI NICCOLO (*c.* 1362–*c.* 1450), whose expressive figure of St John in S. Pietro Ovile, Siena, hesitates upon the brink of the Renaissance. Other prominent Sienese sculptors who occasionally worked in wood included JACOPA DELLA QUERCIA (1374–1438) and FRANCESCO DI VALDAMBRINO (fl. 1401–35).

The richly ornate Gothic of Spain and Portugal was fully exploited by the wood-carver in agonized Christs, dripping with blood, in prettified long-faced Virgins and angels and in massive, intricate altar-pieces. Here again wood-carving follows sculpture in stone, except where a greater delicacy might be achieved in the lighter medium. The most notable sculptor of retables and single figures was DAMIAN FORMENTE (*c.* 1480–1541) who had absorbed a certain amount of Italian influence, but worked in a predominantly Gothic style. In the museum at Coimbra, Portugal, an early fourteenth-century crucifix (Plate 53B) expresses the sharp tormented line of Iberian Gothic. The style remained popular up to the first decade of the sixteenth century.

In the Low Countries an important school of wood-carvers rose to prominence in the middle of the fifteenth century, and was particularly notable for little altar-pieces of oak which were disseminated throughout Europe. Full of life and charm, they have an appealing *naïveté* which has long endeared them to collectors. Most of the artists were anonymous, and many did little but copy the familiar patterns, though some, like the author of the lovely *Meeting of Joachim and Anne*, in the Rijksmuseum, Holland (Plate 54B), were artists of fine sensitivity. In the same collection there is a lovely *Death of the Virgin* and a group of blithe musician angels by ADRIAEN VAN WESEL, of Utrecht, who carved them between 1475 and 1477. Similar carvings of peasants enacting religious scenes – the Nativity, the Flight into Egypt – were executed in the Rhineland.

Towards the end of the fifteenth century tiny tabernacles and altar-pieces a few inches high, carved in exquisite detail with numerous minute figures, became popular for devotional use in the home; though one may suspect that their principal charm lay then, as it does now, in the technical virtuosity of their workmanship. A Flemish tabernacle of 1511, in the British Museum, has a triptych crowded with scenes from the life of Christ and a Last Supper, in the round, all fitted into the compass of 9·9 inches. In the Wallace Collection there is a German box-wood group of St George Killing the Dragon, with the princess standing on a rock and a castle in the background, only 3¾ inches high.

Our knowledge of English wood-carving in the Middle Ages relies principally on the choir-stalls of cathedrals and great churches, for comparatively few independent figures whose origin is certain have survived. At Wells there is an Annunciation group of the fourteenth century, displaying a somewhat alien French elegance. In the next century the dominant influence seems to have been Flemish.

There can be no doubt that the most important school of Gothic wood carving was that established in Southern Germany and flourishing from the early fourteenth to the end of the fifteenth century. In the fifteenth century two cults were productive of particularly fine wooden figures. That of the Schöne Madonna demanded the image of a pretty if somewhat mincing Virgin, holding a lively, kicking child; she was frequently shown standing on a crescent moon supported by cherubim. Early examples are delightfully fresh, but towards the end of the period, the Gothic bend and the elaborately creased draperies became exaggerated (Plate 54D). In direct and pathetic contrast, the very popular Pietà figures, which seem to have been particularly numerous in Germany, showed a grief-stricken Virgin seated with the emaciated dead body of Christ stretched across her knees. One of the best examples of this powerful but not very attractive group is that of about 1400, carved in lime-wood, in the museum at Frankfurt-am-Main. A small Pietà of this kind, for which an English origin has been suggested, is in the Victoria & Albert Museum.

The glory of German Gothic wood-carving is, however, in the large altar-pieces like those executed by Michael Pacher at St Wolfgang, by Viet Stoss at Crakow (Plate 54A) and by Tilman Riemenschneider at Creglingen and Rottenburg. MICHAEL PACHER (*c.* 1435–98) worked in a somewhat prickly Gothic fashion, crowding his figures beneath heavily interlaced tracery and surrounding them with little angels who hold up their garments, sing and trumpet. In the carvings of VIET STOSS (1447–1533) there is a greater simplicity and a closer attention to the naturalism of the heads. His early work was purely Gothic, but his masterpiece, the Annunciation group which is suspended above the choir in the Church of St Lorenz at Nuremberg, has been affected by a strong breath of the Renaissance from Italy. Stoss also worked on a small scale, and is represented in the Victoria & Albert Museum by a little box-wood statuette of the Virgin and Child, who are both as lively as they are plain. The greatest of the three artists, TILMAN RIEMENSCHNEIDER (*c.* 1460–1531) demonstrates a combination of Gothic and Renaissance elements which make it difficult to fit him into either movement (Plate 54C). His beautiful clear-cut faces, beneath their masses of minutely carved locks, are on bodies clothed with rippling Gothic robes; his altar-pieces are crowned by intricate patterns of flamboyant tracery. Among other prominent late-Gothic carvers mention must be made of ERASMUS GRASSER (1450–1526), who made the two lively smirking dancers at Munich; SIMON LAINBERGER (fl. 1475–1503), who is responsible for a lovely walnut Madonna and Child of about 1485, in the Kaiser Friedrich Museum, Berlin; HANS LAINBERGER, the author of the comely peasant-faced Madonnas at Munich, and H. YSELIN (fl. 1478–1513), the carver of the arresting bust of a carpenter, also at Munich. The best of these figures eschew the idealized and somewhat vapid beauty of the late-Gothic Virgin while retaining the traditional poses and crinkly garments. At the same time, and until well into the sixteenth century, an empty and exaggerated Gothic style, devitalized by constant repetition, persisted in conservative studios.

THE RENAISSANCE

The emergence of the Renaissance style in Italy in the fifteenth century did little to stop the production of predominantly Gothic figures for churches. Indeed, the majority of Renaissance sculptors, fired with a zeal for the antique, appear to have spurned so humble a material as wood, though it was used by some of the greatest. DONATELLO (*c.* 1383–1466) carved his Magdalen in the Baptistry at Florence and the St John in the Frari at Venice in wood, which was also used for the St Jerome at Faenza which has been attributed to him. His follower, DESIDERIO DA SETTIGNANO (1428–64), also used wood for the Magdalen in Sta Trinità at Florence. Furthermore, BRUNELLESCHI (1377–1446) carved his great crucifix, in Sta Maria Novella at Florence, in wood, making a figure which, in its accurate anatomy and calm beauty, contrasts with the tortured Christs of the Gothic period. In North Italy, wood-carvers of the early sixteenth century were influenced by their German contemporaries, as is evident in the fine altar-piece of the Crucifixion in pear-wood, in the Victoria & Albert Museum.

Purely ornamental, secular wood-carvings, principally of classical subjects, first became popular in the Renaissance period. It has been suggested that many of these were made as models by goldsmiths and sculptors in bronze. One of the finest, the box-wood *Hercules* in the Wallace Collection, was certainly the work of a goldsmith, FRANCESCO DA SANT' AGATA of Padua (fl. 1520), to whom bronzes have also been attributed on stylistic grounds. Many figures of this type appear to have been carved in Germany, where one of the most notable sculptors was KONRAD MEIT (*c.* 1470–*c.* 1550), who is principally famous for his work in marble at the church of Brou. That he was strongly influenced by Dürer is demonstrated by his box-wood statuettes of Adam and Eve at Vienna, which also show his strict adher-

(A) (Left) The Volto Santo in the Cathedral at Lucca. Late twelfth or early thirteenth century.

(B) (Right) Portuguese Crucifix. Early fourteenth century. *Museu Machado de Gastro, Coimbra.*

(C) Angel of the Annunciation. School of Nino Pisano, mid-fourteenth century. *Victoria & Albert Museum.*

(D) The Falconer (possibly St Bavon). Carved walnut and polychrome. Northern French, fifteenth century. *S. W. Wolsey.*

(E) Christ at the column. Boxwood. German, sixteenth century. *Alfred Spero.*

PLATE 53

(A) Viet Stoss. St James supporting the Virgin. *From the Crakow altar.*

(B) Joachim and Anne. North Netherlandish carving in oak, 1470–80. *Rijksmuseum, Holland.*

(C) Tilman Riemenschnieder. Angel in lime-wood, early sixteenth century. *Victoria & Albert Museum.*

(D) Late fifteenth-century Virgin. *Gerald Kerin.*

CARVED WOODEN FIGURES

(A) Francesco da Sant' Agata. Hercules. Statuette in boxwood, Padua, 1520. *The Wallace Collection.*

(B) Ferdinand Dietz. Boy with a goat. Boxwood, mid-eighteenth century. *Victoria & Albert Museum.*

(C) Johann Baptist Straub. Putto with a book. Painted lime-wood, German, 1767. *Church of Berg-am-Lain.*

Ignaz Günther. St Kunigunde. Lime-wood. 1762. *Church of Rott-am-Inn.*

PLATE 56

To face page 105

ence to the practice of modelling from the life. Flemish and German artists who had specialized in religious *genre* scenes also turned their attention to the carving of individual figures, such as that of an old man in the Wallace Collection.

It was not until the end of the fifteenth century that the Renaissance spirit began to reach Germany, and only in about 1510 did it achieve any prominence. Two of its earliest exponents, Sebastian Loscher (1482/3–1551) and Adolf Daucher (op. 1491–1524), who worked on the famous Fugger Chapel at Augsburg, both carved in wood, tending to use the late-Gothic style for traditional religious subjects, but following the new manner where the occasion allowed, in figures of *putti*, for instance. In Spain the Renaissance style in sculpture seems to have been introduced by Felipe de Vigarni (d. 1543) and, more notably, Alonso Berruguete (1480–1561) who was strongly influenced by Michelangelo. With the growth of Mannerism in the sixteenth century, the style of wood-carvers naturally changed, and from this period we may date the widespread copying in box-wood of Italian bronzes.

THE BAROQUE PERIOD

After something of an eclipse in the later Renaissance, the wood-carver returned to prominence in Italy with the birth of the baroque style. Vast altars crowded with figures of saints and cherubim, demanded a material cheaper and more easily worked than marble. Stucco was used extensively, but in those districts where wood was readily available – Piedmont, for example – figures and sometimes whole altar-pieces were carved in it. A yet uninvestigated school of wood-carvers, the most notable of whom were Carlo Plura (1655–1737), Stefano Maria Clemente (1719–1794) and A. Maria Marigliano (1664–1739), flourished in Piedmont and Liguria throughout the later seventeenth and eighteenth centuries. They executed decorative carvings of angels and *putti*, life-sized crucifixes and images which could be carried in processions. The processional figures were usually made in groups for such lay orders as the *Confraternità della Misericordia*, and represent Saints or scenes from the Passion; their brightly coloured drapery is arranged in baroque flounces, but the figures themselves seem to derive from the realistic terra-cottas in the Sacro Monte chapels.

In the Iberian peninsula somewhat heavy-handed baroque sculpture was very popular throughout the seventeenth century, and many a great altar was enriched with wooden angels attired in billowing drapery. Small box-wood figures were also popular; a fine statuette of Christ at the Column, typically Spanish in the nervous tautness of its line, is in the Victoria & Albert Museum. It also owns a bust of the Virgin of Sorrows in painted wood, attributed to Pedro de Mena (1628–88). The most notable Spanish sculptors in wood of this period include Gregorio Fernandez (1566–1636) and J. Martinez Montanez (1564–1649).

The baroque marks a period of transition between two greater epochs in the history of German sculpture. There is a lingering flavour of Mannerism in the work of Martin and Michael Zurn (op. 1624–65), who carved a number of altar-pieces in Bavaria. On the other hand, a box-wood group of Salome and St John, in the Victoria & Albert Museum, has a touch of fantasy which seems to anticipate the rococo. Most female statuettes have a greater solidity, like those by Leonard Kern (1588–1663). Georg Petel (1590–1633), who is probably more famous for his carvings in ivory, worked in an uncompromising baroque style which he had acquired in Italy.

ROCOCO

In the eighteenth century, the history of wood-carving is dominated by Germany, where a school of unparalleled excellence flourished. The rococo pilgrimage churches of Bavaria, which are among the greatest masterpieces of the period, demanded the most delicate and the most sophisticated ornaments and statues in both stucco and wood. Johann Baptist Straub (1704–

84) worked much for the Bavarian court and employed so large a staff of assistants that his personal style is hard to distinguish. His celebrated *putti* in the church at Berg-am-Lain perfectly express the wit of the rococo in their playful allusions to the statues by which they stand – one child, accompanying the Archangel Raphael, wears a vast hat and sports upon the back of a dolphin, while Gabriel's companion bubbling with laughter supports a book (Plate 55C). Straub's pupil, IGNAZ GÜNTHER (1725–75) is probably the greatest of these sculptors for he alone realized all the potentialities of wood as a medium. Without straining his material he drew from it all that it was capable of yielding. In the large figures he carved for the church of Rott-am-Inn in 1762 one sees the crystallization of the rococo in all its eloquence, grace, wit and supreme elegance. Although his statues are painted, no effort has been made to disguise their medium, which gives the lie to the usual implication in the adjective 'wooden' (Plate 56).

Of the many sculptors who worked on a small scale in box-wood and pear-wood the most important is FERDINAND DIETZ (or Tietz) (1708–77), who also executed larger figures in stone, including those for the gardens of Vietshöchheim; indeed, many little figures he carved in lime-wood are models for garden sculpture. In his work the gay spirit of comedy frequently borders on the grotesque but never approaches the ugly. His lime-wood models have a somewhat sketchy, impressionistic finish, but his figures in box-wood are carved with a nice precision (Plate 55B).

Among the other wood-carvers who worked in Germany in the eighteenth century, the following should be mentioned. AEGID VERHELST (1696–1747), a native of Antwerp, worked principally in Bavaria in a late-baroque style, specializing in large figures, the most notable being those of Peace and Love in the throne-room of the Old Residenz, Kempten, and the fine Pietà group at Friedberg. PAUL EGELL (1691–1752) also worked on a large scale, but is represented in the Wurzburg Museum by a charming little group, possibly a sketch, of St Francis Xavier baptizing a blackamoor. DANIEL KÖHLER (fl. 1751–78) is represented in the same collection by a statuette of St Sebastian. Towards the end of his career, Köhler forsook the rococo for a neo-classical style, which found fuller expression in the work of CHRISTIAN JORHAN (1727–1804).

A flourishing school of wood carving at the end of the eighteenth century existed at Turin, where it centred around GIUSEPPE MARIA BONZANIGO (1744–1820), who was also a cabinet-maker and worked on a very small scale, with the greatest delicacy, treating his medium as though it was ivory.

BOOKS FOR FURTHER READING

CARLI, ENZO: *La Scultura Lignea Senese* (1951).
FRANCOVICH, GEZA DE: *Scultura Medioevale in Legno* (1943).
MASKELL, ALFRED: *Wood Sculpture* (1911).
SCHOENBERGER, ARNO: *Ignaz Günther* (1954).
Rococo Art from Bavaria (1956).

Further information is to be found in general histories of sculpture and in monographs on artists who occasionally worked in wood.

CHINESE MORTUARY FIGURES

By FRANK DAVIS

As soon as man began to speculate upon the possibility of some kind of survival after death, it was reasonable for him to take what steps he could to ensure that, as they journeyed through the shades, the dead would have within reach some of the normal comforts of life, lest their ghosts should be restless and haunt the living. The most obvious and logical method, at moments in time when human life was of no consequence, was to kill the slaves, male and female, and to bury them with their master, together with his horses and a supply of food and utensils. One can imagine without much difficulty what a wrench it may have been to kill a splendid horse in honour of one's father and how small a matter to cut the throat of a groom or two or of a dozen discarded and ageing concubines. Such a procedure was normal enough in many parts of the world in ancient times – at Ur of the Chaldees, for example – but gradually manners became a trifle less barbarous, and at the same time mourners began to wonder whether it was really worth while, for results which could not be absolutely guaranteed, to destroy property which was valuable when alive and entirely useless when dead. Consequently elaborate steps were taken to substitute effigies for bodies and, in general, to persuade the dead grandee that he could get along well enough throughout eternity without involving his heirs in undue extravagance. It is generally considered that in China burial holocausts of living persons and animals were wholly out of fashion by the beginning of the first millennium B.C., and later generations have noted as one of the counts in the indictment against the tyrant Shih Huang Ti, the military adventurer who reigned from 221 to 210 B.C., that the old customs were revived by his express wish at his own funeral ceremonies, when – so the story has been handed down to us – thousands of slaves and all the imperial concubines who had failed to bear male children were buried alive within the walls of the dead Emperor's mausoleum. From then onwards clay models were used, not merely for the tombs of important people but for those of quite modest folk. The Chinese have always scattered their tombs about over the country-side, so that when railway construction began to change the economic life of the land the dead were disturbed wholesale. This was particularly the case during the building of the K'ai-Feng-Hosnan railway, for the line passed through the very heart of ancient China, close to three former capitals and right across the site of one of them. The excavations were not, of course, conducted under archaeological guidance; had this been possible at the time – about 1905 – we should no doubt have a much more precise knowledge of style at various periods. Nonetheless, the results were impressive; here was a hitherto unsuspected underground world furnished with miniature pottery models of the living, exhibiting a wide range of types, some of them minor sculptural masterpieces, many of no aesthetic quality but illustrating the daily life of the people with extraordinary vivacity and humour. When these objects first came to Europe – that is during the first decade of this century – they were greeted first with amazement and then with enthusiasm by a generation which was familiar only with porcelain models of men, birds and animals (some of them produced specifically for export), practically all of them, with the exception of a few vigorous Ming Dynasty roof-tiles in glazed pottery, manufactured to amuse the living during the past two hundred years. But here were some less sophisticated, technically rough figures manufactured to solace the dead, unseen by human eye for more than a millennium and displaying as often as not an understanding of movement and balance and form without obvious parallels in Chinese ceramic history, and far more alive than anything from an Egyptian tomb. As these Tanagra-like terracottas became more familiar, collectors became more critical and began to realize how greatly they can vary in quality, from coarsely designed objects turned out by the thousand from a mould to carefully observed pieces for which it is obvious that a modeller of high talent has been employed; this is specially noticeable in the case of many of the horses. Sometimes these, as the camels, though naturalistic enough, appear to be singularly devoid of all horsiness or – if there is such a word – of camelry; at other times they have clearly been devised by a potter who had not only studied animal anatomy but was able to express animal nature so that the creatures, slightly stylized as they must be for sculptural purposes, take on an extraordinary air of not merely looking like but of behaving like horses. But before dealing further with the character of the figures themselves, whether animal or human, it would be as well to consider briefly the technical development of this type of pottery and the thorny question of its date. So far no figures have been certainly accepted as earlier than the Han Dynasty (206 B.C.–A.D. 220), though a case can be argued in favour of a date of a century or so earlier for a few clay figures of exorcists in Paris, Chicago and London. The general practice has been to place all vessels and figures with a grey body and a green glaze which has become iridescent through burial, in the Han period, those with a dark grey body decorated with touches of unfired pigment in the Six Dynasties period (A.D. 220–589) or the period of the Wei Tartars (A.D. 386–557), and to give figures with a buff-coloured body decorated with coloured lead glazes of grass green, orange, yellow or blue to the T'ang Dynasty (A.D. 618–906). But it has been suggested that some at least of the models of farm animals and buildings could just as well belong to the Ming Dynasty (A.D. 1368–1644), when there was a movement afoot to return to the ancient ways, and that, in any case, an over-rigid classification purporting to cover so vast an area and so many centuries cannot pretend to be more than a very rough-and-ready rule of thumb. Without going into the details of a rather complicated argument, it does, however, seem likely that after learning the use of a green lead-glaze from the West the Han potters employed it consistently, but that during the troubles which followed the collapse of the dynasty the industry reverted to its earlier practice until – with the consolidation of the country under the T'ang Emperors – it was able to improve upon the Han technique and – though this is outside the subject of this note – to make what was, by any standard, true porcelain. What we have from Han times is mortuary ware and mortuary ware only, and this, we can reasonably assume, was of a lower quality than that provided for the living. But dating is not of course purely a question of material; style is not less important, and a comparison between the style of known and dated sculpture for example, or of bronzes, or of objects found in a dated tomb, has by now produced evidence which, within decidedly wide limits, enables us to map out the development during these dark centuries fairly clearly, if somewhat arbitrarily. There are numerous wine and grain jars deriving their shape from contemporary bronzes, with lion-mask and ring handles, and with a horizontal decorative band of hunting scenes or galloping horses. There are cups on a high foot – stem cups – standing on a tray, and cylindrical jars, each type surmounted by a cover in the shape of a range of hills – hill-censers and hill-jars as they are called – the hills representing those Mountains or Islands of the Blest which figure in

Taoist legend and in search of which the Emperor Wu Ti (140–86 B.C.) sent out more than one expedition. Both seem to have been made specially as tomb furniture, neither is of any artistic importance, though the glaze is uncommonly attractive and tends to conceal the poor quality of the potting. There were models of horses and farm-yards and their inhabitants in great variety and profusion; once again there is no great artistic merit to be found in them, but a straightforward naturalism which is very engaging and enough stylization to prevent them becoming niggling – a stylization without which, it should be added, they could hardly have been produced in so rough a material. Not much was omitted which could possibly benefit the deceased – musicians and dancers, fierce guardian spirits, stoves and sheep, dogs and their kennels, oxen in their carts, grooms and labourers, well-heads, mills and barns, pigs and hens and ducks – mostly in dark grey earthenware with traces of red pigment. A rather different type of figure, generally attributed to the Han period, is that of the horse made up of several parts, with a well-modelled spirited head; but it must be admitted that with the collapse of the Han Dynasty in A.D. 220 and the subsequent four centuries of near-chaos until the T'ang Empire was firmly established, there is as much guess-work as knowledge in attempts which have been made to give anything like a precise date to individual pieces; nor, for that matter, can one attain to any kind of precision over dating during the 300 years of the T'ang Dynasty, the Augustan Age of China, which lasted in extraordinary splendour from A.D. 618 to 906. It was during this period that funerary extravagance reached such heights that thoughtful men became alarmed, and in A.D. 713 T'ang Chao sent a memorial to the Emperor in which he declared that 'the princes, the grandees and the wealthy vied with one another in such extravagant display that many families both high and low ruined themselves'. But his protest does not seem to have been taken seriously. The worthy man was probably regarded as a kill-joy; for, in certain stages of the development of civilization, there is nothing the people enjoy so much as a good funeral: it could purge the emotions like a good cry at the theatre. Here is further evidence from a contemporary source: 'Under the Emperor Hsuan Tsung, whose reign was remarkable for great prosperity, those who assisted at the burial ceremonies pitched tents on the side of the road. The usual rites being celebrated, artificial flowers, fruit and cake were distributed. In those days the curtains of the tents did not exceed ten feet square and the tents themselves were but a few feet high; nevertheless, every intelligent man condemned these customs. But after the great civil war, the canopies erected for funerals reached sometimes eighty feet in height and many hundreds of divans were prepared for the spectators'. There were, however, certain sumptuary regulations, but these seem to have been devised not so much to curb extravagance as to preserve the pomp and ceremony of the official hierarchy. For example, in the tomb of a person above the fourth rank his family could place ninety pieces of mortuary ware, above the sixth sixty pieces and above the tenth forty – meaning presumably sixty between the sixth and the fourth, and forty between the tenth and the sixth.

All this must have meant a vast output on the part of the potters who specialized in these wares. It followed also that it was socially important 'to keep up with the Joneses'. Poor families would plunge into debt to give their parents bigger and better funerals; while the rich and powerful would provide more varied and better-made clay figurines to comfort their dead relations in the manner to which they had been accustomed during life. It is doubtful in the extreme whether it is possible to give any very precise account of the beliefs which gave rise to these customs. As far as these beliefs were accorded any articulate expression – and the vast majority of men were probably both unwilling to, and incapable of, rationalizing tradition, and were content to leave such high matters to the astrologers – life and the visible world, and death and the shadow world as well, were seen as the mutual interaction of the two opposite principles: the

Yang and the Yin, male and female, light and darkness, and the individual as possessing two souls, an inferior and a superior. The former was thrust upon him at conception; the latter he could acquire by slow degrees after birth. 'When man's life comes to an end, the purer substance departs from the material substance' is one early definition of death. And again: 'When death comes, the material soul follows the body into the grave, the superior soul subsisting free'. We are also informed that if the soul be provided with food, it is neither noisy nor harmful; if starved, it robs. It is all extremely vague and, we may take it, did not penetrate very deeply into the public consciousness, the majority of the human race being of the earth earthy. But not all the tomb figures were placed there merely for the service of the inferior soul: concubines, servants, horses, yes, but not the fierce soldier guardians or the exorcists, whose duties could presumably be classified as of a higher grade. The exorcist who, in these mortuary wares, appears at least as early as Han times, and very possibly earlier, as a primitive little figure with a hole in his hand which once held a wooden lance and ends up a thousand years later as a well-modelled soldier arrayed in T'ang armour, was an important personage at a funeral. He was the Fang-Hsiang-Shih, wore a bearskin and carried a shield and lance. He walked at the head of the procession, was the first to step down into the grave, and with his lance touched the four sides to banish evil spirits. While such figures are of compelling interest to students of folk-lore, it can hardly be said that, except in rare instances, they have any great aesthetic value. With a few of the humans and certainly with many of the animals, especially the horses, we are in the presence of a higher grade of accomplishment – figures not produced by the thousand but displaying to a marked degree the impress of gifted minds. It is abundantly clear that, as time went on, there was a market for something more lively and naturalistic than the often summary modelling once considered sufficient, and a few of the horses can pridefully take their place among the finest minor sculpture of either East or West; and indeed could not be omitted from any exhibition designed to show how artists have dealt with this animal throughout the ages. The Chinese were a horse-loving people and, in the finest of these tomb figures, they displayed such understanding, not merely of equine anatomy but of equine nature, that one wonders whether they did not produce for the living some horse portraits of even greater quality than those they made for the dead. Certainly, confronted by some of these tomb animals, whether glazed or unglazed, one is reminded of Buffon's famous definition: 'The horse is a noble animal and the friend of man.' It is a well-established fact that the Chinese took to horse-riding about the end of the fourth century B.C., compelled thereto in order to defend themselves against raiding nomads from the north. By the time of the T'ang Dynasty we find them playing polo with enthusiasm, and some of the most vital of the tomb figures are of polo-players – horse and rider – in action, the details of the animal's movements beautifully observed. The earliest Chinese reference to the game occurs in a report written by the Secretary to the Board of Rites in 710 B.C. It says that the fifth Emperor of the T'ang Dynasty, Tai Tsung, 'had given orders that all officials above the third grade were to take part in the game; but certain eminent statesmen were worn out and aged, the consequence being that they were tumbled over on the ground and remained there, unable to rise, to the great amusement of the Emperor, Empress and court ladies, who all shouted with laughter at the sight'. As time went on officials became so fascinated by the game that they were apt to neglect their duties; and small wonder, for skill at polo was a sure means of attracting the imperial favour. Emperors themselves took part, to the pained surprise of their more conservative advisers, one of whom, in the tenth century, ventured upon the following remonstrance:

'Your servant has heard that when two of your majesty's predecessors went out boar-hunting and hawking, and when their ministers remonstrated with them, they joyfully followed the advice given. Now, your majesty takes delight in polo, [literally horse-ball] and your foolish servant has found, on reflection, three reasons why this is not a fitting sport and will state them even at the risk of the axe.'

The worthy man then states his reasons very prosily and by no means convincingly, his reward a commendation for the literary quality of his memorial; His Majesty continuing to enjoy himself as before. One at least of his successors, years later, in 1163, did in fact have a very narrow escape; his pony bolted off the field of play and dashed under a low verandah. The pony got through leaving His Majesty hanging by his hands from the lintel. Later still, under Tartar rulers, 'on festival days, the whole court would appear in full dress on the polo fields, and after worshipping the gods with offerings of food and wine and ceremonials, at the completion of the rituals, the Emperor would change his dress for the various sports. There was archery to begin with, followed by a game of polo'. Horses must have their grooms, and these are nearly always foreigners from the wide-open spaces of the north-west, with some leavening of little men with beards and big noses who would appear to hail from the plains of Mesopotamia – witnesses to the age-old trade route across the Gobi Desert. Camels are fairly numerous, one or two of them as remarkable as the horses, and then – and most charming – there are the women, smiling and long-sleeved, standing immobile or dancing or, standing or sitting, playing musical instruments. Under the T'ang Emperors the imperial seraglio grew to enormous dimensions – a monstrous regiment. In A.D. 813 the land was afflicted by a great inundation, which the Emperor's soothsayers in default of a more likely explanation attributed to an excess of the Yin – that is of the female-principle – in the Empire. His Majesty was persuaded to discard part of this female multitude, and two hundred coaches were required to take them back to the shelter of their parental roofs.

In general, it would appear that dark grey or reddish clays, coloured with unfired pigment, were superseded fairly early in the T'ang period by clays of a lighter tone washed over with a white slip, while a lead glaze was used for many of the finer figures – yellowish, or yellowish brown and green, and occasionally blue. The effect is one of considerable richness and subtlety, especially when handled by a modeller whose eye was sufficiently observant to note with accuracy the natural grace of an animal and to translate what he saw into forms suited to clay. As to the T'ang ladies, Mr Honey has pointed out that 'the best of the many dancers have a rippling grace that is totally different from the grave beauty of the earlier figures of women; fluency of line and a delicate sense of balance in composition are their distinguishing character'.

There is a theory that the practice of placing figures in tombs continued during the Sung Dynasty, and the possibility of some of the homesteads – house, men and women, animals, etc – having been made under the Ming Emperors has already been mentioned. But there seems to be no convincing proof of either of these possibilities, so that – in default of further evidence – we are left with the reasonable assumption that the custom had come to an end by about the year A.D. 1000.

TABLE OF DATES

HAN DYNASTY	206 B.C.–A.D. 220
THE SIX DYNASTIES	A.D. 220–589
NORTHERN DYNASTIES:	
Northern Wei	386–535
Eastern Wei	534–550
Western Wei	535–557
Northern Chi	550–577
Northern Chou	557–581
SUI DYNASTY	581–618
T'ANG DYNASTY	618–906
THE FIVE DYNASTIES	907–960
LIAO DYNASTY	907–1126
SUNG DYNASTY	960–1279

The photographs illustrating the article on Chinese Mortuary Figures, unless otherwise stated, are of pieces which have passed through the salerooms at Sotheby's during the last twenty-five years.

(A) Two chickens. Han Dynasty. Green iridescent glaze. The duck possibly T'ang Dynasty.

(B) Camel and rider. Green glaze with areas of yellowish-brown. T'ang Dynasty.

(C) 'Here comes the bride.' Covered bridal carriage; green and brown glaze over red clay. Probably Sui Dynasty.

PLATE 57

To face page 112

(B) Falconer or conjurer. T'ang Dynasty.

(A) Fowling tower in basin representing lake. Green iridescent glaze. Han Dynasty.

(A) Attendant. Blue and green glazes with silver iridescence. T'ang Dynasty.

(B) Warrior or exorcist. Wei Dynasty.

PLATE 59

Horse. Unglazed. T'ang Dynasty. *Originally in the Eumorfopoulos Collection and now in the British Museum.*

PLATE 60

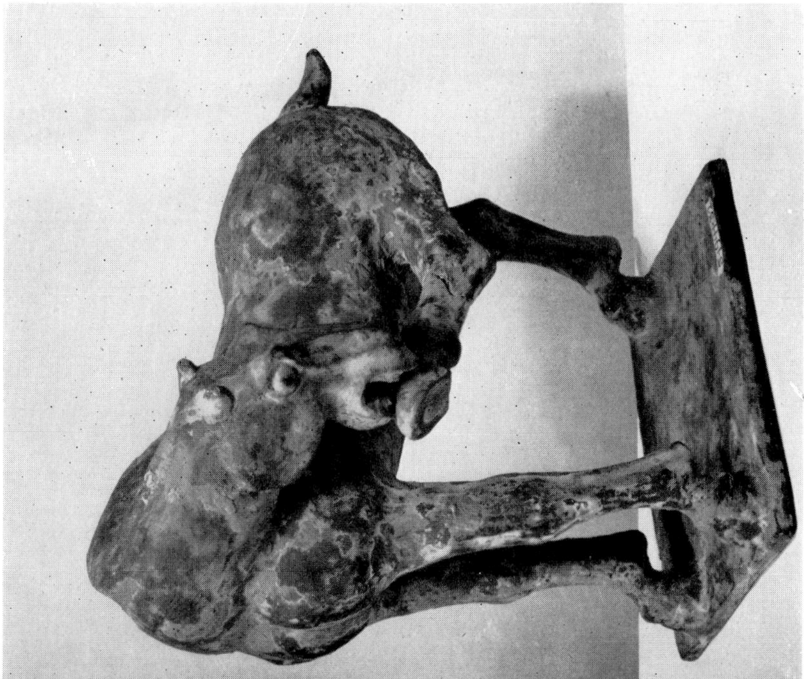

(A) Horse biting near hind foot.

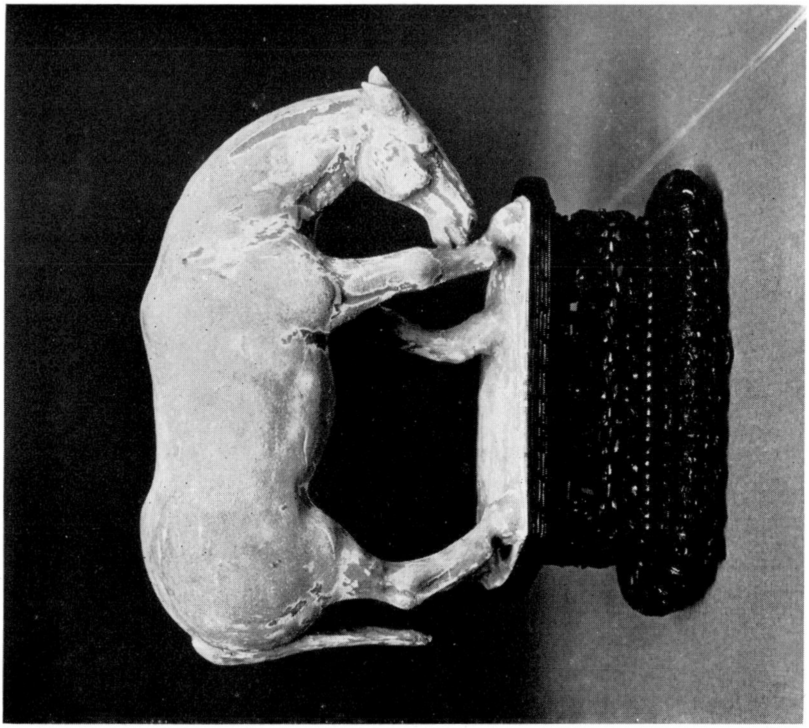

(B) Horse biting off fore foot.

Examples of T'ang Dynasty naturalism.

PLATE 61

(A) Horse and groom. Glazed. T'ang Dynasty. Elaborate trappings.

(B) Wrestler. T'ang Dynasty.

(C) Woman attendants. Green glaze. T'ang Dynasty.

(A) Polo player. T'ang Dynasty.

(B) Dancers in elaborate court dress. T'ang Dynasty.

PLATE 63

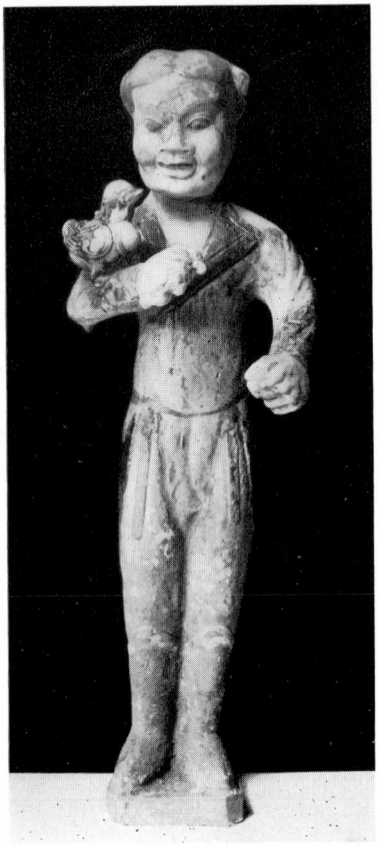

(A) (*Left*): Man with a bird.

(B) (*Right*): Tomb guardian or counsellor. T'ang Dynasty.

(C) Two T'ang Dynasty horses.

PLATE 64

To face page 113

GREEK AND ROMAN STATUARY

By JOHN BOARDMAN

It is unlikely today that major works of ancient Greek or Roman statuary will come the way of the ordinary collector, and in the rare instances in which they are found the advice of an expert must be sought to distinguish originals from ancient, or modern, copies. Minor works are, however, not uncommon, especially in bronze and, to a lesser extent, in marble. These, in detail and style, closely reflect the major sculpture of their day, and can only be appreciated and understood in the light of the development of major sculpture in the ancient world. In this brief sketch it is the major works which provide the framework of the story, but I have included remarks and a number of illustrations of pieces whose like is still often met in sale- or show-room.

Stone Sculpture

The ready accessibility of fine white marble which could easily be quarried from the ground surface was a prime factor in the development of stone sculpture in Greece. As early as the third millennium B.C. marble from the islands of the Cyclades was being used for female statuettes, either of the type illustrated in Plate 65A or of a simple 'fiddle' outline. These had, however, no immediate successors in the Aegean world, and even in the flourishing periods of the Minoan and Mycenaean empires major stone sculpture is so rare that it can be practically ignored. The Mycenae gravestones, and even the famous Lion Gate, give no evidence of any developed style in statuary.

By the eighth century B.C. renewed contact with the Eastern countries, Assyria, Phoenicia and other states comprising modern Turkey, led to a revival of interest in carved work as opposed to the simple clay figurines of animals and human beings which had been made to serve as votive offerings. The main inspiration was the work of ivory carvers, some of whom travelled in Greek lands and no doubt taught their craft there; but in the seventh century the island quarries were also rediscovered and schools of marble sculpture arose, first perhaps on the Cyclades, then on the East Greek islands and in mainland Greece. The island marble was exported to other parts of Greece, but local resources of limestone were often used as well. Simple canons of proportion for the human figure were observed, and the triangular faces with large eyes and the layer 'barrister-type' wigs are distinctive of the style called Daedalic. Male figures (*kouroi*) are generally nude, occasionally wear a belt, and stand with their hands to their sides and one foot slightly advanced in a pose long familiar in Egyptian statuary (compare the bronze, Plate 70C). Women are clothed in simple pleatless dresses (*peploi*). Details of the body are rendered, if at all, in a simple, formal manner, and it is clear that the figures were first sketched on the surface of the unworked block which was then cut back to the outline, for there is no concession to any view other than the strictly frontal, or side – certainly none to three-quarter views (Plate 65C).

By about 600 B.C. a little more realism appears in the carving of head and body, well shown in a fine series of statues from Athens and Attica (Plate 65B). The triangular outline of the face softens into more of an oval, and the corners of the lips are raised in an 'archaic smile'. Body markings are still rudimentary and shown by a formal pattern of grooves or sharply intersecting planes. Through the sixth century the strict frontality of the figures is gradually abandoned and more ambitious poses attempted, particularly in relief sculpture. This was generally reserved for architectural decoration – for the metope panels in Doric buildings or the friezes of Ionic buildings. The use of overlapping figures in such reliefs, together with more skilful carving lends an impression of depth. Frontal figures are attempted but not three-quarter views, and even in profile views of the human head the eyes are shown as if seen from the front (Plate 66B). In the sixth century the East Greek (Ionic) styles of sculpture also become more differentiated from the mainland schools, and generally favour more rounded and fleshy profiles, as on Plate 66A. From the island of Samos comes an important series of marble statues distinguished by their columnar bodies and rounded heads. Around the middle of the century a greater naturalism in the representation of drapery appears, with formal patterns of pleats and hem-line folds. This accompanies the adoption of the more sophisticated Ionic costume, the short-sleeved *chiton*, which replaced the severe Doric *peplos* as the usual dress for women, at least in sculpture. A superb series of maidens (*korai*) from the Acropolis at Athens illustrates the fussy decorativeness of the new fashion. They are the work of both Attic and Ionian artists, and form the most important group of archaic statuary preserved. They owe their survival to the fact that they were broken in the Persian sack of Athens in 480 and, after the battle of Salamis and the return of the Athenians, were buried by them on the Acropolis, where they had once stood. Beside them were statues of horsemen and animals. Plate 66D shows the head of one of these horsemen, and Plate 66C the head of a *kore*, who was dressed in the earlier Doric manner with a foldless *peplos*. Their hair is represented in tight formal curls and crimped waves; the eyes are wide and staring, the lips set in an archaic smile.

With the fifth century, the classical period, almost full naturalism is achieved, at least in the representation of the human body. This generally means the male body which, through the characteristic Greek interest in athletics, presented a more ready model for the artist, and which, in the gymnasium or stadium, offered difficult poses and torsions to tax his skill. The nude female body was hardly ever represented in art before the fourth century. Fuller naturalism in the carving of heads is also apparent, but the features are usually composed and idealized, with no hint of portraiture and little attempt to represent emotion. The hair is carved in more natural, individual locks with a combed crown (compare Plates 70A, B and 72A), and in reliefs the eyes appear now in a properly foreshortened side view.

The decoration of buildings was still a major concern of the sculptor, but occasionally his figures also fulfilled a structural function. Thus the Caryatids of sixth-century treasuries at Delphi and in the Erechtheum porch of fifth-century Athens serve as columns. In the same spirit are the great Atlas-pilasters on the Temple of Zeus at Acragas (Agrigento), and, much later, the crouching satyrs which support the stage of the Theatre of Dionysos at Athens. It is a motif which has long been popular. Of the middle of the fifth century is the sculpture from the Temple of Zeus in Olympia, in which violent action and composed 'classical' features sometimes contrast strangely. Plate 67A, the head of a young Athena on a metope, typifies the new spirit. Now, too, the names of artists can be associated with preserved works or (more often) copies of their originals. Myron's Diskobolos is a good example of a difficult athletic pose successfully rendered. Polyclitus' Diadoumenos and other figures show how well understood now is the anatomy of a relaxed figure standing with his weight on one leg, far removed from the archaic *kouros* pose with straight back and one leg slightly advanced. It is perhaps in the reliefs which decorate the gravestones (*stelai*) of the fifth century that this classical calm is at its most expressive; the dead woman looks for the last time at the jewels her maid has brought her, parents take leave of their son, a girl of her pet doves

(Plates 68A and 69). In the middle and second half of the century falls the work of the school of Phidias, designer of the marble sculptures on the Parthenon at Athens, now largely in the British Museum, and of colossal gold and ivory cult statues, now known only in much reduced and adapted copies. Drapery in particular is now more realistically rendered, and the relief figures from the balustrade around the Nike Temple at Athens show how well it could be carved to reveal the contours of the limbs and body beneath.

In the fourth century there was added to the sculptor's established command in representing the human body an interest in expressing emotion and individuality. Portraits appear, both of dead poets and politicians and of contemporary notables. Portraits of philosophers and orators, for instance the Demosthenes of Plate 67C, are familiar from several ancient copies. Local schools and the work of individual sculptors can again be recognized. To Scopas is attributed the type of head with intense deep-sunk eyes; to Lysippus new canons of proportion, and the expression of incipient movement and contrasting lines of composition in single figures which led to the more complicated and restless groups and figures of the succeeding 'Hellenistic' age. Now, too, the statuary is successfully designed to be viewed satisfactorily from any angle. The nude female body becomes a popular motif for the first time in Greek art, and in the fourth century are evolved many of the Aphrodite types so often copied and adapted in the succeeding centuries (Plate 68B). The name of Praxiteles is particularly associated with these, and his lithe figures created a profound effect on contemporaries and later critics. An original from his hand may be preserved in the Hermes from Olympia (Plate 67B).

The Hellenistic period, of the third and second centuries B.C., sees the logical fulfilment of the novelties and experiments of the preceding two centuries. Portraiture, expression of emotion and violent exertion, compositions of several figures, are developed to a point beyond which there was little more to be attempted in the way of representational plastic art.

The individual styles of local schools can, to some extent, be distinguished. The Pergamene school is thus best represented in the reliefs from the Great Altar of Zeus at Pergamum, where the contorted bodies of fighting gods and giants are closely knit in the composition of a frieze. Rhodes and some of the cities of the Asia Minor coast favour a baroque style of changing rhythms and restless drapery. Two-figure compositions are successfully attempted, of wrestlers, warriors or the like. The bronze boxer and jockey (Plates 70A and 72B) exemplify the new command of movement and expression. No subject is shirked, from old age or deformed grotesques to the mannered prettiness of muses and nymphs, which was more popularly reflected in the 'Tanagra' figurines of clay. Minor works of this period most frequently met in English collections are grave *stelai* crowned with a pediment and with one or two figures in relief, and votive reliefs with groups of worshippers approaching the reclining figure of a feasting hero, or the healer Asklepios with his staff and snake.

The conquest of Greece by the Romans and the emergence of the Romans as art patrons whose tastes created a constant demand for statuary forms a significant stage in the history of ancient sculpture. At the same time it raises the question of originals and ancient copies. Nearly all that is known of archaic Greek sculpture of the seventh and sixth centuries B.C. is gleaned from original works which have been excavated on Greek sites. From the succeeding centuries almost the only originals preserved have been architectural or funerary, and we rely for our knowledge of the most famous works of individual artists on the copies of them made for the Roman market in the first century B.C. and later. Very much of the work of this 'Graeco-Roman' period, both in Italy and in the Empire, can be classed as copy or adaptation of classical or Hellenistic Greek original. It is clear, too, that Greeks were still for the most part the artists; the Roman genius lay elsewhere.

Italy had already some local traditions in statuary which may have conditioned Roman taste. The archaic Etruscans evolved an individual 'graecising' style, but lacking good marble their statuary was virtually confined to small bronzes and impressive but graceless terra-cotta figures, often over life-size. The traditional practice of making portraits of the dead also bred a taste for what often seem cruelly accurate likenesses with none of the idealizing spirit which imbues most Greek work. The most important innovation in the Roman period is the historical, narrative relief, as those of Trajan's column in Rome. Portraiture of both imperial (Plate 67D) and private persons reached its peak in the first and second centuries A.D., although the combination of a matron's head with the copied torso of a buxom Hellenistic Aphrodite sometimes produces a mixture of frankness and flattery which we find unhappily incongruous. The identity of many portraits of the imperial family is determined by comparison with their likenesses which appear on coins. Otherwise an indication of date is given by the elaborate hair styles of the ladies, or by such criteria as the known renewal of the popularity of beards under the Emperor Hadrian. Relief sculpture of the Roman period is probably best known from the marble *sarcophagi*, or coffins, which are carved on one or all sides with mythological scenes (Plate 68C), cupids and the like, often including a medallion with the bust or head of the dead person.

Of the sculpture in this country, and, indeed, in most European collections outside Greece and Italy, most Greek originals have arrived untouched from excavations or enterprising purchase. The Graeco-Roman statues have, however, had a more chequered career. Many were recovered from the soil of Italy in the sixteenth to eighteenth centuries and sold to foreign noblemen, but before they left Italy they were 'treated' in Roman workshops and studios where missing limbs and heads were supplied, pastiches of different originals composed, and original parts often worked over to suit current tastes in 'antique marbles'. Even afterwards they were commonly subjected to repairs, overworking and drastic cleaning, or sometimes, what is worse, neglect. Thus, the Aphrodite of Arles in the Louvre (Plate 68B) had her bust remodelled by Louis XIV's sculptor Girardon to suit the more elegant contemporary fashion. It is often difficult to distinguish even the ghost of the originals which go to compose some of the statuary in public collections and private houses today.

Material and Technique. The white marble of the Greek islands (Naxos, Paros) used for the earliest statuary, but still popular and much exported later, is distinguished by its relatively large crystals which lend considerable translucency. Pentelic marble, from Attica, has a finer grained, 'hard' appearance, while other white marbles from the Asia Minor coast and islands are intermediate. Limestone or other local stones were sometimes employed, especially in the archaic period, but never in later centuries for major works. In Italy the white marble quarries of Carrara were only exploited after the first century B.C., and Greek marbles were still often imported. Carrara marble has very small crystals and a dull white colour which blackens with age; it cannot compare with the Greek marbles for translucency. Only in the Roman period are coloured marbles widely used for statuary. Occasionally in late works the hair is modelled separately in plaster and then painted. It was a common practice, too, in all periods of antiquity, though it is not today, to make statues in separate pieces – head, limbs, etc – which would then be dowelled together.

Traces of working are still apparent on many pieces. The prehistoric statuettes were painstakingly worked with emery. Archaic statuary often shows the marks of claw chisel and rasp, particularly on the backs of figures and in less conspicuous parts of the body. In later times different chisellingwas deliberately employed to give different surface qualities to flesh and drapery. Later classical, Hellenistic and Roman work often carries a highly polished surface which had been waxed to lend added translucency and an almost sensual quality to parts representing bare flesh. In the Roman period the drill and deep undercutting which produce heavy shadows were often employed to excess. The metallic glaze which appears on pieces in many collections is the result of drastic cleaning.

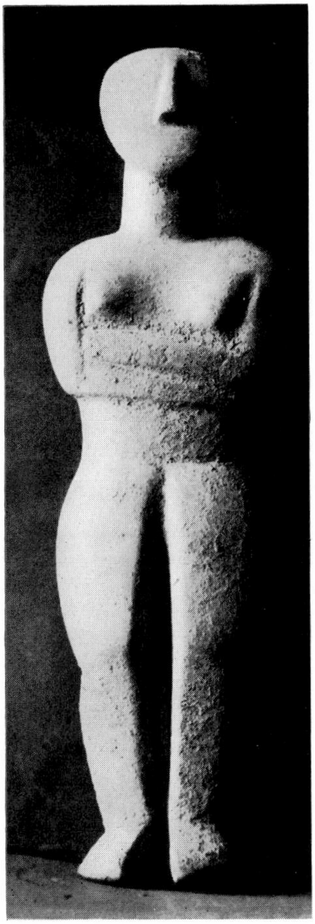

(A) Cycladic marble idol, third millennium B.C.; height 12 in.

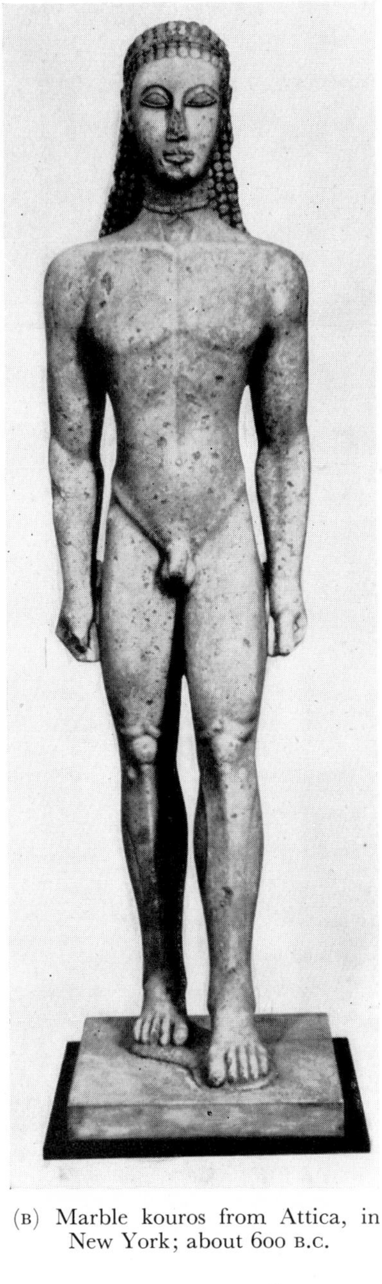

(B) Marble kouros from Attica, in New York; about 600 B.C.

(C) The 'Auxerre statuette' of limestone in Paris. Probably Cretan, seventh century B.C.; height $25\frac{1}{2}$ in.

PLATE 65

To face page 116

(A) Head of a girl, from Miletus (E. Greece), in Berlin; late sixth century B.C.

(B) Metope relief, from near Paestum (Italy); late sixth century B.C.

(C) Head of the Peplos Kore, from Athens; about 530 B.C.

(D) Head of the Rampin horseman from Athens, in Paris; mid-sixth century B.C.

PLATE 66

(A) Head of Athena, from the Temple of Zeus at Olympia; mid-fifth century B.C.

(B) Head of the Hermes of Praxiteles, in Olympia; mid-fourth century B.C.

(C) Head of Demosthenes, in Oxford; copy of a work of the early third century B.C.

(D) Bust of the Emperor Lucius Verus (A.D. 161–9), in Oxford.

PLATE 67

(A) Gravestone of a girl, from Paros, in New York; mid-fifth century B.C.

(B) The Aphrodite of Arles, in Paris; Graeco-Roman copy of a work of the mid-fourth century B.C.

(C) Sarcophagus relief, in Oxford; Hunt of the Calydonian Boar, late second century A.D.

PLATE 68

Gravestone of Hegeso, in Athens; about 400 B.C.

PLATE 69

(A) Head of a boxer, in Olympia; early fourth century B.C.

(B) Head of a charioteer, in Delphi; 480–70 B.C.

(C) Kouros statuette from Delphi; probably Cretan, seventh century B.C.; height 8 in.

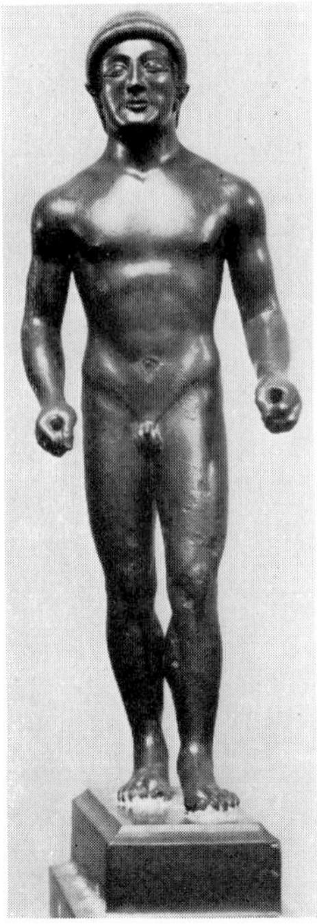

(D) Kouros statuette from Athens; about 500 B.C.

(E) Bathing girl, in Munich; late fifth century B.C.; height 10 in.

(A) Statuette of a horse from a cauldron handle, from Olympia; eighth century B.C.

(C) Late Etruscan statuette of Hercules, in Oxford; height 6 in.

(D) Graeco-Roman statuette of Mercury, in Oxford; height 6 in.

(B) Etruscan statuette of a warrior, in Oxford, fifth century B.C.; height 11 in.

(E) Graeco-Roman statuette of Minerva, in Oxford; height 4 in.

(F) Graeco-Roman statuette of Venus, in Oxford; height 4 in.

(B) Boy jockey from the *Artemision* wreck, in Athens; third century B.C.

(A) God from the *Artemision* wreck, in Athens; mid-fifth century B.C.

PLATE 72

To face page 117

Colour was regularly used on Greek statues for the drapery, eyes, lips and hair. Most of this has usually disappeared with time or cleaning, but traces can still be observed on excavated statues which had not been too long exposed before burial; for example, Plate 66C. The practice continued in Roman Imperial times, and from the second century A.D. the pupil of the eye is regularly also represented by an incised circle. Gilding is often apparent on the hair. We owe most of our misconceptions about the appearance of classical statuary to the disappearance of the colour from the originals. Metal diadems, jewellery, weapons, etc, were also regularly attached, but of these their holes for fastening are usually all that is preserved.

Accurate copies of earlier statues were made in the Roman period by means of the 'pointing' process, which is still practised today. Occasionally the traces of the basic 'points' remain on the surface of the copy in the shape of small pierced mounds. The extraordinary accuracy of this process is attested by the uniform size of many different copies, and by the rare instances in which the original itself is also preserved.

Bronze Sculpture

Because of the value of the material very little bronze statuary has survived from antiquity except for minor objects and some fortunate major discoveries in excavations or wrecks (as Plate 72); the rest went to the melting-pot in the intervening centuries, even more readily than the marble statuary did to the lime-kiln. This easily leads to an under-estimate of the importance of bronzes. The original of a bronze statue, being plastically built up by hand in clay, gave more scope to the sculptor's inventiveness than did the carving techniques required by ivory, wood or stone. It is the plastic quality of the small solid-cast statuettes which is most apparent. In the Late Bronze Age (about 1600–1200 B.C.) minor bronzes representing animals, men and women were being made, notably in Minoan Crete where the distinctive dress is a loin-cloth for the men and flounced skirt for the women. In Geometric Greece of the eighth century B.C. similar subjects are treated in no very different style, the most popular figures being lanky warriors, naked but for their helmets and spears, and bulls which serve as humble substitutes for richer animal offerings. Particularly distinctive horses are made from hammered bronze strips which are welded together; these either decorated cauldron handles (as Plate 71A) or, on flat openwork stands, served as independent votive offerings. Some complicated small groups were attempted, such as a lion hunt or ring dance. With the seventh century the Daedalic style, which we have already met in stone sculpture, is equally well represented in bronze statuettes that observe the same canons of proportion and detail (Plate 70C), but their plastic quality makes them often more satisfying, as they are less rigidly frontal. A small group of bronzes from Crete is executed in the *sphyrelaton* technique of hammered bronze plates fastened on to a wooden core.

The development of major bronze sculpture from this time on runs parallel to that of stone sculpture; in fact, in many ways it precedes it, and in marble statuary many details reveal in their treatment and execution the decisive influence of bronze work. This is particularly true of hair represented in irregular tufts and curls which can be easily modelled in clay but which could hardly recommend themselves to the stone carver otherwise (Plates 67B, 70A and 72B). Bronze also enabled the sculptor to attempt bold compositions of flying figures with outstretched limbs which could not safely be executed in stone. This explains many of the gratuitous tree-trunks and similar supports which appear on Graeco-Roman marble copies of Greek bronze originals whose slender ankles need no reinforcement to carry the weight of the body above.

It is the smaller bronzes which are most likely to come into the purview of the collector today. Through the archaic period, the seventh and sixth centuries B.C., bronze statuettes were made in styles closely resembling the larger marble statuary. As well as independent figures, usually votive offerings, of youths, women or animals, human figures and animals are found serving as the supports for bronze mirrors or the handles of bronze vases. In miniature they reproduce the details of the life-size stone *korai* and athletes of their day. Some local schools and classes can be distinguished among these statuettes, such as the Arcadian shepherds with their pointed caps, and the stocky Spartan warriors. The most important sources of bronzes in this period are the sanctuaries of Zeus at Dodona and Olympia.

From the classical and Hellenistic period there is preserved an occasional statuette which reflects vividly the excellence of the lost major sculpture in bronze of the day. There are some notably fine animal bronzes in this period. The famous bathing-girl in Munich (Plate 70E) is an unusually good example of a type which, in variants, became popular in the fourth century. It is hollow-cast (by the 'cire perdue' method), though most statuettes of all periods are cast solid.

In Italy local traditions die hard in many classes of bronze statuettes, and the Greek motifs are sometimes drastically refashioned. Campania and South Italy have produced important groups of bronzes, but it is in Etruria that most have been found. As well as close imitations and derivations from Greek types, there are individual groups of small 'match-stick' figures, or slim warriors like Plate 71B, which are characteristic of this part of Italy. Later come the common statuettes of votaries wearing radiate crowns and holding bowls (*paterae*) in their hands, of divinities and of heroes. Hercules is particularly popular with his raised club, and lionskin draped over his left arm (Plate 71C). These are types which seem to have been made outside Etruria also, and they long remain popular; their execution is sometimes extremely crude.

The bronze statuettes of the Roman period are often technically superior. The same types are current, especially Hercules, Mercury with purse and caduceus, helmeted Minerva (Athena) and Venus (Plate 71D–F) – all in poses which reflect major Greek originals. These have been found in all parts of the Roman Empire, from England to Egypt.

Material and Technique. For some relevant remarks on the technique of bronze statuary, *see* Mr. Lasko's article in Volume II of this Encyclopaedia (page 222).

Just as the marble statues were usually painted, the bronzes, too, were embellished. Eyes, lips, nipples, finger- and toe-nails could be inlaid with paste, stone or with strips of a contrasting metal like silver. Detailed patterns on drapery and the like might be treated in a similar way, but it is rarely that such details are preserved. When they are, as on the Delphi charioteer (Plate 70B), they are startlingly effective.

Most ancient bronzes have been excavated from the soil, and are consequently coated with a patina and incrustation. In some cases the patina is so light and of so attractive a colour that it enhances rather than detracts from the appearance of the piece. This is, however, rarely true, and much delicate chasing and modelling, to say nothing of incised inscriptions, may be hidden by it. It is clear that in antiquity pains were taken to see that the bronze statues were kept bright and free from rust.

BOOKS FOR FURTHER READING

MISS G. M. A. RICHTER has written a number of well illustrated books which should be consulted: *The Sculpture and Sculptors of the Greeks* (New Haven, 1950); *Kouroi* (New York, 1942); *Archaic Greek Art* (New York, 1949); *Ancient Italy* (Michigan, 1955).

For minor bronzes, *see* W. LAMB, *Greek and Roman Bronzes* (Methuen, 1929), and museum catalogues, as *Greek, Etruscan and Roman Bronzes*, in New York, by G. M. A. RICHTER (New York, 1915).

Other useful works are A. W. LAWRENCE, *Classical Sculpture* (London, 1929), *Later Greek Sculpture* (London, 1927); H. PAYNE and G. M. YOUNG, *Archaic Marble Sculpture from the Acropolis* (London, 1936, 1952); M. BIEBER, *The Sculpture of the Hellenistic Age* (New York, 1955); C. PICARD, *La Sculpture antique* (Paris, 1935—).

For an account of ancient statuary in English collections and its manner of arrival, *see* the introduction to A. MICHAELIS, *Ancient Marbles in Great Britain* (Cambridge, 1882).

ENGLISH COLOUR-PLATE BOOKS 1775–1850

By DAVID BLAND

THE definition of colour-plate books given in Vol. II under *Victoriana* makes it clear how arbitrary are the limits of this category. From it the bookseller excludes flower and bird books, and he would not admit many publications which appeared after Victoria's accession. Blake's illuminated books do not count, although they contained hand-coloured plates. Nevertheless, within a comparatively short period of about seventy-five years a wonderful collection of these volumes appeared, their subject-matter widely varying, their illustrations printed by all manner of processes.

But if different methods were used for printing, the basis of the pictures, the colour, was nearly always applied by the oldest method of all – by hand. This meant that the books were usually expensive, often very expensive, and many of them have remained collector's pieces ever since. It is difficult to believe that there could have been a public for Ackermann's more costly publications, some of which were published at ninety-five guineas a volume; but the steady stream of such books suggests that they must have been bought by members of the new moneyed class which was profiting from the Industrial Revolution. France, recovering from the effects of her Revolution, has little of this sort to show, though at other times she has usually led England in the arts of the book. It is arguable of course that these volumes are not books at all, but simply collections of plates with some explanatory text which is rarely of any importance. Sometimes, indeed, they had no text at all apart from a title-page. The fact remains that the best of them have seldom been surpassed in any period or country.

There was another reason besides the financial one why these books flourished in England. They are, many of them, topographical, and the subject of their plates is landscape. The Romantic revival of landscape painting was just then at its height, and the publishers were able to call on many painters to satisfy a public whose appetite for landscape and for travel had already been whetted. It is significant that the man who introduced aquatint to England was the water-colourist Paul Sandby. He used it for his *Views in South Wales* (*c.* 1775), which is one of the earliest and rarest of the colour-plate books.

It may be convenient here to give a short list of the chief reproductive processes employed during this period. Apart from lithography, these were all intaglio, i.e. they were printed from an incised surface. The time-honoured relief method, which is represented in books of this period by wood-engraving (recently revived by Bewick), is very seldom found in conjunction with colour until Baxter's time. Blake's relief etching had no history outside his own books.

RELIEF METHOD

Baxter Process: *see Victoriana,* Vol. II. This was a method of producing colour-prints from wood blocks, and although book illustrations were often printed by this method, its chief use was for separate prints. It was not patented until 1835, and therefore comes near the very end of our period. Baxter's *Pictorial*

Album of 1837 is one of the best books in which it was used.

INTAGLIO METHODS

Most of the books to be described have plates printed by this method. Very few of their illustrators actually engraved their own plates, although etched work was more commonly done by the artist himself. Generally, however, the drawing was handed to a craftsman, who translated it into the terms of the engraving. Sometimes it was altered considerably in the process, but always in the case of the successful books the engraver deserves more credit than he usually receives.

Aquatint: a description of the technique will be found under *Victoriana* in Vol. II. It was the process *par excellence* for the reproduction of water-colours, not only because it could simulate tone but also because it provided an excellent base for the application (by hand) of colour. Sometimes neutral tints were printed first from the same plate but in almost every case there was touching up by hand. Most of the plates in the more ambitious books with which we have to deal are aquatints. **Coloured Aquatint:** one with more than one colour applied by hand. **Sepia Aquatint:** one printed in brownish ink. **Tinted Aquatint:** one washed over by hand with a water-colour tint.

Chalk Engraving was an etching technique used for making facsimiles of chalk drawings.

Etching: the printed impression results from a line scratched directly on the plate. In this respect it is like line-engraving (q.v.), but the difference is that in etching the line is eaten out by acid. It is therefore freer than line-engraving and more direct than aquatint. It was often combined with the other two intaglio processes on one plate in the colour-plate books, and sometimes it is almost impossible to tell which of the three processes predominates. **Soft-ground Etching** relies on the softening of the ground of the plate by grease. Over this is laid a sheet of paper on which the drawing is made, and when the paper is removed the ground adheres where the pencil has done its work.

Line-engraving: often called copper-plate engraving; it was the favourite method of book illustration in the seventeenth and eighteenth centuries. The design is incised by means of a burin, and a more formal effect than etching is produced. Colour could be added by selective inking of the one plate or by printing from several different plates, but neither method was as much used in books as hand-colouring. **Steel-engraving** developed at the beginning of the nineteenth century, and simply substituted a steel plate for a copper one so that a larger number of impressions could be printed without wear. However, as steel is a more intractable material than copper, the effect on design is one of even greater rigidity. It seems unlikely that 'any book illustrated by this method was issued coloured', though colour has undoubtedly been applied to many since.

Mezzotint is distinguished by its dark tones, which are obtained by roughening the plate all over to produce a black and then smoothing where required for lighter tones. The engraver therefore works from black to white and in tone rather than line. This is the process *par excellence* for reproducing paintings in monochrome, and so it was used throughout the eighteenth century. It is a process that lends itself to hand colouring, and it was often applied over an aquatint ground, as in *The Temple of Flora*.

Stipple is another engraving technique which simulated tone. It did this by means of fine dots, which replaced the lines of line-engraving in rather the same style as the modern half-tone block. France produced a remarkable set of books with illustrations printed in colour by this technique at the very end of the eighteenth century; but the example was not followed in this country, and few of the great colour-plate books use it except incidentally.

SURFACE METHODS

Lithography: the process was invented in 1796 towards the middle of our period, and had an almost immediate impact on the colour-plate book. It is, in fact, the only *new* process with which we have to deal. A definition will be found under *Victoriana*, Vol. II, where the reader is told how to distinguish it from the various forms of engraving. It only remains to stress the autographic quality of the lithograph, which presents the artist's work direct to the reader without any intervention save that of the printing machine. A special skill was necessary to the wood or copper engraver, and the material used partly dictates the design. But the lithographic stone has as few limitations as paper. This facility was partly its undoing in mid-Victorian England, but during the first forty years of the century some magnificent books appeared with lithographic illustrations. Colour in those early days was generally applied by hand. Chromolithography which arrived in the forties and was at first more expensive than hand-colouring, used separate stones for each colour. The first English book with chromolithographed plates was Boys's *Picturesque Architecture in Paris, Ghent, Antwerp, Rouen* (1839), a real *tour de force*, which is proudly advertised as being wholly 'the product of the press'.

Coloured Lithographs were printed in one or two neutral colours with other colours applied by hand. **Tinted Lithographs** underwent two printings, the key in black, followed by a printed tint. **Tinted Lithographs Coloured** were printed in black with a monochrome mechanical tint, other colours being applied by hand. **Chromolithographs** were printed in more than two colours.

Lithotint: this was a forerunner of the chromolithograph, and it was patented by Hullmandel in 1840. The stone was coated with resin, and the result was similar to the aquatint. Usually a second stone was used for printing a flat tint, and from this tint the highlights were scraped out, giving a rather startling white. Another book of Boys's, *Original Views of London as it is* (1842), shows the process at its best. But in spite of a great range of tone, the result is decidedly monochrome.

COLOUR

It is obvious that the distinguishing feature of all the colour-plate books is the use of colour. The various engraving processes by which most of them are printed had, with the exception of aquatint, been used throughout most of the eighteenth century. But colour had not been seen in the book on such a scale since the days of the illuminated manuscripts. The sporadic efforts in the fifteenth and sixteenth centuries to print wood-cuts in colour had been few and limited. When line-engraving ousted wood in the seventeenth century, we find colour-prints being produced by one of three methods: (1) By selective inking of one plate only. This was often done in nineteenth-century aquatint illustration in order to provide a blue sky above a darker foreground. (2) By printing from two or more plates, each plate producing a different colour. This was the method used by Le Blon in *Coloritto* (1723) and by Elisha Kirkall in Martyn's *Historia Plantarum Rariorium* (1728), but retouching by hand was generally necessary. In any case, these books have few successors unless we include J. B. Jackson's essay on the *Invention of Engraving and Printing in Chiaro Oscuro* (1754), which contains wall-paper designs, and some of the plates in *The Temple of Flora.* (3) By hand colouring, far the most popular procedure until about 1830 when the Baxter process and chromolithograph began to supplant it.

It is interesting to speculate why there should have been a desire for colour-plates in the book just at the beginning of our period, not only in England but in France as well and in other European countries, where the little coloured almanacks of the time were so greatly in demand. Now the purist holds that colour is alien to the book because it involves a separate printing from type and more often than not a separate process like lithography, or even hand-colouring which is not a printing process at all. Until about 1775 the book had got on well enough without colour at all, and the whole basis of illustrative design was black and white. Dürer's wood-cuts, the Florentine cuts of the early sixteenth century and the French engravings of the eighteenth not only were uncoloured, they did not need colour, they would have been spoiled by it. Bewick's wood-engravings, which were appearing throughout a large part of our period, were uncompromisingly black and white; the 'colour' of which he spoke was simply their tonal values. But then Bewick saw them as poor relations of copper engraving and never dreamed that they would soon replace it. He was obviously no purist himself.

The reason for the introduction of colour-plates into books must probably be sought in the use to which engraving had been put in the eighteenth century for reproducing paintings. Mezzotint had been found especially suitable for the rendering of oil-paintings because of its tones; and it was natural that the next step should be the reproduction of colour itself. We have already noted the English genius for water-colour painting and how this talent was brought into the book by means of the hand-coloured aquatint. All this helped to build up a sophisticated taste that would not be content with plain monochrome illustration. Many highly trained reproductive engravers were available, too, for work in books. But, as we have seen, the printing techniques were not yet ready for colour and it had to be applied by hand. When chromolithography and the Baxter process were perfected in the 1840s, the result was generally disastrous artistically. The whole palette of the coloured illustration was changed radically for the first time since Rowlandson introduced his delicate scheme of pink and blue washes. But first we have the comparatively short intermediate period of our study, during which many remarkable books appeared.

The best bibliography of the subject is contained in the catalogue of Major Abbey's collection, which limits itself to the years 1770–1860 and of which two volumes have so far appeared; one entitled *Scenery of Great Britain and Ireland in Aquatint and Lithography* (1952) and the other *Life in England in Aquatint and Lithography* (1953). These titles, though not quite accurate, indicate the two main categories – topography and social life – both of them, be it noted, national. In addition, there are a few books on natural history, like Thornton's famous *Temple of Flora* in which the Romantic landscape forms an almost too obtrusive background. But coloured bird and flower books are not generally considered as part of our subject, and information about these may be found under *Victoriana* in Vol. II. Major Abbey's second catalogue, which is entitled *Life in England*, is divided into several subsections, the chief being architecture, drawing books, pictorial collections, high and low life in town and country, and sports. But this last category, into which fall many important colour books, is poorly represented, and the interested reader is referred to Schwerdt's *Hunting, Hawking, Shooting*.

The chief publisher of colour-plate books in the first two categories was Rudolf Ackermann from whose Repository of Arts in the Strand came an endless flow of illustrations and separate prints. He employed many expert engravers, like Stadler, Bluck and Havell, but the colouring was mainly done by children, who seem to have become very skilful. It is interesting to recall that both Turner and Girtin worked at colouring prints in their youth, and in this way the colour print may have had a reciprocal influence on painting. Ackermann's star illustrator was Rowlandson, famous for many fine colour-plate books. Rowlandson's procedure was to etch his design on the plate, leaving it to be aquatinted by someone else. He would then colour a print, and so set the style which the hand-colourists would follow. The cool, clear washes which he used were copied by nearly all his successors, and seem to us to be the hallmark of the colour aquatint. But they also cover up various deficiencies, for the neutral tints (such as blue for the sky), which were printed beforehand from the basic plate, were produced by selective inking, and could not therefore be very accurately registered. Hand-colouring helped to disguise this shortcoming.

TOPOGRAPHY

Among Rowlandson's first books for Ackermann were the famous *Tours of Dr*

Syntax which satirized the topographical books of Gilpin. Gilpin, although most of his early books are uncoloured, is of importance to our subject because he popularized topography and coupled it with the aquatint, for which, incidentally, he favoured an oval shape. He wrote what were really the first popular guide-books, and he illustrated them in accordance with his own recipes for Picturesque Beauty (Plate 74A). The Romantic landscape with its idyllic quality from which every hint of industrialism has been banished, and with its subtle exaggeration that made it just a little larger than life, was by him brought into the book for the first time. His more ambitious coloured books, like *Mountains and Lakes in Cumberland and Westmorland* (1786), gave him even more scope. His great reputation amongst his contemporaries is seen in a later book about his style, J. H. Clark's *Gilpin's Day* (1811), which contains coloured aquatints and is itself a fine production.

Landscape, however, has its dangers as a subject for illustration. For one thing, it requires ideally an oblong page which is not very suitable for text; the unsatisfactory alternative is a conventional page on which the plate is turned sideways. But more serious, a series of landscapes tends to make the book in which they appear into an album. The text, however substantial, becomes a mere excuse for the pictures; and the publishers of those days very seldom troubled to commission a first-class writer to provide it. This is certainly the case with *The History of the Thames*, which Farington illustrated in 1794 and which is filled with many delightful pictures and a substantial but pedestrian text.

That is of course a criticism that can be levelled with more or less justice against all the colour-plate books. It is perhaps a reason though not an excuse for the habit of extracting the plates for separate sale. This has often been done with the smaller, humbler topographical books and it has made good copies very rare. On the other hand, many volumes were issued which are nothing more nor less than collections of plates and which contain no text at all apart from a title-page. Sometimes even that is lacking and the very name of the artist is unknown to us, as in the case of the delightful *Six Views of Plymouth* (1840) with its striking coloured lithographs (Plate 74B).

Topographical books may be divided into the following categories according to their subject-matter:

1. Collections of views within stated limits, e.g. P. J. de Loutherbourg's *Picturesque Scenery of Great Britain* (1801) and T. H. Fielding's *Cumberland, Westmorland and Lancashire* (1822) (Plate 75A).

2. Books dealing with a single house or estate, e.g. J. E. Smith's *A Tour to Hafod* (1810); and Pine's *Royal Residences* (1819), which deals of course with several houses, belong to this class (Plate 80B).

3. Books dealing with a single river, e.g. F. C. Lewis's *The River Dart* (1812) with its coloured etchings.

4. Books dealing with a single town. Spas like Bath or Brighton were especially favoured, and Rowlandson's *Excursion to Brighthelmstone* (1790) and J. C. Nattes's *Views of Bath* (1806) may be cited (Plate 73A).

5. Itineraries following a road or (later) a railway, e.g. A. Robertson's *The Great Road from London to Bath and Bristol* (1792), or the fine *London–Birmingham Railway* (1839) by Bourne and Britton. Some of the later railway guides (usually with lithographic illustrations) are quite delightful, and are perhaps easier to come by and cheaper than most of the other types of colour-plate book (Plate 75B).

Many of the finest books fall into the fourth class, which seemed to offer a more satisfactory framework than the others. T. Malton's *A Picturesque Tour through London* (1792–1801) is a handsome book (Plate 73B). And Ackermann's famous *Microcosm of London* (1808–10), in which Rowlandson collaborated with Pugin, was one of that publisher's earliest ventures into this field. The whole edition contained about 104,000 plates, each coloured separately by hand. Other Ackermann books were Rowlandson's *Oxford and Cambridge* (1809–11) (Plate 76), Pugin's *The University of Oxford* (1814) and *The University of Cambridge* (1815); and finally, an example of tinted lithographs, T. S. Boys's *Views in York* (1841) (Plate 78). But perhaps the most magnificent book of them all had nothing to do with Ackermann. William Daniell's monumental *Voyage round Great Britain* (1814–23) comprises eight large volumes of incomparable aquatints, so delicate that hand-colouring seems to add little to them.

In his later topographical books Ackermann, having perhaps exhausted the native scene, turned his attention abroad. His travel books from 1820 onwards give him great scope for coloured illustration, especially when they deal with tropical countries. *A Picturesque Tour along the River Ganges and Jumna* (1824) is a fine example of this. But these volumes are exceptional among English colour-plate books in that their subject-matter is drawn from abroad.

ARCHITECTURE, ORNAMENT AND THE CRAFTS

We find the great names here – Nash, Wood and Soane – as well as many unknown ones attached to books which are none the less noteworthy. James Malton's *Essay on British Cottage Architecture* (1804) with its coloured aquatints compares well with any book of the period. John Nash's *The Royal Pavilion at Brighton* (1826) gave that architect an opportunity of displaying his own handiwork. Savage's *Hints on Decorative Printing* (1822) is a *tour de force* of colour printing which prepared the way for the Baxter process; and Ackermann's *Upholsterer's Repository* (1830) used various engraving processes for its very numerous illustrations (Plate 80A). But the great Victorian books on ornament by Digby Wyatt, Owen Jones and Noel Humphreys, with their chromolithographic illustrations, fall just outside our period.

DRAWING BOOKS

These were aimed at the great new public of amateur artists, and it is significant that we find many well-known painters producing them. There is a whole series by David Cox containing etchings and aquatints, sometimes coloured, sometimes uncoloured (e.g. his *Progressive Lessons*, 1823) and another series by George Morland. Calvert's *Rural Scenery* of 1825 is somewhat exceptional for its date because it is illustrated by coloured lithographs. The illustration from Morland shows how well suited soft-ground etching is for reproducing drawings (Plate 79A).

PICTORIAL COLLECTIONS

This category consists of volumes of reproductions, and it includes some of the most sumptuous and elaborate books of the whole period. Hogarth's *Works* of 1812, 'one of the most splendid of Regency books', was published at £105 per copy. It contains coloured engravings. *Drawings by Hans Holbein* (1792) is more interesting technically because here the stipple engravings are *printed* in colour. Most of them are by Bartolozzi, whose name will always be associated with this process. Gainsborough's *English Scenery* of 1819 is simply a collection of soft-ground etchings after that painter, without any text. But perhaps the most important colour book in this category is *Imitations de Dessins* (1821–8) by Van Amstel and Josi, which counts as an English book although the text is in French and many of the plates were engraved by Van Amstel in Holland during the previous century. Aquatint, mezzotint and other less familiar processes were used, and the result represents the highest point of the art of colour reproduction before the coming of mechanical methods. Baxter's *Pictorial Album* of 1837 shows a sad falling off, though it is a good example of the Baxter Process. The oiliness of the colour compares unfavourably with the earlier books, though it seems to have chimed perfectly with early Victorian taste.

SOCIAL LIFE

This subject naturally lent itself to caricature, and to the magazines and other ephemera. But so many books were published in monthly parts that the distinction between the book and the magazine meant very little. The same artists often worked for both. Pierce Egan's *Life in London* (1821) and *Life of an Actor* (1825), both with hand-coloured etchings (and wood-engravings) by I. R. and G. Cruikshank, are typical (Plate 77A). Cruikshank, who had already illustrated one

(A) A coloured aquatint. Title page from *Bath* by J. C. Nattes, 1806.

(B) An aquatint by T. Malton from his *Picturesque Tour through the Cities of London and Westminster*, 1795.

PLATE 73

All these plates except No. 80B are reproduced by kind permission of Major V. R. Abbey.

(A) A soft-ground etching by W. Gilpin from *Remarks on Forest Scenery*, 1794.

(B) A lithograph from *Six Views of Plymouth*, *c.* 1840.

PLATE 74

(A) An aquatint from T. H. Fielding's *Cumberland, Westmorland and Lancashire*, 1822.

(B) An aquatint by T. T. Bury from *Six Coloured Views on the London and Birmingham Railway*, 1837.

PLATE 75

An aquatint by T. Rowlandson from *Oxford and Cambridge*, 1810.

PLATE 76

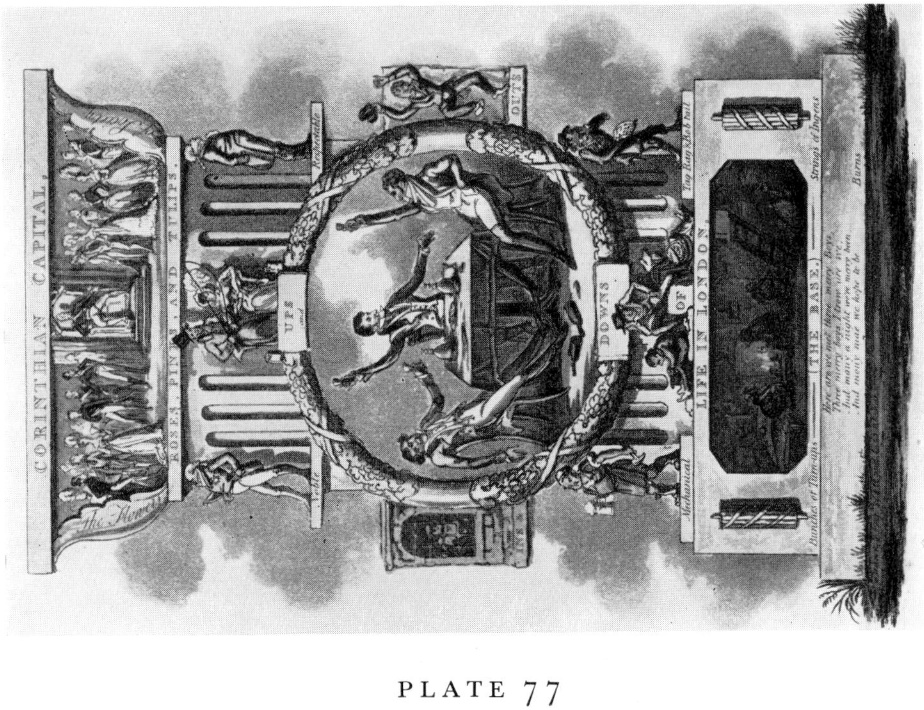

(A) An aquatint by I. R. and G. Cruikshank from Pierce Egan's *Life in London*, 1821.

(B) A binding in green morocco of Gilpin's *Mountains and Lakes in Cumberland and Westmorland*, 1786.

A lithograph by T. S. Boys from *A Series of Views in York*, 1841.

PLATE 78

(A) Title page from Morland's *Sketches*, 1791. A soft-ground etching.

(B) A stipple-and-line engraving from Hincks's *Irish Linen Industry*, 1791.

PLATE 79

(A) A stipple-and-line engraving from Ackermann's *The Upholsterer's and Cabinetmaker's Repository*, *c*. 1830.

(B) An aquatint from Ackermann's *Public Schools*, 1816. *Courtesy of Messrs. Quaritch.*

PLATE 80

To face page 125

of his best books, *The Humourist*, in 1819 thus established himself as one of the great illustrators of the colour-plate book and his favourite method of hand-coloured etching as a rival of the hand-coloured aquatint. But whereas the aquatint was better able to produce the atmospheric effect of the Romantic landscape, the etching, with its spontaneity and freedom, was better suited to caricature.

Leech, the famous *Punch* artist, also favoured etching, and he used it in his first coloured book, *Etchings and Sketchings* (1836). But his best-known illustrations were for Surtees and fall outside our period.

SPORTING BOOKS

The early nineteenth century in England was the great period of the sporting print, and where the print flourishes so usually does the illustrated book. But in this instance the popularity of the sporting print seems to have demanded most of the energies of artists like Alken and Pollard who specialized in it. However, there are several early books of great merit, like the Rev. W. B. Daniel's *Rural Sports* (1805) and Orme's *British Field Sports* of 1807 (which has no text); and later we find a few books illustrated by Alken, such as *National Sports of Great Britain* (1821) and Nimrod's *Life of a Sportsman*, which Ackermann published in 1842. In 1843 Alken illustrated the first Surtees book, *Jorrocks's Jaunts and Jollities*, but thereafter he was supplanted by Leech, who was responsible for the later ones. And Alken's talent compares unfavourably with Leech's.

As many of these sporting books have no text, they have suffered particularly from being broken up into separate prints and are hard to come by. At their best, however, they are worthy to rank with the great books of the other classes, and present a peculiarly English phenomenon that is not to be found in any other country on the same scale.

MISCELLANEOUS

There remain many books that will not fit into any of the foregoing categories (Plate 79B). There are many colour-plate books devoted to the Army and the Navy, and there is also Pyne's *Costume* (1819–20), with its magnificent coloured aquatints. Then there are a few reprints of classics like Bensley's of Thomson's *Seasons* (1797), of which about six copies are known with the stipple engravings printed in colour. There is A'Beckett's *Comic History of England* (1846–8), which Leech illustrated with coloured steel-engravings. And finally there are three monumental books to commemorate George IV's coronation, the best one Whittaker's of 1823, with its gold lettering and its fine series of colour-plates; in 1825 and 1827 two parts of Nayler's edition were published, and in 1837 Bohn combined Whittaker and Nayler. In these plates mezzotint, stipple and aquatint were all used, and two or more colours were often printed, being finished afterwards by hand.

BINDINGS

The outsides of many of the most elaborate and magnificent colour-plates are often quite unassuming (Plate 77B). Simple marbled boards were often used, and the smaller, more modest books were bound in an even plainer manner. Sometimes, more especially in the case of part issues, they have nothing but a printed wrapper, and the flimsiness of this style of binding has led to the disintegration of many and the consequent scarcity of copies in good condition. These wrappers are often delightfully printed, however, and are of some importance typographically. Major Abbey is to be congratulated on having reproduced so many in his catalogues.

Later on elaborately blocked bindings in the Gothic 'cathedral' style appeared, but little consideration seems to have been given to the matching of outside and inside.

BOOKS FOR FURTHER READING

Besides the catalogues of Major Abbey's collection already detailed, the following books may be noted:

BURCH, R. M.: *Colour Printing and Colour Printers* (1910).
HARDIE, MARTIN: *English Coloured Books* (1906).
PRIDEAUX, S. T.: *Aquatint Engravings* (1909).
SCHWERDT, C. F. G. R.: *Hunting, Hawking, Shooting* (1928).
TOOLEY, R. V.: *English Colour Plate Books* (2nd edition 1954).

BIRD PRINTS

By HANDASYDE BUCHANAN

INTRODUCTION

PRINTS or engravings, of all subjects, have always tempted collectors, and it must be realized that the vast majority of all these have been produced as book illustrations, scarcely any solely with the original intention that they should be collected separately for their own merits. All, or almost all, bird prints were to start with part of a book. Now very few trees have been planted for amenity only, but this does not mean that those grown for utilitarian purposes are less attractive in themselves: and bird prints can be viewed in the same way. Whether it is ethically agreeable to pull books to pieces and to sell their engravings separately need not affect the collector so much as the print dealer. And on his behalf it is perhaps fair to say that if he is conscientious he will be more likely to use incomplete or defective copies of illustrated books for his purpose; further, though probably with less justification, that the text of many books, and in particular of bird books, has become valueless or obsolete with the passage of time while the prints have become more valuable; and that some books, like Dr Thornton's *Temple of Flora* or Audubon's *Birds of America*, were in effect collections of prints which have finally found their way into book form.

Bird books with coloured plates make an interesting subject for collectors but they demand a very considerable capital outlay and a library of some size. The individual coloured prints take up little space and can be collected reasonably cheaply. Furthermore, it is possible to specialize and to collect, for example, prints of, say, a robin or a bird of paradise, or to limit oneself to English, French or German prints.

Coloured bird prints started to appear in books around 1730, with hand-coloured copper engravings which continued until about 1830, though at the beginning of the nineteenth century the French produced wonderful stipple engravings of birds and flowers, partially printed in colours by a method unequalled before or since and touched up by hand. Hand-coloured lithographs began to appear around 1830 and chromolithographs, printed in colour, after 1850. All these types have their own special interest, while Audubon's *Birds of America*, giant aquatint engravings which appeared between 1827 and 1838, are unique.

Almost all bird prints come from Germany, France or Great Britain; a few from Italy and Holland, some of very good quality. And a very few, not very interesting, from Scandinavia. The Germans excelled in copper-plate engravings, the French in stipple engravings partly printed in colour and the British in lithographs. Audubon's aquatints stand above all competition, but as loose plates are on sale almost exclusively in the United States, they are not easy to collect as well as being very expensive.

Prices of individual prints naturally vary from a few shillings for the smaller and more common prints up to fifty pounds and more for Audubons; but most other large prints can be bought for well under ten, often for under five pounds.

Most, but not all, prints have the name of the artist on them, usually but not always in the bottom left-hand corner; and again most, though slightly less often, have the name of the engraver, this usually in the bottom right-hand corner. In addition, the name of the printer sometimes appears, under the title or elsewhere. A list of the abbreviations used to indicate artist, engraver or printer will be found below. Meanwhile it must be pointed out that some confusion can be caused to the collector by the naming of complete sets of prints after the author of the book rather than the artist. Thus bird prints painted by BARRABAND are usually referred to as Levaillant's birds, since Levaillant's name is on the title-page of the books in which these prints appeared. Quite often, however, the author was the artist. A catalogue of the principal authors, artists and engravers is given below after the short glossary, catalogued under names, not titles.

GLOSSARY

Aquatint: aquatint is the name given to a process of engraving in which the engraver, instead of scratching lines directly on to the plate, places over it an upper surface of resin or other substance; he now works on this surface, and makes room for acid (aqua fortis, hence the name) to come down on to the plate and eat its way in. Aquatint is therefore not a line process, but produces a more general and softer effect. The most famous of all bird prints, Audubon's *Birds of America* (q.v.), were engraved in aquatint.

Chromolithograph (*see also* **Lithography**)**:** the lithograph only requires one stone for printing, but the chromolithograph needs as many stones as colours are to be used on the finished print. A different colour is applied to each stone, and the various stones are applied in succession to the same paper until the complete picture is achieved. It is obvious therefore that to produce a really fine chromolithograph was both a cumbersome and an expensive process, so that while some magnificent examples appeared, there were far more prints which tended to be cheap and nasty. The very important series of illustrations by Keulemans (q.v.) and others for the works of Richard Bowdler Sharpe were all reproduced in chromolithography, but in most cases the printing and colouring leave much to be desired. A comparison of one of these prints with one of the hand-coloured lithographs from Gould's *Birds* will make this inferiority immediately plain.

Copper Engravings: until the arrival of the lithograph all bird prints, save the few reproduced by aquatint, were taken from copper plates on which the necessary lines had been scratched with an engraving tool. The results naturally varied according to the skill of the artist or the engraver; in many cases the artist was his own engraver. Almost all bird prints, then, from 1730 to 1830 are copper engravings, and some later still, though the hand-coloured lithograph was responsible for the important work in the later period.

Del.: short for delineavit or delineaverunt – Latin for he or they drew. To be seen after the artist's name, usually on the left-hand side of a print.

Dir. or **Direx.:** short for direxit or direxerunt, and means engraved under the supervision of. Occasionally to be seen on bird prints.

Exc. or **Excud.:** short for excudit or excuderunt. Means printed by or engraved and printed by. Sometimes seen on bird prints.

Fe. or **Fec.:** short for fecit or fecerunt. Made by. A less common variant for Del (q.v.).

Imp.: short for impressit, impresserunt or imprimé, in which case it means printed by; or for imprimerie – printing establishment or works. The name of the printer is often found on a bird print, usually under the title.

Lithography: a revolutionary process for reproducing pictures invented at the end of the eighteenth century but not in general use until around 1830, when it quickly ousted the earlier processes. Almost all bird prints after that date are lithographs, and in particular all the prints for Gould's vast series of birds, by far the largest single collection of prints. In lithography a drawing is made upon a stone, levelled and polished with a greasy crayon. The stone is then wetted but the greasy part will not receive the moisture. Next a greasy ink (of any colour) is passed over the stone by a roller or otherwise; only the unwet part of the stone –

Wild Turkey. Hand-coloured aquatint. Drawn by J. J. L. Audubon (*c.* 1830). Engraved by R. Havell.

PLATE 81

To face page 128

Cockerel. Hand-coloured engraving. Drawn by F. H. Frisch (*c.* 1740).

PLATE 82

Wood Duck. Hand-coloured engraving. Drawn by X. Manetti (*c.* 1770).

PLATE 83

(A) The Dodo. Hand-coloured engraving. Drawn by G. Edwards (1757).

(B) Parrakeet. Hand-coloured engraving. Drawn by P. Brown (1776).

(A) Colombe Muscadivore. Engraving printed in colour and finished by hand. Drawn by P. de C. Knip (*c.* 1810). Engraved by C. Macret.

(B) Oiseau de Paradis Rouge. Engraving printed in colour and finished by hand. Drawn by J. Barraband (*c.* 1810).

(A) Finches. Hand-coloured engraving. Drawn by P. Paillou (*c.* 1765).

(B) Der Pirol – Oriolus Galbula. Hand-coloured engraving. Drawn by I. C. Susemihl (*c.* 1800).

(A) Geay Bleu du Canada. Hand-coloured engraving. Drawn by F. Martinet (*c.* 1770).

(B) The Golden Winged Woodpecker. Hand-coloured engraving by M. Catesby (*c.* 1735).

PLATE 87

Avocet. Hand-coloured lithograph. Drawn and lithographed by J. Gould and H. C. Richter (*c.* 1870).

PLATE 88

To face page 129

that already drawn on – will accept the ink. A piece of paper is placed against the stone and receives a reproduction of the drawing. Since the paper does not have to be forced into an engraved plate, a lithographic print has no plate mark such as surrounds all engravings, and so can be easily distinguished. But, of course, apart from this, the whole effect is different too, and it should not be difficult to detect a lithograph at once.

Lith. or **Lit.:** means lithographed by. Follows the lithographer's name on the print.

Pinx.: short for pinxit or pinxerunt. Means painted by. Found after the artist's name on bird prints, but not so often as Del. (q.v.).

Sc. or **Sculp.:** short for sculpsit or sculpserunt, and means engraved by. Usually found after the engraver's name on the right-hand side of a bird print.

Watermarks: it is sometimes possible to date a print which is not otherwise dated by inspecting the watermark. Most hand-made paper had a watermark in it, and this watermark often included the date. It is a fair inference, though not quite always true, that the date of the watermark will be little if any before the time of the making of the print. To inspect the watermark hold the print up to a strong light, when it will at once stand out.

CATALOGUE OF ARTISTS, ENGRAVERS, AUTHORS AND PRINTERS

Albin, Eleazar: author and artist. His *Natural History of Birds*, 3 volumes, quarto, 1731–38, is the earliest of all collections of coloured bird prints, with 306 in hand-coloured engravings. Also produced in 1737, 23 engravings, very small, of British song-birds.

Audebert, Jean Baptiste: author and artist. Produced *Les Oiseaux Dorés ou à Reflets Metalliques*, 1802; 190 very fine engravings printed in colours by a method invented by Audebert himself. There were two sets of these plates, the ordinary one with lettering in black, the superior in gold. Printing in colours had been performed in various ways since 1730. It consists basically only of putting the colours on to the engraved plates and pressing them on to the paper, rather than printing the paper in monochrome and colouring it later. The French, however, performed feats of colour printing which gave us these prints, almost all Redoute's flower books and the illustrations to Levaillant's bird books (q.v.), which have never been surpassed. Most of these engravings, however, were printed in colours and finished by hand.

Audubon, John James Laforest: the author and artist of the most famous of all collections of bird prints, *The Birds of America from Original Drawings made during a Residence of Twenty-five years in the United States*, published between 1827 and 1838 in four volumes, size double elephant folio, easily the largest bird prints ever done. There were 435 hand-coloured aquatints, of which Lucy Audubon drew Plate 64, but Audubon himself the rest. The first ten were engraved by W. H. Lizars, and the remainder by Robert Havell and Robert Havell Junior, who also revised later editions of the first ten plates, adding their name. It is likely that not more than 300 copies of each print were produced. This is by far the most valuable of any collection of bird prints, and a complete set fetches at present (1957) around £10,000 to £12,000. This means that individual copies of the most sought-after prints sell for over £100, while the general level is around £50. For a collection of this size the capital value is therefore staggering, and no other bird prints are in the same class. The most expensive flower prints, the engravings from Dr Thornton's *Temple of Flora*, number only 35, of which the first and only good printing comprised not more than 400 copies of each, but the prints sell for – on an average – £30 apiece. Audubon prints are very rarely on sale individually in Britain, and are, moreover, outside the scope of the ordinary collector.

Barraband, Jacques: artist. Drew most of the pictures reproduced by François

Levaillant (q.v.) in his very important series of exotic birds published between 1796 and 1816.

Bessa: artist, mainly famous for his drawings of flowers, which were almost comparable to Redouté, but drew some of the pictures for R. P. Lesson (q.v.) *Histoire des Oiseaux Mouches*, 1828–33, and *Illustrations de Zoologie*, 1832–35.

Bock, Johann Carl: artist. Helped to illustrate Bernhard Meyer's (q.v.) *Naturgeschichte der Vögel Deutschlands.*

Bolton, James: author and artist for *Harmonia Ruralis*, 2 volumes, quarto, 1794–6, with 80 hand-coloured engravings. Other editions of this well-known collection appeared until 1845.

Bonaparte, Prince Lucien Charles Laurent: author of *American Ornithology or the Natural History of Birds inhabiting the United States not given by Wilson*, 4 vols., folio, 1825–33, with 27 hand-coloured engravings by T. R. Peale, A. Rider and J. J. L. Audubon; and of *Iconographie des Pigeons*, large folio, 1857–9, with 55 hand-coloured lithographs by P. L. Oudart, F. Willy and E. Blanchard.

Borkhausen, Moritz Balthasar: author of *Deutsche Ornithologie*, 2 vols., folio, 1800–17. Illustrated by H. Curtmann and the Susemihl family. A very rare collection, reprinted 1837–41.

Boucquet, Louis: artist. Illustrated L. J. P. Vieillot's (q.v.) *Histoire Naturelle des Plus Beaux Oiseaux Chanteurs de la Zone Torride*, 1805–9.

Brookshaw, George: author and artist of *Six Birds accurately Drawn and Coloured after Nature*, folio, 1817; 6 hand-coloured lithographs. Brookshaw also drew the famous 'Pomona Britannica' series of fruits.

Brown, Peter: part author with Thomas Pennant and artist of *New Illustrations of Zoology*, quarto, 1776; 50 hand-coloured engravings.

Buffon, Comte Georges-Louis Leclerc de: author of the famous *Histoire Naturelle Générale*, 1749–1804. Many editions of this book, a number with coloured plates, were published, but the important illustrations to it are those drawn by François Nicholas Martinet, which numbered 1,008 in all, appearing between 1770 and 1786. Size: small folio, and de luxe edition, larger folio. Attractive plates with a gold-panel line drawn round each, they represent one of the largest of all single collections.

Catesby, Mark: author and artist of *The Natural History of Carolina, Baltimore and the Bahama Islands*, large folio, 1731–43; 220 hand-coloured engravings (109 of which are of birds). These are the earliest of all American bird prints. Reprinted in 1748–56 and in 1771; and in Germany in 1750 and 1757.

Descourtilz, Jean Theodore: author and artist of two works on Brazilian birds. The earlier published in Paris in 1834 with 66 hand-coloured lithographs: the later published both in Rio de Janeiro and London in 1856 with 48 hand-coloured lithographs. Both large folio. These prints are much sought after, as they stand almost alone in portraying only South American birds.

Donovan, Edward: author and artist of several collections between 1794 and 1826; all octavo size and depicting both British and exotic birds.

Edwards, George: author and artist of *A Natural History of Uncommon Birds and Gleanings from Natural History*, in all 7 volumes, quarto. With 362 very fine hand-coloured engravings, mostly of birds. Edwards bird prints are some of the most important, and were reprinted in London, Amsterdam and Nuremberg, the last edition being in 1805. The colouring of these printings varies, but even the later ones are still good, while the printing of 1802-5, which produced only twenty-five of each print, is perhaps the best coloured of all.

Elliot, Daniel Giraud: author and part artist of a number of important collections of bird plates published in New York and London. All hand-coloured lithographs, large folio size, and showing grouse, pheasants, birds of paradise, hornbills and other birds. The other artists were P. L. Oudart, J. Wolf, J. Smit, E. Shephard, W. S. Morgan and J. G. Keulemans.

Frisch, Johann Leonard: author of one of the most enjoyable of all bird books, *Vorstellung der Vögel in Deutschland*, containing 255 hand-coloured engravings, folio size, drawn by F. H. Frisch, P. J. Frisch, and J. C. Frisch. Published Berlin 1733–63, and re-issued 1764 and 1817. These lovely prints are unfortunately very rare.

Gabler, Ambrosius: part artist of Bernhard Meyer's *Naturgeschichte der Vögel Deutschlands*, 1799–1807. (*See under* Meyer.)

Gould, John: author and also largely artist of the most complete and most famous collection of bird books, depicting over 3,000 different birds. All Gould's plates are folio and all are hand-coloured lithographs: the principal subjects are British Birds, European Birds, Humming-birds, Birds of New Guinea, Birds of Australia, Birds of Asia, Toucans, Trogons, Partridges of America and Himalayan Birds. His fellow artists were: his wife, E. Gould; Edward Lear, H. C. Richter, William Hart and Joseph Wolf. The artists did their own lithography, and the printing was done by C. Hullmandel and, to a lesser extent, by Walter and Coln. The dates of the prints, which are all of very fine quality, range from 1831 to 1888. Gould himself died in 1881.

Graves, George: author and artist of *British Ornithology*; 144 octavo hand-coloured engravings, 1811–21.

Gray, John Edward: author of *Gleanings from the Menagerie and Aviary at Knowsley Hall*, containing 79 hand-coloured lithographs. Nine of these are of birds and are drawn by Edward Lear, who was at that time (1846–50) curator to Lord Derby at Knowsley.

Hart, William: artist of a number of the plates in Gould's *Birds* (q.v.).

Havell, Robert, Senior, and **Robert, Junior:** engravers of all but ten of the plates for Audubon's *Birds of America* (q.v.).

Hayes, William: author and, with the other members of his family, artist of *A Natural History of British Birds*; 40 hand-coloured folio-size engravings, 1771–5; and of *The Birds of Osterley Park*; 101 hand-coloured engravings, quarto size, 1794–9. Both very attractive series. Many of the plates are signed in ink by the artists.

Hergenroder, J. M.: part artist of Bernhard Meyer's *Naturgeschichte der Vögel Deutschlands* (q.v.).

Huet, Nicholas: part artist of Temminck's *Nouveau Recueil de Plantes Coloriées d'Oiseaux* (q.v.).

Hullmandel, C.: printer of almost all the lithographs for Gould's *Birds* (q.v.).

Jardine, Sir William: author of Jardine's *Naturalist's Library*, published in 40 volumes between 1833 and 1843. Size small octavo. The first fourteen volumes were devoted to various sorts of birds, and the plates were drawn by Edward Lear, William Swainson, James Stuart and others; each volume contained about 30 plates. Not very exciting to look at, they have been used a great deal in recent years to cover table-mats.

Keulemans, John Gerard: artist and lithographer. Produced about 800 plates of birds altogether during the latter part of the nineteenth century, notably for D. G. Elliot and R. Bowdler Sharpe (q.v.).

Knip, Antoinette Pauline Jacqueline Rifer: artist. Illustrated *Histoire Naturelle des Tongoras, des Manakins et des Todiers*, by Desmarest. With 72 folio plates, 1805, printed in colour. And produced herself *Les Pigeons*. Large folio, 1809–11, with 147 coloured plates. Madame Knip, who was the accredited Natural History Painter to Queen Marie-Louise, produced in *Les Pigeons* one of the finest of all sets of bird prints. The first 87 are printed in colours and finished by hand, engraved by J. C. Macret. The remainder are lithographs, hand coloured except for a few engravings by Dequevaubiller or Guyard. (*See also* Bonaparte.)

Langlois: French printer, who printed partly or wholly in colours, very finely, many books, notably among bird books those by Levaillant and Vieillot (q.v.).

Latham, John: author and artist of *A General Synopsis of Birds*, quarto, 1781–5, with many supplements and reprints. The final total of hand-coloured engravings was 193.

Lawson, Alexander: engraved some of the illustrations in Wilson's *American Ornithology* (q.v.).

Lear, Edward: Lear wrote and illustrated the famous *Nonsense Rhymes*, limericks, etc, and produced many books with topographical plates. He was also famous as a painter of birds. His own illustrations of the family of Psittacidae, or Parrots, folio, 1830–2, with 42 hand-coloured lithographs, are very fine plates. He also did many of the drawings for Gould's *Birds*, for Jardine's *Naturalist's Library* and J. E. Gray's *Knowsley Menagerie* (all q.v.).

Lesson, Rene Primevere: author of many bird books published between 1828 and 1839. All fairly small octavo or royal octavo, and illustrated with plates printed in colour and finished by hand, drawn by J. G. Prêtre, P. L. Oudart, A. G. Bevalet, Bessa and others. In all responsible for more than 700 bird plates, of which the best known are of birds of paradise, fly-catchers and colibris.

Levaillant, François: producer until surpassed by Gould of the largest series of works on exotic birds, including the parrots, birds of Africa, birds of paradise, birds of America, etc. In all nearly 700 engravings, printed in colour and finished by hand. Most of his collections were published in two editions, a folio and a larger folio, the latter 'grand papier' edition being the better coloured. The artists were J. F. L. Reinold and J. Barraband, with various engravers, but almost all were printed magnificently by Langlois.

Lewin, William: producer and artist of several bird books. His *Birds of Britain*, 1795–1801, quarto, with 336 hand-coloured engravings, is of moderate interest, but the first edition of this work, 1789–94, limited to 60 sets, is unique, in that all the illustrations are water-colours drawn and painted by Lewin himself.

Lizars, W. H.: engraver of the first ten aquatints in Audubon's *Birds of America* (q.v.).

Lord, Thomas: artist and author of Lord's *Entire New System of Ornithology*, folio, 1791; 111 hand-coloured engravings.

Lorenzi, Lorenzo: one of the artists for Manetti's *Storia Naturale Degli Uccelli* (q.v.).

Manetti, Xaviero: author and part artist of *Storia Naturale Degli Uccelli.* Large folio, Florence, 1767–76; 600 magnificent hand-coloured engravings. A superb collection of bird prints: the other artists were L. Lorenzi and V. Vanni.

Martinet, François Nicholas: artist. Drew the 1,008 pictures for the great edition of Buffon's *Histoire Naturelle* (q.v.). Martinet also drew and engraved 31 plates for François Salerne's *Histoire Naturelle*, a French edition of John Ray's *Synopsis Methodica Avium.*

Meyer, Bernhard: author of *Naturgeschichte der Vögel Deutschlands*, folio, Nuremberg, 1799–1807. A very fine collection of engravings drawn by A. Gabler, J. M. Hergenroder and J. C. Bock.

Meyer, Henry Leonard: author and artist of *Illustrations of British Birds*, folio, 1835–41; 313 hand-coloured lithographs; and *Coloured Illustrations of British Birds and Their Eggs*, octavo, 1841–50; 432 hand-coloured lithographs.

Miller, John Frederick: author and artist of the *Cimelia Physica*, large folio, 1796, with 60 hand-coloured engravings (41 of birds).

Morris, Francis Orpen: author of *A History of British Birds.* Originally published 1851–7, 6 vols., royal octavo, with 358 hand-coloured lithographs, and reprinted often. The illustrations are disagreeable in all editions.

Murray, G.: engraved some of the pictures for Wilson's *American Ornithology* (q.v.).

Nozeman, Cornelis: author of *Nederlandsche Vogelen*, 5 vols., large folio, Amsterdam, 1770–1829; with 5 hand-coloured title-pages and 250 hand-coloured engravings by J. C. Sepp. A splendid collection of prints.

Oudart, Paul Louis: artist. He did illustrations for Prince Bonaparte, D. G. Elliot, and R. P. Lesson (all q.v.).

Pennant, Thomas: author of the *British Zoology*, folio, 1761–6; with 132 hand-coloured engravings, 121 of birds, all engraved by P. Mazell; drawn by various artists including P. Paillon, and George Edwards.

Reinold, Johann Friedrich Leberecht: artist. Drew the pictures for Levaillant's *Birds of Africa* (q.v.).

Richter, H. C.: artist. Drew some of the pictures for Gould's *Birds* (q.v.).

Rider, A.: artist. Helped to illustrate Bonaparte's *American Ornithology* (q.v.).

Selby, Prideaux John: drew illustrations of *British Ornithology* – 222 huge double-elephant folio hand-coloured engravings (nearly as large as Audubon's *Birds of America*). Issued between 1821 and 1834.

Sepp, Jan Christian: illustrated Nozeman's *Nederlandsche Vogelen* (q.v.).

Sharpe, Richard Bowdler: author of a number of works issued between 1868 and 1898 and illustrated in chromolithography by J. G. Keulemans, William Hart, J. & P. Smit and others. Quarto or folio, they show birds of paradise, kingfishers, swallows, etc. The plates are interesting ornithologically but not aesthetically.

Smit, Josef: artist. Drew some of the illustrations for Elliot's *Pheasants and Birds of Paradise*, for Gould's *Birds* and for R. Bowdler Sharpe (all q.v.).

Susemihl, Johann Conrad, Johann Theodor and Erwin Eduard: drew between them most of the illustrations to Borkhausen's *Deutsche Ornithologie* (q.v.).

Swainson, William: drew many of the illustrations for Jardine's *Naturalist's Library* (q.v.); also produced *Zoological Illustrations* with 334 hand-coloured lithographs, 1820–33 and *A Selection of the Birds of Brazil and Mexico*, 78 hand-coloured lithographs all drawn by himself.

Tanner, Benjamin: engraved some of the pictures for Wilson's *American Ornithology* (q.v.).

Temminck, Coenrad Jacob: author of *Nouveau Recueil de Planches Coloriées des Oiseaux*, a tremendous, but not so attractive sequel to the edition of Buffon's *Natural History*, with plates by Martinet. The plates, 600 hand-coloured engravings by N. Huet and J. G. Prêtre, were issued in both quarto and folio size between 1820 and 1839.

Vanni, Violante: artist. Drew many of the plates for Manetti's *Storia Naturale Degli Uccelli* (q.v.).

Vieillot, Louis Jean Pierre: author of several works published in Paris between 1805 and 1830, with folio coloured plates by P. L. Oudart and J. G. Prêtre. The most important are *Les Oiseaux Chanteurs de la Zone Torride* (72 engravings printed by Langlois), *Les Oiseaux d'Amérique* (131 plates printed by Langlois) and *La Galerie des Oiseaux* (324 hand-coloured lithographs). All very fine plates.

Walter: printed a number of the plates for Gould's *Birds* (q.v.).

Warnicke, J. G.: engraved some of the illustrations to Wilson's *American Ornithology* (q.v.).

Wilson, Alexander: author and artist of the fine folio work in 9 volumes, published in Philadelphia 1808–14, called *American Ornithology*, with 76 hand-coloured plates engraved by A. Lawson, J. G. Warnicke, G. Murray and B. Tanner. Though not comparable artistically to Audubon's *Birds of America*, these plates were considerably earlier and were the first done of American birds in America. Bonaparte's book (q.v.) was a supplement to this.

Wolf, Joseph: artist. Drew many of the illustrations for Gould's *Birds* (q.v.).

BOOKS FOR FURTHER READING

ANKER, JEAN: *Bird Books and Bird Art* (Copenhagen, 1938).

SITWELL, S., BUCHANAN, H., AND FISHER, J.: *Fine Bird Books* (London and New York, 1953).

AMERICAN PRINTS

By HELEN COMSTOCK

WHILE the first American prints naturally belong to the period of discovery and to such glimpses of the New World as are afforded by Lemoyne (1564), John White (1585) and the little bird's-eye view of St Augustine (the first engraved view of a city in the confines of the present United States) which appeared in the account of Drake's expedition, 1588, the subject of American prints for the present-day collector begins with the earliest views of cities advertised for sale in the Colonies. These are the Burgis views of New York and Boston. The few originals of the early states are, it is true, generally unobtainable, having found their way into public collections, but the work of this obscure draughtsman, William Burgis, of whom little is known save that he was perpetually in legal difficulties not to his credit, is the foundation on which a study of American prints rests. His designs were engraved in England, the name *I. Harris* appearing on the panoramic view of New York issued *c.* 1719–21, and of Boston, announced 1722. He also drew a view of Harvard known in only two impressions; a view of the New Dutch Church, New York, inscribed to Governor Rip Van Dam; a *Plan of Boston*; a *View of the Light House* (Boston) and a recently discovered view of Fort George, New York.

Matching the work of Burgis in relation to their respective cities are the *Roberts View of Charleston, S.C.*, 1739, and the *Scull-Heap View of Philadelphia*, 1754, both engraved in London. The importance of the engraved view, in disseminating knowledge of the appearance of cities in distant lands, caused the printsellers to specialize in this popular form of print, and we find Carington Bowles in London including views of Boston, New York and Philadelphia in a collection of city views of Europe, about 1764, designed to be used with the *vue d'optique*. The earliest impressions, although actually not the first state of what have come to be called the 'Carwitham views' of these American cities, because this engraver's name is on them, are extremely scarce and highly desired by the American collector. Later imprints, showing alterations to bring the subjects up to date, are not so valuable.

With the coming of the nineteenth century there was a great increase in the number of town and local views, as a result of the introduction of aquatint. In many instances the artists and engravers had been trained in Europe, particularly England, before emigrating to America. This is the period of the *Hudson River Portfolio*, with aquatints by John Hill; Bennett's nineteen *Views of American Cities* and, with the advent of lithography, the extensive sets by August Koellner and Edwin Whitefield. Views of San Francisco and other cities in California, which experienced a mushroom-like growth following the Gold Rush of 1849, were offered by local lithographers, such as Britten & Rey, or L. Nagel, whose rapid development paralleled the cities they portrayed.

College views form a classification of great interest among prints, the earliest subjects being naturally the most sought. The Burgis *View of Harvard* is known in only two copies, but there has been an excellent re-engraving by Sidney Smith in 1906 which is in itself a rarity (Plate 89A); the Revere *View of Harvard*, 1768, is also scarce; the James Buck *View of Yale*, 1749, the Dawkins *View of Nassau Hall* (Princeton), 1764, complete the most important eighteenth-century views. The nineteenth century offers two attractive views of Harvard in the first quarter of the century after Alvan Fisher; while Dartmouth is proud of one of the most delightful of all college views

(1851), the work of an excellent draughtsman and engraver, Christian Meadows, who unfortunately became entangled in counterfeiting.

Historical subjects are naturally important. Among military actions, priority goes to a crude view and plan of the Battle of Lake George in 1755, drawn by Samuel Blodget, a sutler who accompanied the English and Colonial forces and took advantage of his leisure to draw a sketch of the decisive action which turned back the French and their Indian Allies. It was engraved in Boston in the same year and was published in London in 1756. The painter, Ralph Earl, and engraver, Amos Doolittle, hastened to the scene of the actions at Lexington and Concord in 1775, and having made sketches on the spot, Doolittle made four crude but convincing views which are today very scarce, the most highly desired American historical prints, not excepting the better-known 'Boston Massacre' of Paul Revere in 1770. The latter (a subject also engraved by Henry Pelham) helped to make an unfortunate street fight one of the 'incidents' leading up to the Revolution.

Among naval views there are important English contributions in this class, such as Boydell's *Serapis* and *Bonne Homme Richard*, after Paton, 1780, and the *Phoenix and the Rose engaging the Enemy's Fireships*, which is one of the plates in the *Atlantic Neptune*. The War of 1812 produced the most highly prized subjects for the collector of naval views, painted and engraved in America as well as in England. The actions of the *Constitution* and *Guerrière*, the *United States* and *Macedonian*, *Perry's Victory on Lake Erie* (Plate 94A), *Macdonough's Victory on Lake Champlain* were painted by Birch, Barralet and Reinagle, and engraved by Tiebout, Tanner and Lawson in plates high in artistic and historical importance, with the additional interest of being American work.

Genre subjects, the life of the people, began to interest the print publishers before the advent of lithography in the 1830s and we find such subjects as Krimmel's *Procession of Philadelphia Victuallers* in aquatint, while even after the advent of lithography the American Art Union had Sartain engrave George Caleb Bingham's *Jolly Flatboatmen*, one of the best-known Mississippi river subjects. The same artist's *Stump Orator* and *County Election*, the product of his campaigning in 1840 during a presidential election, are first-rate genre, and these were done in lithograph in France. Lithography saw the appearance of a very characteristic form of Romantic genre, the farm and country scenes of Currier & Ives, of which *Home to Thanksgiving*, *Preparing for Market*, *Autumn in New England*, represent a large class devoted to rural life, the work of George H. Durrie, Fanny Palmer, Louis Maurer and others of the Currier & Ives artists.

Sporting items have an early example in a portrait of the racehorse *American Eclipse*, after Alvan Fisher, 1823, and continue with a series of engraved portraits of blood horses after Edward Troye for *The Spirit of the Times*, 1839–44. Field sports are best represented in the work of A. F. Tait for Currier & Ives; later A. B. Frost offered his *Shooting Pictures*. Baseball has an important item in a lithograph of Sarony, Major & Knapp showing the game played during the Civil War, *Union Prisoners at Salisbury, North Carolina*. The *National Game of Baseball* was offered by Currier & Ives in 1862, long before it had become 'national'. The great period of the printmaker was, however, over before baseball became the absorbing national sport.

The opening of the west in mid-nineteenth century elicited many lithographs from Currier & Ives, very popular with the collector, but these were productions of the studio, the work of Tait, Palmer and others who never saw the west. More important are the 'on the spot' views issued by Britten & Rey, L. Nagel and others in San Francisco.

Transportation prints are concerned with the clipper ship, the coming of the steamship and the development of the railroad. The clippers *Nightingale*, *Sweepstakes*, *Red Jacket* and many more were portrayed by excellent artists, James Buttersworth, Fanny Palmer, Charles Parsons, and lithographed by Endicott as well as Currier & Ives. The coming of steam was marked by H. R. Robinson's lithograph of the arrival of the *Great Western*,

(A) The Burgis View of Harvard, entitled 'A Prospect of the Colledges in Cambridge in New England'. Drawn by William Burgis, engraved in London and published 1726. This is the re-engraving by Sidney L. Smith, 1906. Line.

(B) Revere's Landing of the Troops, entitled 'A View of Part of the Town of Boston . . . and British Ships of War Landing their Troops, 1768'. Showing the Long Wharf, which was an extension of King Street, and the State House, built 1711. Line.

PLATE 89

New York, *c.* 1793. Drawn and engraved by Archibald and Alexander Robertson. This view is known to collectors under the name given by I. N. Phelps Stokes, 'New York as Washington Knew It', because it shows the appearance of the city while the nation's capital. Aquatint and line.

The Congress Voting Independence. Unfinished engraving by Edward Savage after Robert Edge Pine. Franklin is seated in the Windsor chair, centre, and Jefferson, standing, offers his draft of the Declaration of Independence to John Hancock. Line and stipple, *c.* 1794.

Broadway from Bowling Green, New York. Drawn and engraved by William J. Bennett, *c.* 1828; published 1834 by H. J. Megarey, New York. The house at the left, No. 1 Broadway, was Washington's headquarters in 1776, and later occupied by Lord Howe during the British occupation.

Procession of Victuallers. Philadelphia, 1821. After J. L. Krimmel. Aquatint by J. Yeager. Kynett Collection. *Published by courtesy of Philadelphia Museum of Art.*

(A) Perry's Victory on Lake Erie, 1813. Painted by Thomas Birch and engraved by A. Lawson. Published by Joseph Delaplaine, Philadelphia; undated but probably 1813. Shows Perry transferring from the *Niagara* to the disabled *Lawrence* in order to receive the swords of surrender. Stipple and line.

(B) West Point, from above Washington Valley. Painted by George Cooke and engraved by W. J. Bennett. Published by Parker & Clover, New York, 1834. Shows the typical Hudson River sloop and view of the Military Academy in the distance. Aquatint.

(A) The U.S. Naval Portfolio. No. 2. Expedition under Commodore M. C. Perry on the Tuxpan River in the war with Mexico, 1846. Drawn by Lt. H. Walke (later Rear-Admiral). Lithograph of Sarony & Major, New York. *The Mariners' Museum, Newport News, Virginia.*

(B) Wall Street, 1850. Drawn by August Koellner, lithograph by Deroy. Published by Goupil, Vibert of New York and Paris. Shows Trinity Church, the Custom House (at right with flag), the former Branch Bank of the United States (now the façade of the American Wing of the Metropolitan Museum) and other New York banks. *New York Public Library.*

(A) Trotting Cracks on the Snow. Drawn on stone by Louis Maurer, 1858. Published by Currier & Ives. This shows famous trotters including Flora Temple (centre) known for having won purses amounting to $113,000 in her eleven years on the track.

(B) California and Oregon Stage Company. View of Mount Shasta, California, in the distance, with a U.S. Mail Coach in the foreground. This print went through many variants, derived from an original from Britten & Rey, San Francisco, *c.* 1855. Lithograph. Collection of the late Harry T. Peters.

PLATE 96

and also of the *Sirius*, in New York harbour in 1838, and this same astute publisher was one of the first to offer prints of locomotives and railroad subjects, which later became a regular part of the lithographer's output.

Other specialities for the print collector are historical portraits, Indian subjects, whaling prints, the bird prints of Catesby, Wilson and Audubon, and, of course, maps, a fascinating subject in their own right, closely allied to such prints as have been considered here but deserving separate consideration.

GLOSSARY

Anderson, Alexander: 1775–1870. 'Father of Wood Engraving in the United States'; introduced the 'white line' method of Bewick.

Atlantic Neptune: a collection of charts and views of the ports of North America prepared for the British Admiralty by J. F. W. des Barres; first published *c.* 1777; approximately 257 plates.

Audubon, J. J.: 1785–1851. American ornithologist. His *Birds of America* with aquatint plates, elephant folio, by Robert Havell, Sr and Jr, London (a few by Lizars, Edinburgh), was published 1827–38. 435 plates. Also issued in chromolithography by J. Bien, New York, 1860.

Barber, John W.: 1798–1885. Engraver, New Haven, Connecticut; known for historical works on Connecticut, New Jersey, etc. His *View of New Haven Green* with the buildings of Yale College is much sought in the first state.

Barnet & Doolittle: New York; first American lithographic firm (1821–2).

Bennett, W. J.: 1787–1844. Artist and engraver. Born in England, pupil of Westall; sketched in the Mediterranean; emigrated to America 1816; known for Bennett's *Views of American Cities*, the finest aquatint series in existence of this subject; for the three *Street Views in the City of New York*, published by Megarey, New York, 1834; two views of the Great Fire of New York, December 1835, after N. V. Calyo; *The Seasons* after G. Harvey, 1841.

Bien, J.: New York lithographer, active 1850–68. In 1860 issued Audubon's *Birds of America*, elephant folio, in chromolithograph.

Bingham, George Caleb: 1811–79. Artist, known for Mississippi river genre subjects; his *Jolly Flatboatmen*, engraved by Sartain 1847, became one of the most widely known American prints. Bingham's sketches while campaigning for the Whig Party, 1840, resulted in his *County Election*, *Stump Orator* and *The Verdict of the People*, published as lithographs.

Birch, Thomas: 1779–1851. Artist. Worked with his father, William, and later became known for naval subjects of the War of 1812, engraved by Tiebout, Tanner, Lawson.

Birch, William: 1755–1834. Engraver; emigrated to Philadelphia from England 1794 with his son, Thomas, with whom he prepared his *Views of Philadelphia*, 1800, the most important set of engraved views of this city; in 1808 published views of country seats.

Blodget, Samuel: first American-born artist to draw original of an American historical print. His crude, eye-witness view of the *Battle of Lake George* was engraved by Thomas Johnston, Boston, 1755; also published by Thomas Jefferys, London, 1756.

'Boston Massacre': *see* Revere.

Bowen, Abel: 1790–1850. Copper and wood engraver; publisher of the *Naval Monument*, Boston, beginning 1816.

Britten & Rey: San Francisco lithographic firm, *c.* 1849 – *c.* 1880; of great importance for scenes of the Gold Rush.

Brown's Portrait Gallery of Distinguished American Citizens: lithographs from 26 silhouettes cut by W. H. Brown, published, with decorative backgrounds, by Kellogg in Hartford, 1845. Most of original edition destroyed by fire; has been published in facsimile about 1930.

Buck, James: publisher of the first view of Yale College, 1749, engraved by T. Johnston after John Greenwood.

Burgis, William: early eighteenth-century artist whose panoramic views of New York and Boston, published 1719 and 1722 respectively, are the most important of American city views. They were engraved in London by I. Harris. His view of Harvard College, issued 1726, is of almost equal importance.

Carwitham, John: active 1723–41. London engraver whose name appears on three important views after unknown source, showing New York, Boston and Philadelphia in the first half of the eighteenth century; imprint of Carington Bowles, London, *c.* 1764. Scarce in this state, which is probably second; first state unknown; later states up to end of eighteenth century.

Castelnau, Francis: French traveller in America, 1838–40; published *Vues de l'Amérique du Nord*, Paris, 1842, illustrated in lithograph.

Catesby, Mark: English naturalist; in America, 1712–26. His *Natural History of the Carolinas, Florida and the Bahama Islands*, 2 vols., London, 1731–43, with 220 plates, is the first work on American birds.

Catlin, George: 1796–1872. Artist and lithographer; traveller in Far West in the 1830s. Best known for *North American Indian Portfolio*, lithographs by Day & Haghe, England; later published in America. Also known for views in Colden's Erie Canal *Memoir* (1826) with lithographs by Imbert; and the best life-portrait of an Indian, *Osceola*, 1838, put on stone by himself.

Childs, Cephas G.: Philadelphia lithographer, active 1823–58, associated at various times with Pendleton, Kearny, Inman and Lehman.

Clover, Lewis P.: New York publisher of fine aquatints in the 1830s, chiefly town views.

Cockburn, Lt.-Col. James Pattison: 1779–1847. Officer in the Royal Artillery stationed in Canada. Known for Canadian views, particularly *Views of Quebec*; published 1833 by Ackermann, London.

Currier & Ives: the leading American lithographic firm, founded by Nathaniel Currier in New York, 1833. James M. Ives became a partner in 1857. The firm was in existence until 1906. Publishers of popular prints, including sporting subjects, genre, comics, etc, and employing such artists as Louis Maurer, A. F. Tait, Fanny Palmer, Charles Parsons, Thomas Worth and James Buttersworth.

Dawkins, Henry: active in New York by 1754; engraver; his plate showing the earliest view of Nassau Hall at Princeton appeared as an illustration in Blair's *Account of the College in New Jersey*, 1764.

Doolittle, Amos: 1754–1832. Connecticut engraver who did crude but important work, including a set of four views of the Battles of Lexington and Concord (1775) after Ralph Earl; a view of Federal Hall, New York, after Lacour, showing an eyewitness view of the first inauguration of George Washington.

Duval, Peter S.: Philadelphia lithographer, active 1831–79. Associated at times with Lehman, Huddy, Prang and others.

Edwin, David: 1776–1841. Engraver. Went to Philadelphia in 1797 from England. Excellent engraver of portraits in stipple.

Endicott: an important name in American lithography; firm began as Endicott & Swett in Baltimore, 1828, and moved to New York, 1830; active under various names until 1896.

Havell, Robert, Jr.: 1793–1878. After completing the *Birds of America*, Havell went to America, where he painted and engraved views; known for views of New York from the North River (1840) and East River (1844).

Hill, John: 1770–1850. Aquatint engraver known for plates in *Hudson River Portfolio* after Wall, published by Megarey, New York, *c.* 1825; also Joshua Shaw's *Picturesque Views of American Scenery*, Philadelphia, 1819, and other meritorious work.

Hornor, Thomas: artist and engraver, working in New York, 1835–7; known for a *View of Broadway* which Stokes calls the best interior view of the city.

Huddy & Duval: Philadelphia lithographers, 1839–41; published *U.S. Military Magazine*, 3 vols. Prized for costume plates.

Hudson River Portfolio: *see* Megarey, H. J.

Imbert, Anthony: active 1825–35 as pioneer lithographer, New York. His work for Colden's Erie Canal *Memoir*, 1826, is the first outstanding American work.

Jevne & Almini: leading Chicago lithographic firm, established about 1866. Publishers of *Chicago Illustrated, 1830.*

Jukes, Francis: London engraver of Henry Pelham's *Plan of Boston*, 1777; and an important set of four aquatints after Alexander Robertson of which the view of Mount Vernon, 1799, is the most desirable.

Kellogg, D. W. (later E. B. & E. C. Kellogg): lithographic firm of Hartford; also in New York and Buffalo; the most important firm after Currier & Ives; established 1833; subjects included 'sentimentals', portraits, book illustrations.

Koellner, August: 1813–*c.* 1878. Artist and lithographer, best known for 54 well-drawn *Views of American Cities* lithographed by Deroy, Paris; published by Goupil, Vibert, 1848–51.

Krimmel, J. L.: 1787–1821. Painter. His *Election Day at the State House, Philadelphia*, 1815, known in an unfinished engraving by Lawson; *Procession of Philadelphia Victuallers*, 1821, in lithographs by G. Dubois and by A. Clement; in aquatint by J. Yeager (Plate 93).

Lawson, Alexander: 1773–1846. Engraver. Emigrated to Philadelphia from Scotland in 1793. Engraved plates for Wilson's *Ornithology*; War of 1812 subjects.

Longacre, J. B.: 1794–1869. Engraver, chiefly of portraits in stipple. Began his *American Portrait Gallery* with James Herring about 1830.

Maverick, Peter: 1780–1831. Engraver in New York who turned to lithography about 1824. Most famous is his *View of Wall Street*, taken from Trinity Church, after a drawing by Hugh Reinagle.

Megarey, Henry J.: New York publisher of the finest set of aquatint views (twenty in most sets) of New York State, *Hudson River Portfolio*, after Wall. These were engraved by J. R. Smith and John Hill, 1821–5. Also Bennett's *Street Views in the City of New York* (3), *c.* 1834.

Michelin, Francis: lithographer, Boston, 1840; moved to New York 1844. Worked to 1859.

Milbert, J.: French artist in America, 1815–23. Author of the *Itinéraire Pittoresque du Fleuve Hudson . . .*; issued in Paris in thirteen parts beginning 1826 and containing fifty-three numbered views in lithograph.

Nagel, Louis: lithographer in New York, 1844; Nagel & Weingartner, 1849–57. Went to San Francisco in 1862, where he was associated with Fishbourne & Kuchel.

Otis, Bass: made the first American lithographs, Philadelphia, 1818 and 1819, a portrait for book illustration, and a landscape.

Papprill, Henry: one of the last engravers in aquatint, working in New York in the 1840s and known for the Papprill-Catherwood *New York from Governor's Island*, 1846.

Pelham, Peter: *c.* 1684–1751. Earliest engraver in America; came from England to Boston 1726. Known for mezzotint portraits of clergymen.

Pendelton: important lithographic firm; Boston, New York, Philadelphia, 1825–*c.* 1866.

Revere, Paul: 1735–1818. Boston's most famous silversmith, also an engraver known for three highly important historical subjects: (1) a view of Boston (Plate 89B) showing the landing of the British troops in 1768, issued 1770; (2) a view of the so-called 'Boston Massacre' in 1770, in which he plagiarized the design of Henry Pelham; (3) a view of Harvard College, 1768.

Roberts, B.: drew the most important early view of Charleston, South Carolina, 1739. One of the four great eighteenth-century 'prospects' of American cities, engraved in London.

Robertson, Alexander: 1768–1841. Artist, engraver. (*See* Robertson, Archibald.)

Robertson, Archibald: 1765–1835. Archibald and Alexander Robertson were brothers of the Scottish miniature painter Andrew Robertson. They were artists and engravers, established the Columbian Drawing Academy in New York, *c.* 1795; were responsible for important New York and other views, some engraved by Jukes, London. A view of New York waterfront is a prized subject known to collectors by the title 'New York as Washington Knew It' (Plate 90).

Robinson, H. R.: New York lithographer, active 1832–51. Proved the news value of the lithograph with his view of the New York Fire, 1835, issued a few weeks later; also the arrival of the steamship *Great Western* in New York harbour, 1838; his *Peytona and Fashion* was the first print of an American horserace, 1842 (also issued by N. Currier).

Rollinson, William: 1762–1842. Engraver in stipple, best known for portrait of Alexander Hamilton, issued 1804.

Romans, Bernard: 1720–84. Engraver, engineer, cartographer. Best known for eyewitness view of the Battle of Bunker Hill (*Exact View of the late Battle at Charlestown . . .*), published in America in 1775, and in London 1776.

Sarony, Napoleon: 1821–96. Expert lithographer and artist working in New York alone and with others, as Sarony & Major, also Sarony, Major & Knapp; withdrew from lithography about 1867.

Sartain, John: 1808–97. Engraver, working in London before going to Philadelphia, 1830. Mezzotint portraits a speciality, but did general work, about 1,500 plates.

Savage, Edward: 1761–1817. Painter and engraver, generally credited with the first American aquatint, showing a naval engagement in the quasi-war with France, 1798.

Scenographia Americana: a collection of eighteenth-century views drawn by British officers, Paxton, Pownal, Campbell, etc, engraved by Paul Sandby and others, originally 28 in number but extended to 74; issued originally in 1768; publishers – John Bowles, Robert Sayer, Thomas Jefferys, Carington Bowles, Henry Parker, London.

Scull-Heap View of Philadelphia: 1754. Most important early view of city, drawn by George Heap under direction of the Surveyor-General Nicholas Scull, showing the city from the Jersey shore. Engraved in London by G. Vandergucht. Issued in four sections.

Shaw, Joshua: 1776–1860. Emigrated to America 1817. Drew originals for *Picturesque Views of America* done in aquatint by Hill. Later went to the Far West.

Smith, John Rubens: 1770–1849. Engraver. Son of John Raphael Smith. Working in Boston by 1811; later in New York and Philadelphia.

Tait, A. F.: 1819–1905. Leading sporting painter of the nineteenth century; not a staff artist of Currier & Ives, but many of his scenes of field sports were issued in lithograph by them.

Tiebout, Cornelius: *c.* 1770 – *c.* 1830. Engraver in line and stipple. Stauffer calls him 'the first American-born professional engraver to produce really meritorious work.'

Troye, Edward: 1808–73. Artist. Leading painter of American blood horses; subjects engraved for the sporting journal, *The Spirit of the Times*, by Hinshelwood, Dick and others, 1839–44.

Universum: a publication of views and other subjects in lithograph by Hermann J. Meyer, New York, *c.* 1850–7.

Wall, W. G.: 1792–after 1862. Irish artist, in America 1818–36, and returned 1856. Painted in 1820 the water-colours engraved for Megarey's *Hudson River Portfolio*; also known for a pair, *New York from Weehawk* and *New York from Brooklyn Heights*, among most attractive New York views.

Whitefield, Edwin: active 1845–55. Artist and publisher of largest series of American city views in lithograph, printed by various firms – F. Michelin; Endicott & Co.; Lewis & Brown.

TECHNICAL TERMS

Aquatint: a graphic process in which a resin ground is laid on a copper plate either in powdered form with a bellows (French method) or in solution in spirits of wine (English method, used by Paul Sandby, 1775). Both left a granular surface which the acid penetrated, producing a tonal ground in printing and approximating the effect of water-colour. The design was worked into the ground by alternate 'stopping out' and biting areas of the plate. Edward Savage is generally credited with being the first to use this method in America.

Burin or **Graver:** a sharp metal instrument used to incise lines on metal; made in many sizes and forms.

Chromolithograph: lithograph printed in colour from a series of stones.

Del., Delin., Delineavit: drew.

Etching: a print made by covering a metal plate of copper or steel with a wax coat, drawing the design with a needle, and 'biting' the plate by immersion in a weak acid solution, generally nitric. When inked, the bitten lines hold the ink as the plate is wiped, and when an impression is taken the design is transferred, in reverse, to the paper.

Fec., Fecit: made; that is, painted or drew.

Imp., Imprimavit: printed.

Inv., In., Invenit: invented, designed.

Line Engraving: a print made by incising a design directly on a plate with a burin (q.v.), also called a graver. The process was thus an intaglio process.

Lithograph: a print made by what its inventor, A. Senefelder, *c.* 1797, called a 'chemical process', based on the principle that oil and water do not mix. It was a single-plane process. The design was drawn with a special crayon on calcareous limestone, and a film of water passed over the surface. When greasy ink on the roller passed over the stone, the water repelled it, but the crayoned surface took it up, and an impression could be taken.

Lithotint: when the design was washed on with a brush and greasy ink the effect of a water-colour was produced, and this was by some firms named a 'lithotint'.

Mezzotint: an engraving in which an instrument known as a rocker, having many fine teeth, is worked across the plate by rocking and pushing. The fine indentations produce the velvety ground characteristic of mezzotint, which shows no hard lines. The rest of the design is worked in by scraping and burnishing.

Pinx., Pinxt, Pinxit, Pingebat: painted.

Proof before Letters: an impression taken before title, publisher's line, etc, have been added.

Sc., Sculp., Sculpt, Sculpsit, Sculpebat: engraved.

State: each time there is any addition made to a plate, or lithographic stone, between printings, the new form becomes a new 'state' of the print.

Stipple: a process of securing a dotted effect somewhat coarser than mezzotint. The plate is covered with a wax ground and worked upon with a fine-pointed instrument, then biting with acid, and further flecking with a graver where heavier dots are required.

BOOKS FOR FURTHER READING

STOKES AND HASKELL: *American Historical Prints* (New York, 1932).

PHELPS STOKES, I. N.: *The Iconography of Manhattan Island*, 6 vols. (New York, 1915–28).

PETERS, HARRY T.: *America on Stone* (New York, 1931).

PETERS, HARRY T.: *Currier & Ives. Printmakers to the American People*, 2 vols. (New York, 1929).

PETERS, HARRY T.: *California on Stone* (New York, 1935).

FIELDING, MANTLE: *Dictionary of American Painters, Sculptors and Engravers* (Philadelphia, no date).

STAUFFER, D. McN.: *American Engravers on Copper and Steel* (New York, 1919).

Except where noted, the Plates illustrating this article are from The Old Print Shop.

PICTURE FAKES AND FAKING

By BERNARD DENVIR

(Figures in square brackets refer to the Books for Further Reading, page 151.)

It has recently been asserted that 'at the present time the market is glutted with forged paintings, drawings and prints', and there can be little doubt that the nefarious skill of the forger is in greater demand today than at any other time in the history of art. This is due to several causes. The inflationary spiral and the desirability of evading various forms of taxation have made works of art one of the most valued forms of investment. Picture prices are reaching unprecedented heights, and the fluctuations of taste attribute an abnormal importance to the personality of certain artists. In an age of anonymous art, the forger was virtually unknown, and indeed the question of authorship troubled neither artist nor patron. Then, too, the political upheavals of the last twenty years have created an atmosphere of instability amongst the great art collections of the world (Note A, page 151). Works of art have been dispersed through the mishaps of war; collectors have been forced to sell for reasons other than economic ones; certain public galleries have been destroyed, or are inaccessible.

VARIETIES OF MISREPRESENTATION

The misrepresentation of a work of art is therefore today one of the greatest dangers to be faced by any collector, and for the purposes of this article it is assumed that the phrase 'fakes and faking' embraces any transaction in which a work of art assumed to be the work of X, and sold as such, is not in actual fact the work of X. One must also assume therefore, not only that the intentions of the vendor may be honest, but that there may have been nothing sinister in the intentions of the creator of the work of art which has assumed a false identity.

HONEST 'FAKES'

In the case of artists who worked before the beginning of the nineteenth century, the problem is complicated by the studio methods of the time. Not only did most artists employ apprentices who would assist them in their works, painting in backgrounds, curtains, drapery and the like, but most of them employed other artists who specialized in some special aspect of their work. There were figure painters, drapery painters, landscape painters and others, so that when one thinks of an artist like Rubens or Van Dyck, one must always be prepared to acknowledge the fact that even the most authenticated work need not be entirely from the brush of the master to whom it is attributed. Peter Lely, for instance, counted amongst his assistants John Baptist Gaspars (who also worked for Riley and Kneller), P. H. Lankrink, Joseph Buckshorn and Nicholas de Largillière. The system employed by popular artists of the seventeenth and eighteenth centuries had, indeed, many affinities with the assembly-line technique of modern industry.

This system persisted for a long time, and its last vestiges are to be found in the nineteenth century, when, for instance, Millais completed several works which Landseer had left unfinished at his death, notably *Nell Gwynne*, *The Dead Buck* and *Digging out the Otter*. As Millais' son remarked in his father's biography: 'I think it would puzzle even artists to say which was Landseer's work and which was Millais'.'

In a world in which artists had no exaggerated notion of the importance of their actual individual contribution to the creation of a work of art, other complications could arise. A master, for instance, would sign with his own name the work of a brilliant pupil, and there are known instances of this taking place in the case of Boucher. The further back one goes in history, the more complicated does the question of individual authenticity become. In the recently published (1955) catalogue of French paintings in the Metropolitan Museum, New York, M. Charles Sterling of the Louvre, its compiler, draws attention to the important difference between 'studio works' and 'works by the followers' of an artist.

'Studio' works are those done by assistants or at the direction of the artist concerned. Sometimes these consisted of additions to works most of which were the productions of the master's brush, but often, and the possibilities of confusion here are clearly endless, an assistant would produce an actual replica to satisfy another patron. A typical example of this process is the portrait of Cardinal Fleury in the National Gallery (No. 903) from the studio of Hyacinthe Rigaud (1659–1743). In the artist's account book there is mention of ten copies made in 1728, one in 1729, one in 1734 and two in 1735.

It is to be presumed that the 'studio' work is not only close to the master's work in style and execution, but also in intention completely honest. Neither of these suppositions can, however, be relied upon in the case of a follower or imitator. It was for long considered quite natural, in an age which had no strong sense of copyright or of creative 'property', that if an artist had been successful, others who were not, should try to capture his market by imitations of his work. The extent to which William Marlow in the early stages of his career followed Wilson, Giacomo Guardi, or Canaletto can often cause confusion, whilst the possibilities of error are clearly aggravated by the disparity in the prices reached by two such groups of artists. Even when a follower has signed a painting with his own name, subsequent owners may well remove it, and substitute his master's.

In many cases, of course, the original intention was not an honest one, and as early as the sixteenth century there were numerous imitators of Dürer who were clearly producing works which they hoped would pass as original works by that artist. On the whole, however, it may be assumed that when a follower or an imitator produces his work within half a century of the death of the artist to whose style he is addicted, his intentions must be given the benefit of the doubt.

Other 'honest' misattributions of authorship may be described under the following headings.

1. **Instructional Copies.** The copying of old masters was for long considered one of the main methods of art training. There are numerous authenticated copies of the works of earlier artists by Delacroix, Renoir, Van Gogh and others. Often enough these are 'variations on a theme' rather than literal copies, and in any case no attempt is made to simulate the media used by the original artist.

2. **Traditional Errors.** Old inscriptions, either on the painting, or on the frame, can often lead to an erroneous attribution. A sixteenth-century French work in the National Gallery has written on the back 'Leonar de Vincy' though it clearly has no possible connexion with that distinguished Florentine artist. When such attributions are maintained, it is clearly a case of the wish being father to the thought.

3. **Original Errors.** These can be of many kinds. One of the most unusual was the case of a drawing signed by Augustus John, which was in the possession of the Fitzwilliam Museum at Cambridge. The Director was startled to receive a letter from an artist claiming that the work was his and not Mr John's. Apparently the owner of the drawing had asked Mr John to sign a drawing which the artist assumed to be a work of

A work, attributed to Ioni, the twentieth-century forger, in which various elements have been combined to give the impression of an early fifteenth-century triptych. Two obvious failures are the fact that the figures standing on either side of the Madonna are quite incongruous in a painting of this kind, and that a subject such as the Annunciation would never have been depicted on the wings of a triptych.. *Courtauld Institute of Art.*

PLATE 97

(A) One of the many forgeries which came from the collection of 'Corots' amassed by Dr Jousseaume in the last century. The falsity of this one is proved by the fact that the medium—a kind of distemper—was never used by Corot. *British Museum.*

(B) Dürer, supposed self-portrait at the age of twenty-three. Pen and brush on tinted paper. Modern forgery, monogram and date 1494.

PLATE 98

(A) A faked illumination on vellum attributed to the Spanish Forger who worked in Paris in the nineteenth century. It is clearly based on the chromo-lithographic reproductions then popular. *Dr E. G. Millar, F.S.A.*

(B) Acquired by Dr Ludwig Mond in Rome in 1893 and presented by him to the National Gallery as a work by Francesco Francia. The appearance of the authentic version in a London sale room in 1955 led to the discovery that this version was a fake. *National Gallery.*

(A) A painting attributed to Maurice Utrillo (*d.* 1956) *Ohana Gallery.*

(B) Watermill under trees. Oil. Acquired by the Brooklyn Museum of Art (U.S.A.) as a work by Meindert Hobbema. Scientific examination proved that it contained Prussian blue, a colour which had not been invented in Hobbema's time. *Brooklyn Museum of Art.*

PLATE 100

his youth, about which he had forgotten, and so complied (Note B, page 151).

DISHONEST ATTRIBUTIONS

These are many and various, and the motivation complex. Although in nearly every case money comes into the chain of causation, it is not always the predominant factor. Lack of recognition (and it must be granted that many forgers are men of outstanding artistic ability), spite, the desire to do somebody a good turn, a feeling that 'the whole thing's a racket anyway', the delight in sheer virtuosity or mere impishness are all possible causes for embarking on the career of a faker. It must be remembered, too, that people often want to be deceived. For reasons of personal, national or spiritual prestige the owner or possible purchaser of a painting is reluctant to admit errors of judgment (Note C). In execution, in effectiveness and in conspiratorial purpose, fakes vary extensively. These, however, are the major categories.

1. **Inaccurate or Reckless Attributions.** It is impossible in this category to determine at what point the consciousness of deception appears. Dealers, private collectors, even public art gallery curators are all tempted to attribute a work by a minor artist to a major master. The temptation is understandable, and as long as the attribution is not questioned, no harm, presumably, is done to the purchaser – 'where ignorance is bliss, 'tis folly to be wise'. There is, however, an unfortunate tendency for such 'optimistic' attributions to be supported by the testimony of 'experts'. The whole problem is, of course, an involved one and, until every owner of a painting is prepared to have it subjected to exhaustive stylistic and scientific examination, it is largely insoluble.

2. **Alteration of Signatures.** This is the simplest and most naïve form of positive forgery. Most authoritative books on an artist reproduce his signature and its various transformations, but even apart from this, handwriting experts can easily detect a forged signature (Note D).

3. **Alteration of a Genuine Work to Increase its Market Value or for Other Reasons.** Tampering with works of art by other artists has a long, and in some respects a reputable, history. To protect the susceptibilities of a prudish age alterations were often made which are only now coming to light. Foliage was added, portions of the anatomy were painted over and changes of one kind or another made. Works of art have often been 'improved' by subsequent generations. The *Paumgartner Altar-piece* by Dürer in Munich was completely altered in 1614 by the Bavarian painter Johann Georg Fischer, who added landscapes, modernized the dress and completely altered the artist's original intentions. Reynolds repainted a work by Velasquez now in the Wallace Collection, and often the owners of paintings had them altered to suit their changed tastes. From this artistic malpractice to ethical dishonesty was not a great step. Under the all-embracing cloak of 'restoration' paintings were often completely altered. Torn canvas, broken panel, missing paint all offer the opportunity for making a work of art 'more interesting'. It is clearly impossible to restore something which is not there, but there have always been restorers who are prepared to do so, and in [2] Dr Tietze instances and illustrates a panel by Dürer which was virtually rebuilt by reference to another work of the same artist. As restorers are often painters themselves, they are frequently tempted to improve a work in the process of restoring it, and this of course adds yet more to the element of falsity. Even to change the dating of a painting may add to its market value – e.g. a Cubist Picasso of, say, 1902 would be immensely valuable (Note E), but the more usual thing is to alter the subject. When Sir Henry Raeburn was appointed the King's Limner for Scotland he had not painted a portrait of the King, and indeed never did. A few weeks after the event, however, a print of such a portrait was selling on the streets of Edinburgh. The engraver had substituted the King's head for that of the original sitter in an engraving of Raeburn's portrait of a Scottish doctor. Prints and engravings of course particularly lend themselves to this kind of manipulation.

4. **Alteration of Authorship.** This is the form of direct forgery which, after altera-

tion of the signature, requires the least exercise of skill on the part of the forger. In the Walker Art Centre, Minneapolis, U.S.A., there is a painting by Gerbrandt Baen, signed and dated 1651 (*see* [2], p. 43), in which the process can be seen actually happening. When the picture was cleaned in 1945 it was discovered that though apparently a portrait of Henry VIII by a member of the school of Holbein, the work was actually a portrait of an unknown Dutch burgher of the seventeenth century. The museum authorities did not proceed with the cleaning, but left the painting half-Henry VIII, half Dutch burgher, as an object lesson in dishonest ingenuity. Countless works by minor artists are adjusted to suit the style of one more famous. Hack paintings of Venice are converted into Canalettos, works by unknown portrait painters are converted into Gainsboroughs, and some idea of the scale of the industry can be derived from the fact that although Van Dyck died in his early forties there are several thousand paintings attributed to him.

Another advantage of this method from the forger's point of view is that it requires no special treatment of the canvas, as it is to be assumed that the forged work is roughly contemporaneous with the artist which it emulates.

5. **The Creation of a New Work of Art.** This of course is the most fascinating and the most difficult species of faking. It is only resorted to in cases where the eventual price of the painting will be large enough to recompense the 'craftsman' for the pains he has taken, and it is, as a consequence, the rarest type of faking. It is a subject best discussed in a time sequence, for it is obvious that the creation of contemporary fakes is a good deal easier than the creation of old masters. No elaborate doctoring of media is necessary, and the stylistic imitation of a contemporary presents less difficulties than does the copying of the mannerisms of a painter dead some centuries ago.

The simplest kind of fake is a mere copy of a painting already in existence (Note F, page 151). This presupposes that it should be done without the knowledge of the artist or of his heirs, and this may indeed happen more frequently than one would expect. Although it is unusual for a modern artist to produce replicas of his works, the original painting may be inaccessible, in a private collection, in another country, or destroyed. The task of the forger, too, is sometimes made easier by complications connected with the artist's life. This is especially true in the case, for instance, of Utrillo, forgeries of whose works proliferate. Bound by contract to a firm of dealers, more works of his appear on the market than have been sold by that firm. The usual explanation offered is that to make money 'on the side' the artist painted and sold works directly to other contacts. A slightly more elaborate version of this technique of copying already existing works, is to transpose work in one medium into another. A drawing or water-colour may be converted into an oil-painting, or vice versa, and as different media often play an important part in the creation of a work of art, the appearance of the fake does not arouse undue astonishment. A forgery of this kind whereby a drawing of Braque's in gouache was transposed into an oil painting was recently on view at an exhibition in Paris organized by that department of the French police force which is directly concerned with crime in the art market.

This perhaps is the appropriate place to refer to the question of mechanically reproduced prints, replicas and facsimiles. The great improvement in printing techniques, the development of new processes, such for instance as the one whereby a colour plate can be transferred to a canvas and then painted over, have all reduced the gap between original works of art and reproductions of them. As far as old masters are concerned the dangers here are negligible, and a very cursory examination of a modern work will show whether or not it has been mechanically copied. With water-colours and drawings a little more care is needed. The same is true of prints, etchings, engravings or the like. It is worth noting that when a modern photographic block is used the mark of the bevel, never to be found in an original work of that kind, is noticeable on the print.

Next to replicas the easiest form of creating a new work of art purporting to have been done by an artist of recent date is to rearrange elements from other works by that artist in such a way as to create a new, yet vaguely convincing, picture. Even the mere reversal of a pose is enough to suggest the appearance of a new work, and this method of amalgamating existing works not only reduces the amount of actual creation involved, but predisposes a potential buyer – often anxious to prove his connoisseurship – in favour of the work. The Brooklyn Museum in New York possesses a Picasso *Absinthe Drinker* based very closely on the original work which goes by that name and superficially most convincing. The forger, however, has slipped in two quite elementary details, which would be apparent to the veriest novice. The signature is clearly a forgery. In the original work the line beneath the name has been drawn from right to left; in the forgery from left to right; in the one the inclination is towards the top right-hand corner of the picture; in the other towards the bottom left-hand corner. Secondly the painting of the hand and arm is entirely unconvincing. The fingers are too 'fashion plate' in appearance, and the entire limb does not adhere to the body, but gives the impression of being stuck on, in the same way that a child might stick a tail on to a paper donkey.

The fundamental consolation for any collector or connoisseur is that it is absolutely impossible to produce a finally convincing fake. Some of the reasons for this become apparent when we come to consider the question of fakes of living or recently dead artists. A work of art is the creation of a human being, and every brush-stroke reveals the history of that human being as clearly and convincingly as a thumb-print identifies an individual. No outsider can either recapture an artist's feelings as he is painting a picture, or reproduce the actual technique which he used – a forger may come close to imitating the superficial appearance of the work of another painter, but he cannot know, for instance, the exact amount of pressure used on the brush, the sequence of the strokes nor the planning of the entire creation.

In the 'twenties Otto Wacker (his real name was Olindo Lowael), a dancer, produced in Berlin some thirty paintings by Van Gogh. These created a sensation, though possibly by an oversight, their owner forgot that Van Gogh's nephew and legatee, Ir. V. W. Van Gogh, was still alive. Close examination of these showed that, as a result of not knowing *how* Van Gogh produced his effects, the forger imitated ridges of paint without imitating the way in which the artist had built those ridges up; rather as though in copying an aerial view of a street one did not know that there were houses beneath the roofs.

Close identification with an artist and a meticulous imitation of his technique (paying especial attention to the use of the same media) can produce convincing imitations of a work by another man. But there will never be an absolute identity, and in any case fakers are usually either careless or overconfident. A recent case in Germany (cf. [1], Chapter 7) uncovered a forger who had imitated the work of Pieter Breughel, Cézanne, Daumier, Manet, Claude, Turner, Utrillo, Rembrandt, Rodin, Watteau, Vlaminck, Picasso, Delacroix and many others. Largely owing to the connivance of certain dealers he was in many cases successful in his deceptions, especially with reference to some of the more modern works. But it is obvious that nobody could produce convincing forgeries of works by so many different artists working in so many different styles without, sooner or later, being caught out. Always one must remember, however, that anyone who is told that X is X will, under normal psychological conditions, retain a bias towards that belief.

THE FORGERY OF OLD MASTERS

The successful forger of old masters needs to be a scientist, an art historian and a psychologist, as well as an artist of unusual skill and dexterity. That many fakes succeed is not due to the fact that there are many people with these qualifications, but to the intentional or innocent *naïveté* of dealers and would-be purchasers. The tendency of the times, however, is to impel fakers to greater degrees of specialization. In the late nineteenth century a large collection of old masters was offered for sale at a famous London sale-room. After the first day they were withdrawn. Every one was a forgery, the work of Charles Augustus Howell, an intimate of the Pre-Raphaelites and of Whistler, who once passed off a drawing of Brompton Oratory by the latter artist as a preliminary design by Michelangelo for St Peter's, Rome. Brazen attempts of this kind would stand no chance of success today.

In the first place the forger has to pick on an appropriate subject, making sure that the historical accessories are correct. This may be done, as with modern works, by a judicious blending of other works by the artist whose name is to be so invoked. Even then, however, an error of judgment may spell ruin. In 1925 the Burlington Fine Arts Club showed a painting of two women in profile attributed to a fifteenth-century Italian artist (Note G, page 151). It had been concocted by combining two individual portraits by Botticelli and Domenico Veneziano, but the whole conception of this kind of double portrait, and especially the way in which it was done, is entirely alien to the age to which it was supposed to belong.

The right choice of materials did not greatly trouble the very early forgers, but the development of scientific methods of examination has made it a most important item in the counterfeiter's essential equipment. The Curator of the Royal Botanical Gardens at Kew, for instance, was able to prove to the authorities of the National Gallery that a painting attributed to a sixteenth-century artist was painted on a pine board. This wood was not used till much later, and so the work was proved a forgery. The easiest way, of course, to obtain the correct canvas or panel is to buy a work of the right period and either paint over it, or remove the original work and substitute the forgery. As underpainting can always be detected, the latter method is preferable.

The elaborate technical ingenuity of the forger may best be exemplified by reference to one of the most publicized cases of modern times, the productions of the fake Vermeers by Han van Meegeren (1889–1947). Van Meegeren was rightly proud of his skill, and he described his technique at great length (cf. [4], and John Godley, *The Master Forger*, London, 1951). After four years of experimentation he obtained virtually the same pigments used by Vermeer, by making them out of the chemicals used in the seventeenth century, and by grinding these by hand, so that the irregularities which distinguish these old colours from the machine-ground ones of today should be apparent. In the eighteenth century Hogarth had been aware that forgers baked and 'smoked' paintings to get an appearance of age, and to give the medium the hard, compact feeling usually procured by the passage of time. But he did not point out, what Meegeren discovered, that baking a painting tends to produce blisters and to dim the brilliance of the colours. He therefore built an electric oven the temperature of which could be controlled with great accuracy, and used as a medium a resin of phenol-formaldehyde dissolved in liquid, and rendered viscous by the addition of oil of lilacs. This does not blister so easily. To produce the 'crackle' of age he rolled the finished paintings around a cylinder with a diameter of about two feet, having previously varnished them, and covered the surface with black ink. This seeped through into the cracks, and the accumulation of small particles left by the ink when dry gave the impression of accumulated dust. The ink was then removed and another coat of varnish applied.

To produce a convincing fake stimulates a certain kind of person to perform miracles of misapplied ingenuity, but though, in the long run, even the most elaborate technical deceptions can be discovered, the final weakness of every forger is the strength of his own personality which keeps breaking through any false identity which he may assume.

THE DETECTION OF FORGERY

It is certain that no forger has yet evolved a technique which can avoid detection. During the last quarter of a century physics and chemistry have dealt a series of deadly blows to the production of fakes. On the other hand, the ordinary collector is not in a position to apply to a prospective purchase those exhaustive scientific tests which can be utilized by great national galleries. Over and above all the various methods of detecting a forgery which are described here, however, is the fundamental test of judgment by instinct. Most people who have seen and 'handled' works of art on an extensive scale develop an instinct which tells them whether or not a work of art is 'right' or not. Dealers must in many cases rely on such instinct, for they cannot possibly have the time to become intimately acquainted with all the different schools with which they may have to deal. Though this instinct can never be finally relied upon, its warnings should never be disregarded.

(*a*) **Provenance and Documentation.** Before even seeing a work of art, it is possible to discover something about its authenticity. Important works of art are often discovered after being lost for centuries, but there must nearly always be some reference to them in books, literature or periodicals at some point in their career, and such a reference can nearly always be checked. Very often the artist himself kept some kind of record. Claude and Turner, for instance, kept a '*liber veritatis*', in the form of books of sketches. Other artists kept account books, notebooks or records of appointments. Amongst the latter category one may cite the cases of Madame Vigée Le Brun, Reynolds, Joseph Vernet and Delacroix. The account books of agents, of framers and even of transport agents, and the diaries of critics or of connoisseurs may also throw light on the authenticity of a work of art. The *Notebooks of Vertue* (Walpole Society) or the *Diary of Joseph Farington* (Hutchinson) and the account written by the German art scholar C. F. Waagen (*Art Treasures in Great Britain, 1854*) are invaluable in this respect. Scholarly monographs by modern writers are important, and help may also be obtained by reference to collections of prints or of photographs, such for instance as the Witt Collection at the Courtauld Institute.

Of all the documentary sources of evidence mere 'certificates' are the least satisfactory. These are statements by some expert that 'in my opinion so and so is a fine example of a work by X dating from his best period'. Even apart from the fact that an expert's judgment may be warped by the consideration of factors other than artistic ones, human error is an incalculable element and no redress can be obtained from the supplier of the certificate. The Van Meegeren *Disciples at Emmaus* was published in a scholarly article by Dr A. Bredius, an outstanding expert in the history of Dutch art, in *The Burlington Magazine* for November 1937. Yet two months earlier the Paris representative of the firm of Duveen had cabled to the New York headquarters of his firm that the picture was 'a rotten fake' (cf. *The Sunday Times*, 23rd October, 1955). The faked murals at the Marienkirche in Lübeck were discussed at great length by several distinguished scholars. An art historian absorbed in the study of style and relevant characteristic can hardly be expected to assume that a work of art may be a forgery before he sets off on his exploratory investigations.

(*b*) **Superficial Observation.** A close visual examination of a work of art may very often reveal a good deal about its authenticity. The use of a magnifying glass will show all the surface characteristics, cracks, *pentimenti*, unsure brush work, erasures or corrections, mended canvas, suggestions of mechanical reproduction, water-marks, alteration or forgery of signatures. The back of the canvas and the stretcher may also reveal facts of significance.

The analysis of style, the most authoritative check on authenticity, is also a matter for the naked eye. Stylistic analysis depends on the application to a work of art of those methods of investigation first formulated in the nineteenth century by Morelli, who pointed out that an artist's distinguishing characteristics are to be found rather in the details of his work than in the overall impression. An examination of the details of an authentic work will reveal the technical idiosyncracies of an artist – how he paints eyes or fingernails; how he paints leaves or blades of grass; how he distributes his light and shadow. The nearer one approaches to the minutiae of his execution the closer one gets to the so-called 'scientific' analysis of an artist's style. A Rubens, for instance, is generally recognizable by the particular kind of face which he gave his models, suggesting overactivity of the thyroid gland. To give an overall impression of such a face, however, is easy enough. It is only when one comes to examine how the lights are put into the eyes, which way the hair of the eyebrows grows, the amount of red in the canthus and other small characteristics that one approaches the kind of criterion which enables one to differentiate between an original work and an imitation. It has been suggested [5] that this method can be systematized by a simple totting up of points in which a work resembles an authentic masterpiece and then subtracting points of dissimilarity.

Close observation, too, should be given to the subject of a work of art. In the case of a portrait, others of the same subject should be consulted. In the case of a landscape, reference should be made to contemporary accounts whenever possible. Often buildings have been constructed, roads made, field boundaries altered and other topographical changes taken place since the artist's death. Costume, too, changing rapidly with fluctuations of taste, can be a most reliable test. Every incident or detail in a painting should be tested by reference to history. Works by the so-called Spanish forger, who worked in the late nineteenth century, have been detected by his inaccurate rendering of medieval musical instruments (cf. [1], p. 71). The fundamental stylistic weakness of a forger, however, lies in the fact that he sees the world through the eyes of his own age and personality, and in copying the work of another artist he will emphasize those characteristics which appeal to him. That is why a forgery is often more easy to detect in another age than in the age in which it was executed. Many Victorian forgeries, for instance, reveal a sugary sentimentality which the taste of that century demanded.

(*c*) **Scientific Examination.** This can reveal those secrets which the forger hopes are known only to himself. It is known that faked Corots abound. In twenty years more than 103,000 works purporting to be by that artist passed through the New York Customs, and even allowing for superhuman energy, when one adds to that figure the number of Corots already in Europe, one must assume that there is something fishy somewhere. A great number of these fakes, however, can easily be detected in that they have been painted in a kind of gouache, whereas it is known that Corot only used oils and watercolours.

Pigments can nowadays be analysed with the greatest of ease and without doing any damage to the picture. Microchemical and spectroscopic examination can provide details of the age and composition of the medium used. The advantages of this are obvious. Some thirty years ago a painting attributed to Franz Hals was proved to contain artificial ultramarine and zinc white, both modern additions to the artist's palette. A painting acquired by the Brooklyn Museum of Art as being by Hobbema and catalogued as such in the authoritative work on that artist was proved, in 1942, to contain Prussian blue, a pigment only introduced in the nineteenth century.

The application of water and ethyl alcohol, and of strong alkalis and acids, can also help to determine the composition of a pigment, and part of the case against Van Meegeren was that the paints on his 'Vermeers' did not resist these agents and so could not have contained fatty substances.

X-ray photographs can not only reveal the condition of the canvas and the manner in which the artist has applied his paint, but because lead-impregnated pigments are more impervious to the effect of the rays than others, they can reveal the composition of these pigments. Ultra-violet and infra-red rays can also be used to reveal characteristics of the forger's art not visible to the naked eye. Under an ultra-violet light parts which have been repainted show up by differences in fluorescence.

The age and chemical composition of ink and paper, the existence of finger-prints and countless other small loopholes, enable the scientific investigator to worm his way into the shadowy mind of the counterfeiter, who today would need a huge laboratory to be able to produce expert-proof fakes.

NOTES

A. The case of the Vermeers forged by Van Meegeren came to light only because their perpetrator was accused of treason. Heindrich Joerdens, a Bremen dealer, bought large quantities of forgeries from the Lübeck forger Malskat because, he is reported to have said at the trial, 'he believed that the paintings might have come from East Germany, or might be Jewish property' (cf. *Die Welt*, January 1955).

B. In the exhibition *Chefs-d'-Oeuvre de l'Art Français*, held in Paris in 1937, there was a painting by Emile Bernard which was, to the publicly confessed annoyance of that artist, attributed to Gauguin.

C. The position of the dealer who effects the sale of a forgery is a complicated one. It must be admitted that there are certain dealers who are prepared to sell works of art without too close an investigation of their authenticity, and the Malskat case proved how deeply involved they may be. On the other hand, most dealers belong to some reputable trade organization which takes a very severe view of such transactions, and in any case their careers are ruined if they are once detected in passing off, honestly or dishonestly, a forged work. In England the legal position is complicated by the fact that a work of art being a 'document' it does not come under the Forgery Act of 1913, and can only be dealt with under certain minor Civil or Common Law heads.

D. Millet's son used a stencil employed by his father to copy signatures on works faked by an accomplice.

E. Incredible though it may seem, artists occasionally 'forge' their own works. Rubens did, and recently de Chirico has imitated his own early work for polemical reasons.

F. In the nineteenth century F. W. Rohrich produced no less than thirty copies of a portrait of Sophie and Johann Friedrich von Sachsen attributed to Lucas Cranach. It must be remembered, of course, that before the discovery of colour reproductions, rich amateurs often commissioned artists to produce replicas of famous paintings for them.

G. The catalogue of this exhibition, which was devoted to fakes and faking, is invaluable for the study of this subject.

BOOKS FOR FURTHER READING

1. Cole, Sonia: *Counterfeit* (London, 1955).
2. Tietze, Hans: *Genuine and False* (London, 1948).
3. Coremans, P.: *Van Meegeren's Faked Vermeers and De Hooghs* (London, 1949).
4. Graebke, H. A.: *Die Wandmalerien der Marienkirche zu Luebeck* (Hamburg, 1951).
5. Dantzig, H. M. van: *Vincent? A new method of identifying the artist and his work and of unmasking the forger and his products* (Amsterdam, 1953).
6. *Studies in Conservation* (Various numbers, London).
7. Publications of The Fogg Art Museum (U.S.A.).

One of the earliest examples of a wall fireplace, at Rochester Castle, Kent. *National Buildings Record.*

PLATE 101

To face page 152

(A) Palladian carved wood chimney-piece attributed to William Kent. Originally in Brightling Park, Sussex. Now in the Board Room of Hambro's Bank, London.

(B) Carved wood overmantel, surmounting a stone fire-place (*c.* 1620), from an old house in Lime Street in the city of London. *Victoria & Albert Museum.*

(B) Detail of carved wood overmantel at left.

(A) Carved wood mantelpiece and overmantel, originally in Cassiobury Park, Watford (*c.* 1699). *Bert Crowther Ltd.*

The Court Room at the Bank of England, showing the three adjacent fireplaces.

(A) Detail of the central fireplace from Plate 104.

(B) Seventeenth-century carved wood fireplace and overmantel.
Victoria & Albert Museum.

Rare Adam period Bossi inlaid marble chimney-piece—Bossi was an Italian who worked in Dublin 1785–98—with typical Irish 'Adam' engraved gunmetal register grate. *Pratt & Sons.*

PLATE 106

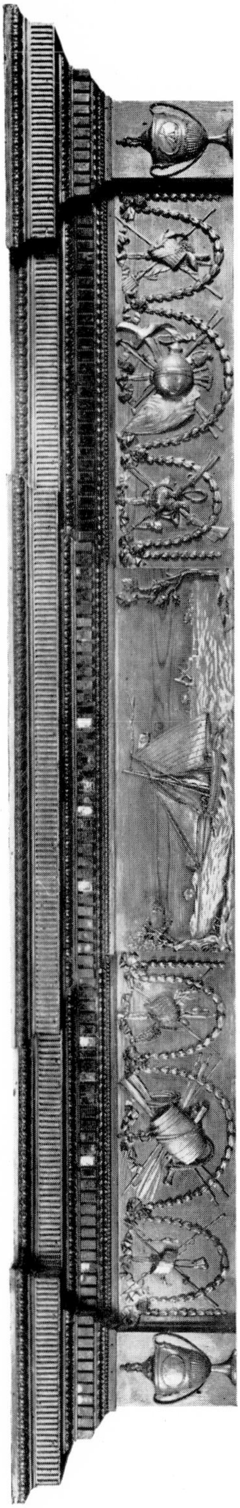

(A) Carved pine mantelpiece displaying a representation of the cup presented by Admiral the Duke of Cumberland in 1776 to encourage yacht racing on the Thames. *Mr A. H. J. Silley and Pratt & Sons.*

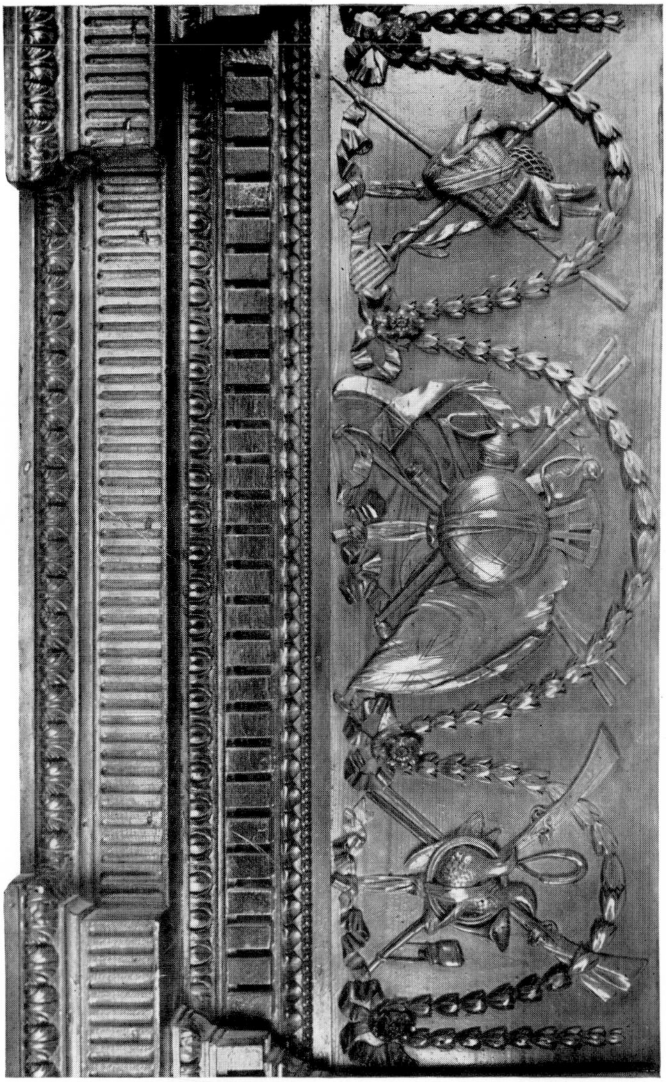

(C) Detail of the 'Cumberland' mantelpiece above.

(B) Detail of cup.

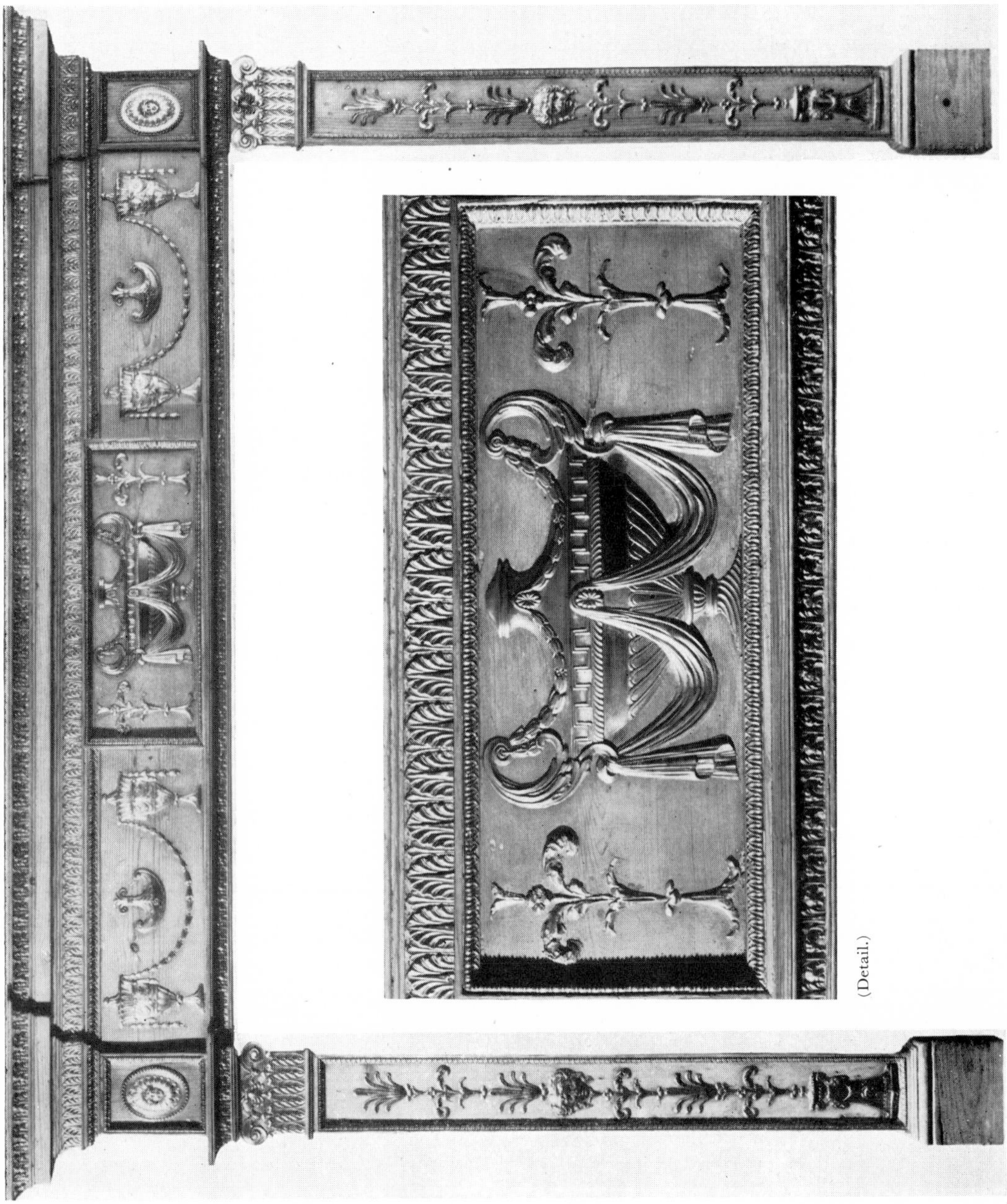

(Detail.)

A wood mantel with decoration in pewter in the style of Robert Adam, *c.* 1775. *T. Crowther & Sons.*

PLATE 108

THE ENGLISH CHIMNEY-PIECE

By SYDNEY J. MAIDEN

THE evolution of the English chimney-piece reached its height in the latter half of the eighteenth century, after which it lapsed into the mediocrity general in an age bemused by material progress. Hitherto it had marched with the development of style and taste through periods in which those things flourished.

Though always governed ultimately by the practical consideration of heating rooms, it had soon become affected by the impulse to embellish and decorate. From the most primitive times the hearth had been the focal-point of domestic life. The cold northern winters made urgently imperative the provision of artificial warmth in living quarters. This need was met at first by the simple and obvious expedient of a fire of available fuel – wood or peat – laid on an open hearth usually set in the centre of earthen or stone floors. Sometimes, as at Penshurst Place in Kent, the hearth was paved with bricks. An outlet for smoke was provided by means of an opening in the roof, known, after the arrival of the Normans, as a louvre (from the French *l'ouvert*). After the Conquest, when buildings of more than one storey were required, chiefly in strongholds for defensive purposes, a fireplace set in a recess in the walls was a logical departure from previous practice. The disposal of smoke from these recessed fireplaces was at first contrived by cutting an opening in the outer wall. Very soon, fireplaces were provided with a projecting hood of wood, lined with clay or plaster and sometimes of stone. Chimneys as we know them were a later development, affecting to some degree the character and dimensions of the fireplace openings as did the introduction of coal as fuel.

In course of time came the chimney-pieces of the eighteenth century which, in line with the architectural achievement of that aesthetically vigorous age, displayed taste and discretion to a degree never again approached. Nor is it likely that modern heating methods and fuel changes and limitations will encourage a return to the high standards once prevalent in England. The most striking examples of eighteenth-century chimney-pieces were naturally to be found in the greater houses, where wealthy and travelled patrons could afford to employ able and imaginative designers. Economic pressure, adaptation and even demolition have of late taken their toll of many features of artistic merit, and much has been lost or, at best, removed to museums. There remain, fortunately, many examples of chimney-pieces of beauty and character in houses which have survived the march of progress. Not a few have found new homes in modern buildings, where they have been intelligently embodied in decorative schemes which reflect the taste of better days. These often eleventh-hour rescues have included chimney-pieces of a more modest scale which serve to challenge contemporary designers and to arrest the impact of self-conscious modernism. None the less, for better or worse the open fire appears to be doomed to extinction.

The wall fireplace first appeared in the twelfth century, and characteristic examples of it are to be seen in many ancient and even ruined buildings. Two such are

Rochester Castle in Kent and The King's House at Southampton. The recesses were arched in a style strongly suggestive of the ecclesiastical architecture of the period. It was some three centuries before the recessed fireplace became general in manors and farmhouses where, no doubt for reasons of economy, the rudimentary central hearth served.

Where stone was not immediately available, lintels of oak beams, as at Stokesay in Shropshire, were resorted to. This gave scope to carvers for the addition of decorative detail varying considerably in refinement until the craft reached a stage bordering on perfection. Minor improvements in design, coincident with changes in architectural outlook, continued until Tudor times. Hitherto Gothic styles had prevailed, finding their highest expression in such fireplaces as may be seen at Salisbury in the Church House and, most impressively, in the ruins of Tattershall Castle in Lincolnshire. But now the effect of the Renaissance made itself felt. Foreign artists, French as well as Italian, found their way to England, encouraged by the urge to express a sense of self-importance, monopolized by King Henry VIII and Cardinal Wolsey. Columns, pilasters and entablatures, characteristic of Renaissance design, appeared in chimney-pieces. Magnificent as much of the work was, it often displayed a not altogether satisfactory mixture of styles. A sense of discreet proportion as yet lay ahead. One of the most impressive compositions, attributable to a notable artist, may be examined in the British Museum collection, but it does not appear to have gone further than the drawing-board. Hans Holbein, the portrait painter, made the design for a splendid chimney-piece, reputedly for the King's Palace at Bridewell. It contains in its detail evidence of royal associations and intention. The Italian designers worked in various media, and showed a strong liking for terra-cotta. Their work occasionally rose beyond mere brilliance of craftsmanship. Standardization of style had not yet hardened, and the identity of particular artists was not then considered as of importance. Patrons were more often concerned with the ultimate splendour of their apartments than with any attribution of credit.

The accession of Queen Elizabeth I signalled a great increase in building, especially to the order of those who had grown rich in the previous reign. Dutch refugees and Germans, skilled in building and the allied arts and seething with the vigour engendered by the classical Renaissance, found scope and patrons for their talents. The new great houses called for chimney-pieces of comparable opulence, and these were forthcoming. With the lapse of Gothic styles went the tacit principle that the chimney-piece should be conceived as an integral part of its setting. In addition to materials locally available, marble of various colours as well as alabaster were imported, giving opportunities to carvers both native and foreign to embody heraldic devices and mythological and Biblical figures in their sumptuously decorated and, it must be said, occasionally overloaded structures.

So far there had been little conscious attempt at stylization. It was, so to speak, a hasty but not invariably unhappy marriage of Continental taste with current English convention. This was a period of transition and a prelude to better things. In the seventeenth century a new force appeared in the person of Inigo Jones, who was to exercise a powerful influence and also to be the initiator of the principle of conceiving a building, interior as well as exterior, as a complete entity. Order and harmony began a rule that persisted for many years. From Jones also sprang the 'signed' work of men whose status as architects was acknowledged by their contemporaries and respected by succeeding generations. The cumbrous and overworked Elizabethan chimney-pieces gave place to simpler conceptions; bolection moulding, for instance, gave a greater sense of dignity and repose to fireplace openings. Jones had enlarged his vision by two visits to Italy, the second being in 1613. He steeped himself in the resurgent classicism of Italy without becoming obsessed by it, and put his knowledge and experience to good use. To his credit are numerous chimney-pieces still to be seen in the settings for which he was also responsible. The effects of his imaginative and creative mind extended well into the eighteenth century, although Christopher Wren who followed him moved forward from the point reached by Jones. Wren, happily at hand when the rebuilding of London after the Great Fire was undertaken, was liberally endowed for the vast amount of work he initiated and controlled. A pronounced change in the character and dimensions of wooden wall-panelling then occurred, and Wren, who was largely responsible for its simplification and greater breadth, treated his chimney-pieces accordingly. Even more than Inigo Jones, he regarded them as incidents, albeit important, in the design of rooms. A cultivated and classical sense of proportion pervaded his work, and the overpowering and elaborate chimney-piece for a time disappeared. Another man destined for great distinction played an important part in the decorative work. Grinling Gibbons was a carver of exceptional skill; in his own domain, an unsurpassed craftsman. John Evelyn, the diarist, recommended him to Wren, with whom he co-operated in the provision of decorative detail of great delicacy and intricate beauty. His impeccable craftsmanship, only questioned by certain critics who detected in it a propensity to over-elaboration – an *embarras de richesses* – earned for him a famous eulogium from Horace Walpole, who proclaimed that Gibbons 'gave to wood the loose and airy lightness of flowers'. Gibbons, who held the appointment of master carver to King George I, employed as assistants foreign craftsmen of the standing of the Belgians Lauret van der Meulen of Mechlin and Dievot of Brussels.

The mantelshelf at this stage was usually upheld by flat pilasters or by caryatids with floral decorations. Rectangular tablets often broke the frieze and carried carved masks. Above the shelf, similar treatment was applied to richly carved frames in which pictures were fixed. Glass mirrors were often enclosed by these frames, for glass manufacture, hitherto almost a Continental monopoly, began to flourish in London under the aegis of the Duke of Buckingham.

Wren's use of broad panelling was not restricted to the great mansions. It was soon adopted for houses of more modest size and character. Their chimney-pieces conformed to the new style.

After Wren and Gibbons, a note of classical severity, to be known as Palladianism, captured and overwhelmed designers. In a measure this was a harking back to Inigo Jones. Lord Burlington, whose claims to fame go further than the influential patronage he exercised, was the titular head of this new cult, and his distinguished protégé, William Kent, was among the most fervent followers of the school of Palladio, Vitravius and Vignola. Others were James Gibbs, John Vanbrugh and William Chambers. Their worship of Palladianism inclined to a rigidity, and led lesser men working to the copy-books to a pedantic dullness which provoked the powerful reaction which followed.

Wainscots and airy carvings gave place to plastered walls, which were painted or hung with damask, leather or wallpaper. Chimney-pieces were now built of moulded plaster or stucco, as well as of wood and marble. Sir John Vanbrugh, noted for his work at Blenheim Palace, is conspicuous more for the weight than for the imaginative nature of his productions, and built chimney-pieces of monumental heaviness. Hawksmoor, another eminent architect with many notable churches to his credit, endowed his chimney-pieces with massive architectural solidity in which grace and proportion were not the chief virtues. James Gibbs, another church architect whose best-known work is to be seen in London at St Martin-in-the-Fields, Trafalgar Square, and St Mary-le-Strand, displayed a sober and cautious classicism in his chimney-pieces which never contained much originality. To Chambers, however, must be given credit for a bold departure from the 'continued' chimney-piece, the oppressive superstructure which had been held in high regard. He occasionally deviated from rigid Palladianism into the Baroque and pseudo-Gothic, but, like James Wyatt, he avoided the excesses which others who were lured into those regions could not resist.

With the disappearance of wood panelling, the fireplace was logically reduced in height;

although Gibbs, Kent and Ware remained for a time faithful to the superstructure, outstanding examples of which are to be seen at Chiswick House and, until recently, at Brightling Park in Sussex. The latter, of carved wood and attributed to William Kent, has lately been re-erected in the Board Room of Hambro's Bank in the City of London, where the size and character of its setting give full value to its nobility of design.

Half-way through the century occurred an outburst of rococo and Chinese styles, the result of visits paid by artists and others to the Continent and the East. Chimney-pieces, often of pine, exhibited these tendencies, which were in a measure a momentary reaction to classical restraint and severity. One bizarre example in the style of Chippendale, who had succumbed to the baleful charms of chinoiserie, is on view in the Victoria & Albert Museum. It has been attributed to W. and I. Halfpenny who, with Thomas Johnson, Ince and Mayhew, exploited this extravagant and restless style. Chippendale himself is renowned for cabinet-making and furniture of greater distinction, and his published work on the subject of chimney-pieces, *The Gentleman and Cabinet-maker's Director*, includes illustrations which show French rather than Chinese influence.

This phase fortunately did not endure, and very soon discretion returned to govern design. Robert Adam, whose name stands high in the history of architecture, supplied the necessary corrective. Like Inigo Jones before him, Robert Adam, a Scotsman, travelled and studied in Italy, where the spell of classicism was laid upon him. He met Piranesi in Italy, and rediscovered the beauty and possibilities of Greek ornament. Adam's mind was powerful and original enough to prevent his becoming overwhelmed by what he saw. He absorbed, classified and adapted the best of Greek design to his own use, and is justifiably respected and admired to this day for his interior decoration and for his elegant and pleasing chimney-pieces. He and his brother did a great deal of work in London and elsewhere. Many of their original designs are included in the collection in the Soane Museum, Lincoln's Inn Fields, London. The outstanding characteristic of Adam's work, as with the best preceding it, is proportion. Such detail as it contains is, for all its delicacy, never obtrusive. In the preface to *The Works in Architecture of Robert and James Adam, London, 1778*, by the Adam brothers, we have their objective clearly expressed with an engaging assurance of its validity. They say, *inter alia*, '. . . we have adopted a beautiful variety of light mouldings, gracefully formed, delicately enriched, and arranged with propriety and skill'. Although these words were intended to cover the Adams' achievement in architecture generally, they apply without question to the chimney-pieces for which they are justly renowned. Throughout, classical Greek influences govern the general design and ornamentation; the latter included such devices as urns, vases, wreaths, floral motifs and medallions, which were painted or applied in relief. A distinguished company of artists co-operated in the familiar decorative detail – Flaxman, Angelica Kauffmann and Cipriani were among the number, and Pergolesi, whom Adam invited to come to England from Italy, also lent a practised hand in certain notable instances. Adam designs were executed in a variety of media, including marble with inlays of contrasting marble or scagliola, as well as wood composition and stucco, the last of which materials he did much to popularize.

Robert Adam was far from being a neglected genius. He enjoyed a high reputation and success in his lifetime. At his death an appreciation in *The Gentleman's Magazine* (1792) spoke glowingly of his influence on design and decoration, saying: 'Mr Adam produced a total change in the architecture of this country: and his fertile genius in elegant ornament was not confined to the decoration of buildings, but has been diffused into almost every branch of manufacture.' This considered tribute proves that Robert Adam moulded and affected taste in his own time and long afterwards to a far greater extent than any other practitioner in his field. But, since he built on the secure foundation of knowledge and tradition, his departures from prevailing modes were more logical and well-founded than the self-conscious innovations of so many modern architects and designers.

The Adam brothers, who for many years dominated interior decoration, including chimney-piece design, were naturally enough subject to imitators as well as serious disciples in whom the 'Adam touch' showed some signs of fatigue in a tendency to overdo ornamentation. It is not remarkable that the fires of inspiration should have burned rather low at the close of a great period of aesthetic endeavour and achievement. None the less, Adam's influence endured, and his status is as unquestionable as that of his eminent predecessors, Inigo Jones and Christopher Wren.

Sir John Soane, the last of the great designers, owed much to Adam, but he was a big enough man to add much from a well-stocked mind and cultivated taste. He is notable for the use he made of pure linear proportion without superimposed decorative detail. A significant example of Soane's work in marble is in the Museum, once his residence, in Lincoln's Inn Fields, London. The moderate height of Soane's chimney-pieces was due to his desire to subordinate them to the general proportion of his interiors, and to permit mirrors or pictures to be placed above them at a lower level than before.

Normally one fireplace was considered adequate to the needs of even large rooms, but occasionally a second was thoughtfully provided. There is, however, a remarkable example of even greater generosity in this respect, and it is unique in its way.

In the City of London, in the original Bank of England, the Court Room, designed by Sir Robert Taylor, had three fireplaces set side by side at intervals in one wall facing the windows. This lavish provision enhanced the dignity of a beautiful and historic room which has yet another claim to our notice. When some thirty years ago the Bank was rebuilt, the Court Room, then on ground level, was reproduced on the first floor. In the process the centre one of the three fireplaces was, with other features, discarded and replaced by one of a different design. Fortunately it was carefully preserved, and some years later Professor Sir Albert Richardson (P.R.A. in 1955 and 1956), who had been empowered to revive the character and detail of the original room, pictorial records of which existed, contrived its return. Together with a wall-clock of exceptional charm, also temporarily in exile, it resumes its rightful position.

The illustrations (Plates 104 and 105) show these fireplaces as they once were and are again. With the wall-clock surmounting the loftier central mantelpiece, they complete a most satisfying arrangement in a setting which bears evident traces of Adam influence.

Whether in these days, with coal almost as precious as the gold in the vaults of the Bank, the three fireplaces actively serve together to give warmth and comfort to the Court in Session is a small matter beside their unusual arrangement and their intrinsic beauty.

With the end of the eighteenth century there set in a decline, gradual at first but gathering momentum as the age progressed. Towards its end and into the present century, style and discrimination in chimney-piece design, as with architecture generally, languished and floundered. Craftsmanship gave place to mass production, with inevitable consequences visible in so much of contemporary work. Although what was called 'old-world' flourished for a time to satisfy the craze for pseudo-Tudor, Elizabethan and other meretricious imitations of distant styles, the latest manifestations even at their most serious are uninspiring. The open fire is unlikely to survive, and the chimney-piece is fast becoming redundant. The best of what was done in the great age is not entirely lost to view, but the impulse to continue a great tradition has gone. The monstrous 'tile surround', as it is called by manufacturers and house agents, is now the average Englishman's idea of the focal-point of his domestic life. The glory has indeed departed; material benefits which have accrued are not to be despised, but they seem to offer little spiritual solace.

ENGLISH WALL MIRRORS

By GEOFFREY WILLS

BEFORE the fifteenth century, in spite of the fact that the process of silvering glass was understood, it would seem to have been little used, and mirrors were made of highly polished plates of metal. Glass had not then the clarity it later attained, and a carefully burnished piece of gold, silver, steel or other metal was likely to provide a more accurate reflecting surface. Limited in size, it is doubtful whether such mirrors were hung on a wall or merely stood on a convenient piece of furniture. In any case, it is conjectured that for a considerable period, along with other comparable luxuries, their ownership was confined to the wealthy.

Glass mirror-plates became a monopoly of the republic of Venice, where Murano was the centre of the glass-making industry on the Continent of Europe and whence knowledge of the process had come from Germany some time about the year 1500. There is no evidence that they were made in England until early in the seventeenth century, when John Aubrey, the antiquarian, noted in his *Brief Lives* that a man named Robson had commenced their manufacture. In 1618 Robson's enterprise was taken over by Sir Robert Mansell, who employed 'many expert strangers from foreign parts beyond the seas to instruct the natives of this Kingdom in the making of looking glass plates', and who by 1623 employed some five hundred men in the 'making, grinding, and foyling of looking glasses'.

Half a century later a glass works was started at Vauxhall by the Duke of Buckingham, and in due course became famous. John Evelyn visited it in 1676, and reported that they made '. . . looking glasses far larger and better than any that come from Venice'. In 1705 another commentator noted: 'The Trade of Looking Glass Plates is so considerably improv'd that they serve not only for Furniture and Ornament, in Her Majesty's Dominions at Home, but are likewise in great Esteem in Foreign Parts; the *Venetians* themselves buying of these *Plates*, and preferring them before their own'. However, it may be thought that this latter statement shows a certain bias on the part of the man who made it – John Gumley, who was himself a prominent manufacturer of mirrors during the reign of Queen Anne and later.

Mirror-plate was first made by what was termed the 'broad' process. In this, briefly, the liquid glass was taken up from the furnace on a blowing-tube and blown into the form of a large bubble. Two opposite surfaces of the bubble were cut off; the tube remaining was then slit along one side and the whole flattened. The sheet of glass was cooled, ground and polished until it was as flat and smooth as possible. In spite of the care it received in the two last treatments, the resulting plate was not always satisfactory. Principally it was found that however skilfully the craftsmen blew the glass, it was extremely difficult to ensure that it was of an even thickness over the entire surface; in addition, there was understandably a limit to the size that could be made in this manner.

Late in the seventeenth century, French glassmakers introduced the process of glass casting. The molten glass was poured on to a bed of metal, was swiftly spread evenly over it and rolled flat while it was still hot. Much larger and truer plates could be made by this method, which was also quicker in spite of the fact that the plates had still to be slowly cooled, and then ground and polished. The casting process was used for a short while in England about 1690, but it did not find favour and for some reason was given up. In

1773 'The British Cast Plate-Glass Company' was incorporated, and factories were opened at Southwark and at St Helen's, Lancashire. The venture succeeded in producing glass to supplant the imported French plates, and the company remained in being until the outset of the present century.

The actual 'silvering' of the glass is misnamed, as the precious metal is not amongst the constituents that were used. A sheet of tin-foil and a quantity of mercury were the principal ingredients, and by their use the English and Continental craftsmen of the past produced the mirror-plates of which so many have survived the wear and tear of the centuries to bear witness to their skill. The tin-and-mercury amalgam remained in general use until about 1840, when it was replaced by a process that does merit the name of 'silvering', for by a discovery of the German chemist J. von Liebig, a coat of the metal is deposited chemically on the glass.

The framing of mirrors during the seventeenth and eighteenth centuries took many forms, and was the subject of careful study from men of artistic talent ranging from Grinling Gibbons and William Kent to Thomas Chippendale and Robert Adam. At the commencement of the period, the pieces of glass were of small size and the frames were usually contrastingly large. Elaborate settings of carved wood, of embroidered stumpwork, coloured beads, ebony and tortoiseshell or of chased plaques of silver, were among the many that surrounded comparatively insignificant pieces of mirror-glass, and were the workmanship of the most skilled craftsmen of their time. No material, save gold itself, was so costly that it is not found to have been formed into a surrounding for the glass that reflected the features of Caroline beauties.

By 1675 the framing had grown less varied and the well-known 'cushion' type was coming into use (Plate 109B). Following the customary rectangular form, it was usually veneered with walnut, often in the form of 'oysters' of selected grain. More decorative versions were heavily inlaid with marquetry, rare examples were of incised Chinese lacquer, and others, rarer still, overlaid with embossed silver may be seen still at Windsor Castle and at Knole.

As it became possible to manufacture glass in sheets of larger size, it was found that not only the frame but also the mirror within it had decorative possibilities, and also that a nearly square shape was not necessarily the most suitable. Perhaps inspired by the *Galerie des Glaces* at Versailles, completed by Le Brun for Louis XIV in 1682, and by the success of the French in casting large plates, English houses began to be ornamented with mirrors in profusion. These mirrors were for the decoration of the rooms in which they were placed, and not primarily for personal admiration as had been earlier examples.

The increase in the size of the glass was countered by a shrinkage in the size of the frame. To such a degree did this change sweep into fashion that for a while, about the years 1690–1700, the frame almost vanished altogether, and was replaced by a surround of strips of glass decorated with cutting or with patterns in *verre églomisé* (Plate 109C). The French may well have inspired the larger mirror, but undoubtedly the Venetians were responsible for this mode of bordering it.

Following the 'frameless' era came the introduction of the gilt frame; in turn following the new taste for gilt furnishings. Whereas polished cabinet-work returned shortly to favour, the mirror frame remained gilt. Few, if any, were in any other finish after 1750, and before that date the exceptions were in a minority. These last comprise the walnut-veneered mirror-frames of small size assigned popularly to Queen Anne's reign, much reproduced in recent years, but, if genuine, dating more probably from the time of George I (Plate 110C); and the larger mirrors of George II date with gilt enrichments on a ground of polished Virginia ('red') walnut.

The placing of mirrors in a room began to assume a regularity that has remained little changed. Above the fireplace was the most popular position, and there the framing sometimes formed an integral part of that most important feature. Some of these overmantel mirrors incorporated within their extensive frames an oil-painting, and examples of the type, dating from about 1740–60,

(A) Carved limewood frame attributed to Grinling Gibbons, *c.* 1700. *Victoria & Albert Museum.*

(B) Mirror in 'cushion' frame, the borders and cresting japanned and decorated with Oriental designs, and inset with panels of rolled-paper work, *c.* 1700. *Victoria & Albert Museum.*

(C) Three-panel 'landscape' overmantel mirror in narrow gilt frame with borders of *verre églomisé*, *c.* 1695. *Mallett & Son.*

PLATE 109

(A) Pier-glass with carved gilt cresting and *verre églomisé* borders, *c.* 1695. *Victoria & Albert Museum.*

(B) Mirror in frame with decoration of gilt gesso, *c.* 1720. *Mallett & Son.*

(C) Walnut-veneered frame with shaped cresting and base, moulded border and gilt-metal candle-holders, *c.* 1720. *Mallett & Son.*

(D) Mirror in frame veneered with walnut, with gilt enrichments, *c.* 1745. *Private collection.*

PLATE 110

(A) Gilt frame carved in the 'Chinese Chippendale' style with exotic birds in the cresting, figure of *Pu-Tai* in the base and rococo ornament, *c.* 1755. *Private collection.*

(B) Oval giltwood frame carved with rococo ornament. About 1755. *Private collection.*

(C) Carved and giltwood overmantel mirror, the cresting formed as Ganymede and the Eagle. After a design by Thomas Johnson published in 1758. *Victoria & Albert Museum.*

(A) Gilt-framed mirror designed by Robert Adam, *c.* 1770. At Osterley Park.

(B) Oval mirror with border of alternate blue and white glass facets. Irish, *c.* 1780. *Cecil Davis.*

(C) Pier-glass with gilt frame and 'back-painted' top panel, *c.* 1810. *Mallett & Son.*

(D) Convex mirror in gilt frame surmounted by an eagle. About 1810. *Private collection.*

PLATE 112

are found usually with landscape or floral pictures. A simpler variation of the large overmantel mirror, the 'landscape' mirror (Plate 109C), came into vogue early in the eighteenth century, gradually grew squarer in shape as the years wore on, and in the succeeding century exchanged width for height (Plate 112C). Upright mirrors were placed on the narrow walls (piers) between windows, and pier-glasses, as they were called, were widely employed from their first introduction about 1700. Further, in those great mansions that boasted suites of state rooms, mirrors were hung at their far ends to reflect one into another and artificially increase their length.

As with the design of furnishings in general, the design of mirror-frames varied almost from year to year and month to month, but they may be grouped conveniently under a number of headings. This is the case with many of the smaller and simpler gilt gesso mirrors (Plate 110B), which are assigned to the period of Queen Anne (1702–14), although most are rather later in date. The larger, more heavily designed mirrors with pediments of classical type, are attributed to one of the foremost architects of his day, William Kent.

Following the vogue of the so-called 'Kent' or 'architectural' frame came the first signs of the combination of French, Gothic and Chinese styles that culminated in the well-known Chinese Chippendale. From a few years prior to 1754, when Thomas Chippendale's volume of designs was published, mirror-frames were modelled elaborately with exotic birds, Chinamen, goats, sheep, sea-shells and flowers (among much else), and the carver was able to give full rein to his agile chisel. Many of these frames were from the designs of Linnell, Johnson, Lock and Copland and others, but all are assigned popularly to Chippendale, whose book conveniently summarized the styles of his time for posterity (Plate 111A, B and C).

The various *motifs* figured by Chippendale, combined or singly, remained in vogue until the introduction of classical themes by Robert and James Adam. In common with the furniture which became fashionable in the 1770s, the mirror-frame was ornamented with urns, honeysuckle, husks and *paterae* (Plate 112A). The delicacy of the work proved often to be beyond the resources of the wood-carver, and many of the detailed and flimsy ornaments were of composition on a wire core or were cast in lead.

By the second half of the eighteenth century the pier-glass had reached very large proportions. Sheets of mirror-glass supplied to the Earl of Mansfield in 1769, and still at Ken Wood, London, measure 74 inches in height, and a plate measuring 91 by 57½ inches was supplied by Chippendale's firm in 1773.

It remains to mention here some mirror-frames that are outside the general classifications. Oval mirrors were made in the 1730s and remained popular throughout the century, during which their framing followed the prevailing patterns in each decade. Distinctive and rare were the Irish mirrors of the last years of the eighteenth century. These were of oval shape, and framed with one or more rows of clear or coloured glass facets (Plate 112B).

Finally, there is the familiar convex mirror (Plate 112D). This was introduced from France, and the majority of surviving examples date from 1800 and later. They had been made several centuries earlier, and one is depicted in Van Eyck's picture in the National Gallery, London, known by the Gallery as 'Jan Arnolfini and his Wife', painted in 1434. Van Eyck's mirror is in a simple gilt frame; its more modern counterpart usually bears a carved eagle above the deeply turned gilt border in which are placed small gilt balls. Usually a ball is suspended from the beak of the eagle, and in some examples the frame is flanked by arms for candles; the arms of gilt brass fitted with cut-glass drops. Rare convex mirrors are more elaborately and individually carved, and are known with the frames surmounted by an ornament in the form of the crest of the owner, or with the side supports in the shape of dolphins.

GLOSSARY

Adam, Robert (1728–92): the eminent architect who, in common with his predecessor, William Kent, paid much attention to the interior decoration of his buildings. He was responsible for the classical revival initiated in the 1760s that ousted the furnishings made popular by Chippendale. Adam designed mirrors, principally pier-glasses, and many of them remain in the houses for which they were made. A great number of Robert Adam's original designs are in Sir John Soane's Museum, Lincoln's Inn Fields, London.

Bevelling: the angular shaping of the surface at the edges of a mirror-plate was performed by grinding and then polishing the glass. A patent for a method of doing this with the aid of water-power was granted in 1678. Much glass for mirrors had the edges bevelled, but the finish was not always employed for large plates after the middle years of the eighteenth century.

Chippendale, Thomas (1718–79): cabinet-maker and designer. Born at Otley, Yorkshire, it is known that he was in London by 1748, and shortly afterwards was established in St Martin's Lane where, at the sign of 'The Chair', he remained until his death. Twice he worked with partners, firstly with James Rannie and later with Thomas Haig. He has attained a world-wide fame from his volume of designs, *The Gentleman and Cabinet Maker's Director*, which was first issued in 1754. The book was reprinted in 1755, and an enlarged edition appeared in parts between 1759 and 1762. (*See* Lock.)

Some of the furniture from Chippendale's workshop has been identified from bills that have been preserved. Two large mirrors at Ken Wood were supplied by Thomas Chippendale in 1769, and were to the design of Robert Adam.

The business in St Martin's Lane was continued on the death of Thomas Chippendale by his eldest son (also named Thomas) in partnership with Haig.

Gesso: *see* Gilding.

Gibbons, Grinling (1648–1720): carver and designer of Dutch birth and English domicile. He was 'discovered' by the diarist John Evelyn. Gibbons's distinctive and realistic carving exists in the form of mirror-frames, but much of the work assigned to him is by his contemporaries and much is of considerably later date.

Gilding: the process of applying gold, beaten into the thinnest of foils, to a surface. It is divided into two types according to the nature of the mordant by which the gold is made to adhere to the article.

Oil-gilding used a preparation of solidified linseed-oil, and the resulting finish was the more durable and least expensive of the two, as it could be employed directly on to the surface of the woodwork. Oil-gilding would not burnish.

Water-gilding required the woodwork to be painted with several layers of a preparation somewhat like plaster, known as gesso. Gesso was made with a base of glue prepared by boiling scraps of parchment or glover's leather in water. To this was added *bole armoniac*, or *Armenian bole* (a fine clay, now known as gilder's red clay), and some tallow, suet or beeswax. The coats of gesso were smoothed to as perfect a surface as possible, and then wetted piecemeal to moisten the glue and cause the gold leaf to adhere as it was applied. After allowing time for drying, the gold was burnished where required with the aid of a dog's tooth or a piece of polished agate.

Water-gilding was the method principally employed for woodwork, but it was sometimes used in conjunction with the oil process; the latter on flat surfaces that did not need to be burnished.

About 1720 the gesso surface was often ornamented by being stamped with a tool that covered it with tiny circles. Shortly after that date a granulated finish was in use; this was obtained by sprinkling sand on the wet gesso before applying the gold leaf.

Gumley, John: glass-maker and furnisher. Some knowledge of the activities of this eighteenth-century London merchant has been gained from frequent notices in the Press of his day. Gumley set up a glasshouse at Lambeth in 1705, and in the following year his showroom over the New Exchange received a commendation from the pen of Richard Steele. A mirror with the name *Gumley* carved on a small gilt plaque is at Hampton Court Palace, and another with *John Gumley 1703* is at Chatsworth. He was in partnership with James Moore, and would seem to have died some time prior to 1729, in which year accounts were rendered by *Mrs. Elizabeth Gumley & Co.*

Ince and Mayhew: cabinet-makers, who published a series of some 300 furniture designs. Entitled the *Universal System of Household Furniture*, they appeared between 1759 and 1763.

Japan and Lacquer: imported in the first instance from the Far East, japanned or lacquered furniture became extremely popular in Europe and was widely imitated. A comprehensive book dealing with the methods of copying the Oriental product appeared in 1688, when John Stalker and George Parker published their *Treatise of Japanning and Varnishing*. Lacquer was not only embellished with painting on the surface, but was also incised with designs; this latter being known as 'Bantam' or 'Coromandel' lacquer. Both types of lacquer work were used in the framing of mirrors. Mostly the lacquering was done in England, but examples are known that were made from Oriental panels, cut to the required size and fitted on a framework.

Jensen, Gerreit (known also as Garrett or Gerrard Johnson): cabinet-maker and 'glasse-seller', who supplied much furniture to the Royal Household from 1680. A tall mirror at Hampton Court tallies with the description on his bill rendered in 1699, and it is assumed that Jensen had the monopoly of supplying overmantel mirrors and pier-glasses to the royal palaces during the reign of William and Mary. The date of his birth is unknown, but his will was dated 1715 and he retired from business in that year.

Johnson, Thomas: designer and wood-carver of London. He published a volume entitled *Twelve Girandoles* in 1755, and a more ambitious work, *One Hundred and Fifty New Designs*, between 1756 and 1758. Johnson's designs are very fanciful, and appear to be almost incapable of realization, however he boasted that they 'may all be performed by a master of his art'. A mirror at the Victoria & Albert Museum (Plate 111C) corresponds with one of his designs, as do a pair of mirrors at Corsham Court, Wiltshire. It is assumed that he worked to his own patterns, but it cannot be taken for granted that anything coinciding with his designs was necessarily from his own hand.

Kent, William (1686–1748): an architect who also planned the landscaping of gardens, painted pictures and was one of the first of his profession to lavish as much care on the interior of a house as he did on the building of it. He was an exponent of the Palladian style, and his name has been given to the mirrors with frames of 'architectural' type that were fashionable in the years 1730–40.

Linnell, John: cabinet-maker and carver, many of whose designs for mirrors and other furnishings have been preserved and are in the Victoria & Albert Museum. He worked in the period 1760–90, and his designs are mainly in the prevailing 'Chippendale' style. He executed work at several of the country mansions that were then building or being refurnished, including Shardeloes, Bramshill and Castle Howard.

Lock, Matthias: a designer who published a number of books of furniture designs between the years 1740 and 1769. He collaborated with H. Copland, and modern research has led to the suggestion that these two men were the true creators of the 'Chippendale' style and were responsible for many of the plates in Thomas Chippendale's *Director*. A number of original drawings by Matthias Lock are in the Victoria & Albert Museum.

Makers and Designers: It is difficult after the lapse of two centuries or more to differentiate between designers, dealers and actual makers of mirrors and mirror-frames. There would seem to have been much intermingling of these three functions, and it is generally not possible to state who did make any particular specimen. This is particularly the case where a designer and carver published his patterns, which were then available for anyone to copy.

In some instances original bills have been preserved, in others the designs of frames have been traced to their originators and in a very few instances the name of the maker (or supplier?) is found on the piece. (*See* Chippendale, Gibbons, Gumley, Ince and Mayhew, Jensen, Johnson, Kent, Linnell, Lock and Moore.)

Mansell, Sir Robert: a financier who organized the English glass industry in the first half of the seventeenth century, and who eventually controlled glasshouses all over the country. He imported skilled workers from Murano, and successfully made mirror-glass.

Moore, James (? 1670–1726): cabinet-maker, in partnership with John Gumley from 1714. Moore is known to have made much furniture decorated with gilt gesso, on some of which his name is incised. He was concerned in the furnishing of Blenheim, and it is assumed that some gilt pier-glasses and tables there were made and supplied by him.

Stumpwork: a type of fine needlework of which much is in relief; figures, etc, being made to stand out by a stuffing of wool or cotton-wool. Caskets were covered with this type of work, and small mirrors were set within panels of it laid down on a wood framework.

Vauxhall: a manufactory of plate-glass was commenced here about 1665 by George Villiers, second Duke of Buckingham. John Bellingham approached the Duke with a secret process for making mirrors, and as a result the Vauxhall factory was started and Bellingham was given the post of manager. Glasshouses continued to operate in Vauxhall until the end of the eighteenth century, and old mirror-plates are often referred to today as 'Vauxhall'.

Verre Églomisé: glass decorated at the back with designs in colour and gold and silver foils. It is a method that has been practised for many hundreds of years, but for some reason is named after an art-collector, J. B. Glomy, who died in France in 1786. Borders of *verre églomisé* in arabesque patterns and with coats-of-arms were used to frame mirrors *c.* 1695 (Plate 109c).

BOOKS FOR FURTHER READING

Almost every book on English furniture devotes both space and illustrations to mirrors. *The Dictionary of English Furniture*, revised by RALPH EDWARDS, 3 vols., 1954, treats the subject comprehensively and illustrates over a hundred examples.

GLASS CANDELABRA AND LUSTRES

By JAMES MELTON

THE strength, yet fairy-like grace of glass makes it ideally suitable for the bearing of candles, wax or electric. Among the first to realize this fact were the Venetians, the foremost glassmakers for many hundreds of years, who made the first chandeliers of the material in the seventeenth century. The French, in costly imitation, made theirs of pure rock-crystal. English versions of these extravagances, the crystal hung on frames of silver, survive today at Hampton Court Palace and elsewhere. George Ravenscroft's development of lead-crystal glass in the last decades of the seventeenth century resulted in the production of a material that lent itself perfectly to every purpose for which glass might be employed. Not the least of its uses was in the making of light-fittings of all types, the brilliance of the glass increasing the power of that comparatively feeble illuminant – the candle. Before the succeeding century was far advanced, the English had ousted all other nations in supplying articles of glass of almost every kind; notable exceptions being plate- and mirror-glass, which the French were able to manufacture in larger sizes.

The English chandelier is not known with any certainty to date before the 1740s, but it is suggested that there may well have been an earlier introduction. The fact that chandeliers of rock-crystal were in the country (there is a record of 'Two chrissal branches' dating from 1650) must have been known to all who were interested in decoration. It would seem most improbable that much time would elapse before copies of them were being made in the closely similar material.

Although the earliest surviving glass chandeliers of English make are not dated earlier than about 1740–50, this fact cannot preclude there having been older examples. It is unfortunate that the discovered evidence of their existence is slight, but there is always the possibility of some further contemporary record being brought forth or, unlikely but not to be discounted entirely, that a surviving chandelier may be found. They were subject to quick changes of fashion as much as other decorative accessories, and would have been liable to be relegated at any time; but it was when gas-lighting was introduced for domestic use in the mid-nineteenth century that those which could not be adapted to the new illuminant must have been discarded in large numbers. If pre-1740 glass chandeliers ever were made, there can be little doubt that they must then have been destroyed, leaving little or no trace of their existence.

CHANDELIERS

1740–50

The very few chandeliers that can be ascribed to the period 1740–50 are of simple design, with curved arms and a series of spheres, half-spheres and baluster-shaped ornaments on the central shaft. The grease-pans are of a moulded pattern, nozzles and arms usually quite plain, but the components of the stem decorated with simple cutting. The general appearance, with the exception of the faceting of the parts of the shaft, is remarkably similar to that of a brass chandelier of earlier date. The fact that brass chandeliers of simple Dutch style were made with few changes from 1670 until as late as 1730 has led to a suggestion that glass chandeliers of the type described may possibly be of an earlier date than 1740–50, but this has not been confirmed.

1750–70

The mid-eighteenth century saw the sweeping success of rococo in every branch of the arts. The chandelier was affected no less than was everything else, and the style, commonly known as 'Chinese-Chippendale', is remarked as obviously in glassware as in cabinet-work and porcelain. Top and base of the chandelier acquired pagoda-like canopies from which cut drops were suspended; the grease-pans became shaped at the edges and cut with patterns and bevelling, and the arms themselves received attention from the cutter as well, bearing their share of pendent drops. Drops were hung also from the pierced points of the grease-pans, and tall spires, sometimes topped with small canopies and 'Turkish' crescents, were placed vertically between the arms.

1770–1800

With the supremacy of Classical styles, introduced and fostered by Robert Adam, came further changes in the appearance of the chandelier. The greatest alteration was in the general form, which grew longer in relation to its width. At the same time the 'ball', so long the principal feature of the central shaft, was replaced by an ornament in the shape of an urn, decorated with cutting and sometimes made in two parts. Additional decoration was in the form of strings of drops, which were placed wherever it was possible to find room for them. By the end of the period it had become quite unnecessary to adorn the arms with cutting, for they were scarcely to be seen in the midst of the welter of glass drapery that surrounded them.

1800–30

By the turn of the century the design of the chandelier began to change completely. The central shaft was no longer encased in glass, but was hidden completely by a screen of long strings of drops. The short arms sprang from a circular band of a larger diameter than the top, and the base was composed of further strings of drops meeting at a central boss. It was described as being of 'tent' or 'bag' shape. The effect aimed at was that achieved in a famous chandelier supplied to the Prince Regent (when Prince of Wales) by Perry and Parker in 1808. This was said to be 'designed to represent a fountain falling into a large reservoir'.

The fantastic chandelier made for the same royal patron by the same firm in 1817 is not dissimilar in general form from other chandeliers of the date, but is embellished with a wealth of Oriental ornament: the lotus-leaf shades round the perimeter being supported by dragon's legs and the whole suspended from the ceiling in the claws of a realistic silvered dragon. This chandelier was seen in 1820 by Princess Lieven (wife of the Russian ambassador), who was visiting the Pavilion at Brighton with the Duke of York. She wrote in a letter: 'We were shown a chandelier which cost eleven thousand pounds sterling – I write it out in full because it is really incredible. The chandelier is in the form of a tulip held by a dragon'. The information given to the Princess is not confirmed by records, which show that this, the principal, chandelier and four smaller ones in the same room cost a total sum of £5,613 9*s*.

Lastly came the chandelier composed of concentric rings of prisms, aptly named 'finger-fringes'. Many of these were designed by J. B. Papworth and made by John Blades of London. It was said that Papworth set a very high standard for any work executed to his order, and if it should fail to reach this excellence it was immediately destroyed under his supervision.

SCONCES AND WALL-LIGHTS

Mirror-backed sconces, very occasionally with glass arms, were in use early in the eighteenth century. They were followed by glass wall-lights of similar design to the chandeliers which were then in vogue. Much the same general changes in style may be observed in the one and the other. Both sconces and wall-lights are scarce today, and the fact that they were so much more accessible than a chandelier may account for many having been damaged and discarded. However, they do not seem to have been as popular as gilt-wood wall-lights, and their present rarity may be accounted for by the possibility that comparatively few were made.

CANDELABRA

Glass candelabra date from the mid-eighteenth century, and again they followed the styles of chandeliers. The same ornaments are to be found on them: stars, crescents, snakes, spires and drops of all shapes and sizes. In the 1770s the vase motif appeared, and space was found sometimes for a classical *patera*, engraved in the glass base or painted on it. Wedgwood's jasper-ware was used to make drum-shaped bases, set in ormolu and embellished with glass. Often confused with this was William Adams' jasper, which served the same purpose and can barely be distinguished from that of his more famous contemporary.

In the Regency, candelabra tended to incorporate ormolu in their construction and decoration, as did the chandeliers of the time, and the glass parts were heavily patterned with elaborate cutting. Ormolu and bronze candelabra were also decorated with glass drops at this date, and the glitter of these additions was added to that of the chased and burnished gold.

LUSTRES

In the middle of the nineteenth century the vase-lustre appeared. Neither a vase nor a candelabra, this was purely a decorative use for glass. Few mantelpieces of the period lacked one at either end, and while many were of poor quality for sale at cheap prices, others were as finely finished as the glassware of a century before.

GLOSSARY

Adams, William (1745–1805): potter, pupil and friend of Josiah Wedgwood (q.v.). Adams helped Wedgwood to perfect and manufacture his famous jasper-ware, and in 1786 opened a factory of his own, Greengates Pottery, at Tunstall in Staffordshire. There he made all types of pottery including jasper, much of the latter being scarcely distinguishable from that of Wedgwood. One of Adams's specialities would seem to have been drums for the bases of candlesticks and candelabra, and as in most cases these are either unmarked or the mark is hidden under a metal mount, they are often mistaken for the work of Wedgwood. In *William Adams: An Old English Potter*, edited by W. Turner (1904), several pairs of the Adams drums are described and illustrated (Plate 115C).

Arm: the 'S'-shaped bearer of grease-pan (q.v.) and nozzle (q.v.), in the latter of which is held the candle. Arms were plain at first and then became the subject of much cut-work, but when the profusion of drops began to obscure almost everything except the candles, they became plainer once again. In the 1800–30 period they were seldom of glass, and were made of gilt metal as a part of the central band of the chandelier.

Betts, Thomas: London glass-seller in business from about 1738 until 1765. On his trade-card he describes himself as: 'Thos. Betts GLASS-CUTTER At ye King's Arm's Glass-Shop, Opposite Pall Mall, Charring Cross'. Among other things he stated that he sold 'Lustres', and that his work was 'Cheaper and Better than hitherto has been done. He being the Real Workman, for many Years'. From which it may be inferred that Betts was the actual cutter and finisher of the goods displayed in his shop. He is known to have died in 1767.

Blades, John: glass-seller of 5 Ludgate Hill, London. He was styled 'Glass Manufacturer to His Majesty King George III'. About 1820 he worked to the designs of John Papworth (q.v.) and made many of his chandeliers.

Branch: late in the seventeenth century and during the first half of the eighteenth, this word was used sometimes to describe a chandelier. That indefatigable traveller Celia Fiennes saw one at Hampton Court Palace early in Queen Anne's reign. She noted: '. . . thence into the dineing roome where hangs in the middle a chrystall branch for candles . . .'. By the mid-eighteenth century the sense of the word would seem to have changed, for Jerom Johnson (q.v.), the glass-seller, advertised for sale '. . . brilliant Lustres, Branches . . .'. A confusing statement in view of the fact that 'Lustre' was a term used also to describe a chandelier.

Canopy: an umbrella-shaped ornament placed at the top and the base of most chandeliers, etc, from 1750 until the end of the century. The points at the circumference were usually drilled for the attachment of pendent drops. Small canopies were often placed at the top of decorative glass spires, which were stood vertically between the arms.

Chandelier: the word was used sometimes in the sense of candelabra or 'table-chandelier'. One of the first noted uses of it in the modern sense, to describe a centrally placed light-fitting with arms, was in 1725. In that year an inventory of the contents of Canons, near Edgware, Middlesex (seat of James Brydges, first Duke of Chandos), listed 'four glass chanderleres'. The word did not come into general use for some time, and the article was referred to variously for the next twenty-five years as a branch (q.v.), a lustre (q.v.) or as a chandelier.

Collett, Jonathan: successor to the business of Thomas Betts (q.v.) in 1765, when the latter retired. Collett is known to have supplied a number of chandeliers for the Assembly Rooms, Bath. These were found to be unsatisfactory, and were replaced by those hanging there today, made by William Parker (q.v.) in 1770–1.

Glass: the material used for the making of English chandeliers and other light-fittings was 'lead-glass' or 'flint-glass', developed by George Ravenscroft (1618–81), who was conducting research on the subject for the Glass-sellers' Company of London during the years 1673 to 1676. This replaced the earlier type of glass with which the English had been unable to compete with Continental products. As a result of Ravenscroft's work, it was found that the incorporation of potash and litharge (oxide of lead), together with calcined flints, in the formula made a glass superior to any from abroad. This 'lead' or 'flint' glass, with its deep transparency, was extremely suitable for cutting, the faceted surfaces increasing its glittering beauty.

Grease-pan: the circular dish beneath the nozzle (q.v.) into which grease from the burning candle might drip. Grease-pans were of moulded pattern with plain edges in the early chandeliers, but by 1750 were of extravagant shapes. The latter were elaborately cut and their pointed rims were drilled and hung with drops.

Johnson, Jerom: London glass-seller who was in business between about 1739 and 1761. His specialities are known from advertisements in the newspapers of his day, and from which it has been deduced that he must have been a prominent man in his trade. A typical announcement of 1752 ran:

> 'For Glass Engraving or Flow'ring, Cutting, Scolloping, and finest Polishing upon Glass in General. At the intire GLASS-SHOP, over-against the New Exchange, in the Strand, IS to be sold all sorts of fine Flint Glasses, brilliant Lustres, Branches, Candlesticks, Dishes, Plates, Bowls, Basons, Cups, and Covers, Saucers, Saltsellars, cut Bottles, Decanters, Rummers, cut and flowered, Desart Glasses of all sorts; scollop'd or engraved Salvers; large Glasses for Cool-Tankards; Cruets and Castors; curious Lamps, wash hand Glasses, most curiously engraved, new-fashion'd or scollop'd; and finest polish'd Moques, and Pitchers, Turkish-fashion Diamond-cut, and Brilliant polish'd, Wholesale and Retail, at the most reasonable Rates, and besure no where else cheaper, in London, being the first Inventor. JEROM JOHNSON.'

Five years later he proposed closing the retail side of his business and announced:

> 'GLASS-SHOP the Corner of St Martin's-Lane, Strand. ALL the Glasses, and Stock in Trade, are to be sold off cheap,

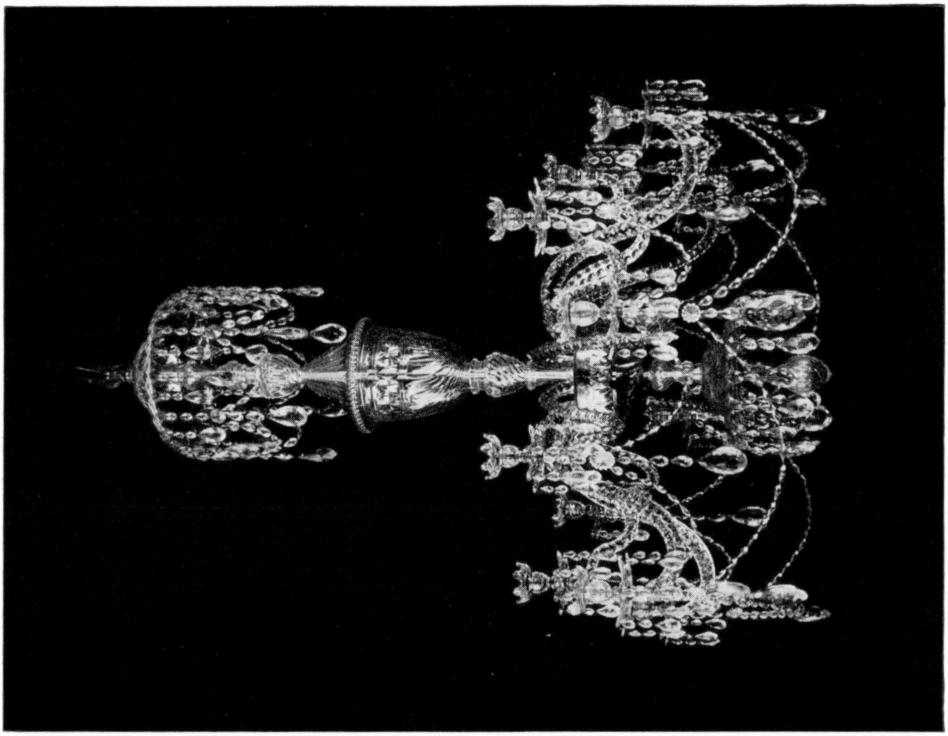

(B) Chandelier showing the classical influence of Robert Adam, a typical feature being the central urn. About 1775. *Delomosne & Son Ltd.*

(A) Chandelier of rococo 'Chinese-Chippendale' design, dating from about 1765. Probably made by Parker of Fleet Street. *Victoria & Albert Museum.*

PLATE 113

(A and B) A most unusual 'bag' or 'tent' shaped chandelier with twelve candleholders round the outside and six within, the base lowering to give access to the latter. About 1810. *Delomosne & Son Ltd.*

(C) Chandelier in the Banqueting Room at Brighton Pavilion. Supplied by Parker and Perry in 1817.

(D) Chandelier with 'finger-fringe' rings of prism drops. About 1830. *Cecil Davis.*

(A) Set of four wall-lights. About 1770. *Delomosne & Son Ltd.*

(B) Candelabrum with canopy surmounting the spire and with 'snakes' set behind the arms. About 1780. *Delomosne & Son Ltd.*

(C) Candelabrum with ormolu-mounted base of Wedgwood or Adams jasper-ware. About 1790. *Cecil Davis.*

(A) Pair of candelabra about 1820, showing the elaboration of the cutting and the employment of ormolu. *Delomosne & Son Ltd.*

(B) Bronze-and-ormolu candelabrum with glass grease-pans, finial and drops. About 1820. *Delomosne & Son Ltd.*

(C) Vase-lustre, of ruby glass with white overlay decorated with cutting, painting and gilding. Mid-nineteenth century. *J. Morland Coon & Son.*

viz. Wine-Glasses at 2s. per Dozen and 4s. the very best; and all the Cut Glasses, Lustres, Lamps, Deserts, Salts, Dishes, Plates, Flowered Glasses, Decanters, &c. in short, the third Part cheaper than usually sold.

'After all are sold, shall remove to the Cock-Pit White Flint Glass-House, near the Falcon-Stairs, Southwark; where I shall beg the favour of the Continuance of my former Customers in the Wholesale Way, By their humble Servant, JEROM JOHNSON.'

From the frequency and style of his advertisements there can be little doubt that Johnson was in the forefront of his business, but it cannot be decided on this evidencc what part, if any, he may have played in shaping the taste of the glass-buying public of his day.

Lustre: nowadays a vase with everted rim from which hang cut-glass drops. At one period it was used to describe a chandelier, and in 1739 Jerom Johnson (q.v.), the glass-seller, advertised for sale 'the most magnificent lustre that was ever made in England'.

The vase-lustre was made in pairs, and came into vogue in the middle of the nineteenth century. Few English houses would appear to have been without at least one pair, and their quality varied in proportion to the fortune of the owner. The most esteemed were of ruby or green glass with an overlay of white, and decoration, in addition to the cutting, in the form of painted flowers or miniature portraits in colours, and gilding (Plate 116C). They were made in Bohemia (now Czechoslovakia), but considerable numbers were manufactured in England, at Stourbridge and elsewhere.

Nozzle: the socket in which the candle is held. Early nozzles were of straight-sided (simple tube) pattern, and un-cut. By the end of the eighteenth century they had become of thistle and other shapes and bore their full share of elaborate cut ornament.

Ornamentation: the earliest lighting glassware was very plain; the transparent material was moulded into suitable shapes and no further embellishment was called for by the taste of the time. By the 1740s the smooth surfaces had begun to acquire ribs and mouldings, and the first appearance of cutting is to be noted. Once begun, this increased in profusion as the century progressed and every change in artistic taste was followed faithfully. The rococo excesses of the 'Chippendale' period were admirably reflected by chandeliers and wall-lights and candelabra resplendent with cascades of small faceted drops, with glittering cutting on every part that showed, and with the prevailing admiration for *Chinoiserie* exhibited in the pagoda-like canopies from which many of the drops were suspended (Plate 113A).

Robert Adam caused a change in the shaping of every article of merit while he held his sway. From being squarish in form, the chandelier became more tall than wide, and the central 'ball' became the familiar Grecian urn. The classical feeling that was so widely admired was further to be seen in table-lights with Wedgwood-style bases, or with severely plain plinths cut with a simple *patera* (Plate 115C).

By the turn of the century a new style of chandelier was in evidence: the central column was no longer visible but bulged out into a 'bag' or 'tent' composed of thousands of small drops, and the glass arms were replaced by metal ones. Instead of the nearly invisible metal supports of former years the gilt-bronze framework was made to play its part in the appearance of the chandelier, and its decorative qualities were put to full use. On other light-fittings of the time glass was often used far less, and bronze and ormolu became the main features, with the glass playing a subsidiary role.

With the introduction of the 'finger-fringe' of hanging glass drops came the wide use of the prism. At first these were mainly with squared or rounded ends, but they later acquired a knop and a spear-point, or were cut with scallops along the edges (Plate 114D).

The successful use of gas as an illuminant, and its replacement of candles and oil, caused the chandelier to become the main lighting feature of a room. Glass table-lights atrophied into ornamental lustres: articles that are a cross between a vase and a candlestick but are the legitimate descendants of neither.

Papworth, John Buonarotti (1775–1847): an architect whose popularity and versatility were such that he did not confine his attention solely to buildings. He painted in water-colours, and designed book illustrations, furniture, silverware and gardens. He designed a glass throne for the Shah of Persia, and is considered to have been responsible for the introduction of chandeliers composed of long 'prism' drops arranged in concentric rings. Many of these were made by John Blades (q.v.), of 5 Ludgate Hill, London, for whose business premises Papworth designed the front.

Parker and Perry: suppliers of light-fittings. The firm was started by William Parker at 69 Fleet Street, London, in 1756. Soon afterwards he took a partner and the firm was styled Parker and Perry. In 1817 premises were taken in New Bond Street, and the style was again changed; this time to Perry & Co. Many drawings made of chandeliers supplied by Parker and Perry in the eighteenth and nineteenth centuries, together with the names of the purchasers and the prices paid, have been preserved. From them it has been possible to deduce something of the successive changes of style that took place in the design of light fittings.

Parker and Perry supplied chandeliers to the Prince Regent between 1789 and 1820, when Carlton House was being furnished, and some of these are now at Buckingham Palace. Chandeliers supplied by the firm when Brighton Pavilion was built include those at present in the Banqueting Room and the Music Room. The central chandelier in the former was made in 1817, weighs not much short of a ton, and together with four smaller ones for the same room cost over £5,000 (Plate 114C).

The meeting-place of the élite of the eighteenth century, the Assembly Rooms at Bath contain some well-known chandeliers, of which one has 'PARKER FLEET STREET, LONDON' engraved on one of the spherical ornaments on the central stem.

Shaft (stem): the central part of a chandelier. This was built up on a metal rod, usually silvered to make it less noticeable, and comprised spheres, baluster-shaped pieces and canopies, together with the bowl containing a metal plate in which the arms were fitted.

Waterford: the Excise Act of 1745 prohibited the export of glassware from Ireland, and it was not until 1780 that trade with England in this commodity was permitted. The well-known Waterford glass factory opened three years later and, in spite of the fact that this is definitely known, is constantly fathered with glass of types that must have been many years prior to that date. The factory was staffed with craftsmen recruited from England, and if chandeliers ever were made there they cannot be distinguished from those from other sources.

Wedgwood, Josiah (1730–95): potter. His world-famous jasper-ware was perfected in 1774, and amongst the innumerable objects made in it may be numbered pairs of small drums for mounting as the bases of candlesticks and candelabra. These were made also by Wedgwood's pupil and friend, William Adams (q.v.).

CHEST FURNITURE

By THERLE HUGHES

TRAVELLING CHESTS

WHEN Charlotte, Princess of Savoy travelled in 1483 her personal luggage filled more than forty chests and coffers; Elizabeth I's retinue counted them by the hundred in her royal progresses. 'Our ancestors' taste for substantialness', that appalled Mrs. Lybbe Powis in 1757, was never more impressively demonstrated than in the chests and coffers, trunks and portmanteaux, standards and arks and fosselets, that delight and bewilder today's collectors. But one has only to read old English inventories – any household, any century – to appreciate the incalculable numbers of lesser specimens that these remaining treasures inadequately and untypically represent. In the 1585 inventory of William Shelley of Michelgrove, Sussex, for instance, the furniture included no fewer than twenty chests. In his wardrobe alone Sir William Ingilby of Ripley in 1617 kept 'one portmanteaux, 3 ould trunkes besides the trunke that keep Sir William's apparrell, an ould counter and 2 great chestes'.

Chest is a term that has been applied to a number of articles more or less box-shaped and opening with a rising lid. Records of the craftsmen who made chest furniture and of the guilds and companies, the churches and great houses, that used them, all contribute terms and definitions but constantly contradict each other. In this survey of chest furniture, this wide application of the word chest is accepted. Even as late as 1730 Bailey's dictionary made no attempt to be specific: a coffer was a chest or trunk, a chest was 'a sort of box, coffer or trunk'. Addison in 1700 used the term for a basket, 'a chest of twining osiers', such as one must assume Lady Grisell Baillie meant by her Dutch basket 'for my cloathes' in 1693. Moreover, chests in their hey-day served a multitude of purposes. Throughout the Middle Ages a man's possessions travelled with him, but when he settled down the chests in which they were packed or trussed became the furniture that displayed them. In later sections of this volume other types of chest furniture are reviewed, but it must be recognized that they, too, had a part-purpose in serving the traveller, whilst what may be regarded as specific travelling chests became accepted home furnishings.

The very word trunk indicates how early and primitive were men's first attempts to make stronger luggage than skin-covered osier baskets. A few ancient dug-outs remain, usually of oak, occasionally, as in Ackington Church, Worcestershire, of elm. The oldest dug-outs were succeeded first by the carpenter's hammered-up constructions, then gradually by the joiner's framed work until the cabinet, the chest at its most refined and most perfectly individualistic, became recognized as the most highly skilled creation in the whole craft of woodworking. But for the travel chest in particular the ancient rounded top of the dug-out was preserved. Since to truss was a familiar word meaning to pack or bundle goods, the traveller's chest was probably most frequently specified by the prefix 'trussing'. Numerous references may be found to trussing chests, such as in 1540, in an Act of Henry VIII. In the early seventeenth-century Howard Accounts, with their frequent references to freight, boat-hire and portage of luggage between London and the North, trunks and trunk chests appeared accepted terms.

The other term particularly associated with travelling chests is coffer. The cofferer was long recognized as the craftsman who covered chests and other furniture with leather. As early as 1483 the Guild of Cofferers protested against the competition of imported Flanders chests, and, until late in the eighteenth century, coffer-makers were listed among the officers of the royal household. But in common usage the term appears generally to have indicated a wide variety of strongly built chests, and will find further mention in later sections.

Boarded Chests: early, poor alternatives to the framed or jointed chest, the horizontal planks of wood forming the front and back being hammered to the vertical end-pieces or flush with heavy corner stiles, and frequently reinforced with corner-pieces of iron. As wood tends to shrink across the grain, the result was never satisfactory, and the horizontal planks usually show signs of splitting. Oak might be used, or planks of elm, large and comparatively little given to warping. The flush construction as contrasted with the loose panels of the mortise-and-tenon jointed chest offered a smooth surface for covering with leather or hair cloth.

Busse Chests: buscarles' or seamen's chests.

Close Nailing: brass convex-headed nails of a darkish tint of brass hammered with great exactitude by the cofferer, head beside head, were used all around the edges of the leather-covered chest and in sufficient numbers over the body of the piece to avoid any loose flapping of the inelastic cover. Similar treatment was given to hair cloth.

Coffers: a term that must be considered also in connexion with Plate Chests, but has always had particular association with the leather-covered travelling chest, the work of the cofferer. Randall Holme, in 1662, made the distinction that a coffer was called a chest if it had a straight and flat cover, a chest being like a coffer 'save the want of a circular lid or cover'.

Fitted Chests: coach travel became more popular and widespread in the seventeenth century, the experienced traveller taking his own fitted chest or case containing drinking glasses and square glass bottles, or a silver dining set consisting of a nest of tumblers, and knife, fork and spoons. Some eighteenth-century cases contained porcelain tea equipages (Plate 117). Doctors travelled with essential surgeons' chests, and craftsmen with tool chests that represented their livelihood.

Hair Cloth: cloth woven with horse-hair was strong and rain-repellent, and was used like leather to cover wooden travelling chests and trunks. As it had no elasticity in the weft threads, it was close-nailed like leather. There is reference in the *Verney Memoirs*, 1653, to 'yelowe haire sumpter trunkes'. Some seventeenth-century writers specified fustian, others merely cloth to cover trunks, sometimes scarlet and even crest-embroidered, requiring an outer casing of leather. In the later eighteenth century hair cloth was available in a wide range of colours and stripes, and many a hair trunk studded with brass rosettes in a somewhat medieval manner was manufactured for the rough and tumble of coach travel in the early nineteenth century.

Hinges: *pin hinges* – the early medieval chest might have a rather clumsy pivot arrangement for opening the canted lid. A pair of horizontal pivots worked in slots cut in the back stiles of the chest. Often small iron plates were introduced, to protect the pivots. *Strap hinges* – these, of iron, were usual after the end of the thirteenth century.

Leather: cowhide close-nailed was the most usual covering for travelling chests, both standards and trussing coffers. Early leather might be enamelled and gilded, imported from Spain and Holland until an Englishman, Christopher, discovered their methods in 1638. Leather treated with oil and spirits was known as *cuir bouilli*, the applications rendering it supple enough to take incised ornament in addition to paint and gilding. The *Dictionary of Furniture* lists Richard Pegge, coffer-maker to Charles II, and Edward Smith, 1750–60, among suppliers of trunks to the royal household, covered in Russia leather (scented with oil of birch-bark). Pegge's were supplied with and without drawers, and included such details as one lined with sarcenet and quilted, and two covered with sealskin and bound with girdles of ox leather.

Linings: trunk lining became a specialized job, and in travelling chests particularly the work was important if the chest contents were to be protected from the drifts of dust that constituted roads and the rushes and rubbish scattered over flagstones or wooden flooring. Linen has always had terminological association with lining, and was the most suitable fabric until eighteenth-century cotton became strong and closely woven enough to be considered as a possible alternative. Paper, hand-made and soft textured, soon rubbed, but was widely used. It may be of particular interest to the collector; for sheets of unsaleable books were used when available, the plain backs printed in wood-block patterns.

Metal-work: travelling chests were frequently iron-bound, sometimes almost covered in iron; but these may be regarded as travelling safes and receive further consideration under the section on Plate Chests. The close nailing that protected the leather covering was reinforced with corner-straps, and often with a massive and handsome lockplate, early work being shaped cold by sawing like wood. Pepys mentioned in 1662 that 'we were forced to send for a smith, to break open her trunk'. Remaining specimens tend to have replacement locks, often with hinge pins too easily removed or damaged for any security.

Panelled Chests: typified joiners' as distinct from carpenters' furniture. The horizontal rails and vertical stiles and muntins that formed the framework to the loose panels of the chest were held together by mortise-and-tenon joints, allowing the wood to respond to atmospheric changes. Joiners' work in 1632 was defined to include dovetail joints, and the wide early style of dovetail may be noted down the corners of some chests in walnut, cypress and other woods that could be undercut in a manner impossible with oak. Plat in 1594 made reference to a 'foure square chest . . . close the sides well with dovetails or cement'. But corner dovetails in view on the outside of a chest are usually taken to indicate Continental work.

Pegged Chests: occasionally a chest is noted which can be dismantled for travelling or store by removing wooden pegs in the style of many early table trestles. Some are authenticated, but obviously the design was very much in the mood of the nineteenth-century's pseudo-medievalism.

Portmanteaux: a term introduced about the mid-sixteenth century, applied to cases specifically for horse travel yet large enough for bulky clothing. In the 1620s, for instance, the Howard Accounts refer to a leather portmanteau priced 10*s.* 1*d.*, and in 1611 Cotgrave noted 'a portmantue with chaine and locke'. There are numerous references to portmanteau saddles, even to portmanteau horses, in the seventeenth and eighteenth centuries. Thus the *London Gazette* referred to 'a coloured leather Portmantle Saddle'. Such a saddle, according to Randall Holme, had 'a Cantle behind the seat to keep the Portmantle . . . off the Rider's back'.

Royal Crown on Travelling Chests: this may be found in close nailing or engraved on metal fittings, and is often assumed to indicate personal association with a monarch. It is thought more likely to indicate that the chest may have been used on Government service or by one of the palaces.

Standards: when a wealthy family travelled, their household goods might be conveyed in huge leather-covered, iron-bound, vividly painted standards. Here again is a term that must receive consideration also among other types of chest furniture.

Sumpter Trunks: a usual term for the pairs of travelling chests carried by sumpter- or baggage-horses or mules, or in the late eighteenth-century sumpter cars. Lady Grisell Baillie paid four pounds for a pair in 1715. Sumpter-horses were comparable with pack-horses. Bailey, in 1730, defined a pack as a horse-load of wool – about 240 pounds. Sumpter-cloths frequently bore the crest or cipher of their owner.

Tills: forerunners of the fitted tray in a modern trunk. Inside many a seventeenth-century chest a small tray was fitted on the right near the lid. Sometimes it was itself lidded, the lid hingeing into the framework of the chest; sometimes it was locked and occasionally had a false-bottomed hiding-place. Catharine of Aragon in 1534 had 'one cofar having four tilles therin, the forefronte of every one of them gilte'. The lidded box-like tills in a chest might be called drawing chests or drawers, although the chest-of-drawers, as a considerable piece of bedroom furniture and as distinct from a cabinet of tiny drawers, was evolved only in the seventeenth century. Thus, in 1599, Minshen referred to 'a great chest or standard with drawing chests or boxes in it'.

Trenails or Treenails: the old term for the cylindrical pins of hardwood used for fastening timber together, mentioned for instance in an inventory of 1571: 'iij houndrethe treenales viijd'. Square wooden pins might be used green, driven into round holes for greater firmness.

Trunks: probably the most common term for a travelling chest, leather-covered and with a rounded top to suffer as little as possible from wet weather. It was used in association with a number of terms regarding such chests. Thus the brass convex-headed nail used by the cofferer was a trunk nail, and there was a trunk saddle recorded as early as 1569. Moxon in 1677 distinguished between trunk locks, chest locks and padlocks.

Trussing Coffers: a frequent term for leather-covered travelling chests, usually implying smaller articles than standards; as, for instance, was indicated in a reference of 1622: 'Commodities packt up in Bundels, Trusses, Cases, Coffers or Packes.'

WRITING-BOXES

Early cabinets were mainly for the dilettanti. The majority of those who worked with their heads as well as their hands sought simpler means of keeping their office work within bounds, using what Cooper in 1584 (*Bibliotheca Eliotae*) defined as 'a littell holowe desk lyke a coffer whereypon men do write'. Old letters and inventories time and time again refer to the small portable desk that rested on a chest or table in the study or parlour, such as the 'wryghtyng box of syprese' in the *Paston Letters*, 1471. They were usually minor pieces; in 1586 Ralph Ewrie of Edgnolle, Co. Durham, had 'j wood deske 2d'. In 1587 William Jeneson, a Newcastle merchant, had two desks valued at 6*s*. 6*d*. in his hall to supplement a 'great counter' valued at 16*s*., three painted coffers and '2 bound coffers for writings, 10s'. The 1545 inventory of Marketon, Derbyshire, gives a vivid little picture of a well-equipped study:

'It' a red cofer bownd with yeron, with evidences, iiijs.
It' a payr balns and a pyle of troye weights vjs.
It' desk a sandbox and a payr golde ballanz xxd.
It' a Standyssh for pen ynk etc of fyrre xxd.
It' a wrytynn bord couered and ij forms j cusshyn ijs. iiijd.
It' a payr table of slate and a combe case ijs.'

In the sixteenth century only a very few specimens of English craftsmanship were ornate in the Continental manner, painted inside and fitted with compartments, like the 'desque with a Cabonett therein of crimson velvet laced xls', in the Earl of Northampton's inventory (1614). Not until late in the seventeenth century were larger units of furniture developed in any quantity comparable with modern desks, bookcases and filing cabinets. Thus, throughout the centuries dominated, though not monopolized, by oak furniture with its carving and panelling, inlays and glued embossments, its emphasis on massive effects in ornaments and mouldings and iron mounts, the writing-box was the one piece of furniture more specialized than a plain chest for a man of the standing of squire or farmer or lesser merchant. Here he kept his papers and his few, heavy books, and inscribed his records in the family Bible. It is this personal association with past owners that gives writing-boxes their peculiar appeal.

As they were placed on tables or chests, they were ornamented on all sides, but usually lacked legs, being based on wide convex mouldings. Such a box, perhaps as much as 2 feet 6 inches or 3 feet wide, frequently, though not always, had a sloping lid, the slope slight in early specimens, and the hinge at the top, desk fashion. In some instances a shallow box for quills or ink with a separate lid was included in the design, to the right of the main writing-box and mounted on the same reeded base moulding. By the later seventeenth century the style was changing, with a more steeply sloping front that might be hinged at the bottom to open down for writing with the interior fittings accessible. These at their most elaborate included small drawers with concave fronts shaped from the solid wood flanking pigeon-holes, and a central domed cupboard perhaps with secret compartments behind its tiny decorative pilasters. In the provinces it continued in popular use throughout the eighteenth century, and in Wales in particular its individuality has been demonstrated in an exceptionally handsome style of country furniture. But many more were sophisticated little pieces. *The Cabinet-Makers' London Book of Prices* (1788) put a price of 30*s*. for a traveller's specimen fitted for shaving as well as for writing.

By the beginning of the nineteenth century every kind of compendium, for the writer, artist, needlewoman was being made as dainty and elaborate as highly competitive ingenuity could devise. Thus by the mid-nineteenth century there were yew-tree writing-boxes with fittings of ebony and mounts of bronze, ebony boxes with 'medieval mounts', and every kind of lavish but finely made compendium under the general classification of 'elegancies for presentation'.

Bonheur du Jour: a dainty piece of furniture derived from the writing-box that enjoyed a short spell of popularity in France around 1760 and was copied in England. It suggested a shallow writing-box backed by a small cabinet and mounted on the period's slender, unencumbered legs. The top might be surrounded on back and side edges with a low ormolu gallery. When the cabinet portion rested on a slightly more extensive stand, there might be small wooden fences of spindles at its sides as letter racks (Plate 124B).

Bureaux: a term sometimes applied to writing-boxes before they became established as full-sized desks. It was derived from the colour of the rough woollen forerunner of baize commonly used for writing-tables – *burrus*, Latin for the colour of fire.

Coffor Bach: the Welsh Bible-box, peculiar to the Principality and an attractive little piece of furniture, suggesting a diminutive mule chest. The authors of *Welsh Furniture* state that it was usually made of oak or elm, occasionally inlaid with holly, and most commonly dated from the second half of the eighteenth century onwards, including many twentieth-century copies. The upper chest portion was intended for the Bible, and the two small drawers below for family papers.

Compendiums: *see* section on Cabinets.

Counters: frequent accompaniments to writing-boxes in homes of merchants and the like. In 1459 Margaret Paston wrote to her husband regarding 'your coffers and your cowntewery'. They were distinguished from other flat-topped storage chests by being scored for reckoning.

Crofts: Seddon, Sons and Shackleton in the late eighteenth century manufactured and sold an attractive little piece of desk furniture that they claimed would serve 'men of method' and particularly those who had to travel and wished not to disarrange their business papers. A small table top with D-shaped drop-flaps was fitted over a partitioned drawer with a sliding lid for writing on while the drawer was extended. Below were small drawers and partitions enclosed by a wide door. The makers claimed that corners, hinges and so on were finished so as to cause the minimum of inconvenience if the owner travelled with it in a post-chaise. Sir Ambrose Heal has traced the name to the Rev. Sir Herbert Croft, Bt., who at one time proposed to issue a revised version of Johnson's dictionary.

Cypress: hard, durable, coniferous wood almost imperishable and used for writing-boxes, coffers, etc, sometimes bearing incised ornament that suited its close grain. It was usually assembled by dovetailing.

Derbyshire Desks: term for oak writing-boxes, carved and sometimes dated.

Lace Boxes: many delightful boxes now go by this name, although their original purpose must have been less restricted. They became most conspicuous in the late seventeenth and early eighteenth centuries when bedroom furniture was being given the handsome treatment fitting the furnishings of what was often in practice an office, study and reception-room for the head of the household. These boxes frequently bore floral marquetry patterns that originally must have matched similar work on the chests of drawers they accompanied. Lace was, of course, vastly important at a period when William III could spend £290 on the lace for half a dozen razor-cloths, but obviously the shallow box had many possibilities, for the family Bible and often as a fully adequate writing-box (Plate 120B).

Ladies' Work-boxes: the implication that such boxes were solely or mainly associated with needlework is comparatively new. Even in the early nineteenth century they were usually equipped for writing, often also for drawing and painting as well as for needlework. Inkpots might be contained in a special drawer at the right side of the box that could be kept open during use. Such boxes were intended to meet their users' every imaginable need at a period when fierce competition made every manufacturer struggle for novelty and elaboration. The box might be covered in satinwood, more often pre-dating 1800, rosewood, tooled and gilt-stamped leather, tortoiseshell veneer. Fittings might be of gold and mother of pearl, the mounts brass or steel (Plate 120A).

Ornament: applied on all sides since the box might rest on a centrally placed table. It included simple repetitive carving, such as deep lobe mouldings, guilloche braids, etc; inlay in green and brown stained holly, box, sycamore and bogwoods; even intarsia work in the manner of large Nonsuch chests (p.185). The base moulding usually received careful treatment, whether in the plain wide thumb moulding of an early Stuart table or in more elaborate egg-and-tongue outline. Eighteenth-century work included the expected range of japanning and marquetry in the early years and satinwood in solid and veneer late in the century, ornamented with the marquetry ovals and fan shapes and the box and ebony stringing associated with this wood. By the early nineteenth century rosewood was supplemented by the wealth of ornament – japanning, Tunbridge ware and even glue-on varnished prints—that in early Victorian days so easily descended into tawdriness.

Papier Mâché: by the early nineteenth century writing-boxes were made in this amenable material, their highly decorative surface finish requiring only a simple design of box. The pulped paper, like the layered construction of earlier 'paper ware' made before the 1840s, was given its superb silken finish with numerous varnishings, long, slow stovings in a japanners' oven and hand rubbing with bare hands occasionally dipped in cold water. Ornament most usually took the form of flowers and butterflies, hand-painted in the crowded manner of the period (Plate 121D). Slabs of nautilus shell might be introduced by other firms, while the Birmingham japanners, Jennens and Bettridge, held the patent for grinding shell paper-thin and shaping it delicately with acid. Some boxes had a suggestion of Oriental lacquer work, part of the ornament being in raised composition covered with gilding – but never gold paint. Some were competently painted with souvenir views, such as the many Oxford scenes issued by Spiers and Son of that city.

Reed Top: whereas a large desk might open with a solid cylinder lid, a writing-box might have the space-saving opening associated with tambour tables. In this the rounded top could be pushed out of sight inside the box, being constructed of lengths of thin moulded beading glued side by side on to a back of strong canvas, pliable enough to move in curved runners.

Satinwood: some delightful writing-boxes appeared in this wood, either solid or in veneer, early imports before about 1795 being comparatively unfigured. While demand exceeded supply, sycamore and chestnut were substituted. The greenish wood known as harewood was sycamore suitably tinted. Often these little boxes were tall, the upper half rounded at the front, somewhat in the manner of contemporary knife-boxes. This uprising portion was often ornamented with a fan or shell motif, such as specialist marquetry men prepared and sold in quantity to furniture makers. Inside, the box was divided into compartments.

Screen Writing-tables: late eighteenth-century devices by Gillow and others with adjustable screens of pleated silk.

Sheverets or Chevrets: A late eighteenth-century term used by Gillow and others for small pieces of table furniture associated with writing. The back half of the top offered housing for books, while the front might open forwards to serve for writing.

Tunbridge Ware: early Tunbridge-ware writing-boxes were often in attractive parquetry patterns, such as shaded cubes and the deep vandykes suggested by the backgammon boards that were another Tunbridge-ware speciality. In the subsequent mosaic veneers a writing-box might carry a picture on its upper front or sloping lid, such as a view of Hever, Eridge or Tonbridge castle, or some similar local sight of souvenir value. Such mosaics were built up from the various local woods, only their natural colours being approved and the greenish shade caused by the local spring water. Strips of these woods in appropriate colours were assembled by hand like so many matchsticks, fastened together by their sides so that the tiny squares of their ends together formed the picture. These could then be thinly sliced across their length, so that every slice would bear the same mosaic picture ready for mounting on the box. Occasionally one sees a marble box, the veneer consisting of a haphazard assembly of the various coloured shavings glued and sliced in the same way as the mosaic pictures (Plates 121A and B).

Writing-box Stands: The post-Restoration writing-box might be placed on a stand instead of a table. This had gate-legs and the fall-down flap of the box opened on to them for writing. Even towards the end of the seventeenth century box and stand might be separate, although the box was acquiring the characteristic shape of the more elaborate desk, with the writing portion based on a chest of drawers. The simplest stands were without drawers, and resembled some of the first toilet looking-glass boxes. Early legs were turned and tapering, linked by flat, waved stretchers. By about 1705 simple cabriole legs were coming into use.

CABINETS

To this day the most expert furniture craftsman is the cabinet-maker, and cabinets are unquestionably the most fascinating as well as the most technically perfect pieces of furniture ever evolved. They represent the chest at its most refined and personal, the antithesis of the old clumsy chest with its casual disregard for orderliness. Their very perfection rules out any very ancient pedigree for English work. The Earl of Northampton was ahead of his times in his collection of lovely furniture, and the inventory taken in 1614 lists no fewer than eight – ebony inlaid with white bone, crimson velvet laced with silver and gold lace and similar exotic beauties. But only twenty years before the very term cabinet had been a rarity and the Dean of Durham's wife, for instance, referred in her will to 'one coffer with boxes in y[t] standinge onn a frame'. In 1620 Lord William Howard bought what had to be described as a 'cabbinnit with 21 drawboxeis' for 7*s.* 3*d.* As late as 1730 Bailey's dictionary defined a cabinet first as a closet in the king's palace, and only secondly as 'a sort of chest of drawers, also a kind of little trunk to put things of value in'.

In late Stuart and early Georgian days, however, for china, shells, coins, curios, cabinets achieved a remarkable maturity and range of design and material, and even in the nineteenth century new treatments were being evolved. In silver and papier-mâché, in lacquer, tortoiseshell and ivory, in needlework, straw-work, paper filigree and every delicate and decorative treatment of woodwork – inlay, marquetry, carving and paint – the cabinet declared man's admiration for patient, exquisite craftsmanship. Basically it was the development of hardwoods that enabled craftsmen to accomplish the small-scale joinery of countless fitted drawers and compartments, this necessarily limiting its execution to the most skilled.

The idea of immensely valuable, ornate chests for storing one's treasure is almost as old as the valuables themselves, but early specimens might be classed as caskets. The costly brilliance of such work may be visualized from such contemporary sources as the summary of the 'chests' in the 1536 inventory of Salisbury Cathedral. These included: 'A fair chest, curiously and cleanly made, covered with cloth of gold, with shields of noblemen, set with pearls, with lock, gemmels and key silver and gilt. Item one fair chest, painted and gilded, with precious stones and knops of glass, broidered with coral, seven of them wanting, and painted within like silver. Item, three other chests, very fair, and ornate with precious stones, with gemmels of silver and gilt. . . . Also divers chests . . . some covered with cloth of blue and silver, and others ornate with ivory and gemmels and locks.'

Even by the date of this inventory cabinets with small compartments for jewellery had a considerable history in Italy, and they had become extremely ornate before English craftsmen began to give much attention to such work in response to seventeenth-century demand. Ivory inlay was associated with Milan, damascened iron with Milan and Florence, glass encrustations with Florence, mother of pearl with Venice. The *varguenos* of Spain were conspicuous for their characteristic horizontal shaping, long hinges and other gilded ironwork. But before the end of the seventeenth century men were looking beyond these lovely creations. Charles II's queen brought Bombay as her scintillating dowry, and the so-called Portuguese cabinets that the king presented to his favourites – ornate gold-mounted treasures incrusted with mother of pearl or ivory – came mainly from India, from the Portuguese colony at Goa. And even these could not compare with the wealth of magnificent colour and fantastic design displayed by some of the cabinets introduced in the seventeenth century from China.

By the late seventeenth century English cabinet-makers were devising a range of furniture variously termed cabinet bookcases, desks, scrutoires, bureaux and so on in which the cabinet-maker's skill was tested to the full on the small compartments, drawers, shelves and hiding-places that constituted the cabinets themselves. But in this brief survey such furniture can receive only passing mention. During the eighteenth century the tendency was to develop smaller pieces that possessed the dainty charm of early table cabinets yet which were complete in themselves.

Cabinets on Stands: large cabinets mounted on stands are especially associated with the late seventeenth and early eighteenth centuries. Early specimens retained the rectangular outline of the chest on stand, becoming less massive after about 1670, but with a heavy, straight cornice and often a drawer in the swelling frieze, and another in the tall table-like stand. Two vertical doors usually embraced the whole front of the cabinet, finely ornamented and with handsome lock-plates. Inside, the space was filled with drawers, cupboards, pigeon-holes.

Alternatively the cabinet was combined with a bureau, the doors replaced by a wide fall-front hinged at the bottom to provide writing space when open. Such a piece was most usually mounted on a chest of drawers. By the late seventeenth century there were numerous variants. There were even a few display cabinets with glazed fronts, plain rectangles of glass being framed in heavy glazing bars. From the 1680s a china or book cabinet might be mounted over a bureau with a slanting fall-down flap, charming interior fittings and deep drawers below. Some were narrow, to fit against the piers between the windows, and all lent themselves to the architectural furniture treatment of their day. A few were of oak, many more in veneer, such as walnut, burr elm banded with foreign wood, or mulberry, associated with stringing in pewter.

Mahogany appeared more widely once the import tax was removed in 1733, and was used in the early Georgian style associated with William Kent, followed by lighter mid-century work with rich naturalistic carving. Some had fret-cut, pierced cresting boards, several thicknesses of wood being glued together in different ways of the grain to avoid warping. There was more use of clear glazing in place of heavy mirror-plate fronts, the lighter glazing bars that could be cut from mahogany dating from about 1750 onwards. But shapes and styles in the mid-eighteenth century were numerous, followed by the more restrained, formal designs of the neo-classic mood. In the late eighteenth century a delightful style of little cabinet consisted of about six graduated drawers beneath a lifting top rebated on a plain stand with the entirely unencumbered legs, tapering only on their inner sides, associated with Hepplewhite's day. Such a cabinet was typically of satinwood, with simple but precise bandings of richer tulip-wood.

Caskets: a frequent term for small decorative chests that contained jewels, letters and similar highly valuable articles with some degree of security and with great decorative effect. Until the term cabinet became widely current, caskets and chests of draw-boxes were in common usage. References are endless. As early as 1467 a guild record was 'to be put in a boxe called a Casket'; in 1471 in the *Paston Letters* there is allusion to 'Syche othyr wryghtynges and stuff as was in my Kasket'. Some extremely finely made caskets date to the first quarter of the nineteenth century, when they might be known as compendiums, with lift-out fitments for a wide variety of purposes. Treatments varied endlessly, but a typical specimen might be of rosewood, perhaps pearl-mounted and with interior mountings of gilt-stamped leather and fittings of cut steel.

Compendiums: *see* Caskets.

Drawer Construction: by Tudor days the early wide dovetail was in widespread use in England, but by about 1695 the lap dovetail was preferred under veneers, as the old through dovetail exposed too much end-grain for satisfactory glue-work. Some Dutch work continued the earlier style. Oak was used for drawer linings to take the rub of wear. As early as 1655 the Marquess of Worcester patented 'a total locking of Cabinet-boxes'.

Ebony: this brittle, difficult wood was first employed to supplement the native woods used for decorative inlays, but it so fascinated the early cabinet-maker that it prompted the development of the veneer technique. Corfe Castle in 1643 was typical of wealthy establishments in containing a 'rich ebony cabbonett with gilded fixtures', and a very large ebony cabinet, in contrast to a more simply constructed casket covered with mother of pearl that was catalogued as a trunk.

Filigree Cabinets: throughout the 18th century filigree was a popular amateur ornament for small cabinets, calling for neat fingers and considerable patience. The ornament entirely covered the main panels of the cabinet, creating pictorial designs and arabesque patterns in an effect of metal filigree. This was achieved solely with tiny rolls of paper arranged so that they projected edgeways from their background. To complete the effect, they were gilded or coloured on their exposed edges (Plate 124A).

Forsets, Fossets, Fosselets: terms defined by Bailey in 1730 as small chests or cabinets. They were smaller versions of the forser or fosser, an early form of strong box such as the Cockesden 'waynscott fosser' (1610) and the 'grete joyned forser' with two keys owned by the Pewterers' Company in 1488–9.

Handles: the quality of the work depended more upon cost than period. Early cabinets might have turned ivory or wood handles, or solid, pendant 'knobs of tin' or iron. The brass handles of the later seventeenth century most often consisted of slender loops, rings, stirrup and ellipse shapes on circular plates and held by strips of metal folded outwards at the back in the manner of brass paper-clips. The wide, low, loop handles of Queen Anne cabinets might have their back-plates incised, but piercing for such work dates mainly from about the 1720s. They hung on the nutted bolts that held the back-plates. By the 1730s heavier drop loops had their bolt heads mounted on separate moulded circles. Showy, asymmetrically shaped 'French' mounts were popular around the mid-century, followed by the austere circles and ellipses of Adam's day, cast until about 1777 when stamping was used in Birmingham to make back-plates with patterns in relief. From about 1790 many heavy cast handles were used, including wreaths of flowers and the most familiar ring-holding lion heads.

Inlay: *see* the section on Blanket Chests.

Japanning: *see* Lacquer.

Lacquer: 'Right Indian' and 'Right Japan' were indiscriminate terms for Oriental lacquer to differentiate it from the poorer paint and varnish imitations executed in England. Many Oriental and Dutch cabinets were made in a distinctive plain rectangular silhouette notable for elaborate lock-plates and many fine hinges. Their crestings, like their stands, were English, carved and gilded or silvered; first in the florid Renaissance style, and then more restrainedly, with tapering trumpet legs. Stands ornamented with low-relief gilded gesso were followed by early Georgian stands like contemporary side-tables. Good-quality English japanned imitations of Oriental cabinets were frequently based on the gesso process of building up a ground of whiting and size that would be coloured, lac varnished and gilded. Sometimes the cabinet's softwood carcase was veneered – inside and out of the heavy doors – to provide a lastingly smooth surface to the lacquer substitute. Black was the most usual ground, red rarer, blue and white still rarer. Black and red were sometimes used for 'counterfeit tortoiseshell'.

Marquetry: *see* under Blanket Chests, p. 185 (Plate 122).

Needlework Cabinets: 'A coffer maid in broderie upon reid satine' was listed among Elizabeth I's movables in 1561. This was a forerunner of innumerable examples characteristic of English needlework around the mid-seventeenth century. Every well-to-do young lady, it would appear, then embroidered a set of satin pieces for mounting on a little wooden cabinet fitted either with doors or with a fall-front to allow access to jewellery drawers and toilet compartments. In some examples the interior above the drawers consisted of a little well surrounded by lidded boxes for toilet accessories, and ornamented with pieces of the still-novel looking-glass and perhaps carpeted with a hand-coloured print. But the major work went into the exterior mountings, usually embroidered on the narrow rich satin, then newly available, that allowed the embroidery to break away from the customary ground-covering tent stitch into speedier ornament that left some of the ground visible.

Most often the main embroidery was scenic, such as one of a few favourite scriptural scenes—the story of Rebecca, or Jephthah and his daughter, perhaps. Always the tendency was to crowd the scene with fascinating, disproportionate detail in the Elizabethan manner. Often some of the main figures were padded and stitched separately, their faces and hands of wood, silk covered, their clothes exquisitely wrought with minute lace stitches and decked out in all the trinket ornaments that age has rendered somewhat tawdry. Beads and coral, feathers and tinsel, were freely used in what was then termed raised work but has become known as stump work.

Those who condemn the extraneous ornament on the raised work must remember that its creators were usually girls barely into their teens, who had graduated to this fanciful exercise through the rigours of an elaborate sampler of flat coloured stitches and another of alphabets and cut-works in white. And even the most frivolous are usually in meticulous stitchery.

Such conspicuous trifles have tended to overshadow the many cabinets mounted with flat embroidery, either in a wide variety of stitches or in the fine unemphatic grace of tent stitch, known also as *petit point*, although this term has now been transferred by some collectors to the comparatively clumsy cross stitch (Plate 119B).

Ormolu: originally gold ground to powder for gilding metals, and hence the gilded bronze that decorated fine furniture, so that the term came to mean an alloy of copper, zinc and tin, gold coloured. Ure's *Dictionary of the Arts* (1875) defined it as 'a brass in which there is less zinc and more copper than in ordinary brass, the object being to obtain a nearer imitation of gold than ordinary brass affords'. English manufacture was launched by Matthew Boulton; in 1778 the *English Gazetteer* referred to Birmingham ormolu as highly esteemed all over Europe.

Painted Cabinets: some of the earliest English casket cabinets were painted inside and out, often with heraldic motifs. But it was about 1780 before this again became an important medium. Then the cabinet was often of satinwood, solid or in veneer, and slightly painted with ribbons and swags of flowers. Some cabinets were painted all over, either white in the Pergolesi manner or a pale straw colour to suggest a satinwood background to painted medallions of cupids and the like in the Cipriani-Kauffmann style. After about 1800 exotic wood veneers were generally preferred.

Parquetry: some attractive small cabinets were veneered in regular patterns created with squares, diamond shapes, triangles, etc, of matching and contrasting grain patterns.

Porcelain Cabinets: Mary II owned several for Chinese porcelain and Delftware, but they are associated especially with the mid-eighteenth century when English porcelain was a spectacular novelty. They offered wide scope for fantastic 'Chinese' designs, some in fine mahogany and many more in softwoods, japanned and painted or partly gilded. Then followed slighter, classic carving with much use of peardrop cornice mouldings, after 1770, on straight cornices, urn-crested.

Straw-work: professional as well as amateur ornament on small cabinets, achieved with delicate and precise arrangements in split and variously coloured straws. These might be red, green, blue, as well as buff and black and white. The colour has proved fleeting, but cabinet interiors are often bright. Crude little pictures in this straw parquetry, often of buildings, are usually ascribed to French prisoners of war around 1800 (Plate 121C).

Stump-work: late nineteenth-century term for seventeenth-century raised or embossed work. (*See* Needlework.)

Tills: term occasionally noted in connexion with cabinets as well as chests. In 1561 Elizabeth I was presented with a 'cobonett full of tylls'.

Tunbridge Ware: small fitted cabinets were largely made in the styles of parquetry and wood mosaic that formed a distinctive craft in the Tonbridge and Tunbridge Wells area. (*See* the section on Writing-boxes.)

Walnut Cabinets: in 1687 the *London Gazette* referred to 'a drawing Walnut Tree Box, with two Drawers in it . . . to put Mathematical Instruments in'. This might have been in solid walnut with rich undercut and cross-grained carving. Or it might have been in walnut veneer, hand-sawn, one-sixth or one-seventh of an inch thick, to display the beautiful pattern of the grain without regard for strength, and glued to a deal framework. Burr walnut, most difficult to lay, came from the tree stump where the roots showed as minute veins. The plumed effect was obtained from crotches or branch junctions; the 'oyster' was sliced across a small branch, often of laburnum or olive wood instead of walnut. Some walnut veneers were further enriched with marquetry. Suggestions of panelling on the flat surface might be achieved with narrow lines in contrasting veneers, mitred at the corners in high-quality work; diagonal grain especially between 1680 and 1705; cross grain with the herringbone or feather grain especially 1695–1715; cross grained alone especially after 1710. English, then French, then the 'black' Virginia walnut was used for cabinet work.

BLANKET CHESTS

'In ivory coffers I have stuff'd my crowns,' declared Gremio in *The Taming of the Shrew:*

In cypress chests my arras, counterpoints,
Costly apparel, tents, and canopies,
Fine linen, Turkey cushions boss'd with pearl,
Valance of Venice gold in needle-work,
Pewter and brass, and all things that belong
To house or house-keeping.

Heavy and rich, laboriously woven or embroidered, sumptuously lined and trimmed, the fabrics of earlier centuries were made to last for generations – and presented the housekeeper with the monumental problem of their safe keeping from the ravage of moth and the tarnish of damp. Chests were evolved as a refuge centuries before wardrobes became pieces of furniture instead of rooms, or chests of drawers broke free of the lidded-box design, and they have never entirely disappeared from use.

Very many of the splendid chests in churches were required for robes and vestments, even to the inclusion of a few quarter-circle and half-circle designs for most highly treasured copes. In 1480 the Pewterers' Company had streamers made to decorate their barge in a water pageant, and at once the accounts recorded the consequence: 'Item, payed for a cofyn for the sayde strem^{r}s xijd.' In 1550 this typical guild owned a wainscot chest for napery, and their records even included occasional payments for 'bagges of Rose leaves and lavender ffor tje chest of lynnen xviijd.'

As late as Tudor and early Stuart days, every room in the old rambling self-sufficient house might have its bed pitched like a tent and with a tent's semi-privacy among the tools of the establishment's innumerable trades, and more often than not every bed had its own accompanying furnishings, a blanket chest at the foot and probably another alongside serving instead of chair or table, such as Robert Belassis of Morton recorded, 'the great Danske chest at the bedde feete and a littell Chest at the bedd syde'. Inventories give fascinating glimpses of this confusion. They also testify to the importance of chests as furniture. Robert Barker, for instance, mayor of Newcastle from 1577 to 1585, had two danske chests in the nursery in 1588, a danske chest and a danske coffer in the fore parlour, and two more danske chests, one of fir, a little counter and a banded chest in the back parlour. In the previous year an inventory of a Newcastle merchant, William Jeneson, furnished a servants' chamber solely with two beds, four cupboards and five danske chests.

The mid-seventeenth century introduced mule chests and the gradual evolution of the big chest of drawers, but even in the eighteenth century's more polished household blanket chests received the consideration of good design and excellent workmanship. Evelyn and his daughter, in *Mundus Muliebris*, described the bed-chamber of a late Stuart society lady, and among the expected cabinets, tea tables, and all the rest she was furnished with 'trunks on stand'. It must be remembered, of course, that household linen was stored in immense quantity by every lady of any substance, and handed down from generation to generation.

The contemporary names of many of these chests indicate that they were imported from abroad—Danske, Spruce, Flanders and so on. The Act of Tonnage and Poundage, 1689, indicates that they came in nests of three, fitting inside each other, and duty rates were calculated on this assumption; whereas chests of iron were dutiable singly, and small painted chests and gilt-leather covered coffers by the dozen. The duty on cypress-wood chests was more than five times as great as on spruce or danske chests or iron-bound coffers. While many were specifically for blankets, linen or napkins, this style of chest was widely used for household storage. Cedar-lined chests have never been ousted for protection against moth and damp.

Armour was stored in chests, as described in Chambers' *Cyclopaedia*, 1751, and in 1789 Dr Burney referred to the custom in music-loving families of possessing chests of viols – two trebles, two tenors and two basses. Various food chests were developed with local names: in the north-east, for instance, an ark was often a ventilated chest. 'The cheese in arke, the meill in Kist' (Henryson, 1450) was reiterated in innumerable later inventories. But Warwick's St Mary's Church in 1464 listed 'i grete olde arke to put in vestyments &c'. In East Anglia the term hutch was widely used for a kitchen chest. Spices, salt and candles all had their own chests. Some idea of the widespread demands may be gained from a wholly typical late sixteenth-century inventory: in 1580 John Lawson of Chester had a counter, a salt kytt and a danske chest in his hall; two old chests and a leather-covered chest in his chamber; a chest, a coffer and another little chest in his parlour – no chairs, no tables – and a 'great arke' in the kitchen.

Carved Chests: it is impossible to differentiate entirely between ecclesiastical and domestic chests. Surviving medieval specimens probably represent only the finest work. Some of the earliest ornament consisted of chip-carved roundels. Always the tendency has been for the ornament to suggest, superficially, the architectural construction of building in stone: thus an early panel would have chamfering on the top edge of the lower rail because this allowed water to drain off a stone sill. Until well into the sixteenth century foreign influence was mainly Flemish. Some of the richest remaining fourteenth- and fifteenth-century chests are 'Flanders chests' carved with representations of 'Gothic window' tracery, although attention has been drawn to the fact that in some instances a chest's frontal carving may originally have formed the reredos associated with a church's stone altar (Plate 126F and B).

Other low-relief carving more simply followed linenfold and similar fabric patterns. High-relief carving was used for naturalistic ornament. In medieval and early Tudor chests various real and mythological creatures were carved and occasionally there were even pictorial scenes, followed by more sophisticated pilaster figures, caryatides and the heavy round-headed Roman arch that has become symbolic of Renaissance decoration. Soon this Roman arch was surrounding panels of inlay instead of carving. In the seventeenth century there was a vast amount of dull repetitive work, much of it lacking even surface modelling. After the interruption of smooth-faced veneers and lacquers there came a return to some heavy architectural carving in early mahogany and by the mid-eighteenth century some good cut-card work was appearing on mahogany chests, but it became more usual to fret-cut and apply it, instead of carving from the solid and smoothing the background. Late-eighteenth- and nineteenth-century oak chests were often coarsely carved, being only faintly reminiscent of simple work of earlier centuries (Plate 126).

Cassoni: a pair of Italian dower chests constituted important furnishings in the sixteenth and seventeenth centuries. Some were elaborately painted, the wood covered first with glue-on canvas, then perhaps with gesso, then with paint. Others were richly carved or decorated with marquetry. The Earl of Leicester in 1588 had 'fower faier flatt [i.e. not rounded trunk-tops] Venetian chests of Walnut tree carved and gilte'. English work is occasionally noted in similar vein.

Cedar Chests: Cedar veneer made an excellent lining for a blanket chest. John Houghton stressed in 1727 that the wood 'is of so very dry a nature that it will not endure to be fastened with *nails*, from which it shrinks, therefore *pins* of the same are better ...' Cedar chests were extensively imported from Holland in Queen Anne's reign.

Chest Stands: towards the end of the seventeenth century many blanket chests were fitted with stands. These resembled their period's side-tables, with trumpet-shaped legs, waved diagonal stretchers and heavy ball or bun feet. Soon after the turn of the century, low cabriole-legged stands might be used, or a chest might be mounted merely on plain bracket feet. Oriental lacquered chests were mounted on stands made in England, first with heavy naturalistic carving and then in more formal designs. Some were gilded but many more were silvered to accord with the late seventeenth century's craze for silver furniture, and only assumed a golden tone as the protective varnish lost its original clarity. Around the mid-eighteenth century some blanket chests were mounted on straight-legged, fret-cut stands in the English 'Chinese' manner.

Commodes: Sobry in *Architecture* (1718) stated that 'coffers and arks are commonly called commodes. Some have a lid, others have drawers'. But the term is more usually restricted to a cupboard design with doors and drawers. While bedrooms remained customary visiting and reception rooms, all bedroom furniture tended to be disguised and some bedroom commodes were constructed to resemble chests or trunks.

Construction: *see* section on Plate Chests.

Counters: *see* section on Plate Chests.

Cypress Chests: introduced early in the sixteenth century, but by the late seventeenth century were subject to heavy import tax. Some bore all-over ornament in low relief, incised or in cheap poker work. John Houghton reported in 1727 that such chests were made in Venice for the wood 'resists the *worm* and *moth*, and all putrefaction to *eternity* . . . nothing outlasts it, or can be more beautiful, especially than the roots of the wilder sort, incomparable for its *crisped undulations*'. Houghton also referred to the use of juniper wood for chests (Plate 127E).

Danske Chests: frequently appear in Elizabethan records and might be assumed to be imports from Denmark, but probably there was more or less generalized use of the terms spruce (Prussia), danske and danszig for chests of Baltic fir wood.

Dowry Chests: for centuries a chest of linen was a bride's usual contribution to her new home, but the term dowry chest appears of comparatively recent popularity.

Feet: early chests merely had their corner stiles prolonged to raise them from the floor, a frequent detail consisting of a semicircular shaping on the inner side of each front stile partly filled with a turned spindle or a vestige of such ornament. In heavily carved Elizabethan chests, the feet might continue the pillar motif. But during the seventeenth century separate feet were often applied, consisting of balls or bun shapes. In 1633 the turners complained that the joiners were wrongfully making their own. Low cabriole and simple bracket feet, sometimes on a separate stand, came with the eighteenth century (Compare Plates 126A, 126F, 127B and 127F).

Flanders Chests: more vaguely defined as overseas work in some inventories. They were in great demand by the sixteenth century; as early as 1483 the Cofferers' Guild was protesting at their importation. Inventoried specimens were generally priced at about five shillings in the late sixteenth century, and were in general use throughout the house. Some remaining specimens may have been preserved because of the exceptional richness of their traceried 'church window' carving, attached sometimes instead of carved from the solid. In the seventeenth century the ornament associated with Flanders included a range of unambitious glued-on decoration intended to simulate elaborate constructional work.

Gesso: among the richest, most ornate furnishings of many a flamboyant late Stuart and early Georgian household were chests covered with gilded gesso. These tended to follow the heavy baroque designs of other gesso furniture, contrasting with extremely delicate work in low relief on the lid where intertwining arabesques shaped by brush in the gesso composition were set off by the customary ground of subdued matting. The gesso was suitably coloured and then covered with gold or silver leaf, and this protected with varnish.

Inlay: pieces of contrasting wood about one-eighth of an inch thick sunk into the solid oak or walnut of the chest. It was associated especially with the seventeenth century, but introduced much earlier, at first with native wood, then with ebony, with ivory and mother-of-pearl fostered by the monarchs' associations with Spain in Mary's and James I's reigns, with silver, pewter and the ubiquitous tortoiseshell. John Houghton in 1727 referred to the practice of inlaying holly under ivory 'to render it more con-

Chest fitted with a tea equipage in Dresden porcelain. Eighteenth century.

PLATE 117

Writing box or table desk covered with painted and gilt leather and bearing the heraldic badges of Henry VIII and Katherine of Aragon. 16 × 11½ × 9½ in., *c.* 1525. *Victoria & Albert Museum.*

PLATE 118

(A) A fitted compendium, second quarter of the nineteenth century. Rosewood inlaid with pearl. Red leatherwork, stamped in gold, the fittings are of cut steel. *Presented to Bethnal Green Museum by Her Majesty Queen Mary.*

(B) Cabinet covered in raised needlework known as stump work. On the left Eliezer offers betrothal gifts to Rebecca, and on the front Abraham kneels to an angel. An unusual feature is the tray set out as a formal garden. Late seventeenth century. *Victoria & Albert Museum.*

(A) A superb casket equipped for various hobbies, covered with pearl and ormolu, made by Nicholas Rozet at Vienna in the first half of the nineteenth century. *By gracious permission of Her Majesty the Queen.*

(B) 'Lace box' covered with floral marquetry of a shape that would have proved equally convenient for writing equipment. Early eighteenth century. *Victoria & Albert Museum.*

(A) Cabinet and boxes in Tunbridge ware marquetry showing the shaded-cube effect and vandykes, and, at the back, the marbled effect created by cutting the veneer from the glued-together shavings of the variously coloured natural woods. *Tunbridge Wells Museum.*

(B) Writing-box and associated woodwork decorated with elaborate Tunbridge ware, the mosaics of naturally coloured woods worked into popular souvenir views. The writing box shows Battle Abbey, the tray Hever Castle before restoration, the boxes, below, Eridge Castle and Penshurst Place. *Tunbridge Wells Museum.*

(D) Writing box of papier-mâché with a sloping hinged lid most delicately painted. *Victoria & Albert Museum.*

(C) Cabinet or casket ornamented with straw-work in dark and light tones of green, red and blue. Attributed to French prisoners of war, *c.* 1800. *Bethnal Green Museum.*

(A) Cabinet enriched with oyster veneers and the early naturalistic style of marquetry. Below the frieze drawer the front opens downwards, hinged at the bottom, to reveal eighteen short drawers and one long one for coins or similar curios. *Mallett & Son.*

(B) Cabinet enriched with oyster veneers and marquetry; another view, showing the front open. *Mallett & Son.*

(A) Writing-box, of ash, decorated with glued pear-wood, bog-wood, etc. Length 30½ in., depth 22 in., height 10 in. Early seventeenth century. *Victoria & Albert Museum.*

(B) Blanket chest in the mule chest tradition made of mahogany, on its own cabriole legs. Early Georgian. *John Bell Collection.*

(D) Papier-mâché cabinet of the early nineteenth century. Decorated with gold and slabs of shell tinted with transparent paints.

(C) Travel chest that expands into a writing desk. The lid may be opened to make two table flaps and the legs fold flat. *John Bell Collection.*

(A) Cabinet in filigree paper work. Both cabinet and stand are covered in designs created with rolls of paper around pictorial medallions. Late eighteenth century. Height

(B) Writing equipment at its most elaborate – a charming little *bonheur du jour*, the pull-out writing drawer fitted with a tiny ink-well drawer, painting equipment at the side and the table section topped by a fall-front cabinet. *Mallett & Son.*

Mule chest covered with brown leather, finely close-nailed and with notable pierced mounts. This bears the monogram of William III and Mary. Late seventeenth century. Measurements 3 ft. 2 in. × 1 ft. 10 in. × 2 ft. 3 in. *Victoria & Albert Museum.*

PLATE 125

(A) Chest for storage, early Stuart period. The chest ends slide in grooves and when drawn up show two drawers beneath a false bottom. Measurements 3 ft. 11 in. × 2 ft. × 2 ft. *Victoria & Albert Museum.*

(B) Beautifully carved walnut chest, late fifteenth century. *Victoria & Albert Museum.*

(C) Late fifteenth-century chest, carved oak banded with iron. Measurements 6 ft. $11\frac{1}{2}$ in. × 2 ft. 3 in. × 1 ft. 11 in. *Victoria & Albert Museum.*

(D) Seventeenth-century oak mule chest. Low-relief carving mainly lacking surface modelling. Lower part contains only one small drawer, flanked by two cupboards. Measurements 5 ft. × 2 ft. × 3 ft. *Victoria & Albert Museum.*

(E) Chest of very simple nailed-up construction, the vertical ends continued and shaped to form legs. Elm, *c.* 1630. Measurements 3 ft. 3 in. × 1 ft. 3 in. × 1 ft. 8 in. *Victoria & Albert Museum.*

(F) Thirteenth-century chest, chip-carved in roundels. Measurements 3 ft. 7 in. × 1 ft. 7 in. × 1 ft. 8 in. *Victoria & Albert Museum.*

(A) Leather-covered chest with brass lockplate and close-nailing. Dated 1666. Measurements 4 ft. 6 in. × 2 ft. 6 in. × 2 ft. $7\frac{3}{4}$ in. *Victoria & Albert Museum.*

(B) Mule chest, early eighteenth century, the front of burr walnut veneer with wide herringbone bandings. *Victoria & Albert Museum.*

(C) Nonsuch chest of oak ornamented with various woods. Late sixteenth century. Measurements 5 ft. $11\frac{1}{2}$ in. × 2 ft. 3 in. × 2 ft. 2 in. *Victoria & Albert Museum.*

(D) Oak panelled chest painted with formal flower groups. Seventeenth century. Measurements 4 ft. 10 in. × 1 ft. 10 in. × 2 ft. 2 in. *Victoria & Albert Museum.*

(E) Chest of cypress wood, incised on front with grotesque birds and dragons among formal ornament. Early seventeenth century. Measurements 5 ft. 3 in. × 1 ft. 10 in. × 1 ft. 11 in. *Victoria & Albert Museum.*

(F) All-over strapwork in low relief around panels finely inlaid with flower-and-vase motifs on an early seventeenth-century chest. The feet are formed by the corner stiles, overlapped by the applied base moulding. *Hotspur Ltd.*

(A) Chest decorated with Japanese lacquer in relief. Gilded base and engraved brass mounts are English, *c.* 1750. *H. Blairman & Sons.*

(B) Chest of carved mahogany, design taken from Verrocchio's tomb of the Medici in St Lorenzo, Florence. 5 ft. long × 2 ft. 9 in. wide × 2 ft. 10 in. high, *c.* 1730. *Victoria & Albert Museum.*

(C) Plate chest of oak veneered with lignum vitae. Seventeenth century. Measurements 14¼ in. × 9⅜ in. × 8½ in. *Victoria & Albert Museum.*

(D) Chest of camphor wood from the Dutch East Indies, the brass mounts cut and chased. Late seventeenth century. Measurements 5 ft. × 2 ft. 4 in. × 2 ft. 6 in. *Victoria & Albert Museum.*

(E) Wrought-iron plate chest with painted ornament, dated 1597. Mounted on iron wheels. 4 ft. 5¼ in. long and 2 ft. 8¾ in. high. *Victoria & Albert Museum.*

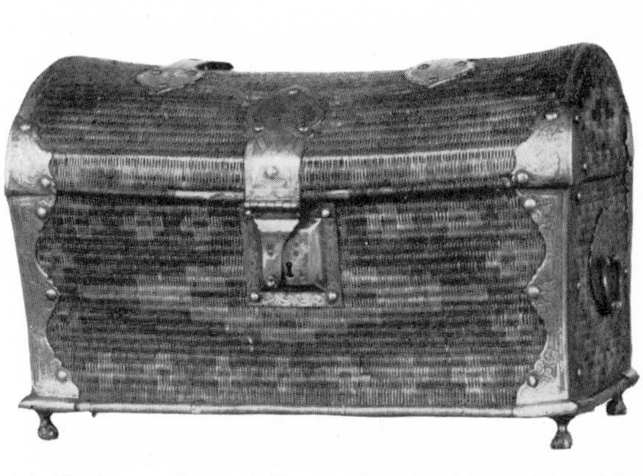

(F) Casket, substantially made of wickerwork with ornamental brass mounts. Eighteenth century. 22 in. × 12 in. × 14¼ in. *Victoria & Albert Museum.*

PLATE 128

spicuous'. An alternative term was set-work. Thus Robert Atkynson, a former sheriff of Newcastle, owned a 'great Danske Chyste with sett wourke'. valued at £5 in 1596 when a more usual valuation of a danske chest was five shillings (Plate 127F).

Joined Chests: *see* section on Plate Chests.

Jousting Chests: an attractive name given to chests carved in high relief with naturalistic scenes of secular subjects, such as jousting and hunting. These may have been created as early as the fourteenth or fifteenth century, but they have prompted many nineteenth- and twentieth-century copies.

Lacquer: first the Dutch and then the English East India Company imported great quantities of Oriental lacquer boards in the later seventeenth century, and these were often made into handsome blanket chests. Pepys in 1661 wrote of the Duke of York's 'many fine chests covered with gold and Indian varnish given him by the East Indy Company of Holland'. Lacquer trunks were listed in 1700 among the goods sold at East India House. But many more were made up in England. Some Oriental lacquer panels were framed up in English japanned work, usually an unattractive combination. Others were wholly of English japanning. 'Lackered Ware Truncks' were advertised in the *London Gazette* in 1687. (*See* section on Cabinets.) The liking for Chinese work never entirely disappeared, and around the mid-eighteenth century many Chinese rooms were created with lacquer or japanned chests among their handsome furnishings.

Leather: some blanket chests were covered with leather, closely studded with nails but lacking the metal angle-pieces and bandings that would fit them for travel. Some were mule chests.

Lids: for household use chests had flat table tops, the flat boards secured by cross battens fitting outside the chests themselves. Stuart chests had thinner lids from about 1600, and they might be framed up in loose panels after about 1625.

Mahogany: by George II's reign these chests ranged from extreme plainness to the most richly carved work. A mule chest, for instance, might be entirely plain save for the metal mounts and the cock's head beading around the drawers, and many depended upon the beauty of their rich Cuban veneers (Plates 123B and 128B).

Marquetry: achieved much the same effect as inlay (q.v.), but the contrasting pattern and its background were both created in wood veneer thinly covering the wood that formed the chest. Veneering proved the most successful method of using the hard, brittle ebony that came into fashion in the seventeenth century. Inlay usually appeared on panelled chests and in association with carving; marquetry required a flat, unbroken surface. Nothing elaborate was attempted on chests and much of the naturalistic flower-and-bird work that remains appears to be Dutch.

Metal Mounts: Wrought-iron, often gilded, largely ceased to ornament chests during the fourteenth century, apart from security bandings and heavy lock-plates, and the strap hinges that were replacing wooden pin hinges. Iron was costly and the wood was smooth enough for carving. Some Elizabethan hinges were decoratively shaped to form a pair of rounded Es, one in reverse. Handles were of iron until the mid-seventeenth century when brass might be used. Screws were cut and filed by hand, and were rough and less perfectly regular than modern machine work. Their heads varied perceptibly in size and their ends were blunt.

Mule Chests: here the usual box construction was combined with one or two drawers below. Some were of oak, many more of walnut; mid-eighteenth-century work might be in mahogany. For drawer construction, *see* the section on Cabinets (Plate 123).

Nonsuch Chests: decorated with a kind of wood mosaic known as intarsia, a geometrical inlay prepared in bulk and cut off into lengths as required to fill hollows sunk in the wood. This work possibly dated to about 1500 onwards. In the Nonsuch designs quaint buildings were portrayed, perhaps, as Fred Roe has suggested, intended to represent the Nonsuch House on old London Bridge, a timber construction brought over from Holland in prefabricated sections early in Elizabeth I's reign (Plate 127c).

Ornament: probably the earliest chests were brightly painted: the Carpenters' Company paid 13*s.* 4*d.* for a chest to be painted and gilded in 1484. Carving observed a sequence of modified Gothic and Renaissance Greco-Roman styles followed by much raised applied ornament. Inlay appeared in the sixteenth century and was developed in the seventeenth, and there was some intarsia work in the Continental manner. There was some simple marquetry, and a little sumptuous silvered or gilded gesso, as well as much English japanning. Early Georgian mahogany might bear such simple classic enrichment as dentil moulding, and there was some mid-eighteenth-century pseudo-Chinese cut-card work.

Settles: often merely chests with tall panelled backs and arm-rests, and sometimes placed at the bed-foot. Sir Thomas Ramsey in 1590 possessed several, their style indicated by an entry 'a wainskot settle wth two locks vs'.

Spruce Coffers: *see* Danske Chests.

Trunks: this term is so usually associated today with travelling that it is well to realize its wider implication, as in G. Greene's reference, 1591: 'At the bed's feete stood a hansome truncke, wherin was very good linnen.' Even the Carpenters' Company in 1648 used it as a term for linen chest, and the Company's writings, too, were 'locked up in a trunke'. (*See* the section on Travelling Chests.)

PLATE CHESTS

Chests were the forerunners of the modern safe throughout century after century of pillage and pilfering, of unbridled violence and the petty tricksters who, one suspects, must have been major pests in the big households that dominated Tudor and Stuart life. As early as the thirteenth century the majority of towns were acquiring self-rule and arranging that city dignitaries should be responsible for the keys that trebly locked each muniment chest and iron-bound coffer. A number of churches testify to the security of their thirteenth-century treasure chests. Liveried companies record many among their possessions, such as the Pewterers' in 1488–9: 'A grete joyned forser peintyd w^{t} the armys of the crafte and lockyd w^{t} ij keys pryc viijs.'

This Company's records at this time indicate the range of chests used for safe keeping; consecutive items in their books included 'boxis contayning dyverse evydences', 'a Casked lokt with the jury booke', and other documents (this had become 'an olde boxe or Casket' by 1549, and was supplemented then by a black, leather-covered chest bound with iron), 'a box with xxiiij byllys of paper' and other documents, 'a blak cofyr containing iij chapelets of Rede Saten, ij lelypottys' and other silver, and 'a grete Chest bounde with Iren called a standard'. Another chest with two locks was acquired seven years later. But it is not always remembered that this problem of safe-keeping continued far beyond the troubled days of medievalism. Henry VIII commanded that parish registers should be kept in coffers with two locks and keys, and valuables in chests of iron. Some early specimens found in old churches may date to the day when Edward VI commanded every parish to supply a strong chest, trebly locked and with a hole in the top for collecting money for the poor. But it was by no means unusual for a church to have custody of a family's plate chest.

By Elizabethan days a man of considerable wealth would have a jewel coffer such as was owned by the Earl of Leicester in 1588: 'A jewel coffer, with sundry boxes and partitions of redd leather, guilte, covered with fustian of Naples, nailed all over with yellow nails, barred with iron and w^{t} iij lockes and keies.' But for larger articles of plate he might use his 'great redd standard bound with iron, with lock and key'. The Earl at this time possessed nine other chests, covered with leather or Naples fustian, and also four Venetian chests, of carved and gilded walnut. The 1666 fire in London resulted in a great demand for new and stronger boxes for documents and valuables: the Pewterers, for instance, resorted to the purchase of two 'Sea Chests to secure ye Books, Deeds and Records.' Still later, the end of the seventeenth century witnessed an extreme intensity of hoarding, and Georgian furniture with its many hiding-places testifies to the continuance of the nagging anxieties of possessions. Some extraordinarily elaborate strong-boxes date to the seventeenth and eighteenth centuries.

The collector traces the development of the plate chest from the earliest dug-out through the medieval thick-planked trunk, the wood as much as 2, occasionally 3, inches thick, too heavy to move, doubly or trebly locked, banded with iron and perhaps guarded at the hinges with iron chains or perhaps chained to the wall. The chest, 11 feet long, in Chipping Sodbury (Gloucestershire) town hall, dating to about 1500, is so heavily banded with iron bolted to the thick oak that its weight has been calculated at one and a half tons. Ironwork ornament had been superseded by cheaper alternatives by the fourteenth century, but the idea of chests constructed wholly of metal is not so ancient. Even the Blacksmiths' Company themselves in 1496 kept their valuables in 'a gret Cheste of elme in length VII fote di w^{t} a box Thereynne w^{t} III lokks and III keies'. Some chests were banded with iron in both directions. When this developed into the chest wholly of iron this so recommended itself to the rich liveried companies that even such craftsmen in wood as the Carpenters bought an iron chest in Charles I's reign for keeping their stocks and bonds, worth over £4,000 (Plate 128E).

By the late seventeenth and throughout the eighteenth century many of the most elaborate strong-boxes were imported from Germany. These were long associated, erroneously, with the Spanish Armada, and are described under the usual popular name of Armada chests.

Adze-surfaced Wood: some late medieval and early Tudor chests of heavy, strong construction show a pleasing irregularity of surface under the metal bandings, due to being faced with an adze. This tool, resembling a hatchet but with the blade at right angles to the shaft, inevitably left the surface faintly patterned with ridges and saucer-shaped hollows.

Armada Chests: these iron strong-boxes were imported from Germany in the late seventeenth century and throughout the eighteenth, and have no association in fact with the Spanish Armada. They were copied by English craftsmen, but not usually in such elaboration. In the typical design the whole lid was a gigantic lock, with as many as a dozen bolts – occasionally twice that number – which when shot caught under the turned-in edges of the sides. A false keyhole was usually included in the front, although this must have been too well known to any potential cracksman to have any security value; the real keyhole was in the lid hidden by a small plate that sprang up when a knife was pushed under one of the metal straps. For further security there might be looped hasps or staples for fastening with padlocks. But the metal itself was thin and would not offer much resistance to a modern safe-breaker. The lock often had a highly decorative plate, engraved and pierced, and in some instances the whole chest was ornamented with wrought-iron scrolls. Further decoration was provided with painted pictorial work.

Coffers: term frequently applied in circumstances that indicate a strong-box, and in the plural bearing a direct association with money, as for instance Dryden's 'Money in our Coffers'. In the king's household, Bailey's dictionary (1730) points out, the cofferer was the name for the second officer under the comptroller, responsible for paying the other officers their wages. Early references are numerous. Beket in 1300 had 'a lute cofre' in which at least £800 was kept, and as late as 1732 Lediard referred to 'several coffers and cabinets filled with stuffs and gold'. But here again it is unwise to be over-precise; for one finds, for instance in a Bury will of 1463, a more general and typical application – 'a lityl grene coffre for kerchys'.

Compartment Chests: when safe keeping was the main preoccupation, a large chest or standard, and its lid, might both be divided into two or more parts, each fitted with its own lock.

Construction: it is important to recognize that primitive construction is no guarantee of age. The first advance from pegged or hammered-up plank construction towards a framed style may be dated to as early as around the mid-fifteenth century; the four big upright pieces, stiles, were grooved to receive one or more tongued horizontal side planks placed flush with the stiles and often cross-banded at the corners with iron. But village carpenters and other craftsmen continued to meet local needs long after the joiner became established in England making his joined chests (q.v.). It is interesting to note that in 1500 the Carpenters' Company went to a joiner to make them a chest. In the early seventeenth century many of the elaborate effects of panelling were achieved merely with glued-on ornament, and decorative panelling gave place to veneering. By the eighteenth century all constructional methods were in use. As an additional security, a plate chest might have its ends drilled with vertical holes so that it could be screwed to the floor.

Counters: usually large, strong chests, found especially in merchants' houses, with their flat lids scored for reckoning. They are often noted in inventories of the main halls in Elizabethan houses.

Ironwork: some of the most interesting early work was fashioned by hammering the hot iron into chilled iron dies. Some extremely attractive flower-and-leaf patterns were achieved in this way, which may be compared with the grille on the tomb of Queen Eleanor in Westminster Abbey dating to 1292. Otherwise the bands were wrought by the blacksmith in a manner so traditional that it is virtually impossible to date it. The metal itself, of course, may be distinguished from modern iron, but not easily from Tudor or early Stuart work. Charcoal-smelted iron has a black tone, and never the fresh bright rust of modern work. Some bands were let into the wood of the chest to their full thickness, but more usually projected to take the rub of wear, especially on their massive nail heads. The majority were plain or had simply ornamented terminals. Iron ornament returned only with the pseudo-medieval castings of the nineteenth century. Even apart from any question of security, the everyday usage of earlier, rougher centuries demanded strong construction. Catherine Parr complained that the royal children Mary and Elizabeth smashed all the furniture in their Hatfield apartments except what was made of cast-iron or massive oak (Plate 128C).

Jewel Chests: in some instances a chest of the so-called Armada type would hold a rich family's jewels, although these are more particularly associated with companies and official holders of securities. Ralph, first Earl Verney, in his will in 1752 referred to his wife's little iron jewel chest, but indicated that more jewels and money were concealed in a cabinet in the trunk-room. Obviously one of the major requirements of the small many-compartmented cabinet was as a container for jewellery, handsome enough to be worthy of its contents. These are considered under the section on Cabinets.

Between these extremes, very many small chests were made of other sturdy materials for jewellery. Often they were trunk-shaped with rounded lids, substantial lock-plates and heavy metal corner-pieces. The earlier iron-work was replaced by brass in the course of the seventeenth century, this often being engraved in the eighteenth century and sometimes including four small brass feet. The trunk itself, perhaps 18 inches wide by 12 inches high, might be veneered in decorative burr or oyster walnut, or covered in leather or japanning, or even made of wicker-work (Plate 128C and F).

Joined Chests: few survivors may be dated earlier than the sixteenth century. In these the horizontal rails and vertical stiles and intervening muntins were secured with mortise-and-tenon joints, often by the draw-bore process, and grooved on their inner sides to hold loose panels allowing for the wood's reactions to changing atmospheric conditions, especially important in the tough, widely used oak of standard and coffer. Panels tended to be small to minimise joining and yet avoid cutting into the centre of the tree's heartwood, most liable to warp. In 1632, when some sort of agreement was attempted between carpenters and joiners, the joiner's work was defined to include 'all Sorts of Chests being framed duftalled pynned or Glued' (Plate 127D).

Locks: these followed the styles used on other contemporary woodwork, early specimens depending on quantity rather than intricacy, although the provision of a number of locks on a parish or company chest was mainly a safeguard against a dishonest or careless key-holder, different officials each being responsible for one key. In some instances a plate or muniments chest with three locks had iron staples so arranged that a bar run through them would make it even more difficult to prise open the lid until all were unlocked.

Locksmithing was a well-established craft in London by the twelfth century, the principle of the warded construction remaining unchanged until late in the eighteenth century. Plate locks were the rule until the late fifteenth century, and continued in most general use until mid-Victorian days. The exposed working parts, perhaps slightly ornamented, were riveted to a heavy hatchet-shaped plate of wrought-iron fixed flat against the wood. While iron and steel were very costly, the comparative cheapness of plate-locks was a strong recommendation. It must be stressed, however, that there was an Early Victorian craze for reproducing early plate-locks, distinguishable by the fact that they were riveted to rolled or cast-iron plates instead of hammered iron. Improvements in the locks' appearance were made in the sixteenth and early seventeenth centuries, but the metal itself wore badly. The most decorative might bear hand-sawn Gothic pierced ornament or coats-of-arms, and were bright with paint and gold leaf. Damascening on steel lock cases was introduced in the late sixteenth century and by the 1620s lock-cases were being engraved as a specialist trade, and afterwards fire-gilded to prevent rust.

Meanwhile lock-cases of latten had come into use, mostly Dutch metal until the 1730s, except for a period of monopolistic action when flawed English metal had to be used; such locks usually dated between 1660 and 1675. Early decoration on brass locks was punched. By the end of the seventeenth century locks were sometimes sold with matching accessories, such as hinges and key escutcheons. Greatly improved English brass replaced the latten in the mid-eighteenth century. In considering late locks, the collector may note that cases and parts for cheap locks were first cut from sheet iron by fly press, punched and bolstered, in 1796. Keys were hand-forged until 1812, and thereafter might be of stamped wrought-iron or, after 1816, might be cast.

Riven Wood: this was much used in early strong chests, saving labour although wasting wood, and ensuring enduring work, little subject to warping and splitting that would render a plate chest useless. The tree trunk was split or riven along the natural growth lines of dense, non-cellular tissue radiating from the tree centre. These rays show a relief on old, weathered, riven timber, and probably suggested the early linenfold patterns.

Silver: at periods when silver was lavishly used as a fashionable medium, silver caskets for jewels were devised. As early as 1494 Fabyan in his *Chronicles* wrote, 'he ordeyned a cheste or Trunke of clene sylver, to thentent yt all such juells and rych gyftes should be kept'. More date to the late seventeenth century, or to the 1820s onwards, when they suited the vogue for loading silver vessels with impressively heavy ornamental castings.

Standards: the most frequent term for large plate chests, described, for instance, in an inventory quoted by T. H. Turner: 'A square standard & covered with black letheir, & bowden with yrne, with 2 lokys. . . . A great red standard, full of stuff . . . a gret standard bound with ierne, with 2 lokks.' Many references might be noted, usually concerning wealthy households with considerable possessions. For instance, Henry VIII's privy purse expenses in 1530 included: 'for ij standards for to carry plate from yorke to hampton courte'. Wolsey in 1526, according to a quotation by Cavendish (1893), was sent three or four cartloads of stuff by the king 'and most parte thereof was lokked in great standerds'. (*See* also the section on Travelling Chests.)

NOTTINGHAM ALABASTER CARVING

By C. F. PITMAN

SPEAKING chemically, alabaster, commonly called gypsum, is only sulphate of lime which, crushed and calcined, makes admirable plaster. At the Reformation this fact doubtless facilitated the destruction of the images and altar-pieces produced in this material which, however, were sometimes, more or less surreptitiously, exported abroad [1] for private gain. (See Notes on pp. 195–6.)

In England alabaster was first used *decoratively* [2] round about A.D. 1160 on the west door of Tutbury's Norman parish church in Staffordshire. The parish church of Hanbury in the same county provides the earliest datable example of alabaster *figure* [3] *carving*; namely, the tomb-figure of a knight of *c.* 1280–1300. The alabaster used was quarried at Chellaston, Derbyshire, and at Tutbury, Staffordshire.

From the former site alabaster, both worked and unworked, was sent abroad [4] and to other parts of England – London,[5] for example. The affinity between tomb-carvers and these medieval workers of alabaster images, altar-pieces and residual plaques is very marked. The exact nature of the contact is, however, still unestablished, though undoubtedly related to changed conditions brought about by the Black Death of *c.* 1350.

It is quite possible the altar-piece and plaque carvers sprang from the carvers of 'tomb-weepers', clearly inferior craftsmen to the effigy-carvers whose apprentices they could have been.

In any event, the carvers of plaques and altar-pieces were originally attracted by the semi-translucent, creamy whiteness of this English alabaster, and the aesthetic appeal of the vellum page bedight with gold, red, blue and green accented by the packed 'black letter', quill-pen, Gothic writing (Plate 132A) of the period under review – *c.* 1340 to the Reformation.

During this fourteenth century, even when the influence of French ivories (Plate 129C) seems to be felt, the sculptor is always aware that his medium is stone and respects it. Nevertheless, by the mid-fifteenth century this approach is being rapidly superseded by much blunter carving (Plate 129B) and, as far as 'the images' are concerned, all-over colouring, thus producing an effect very similar to that of the great Flemish and German polychromed and gilded altar-pieces of carved wood, their contemporaries. Was this the outcome of foreign competition or an example of enhancing profits by ruthlessly reducing production costs by means of shoddy workmanship? An inextricable combination of both factors is probably the true answer.

Anyway, in the Victoria & Albert Museum alone, sufficient ferruginously [6] stained alabaster plaques can be seen both to justify this speculation and to make it clear that, by about 1450, these alabaster craftsmen were in any event rapidly becoming less selective with their material.

Alabaster – Clientele and Transport: (*a*) *The Home Market.* Let us examine the home and foreign markets, in that order. The material sold was composed of 'images' (Plate 129A, B, C), individual plaques in painted wooden shrines and, by the late fourteenth century, altar-pieces at which point in time the foreign trade rapidly increased. Nevertheless, the only properly documented home commission is Edward III's [7] to Peter the Mason of Nottingham for an altar-piece of the life of St George for St George's Chapel, Windsor. This no longer exists.

Records of two important commissions from Durham and Ripon [8] and the Suppression Inventory of the London Charterhouse (1538–9) show that, at one time or another, these monasteries had acquired both alabaster 'images' and altar-pieces. Wills, bequests and individual church inventories also show the consumption level of these objects, and considerably justify calling this craft a Nottingham one, despite production at York, Burton-on-Trent and Leicester. On this last point the existing vagueness is considerably the outcome of referring in legal [9] documents to any and everybody involved in this craft, from the actual alabaster carver to the mere travelling salesman, as an 'alablasterer'.

The Rivers Trent and Leen were the basic transport assets, though transport by land was not excluded, as the Edward III commission, just referred to, shows. It took ten carts with eight horses apiece and seventy days to get to Windsor and back. Nevertheless, today there are only five altar-pieces in England – three [10] in the Victoria & Albert Museum and two [11] in private collections.

(*b*) *The Foreign Market:* Foreign trade, on the other hand, is better documented. First there is Richard II's permit of 1382 to Cosmato Gentilis – Pope Urban II's agent for collecting Peter's pence – to take out of England an 'image of the Virgin, St Peter,[12] St Paul and a small Trinity'. This was via Southampton.

Then there is the famous altar-piece of 1456 (Plate 131) given to the Cathedral of St James at Compostella [13] by a priest named John Goodyear, Rector of Chale, Isle of Wight. There are also references to alabaster 'images' in the medieval import tax returns of Iceland. There is also one mid-fifteenth-century five-plaque altar-piece [14] in that country.

The further extent of this trade is measured by there being at least fourteen complete altar-pieces in France (Plate 132A and Plate 134), three in Italy (Plate 130), two in Denmark and one in Holland and Germany, not to mention many detached and widely dispersed plaques contributing to the approximately estimated total of 4,000.

Since single figure carvings have not as yet been definitively collated, it will here suffice to refer the reader, by way of a reminder of their existence, to the Boston *Trinity* (Plate 129A) found in Spain and *St Anne instructing the Virgin* (Plate 129B) found in Portugal in 1934, and the Flawford *Madonna and Child* (Plate 129C).

In short, it was no mean trade which extended from Iceland to Italy and from Portugal to, maybe, as far east as Russia (Plate 132C). The success of this trade in France was of course related to the facts that England controlled Aquitaine from 1355 to 1368 and, later, most of France from the victories of Henry V until the collapse of English power, so successfully opposed by St Joan of Arc.

In France the distribution centre seems to have been Bordeaux and the main transport route the River Garonne. Germany and the Netherlands were doubtless contacted through the Kentish ports and over the trade routes of the Hanseatic League. Trade with Scandinavia, many of whose medieval bishops were English, was apparently conducted through Yorkshire ports.[15]

Dating of Images, Plaques and Altar-pieces. Unless these are documented the dating is perforce deductive, partly stylistic, in any event tentative and mainly based on the principles laid down in 1913–14, and even now more or less unquestioned, by Professor E. S. Prior.[16] It is rarely that an accurate rendering of costume – as in the *St Anne instructing the Virgin*[17] (Plate 129B) – solves one's dating problems.

Prior's First Period is from about 1340 *to* 1380: To it belong such superb carvings as the Boston *Trinity* [18] (Plate 129A) and *The Madonna and Child* (Plate 129C), found in 1779 at Flawford, near Nottingham.

Both give the impression of serene happiness, smiling through that complete sculptural integrity destined to disintegrate during the fifteenth century. In this period individual plaques of various shapes were also made

(A) Holy Trinity, *c.* 1380–1410. *Museum of Fine Arts, Boston.*

(B) St Anne instructing the Virgin, *c.* 1436. *National Museum, Lisbon, Portugal.*

(C) 'Flawford' Madonna and Child, *c.* 1380. *Nottingham Castle Museum and Art Gallery.*

PLATE 129

Passion altar-piece. Between 1470 and 1500. *National Museum, Naples.*

Triptych (Life of St James of Compostella), 1456. *Cathedral of St James, Compostella, Spain.*

(A) Resurrection, etc. (Detail from right half of altar-piece at Yssac-la-Tourette, Puy de Dôme, France), *c.* 1450.

(B) Annunciation. Between 1380 and 1400, in a German painted wooden shrine. *Victoria & Albert Museum.*

(D) Adoration of the Kings. Between 1350 and 1400. *Long Melford Church, Suffolk.*

(C) Christ as King (also side view), *c.* 1400. *Stieglitz Museum, Leningrad.*

Coronation of the Virgin. Between 1420 and 1440. *Mrs Anthony Norman Collection.*

PLATE 133

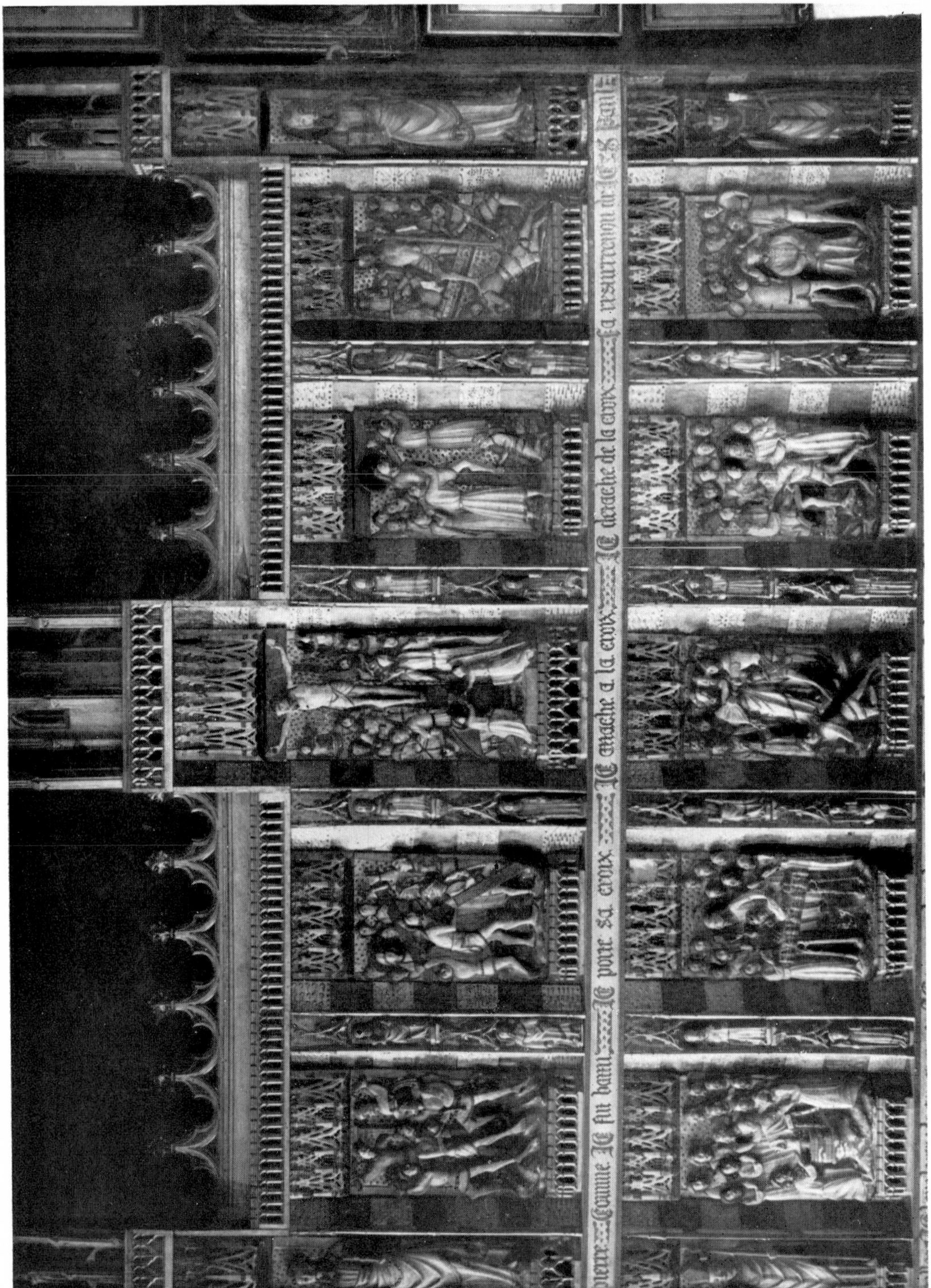

Passion altar-piece. Between 1475 and 1500. *Musée Vivinelle, Compiègne, France.*

(B) Coronation of the Virgin. Between 1460 and 1500. *Nyköping Museum, Sweden.*

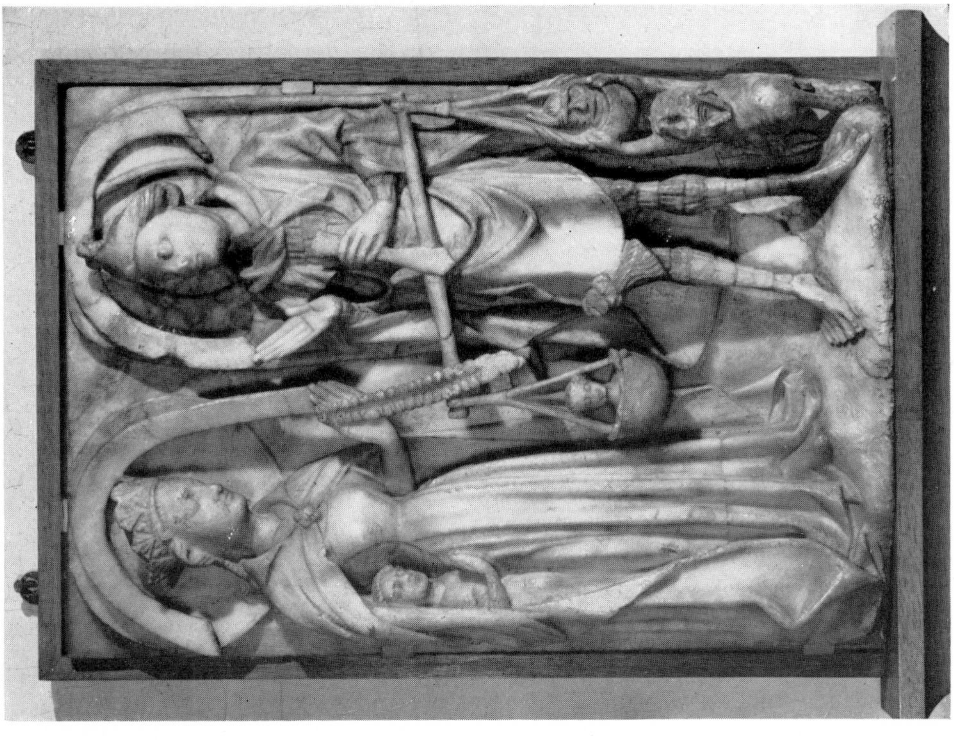

(A) The Judgement of Souls, *c.* 1450. *Sir Ronald Storrs Collection.*

(A) Adoration of the Kings. Between 1420 and 1460. *Sir Alfred Bossom, Bt. Collection.*

(B) The Resurrection. Between 1420 and 1460. *National Museum, Stockholm, Sweden.*

(C) Head of St John the Baptist on a Charger. Third quarter of the fifteenth century. *Municipal Museum, Leicester.*

PLATE 136

To face page 193

(Plate 132) – apparently more horizontals than uprights. Their carving is in low relief with an 'edging' suggesting a frame (Plate 132A). Such plaques have also been found pierced and with latten[19] attachments for hanging. It is therefore reasonable to assume that such work was inspired by private devotion.

Aesthetically, the fourteenth century is the best period, the easiest to identify, the most rare and, consequently, the most costly to acquire.

Prior's Second Period, c. 1380–1420: In it plaques become permanently upright with average size 17½ inches high by 10½ inches wide, and, when not the central plaque from an altar-piece, often much larger. Further, the 'picture-frame' edging is replaced by a thin edge sometimes bevelled (Plate 132C). This facilitated the placing of these plaques side by side in a painted and gilded wooden framework. Add a saint at each end, and phase one of the altar-piece has been evolved, probably around 1400. This was also stage two in building up a foreign market, the 'images' being most probably the first objects to be sold abroad in any quantity.

Low relief is now replaced by shallow carving rather than deep, and the plaques or 'tables' now have gilded backgrounds diapered with studs and 'embattled' tops. Finally towards 1420 five of these plaques are now assembled with an extra large one in the middle: stage two in the evolution of the altar-piece (Plate 130).

Prior's Third Period, c. 1420–60: In this period the altar-pieces are more and more characterized by uprights dividing the panels, the former rapidly becoming ornately decorated with small saints under canopied niches (Plate 132A). This last feature is certainly a reaction to the similar decorative features engraved on late fourteenth- and early fifteenth-century imported Flemish brasses.[20]

Hitherto the subject-matter has been mainly 'Scenes from the Passion' and from 'The Life of Our Lady'. Now lives of the saints are added, those of St Thomas à Becket and the very apocryphal St George being the most popular. Finally, shallow carving is replaced by very deep cutting; large 'floppy-hat' haloes (Plate 135B) become the vogue, together with much painting of flowers, sprigs and general decoration on dresses and furniture.

Prior's Last Period, c. 1460–80: This period could just as well be called 'from 1460 to the Reformation'. It is a period of rapidly degenerating craftsmanship, over-crowded compositions, general bad taste and, even, total iconographical confusion. The only triumph is the 'two-row' altar-piece (Plate 134), such as the superb example now in the Musée Vivinelle at Compiègne and, until the French Revolution, in the Church of St Germain l'Auxerrois, Paris.

INDIVIDUAL PLAQUES

St John Baptist Heads. There now remain for consideration a few representative 'tables', to use the medieval terminology of these makers of plaques.

Most distinctive of these plaques are 'The heads of St John Baptist on a charger'. Every one of them was originally in a painted wooden shrine (Plate 136C), like the one at Leicester, and none of them was ever at any time part of anything else. Nevertheless, they did not completely supplant other single-plaque subjects (Plate 132B) so popular in the fourteenth century.[21]

What is virtually the earliest documentary reference to a 'St John Baptist head' occurs in the 1417 inventory of St Kerrian's Church, Exeter, where an example is referred to in connexion with 'ij images de alabastre'. But no doubt exists in the 1432 will of Isabella Hamerton of York bequeathing there 'unum lapidem alabastri secundum formam capitis Sanctis Johannis Baptistae, and, of course, *The Nottingham Borough Records*[22] contain more references to this kind of plaque than to any other – whatever York[23] may, or may not, have contributed to their inception. These 'heads' were certainly on the market early in the fifteenth century, if not earlier, when phase one of their evolution was *either*, though doubtfully, the head alone in the round, as on the Continent,[24] *or* the head of the saint alone on a charger, carved in comparatively low relief on a plaque. There is such an example in the Metropolitan Museum, New York.

The next phase of their presentation represented, above the saint's head, his soul born in a napkin held by an angel (or two) with, to left and right, Saints Peter and Thomas à Becket. Nevertheless, 'the soul' was sometimes omitted, as in the Leicester Museum example here illustrated (Plate 136C). This formula is then developed by placing an 'Agnus dei' beneath the charger. Between 1444 and 1450, perhaps due to Franciscan influence, the final phase is reached by replacing the 'Agnus dei' with a demi-Christ (Plate 136C) 'displaying' his wounds in a tomb. This detail the Middle Ages called a 'Jesu's pity'.

The primary object of these plaques was to visualize a meditation on the sanctity of martyrdom, perchance to provide a calendar [25] and, incidentally, a 'sickness insurance' in days when St John the Baptist was invoked against all maladies of the head, from sore throat to headache and erysipelas. In England this saint was also the patron of the wool trade. This latter included everyone from wool-seller to cloth vendor, and medieval Nottingham was in the very centre of such activities.

The remaining plaques to be discussed are, or the majority of them, survivals from long-since dismembered altar-pieces, and will be considered iconographically.

ICONOGRAPHY

At this juncture it should be remembered that during the Middle Ages some ninety per cent. of mankind was totally illiterate, theocentric and acquiring its information from word of mouth when not from works of art. In addition, some of their religious beliefs were acquired both from, and expressed through, a dramatically presented liturgy.

It was, therefore, virtually inevitable that Mystery [26] and Morality plays, at the height of their influence in England by about 1450, should have contributed so much, though not everything, to the iconography of these particular medieval craftsmen. For example, the Crucified Christ on a lily stem (Plate 132B) is purely English symbolism. But its source – some hymn now lost? On the other hand, the three-flowered lily consistently rendered in 'Annunciations', is a clear allusion to Christ as a Person of the Trinity. Such an adequate symbol as this must surely have grown from direct clerical inspiration.

The two illustrated 'Coronations of the Virgin' (Plates 133 and 135B) show two other methods of symbolizing the Blessed Trinity. The Nyköping Museum 'Coronation' has a dove above the Madonna's head, and to the left Christ, enhaloed, wearing only the crown of thorns, whereas God the Father to the right has a golden crown. In the very lyrical 'Coronation' (Plate 133), owned by Mrs Anthony Norman, all three persons are identically crowned, though God the Father is the least in size.

Since size and lack of it were both symbols, the diminutive God the Father was clearly embarrassing, and this Trinity problem was never really satisfactorily solved despite the frequent presentation of all three persons on the same scale. The rest of the convention, figures on raised seats, is clearly a mystery play and stained-glass derivative not unallied, maybe, with harsh considerations of cost price, since we are not dealing with Fra Angelicos but 'hard-boiled' artisans out for a living and with spiritual aspirations as dulled as in most of us.

Another subject popularized through stained glass and painting, especially that of the fourteenth century, is *The Judgement of Souls by St Michael.*[27] But at that date and in those media the Madonna does not cast her rosary over the beam of the Archangel's scales. This is undoubtedly a dramatic contribution from the mystery players. St Michael's scaly legs should be understood as feathered tights recording a theatrical convention so ubiquitous as to figure in the presentation of him on those coins of Henry VI called angels. This subject in alabaster is comparatively rare. However, the two subjects with the best documented evidence of mystery play influences are *The Adoration of the Magi* and *The Resurrection.* All 'Adorations of the Magi' are from 'Life of the Virgin' altar-pieces, and the one illustrated (Plate

136A), because of the surviving colour and good condition, is a particularly fine example of its kind.

In medieval Coventry the Guild of Shearmen and Tailors undertook the Christmas cycle of plays, which included the *Adoration of the Kings*. Elsewhere this episode was frequently allocated to the Goldsmiths' and Silversmiths' Guilds. However, in the Coventry play St Joseph is described as 'an old man sitting at the Madonna's Knee' and one of the kings is told to point to the star. Then the Madonna speaks: 'I have a sonne . . .', followed by the instruction 'then the star will appear' which, if all went well, it doubtless did, being drawn across the little stage on a wire.

The iconography of the Resurrection, very frequently a plaque from a 'Passion' altar-piece, is provided by the Chester [28] mystery plays in the following instruction (in Latin) to the 'Christus' player: 'Jesus rising crushes the soldier with his foot'. The complaining words from the soldier which follow make this gesture quite clear and that the emphasis is on a corporeal resurrection. This particular convention, of a foot placed directly on a sleeping soldier, is extremely rare in Continental art.

One also wonders whether or not the royal regalia in any way contributed to the current iconography. The crowns worn by the Trinity (Plates 129A and C) and the Madonna in *St Anne instructing the Virgin* (Plate 129B) are, for example, very close to those on some of the contemporary coins; and when crosses on orbs have survived they are usually very long stemmed, as in the portrait of Richard II in Westminster Abbey.

The invariable 'daisy-dotted' green foregrounds began as decoration derived from manuscripts such as the fourteenth-century 'Queen Mary Tudor psalter' in the British Museum. When, however, this decoration occurs on the Cross [29] itself it may well be an allusion to the medieval [30] legend that the wood of the Cross was of the dead wood from the forbidden tree in Eden and that it flowered anew at the Redemption.

By way of conclusion one must add that there is a considerable Continental bibliography on the subject of alabasters and that the English contribution only seriously began in the opening years of this century with the writings of the late Sir William St John Hope. Since then some fifty per cent. of it has been the work of the American-born, English-residing, Dr W. L. Hildburgh, F.S.A., who died on 25th November, 1955.

Finally, the present state of our alabaster knowledge suggests that further documentary information is now much more likely to be found abroad than at home, and that a thorough and systematic stylistic analysis of the known material of all types would very probably lift much of the mist of uncertainty still overhanging this aesthetically erratic, though historically important, medieval English craft.

NOTES

1 Calendar of State Papers, Foreign, 1547–53, p. 55 – i.e. a letter dated 10th September, 1550, from Sir John Mason, English Ambassador to France, addressed to the Privy Council: 'Three or four ships have lately arrived from England laden with images, which have been sold to Paris, Rouen and other places, and being eagerly purchased, give to the ignorant people occasion to talk according to their notions; which needed not had their Lordships command for defacing of them been observed.'

2 (*a*) The whole door in *Staffordshire*, by Arthur Mee (Hodder & Stoughton, 1937), p. 209. (*b*) The alabaster detail in *English Mediaeval Sculpture*, by Gardner (Cambridge University Press, 1951), p. 315, Fig. 619.

3 *English Mediaeval Sculpture*, by Gardner (Cambridge University Press, 1951), p. 324, Fig. 641.

4 For export to Nantes *vide* T. Rymer, *Foedera*, O. VIII, 540; for export to Fécamp *vide* Bilson, *Archaeological Journal*, Vol. LXIV, pp. 32–7 (1907), and the same in *Transactions of the Thoroton Soc.* (Nottingham), Vol. XIV, 1910.

5 For examples of worked alabaster sent from Derbyshire to Newcastle via London *vide Historiae Dunelmensis Scriptores, tres* (Surtees Soc. 9), 135, 136.

6 For example, a *Flagellation* (No. 1572–1902); *Christ in Majesty* (No. A169–1946) and *Adoration of the Magi* (No. 95–46) in the Victoria & Albert Museum.

7 Issue Rolls of 42 Edward III (1367/68–68/69) and 45 Edward III (1370/71–71/72).

8 For Durham, see *Historiae Dunelmensis Scriptores, tres* (Surtees Soc. 9), 131, 135, 136. For Ripon, see *Memorials of Ripon* (Surtees Soc. 8), III, 18, 38, 39.

9 *Vide* the references to these craftsmen in *Nottingham Borough Records*, II & III.

10 (*a*) *The Last Supper*, Victoria & Albert Museum (48–1946). (*b*) *The Five Joys of Mary* (also called 'The Swansea' altar-piece) – from Singleton Abbey, though bought in Munich – Victoria & Albert Museum (89–1919). (*c*) *The Twelve Apostles* (an altar-piece that has lost its 'howsing'). Victoria & Albert Museum (148/59–1922).

[11] One of these, the mid-fifteenth-century altar-piece in the chapel of Haddon Hall, Derbyshire. *Vide Antiquaries' Journal*, XVII, Plates 49–51.

[12] T. Rymer, *Foedera*, O. VII, 357.

In *Antiquaries' Journal*, Vol. XXV (1955), p. 185 (with reproductions) Hildburgh argues convincingly that this St Peter and St Paul are now in the Church of Santa Croce in Gerusalemme, Rome. His arguments would have been conclusive had he contrasted this St Peter in Rome with the Flawford *Madonna and Child* (Plate 2). The cutting of the heads of both is identical and therefore the work of the same hand. Further, this St Peter holds a small symbolic church identical with that held by the (Nottingham) Flawford *St Peter as Pope*, reproduced in *The Connoisseur*, May 1954, Fig. 4. It can also be remarked here that the seated *Madonna and Child* in the Burrell (Glasgow Gallery) Collection (reproduced in *Scottish Art Review*, Vol. V, No. 4, p. 4) is also, on technical grounds, quite clearly from the same hand.

[13] *Vide Antiquaries' Journal*, Vol. VI (1926).

[14] Reproduced in *The Connoisseur*, Vol. 133 (May 1954), p. 226, Fig. xxiv.

[15] The whole transport question is variously discussed in (St John Hope) *Archaeological Journal*, Vol. LX (1904); (Destrée) *Annales de la Société d'archéologie de Bruxelles*, Vol. 23 (1909); (Nelson) *Archaeological Journal*, Vol. XXV (1918); and (Rostand) *Bulletin Monumental*, Vol. 87 (1928).

[16] *Illustrated Catalogue of the Exhibition of English Mediaeval Alabaster Work*, by W. St John Hope and E. S. Prior, held in the Rooms of the Society of Antiquaries, 26th May to 30th June, 1910, printed by H. Hart at Oxford in 1913 for the said Society.

[17] This attire, the adapted habit of a religious, was worn by 'vowesses', i.e. women vowed to maintain their widowhood. See, for example, the brass of Matilda Burghurst (1436) in Ewelme Church, Oxfordshire, reproduced on p. 252 *English Church Monuments*, by F. H. Crossley, F.S.A.

[18] Boston Trinity: whether, or not, such figures *without* a dove and *with* souls in a napkin can rightly be called 'Trinities' is discussed (Hildburgh) in *Folklore*, Vol. XLIV, March 1933, pp. 50 et seq.

[19] See authority referred to under note 15, and a fifteenth-century 'Trinity' in a shrine with such attachments in the Burrell (Glasgow Gallery) Collection.

[20] For example, the 1360 brass in St Alban's Abbey of Abbot Thomas Delamere d. 1396 – reproduced in *Costume in Brasses*, by Herbert Druitt, p. 46 (Alexander Moring Ltd, 1906).

[21] This late fourteenth-century plaque found in Cologne, once in the Kunstegewerbe Museum and now in the Victoria & Albert, is discussed by Hildburgh in *Folklore*, Vol. XLIV, March 1933, pp. 46–8. *Archaeologia*, Vol. XLIX, and *Archaeological Journal*, Vol. XXIV, p. 209, and *Antiquaries Journal*, Vol. XII, p. 24. There is a fifteenth-century single-plaque 'Ascension' in a shrine in the Victoria & Albert Museum.

[22] *Nottingham Borough Records*, II & III.

[23] See (St John Hope) *Archaeologia*, Vol. LII (1890), p. 707; Jacob, foreword to 'York Festival (Alabaster) Exhibition' Catalogue, 1954.

[24] See (St John Hope) *Archaeologia*, Vol. LII (1890), p. 707; (Hildburgh) *Antiquaries' Journal*, Vol. XVII, No. 4, March 1937.

[25] See (St John Hope) *Archaeologia*, Vol. LII (1890), pp. 669 et seq.; (Hildburgh) *Folklore* (June 1933), pp. 143 et seq.; (Hildburgh) *Folklore* (June 1949), pp. 261 et seq.; (Pitman) *Connoisseur* (May 1954), Vol. 133, pp. 222 et seq.

[26] *Re* mystery plays – in France: Emile Mâle in *Gazette de Beaux Arts* (1904); in England: (Hildburgh) *Archaeologia*, Vol. XCIII (1949), pp. 51–101.

[27] See (Hildburgh) *Folklore* (March, 1933), p. 48; (June 1949), p. 260.

[28] *Chester Plays* (Shakespeare Society) (London, 1843–7), Vol. II, p. 89.

[29] Such a 'daisy pattern' cross occurs on *Christ Carrying his Cross* in York Museum, for example (reproduced in *Preview*, No. 54, July 1954), and on central 'Trinity' on *The Swansea Altar-piece* (Victoria & Albert Museum, 89–1919). The practice is not extremely rare and leaves the impression that originally it was the norm.

[30] The legend referred to discussed in (Miss M. R. Bennett) *Archaeological Journal*, Vol. LXXXIII. *The Kettlesbaston Trinity* (fragment) in the British Museum has only a green cross.

BOOKS FOR FURTHER READING

The desired information is large and, unfortunately, very scattered, consequently has mainly to be garnered from the learned periodicals cited below. The foreign bibliography is smaller, equally scattered and involves most European languages. It is certainly of importance to a student to be soaked in the English bibliography before becoming involved in the Continental. America has also contributed sporadically to research in this subject, but it is never the most easily accessible material.

BOOKS

Evans, Joan: *English Art*, 1307–1451 (Batsford, 1921).

Gardener, A.: *Alabaster Tombs* (Cambridge Univ. Press, 1940).

Gardener, A.: *English Mediaeval Sculpture* (Cambridge Univ. Press, 1951).

Prior, E. S. and Gardner, A.: *Mediaeval Figure Sculpture in England* (Cambridge Univ. Press, 1912).

PERIODICALS

Numerous articles and references contributed to *The Antiquaries' Journal*, *The Archaeological Journal*, *Archaeologia*, *The Burlington Magazine* and *The Connoisseur*.

CATALOGUES

Prior's preface to illust. cat. "English Mediaeval Alabaster Work" (Soc. of Antiq. 1910), London, 1913.

Introduction (J. Jacob) in cat. "English Mediaeval Alabaster Carvings"—York Festival Exhibition, 1954.

CHESS-MEN

By G. BERNARD HUGHES

'KYNG RYCHARD stode and playe At the Chesse in his Galley' records a manuscript in the British Museum describing the Third Crusade (1189–92). For long chess was considered a royal and noble accomplishment, to be played with costly chess-men of ivory enriched with gold and jewels. The less illustrious eventually became devotees, and by 1474 the game was sufficiently popular in England for William Caxton to publish *The Game and Playe of Chesse*, with twenty-four woodcuts illustrating the type of men then in use. The book was profitable, and two years later Caxton published a further work on the game.

Chess-men by then were for the most part shaped by the turner in his lathe from hardwood in two contrasting colours, or in beech and ash, one side in natural colour, the other stained or painted, usually in red. Such a utility set is recorded in the Howard Household Accounts, 1481: 'Pay^d^ to the chess-maker for chess-playes viij^d^'. A century later a simple, turned set usually cost three shillings, the board eightpence.

Cabinet chess-men were highly prized possessions, and might be in finely carved ivory enriched with gold. Many fifteenth-century examples are recorded. Such a set might be enclosed in an ivory chest, the lid designed as a chess-board. The Earl of Northampton played on 'a table of Ebonie inlaid with Ivorie and men suteable'. Board and men were valued at five shillings after his death in 1614. More sumptuous was the earl's fashionable set, displayed in a 'cabinett of purple velvett with men suteable, laced with gold lace': this was valued at ten pounds.

Although ivory, ebony and wooden chess-men have always been preferred, there was a vogue in the seventeenth century for sets cast in metal, turned in the lathe and hand-finished. These might be in bronze or brass, one side enriched with bright colours and gilding; in burnished pewter, one side gilded: or in lead with one side tinned and burnished. Records of such sets are frequent, particularly with one side in bronze, the other in pewter. Other contrasting materials include light and dark amber, pink and white alabaster, Scottish pebble and agate, Derbyshire spars and marbles, horn and ivory, the latter being a favourite combination with Stuart chess-players.

GLOSSARY

Alphin: the old name for the bishop, derived from the Italian *alfieri* or standard-bearers who administered the king's laws. English players eventually altered these pieces into cross-bearing bishops, supporting the king as immediate upholders of law and order.

Boards: at first chess-boards were oblong with ninety-six squares in a single colour, as against the later square board with sixty-four squares in alternating colours. The ninety-six-square chess-board, twelve squares by eight squares, brought into use pieces now unknown to the chess-player – camels, horses and elephants. Caxton in his *Game and Playe of Chesse* noted that the square chess-board was designed 'after ye forme of ye citie of Babylon'. The squares might be marked on leather, heavy textile, wood or tables of baked clay.

Fashionable chess-boards in England alternated ivory and ebony, or a natural ivory with stained ivory, and each square might be engraved with a pictorial scene. Others were of coloured hardwoods: mother of pearl was also used, white nacre alternating with green or other dark-hued shell. For everyday use a wooden board was preferred. This might be inlaid with woods of contrasting colour or a solid board might have the alternate squares coloured with red lead or stained or burned to a dark hue.

After the restoration of the monarchy in 1660 fine chess-boards, exquisitely enriched with parquetry work in exotic woods and ivory, were made. The design might consist of two shallow box-like sections hinged together to contain playing chess-men. The squares were veneered with burr or oyster walnut alternating with holly, lignum vitae or other distinctive wood. Boards set with coloured leathers were also used.

Makers of chess-boards might also turn wooden sets of chess-men: records show that the trade was well-established in Tunbridge Wells by the late seventeenth century. Georgian chess-board makers might advertise themselves as turners in ivory, joiners and turners in wood, but more frequently as makers of Tunbridge ware – not to be confused with nineteenth-century wood mosaic work.

Castleford: chess-men in vitrified stoneware were made here between 1795 and 1821 by David Dunderdale. Opposing colours were at first black basalts and white stoneware, then coloured slips were used and sets might be in chocolate brown and greyish green, or greyish blue and white. The king and queen represent George III and Queen Charlotte, both in their state robes and crowned; the pawns are kilted Scots Guards, and the rooks are elephants carrying square castellated towers. Both sides were made from the same moulds. These have been widely copied.

Doulton: George Tinworth designed a brown and white mouse chess-set for Doultons in 1887. These were hand-modelled throughout in bone china. The castle depicts a mouse within a barred dungeon.

East India Company: for more than a century the company imported sumptuously carved ivory chess-men in a number of ornate designs. One considerable issue depicts India and the Company as opponents, both sides being left white, the Indians standing on black or coloured bases. Rajahs and viziers – queens are unknown in Eastern sets – are represented by laden elephants, the former carrying howdahs. Bishops take the form of lions for the Company, red bulls for India; Company knights ride horses, the Indians are on dromedaries.

Ivory: English workers in ivory were considered inferior to Continental ivory carvers and turners until early in the eighteenth century when fashion demanded exquisitely carved and fretted fan-sticks. Soon English craftsmen engaged in this work were also fulfilling a demand for intricately carved and turned chess-men, competing successfully with sets imported by the East India Company. The ivory might be tinted red, green or blue.

There was a vogue for chess-men mounted on pedestals having as their main feature several free concentric hollow fretted balls. The king and queen might each contain as many as seven of these delicate, loosely revolving balls in their pedestals. Contrary to general opinion, much of this delicate turning and carving was carried out in England, particularly in London and Wolverhampton. Technical works, such as C. Plumier's *The Art of the Turner*, 1701, gave fully illustrated instructions regarding such turning in ivory.

Minton: in 1850 Herbert Minton issued chess-men in Parian ware, designed by the celebrated sculptor, John Bell.

Pawn: the name is the old English form of peon or day labourer, and in old English chess-sets they were carved to represent eight occupations: the king's pawn, a banker-merchant; the queen's pawn, a physician-apothecary; bishops' pawns, notaries, inn-keepers or provision dealers; knights' pawns, keepers of the king's highway or workers in stone, iron or wood; rooks' pawns, letter-carriers and farm labourers. Not until the late eighteenth century was it usual to carve eight identical pawns for a cabinet set.

Pipe-clay: chess-men in pipe-clay are exhibited in the London Museum.

Rockingham: chess-men were made in bone-china between 1822 and 1826. Exact copies of an earlier Meissen set, with figures wearing Tudor clothing, were made, as well as conventionally turned sets. The opposing sides were in apple green and periwinkle blue enriched with gilding.

Rook: derived from the Italian *rocchi* meaning towers or castles, which were the king's outposts maintaining his authority in distant parts of the kingdom.

Silver: chess-men in silver were made throughout the eighteenth century modelled as opposing armies such as the Romans *v.* Barbarians, Frederick the Great *v.* Maria Theresa and Napoleon *v.* the Mamelukes.

Staunton: these very popular chess-men were designed by the Hon. Howard Staunton, son of the Earl of Carlisle, and registered by him at the Patent Office in 1849. Their makers then, as now, were Messrs John Jacques & Son, London. The conventional king and queen are crowned, the bishop mitred and the rook a castellated tower. They are found in boxwood, natural colour and dyed red or black.

Wedgwood: Josiah Wedgwood in 1783 commissioned John Flaxman to design a set of chess-men for production in blue and white jasper. Flaxman modelled his men as actors playing Macbeth, each armed with a primitive weapon, such as stones, bows and arrows, battle-axes and daggers. Charles Kemble is depicted as Duncan, King of Scotland, and Mrs Siddons as the queen, each in three different models. The remaining pieces were issued only in one model, the rooks with square crenellated towers, the knights on prancing horses, mitred bishops draped in copes. In chess sets intended for the French market the bishops were replaced by jesters, known to the Wedgwood potters as Tom Fools.

Wedgwood chess-men were made with three types of bases: rough mounds indicate the 1784 edition issued only in blue and white. These were superseded by flat, wafer-like bases, in their turn superseded by short, plainly turned attic plinths. Colours were grey, mauve, dark biscuit, blue, Flemish green, buff and white; a few in white were on blue dipped bases. Pieces were usually of a single colour, occasionally enlivened with a touch of gold. They sold at five guineas the set.

Jasper chess-men were again issued during the mid-nineteenth century, blue with bases of black and natural boxwood distinguishing the opposing sides. These sold for £3 10*s.* 6*d.* the set. Stoneware chess-men of the same period cost £3 1*s.* 6*d.* the set.

All Wedgwood chess-men are impressed WEDGWOOD: early examples also bear model numbers and workmen's marks in the form of single initials or fine lines.

BOOKS FOR FURTHER READING

BEALE, FRANCIS, translated from Greco Gioacchino: *The Royall Game of Chesse-Play* (1656).

HAMMOND, ALEX: *The Book of Chessmen* (1950).

MURRAY, H. J. R.: *A History of Chess* (1913).

Chess-set in gold and silver filigree; formerly in the possession of Madame de Stael. *Alex Hammond.*

PLATE 137

To face page 200

(A) Chess-set in ivory, Mortals and Immortals including (top) Mercury, Minerva, Jupiter, Mars, Zeus. The king and queen of the Mortals (below) represent King David and the Queen of Sheba. *Alex Hammond.*

(B) Ivory chess-set carved in Delhi to the commission of the East India Company, *c.* 1790. *Alex Hammond.*

(A) Two knights and two pawns from a set of silver and silver-gilt chess-men representing a battle between the Romans and the Barbarians. Possibly designed by the German architect and sculptor Andreas Schluter, *c.* 1700. *Metropolitan Museum of Art.*

(B) Two kings and two knights representing Frederick the Great (back to camera) in opposition to Maria Theresa with Hungarian troops, *c.* 1750. *Metropolitan Museum of Art.*

(C) King and Queen and two pawns of a Cantonese chess-set in ivory. *Alex Hammond.*

(A) Wood-cut and stencil pack, with wrapper of second-quality playing-cards known as 'Harrys', 1807–10. *Victoria & Albert Museum.*

(B) Typical court cards from a pack dating to about 1810. The outlines are from woodcuts and the colouring has been added by stencils. *Victoria & Albert Museum.*

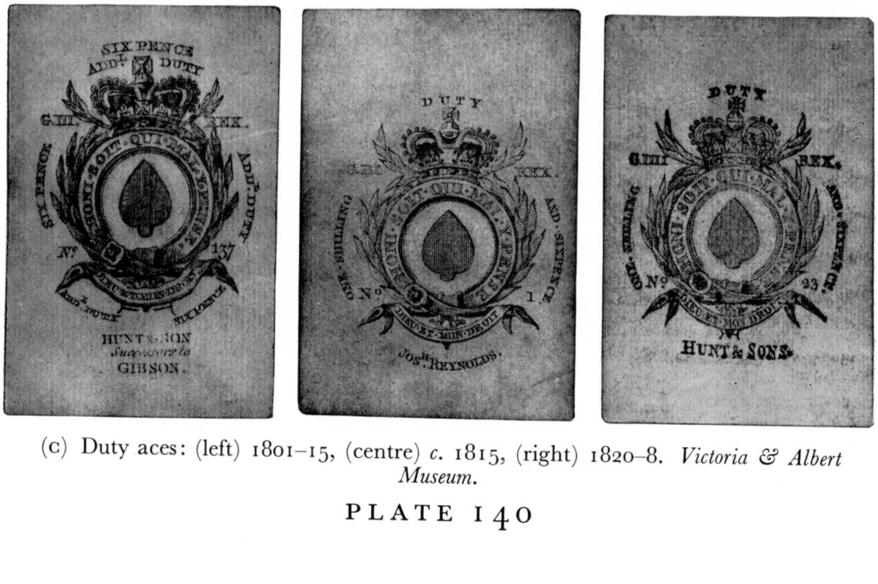

(C) Duty aces: (left) 1801–15, (centre) *c.* 1815, (right) 1820–8. *Victoria & Albert Museum.*

PLATE 140

(A) Duty aces: (*Top left*) 1789–1801; (*Top right*) after 1862; (*Lower left*) 1789–1801; (*Lower right*) 1765–76. *Victoria & Albert Museum.*

(B) Marlborough's victories, the disputes regarding the Spanish succession, and other events in the reign of Queen Anne are elaborated on this pack, 1707–8. *Victoria & Albert Museum.*

(C) Cards from a pack dating to George III's reign, showing one of several unsuccessful attempts to change the conventional suit marks and court cards; here the two suits are clovers and topaz. *Victoria & Albert Museum.*

A backgammon board of inlaid walnut of the type made at Tunbridge Wells in the late seventeenth century.
Victoria & Albert Museum.

Games board marked inside for backgammon and outside for mereles and fox and geese, and for chess and draughts. Framed in ebonized pearwood and decorated with marquetry of satinwood, boxwood, tulip and other woods. Early seventeenth century. *Victoria & Albert Museum.*

(A) Sheraton sofa table in satinwood, with edges cross-banded in rosewood. The reversible top slide conceals a tric-trac board.

(B) Games table in amboyna wood, with single drawer and slide below marked for chess on one side and backgammon on reverse. The top opens, turning on a swivel, to form card table with central panel of green leather.

(C) Combined games, reading and work table, the top section in burr yew, the lower in straight-grained yew. *Judge Jeffreys Antiques.*

(D) A games table made at Tunbridge Wells, *c.* 1845, for the Prince Consort. Decorated with mosaic. In Kensington Palace. *By gracious permission of Her Majesty the Queen.*

PLATE 144

OLD ENGLISH PLAYING-CARDS

By G. BERNARD HUGHES

FOR more than five centuries English modes and manners have been recorded with uninhibited enthusiasm, not in books or pictures prepared with some thought for posterity, but on innumerable thousands of playing-cards. Even by the later fourteenth century card-playing commoners were so neglectful of their work that a law was passed confining such activities to holidays for all but the nobility. In 1532 fifteen-year-old Mary, future Queen of England, was granted a monthly allowance for her play. Elizabeth I in her turn earned a reputation for being a bad loser. Our court cards still bear representations of Henry VIII and his mother.

Where royalty led, the people followed,

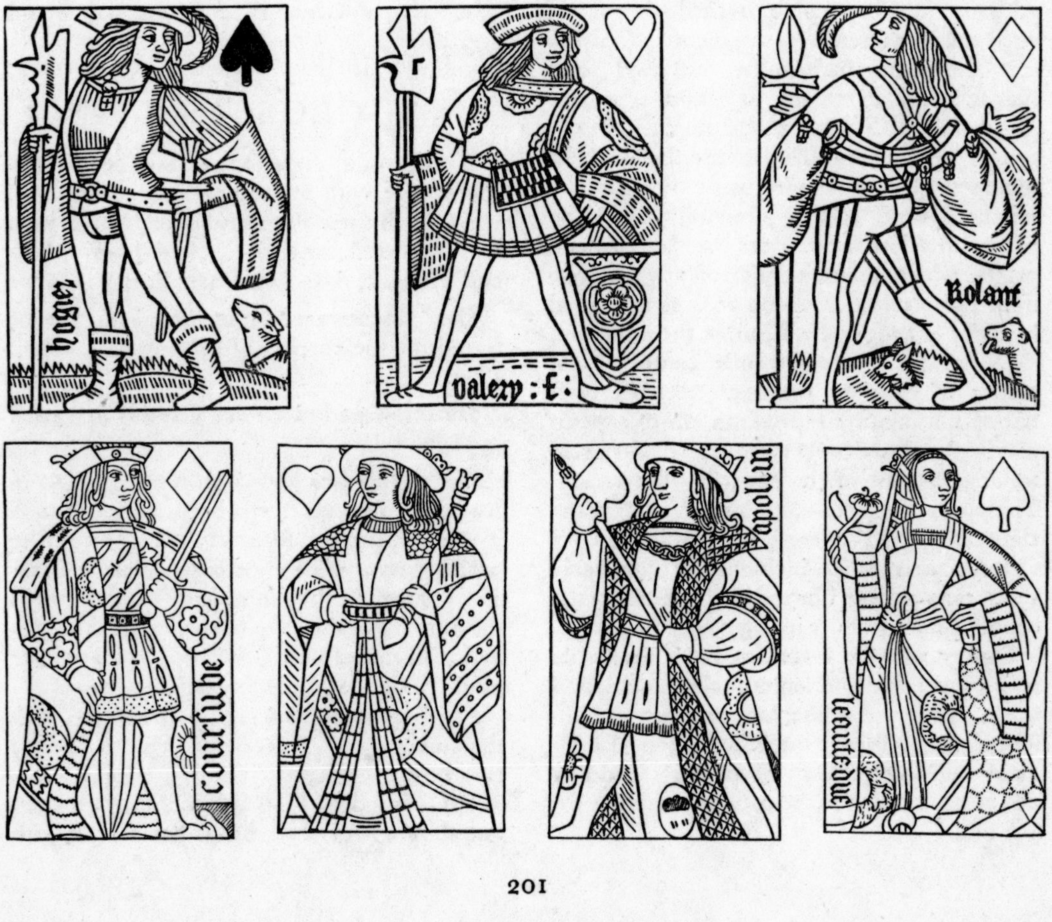

the magnificent packs of cards created in gold and colours by the manuscript illuminators supplanted and replaced by an endless range of packs less ambitious but almost as alluring. In addition to the more decorative cards far greater quantities of purely utilitarian cards were manufactured. Shop inventories show that by Elizabethan days the general merchant might reckon his stock at two shillings for a dozen packs. Elizabethans referred to a pack as a bunch of cards, and during the following century it was known as a 'pair of cards'.

At first playing-cards were made of parchment or varnish-stiffened fabric; paper came into use at the end of the sixteenth century. Once paper became common, cheaper methods were applied, with crude hand-colouring over printed outlines, at first made with wood blocks and later with copper plates. Even the ornate cards fashionable by Charles II's reign were often crude enough. Although they were plain backed, the face of each was so elaborately ornamented that the suit and value had to be restricted to a narrow strip across the top, and even this strip might include an arabic numeral in the centre relating to the picture below. On some seventeenth-century packs the suits and numbers were tucked obscurely into the corner to allow more space for the pictorial prints, which might consist of any subject, from the crudest lampoon to instruction in heraldry or geography, Latin or the alphabet.

Often, by the eighteenth century, one corner of such an ornamented card contained a miniature representation of a plain playing-card to denote its suit and value, still leaving the rest of the card for illustration. The outlines of such popular subjects as the elaborate series recording Marlborough's victories and other incidents of the early 1700s may appear blurred, so worn were the copper plates from printing many packs.

Ombre was the favourite game for ladies and piquet for gentlemen; clergymen and squires preferred whist; and commoners all-fours, put, cribbage and contraloo. Landlords used to send a string of hog's pudding and a pack of cards for a Christmas gift for tenants.

When a *duty* was placed on playing-cards, no person was allowed to manufacture them except in London and Westminster, and in Dublin; manufacture was prohibited in Scotland. Every card manufacturer was required to give two securities for £500 before a licence could be obtained. The duty and export aces were printed at Somerset House, on paper furnished by the card-makers who also had to pay £30 for every ace-plate, on which were engraved twenty aces.

Collectors' packs of the eighteenth century include 'Proverbs and Witty Sayings' issued intermittently from 1710; 'Aesop's Fables', 1759; 'The Rulers of Europe' by Rowley & Company, 1769; and 'London Street Cries' after Wheatley's engravings, 1795. In 1781 Rowley & Company issued playing-cards in which spades were replaced by blue pike heads, clubs by green trefoils, hearts by red chalices, and the diamonds by yellow faceted topaz. The court cards showed the reigning monarchs of Great Britain, France, Spain and Prussia.

GLOSSARY

Backs: until about 1840 backs of playing-cards were with few exceptions quite plain, with rough surfaces easily soiled. Cards with highly glazed, enamel-finished backs, difficult to mark, date from early in the 1830s.

Cut Corners: it was illegal to cut or round off the corners of playing cards until 1862.

Double-headed Court Cards: first used in 1867.

Duty: this was levied on playing-cards in August 1712, and from that date until 1862 it was compulsory for every ace of spades to bear a duty mark indicating payment of tax. The changes in the reigning monarchs and in the amount of the tax are shown in a chronological series of aces, making it an accurate guide in the dating of packs:

1712–14: duty sixpence. A red stamp with the monogram A.R. (for Queen Anne) crowned.

1714–65: duty sixpence until 1756, then one shilling. A red stamp as before, but with the letters G.R. (for all three Georges). The red ink used for the stamp has usually faded and is sometimes scarcely visible.

1765–76: duty one shilling, half of this being levied by a stamp on the pack's wrapper. The monarch was signified by the letters G. III Rex, and the design on the card consisted of a Garter surrounding the ace of spades, wreaths at the sides, surmounted by a crown, and with DIEU ET MON DROIT on a ribbon below.

1776–89: duty raised to one shilling and sixpence, the previous stamp surmounted by the words SIXPENCE ADD[L] DUTY.

1789–1801: duty raised again, to two shillings. This time SIXPENCE was printed to the left and ADD[L] DUTY to the right.

1801–15: duty two shillings and sixpence. There were now three indications of sixpenny increases, the third – ADD[L] DUTY SIXPENCE – appearing below the design.

Circa 1815: duty continued to be half a crown, but the wording was changed on the stamp to DUTY at the top, ONE SHILLING to the left and AND SIXPENCE to the right. The other shilling was made up by two embossed sixpenny stamps on the wrapper.

1820–8: duty half a crown, with the stamps as before, but the monarch was changed to G. IIII.

1828–62: duty down to one shilling, with a new design of ace, so intricate that it was known as Old Frizzle, surmounted by the words DUTY ONE SHILLING. This ace contained the royal heraldic quarterings and was supported by a lion and unicorn.

1862: duty down to threepence, levied on the wrapper. There was thus no duty ace, but card manufacturers continued to produce elaborate aces of spades, and some late-nineteenth-century and early-twentieth-century aces carry the words DUTY THREE PENCE WHEN USED IN GREAT BRITAIN AND IRELAND.

Figure Indices: these date from 1862.

Fortune-telling Packs: first issued in 1665. They consist of fifty-two cards with two others of complicated instructions. In the upper left corner of each is a suit sign and the cards in each suit are numbered I to XIII, the odd numbers bearing a circle with signs of the zodiac, the even-numbered cards each holding answers.

Geographical: the earliest were issued in 1665 by H. Winstanley, Lothbury. Hearts represent Europe, diamonds Asia, spades Africa, clubs America. Packs illustrating the fifty-two counties of England and Wales were popular.

Letter Values: first used in 1884.

Oil-colour Printing: this process was patented by the firm of De la Rue in 1832, a quick-drying printing ink not liable to rub off in glazing being applied by metal or wooden blocks. This method gave a sharper impression, and colours were more vivid than formerly.

Paper: until the 1790s Genoa paper was used exclusively because of its silkiness and power of receiving colour freely. It took the glazing flint better than did the harsh English paper. Later cardboard was used consisting of four sheets of paper: two strong sheets of cartridge-paper were pasted together and covered on each side with strong, roller-sized paper.

Quality: three qualities of playing-cards were sold. The best were labelled 'Moguls', the slightly defective 'Harrys', and the defective 'Highlanders'. Each pack was placed in a wrapper with a thread tied around it, and sealed by a revenue officer when required.

Second-hand Packs: the reissue of second-hand packs was common, enabling once-used packs to become servants' perquisites. They were then sold to the original vendors: this resulted in the production of forged aces, now collectors' prizes.

Stencilling: from the late seventeenth century to the 1830s the majority of cards were stencilled. Court-card outlines were printed from two pear-wood blocks, the designs so arranged that the figures on the one block were coloured red, yellow, blue, grey (a dilute blue) and black; the figures in the second block contained no black. These produced court cards for ten packs. The pips had a printing block for each suit, each containing cards for two packs. The colours were applied to the blocks by means of a paper stencil stiffened by painting each side with several coats of oil paint. The cards were then well-dried, aired and then rubbed with Castile soap, which enabled the glazing flint to be operated without damaging the card.

Transformation Cards: first issued in London, 1808. In these pictures the requisite number of suit signs served as prominent features, such as hearts for men's faces, diamonds as parts of feminine dress, clubs and spades as carved motifs in pseudo-Gothic furniture. Making transformation cards from ordinary packs became a fashionable pastime, pen and ink converting cards into designs of topical or personal association. It is difficult for the collector to recognize recently transformed cards unless the artist has inadvertently used a pack of later date.

BOOKS FOR FURTHER READING

BENHAM, W. G.: *History of the Pack and Explanations of its many Secrets* (1931).
CHATTO, W. A.: *Origin and History of Playing Cards* (1848).
MORLEY, H. T.: *History of Old and Curious Playing Cards* (1931).
TAYLOR, REV. E. S.: *History of Playing Cards* (1865).

GAMES TABLES AND BOARDS

By G. BERNARD HUGHES

GAMES of hazard, chance and skill have occupied the leisure moments of Englishmen since knuckle-bones, jack-stones and dicing became prevalent. Gaming boards, dice and counters discovered in tombs of early Christians differ little from those illustrated in medieval illuminated manuscripts.

Board games have more than a thousand years of history in England. Indoor amusements were few, and board games, seldom intended for more than two players, fascinated during long winter evenings when illumination was poor and costly. The board itself was known as a table board, the player as a tabler and the pieces as tablemen, at a period when the table in its modern sense was termed a board. *Chess* and *backgammon* are numbered among the earliest tables, one side being marked in 64 squares, the other with two sets of 12 points. Such a double-sided board was known as a pair of tables; in 1519 Horman recorded that he had 'bought a playing tabull with poynts on one side and *checkers* on the other'.

In Tudor days these might be highly costly in beautiful hardwoods set with ebony, ivory, mother of pearl and tortoiseshell, sometimes ornamented by small paintings in full colour and gold, with men wrought in precious metal; or in common wood costing fourpence in the time of Henry VII (1485–1509) or eightpence a century later. A pair of tables might be accompanied by a three-legged table upon which it rested during play. This was described as 'a paire of Tabyles tabelle'. Inventories taken during the sixteenth century demonstrate that most well-established families possessed at least one pair of tables. That at Marketon, Derbyshire, was described in 1545 as 'a square payr of tables with the men of boxe red and white XIJ^{d}'. The lid of an oak chest might have the top laid out as a games board, chess at one end, backgammon at the other and merelles in the centre.

In the Victoria & Albert Museum is a superb pair of hinged tables in marquetry of various woods, with carved, painted and punched ornament. This is marked inside for backgammon and sunk for *tric-trac*, and outside for *merelles* and *chess*. Illustrations carved on the inner border represent other popular games of the period – *shovel-board*, bat-and-ball, quintain, kayles, bagatelle, knur-and-spell, nine-pins and tennis (Plate 143).

Lavishness in furnishings which accompanied the restoration of Charles II included handsome card tables in walnut in which tables for backgammon and chess were combined. Lockers for playing-cards and games pieces were devised in the underframing and later replaced by drawers. Tric-trac again became a fashionable amusement, and games tables, still square, were made with a wide carved or moulded underframing, the top containing a movable panel secured by trigger catches resembling drawer knobs. The upper surface was veneered: on the reverse it was inlaid as a chess-board, with a small, ivory, rectangular inset on either side, pierced for pegging the score at cribbage. Removal of the panel revealed a shallow recess inlaid for backgammon and tric-trac. Beneath this was a deep drawer extending the full width of the table. This contained a set of matching boards for other games, such as *agon*, *solitaire* and *nine men's morris*. The trigger mechanism was abandoned in about 1770 in favour of a central leaf running the full length of the now rectangular table top, and sliding into position on tongues and grooves so skilfully worked that joins were visible only on close inspection. The beautifully figured mahogany of the period produced some lovely colour shadings in the best work. By the end of the century the noise associated with the playing of tric-trac was lessened by lining the backgammon recess with leather, the points being marked in colour and gilding.

GLOSSARY

Agon or **Queen's Guard:** a hexagonal board divided into 91 equal hexagonal compartments arranged in concentric bands of two contrasting colours, such as ivory and ebony or mahogany and satinwood. The numbers of hexagons contained in the bands were 30, 24, 18, 12, 6 and one in the centre. Each of the two players had seven men, a queen and six guards of distinctive colour.

Backgammon: played on a square *board* painted or inlaid to mark 24 points, 12 on each side. The pieces were draughtsmen moved in accordance with the throw of dice. (*See* Tric-trac.)

Board: a tablet or frame, almost invariably of wood, upon which several indoor games are played, such as *chess*, *backgammon*, *merelles* and *solitaire*. These might be costly objects of ivory or ornamental woods, and exquisitely decorated with marquetry of satinwood, tulip, ebony, holly and other woods, sometimes set with jewels or precious metals. Others were of hard native woods painted with the required markings. The frame used for scoring at cribbage is also known as a board. The making of games boards and pieces was a specialist occupation. John Gough, for instance, advertised in the *London Gazette*, 1686, that he was a maker of chess-tables, chess-boards and chess-men, at The Sugar Loaf and Tables, near Serjeant's Inn, in Chancery Lane. They were also made as a hobby by early Georgian men and women. The Duchess of Portland in 1752 turned a set of draughts in jet and ivory. The hand-made board of wood is fast becoming outmoded by plastics.

Checkers: *see* Draughts.

Chess: *see* article on Chess-men.

Counters: used in lieu of money for keeping an account or reckoning in games of chance, especially cards. Until the seventeenth century any small object, such as shells or cherry stones, might be used; then thin discs of precious metal, ivory, tortoiseshell, bone stained in various colours, brass, tin or pewter were introduced. In the eighteenth century mother of pearl was preferred in various shapes – round, oblong or fish shape with surfaces exquisitely carved or finely engraved. From 1820 metal counters simulating gold coins were made by the button-men of Birmingham, such as imitation guineas and pattern three-halfpenny pieces. For a description of the early counter-board and its use, *see* R. W. Symonds in *The Connoisseur* (December 1951).

Draughts or **Checkers:** the board is the same as for chess with sixty-four squares, and each player with twelve men in contrasting colours. The earliest English description of the game dates to 1566, but not until the early 1800s did the game become standardized as played today. Polish draughts was popular in the eighteenth century, the board having a hundred squares and each player twenty men.

Fox and Geese: played on a square board, usually of mahogany, inlaid or painted with thirty-three spots arranged in the form of a Greek cross. There are twelve or seventeen pieces known as geese and a larger one, the fox, distinguished also by shape and colour. The spots on early boards were perforated, and the fox and geese turned with pegs to fit. Edward IV (1461–83) was a devotee of this game, and ordered '2 foxes and 46 hounds of silver overgilt' to form two sets: these were modelled to represent foxes and hounds. Geese appear to have replaced hounds in the seventeenth century.

Halma: invented by George Monk in 1883.

Men: *see* Pieces.

Merelles, Nine Men's Morris or **Five Penny Moons:** dates from the fourteenth century. The square board was painted or incised with three squares drawn one within the other and with cross lines connecting the squares. Each player possessed nine men in sets of contrasting colour. These might be thick discs or pegs inserted into twenty-four holes sunk into the cross points. Machine-made boards have been made from about 1860, when the game enjoyed a quarter century revival.

Nine Holes or **Trunks:** a table game revived periodically from the thirteenth century to the present day. A long piece of thick wood cut with nine small arches in the shape of trunks, all of them numbered, was set upright. Each player possessed two flattened balls which he aimed to bowl edgeways beneath the arches. From the nineteenth century marbles have been used. Phillips in 1706 defined trunks as 'a kind of play other wise call'd Troll-Madame and Pigeon-Holes'.

Philosopher's Game: the board is a rectangle as long again as wide, with eight squares the narrow way and sixteen vertically – two chess-boards joined, the squares alternating in contrasting colours. Each of the two players had twenty-four men: eight each circular, triangular and square. The game was made more difficult by engraving each with numerals, one side even, the other side odd.

Pieces or **Men:** originally known as table-men are the combatants used in playing most board games, and might be in silver-gilt, silver, ivory, ebony, bone stained in various colours, jet or hardwoods.

Slide Groat or **Shovel-board:** dates from Tudor days and was played on a long board of elm which, if rightly seasoned, could be given a highly lustrous sheen and was not subject to warping. Examples have been noted in mahogany. On this board was marked a rectangle, either inlaid or more usually painted or gilded, measuring three or four feet long and twelve or fourteen inches wide and divided laterally into nine or ten equal sections, each numbered. Each player possessed a smooth silver groat – later a copper halfpenny was used – and placing it on the edge of the board drove it towards the marks by striking it with the palm of the hand. In the eighteenth century a thin, flat shovel-shaped slider was used, looped for hanging when not in use and engraved with its owner's name. These were used by regular customers in taverns, coffee-houses and so on. The Maldon Borough Deeds for 1635 record that two games of slide groat would occupy three-quarters of an hour.

Solitaire: dates to the eighteenth century and was then known as the 'solitary game'. It was played on a thick circular board drilled with fifty or sixty holes half an inch apart, each being fitted with a turned peg, often in ivory or ebony, more usually in wood. Alternatively, in the nineteenth century the holes were made saucer-shaped and each contained an ornamental glass marble. The men were removed one at a time by jumping as in draughts.

Tric-trac: a complicated form of *backgammon*, so-called from the clicking sound made by the *pieces* during play. Boards intended for tric-trac are distinguished by a shallow gallery surrounding each of the two playing areas, a feature found in most games tables from the late 1760s.

BOOKS FOR FURTHER READING

PICK, J. B.: *Dictionary of Games* (1952). (This gives instructions for playing the above games.)

STRUTT, JOSEPH: *Sports and Pastimes* (1838).

(A) A German set of flats, Frederick the Great and His Troops. Based on Hilpert's models, *c.* 1920–30, Nuremberg. *Collection: T. Sutton. Photo: T. Sutton, A.R.P.S.*

(B) Nuremberg set of Ancient Assyrians, flats 30 mm., *c.* 1920–30. *Collection: T. Sutton. Photo: T. Sutton, A.R.P.S.*

PLATE 145

(A) German or Austrian flats. Three Grenadiers of unusual size, presumably about 1840. The stand is shaped as though it might have fitted into a movable base. *Collection: T. Sutton. Photo: T. Sutton, A.R.P.S.*

(B) Dragoons and Zouaves. Typical flat figures, *c.* 1870. Size (foot) 30 mm. *Photo: F. Wackett.*

PLATE 146

(A) French Revolutionary Soldiers by Lucotte, *c.* 1870. Size (foot) 2½ in. *Collection: J. Grafton.*

(B) Various Regiments of the British Army. Solid lead figures by Heyde, *c.* 1890–1900. The alignment of the legs of the camels and certain of the horses and the blob of smoke at the end of the rifle of the kneeling infantry-man will be noted. *Collection: G. A. Jewson. Photo: F. Wackett.*

Medieval Knights. First two dismounted figures on left and mounted knight (Black Prince) extreme right by Courtenay, *c.* 1935. *Collection: J. Grafton.* Others all Messrs. Britain's 'Knights of Agincourt', 1954. Size (foot) $2\frac{1}{2}$ in. Repainted. *Collection: Author.*

PLATE 148

To face page 20

MODEL SOLDIERS

By J. G. GARRATT

THE collector of model soldiers cares little for any arbitrary and artificial barrier of time: he is generally as eager to acquire a contemporary specimen as a product of an earlier age. For whilst the societies founded in Germany in the 1890s did indeed concentrate on the collection and preservation of historic pieces, the present leaning is rather towards later accuracy of representation, and in this the collector has been well served in recent times, especially since the end of the Second World War. Some of the craftsmen working today are producing superb figures, and there seems to be no limit to the ingenuity and effectiveness of the new materials which are constantly being developed.

The original 'model' soldier was, of course, a toy, in the same way as a Georgian table-game or a doll is a toy; as a toy it was made to be played with, and thousands must have been played out of existence. Everybody at one time or another has owned a collection of soldiers, and every now and then the battered veterans, scarred and sorely distressed, their ranks decimated from the constant skirmishes on the drawing-room floor, surrender to the unequal struggle and are consigned to the dustbin, or die more theatrically in the heat of the kitchen fire. That so many have survived is due to the efforts of serious-minded adults who take over where their sons leave off and achieve a praiseworthy object while satisfying their own innate interest in playthings. Thousands of soldiers still made yearly as toys are of such high quality as to rank as 'models' (or shall we say superior toys), and as far as the collector is concerned there is no dividing line.

Warfare, or the threat of war, being as much part of life in ancient times as it is today, it is obvious that the model soldier has a long history. Specimens dating from Egyptian, Rhodian, Grecian and Roman times are known, and we have evidence in the form of illustrations and the actual models themselves of model medieval tilting knights. All these are, of course, almost impossible to find outside museums, and are as outside the range of the average collector as the models made for the various nobility of Europe, which were of gold or silver, or which consisted of specially made automata. Complete regiments printed on paper, coloured by hand and then cut from cardboard, were known as far back as the childhood days of Louis XIV, who had a collection costing 6,000 francs, but the very frailty of these has rendered them very difficult of acquisition. Even more so are the curious, not easily recognizable, soldiers made of pinched paper, about 2¼ inches high, which were popular about 1820, and can be seen in some Continental museums.

Peasant-carved figures of wood were made extensively all over Germany, especially in Bavaria, but are not often seen today. These attractively painted figures vary from under 2 inches to 20 inches high, and include examples set on springs and on wheels, and groups which perform evolutions on the trellis-tongs principle. Most curious of all are the models made in Swabia from a mixture of sugar, meal and gum-tragacanth, which, having set in a mould, could be hardened and painted. The result is a 2–3-inch high figure with a porcelain-like appearance.

FLATS

Whilst many of these models can undoubtedly be classed as commercial products, there was nothing approaching uniformity about them, but somewhere in Germany in the early part of the eighteenth century some unknown and unhonoured genius produced a few 16-cm. high grenadiers of flat, embossed tin, clumsy, awkward, as primitive when compared with later productions as the first gropings of primordial man with Athenian sculpture. This, then, was the first commercial tin soldier, and it was timorously and tentatively developed until about 1740 quite passable figures, some 6 cm. high, were being produced. The real developers of the art were Andreas and Johannes Georg Hilpert, who settled in Nuremberg in 1760, and gradually produced figures in vast quantity, varying in height from 5 to 12 cm., mounted on little stands and in the main restricted to the regiments of Frederick the Great. Special models were also made to order, notably that of Frederick himself, 5 inches high, and signed and dated 1775.

The example set by the Hilperts was soon followed by other makers, who were so active in exporting their goods that by the middle of the nineteenth century they were to be found in every corner of Europe. Allgeyer of Fürth (1812) and J. G. Lorenz of the same town; Heinrichsen of Nuremberg; M. and A. Ruckerts of Würzburg; Deneeke of Braunschweig; Wegmann and Von Haselbach of Berlin; du Bois of Hanover; Gottschalk and Wehrli, were all responsible for expanding the range of products, and not only were all the contemporary European regiments manufactured, but also Romans, medieval knights and Saracens. That many of the figures are crude, inaccurate and inartistic can be readily seen when comparison is made between a fine Hilpert or Heinrichsen and one of the lesser German factories. Generally speaking, however, the European troops are well-made, and the varied action (including such things as mounted hussars leaping over dead horses) is good; but the models of ancient civilizations and of knights exhibit all the typical Germanic exaggeration of the Romantic period, evinced in another art by the stage costumes of *Der Freischütz* and *Oberon*, and paralleled in England by tinsel pictures and the 'Penny Plain, Twopence Coloured' of the juvenile theatre.

Hilpert was succeeded by Allgeyer, Allgeyer by Heinrichsen, as the outstanding manufacturers of their age; and the two latter firms were particularly active in exporting their wares to France, and in 1890 Heinrichsen seems to have entirely captured the market. This firm, to quote a French authority, 'pursued a clear aim, that is, to place in the hands of boys the instruments of aggrandisement, the boxes in which the toys were packed bearing plans of battles representing the Prussians in the most victorious and favourable aspects possible'. The moulds of this firm were melted down during the First World War, and the existing models were taken over by the firm of Ochel of Kiel, who also marketed their own products under the name of Kiel. They have developed many new styles since 1945. Rieche of Hanover and Neckel of Stuttgart, Gottstein, Eulner, Biebel and others were producing flat figures up to the Second World War, and some of these can still be obtained from Germany and Switzerland at a reasonable price (usually unpainted). The only French manufacturer was the firm of Mignot, who in 1930 created a distinct range, but they now appear to have abandoned these in favour of the solid lead models.

Besides the usual impedimenta of an army, the cannons, and the baggage-wagons, even the *vivandières*, the late nineteenth-century manufactures added such things as tents, with feeding horses and soldiers smoking at ease, so that the purchaser could arrange his army either in action, on the march or in bivouac. The great appeal of the flat tin soldier was its lightness and portability, its speedy arrangement for the 'war game', and perhaps, above all, its use in the making of dioramas, in which the Germans excelled themselves. At an exhibition held at Nuremberg in 1930, there were hundreds of tableaux, all made from flat models and ranging over every period. The majority of the figures were by Heinrichsen. Those in the Royal United Services Museum in Whitehall should be seen, with models by Blum, Müller, Kiel and others.

The actual manufacture of these delightful little soldiers is simplicity itself, once careful engraving has been done, and the hardening of the moulds by bronze ensures that many hundreds of models can be produced. The earlier specimens were sometimes only half painted, the figures only being treated, whilst the horses were untouched by colour. Sometimes they are found in a darkened condition, due to insufficiency of care in mixing the alloys to ensure continued brightness. The size varies from 20 to 40 mm., but, exceptionally, and only in very early models, from 5 to 6 inches: and about 1850 the most important firms, led by Allgeyer and Heinrichsen, agreed to a standard size of 33 mm. for a foot soldier, with a corresponding scale for cavalry. One amusing little characteristic of models of the later part of the nineteenth century was a little blob at the end of a rifle to represent a puff of smoke. Many are engraved with the name or initials of the maker, and they were packed in decorated boxes of thin wood, sometimes with a label bearing a title, such as 'The Sham Battle', of which the author has seen a specimen of about 1870.

Many sets were reissued to serve different functions, and the main guide in distinguishing them is a study of the military costume of the period represented. As an example, in 1864 Heinrichsen issued a set of Danes defending the Duppeler fortifications, and after 1870 repainted them for the Defence of Paris. The coats, caps, etc, although repainted, are easily distinguishable as Danish and not French.

SOLIDS

What would appear to be a natural development of the flat was the 'semi-flat', or 'semi-solid', consisting of a figure made of lead which follows the main lines of the flat inasmuch as the feet, whether of man or of horse, are in the same plane but the body swelled out. In actuality, however, they do not pre-date the solid figure, and examples dating from 1820 right up to the 1900s are known. Indeed, there are several dioramas on the Continent made with these figures as late as 1901. Generally speaking, they are about 1 inch in height, but later examples can be of larger size. The accoutrements are sometimes made of tin.

It is perhaps surprising to note that solid figures of lead were being made as far back as the sixteenth century. (One excludes the special models made for wealthy patrons.) Certainly they were being manufactured, probably in very small quantities, in Germany as early as about 1730, and with these figures the interest of most present-day collectors may be said to commence. The word 'solid' is self-explanatory – they were made of solid soft lead, the heads, arms, legs and accoutrements made separately and welded on or plugged in. In many cases the weapons they bore were made of tin. It is to the French that credit may be given for really manufacturing solids for commercial purposes, and it is known that the firm of Mignot created in the 1820s a range of solid lead soldiers which formed the basis of their present great collection. They later bought up the moulds of the house of Lucotte (marked on base with the Imperial Bee flanked by the initials L and C). Their natural tendency was to specialize in troops of the Revolutionary and Napoleonic periods, but they also made ancient races, soldiers of the Middle Ages, double-figure groups, artillery and chariots. The figures are the normal size, the heads occasionally badly plugged in, giving the figure the appearance of having an overlong neck. Their 'Ancients' and 'Medievals' have a certain naïve quality of stiffness reminiscent of French medieval statuary. There are certain small differences between the two ranges which will be of interest to collectors. The Lucotte bases are generally rather longer and narrower: the horses have longer tails, and not only are equestrians detachable but also the saddles and the horse-clothes. The bases of the figures are uniformly painted a biscuit colour. A very large range at a fairly reasonable price is still obtainable from the firm in Paris, but dealing with any French dealer requires much patience before any order is fulfilled.

Other Continental firms have engaged in the manufacture of solids, of whom the most likely to interest the collector is that of George Heyde of Dresden. Their figures have much in common with Mignots, both in the method of manufacture, the colour of the bases and the general appearance. Their range was wider, and they issued a vast number of models, of all conceivable types, including complete bivouac scenes of the American War of Independence, a North American Indian encampment with natives bringing in bound prisoners, a complete set of Greeks and Trojans, with chariots and females and children, and Arab scenes with palm-trees and camels. One very scarce model is that of the State Coach of the Elector of Hanover. They made their models in three sizes, 1 inch, 2 inches and 3½ inches high, and their wares are distinguished by their superior quality and finish, and the diversity of action of the figures. Generally speaking, the bases are smaller than those of the French manufacturers. Early models retain the conventional blob at the end of the rifle. The firm went out of existence during the Second World War, but has now started functioning again in Russian-occupied Germany (Plate 147B).

Like most innovations, the solid figure was received but slowly in France and in Germany, riveted as the latter was to the traditional tin soldier; but by the 1890s they had become so popular that the world export market had been completely captured by the Germans. However, in 1893 an English toy-manufacturer – the appropriately named William Britain – placed on the market his new invention, the slightly smaller and lighter hollow-cast figure, and within the space of a few years had entirely swept the Germans from their long-established pre-eminence. This firm is still in existence, and has indeed become a household word. Their range, whilst not so intelligent or embracing as those of the Continental firms, is comprehensive, with a natural leaning towards British and Colonial regiments. The bases have always been painted a uniform shade of darkish green, and the early ones are round or near round. The horses in early models are smaller than those of the present day, and in some cases all four legs of a galloping horse are outstretched. A curious model is that of a lancer in which the horse has a twisted rear leg. Early cavalry officers have swords made of tin. Their products were first stamped with their name in 1900, probably to combat the many pirate firms which had sprung up (two at least, indeed, having been founded by former Britain employees).

A Britain rarity is a box of four kneeling firing British infantrymen, in which a short, broad piece of flexible metal is attached to the rear of the figure, which can be bent backwards and which, when released, propels a projectile through the hollowed rifle. The 'plug-handed Highlander' is well-known and sought after, and very scarce sets are those of the Boer War infantry and cavalry, the Jameson Raid, the Middlesex Yeomanry, the West Indian Regiment and the South Australian Lancers, early Hussar Regiments (with smaller heads) and the six-gun team of the Royal Horse Artillery with bucket seat and shafted limber. Indeed, early Britain's are a study in themselves.

It must not be imagined that Britain's are the only firm of manufacturers of model soldiers in England. There have been and still are many others, some good, some bad, but Britain's have never been superseded. But the latest material in use, polythene, made from standard I.C.I. Alkathene, generally known as 'plastic' or 'unbreakable', may revolutionize the model-soldier world as much as did Britain's hollowcast. Certainly the ranges so far issued are of exceptional quality and beautifully painted (Plate 148).

SPECIALIST MAKERS

The growth of model soldier societies all over the world has resulted in the change of name from 'toy' to 'model', and has thereby created a special demand for the individual figure made by a craftsman and correct in every detail. This is perhaps due in a measure to a certain monotony of the attitudes of the boxed figures issued by commercial firms. Present-day manufacturers are becoming aware of this, and are now issuing single figures, in varying postures, at a price which attracts not only the average individual but also the connoisseur. (*See*, for instance, the recent set of 'Agincourt Knights', by Britain, which, when skilfully repainted, are hardly inferior in finish or action to the much more expensive models made by Courtenay.)

To satisfy the demand, there has arisen a

group of craftsmen whose products are of superb quality, capable of classification as works of art in their own right. One has only to mention a Courtenay or a Stadden, a Ping, a Greenwood, a Metayer or a Berdoux, to raise enthusiastic applause from the knowledgeable collector. Not only can these artists produce models of every known regiment, but they will supply to order a representation, accurate to the last detail, of any monarch known to history, or a humble hoplite, or a private of some obscure regiment of the Napoleonic Army. In any of their productions are to be found a blend of artistry as to the posture and proportion of the figure itself, a profound knowledge of costume, whether military or civil, an accuracy of heraldry or military accoutrements and a most skilful use of colour. It is only to be expected that these specialist models are expensive.

Within any small group of collectors will be found one who specializes in 'Ancients' – i.e. Egyptians, Greeks, Romans, etc – complete with chariots and siege engines; and another who collects another type of 'ancients', as early Britain models are colloquially known. There will be one whose range is limited to medieval knights, another whose collection comprises British Army figures from Cromwell's time to the present day. What the collector cannot buy he very often creates, either by moulding or casting, or by 'converting' existing models into something quite different. The humblest chain-store product has been known to undergo some Protean, and progressively improved, changes; and Britain's products have always been favourites for repainting for the creation of different regiments. The French and German figures, being of solid lead, lend themselves not so much to conversion as to reconstruction, as the arms and legs can be gently eased without breakage to another position. The new plastics are a boon to the converter, as they can be cut about in the most extraordinary and ingenious ways for the creation of new figures.

HINTS ON PURCHASING

Collections rarely appear in the auction-rooms (indeed, the two leading London houses state that they have never had any through their hands), and the normal source of supply for the out-of-manufacture ranges is the British Model Soldier Society, whose members either sell or exchange their pieces, either by personal contact, or through the medium of their journal, or by auction sales at their London headquarters. In provincial towns much the same system applies.

Continental flats, in groups, generally of about 500 pieces, are occasionally met with in antique-dealers' shops, where the prices range from the reasonable to the ridiculous. A considerable variety is still obtainable from the British Zone of Germany, from France and from Switzerland, at the equivalent of about one shilling and eightpence each unpainted. Dealers in general know little of the model soldier, especially the solid variety, and it is occasionally possible to buy a small group of Courtenays or Mignots at a very cheap price.

But the average beginner of small means cannot rely on these sources, nor can he afford the specialist models, and therefore nothing could be better than the contemporary commercial ranges, from which he will be able to build up a comprehensive collection of well-made figures, to be added to from time to time by the special item, or by purchases from friends, leading perhaps to membership of a society, with wider scope for barter or purchase from other members. Finally, to repeat what was said at the beginning of this article, this is a branch of collecting that has no ending.

GLOSSARY

Castings: lead or tin models before paint has been applied.

Conversion: an adaptation from an existing model.

Diorama: A spectacular scene made of models, usually a battlepiece, in which hundreds of soldiers are placed in appropriate surroundings, the whole enclosed in a glass case. The soldiers may be flat, semi-flat or solid. Excellent examples are at the

Royal United Services Museum and the museum at Compiègne.

Flats: the thin, tin Continental soldiers made in the flat, with an engraved surface which gives them almost a three-dimensional appearance. They range in size according to age, but normally are about 30 to 33 mm. high. (French: *Plats d'étain*; German: *Zinnsoldaten.*)

Hollowcast: a model which has a thin casing of lead as against the solid and heavier model. Invented by William Britain.

Plastics: unbreakable models made of a chemical substance with a solid rubber-like appearance.

Semi-flat (semi-round, semi-solid): a small model (usually about 33 mm., occasionally larger) in which the legs of man or horse are in the same plane (as in 'flats') but the body swells out on both sides. (French: *Demi-Ronde-bosse*; German: *Halbmassif.*)

Solids: models made in the round of solid lead. (French: *Ronde-bosse*; German: *Bleisoldaten; Metallsoldaten; plastische figuren.*)

SELECTED LIST OF IMPORTANT MANUFACTURERS

FLATS

Eighteenth-nineteenth century

Allgeyer (Fürth); Ammon (Nuremberg); Deneeke (Braunschweig); Du Bois (Hanover); Haffner (Nuremberg); Heinrichsen (Nuremberg); Hilpert (Nuremberg); Lorenz (Fürth); Ruckerts (Würzburg); Wegmann and Von Haselbach (Berlin).

Twentieth century

Ballada (Paris); Douchkine (Paris); S. Frk. K. (Nuremberg); Mignot (Paris); Müller (Erfurt); Neckel (Stuttgart); Ochel (Kiel); Rieche (Hanover).

SOLIDS

Nineteenth–twentieth century

Britain (London); Heyde (Dresden); Hill (London); Mignot (Paris, incorporating Lucotte); Timpo (London); Authenticast (U.S.A); Bussler (U.S.A.).

MAKERS OF INDIVIDUAL MODELS

Arthur (English): Carved wood, 13 inches high, wide range.

Ballada (French): All types, especially artillery.

Berdoux (French): Splendid models.

Bittard (French): 1900–14 period, and Second Empire.

Courtenay (English): Medieval knights, very fine quality, but early ranges not remarkable.

Gamage (English): As yet a limited range, but fine quality.

Greenwood & Ball (English): Very large range English and German regiments, Highland Clansmen, 3 inches.

Matchlock (English): British Regiments, 7 inches.

Metayer (French): French Revolution; Louis XV–XVII; First Empire.

Ping (English): All periods, 3 inches. Perhaps the finest modeller in existence.

Sentry (English): Large range British and Scottish regiments, 7 and 9 inches.

Stadden (English): Most regiments, three distinct ranges, single and groups, two sizes. Fine, but legs perhaps a little heavy.

BOOKS FOR FURTHER READING

There is, at the moment, no complete history of the model soldier in the English language. This, however, is being remedied. Meanwhile, the following contain chapters of more or less value:

Bulletin of the British Model Soldier Society. Surprisingly little historical information, being in the main devoted to the activities of the group, and with a distinct leaning towards purely military matters.

Daiken, Leslie: *Children's Toys Throughout the Ages* (Batsford, 1953). Discursive, and not very rewarding chapter on 'solids', mostly of Britain's manufacture.

Gröber, Karl: *Children's Toys of Bygone Days* (Batsford, 1928). Excellent for early models, but deals mainly with pre-1900 'flats'.

Holme, C. G., *Editor: Children's Toys of Yesterday* (1932). No text, but good illustrations.

Jackson, Mrs Neville: *Toys of Other Days* (1908). Covers mainly the same ground as Gröber.

CHARTERS, SEALS AND PARCHMENTS

By NOEL BLAKISTON

The objects now briefly described differ from all or most of the others mentioned in this Encyclopaedia in that they rarely appear in the sale-rooms. Private collectors of medieval deeds and seals must indeed be few nowadays. Moreover, it is widely felt that these things, which are the stuff of history, should not be in private hands, or, if they are, should be generally available for research. The tendency therefore is for such objects to find a home in some public repository, whether one of the great national collections or some provincial muniment room. Whoever would study the subject, then, could not do it better than at the Public Record Office or the British Museum in London or at a County record office.

Before going any further, a definition is necessary. What are we talking about? We are *not* talking about any of those parchments, mainly in book form and often beautifully illuminated, such as missals, lectionaries, chronicles, etc, that were compiled in monasteries or cathedral chapters for literary or liturgical purposes. We are talking about legal and administrative documents. These documents can be divided into two groups: on the one hand the roll or the book, in which were entered or registered mandates to officials, such, for example, as royal letters close upon the Close Rolls, or records of the proceedings of courts of law, as those of the King's Bench upon the King's Bench Plea Rolls or of a manor court on the manor-court rolls, or registers of title deeds such as are found in monastic cartularies. On the other hand, there are the original mandates themselves, warrants, precepts, letters patent, treaties, contracts, conveyances, indentures, receipts and what are in a general way known as deeds. The common feature of this group is that the documents usually bear seals. It is with this group alone that we are here concerned.

The great period of seals was the twelfth to the fifteenth centuries, great whether from the point of view of their beauty and magnificence of design or of their importance in the processes of business and administration. The first purpose of a seal was to authenticate a document. In the days when so many of those who had to authenticate documents, from the King downwards, were unable to write, the application of a seal was the only way of authentication. In that period, then, the seal had an importance which, with the spread of literacy, it began to lose; though even now, such is the power of tradition, a memory is preserved, in that little fretted circle of red paper against which we sign our name on a legal document, of the wax seal, with a device or a coat-of-arms upon it, and a motto or the name of the owner around the edge, which our medieval ancestor would have appended to a deed.

The word 'append' reveals one of the distinctions between medieval and modern sealing. Most modern sealing is done with the substance known as sealing-wax. This is made of shellac, a material that began to be imported from the East in the sixteenth century. It is suitable for the applied seal, being melted on to the parchment or paper, to which it readily adheres, and receiving the impression while still liquid. In the Middle Ages seals were made of beeswax mixed with resin. Though they were frequently applied to the surface of the document they more normally hung from the deed by a tag of parchment or, in the case of certain grander sorts of document, by coloured silk cords and gold braid, that passed through the middle of the wax. A lump of beeswax, that is to say, having been warmed until it was malleable, was made to surround and grip the tag or cord and then pressed by the fingers into the matrix or metal mould from which it was to take the impression. The finger-prints upon the backs of medieval seals are not the least part of their appeal.

On double-sided seals, of course, there are not these marks of fingers. Such are the great seals of England, of which a continuous series of impressions survives from the time of Edward the Confessor. The second great seal of Elizabeth I is reproduced here (Plate 149). The matrix of the great seal, generally of silver, consisted of two moulds that were pressed upon one another, with the wax between. Impressions of great seals, back at least to the fourteenth century, are by no means rare. For the great seal was attached, at least in the later Middle Ages, to many thousands of administrative documents every year. What a humming of bees in medieval England to make all that wax!

Queen Elizabeth's seal has been chosen for reproduction as it is a particularly distinguished one in the series, being from the design of Nicholas Hilliard. It shows the convention of the great seal by which the sovereign was represented enthroned on one side (known as the obverse) and on horseback on the other (the reverse). Fine though this seal may appear to us, it has been found from Exchequer accounts and other documents that the Queen was far from pleased with it, and for the rest of her reign Hilliard was busy trying to make another design that should satisfy her. She was over fifty when this seal came into use. He has made her look perhaps thirty-five. No doubt he should have made her seventeen.

The shape of royal seals, which, in addition to the great seal, included the privy seal and the seals of the Exchequer and the common law courts, was round. The seals of bishops and of monasteries were normally pointed oval, or, as it is called, vesica shaped; those of cathedral chapters round. Round, too, was the normal shape for the seals of towns, corporations and colleges, and for equestrian seals. Personal seals might be either round or pointed oval, or, less commonly, rounded oval, square or polygonal.

Vermilion or verdigris were used for colouring seals red or green; many seals, however, simply have the natural colour of the wax. Most impressions of the great seal were in natural-coloured wax, red being used only on diplomatic and other documents of great importance, and green, it has been said, for grants in perpetuity. The rules governing the use of green wax in great seals, however, still seem to await elucidation. At Eton College there are various patents, including the foundation charter, of which two copies exist, one bearing a green and one a natural-coloured impression of the great seal. Perhaps green cost more and you simply got what you paid for. Seals of ecclesiastics, boroughs and corporations are generally in red wax, those of persons in red, green or natural colour. Colouring appears to act as a preservative to the wax and to prevent it crumbling away. Anyone who has worked much on thirteenth-century deeds will agree that the best impressions are found among the red and green seals.

The study of the designs upon medieval seals is one of inexhaustible fascination. For the art of seal designing, like Gothic architecture, was always on the move. The dead hand of routine never lay upon it. The artists' fancy, you always feel, was given the fullest freedom, and it is a delight and an astonishment to see how they could fill the awkward little space at their disposal with some glimpse of the pageantry of medieval life, with saints, kings, queens, prelates, knights on horseback, tenuous ladies in high head-dresses, monks at prayer and ships at sea, with hounds, birds, bears, boars and every sort of animal, real or imaginary, with scenes of action such as the murder of Becket or the slaying of a dragon, with cities, castles and, of course, Gothic church architecture, from the single arch or canopied

The Great Seal of Elizabeth I.
(Obverse.)

(Reverse.)

PLATE 149

To face page 216

(A) Roger de Quinci. (Obverse.)

(Reverse.)

(B) William de Sleford.

(C) Ingelard de Warlee.

(D) Lord Berners.

(E) Thomas de Chaworth.

(A) The City of Rochester. (Reverse.) (Obverse.)

(B) Letters Patent of Henry VIII.

PLATE 151

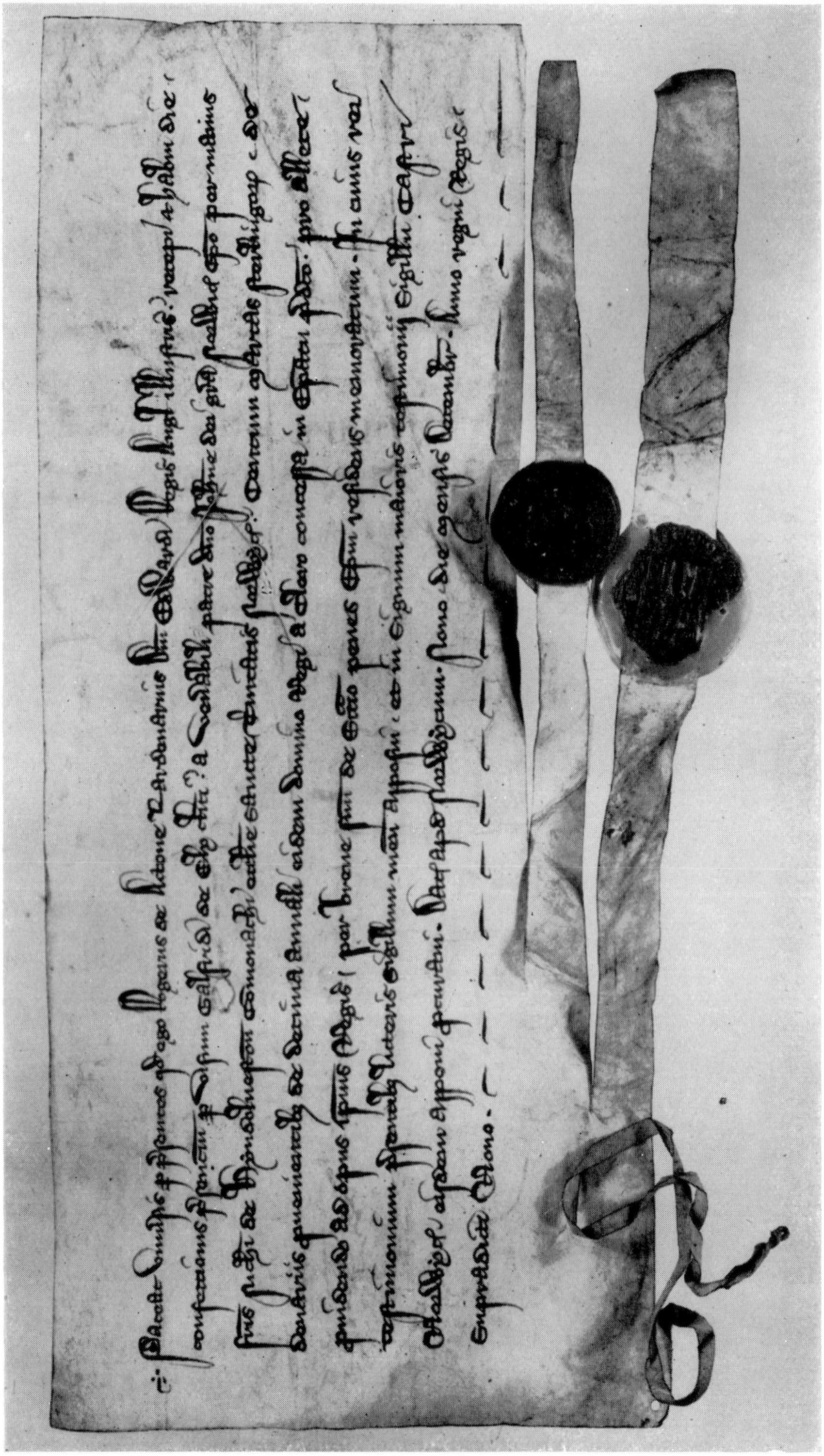

Receipt of Roger de Actone.

PLATE 152

niche to the entire cathedral. If all medieval churches in England were to be destroyed, a very fair idea of what had been lost could be obtained from seals alone.

The tiny selection of seals here reproduced shows, in addition to the great seal already mentioned, three armorial seals and the seals of two minor officials and of a municipality. The seal of Roger de Quinci, Earl of Winchester and Constable of Scotland, is of the middle of the thirteenth century. On the obverse (Plate 150A) it shows the earl in mail and helmet and surcoat, with shield and drawn sword galloping to the right. On his shield and on the trappings of the horse the earl's arms appear, seven lozenges voided. (The student of seals will quickly find himself also a student of heraldry.) Below the horse is the monster known as a wyvern. The legend reads SIGILL ROGERI DE QUINCI COMITIS WINCESTRIE. The Latin for seal is *sigillum*, for earl or count *comes*. The reverse shows the earl defending himself against a lion. In the legend on this side he is described as CONSTABULARII SCOCIE.

A fine heraldic seal, that of Thomas de Chaworth, dated about 1300 (Plate 150E), shows a shield of arms, slung from a hook, between two wyverns. The arms are two chevrons. Below the shield is a lion. More elaborate arms, quarterly, appear on the mid-fifteenth-century shield of John Bourchier, Lord Berners (Plate 150D). Here the shield is surmounted by a helmet with mantling, from which issues the crest, an old man's head. The seal of Ingelard de Warlee, Keeper of the Wardrobe in 1310 (Plate 150C) shows, within a quatrefoil, the profile of Ingelard facing to the left. Above his head is the hand of God, to the left is a castle, to the right a lion. The legend, which starts, as they normally do, at the top, reads LE: SEAL: INGELARD: QUE: DIEU: GARD. The seal of William de Sleford, clerk of the works at Westminster (Plate 150B), shows a half-length figure of a clerk in a gown, holding a book before him, beneath a triple Gothic canopy with panelled side shafts. The legend reads SIGILLUM: WILLI: DE: SLEFORD.

The seal of Rochester (Plate 151A), which is dated about 1210, shows, with an extraordinary sharpness of impression, on the obverse St Andrew, the patron of the city, being tied to his cross, and on the reverse the castle, with a banner flying and a herald on a turret. The reproduction is the same size as the original, as is the case with the heraldic seals here reproduced. The seals of Warlee and Sleford, however, are slightly enlarged; the great seal of Elizabeth I is reduced from a diameter of 5·9 inches.

A word now about the documents to which seals were attached. These range from royal letters patent to deeds executed by some of the humblest subjects of the Crown. It is natural that documents which have been brought into being for a utilitarian rather than an aesthetic purpose should not, as a rule, contain more appeal to the eye than can be found in the handwriting; though this is by no means small and grows with a growing knowledge of the various styles of what is known as court hand. Some of the more important royal and ecclesiastical documents, however, were, from the fifteenth century, often embellished with elaborate penwork on the initial letters of the top line and, from the time of Henry VIII, it was not uncommon for a royal patent of nobility or charter of incorporation to bear an illuminated portrait of the monarch within the first initial. Such is the grant to William Rede, mercer of London, of certain lands in Suffolk and Norfolk (Plate 151B), in which Henry VIII, enthroned and surrounded by his courtiers, is seen handing the charter to Rede, who kneels with his wife and child. Letters patent, by the way, are so called because they were open, for all to read, in distinction to letters close which were directed to a particular person and closed.

The other parchment reproduced (Plate 152) is a receipt from Roger de Actone, the king's larderer, for 100 marks from the Bishop of Norwich, out of the taxation of the clergy. An examination of this little document will show some of the interest, and some of the problems, attaching to the understanding of a medieval deed. The first line reads as follows: *Pateat universis per presentes quod ego*

Rogerus de Actone Lardenarius Domini Edwardi Regis Anglie illustris recepi et habui die. . . . That is to say, Be it known to all by the present (letters) that I Roger de Actone, larderer of the lord Edward, illustrious king of England, have received and had on the day (of the execution of the present, etc). Observe in the first place that the document is in Latin, the normal language of a medieval deed. Observe more closely, how the writing makes use of abbreviations, for example *per* is written *p*, with a line through the lower stroke of the letter to indicate *er*; *presentes* is written *psentes*, with a loop above the *p* to indicate *re*; *quod* is written *qd* with a line through the *d* to indicate that some letters have been omitted; similarly *Domini* is written *Dni* with a line above to show omission. The student will find that he quickly learns the simpler abbreviations.

A problem often attaching to medieval deeds is their date, and this particular document has its dating problem. It was rare for deeds before the fourteenth century to be dated by the year of the Lord. Indeed, the regnal year, or year since the accession of the reigning king, was the normal way of dating a secular document throughout the Middle Ages – when it *was* dated, for a twelfth or thirteenth-century deed may well not be dated at all, and the date can often only be approximately arrived at from the style of the writing and the evidence provided by what may already be known about the parties and the witnesses named.

Roger de Actone's receipt is dated on its last line as follows: *Datum apud Norwycum nono die mensis Decembris anno regni Regis supradicti Nono* (Given at Norwich on the ninth day of the month of December in the ninth year of the reign of the above-mentioned king, i.e. Edward.) The question is, which Edward? Edward I was normally called either plain 'Edward' or 'Edward, son of Henry'; Edward II was normally called 'Edward, son of Edward', but might be called simply 'Edward'; Edward III was normally called 'Edward the third since the Conquest'. The first supposition, then, in the case of this deed, in which on the first line the King is simply called 'Edward', is that it belongs to the ninth year of Edward I. The writing, however, suggests, but not conclusively, Edward II. What of the internal evidence? An attempt to identify Actone in various printed sources is not at once successful. Then, from the second line of the receipt the answer is given. The larderer is receiving his money from John, Bishop of Norwich. Le Neve's *Fasti* shows that a John was Bishop of Norwich in the ninth year of Edward II and not in the same year of Edward I. Edward II came to the throne on 8th July 1307. The date of this document is therefore 9th December 1315.

We have been spared one dating problem with regard to this document. The day of the month is given. It was more usual at this time to date a deed by a saint's day. Thus, for example, a deed might be said to have been executed on Sunday before the feast of St Simon and St Jude in the ninth year of the reign of Edward son of Edward. Now the feast of St Simon and St Jude was 28th October. From a book of reference, it is found that 28th October in the ninth year of Edward II was a Tuesday. The Sunday before will therefore be the 26th, and the date of the deed will be 26th October 1315.

BOOKS FOR FURTHER READING

It will be clear that certain books of reference are indispensable to anyone studying medieval deeds. I note a few of such, together with some literature on the subject of seals: For general study of court hand, C. Johnson and H. Jenkinson, *English Court Hand, 1066–1500*, one volume of text and one of illustrations. *The Record Interpreter*, by C. T. Martin, contains both a glossary of medieval Latin words and a key to abbreviations used in court hand. *The Medieval Latin Word-List* is a dictionary of medieval Latin. For the elucidation of dates, C. R. Cheney's *Handbook of Dates for Students of English History*. The British Museum *Catalogue of Seals*, in six volumes, contains descriptions of several thousands of seals and many illustrations. See also H. Jenkinson's *Guide to Seals in the Public Record Office*.

[*The seal of Rochester is reproduced by kind permission of the Town Clerk of Rochester, the others by that of the Public Record Office.*]

ENGLISH BOOKBINDINGS

By HOWARD M. NIXON

Collecting bookbindings is generally thought to be a rich man's hobby, and a long purse is certainly needed to form a truly representative collection containing the most beautiful and the most interesting bindings of all periods. Yet by intelligent specialization in a limited field, such as the blind-tooled bindings of the sixteenth century, the less elaborate gold-tooled work of the eighteenth century, early nineteenth-century signed bindings or the plainer trade bindings of any period, an interesting, attractive and historically valuable collection can be brought together by the ordinary impoverished British citizen of today.

Condition: as in any form of book collecting, condition is an all-important consideration. The aspiring collector must set himself standards of condition which accord with his bank balance, bearing in mind that he will probably derive more pleasure from the possession of a humble trade binding in mint state, almost as fresh as when it awaited a purchaser in a seventeenth-century bookshop, than from a soiled example from a famous collection, lavishly gold-tooled but so badly worn as to be beyond restoration. The more ambitious collector will, when possible, avoid acquiring any binding that has been at all extensively repaired, but the leathers used in England, with the exception of the best moroccos, have not lasted very well and some compromise may often be necessary. The decorated calf bindings which survive from the library of Thomas Wotton, the 'English Grolier' (1521–87), seldom retain their original backs; but as long as they have been suitably rebacked in a close imitation of the original style, they need not be excluded from a collection of the first rank – except by the purist who wishes to collect English bindings only and not bindings produced for Englishmen in France. The morocco of Charles II's reign, on the other hand, has usually lasted excellently, and for this period it should not normally be necessary to accept anything that has undergone more than a little judicious titivating of the caps at head and tail or a very skilful repair of a joint.

Leathers: the leather used for a binding will give the first clue to its date. On a medieval manuscript, sheep or deerskin (either white or pink) is the commonest material, while what is customarily described as calf (but is more probably cowhide) runs a poor third until the last quarter of the fifteenth century. Throughout the sixteenth century this so-called calf was the normal covering of all decorated bindings, whether blocked in blind or tooled in gold. From 1525 onwards, however, limp vellum (or its cheaper form known as forel) became increasingly popular for smaller undecorated books. Morocco (tanned goatskin) was very rarely used before the reign of James I, and in the first half of the seventeenth century it was usually brown or olive green. Red and blue moroccos began to appear after 1650 and were the normal material of the finest bindings of the Restoration, which were often further adorned with thin onlays of different-coloured leathers. Gold-tooled vellum bindings were fashionable in the first half of the seventeenth century, but the material was gradually ousted on the plainer bindings by sheep or calf. In the eighteenth century sheep was relegated to the cheapest work—school books or the chapbooks peddled round the country by itinerant chapmen – and was in turn replaced from 1770 onwards on these books, by the earliest form of bookcloth, a rather coarse, brown canvas. Vellum or parchment was only found on the elaborate Edwards of Halifax bindings, which have designs painted on the under-surface of transparent vellum, or on half-bindings such as Newbery's 'vellum manner' of the 1770s.

For the better class of book, calf was the most popular material until the introduction, also in the 1770s, of paper-covered boards – a style which was intended to give the book temporary protection until the owner should have it properly bound to his personal taste. The moroccos in use in the first half of the eighteenth century were still generally dyed red or blue, and were often of poorer quality than those tanned in Charles II's reign. About 1760, however, new and more delicate shades of colour were introduced, and about ten years later 'straight-grain' moroccos, with an artificial surface pattern of raised parallel lines, came into fashion. In the 1820s came the rise of edition binding, when the publisher, rather than the bookseller or the purchaser, took over the responsibility for having the book bound. Bookcloth was introduced about 1823 by Archibald Leighton at the instigation of William Pickering, the publisher, and when casing replaced binding for cloth-covered books about 1830 the modern era had arrived.

Blind-tooled Bindings: the earliest known English decorated leather bookbinding is that on the Stonyhurst Gospel, which was removed from the tomb of St Cuthbert in 1104 and probably dates from the seventh century. One other binding that may be English is now at Fulda, having belonged to St Boniface, the eighth-century English missionary to Germany. These, however, are fabulous rarities, and hardly more accessible to modern collectors are the small group of 'Romanesque' bindings of the twelfth and thirteenth centuries decorated in blind with beautifully engraved tools. London, Oxford, Winchester and Durham may all have had binders working in this manner, but it is now clear that the great majority of these Romanesque bindings – once all confidently assumed to be English – were produced in Paris. Hardly any decorated leather bindings were produced in England in the fourteenth century, and the earliest examples likely to find their way into the antiquarian book market are the blind-tooled bindings of the second half of the fifteenth century. At first, single tools only were used on these 'calf' bindings, although one enterprising craftsman, known as the Scales binder, essayed some naïve cut-leather bindings in feeble imitation of the splendid works of art being produced in this technique in German-speaking lands. The first labour-saving decorative device – the panel stamp – was probably introduced into England by William de Machlinia about 1487. It enabled the decoration of the cover of a book to be completed at one operation in the binder's press. These panels are often signed with initials or names, but these are normally those of booksellers rather than binders. Many of them, particularly those decorated with figures of saints and Biblical scenes, are of Continental origin. There is, however, an interesting series of panels decorated with the royal arms and Tudor rose (used decoratively by booksellers and not as a mark of royal ownership) which are distinctively English (Plate 156A). Panel stamps continued in use until about 1550, and there seems to be a gap of ten years or so before they were replaced by new designs, blocked in gold, which remained a popular form of decoration for smaller books throughout the Tudor and Stuart periods. A second short-cut to decoration was the roll, engraved with a wide band of ornament, which came into use in England about the year 1500. Tooled in blind, it remained in vogue for a long period, being *de rigueur* for the heavier theological tome well into the seventeenth century. One very late example (characteristically produced in Oxford) dates from 1654. From the Restoration onwards, blind-tooling was usually restricted to the delineation with a fillet or a very narrow roll of a rectangular panel on the covers and the back of a calf binding until it was revived in the 1790s for use in conjunction with gold-tooling on bindings of the highest quality.

Gold-tooled Bindings: the earliest English gilt binding (now in the Bodleian) was probably bound for Cardinal Wolsey in 1519; it is decorated with what appears to be a wooden block, with panels of St George slaying the dragon and Tudor emblems. A unique example of one of John Reynes's royal arms panels blocked in gold survives in the Paris Bibliothèque Nationale on a book presented to Henry VIII by Thomas Linacre, who died in 1524. The use of small tools impressed in gold by hand, however, does not appear to have been introduced much before 1530. From the next twenty-five years quite a number of bindings have survived bearing the royal arms, which were formerly all ascribed to Thomas Berthelet, the king's printer in Henry VIII's reign. He certainly supplied fine bindings to the king, but there is no evidence that he had his own binder's shop. The bindings undoubtedly came from a number of different shops, at present distinguished by names such as King Henry's binder (the earliest, who based his designs on Italian models), the Medallion binder, and King Edward and Queen Mary's binder (whose work seems the least rare and who copied the French bindings of his day) (Plate 154A).

Queen Elizabeth I showed a marked partiality for embroidered bindings, and this probably retarded the progress of gold-tooling in England. In the 1560s and 1570s some interesting bindings, decorated with small tools of French design, were produced in London for Archbishop Parker, who at one time had binders working for him at Lambeth Palace. Some bindings from the same shop were, however, also executed for Parker's enemy, Robert Dudley, Earl of Leicester, so that it is unlikely that all this group was bound at Lambeth. The most typical Elizabethan fine leather bindings are in the international style known as Lyonese, on which heavy centre- and corner-pieces were blocked in a press, and this style continued in use until about 1640. Some imitations of the French *fanfare* style (Plate 154B) were made in the last few years of the reign of James I, but distinctively English bindings now began to appear. Among these are versions of the centre- and corner-piece style, to which has been added an outer frame decorated with impressions of large tools, often wedge-shaped pieces of conventional foliage. Cambridge produced some characteristic bindings in the twenties and thirties of the seventeenth century which have small tools arranged in a circle in the centre and quarter-circles in the angles. It is at this period that we can begin to identify some of the binders by name, and these bindings are probably the work of Henry Moody and Daniel Boyse.

From Cambridge also came some of the earliest mosaic bindings of the Restoration period – the golden age of English bookbinding – and these can be attributed to John Houlden. He had been preceded in London by the brothers Stephen and Thomas Lewis and by Henry Evans, both of whom produced unexpectedly gay work in the last years of the supposedly gloomy Commonwealth period. Fletcher and Samuel Mearne were prominent in the 1660s, and the latter's shop was probably one of the most important in London until the death of his son Charles Mearne in the 1680s. To Mearne were long attributed all the decorative leather bindings of this period; it was then asserted that, although he held the office of Royal Binder, he was not a binder himself and only commissioned bindings from others; it is now known that he was apprenticed to a bookbinder and that he had a binder's shop attached to his bookselling business, and a considerable number of bindings from his shop have been tentatively identified. Other binders whose work can be recognized include Samuel Mearne's apprentice, Robert Steele; Richard Balley who was trained under Suckerman 'at Mr Mearne's'; and Roger Bartlett, who retired to Oxford after the Great Fire. There are still, however, some distinctive groups of important bindings which cannot be ascribed to any known craftsman, and can only be attributed to the Queen's binder, the Devotional binder and the Naval binder (Plate 153). During the reign of Charles II new and distinctive English binding designs were developed, including the Cottage style and the all-over pattern with drawer-handle tools, although some of the decoration was still based on the French *fanfare* style of a hundred years earlier.

The first half of the eighteenth century proved rather dull, exhibiting debased versions of the Cottage style and the rather insipid Harleian bindings. Some rather tasteless examples of mosaic binding came from Oxford in the 1720s. Others were produced in London between 1741 and 1745 on a group of bindings which includes three presentation copies of the illustrated edition of Faerno's *Cent Fables* printed at London in 1743. Andreas Linde perpetrated some Teutonic excesses for the future George III, *c.* 1751, but it was not until the next decade that any really important bindings were executed. The finest of these were designed by Robert Adam and by 'Athenian' Stuart for books intended to popularize their architectural styles and theories, and neo-classical decoration of the same type appears on an attractive binding on a book printed by Horace Walpole at Strawberry Hill, which is now in George III's library (Plate 155A).

Two interesting eccentrics now enliven the collector's scene – Thomas Hollis, an ardent republican in theory and a dutiful subject of George III in practice, and Jonas Hanway, founder of the Marine Society, opponent of tea-drinking and protagonist of the umbrella. Unfortunately the more elaborate Hollis bindings, the work of Richard Montagu, were only executed for presentation to Harvard, or to Swiss or Italian public libraries, where they still remain. In the 1700s rococo decoration made a tardy appearance on a number of unsigned bindings, but the best known of these are the work of James Scott, of Edinburgh where, as in Dublin, the binders outstripped their London rivals for much of the century. The eighties and nineties were marked by the rise of Roger Payne and by the flourishing school of German immigrants, including Baumgarten, Kalthoeber, Hering, Staggemeier and Welcher, Benedict and Bohn, who were attracted by the boom in English book collecting and the passion of the collectors of the period for full morocco. They were responsible for popularizing in England the admirable practice of signing bindings. Generally this was done with an engraved ticket, but not infrequently the binder's name was tooled on the leather or on a fly-leaf. Payne, notorious for alleged insobriety and for his endearingly verbose bills, worked almost single-handed, but in the last decade of the eighteenth century he set new fashions in design with his elaborate 'gold-studded' backs (Plate 155B). These were not only copied by his German contemporaries in London, but also achieved the unusual distinction of being imitated (not very successfully) in Paris. Egyptian and Pompeian motifs are found on some of the bindings of the Regency period, and soon after 1810 'Cathedral' bindings appeared on a number of the large books on ecclesiastical antiquities popular at the time. Some of the cheaper bindings decorated with the fly-embossing press introduced about 1830 were also decorated in this Cathedral style (Plate 156B). The 1820s, however, saw the introduction of a nearly fatal influence on English binding design – the copying of an historical style such as the 'Grolier' or 'Cottage'. For the next sixty years magnificent workmanship was lavished – and wasted – on the production of dreary pastiches, and it was not until the mid-1880s that the ex-barrister T. J. Cobden-Sanderson injected new ideas and new enthusiasm into his adopted profession.

The Patrons: some of the finest English bindings were no doubt ordered by collectors like Pepys, who visited Nott in Westminster in 1669 'to bespeak a book to be bound, only that I might have one of his binding'. More, however, probably cover Bibles or Prayer Books intended for a church or nobleman's private chapel. A third group – particularly the bindings on the various works of the author of *The Whole Duty of Man* – were evidently bought ready-bound as presents. The most numerous class, however, is that of dedication and presentation copies from the proud author, and the more obscure the author the more lavish is the binding.

GLOSSARY

Many of the definitions given here are based, with Mr John Carter's permission, on his invaluable *ABC for Book-Collectors*, published by Rupert Hart-Davis. A number of relevant entries will also be found in the glossary of Mr Carter's article on Book Collecting in the first volume of the *Concise*

Encyclopaedia of Antiques, pages 200–9. These include: Armorial, bevelled edges or bevelled boards, blind, calf, Cottage style, dentelle, doublure, endpapers, fore-edge painting, half-bound, Levant, morocco, re-backed, re-jointed, roan, russia leather, sheep, signed bindings, Spanish calf, sprinkled, tree calf and wrappers.

All-over: a style of decoration in which the same motif is repeated at equal intervals all over the covers; particularly used to describe late seventeenth-century bindings with 'drawer-handle' tooling (q.v.).

Azured: descriptive of tools decorated with a series of slanting parallel lines. (From the method of depicting azure in heraldic engraving.)

Backless Bindings: a whimsical style of the sixteenth and seventeenth centuries in which the spine of a binding is replaced by a fabric which is covered with gilt paper, so that the book appears to have four gilt edges.

Bands: horizontal projections on the spine where the leather crosses the cords on which the book is sewn. On a hollow-backed book or one with sewn-in cords the same effect can be obtained with *false bands*.

Binding: involves the cords or tapes on which the book is sewn being securely fastened into the boards, which are then covered with leather or other suitable binding material. Cf. Casing.

Block: a piece of wood or metal, without a handle, being an engraved design for decorating the cover of a book, and intended to be used in a press.

Casing: involves the preparation in quantity of the boards and covering material (usually cloth) to form ready-made cases. These are attached by gluing a strip of mull to the back of the book, gluing the overlaps of the mull to the case and pasting down the endpapers.

Cathedral: applied to bindings of the period 1810–40, decorated in gold or blind with Gothic architectural motifs, which often include a rose window.

Chemise: a prolongation of the covering material at the foot of a binding. Existing examples (in leather and velvet) date from the fifteenth or early sixteenth centuries. Cf. Girdle-book.

Chinoiserie: most English bindings in the Chinese taste date from the 1770s and 1780s, Chinese figures mingling with rococo shell ornaments and C-shaped curves.

Dos-à-dos: a style of binding used mostly for small devotional works in the sixteenth and seventeenth centuries in which two volumes are bound back-to-back with a common lower board.

Drawer-handle Tool: an ornament in the shape of an Ionic capital, first used on binding tools in the second half of the seventeenth century.

Etruscan Style: descriptive of bindings in calf (*c.* 1780–1825) decorated by acid staining with classical decoration.

Fakes and Forgeries: most of the well-known bookbinding forgeries purport to be foreign examples. In the British Isles – apart from a brisk production of fore-edge paintings – activity seems to have been limited to the addition of royal arms or ciphers (particularly that of Mary Queen of Scots) to otherwise genuine bindings. Two well-known bindings with the arms of Henry VIII of England in the centre, surmounted by the Virgin and Child and surrounded by a motley collection of armorial escutcheons, were probably produced in France in the nineteenth century.

Fanfare Style: originated in Paris, *c.* 1565. Copied in England from 1620 onwards. Interlacing ribbons, bounded on one side by a double line and on the other by a single line, outline geometrical compartments of varying shapes which (with the exception of a large central one) are filled with conventional floral ornament. The English imitations often have the interlacing ribbon bounded by a single line on each side.

Fillet: a wheel tool used for impressing one or several parallel straight lines; applied also to the lines produced by the tool.

Gauffered (of the gilt edges of the book): decorated with the impression of a heated tool.

Girdle-book: some pre-Reformation service books were bound in a chemise (q.v.) gathered into a knop or button which could be attached to the owner's girdle. Small folding almanacks were similarly attached with a cord.

Harleian: in the manner of the eighteenth-century bindings executed for the library of Robert Harley, Earl of Oxford, and his son, Edward. They were usually of red morocco, with a border made up of one or more rolls (or rows of single tools), and often had a large central lozenge made up with small tools. They were the work of several different binders, including the rival firms of Thomas Elliott and Christopher Chapman.

Inlaid Bindings: *see* Mosaic.

Masonic Bindings: the earliest English bindings decorated with Masonic emblems date from the second half of the eighteenth century. Robert Black and John Lovejoy specialized in their production.

Mosaic Bindings: bindings with polychrome decoration, produced by using: (i) paint; (ii) onlays of very thinly pared leather applied on top of the leather of the covers; (iii) genuine inlays of different-coloured leather inserted into the leather of the covers. Onlay is very much more common than inlay.

Onlaid Bindings: *see* Mosaic.

Pallet: a tool with a short strip of decoration designed primarily for decorating the panels of the back of a binding. Specialized kinds can be used for lettering or signing bindings.

Panel-stamped: a term used by writers on bookbinding (but not bookbinders) to describe leather bindings of the fifteenth and sixteenth centuries decorated in blind with engraved blocks.

Pointillé: used of tools, first introduced in France *c.* 1640, having a dotted and not a solid outline.

Remboîtage: the transference of a book from one binding to another or the result of this nefarious practice.

Rococo Bindings: rococo decoration was surprisingly late in affecting bookbinding design, and most English bindings with the typical asymmetrical ornaments, C-shaped curves and fantastic shells of the style date from the late 1770s and the 1780s.

Roll: a tool (or the impression of a tool) leaving a continuous or repeated design engraved round the edge of a wheel.

Royal Bindings: any binding blocked with the royal arms. Very often these do not denote royal ownership, but are used purely decoratively, e.g. the blind-stamped panels of Henry VIII's reign or the calf bindings, *c.* 1600, with Queen Elizabeth I's crowned falcon badge; both of these groups are trade bindings. Bibles and Prayer Books with the royal arms are very unlikely to have been personal possessions of the sovereign. They may have been part of the chapel furniture issued to all English ambassadors abroad; they may have come from a royal chapel; or they may even come from a parish church. Even books in an elaborate binding with the royal arms and a dedication to the king may never have been in royal possession, for sometimes an author seems to have had identical bindings made for his presentation copies. The dedication copy of Robert Adam's *Ruins of the Palace of the Emperor Diocletian at Spalatro*, 1764, is one of six copies known which bear the royal arms. (See Plate 117 in Volume I of the *Concise Encyclopaedia of Antiques.*)

Semis: a repeating pattern of small ornaments 'sown' over the covers.

Sombre Bindings: bindings of black leather, tooled in blind and often with black edges. The style (no doubt connected with mourning observances) was much in use on devotional books between 1675 and 1725. They were produced by all the important binders.

Trade Binding: executed for a retail or wholesale bookseller prior to the development of publishers' bindings in the nineteenth century. Before 1820 ready-bound books

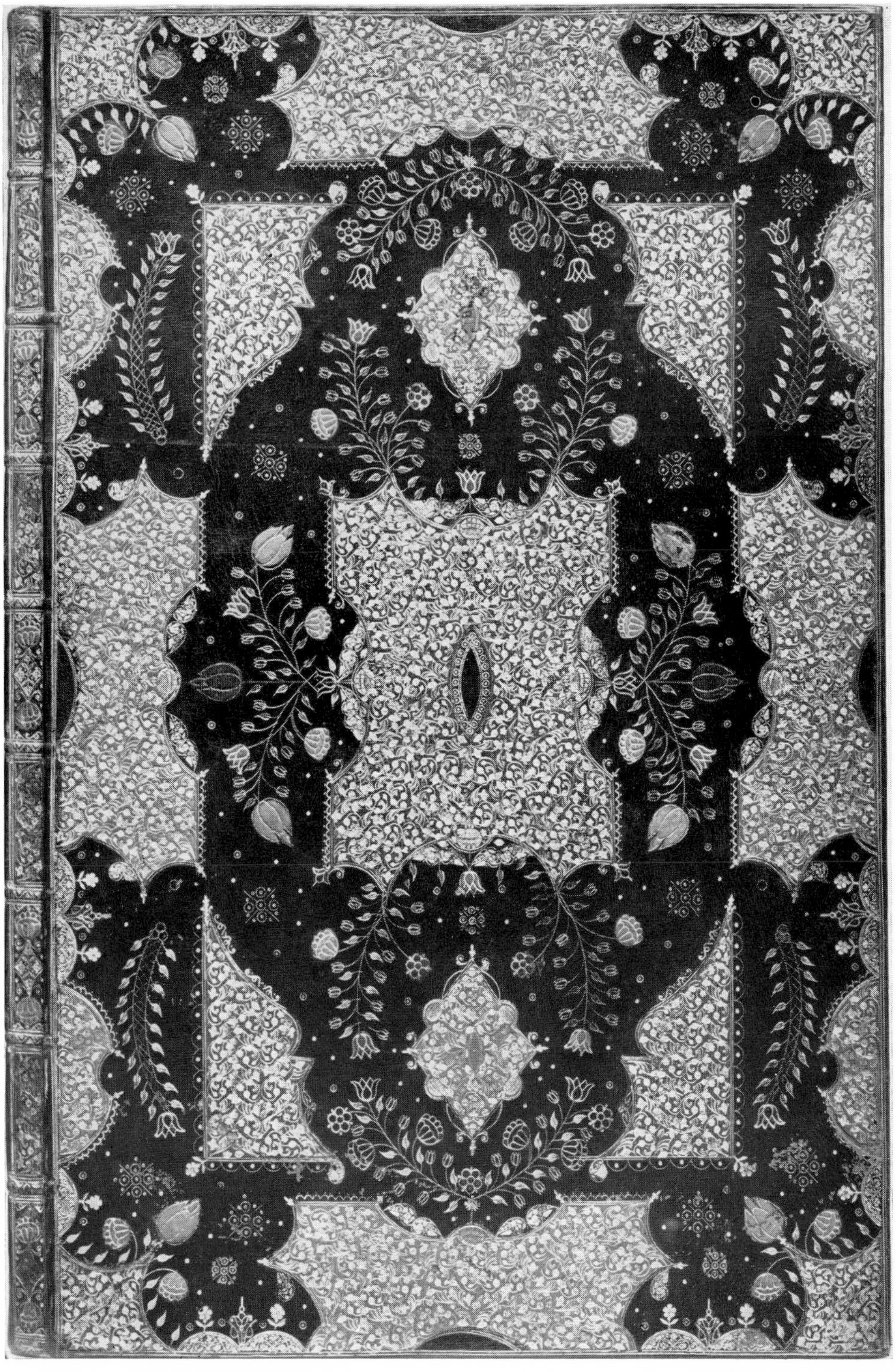

A binding by the so-called Naval Binder, *c.* 1675. *Abstract of the Accompt of Payments made by the Earle of Darby . . . as Treasurer of His Majesty's Navy* . . . 1671–3. Black morocco, with red and orange onlays, tooled in gold. *British Museum.*

PLATE 153

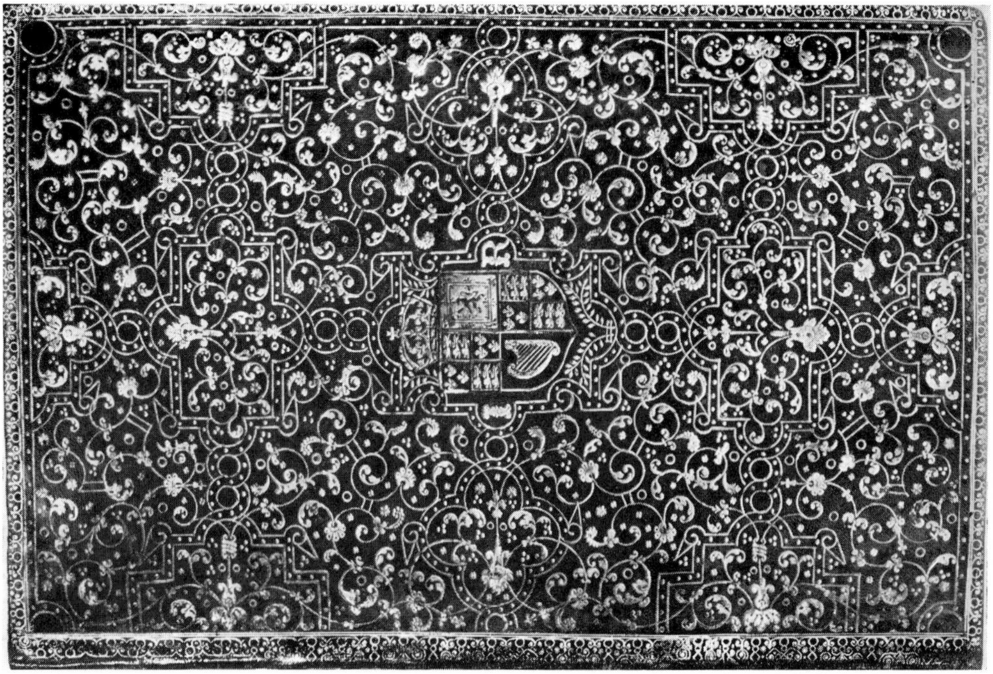

(B) A London binding in the fanfare style for King James I, *c.* 1620. Thevet. *Pourtraits et Vies des Hommes Illustres.* Paris, 1584. Dark green morocco, gold-tooled, with the royal arms inlaid in colours. *British Museum.*

(A) A London backless binding for King Edward VI by the so-called King Edward and Queen Mary binder, 1552. Bembo. *Historia Veneta.* Venice, 1551. Brown calf with gold-tooled interlacing strapwork enamelled black. *British Museum.*

(A) A London binding with classical ornament, *c.* 1764, from the Library of King George III. *The Life of Herbert of Cherbury*. Strawberry Hill, 1764. Red morocco, gold-tooled. *British Museum*.

(B) A binding by Roger Payne for C. M. Cracherode, *c.* 1796. Cicero. *Officiorum libri III*. Venice, 1545. Olive-brown morocco, gold-tooled. *British Museum*.

(B) A trade binding, *c.* 1830, blocked in blind with a cathedral design. *Holy Bible*, 1828. Red morocco. *Chas. J. Sawyer Ltd.*

(A) A trade binding, *c.* 1530, blocked in blind with the arms of King Henry VIII impaling those of Anne Boleyn. Whitinton. *Grammatical Tracts*, *c.* 1530. Brown sheep. *British Museum.*

PLATE 156

To face page 22

formed only a proportion of a bookseller's stock, much of which would be in sheets (or after 1770 in paper-covered boards, uncut ready for binding to the customer's order).

Waste: spoiled or surplus sheets of printed matter, often used before 1650 by binders for lining the back of a book, making boards of compressed layers of paper or as endleaves. *Bookseller's waste* – surplus quires of recent books or discarded fragments of old ones – is of little value in localizing a binding. *Printer's waste*, however – proofs, trial sheets, overprintings, etc – is not so likely to travel as sheets from a completed book, and may give a clue to the place of binding.

BOOKS FOR FURTHER READING

HOBSON, G. D.: *English Bindings in the Library of J. R. Abbey* (1940); *Bindings in Cambridge Libraries* (1929).

NIXON, H. M.: *Broxbourne Library. Styles and Designs of Bookbindings* (1956); articles on English bookbinding in *The Book Collector* (quarterly).

OLDHAM, J. B.: *Shrewsbury School Library Bindings* (1943).

Earlier books with useful plates, but much of the text now proved inaccurate are:

DAVENPORT, C. J.: *Royal English Bindings* (1896); *Thomas Berthelet* (1901); *Samuel Mearne* (1906); *Roger Payne* (1929).

FLETCHER, W. Y.: *English Bookbindings in the British Museum* (1893).

Valuable specialist studies include:

GIBSON, STRICKLAND: *Early Oxford Bindings* (1903).

GRAY, G. J.: *The Earlier Cambridge Stationers and Bookbinders* (1904).

HOBSON, G. D.: *Blind-stamped Panels in the English Book-trade* (1944); *English Binding before 1500* (1929).

OLDHAM, J. B.: *English Blind-stamped Bindings* (1952).

There are three dictionaries of binders:

HOWE, ELLIC: *A List of London Bookbinders, 1648–1815* (1950).

RAMSDEN, CHARLES: *Bookbinders of the United Kingdom (outside London), 1780–1840* (1954); *London Bookbinders, 1780–1840* (1956).

MAPS AND GLOBES

By JOHN MUNDAY

If you choose to surround yourself, to whatever extent, with examples of the beauty to be found in the almost limitless products of craftsmen of the past, maps, not less than other works of art, will provide decoration, interest and often pieces of high artistic merit. This article does not attempt a history of cartography, for there are several excellent published works which will guide the collector with authority; but some of the names and styles which are most frequently met, and some of the terms used, are here set out. English map-makers have reached their own peculiar heights of achievement, but the influence of Continental styles and cultures has been both felt and reflected. The rise of national schools or tendencies in map-making accompanied an ascendancy in maritime affairs. Sea-power and the consequent prospering of seaborne trade have a close bearing on the production of both land maps and sea charts. Ocean voyages of discovery, embarked upon by thriving and questing peoples, brought forth pictures, cartographic pictures, of new lands and new seas.

We may leave aside technical considerations of surveying, which were often not of paramount importance nor of remarkable accuracy, even into the eighteenth century. The processes by which maps were reproduced are one of their most interesting aspects, and much of what has been said in this Encyclopaedia relating to prints and books is applicable here. Many maps found by collectors today have come from books, either as illustrations to a text or from an atlas; a sobering thought that so many handsome volumes have been broken up. However, without it the beauty, interest and consequent pleasure of their contents would necessarily have been lost to thousands of people. Sometimes, it is true, the books themselves were nothing but collections of maps by different engravers and publishers, so perhaps from one point of view the process is not without a certain reason. The names of engravers and publishers as well as of cartographers and surveyors are all signposts to the collector; indeed these functions were frequently combined by one individual.

PROCESSES

Manuscript maps, the beginning of everything in this field, are a special study; their discovery is a matter for consultation with the expert.

Engraved maps: the *copper plate*, taking the 'scratch' of the craftsman's graver, is the chief means by which maps were reproduced. The etched line, bitten into the plate by acid and having its own qualities, was also used, but to a lesser extent. In the nineteenth century *lithography* (printing from stone) was used, while the advent of steel in place of copper for engraving generally, although resisted by some craftsmen, was also applied with success to map-making. The *woodcut*, a reversal of the engraving process, in which the ink was carried on the surface left standing and not in the groove left by the tool, was the other important early medium. The quality of the woodcut is recognized in a heavier, less flexible line and a more compact or sculpturesque treatment of ornament. The block leaves no impression of its dimensions on the paper, whereas the copper plate, its edges rounded off to prevent tearing, leaves a shallow depression in the paper as it passes through the press. This depression is known as the *plate-mark*, the presence of which is a guide to the beginner that the map is in the first place printed and secondly that it is complete.

Beyond the plate-mark, the *margins* or spare paper are generally preferred as large as possible, for apart from setting-off the engraved surface of the map, they are some indication that it is in a reasonably unspoilt state. Though desirable, wide margins are neither essential nor inevitable, and a scarce map trimmed to its border or with very small margins is not to be passed by. The possibility of acquiring the better example is present in the minds of all collectors, not only of cartophiles. Within the plate-mark is the *border*, confining the detail of the map itself. From a single line, on some examples, the border may vary in others to an elaborate pattern in imitation of a carved picture frame. Within the border may occur a scale of miles or of units of latitude and longitude, although other uses such as a numero-alphabetical system for map references are to be seen. It should also be remembered that longitude, in times past and in other countries, has been measured from several places other than the now familiar Greenwich.

The folding of maps of large size into a volume of smaller dimensions can have caused wear, which is not a bar to good condition unless of serious extent. The way in which double-page maps were hinged to a stub of paper in the binding of a book and not sewn in, enabled them to lie flat, and has had the admirable effect of preserving them whole to this day.

To return to the inner surface, ornament, reflecting all the styles and decorative fashions of its period, and one of the attractive features of maps as a whole, is found on the *title*. This sometimes contains in addition to the necessary descriptive details, particulars and place of publication (the *imprint*) and the date, although the last is frequently omitted, adding to the interest of the collector and sometimes to his undoing! These details are usually enclosed in a *cartouche*, perhaps architectural, in imitation of carving (Plate 158A) or drapery. Scenic titles (Plate 162B) or figure pieces (Plate 161A) give some of the most interesting and decorative additions to the purely topographical features. *Insets* such as descriptive notes, armorial bearings, views, town-plans or 'close-up' details on a large scale, are other points of embellishment. *Vignettes* occur in the form of land and sea battles, shipwrecks, beasts, sea-monsters and families of mer-folk; also groups of inhabitants pursuing their occupations and practising their customs (Plate 160B). *The Scale*, sometimes comparing various measures of distance, is frequently the subject of artistic elaboration too. Plate 161B shows the ubiquitous cherub; Plates 158B and 159B navigator's and surveyor's instruments, the dividers and compass. The *Compass Rose*, with its own long history of design, is a necessary feature, for the orientation of a map was not always with north at the top.

The wide use of Latin for the titling especially of early maps, gives often in abbreviated form, the 'Sculp^{t}.' or 'Fecit' of the engraver, the 'Delin:' or 'Inven^{t}.' of the draughtsman, and the 'Excud:' 'Apud' or 'Sumptibus' of the publisher. The *Lettering* employed, apart from its obvious function of identification, has an important decorative part to play. Gothic, Italic and Roman, plain and flourished, handsomely tailed or classically serifed, they are found to have a considerable effect on the surface pattern; the choice of certain styles and sizes of letter to denote particular features had early been made (Plate 157A). In later times a marvellous variety of lower-case as well as capital letters 'hollow', 'shadow', upright and italic, not to speak of several sorts of scripts, were the visual vocabulary of the map-maker.

The stages in the reproduction of a map are of importance from the time the first proof is taken. Two copies of what is seemingly the same item can, on inspection, reveal differences of greater or lesser extent, by which it is often possible to date them. Since the life of a copper plate was frequently surprisingly long and its ownership diverse, the range of possible variations is wide.

Colour is a matter of great interest and importance, for while the engraving was black and sharp on the white paper when it came off the press, and it was sold in that form, a large part of the map-seller's business was the colouring of his wares. There are preferences today for the uncoloured specimen, but good original colour is so much a distinctive period feature that understandably it greatly enhances the value of many types of map. The specialist who applied pigment to the map, following certain time-honoured conventions, gave us those glowing, exciting and perhaps vivid effects which are a feature of 'Contemporary Colouring'. Old maps are coloured for sale today, often in skilful imitation of the proper styles. Colour which has been a long time on the paper will have made a darkening stain right through; some tints, green in particular, have had a corrosive effect which now renders the map brittle where it was applied. The actual pigment used to colour early maps was often more or less opaque, concealing the engraving, and the way in which it was applied was frequently more spirited than meticulous.

Rarities, for which the collector naturally hopes but does not necessarily pursue, are best treated in the books of reference quoted on p. 237; many famous maps, desirable in any collection, are, however, quickly reaching that category. Collectors have a broad field for their hunting, and whatever the nature of their quarry they can be sure of some fascinating discoveries. The wealth of historical detail to be found in old maps of your own part of the country, the sure reflection of changing tastes in ornament and the delight of making your own tours and voyages in an older world, are a few of the recommendations.

MAKERS, ENGRAVERS AND PUBLISHERS

The names which form a monumental foundation for this subject are still to be encountered in the map-seller's on terms of comparative familiarity. The great ones of cartography are still attainable by the humble collector, the Old Masters here being far less the companions of rich collectors than in almost any other branch of the Arts.

Claudius Ptolemy of Alexandria, who worked in the second century A.D., was brought to light again in the Renaissance, when an edition based on surviving manuscript copies of his *Geographia*, with maps, was published (Bologna, 1477). These maps were printed from copper plates, but some of the most famous early editions of the same book came from Germany, notably Ulm, 1482 (Plate 157A), and Strasbourg, 1513, in which they were printed from wood blocks. Here we have the two schools almost typifying the cultures on either side of the Alps. Ptolemy, with modern additions, was much reprinted and edited in both countries; here is the world as understood by the Ancients, approximate but recognizable, and with it visions of new continents as yet unexplored.

In Italy, the map-sellers of Venice and Rome, such as Forlani and Lafreri, produced maps ranging from continents in several sheets to small ones of islands on a single leaf, all from copper plates. They gathered together selections of the works of their competitors and contemporaries, into volumes of maps which were the forerunners of what we mean by the term Atlas, although that word was first used to personify a collection of his own maps in 1585, by Mercator, whose title-page showed the mythical king. The *Italia* of G. A. Magini (Bologna, 1620), which contains some plates from the hand of Benjamin Wright, an English engraver working on the Continent, presents a detailed series of elaborate maps of the country with crowded topographical pictures and but little added embellishment. Round about the end of the seventeenth century, Venice was the scene of the remarkable activity of M. V. Coronelli (1650–1718), Cosmographer to the Republic, who conducted the Academy called *Gli Argonauti* and produced maps of a grand and ornamental nature.

One of the most important names in cartography, and probably the most generally familiar, Gerhard Mercator, lived from 1512 to 1594, and his *Atlas Sive Cosmographicae Meditationes* (1585–95) contains the work of one who had been an instrument maker and an authority on the italic script in which he inscribed the place-names, as well as a draughtsman and engraver. The map-makers of the Netherlands were a closely knit fraternity, and it is of interest and importance to note how their stock-in-trade was passed from father to son and from publisher to successor. This is why the same map may carry several different imprints at various times; the plate was handed over to a new proprietor, and a new name and date appeared. As the plates wore, the lines were strengthened, new information was included and often a new dedication to some more recent notability replaced the older. Mercator's business passed to sons and grandsons, but soon after 1600 it went to JODOCUS HONDIUS (1563–1612), who had spent some ten years of exile in England. He published further editions of *Atlas*, with his own contributions, and his son Henricus also continued the work (Plate 159A). Another famous name was brought into the business by marriage, in JAN JANSSON (1596–1664), who became Henricus' brother-in-law and took control in about 1657.

ABRAHAM ORTELIUS of Antwerp (1527–98), friend of Mercator, collected from many sources and used the work of most of the known figures of cartographic and geographic repute. Having begun as a colourer and map-seller, he produced in 1570 his great *Theatrum Orbis Terrarum*, a step nearer the atlas of uniform maps which we know today. Examples, such as Plate 158A, particularly when in original or near-contemporary colouring, are among the most highly evocative of the spirit and decorative style of that age. The names of FRANS HOGENBERG the engraver and GEORGE BRAUN his editor are linked in their wonderful *Civitates Orbis Terrarum*, published at Cologne between 1573 and 1618. The six books contain several hundred plan-views of important cities, many including costume figures, coats-of-arms and scenes of historical incidents, which make the series a valuable work of reference; the individual plates, which are reasonably common, are a source of more than ordinary interest. One of the links between our native map-makers and these great names on the Continent occurs here, for Frans Hogenberg, who was also responsible for putting on to copper the maps of Ortelius, had a brother Remigius who came to England and contributed nine of the plates to Saxton's atlas.

Early maps of England were manifestly unsuited for the comings and goings of the Elizabethans, and the peril in which this country stood from foreign invasion hastened the realization that better surveys were needed. GEORGE LILY, another English exile abroad, had produced the first engraved map of Britain in two sheets printed at Rome in 1546; also Mercator had a map of England and Wales in 1564, and Ortelius included maps of England and Wales in his 1573 edition and later. It was, however, CHRISTOPHER SAXTON, a Yorkshireman, who proceeded under the Queen's mandate to make his survey of the counties of England and Wales, and so produce the first collection of its kind in the world. The results, to the extent of thirty-four county maps and one of the country in general, appeared between 1574 and 1579, and were engraved by Netherlanders like HOGENBERG and TERWOORT, and by Englishmen like AUGUSTINE RYTHER, another Yorkshireman. The latter's signature carried the qualification 'Anglus' to differentiate between the true-born English, of whom his contemporaries and we, too, have every reason to be proud, and on the other hand the Dutch and Flemish masters from whom we learnt. In style, however, there is little such difference; Plate 158B shows the work of Ryther, who will be noticed again later. While a complete Saxton atlas is now something of a rarity, and maps from it in contemporary colouring are not exactly cheap, they are still obtainable. The graceful and sometimes elaborate script used is an ornament in itself; the Latin titles within their cartouches of fruit, flowers and bird-life, the Queen's arms with the fleurs-de-lys and the Tudor dragon, give us the England of nearly four hundred years ago in spirit as well as name and appearance. The late Edward Lynam wrote: 'Saxton deserves a place beside Shakespeare as an interpreter of the national consciousness, unity and pride which were the greatest achievements of Elizabethan England' (*British Maps and Mapmakers*).

Saxton's plates, in the hands of PHILIP LEA (d. *c.* 1700), who made considerable alterations, had a new lease of life, and later appeared under the Bowles's name, also under that of Sayer (1763). Lea was a busy cartographer, globe-maker and publisher who also constructed and sold instruments.

Use was made of the word 'Theatre' for a display of maps, by JOHN SPEED (1552–1629), who in 1611 issued the renowned *Theatre of the Empire of Great Britain*. This bore similarities to Ortelius' *Theatrum* besides its title. Speed cast wide for his sources, and acknowledged the fact on many of his plates, which were engraved not in England but by Jodocus Hondius in Amsterdam. The book was a great commercial venture, not sheltered by royal or noble patronage, but well justified by its popularity, which called for many editions in the succeeding century. The maps, favourites today among collectors, owe a great deal to Hondius's art. His masterly ornamentation of the groundwork with which Speed supplied him is to be recognized in the borders, titles and lettering. Speed's own antiquarian fancy has given us the historic heraldry of the families which bore county titles, and the city plans, views of notable mansions and churches, etc (Plate 159B). Compared with Saxton's county maps, examples of Speed's in early state are generally a little less expensive; the editions of the complete work were numerous and the life of the plates in the hands of successive publishers was long, copies bearing an imprint of about 1770 being known.

JOHN NORDEN (1548–1625) was a rival of Saxton's, and while his smaller output did not share the popularity of the latter's, his maps in some instances take pride of place, as for example in the delineation of the chief roads. The face of the countryside as it then was has assumed a lasting significance by the distinguishing of parks, noblemen's seats, gentlemen's houses, castles, market-towns and many other features not before shown, while the borders include a simple system of letters and figures for map references. WILLIAM CAMDEN'S *Britannia* contained, in the Latin edition of 1607, some county maps engraved after Saxton and Norden, but smaller in size than their originals. The same work, in its English translation of 1695, contained some fifty county maps fostered by ROBERT MORDEN (d. 1703), not to be confused with Norden. These, of rather inferior and coarser style, are nevertheless interesting and quite common.

In the later seventeenth and eighteenth centuries, families like the OVERTON'S, J., H. and P., and the BOWLES'S, T., J. and C. (who were print- as well as map-sellers) handled other men's plates, so that impressions of earlier works lived on under their ownership and passed to their heirs and successors down into the nineteenth century (*see* SKELTON, *Decorative Printed Maps*, Chapter 8). Pursuing the connexion between England and the Netherlands, we find that J. Hondius and his brother-in-law PIETER VAN DEN KEERE, who by the same token should perhaps be called by the Latin form Kaerius, settled in Amsterdam on leaving England in the 1590s. As we have seen, Mercator's Atlas continued to appear with many and valuable additions by Hondius, so that his name and that of his son Henricus, is rightly connected with the editions published after 1606. Their successor, Jansson, had a formidable rival in the famous house which produced some of the finest maps of the seventeenth century, BLAEU of Amsterdam, the history of whose members and their contributions to both cartography and printing is fascinating. WILLEM JANSZOON BLAEU (1571–1638) made confusing use of several variants of his name in signing and publishing his maps, and Gulielmus Blaeu and Gul. Janssonius are two of them, the latter apt to be mixed with Jan Jansson. In style, many of the Blaeu maps show a more open design, with restrained Roman lettering which appears severe by contrast with earlier forms. Decorative heights were, however, reached with some plates, and the figures, Plate 160A, are characteristic. At the present time county maps of England, Wales and Scotland from Blaeu atlases, copied it must be admitted from Speed, are to be found in the map-seller's, as well as handsome representations of a great many other parts of the known world. The work, which must be considered a summit of achievement, and in which so many of these fine maps are gathered, is something once seen not easily forgotten – the *Atlas Major* or *Geographia Blaviana* of 1660. The imposing folio size, the lustrous vellum-gilt binding (also part of the Blaeu business) and its extent, in as many as twelve volumes, constitute a monument far outside the reach of the ordinary collector, who can, however, possess individual maps from it in contemporary colouring, heightened with gold and on paper which it is an inspiration to handle. In England RICHARD BLOME (d. 1705) made county maps for his own *Britannia* of 1673 and his *Cosmography* 1693, as well as *Speed's Maps Epitomised* in a small size, 1685. Here again we have honest period decoration but somewhat rough workmanship. JOHN OGILBY (1600–76) conducted the first systematic survey of our roads and published *Britannia . . . Description of the Principal Roads Thereof* . . . in 1675, a work both ingenious and practical. The chosen highway, drawn as on a long scroll or strip which appears to be folded down across the page, leads the traveller from left to right, from bottom to top, up hill and down dale through hamlets and towns, past houses and halls. The nature of the country is shown by clusters or strings of hills, and such terms as 'arable' and 'pasture'; inns are well noted and the mileages from the starting-point, with intermediate furlongs, are all set down. Its folio size, which makes plates from it such admirable decorative features today, was unhandy for travellers and later versions of the road atlas took on a smaller form. Ogilby's activities were by no means confined to the *Britannia*; he published handsome folio accounts of *Africa* (1670), *America* (1671) and *Asia* (1673), which all contain maps and views of a most decorative nature.

The Netherlands with its great output of maps catered by translation for the other nations of Europe, the same maps serving England, Spain, France, Italy and Germany with appropriate texts. The famous Dutch makers, already mentioned, were followed by successors to both their fame and their business – the DE WIT'S, the VISSCHER'S, the DANCKERTS'S, SCHENK, the MORTIER'S, ALLARD, whose maps are rich in style and full of detail.

The eighteenth century, at the beginning of which great use was still being made of the older authorities, saw throughout its course a series of important discoveries which enlarged the face of the globe; great advances in surveying practice and withal a rather bewildering process of amalgamation and succession on the part of the publishers and map-makers themselves.

France under Louis XIV had as Geographer Royal NICOLAS SANSON (1600–67), who with his sons, grandsons and successors, represents a major source of French cartography from the appearance of his first atlas in 1654, until about 1780. A. H. JAILLOT (1632–1712), Sanson's successor, and P. DU VAL, his son-in-law, are other names to be noted. French maps, like so many other aspects of French art, display a beauty and elegance in all their characteristics. Many are large, but with fine lettering and unobtrusive though fitting decoration. Lovers of French furniture and pictures will recognize many of the traits which please them in maps from the DE LISLE'S, the DE VAUGONDY'S, J. N. BELLIN (d. 1772) and J. B. D'ANVILLE (d. 1782).

As in the Netherlands and France, so in England important businesses were quickly taken up on the death of the principal by enterprising rivals and relatives. Reference to the standard works will give the collector the sequence and help him to identify and date his maps. Foreign talent was still much in evidence in this country; HERMAN MOLL (d. 1732), an *émigré* from Holland, published several collections, e.g. *New and Complete Atlas* (1719), from which individual plates are quite common. From highly decorative in the style of the time, they range to a type which almost dispenses with ornament in favour of maximum topographical information. A breath of the map-selling world of the day is given in this extract: 'Since the beginning of this New Set of Maps, now compleatly finished, several ignorant Pretenders have started up, and with great Shew and Noise frequently advertised their trifling performances, calling them Cheap, Curious, Useful and Correct; As to the first Epithet, they are really Dear at any price; in the second place, every Body may see they are Wild, Confused and Poorly Engraved; as for their Usefulness they tend only to lead

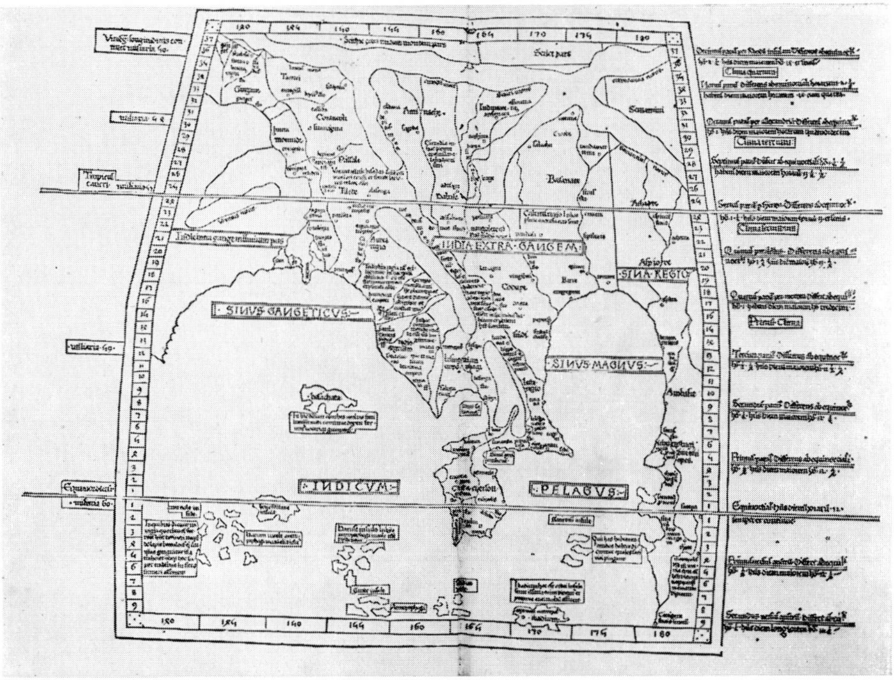

(A) India and beyond. Ptolemy, 1482. Uncoloured woodcut, about 15 × 15 in.

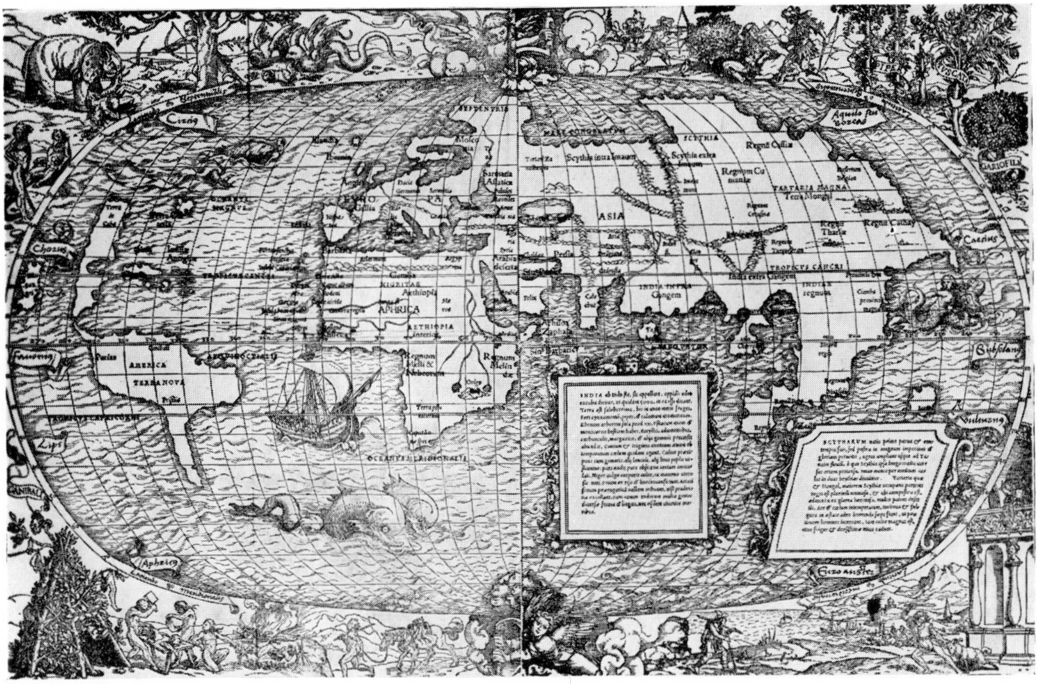

(B) The World. *Typus Cosmographicus Universalis*, Basle, 1555. Woodcut in two sheets 14 × 21 in. from Grynaeus: *Novus Orbis regionum ac insularum.*

PLATE 157

Plates 157–164 are reproduced by courtesy of the Trustees of the National Maritime Museum, Greenwich.

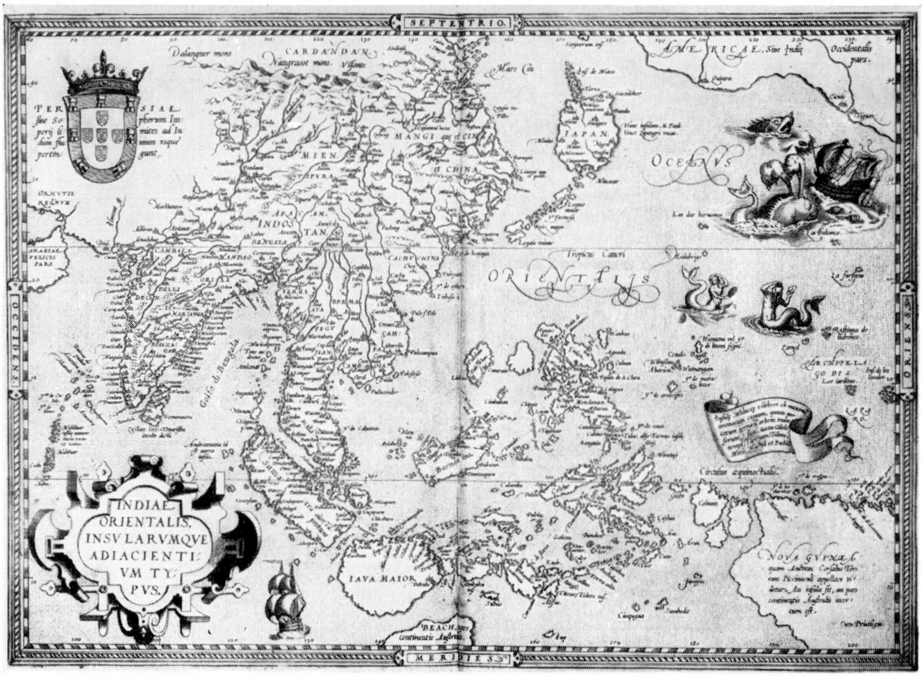

(A) The East Indies. Ortelius, 1570. Uncoloured engraving, 14 × 17½ in.

(B) Durham. From Saxton's atlas, engraved by A. Ryther, 1576. Coloured, 15 × 19¼ in.

(A) Virginia. H. Hondius, 1636. Uncoloured engraving, 15 × 19 in.

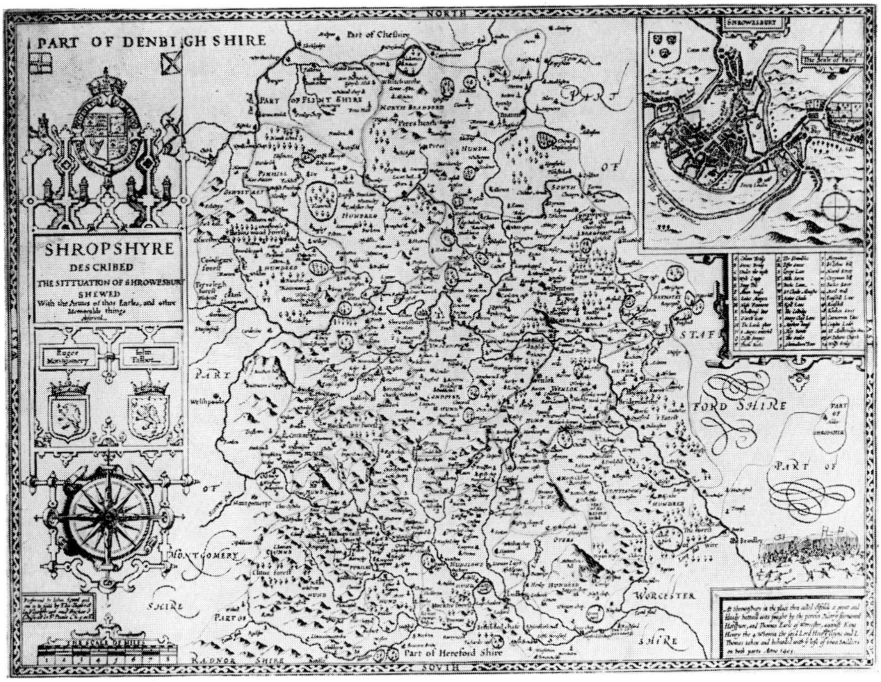

(B) Shropshire. J. Speed. Uncoloured engraving, $15\frac{1}{2}$ × 20 in. A late edition with the imprint of Bassett & Chiswell, 1676.

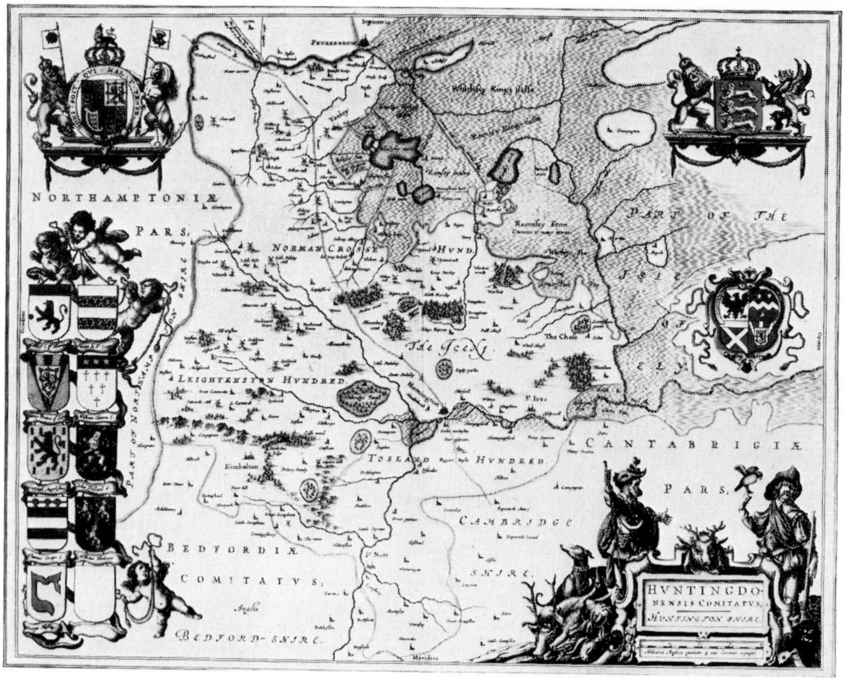

(A) Huntingdonshire. W. J. Blaeu, 1645. Coloured engraving, $15\frac{1}{2} \times 19\frac{1}{2}$ in.

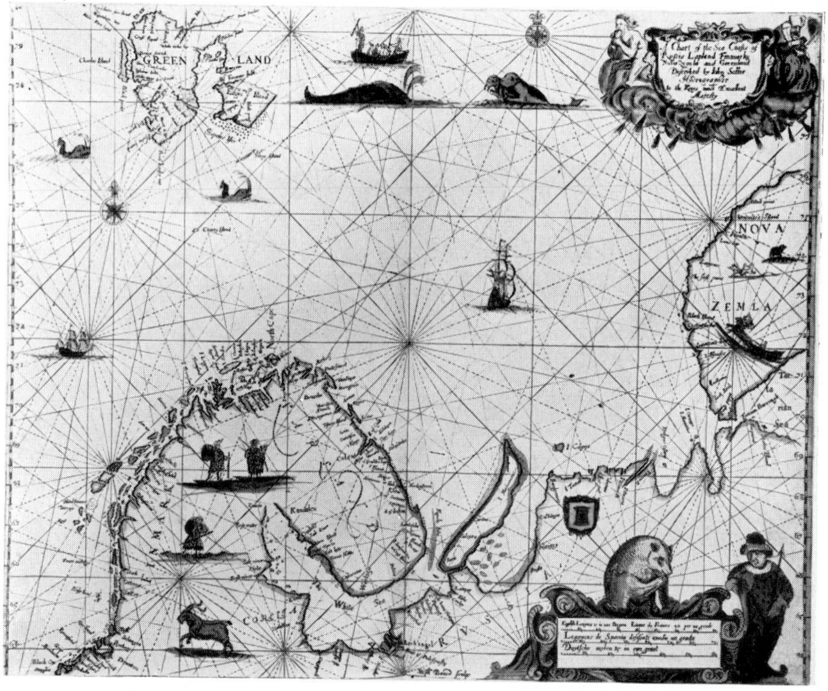

(B) Russia and Finland. Chart, J. Seller, *c.* 1675. Coloured engraving, $17\frac{1}{4} \times 21\frac{1}{2}$ in.

(A) The River Dvina. Detail (Title) J. van Keulen, 1683. Coloured engraving.

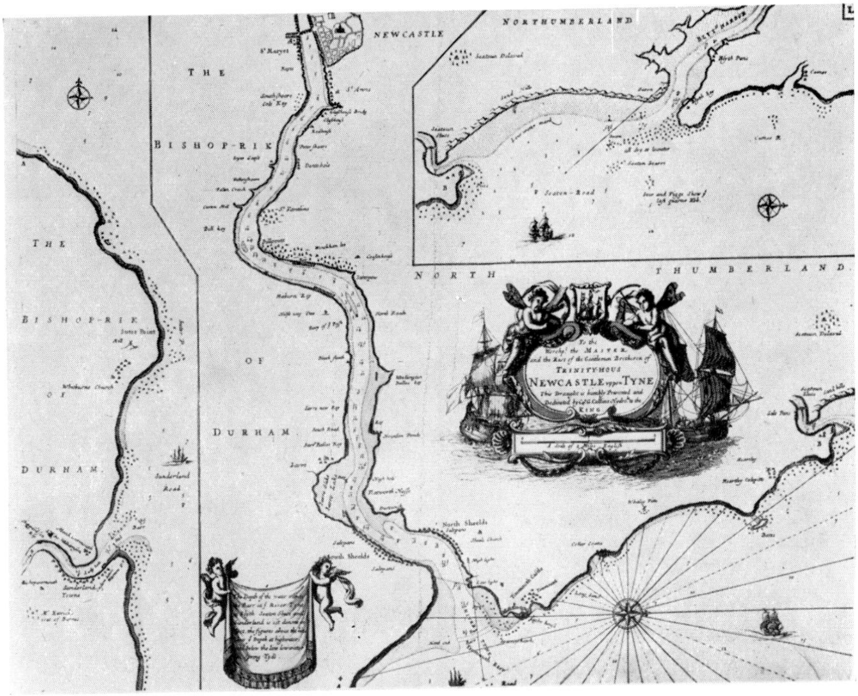

(B) The River Tyne (part). Chart, 1693. Greenvile Collins. Uncoloured engraving.

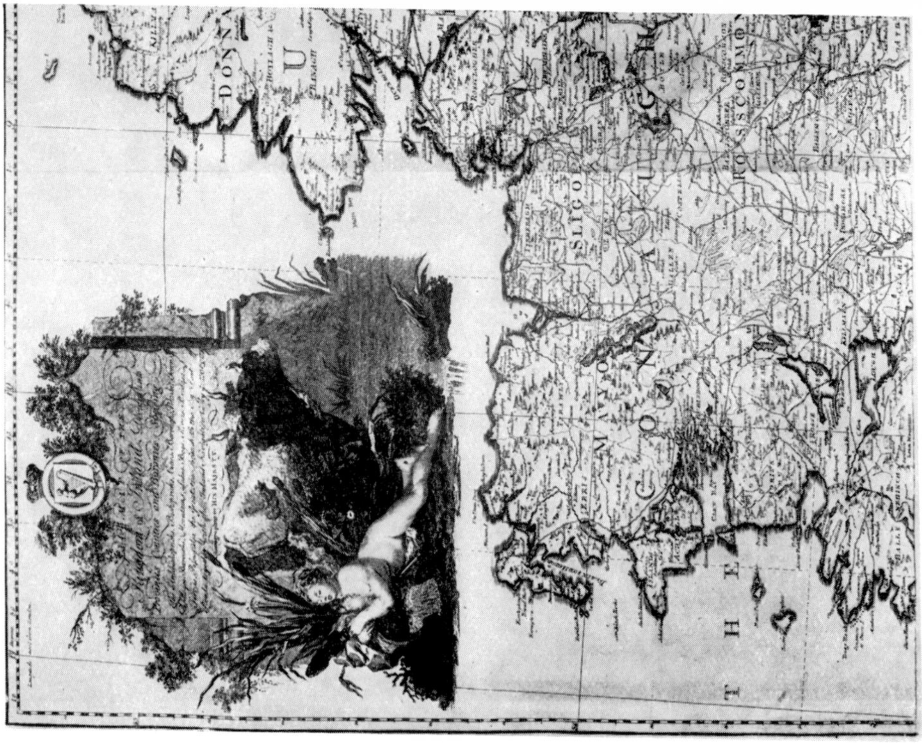

(B) Ireland (part). J. Rocque, 1773. Uncoloured engraving.

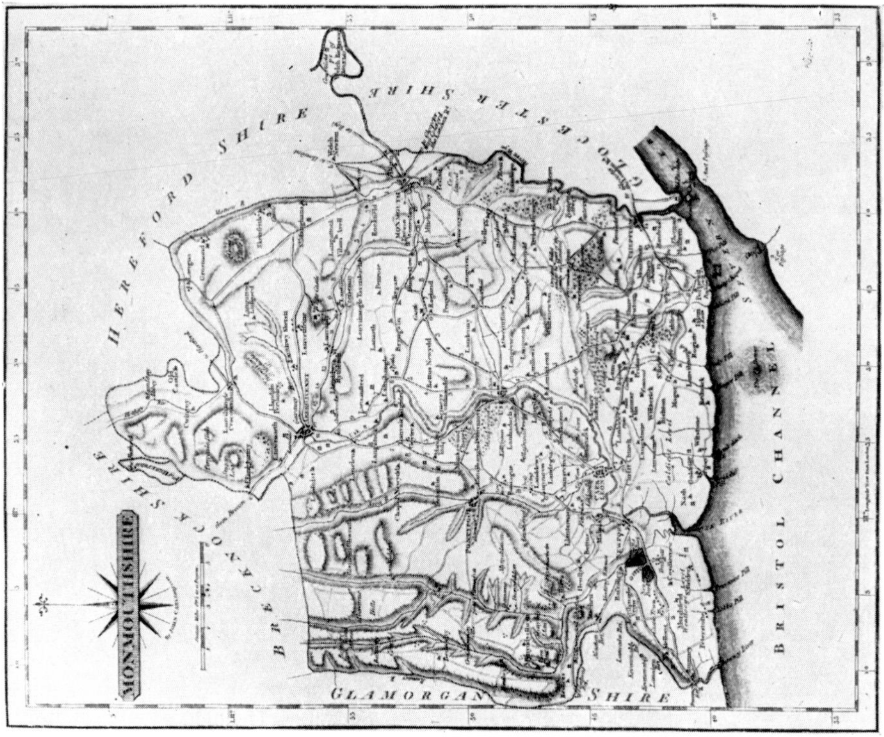

(A) Monmouthshire. J. Cary, 1787. Uncoloured engraving, $10\frac{1}{4} \times 8\frac{1}{4}$ in.

(A) Scotland, James Wyld, 1836, tinted engraving. Wyld was successor to Faden who had succeeded Jefferys.

(B) Plate from Doppelmayr's *Atlas Coelestis*, 1742. Tinted engraving. Note representations of famous observatories; Greenwich, top left.

(A) Terrestrial Globes.

Left to right: (*a*) French by Abbé Nollet, 1728, 11 in. diameter. On painted and lacquered pedestal.
(*b*) French, Lapie-Langlois, 1815, 9 in. diameter. Supported in stand resting on black and gold caryatides. A compass is inset at centre of base, which has brass paw feet.
(*c*) English, by Malby, 1845, 12 in.
(*d*) German, by Klinger, 1792, 12 in.
(*e*) English, by N. Hill, *c.* 1750, 5 in. The hour-circle is seen fitted in this example.
(*f*) English, one of a pair, by Newton, 1836, 18 in. Compass beneath.

(B) Celestial Globe, G. Mercator, 1551. Diameter about 16½ in.

People into Errors and Dangers; lastly they are so far from being Correct that the Fundamental or Projection of their Principal Maps is Notoriously False' (from Herman Moll's advertisement, *c.* 1717). Moll's titles give a composite arrangement of architecture, figures, animals and floral settings, with frequent inset views and, for example in a map of England, an edging of complicated tables of distances from London, market-days, map references and 'eastings and westings' from the capital. His lettering is clear and frequently the only colour introduced is a tinted outline.

JOHN ROCQUE, a Frenchman (d. 1762) (Plate 162B), has amongst others to his credit a large-scale map of London in two dozen sheets, an extensive and splendid work, and particularly when seen in original colour a feast of intimate detail.

EDWARD WELLS's *New Sett of Maps of Ancient and Present Geography*, about 1700, carries on nearly every plate a dedication to the short-lived son of Queen Anne, William Duke of Gloucester. The maps, although not in the highest class of workmanship, are good decoration.

JOHN SENEX, F.R.S. (d. 1740), produced such works as the *New General Atlas of the World*, 1721, which has some pleasant scenic cartouches. He also printed and engraved a new edition of Ogilby's road maps, which was still being issued as late as 1775. His work is like Moll's, but with generally less elaboration.

THOMAS KITCHIN (d. 1784) was very active, and with EMANUEL BOWEN (d. 1767) likewise highly productive, they printed, for example, the *Large English Atlas* in 1755. Maps from this are handsome pieces of engraving with much light rococo ornament. Bowen also illustrated his own *Complete System of Geography*, 1744, and with J. OWEN brought out a smaller version of Ogilby called *Britannia Depicta or Ogilby Improv'd*, 1720, and subsequent editions for the next forty years.

Another notable figure was the prolific JOHN CARY (d. 1835), whose imprint will also be found on road maps, and who published a *New and Correct English Atlas* (1787) (Plate 162A) (still being issued in the 1830s), containing pleasant county maps without the large decoration of previous periods. Maps from it are generally cheap.

THOMAS JEFFERYS, Geographer to the King (d. 1771), collaborated with Kitchin in a *Small English Atlas* (1749), and also compiled a finely engraved *American Atlas*, which was not, however, published until 1776.

WILLIAM FADEN (d. 1836) succeeded Jefferys and continued to make the American continent the subject for his maps. *North American Atlas* (1777) and other collections contained views, plans and maps from original surveys, which are of great interest today.

A large output from the ARROWSMITH's (father and son), Aaron and John, bridges the late eighteenth and early nineteenth centuries. With BRYANT, GREENWOOD, PIGOT and lastly MOULE, we find ourselves entering the Victorian era, with different standards and different processes. Moule's county maps, 1836, from his *English Counties Delineated*, are still decorative with vignettes and ornamental titles, but have the somewhat studied elegance of the time.

The celestial or star map, often included in general atlases, can be a thing of great beauty; the imagery of the constellations, always a little baffling, was sometimes brought to a high degree of complexity. There were a number of star atlases of note, and the seventeenth century alone saw such as BAYER (1603), SCHILLER (1627), CELLARIUS (1660), HEVELIUS (1690); also CORONELLI and the Englishman SELLER, whose *Atlas Coelestis* is another of his 'pocket-size' publications.

In later times there were, FLAMSTEED, the first Astronomer Royal, with his *Atlas Coelestis* (1729); J. G. DOPPELMAYR (1742) (Plate 163B), etc. The stars were not always marshalled into the familiar shapes of deities and objects, schemes of Biblical figures and of heraldic arrangements being also proposed. Examples of coloured star maps can be striking, while the decorative possibilities of large photo-copies of uncoloured examples are considerable.

CHARTS

The subject of maritime maps or charts is something of a speciality, although the essential differences are easily discernible. The oceans of the world on early maps received a treatment designed to fill up a blank space, but for the seamen whose path lay across these spaces there were dangers far more real than sea monsters, and lines which had a use quite different from the 'Moire' pattern of pure decoration. Manuscript charts, Portolani, examples of which from the early fourteenth century have survived, are of course great treasures. Written on vellum, finely coloured and gilded, they are essentially a mariner's aid, although a great many of the examples now known must have been the object of some special presentation. The Portuguese, Catalans and Italians had traditions in the production of such charts, and their form seems to have been either mounted on hinged boards or in the form of a roll, or again with several charts bound as a book. Their arrangement of a formalized coastline with name of the coastal towns and seaports, the provision of elaborate compass and wind roses with lines radiating into a complicated network, were also features of later printed charts based on such rudimentary knowledge. Their production continued into the seventeenth century, and English makers are known. The Dutch, our maritime rivals in the later sixteenth and seventeenth centuries, were among the first to print charts, and these, although showing much of the decorative engraving we have noticed on their maps, also contained serious details necessary to mariners. The name of LUCAS WAGHENAER has a double significance, as the author of the *Spieghel der Zeevaerdt* (1584–5), and its Latin version *Speculum Nauticum* (charts engraved by J. VAN DOETECUM), and because the English corrupted his name into 'Waggoner' and used it to describe a book of charts and sailing directions. In 1588, the memorable year of the Spanish Armada, this work was translated by SIR ANTHONY ASHLEY, and the charts were re-engraved by Flemish craftsmen and the Englishman Augustine Ryther, appearing as the *Mariners' Mirror*. The features of charts from this, the first printed marine atlas in England, are the soundings, banks and shoals, the little anchor symbols denoting good ground for anchoring and the 'Views' or outlines of the coastline with its landmarks as seen from the sea. W. J. BLAEU was also noted for his charts and, like his land atlases, his sea books were sent into other countries, with translations of the text, e.g. the English *Light of Navigation* (1612).

This idea of the guiding light at sea was an obvious and universal favourite, and was perpetuated in such collections as the *Sea Beacon*, and *Fiery Column*, *Lighting Colum*, *Lightning Columne*, *Flambeau de la Mer*, etc. So, too, the conception of a revealing looking-glass in the *Sea Mirror*, *Mariners' Mirror* and the various *Spieghels*.

The DONCKER, GOOS and VAN KEULEN families, flourishing from the latter half of the seventeenth century, published large numbers of charts which are still to be found in plain and coloured states. Their aspect naturally differs from land maps in that large areas are water and show only the compass roses and lines with the occasional ship. Their titles, however, are often fully as ornamental, and those of Van Keulen in particular contain some of the most beautiful groups of figures and beasts of the period (Plate 161A). As decoration, these charts have their own personal appeal, and in the picture they give of foreign parts (and they include the coasts of all the known world) there is a little of fancy, much truth and some splendid 'atmosphere'. The Englishman SIR ROBERT DUDLEY lived and worked in Florence. He had been on ocean voyages and published, in Italian with the aid of an Italian engraver, a spectacular book of sea charts called *Dell' Arcano del Mare*, the 'Secret of the Sea' (1646 and 1661). Still reminiscent of the Portolans, these charts are, however, made on Mercator's projection, and are decorated with flourished lettering of notable ornateness. The atlas in its entirety is another treasure, but single charts are still sometimes to be had. The business of JOHN SELLER (d. about 1700) and his associates and successors, like JOHN THORNTON and RICHARD MOUNT, provided the majority of the charts published in Restoration England.

Samuel Pepys had it that Seller imported Dutch copper plates, which had already seen service with Danckerts, Visscher and others, and although it is unwise to generalize, the workmanship of his own maps and charts may be said to be somewhat crude (Plate 160B). His project entitled the *English Pilot* (1670), included charts and sailing directions for the 'Southern Navigation' (England to the coast of Africa), 'Northern Navigation' (Northern England and Northern Europe), as well as the Mediterranean, Orient and the Americas. These charts have each their titles, their dedications and other embellishments, but even when coloured can hardly compete with Dutch works of a similar sort. Seller's business was not confined to charts and instruments, for he produced county maps and star maps and some charming little epitomes like his *Atlas Minimus* (1679).

CAPTAIN GREENVILE COLLINS began, by command of Charles II, a survey of the coasts of the realm in 1681, and the result, published by Mount in 1693 under the title *Great Britain's Coasting Pilot*, was a well-engraved series of charts with true mariners' marks and bearings (Plate 161B). They are all furnished with appropriate dedications in the title; for example that of Harwich, to Samuel Pepys, Esq., Member of Parliament for that place, humbly dedicated and presented by the 'Hydrographer to the King'. The *English Pilot* in the hands of the MOUNT and PAGE families and their successors, who can be traced to a printing house that still flourishes, continued in its familiar form with additions and corrections even into the nineteenth century. For a long time, however, it had been far surpassed by other works, handsomely engraved in a business-like style, suitable for carrying the proud trading ships of the Honourable East India Company to their varied destinations in the Orient. These charts were kept up to date by reports from the ships themselves, and the Hon. Company had its own hydrographer and map-sellers. SAYER and BENNETT, DUNN, HERBERT, HEATHER, LAURIE and WHITTLE, these names appear on such works as the *Oriental Navigator*, *New Directory for the East Indies* and *Complete East India Pilot*. Charts from these atlases are mostly large, severe and purely practical, and would not ordinarily be found in colours. The fineness of their engraving is, however, noteworthy. The route to the West Indies is likewise covered by Sayer and Bennett, SPEER, T. JEFFERYS and the famous *Atlantic Neptune* of J. W. DES BARRES (1777). These, too, are very much the navigational tool, decoration being subordinated to the essentials of hydrography; the *Atlantic Neptune*, a highly scientific work produced under Admiralty patronage, contains charts and lovely views of great antiquarian interest for Americans.

Among curiosities, maps printed on silk are worth a word. Examples exist of a map of England and Wales in four parts, by Philip Lea, printed from copper plates on both sides of a white silk ribbon some 6 inches in width. This, with all the decorative features of an ordinary map, including roads and a table of counties with map references, is about 40 inches long and travelled (for this must have been its function) in a turned ivory cylinder which unscrews in the middle. A later version of a similar sort is Bowles's *Pocket Plan of the Cities of London and Westminster* (1777); this was also printed on silk and tinted. It bears a resemblance to the modern decorated silk 'squares', and had of course a very practical use.

The geographical game, in various forms, was quite a favourite educational toy in the later eighteenth and nineteenth centuries, although the pack of geographical playing-cards dates back to the end of the sixteenth.

The inflatable paper globe often had an understandably short life, but examples are sometimes met with. A German version by Cella (Munich, 1831), with its detail boldly engraved on crisp, tinted paper, measures nearly five feet in length when folded flat. 'Pocket sets' of cardboard and paper terrestrial and celestial collapsible globes, with a planetarium, are another interesting educational curiosity.

GLOBES

The suggestion that the world was in fact round was expressed in world models at an early date, and Columbus has to share the fateful year of 1492 with Martin Behaim, who made at that time a famous globe. This still exists, a venerable monument of geography, and since then most of the great figures in map-making have also produced world maps 'in the round'.

Globes 'fit to adorn the Libraries of the curious' are still thought of as desirable decoration, although the day has gone when 'The necessity of the Knowledge of the Use of the Globes for easy conception and due understanding of . . . Geography, Astronomy . . . Navigation, Chronology and other liberal sciences is known to everyone, and is the first consideration among those Qualities requisite for forming the Scholar and Gentleman' (BENJAMIN MARTIN in *Description and Use of Both the Globes*, about 1758).

Terrestrial globes paired with their celestial counterparts, if really old, are today museum pieces: fragile, worn and glass-encased. The later globe, say from the mid-eighteenth century onwards, comes rather near the category of antique furniture, and is sought almost as much for period furnishing as for its geographical significance. Mercator, Hondius, Blaeu, Jansson and Coronelli all constructed remarkable globes, and there were other specialists, like MATTHEUS GREUTER (d. 1638). In England EMERY MOLYNEUX completed a pair in 1592, and some of the better-known later makers are JOSEPH MOXON, F.R.S. (d. 1703), PHIL. LEA (d. 1700), R. MORDEN (d. 1703), E. and also R. CUSHEE (*c.* 1730–40), JOHN SENEX, F.R.S. (d. 1740), N. HILL (*c.* 1750), J. FERGUSSON (d. 1776), GEORGE ADAMS (Snr. and Junr.) and also DUDLEY ADAMS (*c.* 1750–1810). The CARY family, Johns, Georges and William, from 1791 to *c.* 1850, were one of the chief globe-makers, as indeed they were map-makers. Also prominent were the firms of NEWTON and STANFORD.

The parts of the globe in its entirety are first the *Sphere*, constructed in a number of different ways, perhaps turned wood, or lath and plaster, or some metal like copper or brass. The *Meridian* is a flat graduated hoop of metal or wood which encircles the orb, and into which the poles of the axis are set, permitting rotation. This meridian, borne on a short column or similar support beneath, can itself be turned to raise or depress the poles. Around the upper end of the axis is frequently found a metal *Hour Circle* graduated, with a pointer or *Index*. The framework of the stand carries on its upper surface, surrounding the globe, the *Horizon*, on which is presented a perpetual calendar, with day of the month, the sun's place in the zodiac, the points of the compass, fixed feasts and winds. A mariner's compass was often introduced on the stand. The surface details were printed on paper, which, divided into *gores* or shaped sections, was pasted down on to the orb; the horizon was also usually printed. While a pillared stand with the globe set into the encircling horizon was the chief method of presentation, the 'sickle' shaped support consisting of a brass half-circle mounted on a turned column and base, was later common, especially for small globes. The half-circle or semi-meridian, is sometimes graduated, or there could be an independent flat brass half-hoop so marked and hinged at the poles. The style of the stand varied with furniture fashions; the turned pillar supports of Plate 164B contrast with the fluted legs or the caryatides seen in Plate 164A. The use of varnish to protect the globe is often the cause of a darkening and crackling which obscure the detail. Cleaning, or advice on cleaning, is the work of an expert, and the opinion of a museum or of one of the firms still making globes should be sought.

Another instrument which is sometimes found, and is decorative besides being of considerable interest, is the *Armillary Sphere*, looking like a skeleton globe, but which is actually a construction of rings showing the paths of the heavenly bodies.

In about 1700 Philip Lea was advertising a pair of 26-inch globes for £20. Martin's *Description and Use of the Globes* (1758) also contains an interesting advertisement of his wares. He was selling the famous Senex globes, made with 'exquisite skill, taste and elegance', and a pair of 28-inch globes in mahogany frames, with carved work and silvered meridians, cost £35. Others could be had in 17-inch, 12-inch, 9-inch and 3-inch sizes, the last being in a case, on the inside of which was shown the celestial part (price 10*s*.). In 1792 J. Cary advertised 21-inch globes in 'Pillar and Claw Mahogany Frames, with Mariner's Compass' at thirteen guineas the pair.

BOOKS FOR FURTHER READING

The bibliography of maps and map-makers is extensive, but for the new collector perhaps the kindest advice is that he should equip himself with such a work as:

SKELTON, R. A.: *Decorative Printed Maps of the 15th–18th Centuries* (Staples Press, 1952) or TOOLEY, R. V.: *Maps and Map Makers*, second edition (Batsford, 1952).

Both contain bibliographies of the utmost value, and both are sumptuously illustrated, including colour plates. Their references for casual inquirer and serious collector alike are ample, and so much admirable guidance is contained in them that they might almost come before actual specimens of maps.

Also LYNAM, E.: *British Maps and Mapmakers* (Collins, 1947), and the same author's *The Mapmaker's Art* (Essays) (Batchworth Press, 1953), together with CRONE, G. R.: *Maps and Their Makers* (Hutchinson, 1953), are useful and interesting reading.

CHUBB, T.: *The Printed Maps in the Atlases of Great Britain*... 1579–1870 (London, 1927) is a great reference book, and BROWN, B. J. W.: *Astronomical Atlases, Maps and Charts* (London, 1932), will also be of use.

STEVENSON, E. L.: *Terrestrial and Celestial Globes*, published in America in 1921, is a standard work, but there is nothing comprehensive yet in print.

There is a valuable small publication issued by the Library Association, Number 13 in their series of pamphlets:

LEE, R. J.: *English County Maps, the Identification, Cataloguing and Physical Care of a Collection*, 1953.

Some county authorities have compiled handbooks on local maps; these with other specialized regional studies are detailed in Tooley.

A most scholarly international annual on cartography is *Imago Mundi*, published in Holland, to which the collector of wide interests might subscribe.

FIRE-BACKS AND DOGS

By J. K. MORRIS

UNDERSTANDABLY, the fireplace has been the focal-point of domestic life down the ages. In cave and castle, from primitive man to Dandy, the Englishman, no less than the inhabitant of any other land, has regarded his hearth as the centre round which much of his comfort and much of his happiness revolved. It is no wonder that time and ingenuity have been spent in devising economical methods of using the available fuel and in evolving the most suitable tools with which it might be handled.

The equipment of the old English fireside may be divided conveniently into two sections: articles used in the living-room and those for use in the kitchen. In the mansions and houses of the well-to-do these were quite apart, but among the poorer people there was no distinction. In many cases, especially in country districts where it is not uncommon to find it still in daily use, the one room – kitchen-cum-living-room – served a dual purpose; the one simple 'down hearth' providing the only heating, both for warming the room and for cooking the food of those occupying the cottage.

In the buildings of the Middle Ages the source of heat was to be found in the centre of the room, large or small, and the smoke rose to find its way through louvres or holes in the roof, or through the small unglazed windows. By the advent of the thirteenth century the fireplace was usually placed to one side, and a flue incorporated in the wall.

As Continental sophistication spread to England and the houses of the great and wealthy began to vie with each other for splendour, the fireplace became no less a subject for decoration than the rest of the contents of a room. Silver, bronze and polished steel played their part in the embellishment of grate and fire-irons, and by the end of the seventeenth century the fireplace and its accessories were as much subject to changes of fashion as everything else.

The cottage fireplace or 'down hearth' was a cavity some 6 feet in width, as much in depth and rather more in height. The floor of it was raised a little above the level of the floor of the room, and the hearth, lintel or mantel and the side-posts were usually of stone obtained in the locality. Most of the few luxuries of the cottager's life were obtained from the fire, which was kept burning continuously, night and day and year in and year out.

In contrast to those used in drawing-room and parlour, the various implements for tending the cottage fire remained unchanged and simple; they had developed slowly during the centuries and once proved they stayed unaltered. Of purely functional character they bore usually little in the way of ornamentation, although in rare examples the individual smith has imprinted his personality by some personal touch. Unlike the modish accessories in use elsewhere, the equipment of the cottage hearth remained in use until completely worn out and useless, however long that might take, and it was not likely to be discarded because it had become unfashionable.

Coal, referred to as 'Sea Coal' from the routes by which it reached the consumer, did not come into use very much until the second half of the sixteenth century, and not at all widely until a hundred years later. It was burned principally in the towns and the great houses; the price being too high for the cottagers, who obtained their wood, furze or peat mostly free of cost. The introduction of coal saw also that of the grate in which to burn it, and at the same time a change was made in the design of fire-irons. The fire-fork was replaced by the poker, the shovel was added to their number, and the first sound of the long-lasting outcry against smoke in cities was heard.

Almost every article used by the fireside enjoys more than one name. Every region of England in each succeeding century seems to have had a particular word with which to describe each accessory, and few writers can agree on any single definition. An implement may differ only minutely in appearance from one made in another locality, but it will be found that it bears a very different name. In the Glossary which follows all the variants brought to notice are recorded, but it cannot be decided which is the more correct of the numerous alternatives.

GLOSSARY

Andiron (Fire-dog, Brand-iron): a pair of andirons standing in the open fireplace was the general practice while wood was the staple fuel for heating the home. The irons varied in elaboration according to the wealth of their owner, but each consisted essentially of an upright terminating in two feet, with a horizontal bar projecting behind and bent downwards to form a third foot. The decoration was confined to the upright member, and the logs were burned while resting on the horizontal part, known as the 'billet bar'. In all cases the latter was of iron, but the ornamental portion was of iron, brass, bronze or silver. Exceptional examples, dating from the seventeenth century, are of metal inset with coloured enamel; silver examples may be seen at Ham House, Knole, Hatfield House and in other mansions of importance; at Windsor Castle, Hampton Court and Knole are pairs of silver gilt.

While the fireplace remained in the centre of the hall of the house, the andirons were strictly utilitarian and usually undecorated. The common form was double-ended, with the billet bars connected by a further bar (Plate 165A). With the removal of the source of heating to the side of the room and the subsequent decoration of this feature, andirons also began to receive attention. The earliest ones were of wrought-iron, and these were followed early in the sixteenth century by examples cast with raised designs of running scrollwork, crests and coats-of-arms. Later in the century were made tall andirons, some standing over 4 feet in height, but many of the more artistic examples were imported from Italy and elsewhere. With the introduction of coal for household use and the adoption of the grate, andirons became superfluous; in some instances they acted as supporters for the early grates, but it was not long before the latter were made with their own feet. Andirons were made in an atrophied form late in the eighteenth century and in Victorian times, and served as fire-iron rests.

Bellows: contrivances for making a draught artificially, dating from very early times. Mention is made of bellows in wills from 1500 onwards, but as they suffered hard usage, survivors are seldom earlier than the seventeenth century; and any of that date are a great rarity. They received their due share of attention and were decorated in many styles. Carved and inlaid wood, wood overlaid with leather or silver, and even finely stitched needlework were used to ornament them. Lacquered examples were made in the first quarter of the eighteenth century. Apart from the small hand-bellows, which were often decorative rather than useful, more business-like machines were made; doubtless for the use of those servants on whom the warmth of the house depended. These standing-bellows were in heavy wooden frames, and rested on the ground firmly, to be worked by means of a lever. Another type, lighter in weight, was operated by turning a wheel which was linked to the mechanism by a cord. This last type dates from the early nineteenth century.

The construction of the bellows has not changed in the course of the centuries. It comprises two shaped boards with a spring to keep them apart, held together by a loose leather hinge. One of the boards is pierced in the centre and fitted with a flap of leather on the inside, which acts as a valve, letting air enter but not allowing it to escape except by way of the nozzle.

(A) Central Hearth with double-ended Andirons.
Penshurst Place, Kent.

(B) Fire-back of floral design, Cobirons and Basket-grate. *Penshurst Place, Kent.*

(C) Fire-back with mythological scene, and Basket-grate supported by cast-iron Andirons. *Sutton Place, Guildford.*

(D) Cast-iron Fire-back and Andirons; the former dated 1706.

PLATE 165

(A) Fire-back with the Royal arms of James I and dated 1604.

(B) Cast-iron Fire-back composed of movable ornaments, Sussex, seventeenth century. *Victoria & Albert Museum.*

(C) Dutch cast-iron Fire-back, inscribed 'Hollandia' and dated 1644.

(D) Cast-iron Fire-back moulded with a group representing 'Charity'. Probably Dutch, early eighteenth century.

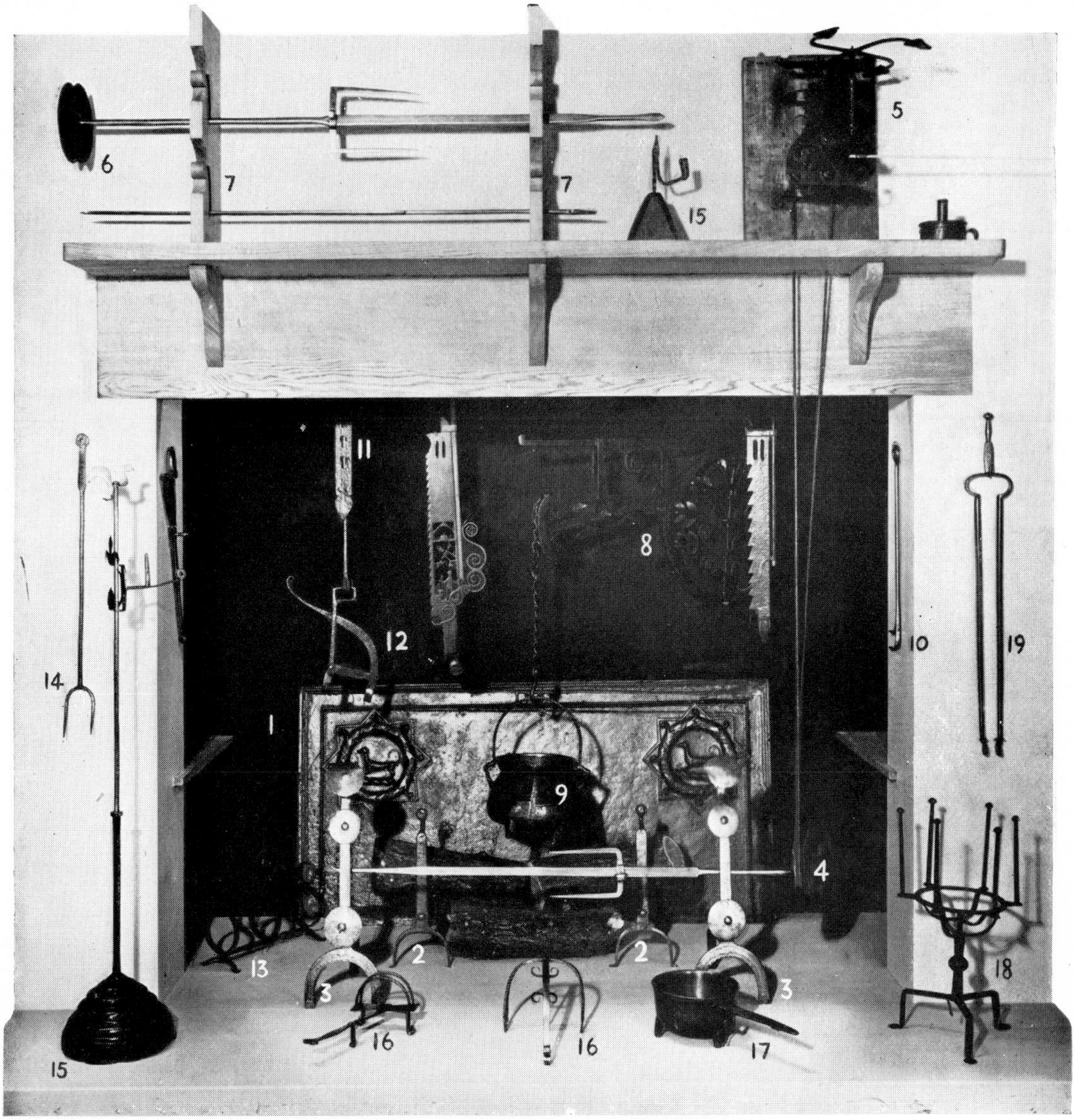

A 'Down-Hearth' and its equipment. *Victoria & Albert Museum.*

(1) Fire-back dated 1584; (2) Pair of Andirons; (3) Pair of Cobirons; (4) Spit; (5) Spit-jack; (6) Spare Spits; (7) Spit-rack; (8) Chimney-crane; (9) Cast-bronze Cauldron; (10) Hook for moving Chimney-crane when hot; (11) Pot-hooks; (12) Kettle-tilter; (13) Pipe-kiln; (14) Meat Fork; (15) Rush-light Holders; (16) Toasters; (17) Skillet; (18) Plate-warmer; (19) Hearth Tongs.

The Fireplace in the kitchen of the Royal Pavilion, Brighton.

PLATE 168

To face page 241

Blowing-tube: forerunner of, and contemporary with, the bellows was a long metal tube widening from a mouthpiece and

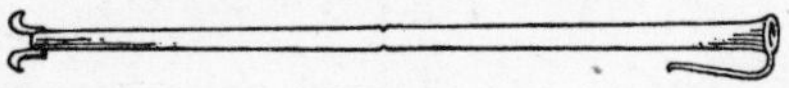

FIG. 1

with a short projection at the base to raise it from the ground. The tube was placed where the draught was needed, and the user simply blew down the mouthpiece.

Brander: a pierced metal plate, with a half-hoop handle by which it was suspended

FIG. 2

from a pot-hook. It was used principally in Scotland for the making of brander bannocks – oatmeal cakes.

Brazier: in place of, and in addition to, a fireplace, heating was sometimes provided by a portable iron brazier which burned coke. At a later date the fuel was charcoal. A brazier was at Trinity College, Cambridge, in 1866, and had been in use there 'for upwards of 160 years'.

Carron: the Carron Ironworks, Falkirk, Scotland, opened in 1759 and was responsible for the making of much fireside equipment. Small andirons (or rests for fire-irons), of early nineteenth-century pattern are found with the name of the firm cast on the fronts. Many of these have been re-cast from the original moulds, in the present century, but it is stated that in these instances the name 'Carron' appears at the back of each piece.

Cat: *see* Plate-warmer.

Cauldron (Kettle): one of the oldest of all cooking utensils and recorded from the earliest times. They were first made of sheets of bronze, hammered to shape and riveted together; later they were of cast bronze. From the sixteenth century they were made of cast-iron, and formed an important item in the equipment of the 'down hearth'. Small-sized cauldrons were known in some regions as 'crocks'.

Chimney-crane: known in Scotland as a 'Swey', this was a bracket of wrought-iron from which a cauldron or tea-kettle was suspended. Cranes were of many types; large and small, simple and complicated. In the case of the latter the pot could be raised or lowered and swung to any position over the fire.

Coal-containers (Coal-box, Hod, Purdonium, Scuttle): it can be well understood that owing to the hard usage they received the life of these was short. There appear to be no examples surviving from before about 1800, and most of them have been reproduced in quantity in this century.

Scuttles made of sheet copper are described as being of 'bucket' or 'helmet' shape; the latter modelled on the fifteenth-century helmet, the *salade*, inverted, and with a moulded base and swing handle.

Covered boxes of mid-nineteenth-century date were of japanned metal with gilt decoration, and the hinged lids were often fitted with a panel of shaped glass with 'back-painting' of flowers or landscapes. The handles of these boxes and their accompanying shovels were often of white china.

Cobirons: these are similar to andirons, but are usually quite plain in design and have rows of hooks on the standards on which spits could be placed. Some examples of cobirons have basket-like tops, and it has been suggested that they are 'cressets' for holding a light. Alternatively they may have been intended for containing a cup used in basting meat.

Cran: an iron trivet fitted over the fire for supporting a kettle, girdle-plate, etc.

Creepers: these, in pairs, were small irons of similar shape to andirons, between which they were placed in the hearth. Creepers were of very simple design, and they came into use when andirons grew elaborate and costly. A pamphlet of 1642, entitled *Threefold Discourse between Three Neighbours*, speaks of bishops and the lesser clergy, and compares the former to 'andirons of state, standing in a chimney but for show; but if a heavy block or red billets are brought to the fire there are poor little creepers or cobirons underneath that must bear all the weight'.

Curfew (*Couvre-feu*): to enable the fire to be kept alive during the night or when left unattended, a metal cover was placed over it. This cover, known as a 'Curfew', was roughly

FIG. 3

in the shape of a quarter-sphere and had a handle affixed to it. Old specimens are very rare, and existing ones are of brass or copper with embossed ornament.

Dangle-spit: a non-mechanical type of spit which operated in the manner implied by its name. It hung downwards, twisting one way and another on a rope as the latter wound and unwound itself, clockwise and anti-clockwise, sometimes with the aid of two weighted arms.

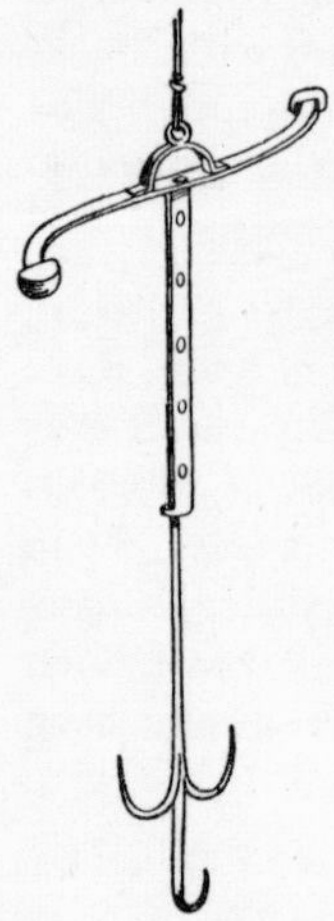

FIG. 4

Down-hearth: a slab of stone or metal raised slightly above the level of the floor of the room, forming the earliest and most simple type of fireplace. The first versions were centrally placed in a room, and smoke rose to escape through a louvre in the roof. The down-hearth built in one side of the room with a flue communicating with the outside has remained in use in cottages to this day.

Dutch-oven: an open-fronted oven, usually raised on legs, placed before the fire and used for cooking. Dutch-ovens were made of sheet-iron, brass and even of pottery.

Fire-back: this slab of cast-iron, sometimes referred to as a 'Reredos', stood at the back of the fireplace, protected the wall and reflected the heat of the burning fuel. Fire-backs were made by the simple means of pouring the molten metal on to a prepared bed of sand in which a pattern had been impressed. The patterns were carved in wood, and were either of a full-sized design or in the form of single ornaments which were composed into a whole to suit the taste of the maker or his client.

The iron fire-backs of Sussex are the best known; others were made in Yorkshire, Derbyshire and in the Forest of Dean. Many were imported from Holland late in the seventeenth century and onwards. It is often difficult to determine the origin of one from another; the fire-backs with scenes from the Bible or mythological subjects are usually said to have been of Dutch make, but these were copied in England and there is no certainty on the point. In Holland the castings were made thinner than in England, but this feature also was adopted here. The earliest English fire-backs were of a wide, low shape, but by the mid-seventeenth century tall ones, of 'Tombstone' style, were introduced.

Fire-backs are recorded which bear the coats-of-arms and initials of English sovereigns from Henry VII to James II (Plate 166A); others commemorate the defeat of the Spanish Armada (1588), Charles II and the Boscobel Oak (1651), and similar personages and events of widespread contemporary interest.

Fire-board (Fire-screen): a decorative panel used to conceal the fireplace cavity when no fire was burning. In the Victoria & Albert Museum is one of wood painted with a vase of flowers, and at Osterley is another covered with tapestry to match the hangings of the room in which it stands.

Nineteenth-century examples in the French Louis XV style were of gilt metal, chased and pierced, in the form of a fan which folded up when not in use.

Fire-fork: an instrument made of wrought-iron, some 4 feet or more in length in order that the user would be away from the heat when moving burning logs in the hearth. Usually it had two stout prongs, but some examples have a spike at one side about

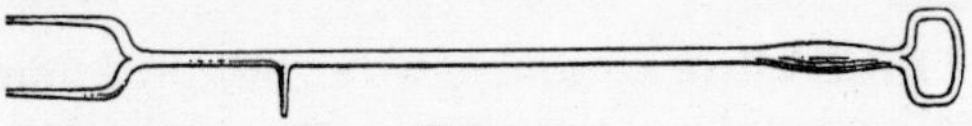

Fig. 5

three-quarters of the way down from the handle. The fire-fork was the forerunner of the poker, and it went out of general use when coal replaced wood as a fuel.

Fire-guard: metal screens to prevent damage from a fire in the fireplace to the contents of a room are seldom mentioned in eighteenth-century memoirs, nor do they seem to have endured as evidence of their one-time existence. Mrs Lybbe Powys, a much-travelled lady, noted in her diary for 23rd March 1767, while on a visit to Buckingham House (now Palace): 'It being at that time the coldest weather possible, we were amazed to find so large a house so warm, but fires, it seems, are kept the whole day, even in the closets, and to prevent accidents to furniture so costly from the neglect of the attendance, there is in every chimney a lacquered wire fireboard, the cleverest contrivance that can be imagin'd, as even the smallest spark cannot fly through them, while you have the heat, and they are really ornamental'.

Fire-irons: in the days of wood fuel these comprised tongs, brush and fire-fork. For coal, the principal addition was a shovel, and the poker was substituted for the fire-fork. The shovel was often pierced so that the coal might be sifted, and the smaller pieces chosen for starting the fire. Late in the eighteenth century the pierced designs were still current, but their retention had become no more than a decorative feature.

The implements were variously ornamented, and although the working parts were of steel or wrought-iron, this did not preclude the craftsman from making the handles of more costly metals. The sets of fire-irons enriched with silver, at Ham House, have been described and illustrated frequently since they were seen and commented upon by John Evelyn when he was there in 1678.

Steel fire-irons of eighteenth-century pattern have been much reproduced in the present century.

Footman: the name given to a four-legged trivet made to stand in front of the fire in the sitting-room or parlour. They were made of wrought-iron or brass, or partly of

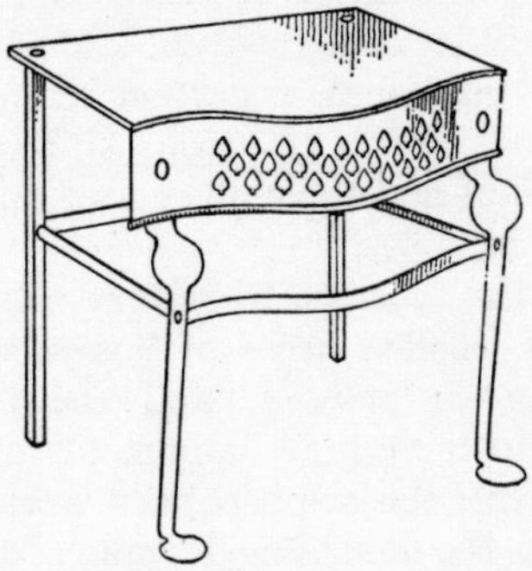

Fig. 6

each, and commonly had front legs of cabriole design. The top was often pierced with a central hole so that it could be carried. The footman dates from the second half of the eighteenth century onwards.

Girdle-plate: a flat iron sheet on which oat-cakes were baked in Scotland. They were of two types: those with a half-hoop handle which were attached to the pot-hook and the cakes cooked while suspended; and those with a small handle projecting at one end for manipulation. The latter type was placed on a cran.

Grid-iron: this was placed over the centre of the fire for cooking, and comprised a number of parallel bars on which meat, etc,

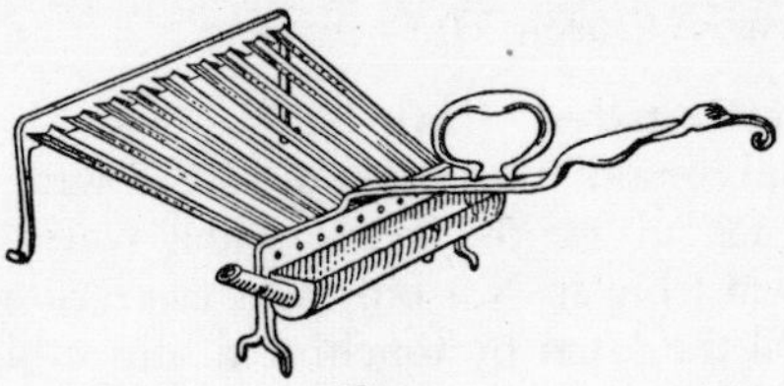

Fig. 7

rested during the process. Early grid-irons were of simple pattern and made of wrought-iron. Later ones sometimes had the bars channelled and leading to a trough at the front, which had a spout for pouring out the gravy and fat collected in it (*see* Fig. 7).

Iron and steel: the English iron industry, to which the fireside owes so much of its equipment, was centred on those places where there was assurance of ample supplies of wood – the essential fuel for melting the ore and for causing chemical changes in it. Iron is divisible into two distinct types: with little carbon content it becomes malleable and is steel or wrought-iron, and with more than the minimum of carbon remaining in its composition it is cast-iron. All three forms of the metal had their place and purpose at the fireside.

From the fourteenth century until about 1800 the wooded areas of Sussex were the seat of great activity, and the foundries established there grew famous for their products. While the ore had been worked from as early as the time of the Roman occupation, it was in the fourteenth century that a great expansion took place and new methods were brought into use. Today there remain traces of slag ('cinder') from the long-dormant workings, sited near streams which once provided power for the needed draught.

In the sixteenth century, Buxted was noted for the making of cannon of cast-iron, which were first produced in 1543, together with the ammunition. No less well-known were the Sussex fire-backs, and a number of these have been identified with certainty as having been made in that area. One, inscribed 'Richard Lenard Founder at Bred Fournis' (*Bred:* Brede) is dated 1636, and another depicts the burning at the stake of an earlier ironmaster, Richard Woodman, and his wife; a couple who suffered that fate in the religious persecutions of Queen Mary in 1557.

Kettle-tilter ('Idle-back', 'Lazy-back', 'Handy-maid'): a simple device of wrought-iron for tilting the kettle when water was wanted from it. Not only was there no need to soil the hand by touching a smoke-blackened kettle, but the handle of the tilter projected outside the fireplace, was cool and there would be no risk from scalding steam or water. The kettle was suspended over the fire in the tilter, which in turn hung from a pot-hook or crane.

Meat-fork: used at the fireside when cooking. It usually had two prongs and was very little (if at all) different from a toasting-fork.

Pipe-kiln: a tubular wrought-iron frame with a handle at the top and feet at each end. Clay 'churchwarden' pipes were placed in the kiln in order to clean them when they

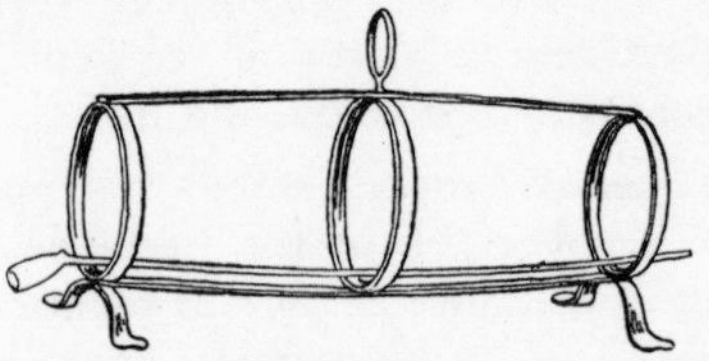

Fig. 8

had become foul, and the pipe-kiln and its contents were then put into an oven. It is said that in country districts the local baker performed this task.

Plate-warmer: this stood before the fire in kitchen, living-room or dining-room, to heat the plates preparatory to the serving of a meal. Several types of plate-warmer have been recorded; all date from the eighteenth and nineteenth centuries, and the surviving examples are not numerous. One variety is in the form of a wrought-iron revolving

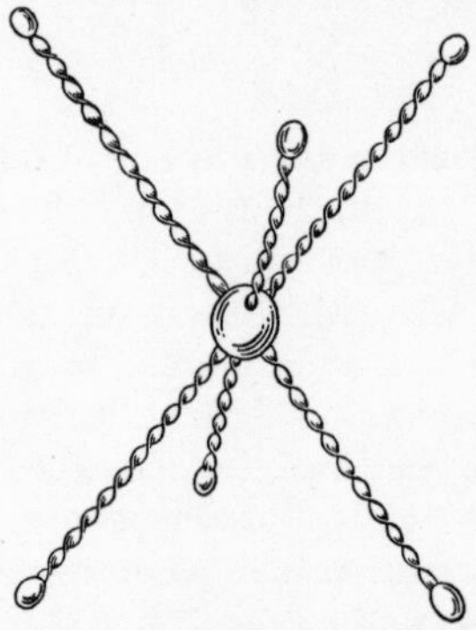

Fig. 9

stand on a tripod base with upright bars to hold the plates in position. Another kind is similar to a Dutch-oven, and has a handle so that the whole apparatus, complete with warmed plates, might be brought from the fireside to the table. A third type is the cat: an ingenious arrangement of three turned wood or metal rods, arranged cross-wise to form a double-ended tripod that could stand either way up.

Pot-hook (Cottrall, Jib-crook, Hanger, Tramelle, Hake): a wrought-iron device that was in use from medieval times for suspending a pot over the fire. By means of a ratchet it could be adjusted for height. In Scotland the same means was attained by using a chain and hook, known as a 'Jumping Rope'.

FIG. 10

Salamander: a bar of wrought-iron with a thick round or oblong piece at one end; somewhat like a long-handled shovel

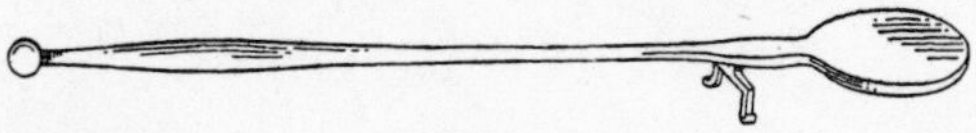

FIG. 11

in appearance. The larger end was heated until it became red-hot, and then held near bread, cake, etc, in order to brown it.

Skillet (Posnet, Pipkin): medieval skillets were shaped like cauldrons, and it was not until the sixteenth century that this ancestor of the modern saucepan became recognizable. These later skillets had no feet, but were made with the sides sloping outwards so that the circumference of the top was greater than that of the base. The handle was popularly used for advertising the name of the maker or for the spreading of texts such as 'Ye Wages of Sin is Death'. They were made of bronze.

Spit: a metal bar with which meat was pierced and placed on cobirons before the fire for roasting; as the bar was rotated all sides of the meat received the heat equally. The spit had prongs in the centre, and a grooved pulley at one end to connect by chain or rope to some sort of motive power: human, animal or mechanical. This motive power, if human or animal, was termed a 'turnspit', and if mechanical a 'Jack'. Illustrations in early manuscripts show that boys were employed as turnspits, and by the sixteenth century spit-jacks were in use. These latter were made of brass and iron, and were driven by large weights of stone or metal, which descended slowly into pits dug for the purpose to increase the length of fall. Like the weights of a clock, once they had completely run down they were wound up again. Another mechanical method of turning the spit was by a fan fitted in the mouth of the chimney, which was operated by the rising draught. A further method was the employment of dogs, specially trained for the purpose, which were confined in a small treadmill fixed to the wall of the kitchen. At the end of the eighteenth century, spring-driven jacks were in use, and culminated in the neat bottle-jack, brass-cased and driven by clockwork.

When not in use the spits were kept in the spit-rack: a row of hooks at either end of the space above the fireplace.

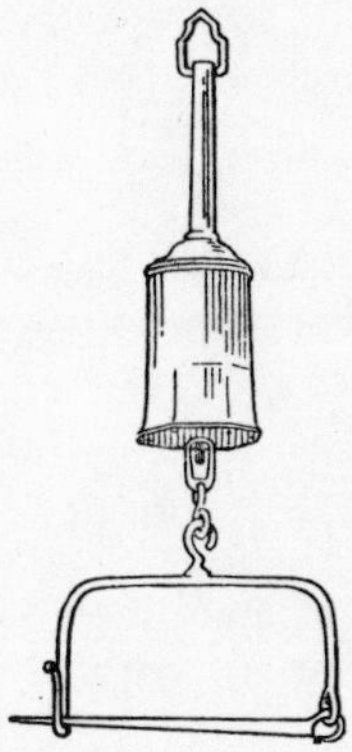

FIG. 12

Toaster: these were either in the form of standing toasters or the familiar fork, and were used for the toasting of both bread and meat. The fork needs little mention beyond pointing out that it almost always has three prongs. A variation of it is the toast-

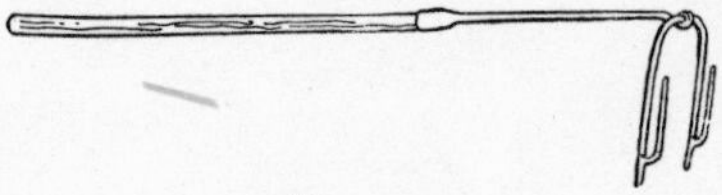

FIG. 13

holder, which has two short upcurved arms at the end of a long handle.

Standing toasters are rare and vary much in design. Four in the Victoria & Albert Museum are worthy of description. Two of them have simple tripod bases and central pillars with turned finials. On each pillar is a bell-shaped fitting with three prongs for holding the food to be toasted, and these are adjustable for height. Another is in the form of a circular trivet with a three-pronged fork, also adjustable up and down. The fourth type stands on the ground and is like a table toast-rack for only one slice of bread, and it has a long handle projecting at the back. The latter type was for use at a down-hearth, and all four were of wrought-iron.

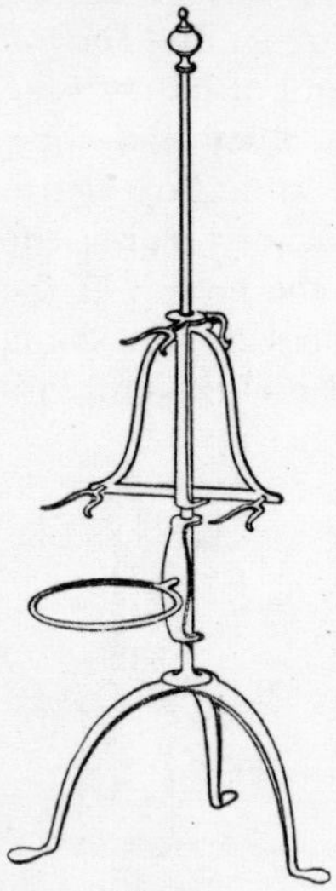

Fig. 14

Trivet (Brandis(e)): strictly a three-legged stand on which utensils might rest before the fire, but the word is used to cover many types of stand. The trivets of the seventeenth and eighteenth centuries were usually circular and of wrought-iron; sometimes they had a projecting handle. Later versions, also on three legs, were of an oblong shape with one end curved and fitted with a handle, while the far end had curved projections to fit over the fire-bar of a grate. Others dispensed with legs, and were made to hang on the front of a stove; of this last type many were made in the nineteenth century of cast-iron with pierced brass tops.

Fig. 15

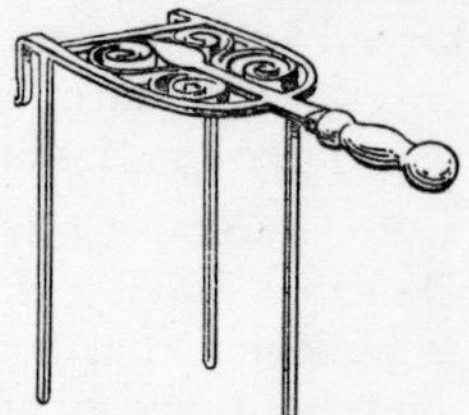

Fig. 16

BOOKS FOR FURTHER READING

Lindsay, J. Seymour: *Iron and Brass Implements of the English House* (1927).
Shuffrey, L. A.: *The English Fireplace* (1912).

WALLPAPER

By E. A. ENTWISLE

DURING the past few years wallpaper has been very much in the news, and most of us have a good idea of the types available today and also of the kind of wallpaper we prefer. But the facts about its origins and early development are not so widely known. Contrary to popular belief, the Chinese, inventors of paper A.D. 105, were not the first to use paperhangings as such, and the idea of pasting paper sheets on the wall as a means of decoration seems rather to have been of European origin, dating back roughly to the time when papermaking became an established industry in Europe during the fifteenth century.

The earliest designs of wallpaper were inspired by the more costly hangings they superseded, and it is not surprising to find, therefore, that one of the oldest wallpapers to be discovered *in situ* (at Christ's College, Cambridge, in 1911) has a textile pattern resembling those seen in the silk hangings and brocades of the Italian Renaissance. This particular wallpaper, generally known as the 'Cambridge Fragment' (Fig. 1), was printed by means of a wood block on the back of a Royal Proclamation of 1509, and evidence points to its being the work of a letterpress printer, Hugo Goes, of Beverley and York. It is probable that painted or stencilled sheets were in use in England and abroad even before this date; in England, certainly during the sixteenth and seventeenth centuries, there was a vogue for letterpress printed sheets, which were often used as linings for chests and cupboards. These are sometimes referred to today as 'black and white' papers because the design (floral, conventional or heraldic) was hand-blocked on to the paper in black printers' ink, though on occasion variations are to be found printed in colour, the commonest of these being red ochre.

The most important development in the history of wallpaper was the introduction,

FIG. 1. RECONSTRUCTED DESIGN OF THE WALLPAPER DISCOVERED AT CHRIST'S COLLEGE, CAMBRIDGE

during the first half of the seventeenth century, of the flock papers, claims for the discovery of which were advanced equally convincingly by both France and England. Flock is the minute shearings of wool left over as waste in the manufacture of cloth, and the skilful application of this medium to a paper on which the design had been drawn or printed with an adhesive medium resulted in a near imitation of the rich cut velvet hangings in use at this period (Plate 170c).

FIG. 2. TYPE OF FLOCK BOX IN USE DURING EARLY VICTORIAN PERIOD

The connoisseur of wallpaper will be familiar with this form of production, and we are indeed fortunate that this handsome wallpaper is the kind most frequently found by those engaged in the renovation or demolition of old property. With the possible exception of the Chinese painted papers which began to be imported into Europe from the end of the seventeenth century onwards, no wallpapers have enjoyed such an undisputed run of popularity as those in which flock has been employed. It is reassuring to know that the art has not been lost, and that in addition to reproducing to perfection designs of the past, present-day manufacturers of wallpaper are now regularly producing flock papers in up-to-date designs and colours.

The eighteenth century saw the establishment of wallpaper making as an important industry in England, America and France and, of course, an increase in the various types available. In addition to the flock papers, there were the gay chintz patterns, the stripes, the marbled varieties and the arabesque designs of the French, later to become famous for their panoramic designs known as *paysage* papers. Wallpaper borders in great variety were freely used, at first of the narrow 'gimp' type and later forming part of elaborate pilaster compositions (*see* Glossary); various forms of embossed papers (though few of these have survived); spangled papers, in which talc or mica was used, and also 'chinoiserie' designs in which English, French and German makers attempted to rival, with sometimes ludicrous results, the serenely beautiful drawing of the original Chinese painted papers.

Meanwhile, and because of increasing demand, makers were constantly seeking ways and means of producing wallpaper other than by hand processes. Successive patents to this end were taken out during the latter part of the century, and machinery was, in fact, used at some stages of manufacture with indifferent success until an English patent (1839) taken out by Harold Potter, a calico printer of Darwen, Lancashire, provided the solution in the shape of a machine based on calico-printing principles.

About this time the duty on wallpaper, which had to some extent burdened English makers since the reign of Queen Anne, was repealed (*see* page 252), and the industry, though losing ground in design standards, showed a phenomenal increase in production, outstripping at last that of any other single country in the world. It says much for the merits of wallpaper that its popularity has never waned, and that today the design and quality of machine printed papers is comparable in certain respects with that of the more expensively produced types.

The subject of wallpaper, as the list of books on page 254 shows, has not been neglected during past years, but few, if any, of these books deal with the collectors' interest in what has been described as perhaps the most perishable form of decorative art. This is probably due to the fact that knowledge of the characteristics of old wallpaper has been shared, up to now, by a comparatively small number of experts; and it may be, too, that for a long time it was the practice to destroy inadvertently valuable material in the course of stripping walls down to the plaster preparatory to repapering. There is little time even today for the examination of damp fragments of wallpaper that have escaped the worst depredations of the paperhanger's stripping knife, and there must be innumerable cases where the unusual character or

(A) Early black and white lining paper. English, probably seventeenth century. *Mrs Ruth Pollard*

(B) Block-printed border. English, *c.* 1800. 9 in. long by $2\frac{3}{4}$ in. *Author's Collection.*

(C) English Duty Stamp on the back of flock paper, *c.* 1750.

(D) French wallpaper cover used as a book cover, *c.* 1780. *Author's Collection.*

(A) Eighteenth-century Chinese wallpaper from Clytha Park, Abergavenny. *Pratt & Sons, London.*

(B) Two lengths of a hand-printed wallpaper by Réveillon, Paris, *c.* 1780–90. *Victoria & Albert Museum, London.*

(C) Flock wallpaper at Clandon Park near Guildford, Surrey, *c.* 1785. *The Countess of Onslow.*

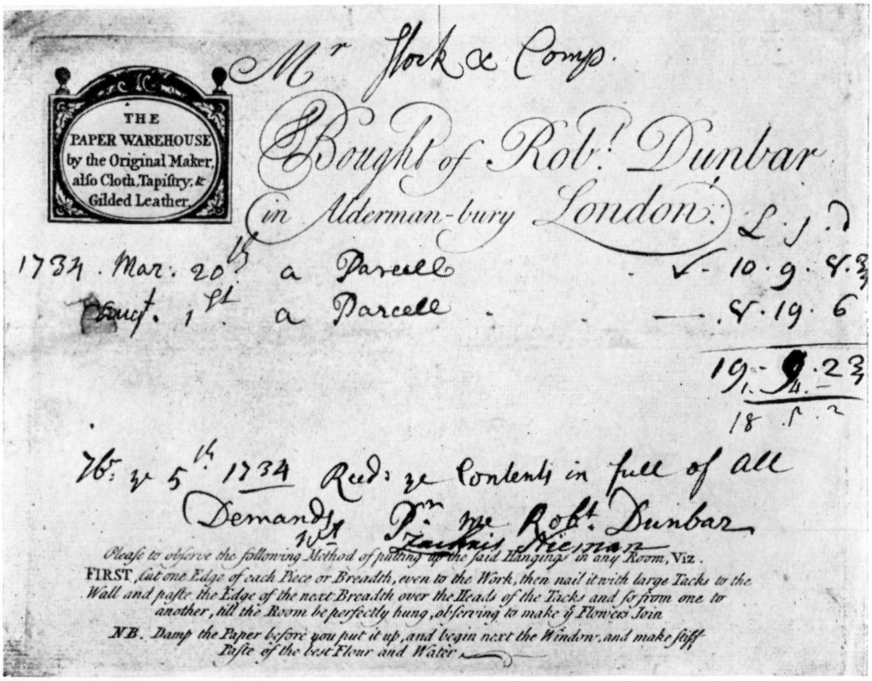
THE PAPER WAREHOUSE by the Original Maker, alfo Cloth, Tapiftry, & Gilded Leather.

Mr Stock & Comp.

Bought of Robt. Dunbar in Alderman-bury London. £ s d

1734. Mar: 20th a Parcell 10. 9. 8¾

Aug. 1st a Parcell 8. 19. 6

Feb: ye 5th 1734 Recd: ye Contents in full of all Demands Pr me Robt. Dunbar

Pleafe to obferve the following Method of putting up the faid Hangings in any Room, Viz.

FIRST, Cut one Edge of each Piece or Breadth, even to the Work, then nail it with large Tacks to the Wall and pafte the Edge of the next Breadth over the Heads of the Tacks and fo from one to another, till the Room be perfectly hung, obferving to make ye Flowers Join.

NB. Damp the Paper before you put it up, and begin next the Window, and make ftiff Pafte of the beft Flour and Water.

(A) Bill issued by Robert Dunbar, 1734, with instructions for hanging wallpaper.
Author's Collection.

(B) English wallpaper used as a cover for a book issued 1760.

(C) Bandbox covered with American hand-printed wallpaper, *c.* 1820.
The Cooper Union Museum, United States of America.

(A) Two lengths of French scenic wallpaper, 'Les Incas', printed in 1832 by A. Leroy, successor to Dufour, Paris.

(B) Machine-printed wallpaper commemorating the investment of Cyprus, 1878. *Victoria & Albert Museum.*

PLATE 172

rough printing of a design has failed to arouse sufficient curiosity to prevent, or at least defer, its eventual destruction. Perhaps a brief account of some recent discoveries will be of interest as indicative of the rewards awaiting those who know what they are about and who appreciate the value and interest of old wallpaper.

Just over three years ago the existence of an unusual paper was reported at Overton-on-Dee, near Wrexham, in a room of a house built during the seventeenth century which was about to be pulled down owing to its dilapidated condition. On visiting the place it was noted that the room had once been wainscotted and the wallpaper, already badly damaged and torn, had obviously come to light with the removal, probably unauthorized, of the wood panelling. This paper, the discovery of which was reported in *Country Life* (16th July 1953), turned out, after careful examination, to be the second oldest printed wallpaper to be discovered *in situ* in this country, the other being the so-called Cambridge Fragment (*see* Fig. 1). The ruins of Holland House, recently pulled down, revealed an old wallpaper buried under a heap of rubble, almost a complete length, exquisitely printed by the famous French maker Réveillon, during the late eighteenth century. Again, a finely produced multi-coloured flock wallpaper was preserved intact for two centuries under a mirror at Mount Clare House, Roehampton.

Another interesting 'find' relates to a painted paper which had hung for years on the staircase wall of an old house in Sussex. It had been there for so long, in fact, that its owners had accepted its presence in much the same way as they would have grown used to a pleasant piece of linenfold oak panelling. But when the house changed hands the new owner expressed a desire to know something about it, and was delighted when, by a happy chance, a loose corner of the paper was turned back to show the clear impression of an English duty stamp which confirmed its origin and provided valuable information as to the date of manufacture. (*See* Glossary, Duty Stamp and Plate 169C.)

FIG. 3. VARIETIES OF DUTY STAMPS. TOP STAMP IS WHAT IS KNOWN AS A 'FRAME MARK', SHOWING DATE OF MANUFACTURE AND OTHER DETAILS IN CODE

Yet another case was the discovery of a seventeenth-century lining paper (*see* Glossary, 'Black and White' papers), firmly adhering to the bottom of a drawer of a chest which had been in constant use for as long as anyone could remember (*see* Plate 169A). All these discoveries assumed special importance when it was found that with very little trouble it was possible to restore these fragments to something like their original condition.

Today with increased building activity on every hand, more old houses are being demolished or renovated than ever before, and there must be many similar discoveries being made every week in various parts of the country. The point is, of course, how many wallpapers found in this way are considered worth keeping, how many are identified correctly if and when preservation is agreed upon?

What are the characteristics of those wallpapers that are worthy of the antiquarian's or the collector's notice? To begin with, they must inevitably be painted or printed by hand processes. As stated elsewhere, the wallpaper printing machine was invented just over a hundred years ago. There are very interesting wallpapers in this class, particularly up to about the middle of the nineteenth century, but the machine brought mass production and, compared with the hand-made article, inferior design and printing technique. Interest in the machine-made goods can only be academic, and if the value of a wallpaper is to be judged by its rarity or the character of its design, the machine-made article can be safely left alone for the time being. Of the painted papers, few will be found today (compared with the number of wall-paintings, for example), but discovery of the hand-made or block-printed papers, including the lining papers, may be considered to have by no means come to an end. Not only may we expect to find a number of letterpress-printed varieties, but also flocks, distemper coloured papers of fine design, embossed types and pretty borders which every self-respecting maker produced in large variety during the eighteenth century. It is unlikely that the Chinese painted papers will lend themselves to dramatic discovery, for these have been cared for by successive owners who have appreciated their beauty or their cash value, with the result that they may still be admired often in the positions they have occupied for centuries. These attractive papers, and also the French scenic wallpapers of the early nineteenth century, are collectors' prizes of considerable value, more often to be seen *in situ* than in their original form consisting of a number of rolls per 'set'. To appreciate the current values of these sets one must watch the auctions, when it will be found that they are being bought, when they come on to the market, for sums varying from a few hundred pounds to as much as a thousand pounds for a particularly rare or beautiful series, or depending on how much time and money has been spent on, say, removal or renovation. Incidentally, the French and Chinese wallpapers can present many problems even for the expert. The best of the French scenic wallpapers were produced at the beginning of the nineteenth century, but reprints have been made in fair quantity since. One indication of reprinting is that the colouring of the reprint is generally much less subdued and subtle than the original. Reprinting from old blocks of the Regency period is commonly carried on today, and designs printed in the 1860s by a London manufacturer for William Morris can be similarly reproduced today on request. It is generally supposed that Chinese painted papers were never duplicated and that every set was unique, whereas it is known, by dealers especially, that some at least were drawn and painted as required from one master cartoon. It is therefore possible to find two identical designs, though perhaps different in colour detail. The English imitations can be quite baffling on occasion, particularly in the case of the better varieties. Usually, however, pictorial incongruities – European apparel, faces or furniture – will help to identify the English production. It is interesting to note that these papers, if imported by the East India Company, were exempt from the duties imposed on similar goods made by English manufacturers.

There are many other aspects of wallpaper in which the collector may develop an interest. In America there is a great fondness for the wallpaper-covered bandboxes of the early nineteenth century (*see* Plate 171C). On the Continent many people specialize in the marbled or otherwise decorated papers to be found as end-papers or coverings of old books (*see* Glossary, Marbled Papers, page 253), and in England a few experts have contributed a store of information relating to the letterpress-printed papers which were used as lining papers for chests, cupboards, coffers and boxes of various kinds. Pictorial wallpapers, as distinct from those of the French type, have always claimed attention – even those of the early machine age of which many interesting and amusing examples are included in the Victoria & Albert Museum collection (*see* Plate 172B).

Further lines of inquiry which the collector may find worth-while to pursue are as follows: firstly, the small fragment of wallpaper which, while it reveals as much as is necessary of the design and colour, yet leaves something to be imagined, is easily handled and can be studied or shown to others without undue inconvenience; small strips of wallpaper borders (*see* Plate 169B) are well worth collecting since the 'repeat' being a matter of a few inches, only a small length is needed to convey an idea of the effect; pieces of wallpaper that have been stamped on the back by an Excise Officer; scraps which contain a single motif of attractive design enough to suggest the character of the full repeat; a book-cover chosen for its decorative quality (*see* Plates 169D and 171B); a sample cutting which long ago enabled someone to decide his or her scheme of decoration. There is, too, an absorbing side in the gradual accumulation of wallpaper makers' bills, trade cards and advertisements, of which there is no doubt the private archives of the big estates all over the country still contain many unsuspected examples. A particularly interesting bill of 1734, which the writer came upon by accident in a second-hand book shop, is shown on Plate 171A. It will be noticed that included at the foot of the document are instructions for 'putting up the said Hangings in any Room'. Many similar reminders of the importance of wallpaper in bygone ages are to be seen today in museums or private collections, and fresh additions are continually being made.

Wallpaper is necessarily a somewhat ephemeral thing, and we do well to prize the examples that come our way. Every additional discovery contributes to the history of the subject; from these we learn something of social conditions and taste throughout the centuries. The popularity of wallpaper has been increasing ever since it was first invented, and, who knows, there may be a profitable side for the discerning connoisseur, in collecting some of the finer types that are being produced today.

GLOSSARY

'All-over' Designs: a pattern of close character which, conventional or abstract, and of large or small repeat, gives an all-over coverage.

Arabesque Design: originally inspired by Arabian design, but during the eighteenth century typical of the rich ornamentation seen in contemporary mural painting and woodcarving. Arabesque wallpapers said to have been originated by Sherringham of Chelsea (*see* 'Designers') and carried on in France by Réveillon of Paris (*c.* 1780).

'Black and White' Papers: modern name given to the sixteenth- and seventeenth-century letterpress-printed papers, many of which were designed in imitation of the black-thread embroideries of the Tudor period.

Block Printing: most early wallpapers were printed by wood block, the engraving of which was a skilled craft owing its origin to the wood engravers of medieval times. The size of block varied according to the size of design, but was usually governed by the ease with which the operator could handle the block. Hand-printed wallpaper is produced today according to traditional methods.

Borders: narrow strips of paper in use from earliest times, giving an additional embellishment in the same way as upholsterers' gimp. Made in a variety of sizes, designs and colours, 'cut-out' or scalloped. Still popular today.

Chinoiserie Papers: 'Mock India' (eighteenth century). Imitations and variants of the beautiful painted Chinese wallpapers so popular during the eighteenth century. A notable English example from Wotton-under-Edge (*c.* 1740) is to be seen in the Victoria & Albert Museum. France and other European countries also made chinoiserie papers (*see* Plate 170A).

Colours: early wallpapers were mainly black and white, but were eventually succeeded by the coloured papers printed or stencilled in earth colours, such as ochres, etc. These in turn were succeeded by colours which were mixed with whiting and size. There were also colours mixed with certain drying oils. Today most of the colours used are lake colours mixed with a china-clay base and a gum adhesive.

Damask Pattern: imitation of the costly silk hangings of Italian origin, obtained in wallpaper by contrasting a polished ground with a pattern printed in matt distemper perhaps of the same shade as the ground colour.

Designers: names of the designers of early wallpapers in England are not known. The names of Papillon and Réveillon (Plate 170B) are linked with the eighteenth century in France, and the Eckhardt Bros and Sherringham were eulogized by critics in England when referring to eighteenth-century design. Many interesting names are associated with English wallpaper during the nineteenth century, including William Morris, Walter Crane and C. F. A. Voysey. Among famous artists who have designed wallpapers today are Edward Bawden, John Aldridge, Lucienne Day, Eduardo Paolozzi, Salvador Dali, Roger and Robert Nicholson, etc.

Duty Stamp: by an Act of Queen Anne (1712) every square yard of paper 'printed painted or stained' was subject to a tax of 1*d.*, increased two years later to 1½*d.*; the excise officer had to stamp the paper with the appropriate stamp and attended the factories regularly for this purpose. The duty was repealed in 1836.

Embossed Papers: 'Stamp'd' or 'Embost' wallpapers (eighteenth century). Description given to an after process involving the use of block or roller under pressure which gives to the paper an embossed finish resembling leather, textiles or plaster. Embossing was practised at an early date in the manufacture of wallpaper, though the date cannot be ascribed with certainty (*see* 'Stucco' Papers).

Flock Papers: powdered wool applied to the paper on which the design is first printed, painted or stencilled with a slow-drying adhesive. A process known to antiquity especially associated with early clothworkers (*see* Fig. 2).

'Gothic' Papers: style of design favoured, if not innovated, by Horace Walpole for Strawberry Hill. Inspired by certain features of medieval architecture. A second Gothic period occurred in England during the 1850s.

Grounded Papers: the overall application of colour to the paper before printing. A hand process up to within recent times, including various types, polished, lustred (with the use of mica), metallic, flock, etc.

Historians of Wallpaper: *see* article on this subject in *The Connoisseur*, March 1945, E. A. Entwisle.

'India' Papers: Eighteenth-century name given to many articles imported from the Far East, including paperhangings specially made for the European market.

Lining Papers: the sixteenth and seventeenth centuries saw a great variety of these papers, usually printed in black ink on self-coloured paper. Designs were floral, heraldic and conventional, and while generally produced specifically for lining boxes, coffers, etc, were sometimes used as wallpapers, particularly those designs capable of 'repeat'.

FIG. 4. TYPICAL 17TH-CENTURY LINING PAPER

Machine Printing: the first successful wallpaper printing machine was in operation in England about 1840. Based on calico-printing principles, it was dependent on the invention and supply of paper in 'continuous' lengths.

Marbled Papers: made in France by the Dominotiers as early as 1580, makers of small pictorial sheets for books, etc. Essentially a hand craft of Turkish origin, it was introduced to England early in the reign of Charles I. There was a vogue during the late seventeenth and early eighteenth centuries for decorating the walls of halls and staircases with marble papers printed by wood blocks.

Moiré Papers: printed or embossed wallpapers imitating watered-silk effects.

Ogee Pattern: geometrical device based on circles much favoured by wallpaper designers.

Overdoors (Supraportes): painted or printed papers suitable for the decoration of the space between the top of a door and cornice. A speciality of the wallpaper maker in England, France and America during the eighteenth century. Similar decorative panels were made to fit empty chimney-places in summer months.

Painted Papers: probably used in England as early as the end of the fifteenth century, though few if any of these have survived. Painting of 'perspectives' was undertaken by eighteenth-century paperhanging makers, frequently after the plain paper had been hung.

Paperhanging Maker: seventeenth- and eighteenth-century term describing the maker of wallpaper, superseded by 'paperstainer' until 'wallpaper manufacturer' became generally used within the present century.

Pilaster: a richly patterned paper suitable for use in elaborate schemes of panelling (*see* Fig. 5). Sets of papers containing units of the complete scheme were made in France and in England during the early part of the nineteenth century.

Print Rooms: a fashionable form of mural decoration in England during the mid-eighteenth century. Prints were pasted on to the wallpaper and framed in paper. Chippendale and Horace Walpole both adopted this manner of decorating rooms.

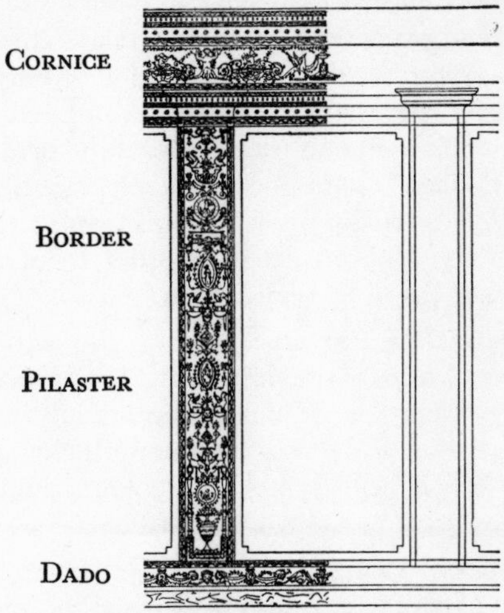

FIG. 5. PILASTER DECORATION

Repeat: a characteristic of most wallpaper designs which enables these to be repeated when the sheets or lengths are placed in juxtaposition. English makers well understood this principle as early as the sixteenth century, and the idea goes back probably farther than this in textile production.

Reprints: where the original blocks of an old design have been preserved, it is sometimes feasible to reprint. In cases where an excessive number of blocks make up the original design, reprinting (owing to the labour involved) will not be lightly undertaken – as in the large French panoramic sets, for example. It is advisable to seek the advice of an expert before purchasing the latter, as the difference in price between the original and the reprint may be considerable.

Roll or Piece of Wallpaper: early paperhangings consisted of a number of sheets (generally a dozen) joined together end to end. Each sheet was roughly $22\frac{1}{2}$ inches wide by 35 inches long (double demy), giving a length of about 12 yards. Today the British Standards Institution length of a piece of wallpaper is $11\frac{1}{2}$ yards.

'Scenic' Papers: exemplified in their most attractive form by the French panoramic types sometimes known as *paysage* or landscape papers. Among the first of these to be produced was *Vues de Suisse*, by Jean Zuber, Rixheim, in 1804.

Selvedge: most wallpapers made during the past 150 years have a selvedge or edging on either side of the roll which is not printed upon and serves as a protection to the printed roll. In hand-made goods the selvedge bears the impress of the pitch or register pins with which the block is fitted in order to obtain accurate printing registration.

Stencilled Papers: one of the earliest forms of wallpaper making and a ready means of repeating the design automatically over large surfaces. It was common during the seventeenth century to add colours in this manner to a block-printed outline.

'Stucco' Papers: wallpaper imitating the effect of stone or plaster. During the eighteenth century the term was generally descriptive of papier-mâché, with which industry the paperhanging maker was then closely associated.

'Verditure' (or Verditer (*Verd de Terre*) Papers): eighteenth-century name for plain bluey-grey wallpapers.

BOOKS FOR FURTHER READING

The most useful books, all fully illustrated, on the origins and history of wallpaper published during the present century are as follows: *Historic Wallpapers*, Nancy McClelland (1924); *A History of English Wallpaper*, A. V. Sugden and J. L. Edmondson (1926); *Catalogue of Wallpaper*, C. C. Oman (Victoria & Albert Museum) (1929); *Histoire du Papier Peint en France*, H. Clouzot and Ch. Follot (1935); *The Book of Wallpaper*, E. A. Entwisle (1954), and the *Catalogue of the Deutsches Tapeten Museum, Kassel* (1955). Earnest readers are also recommended to turn up the old numbers of the following magazines, which contain a wealth of information on the subject in the form of articles, generally well illustrated and documented: *The Connoisseur; Burlington Magazine; Country Life; The Journal of Decorative Art* (now *Painting and Decorating*); *The Decorator; Tapeten Zeitung; The Wall Paper Magazine* (U.S.A.), etc. Brief but informed articles on the subject are also to be found in the various encyclopaedias, notably the *Encyclopaedia Britannica*, to which William Morris, Nancy McClelland and the present writer have contributed in turn.

Other references of importance which will repay consultation are: *English Wallpapers of the Sixteenth and Seventeenth Centuries*, Hilary Jenkinson, F.S.A. (a paper read to the Society of Antiquaries, 1925); 'Studies on Wallpapers in Ireland' (*Journal of the Royal Society of Antiquaries in Ireland*, Vols. 77, 78, 80), Mrs Ada Leask; *The Crace Papers*, a paper read by J. G. Crace to the Royal Institution of British Architects in 1839, with notes by A. V. Sugden and E. A. Entwisle (1939); various articles in the *Journal of Design and Manufacture*, 1849–52.

MASTERPIECES OF THE PUPPET-MAKER'S ART

By ERIC BRAMALL, F.R.S.A.

PUPPET-making is one of the oldest arts in the world. Long before the first puppet show as a form of entertainment came into being, temple idols, activated by hidden priests, moved mysteriously to impress and awe worshippers, and the fate of the craftsmen who fashioned the idols and knew the secret of their 'supernatural' life is a matter for speculation. That an incredible amount of ingenuity and skill went into the figures, however, is certain, and throughout succeeding centuries artists and craftsmen lavished their talents on puppets of all kinds. The writers of Ancient Greece described the most elaborate displays, incorporating figures half puppets and half automata, used either in religious or semi-religous rites which may or may not have been credited with supernatural associations by the beholders, and from these mysterious and somewhat deceitful beginnings the puppet show proper evolved. Into what was at first a repertoire of purely religious drama profane characters crept slowly, until offshoots of the temple-puppet performance became entirely separated from it and were concerned solely with entertainment. A close association of puppetry with the Church, both pagan and Christian, has, however, been maintained until the present day, and indeed the Christian Church is by no means innocent of using puppets for fraudulent practices, for phenomena associated with certain statues have been due not to supernatural intervention but to puppetry of neither so pure nor so simple a nature.

The word 'puppeteer' is used somewhat vaguely and indiscriminately with reference to anyone who happens to 'dabble in puppets'. A word of American origin, it has almost superseded the older term of 'puppet-master', sounding perhaps less pretentious, but its true meaning remains the same. The puppeteer is the showman, the creative artist and craftsman combined; firstly the showman, for puppets are made to be shown in a performance of some description; secondly the creative artist, for to be true to himself the showman must create his own characters; and lastly the craftsman. A brilliant puppeteer does not of necessity have to make first-class puppets, for, as has been said often before, a skilled puppeteer can hold an audience with a puppet made from firewood and rags, though invariably he prefers to work with perfectly made figures and is fully capable of making them. Happily the technical ability and imagination necessary to the creation of puppets and the senses of rhythm and drama, coupled with the manual dexterity necessary for their accomplished manipulation, are sometimes found in the one individual, and where such a combination exists the final results are generally the most satisfactory, for they represent a solo performance, a true and unadulterated form of artistic expression. To portray skilful manipulation in words or a still picture is, however, impossible, for it is essentially something to be seen in movement; but without it the puppet-maker's efforts are wasted. The finest puppet in the world is useless as such without the magical life which only the manipulator can give, for its true function, and indeed the very reason for its being, is the fantastic – or realistic – interpretation of living movement of which it is capable. Some of the finest puppet characters extant are too grotesque to be appreciated at close quarters or successfully photographed, though seen from stage distance and in action, are undoubted masterpieces of artistry; but the puppet-maker is also responsible for creations so beautiful that they rank high as works of art even in the stillness of 'puppet-death' to which inactivity or a photograph condemns them.

The Far East, so rich in its heritage of art, produces some of the world's most beautiful puppets, and while these are often overloaded with jewellery and decoration, they display nevertheless an intrinsic refinement and economy of line which is rarely found in Western work. Most delicate and fragile of all are the shadow-puppets of China, cut from paper or vellum and tinted with transparent colours. In use, they are held, from behind, against a thin screen of paper or fabric, by means of wires, and a light casts their shadows on and through the screen for the benefit of the audience seated on the other side. A great many traditional plays are shown, interspersed nowadays with Russian fairy-tales and propaganda plays. The shadow play was well known in the Sung Dynasty (A.D. 960–1279), and doubtless dates back to far earlier times, and although it is primarily a folk-art, having at all times been most popular among village communities, the great beauty of the shadow-puppets, with their incredibly fine open-work patterns and exquisite colouring, has never been bettered anywhere in the world.

The shadow-puppets of Java and Bali are of more robust construction, fashioned as they are from leather and punched with thousands of holes representing the patterns, and even the textures of imitated fabrics. Sometimes the perforations are covered with dyed skin, and the finished puppet casts a strong shadow suggestive of a stained-glass window. Many of the characters are, to Western eyes, magnificently grotesque, the good characters having long, thin features and bowed heads, suggesting refinement and humility, and the evil characters gross features, fat bodies and heads held erect, suggesting coarseness and pride.

The rod-puppet is popular throughout the Far East. This is a puppet supported and activated from below by means of slender rods, movement being restricted usually to head and arms, the puppets rarely having legs at all, though this fact is concealed by their long dresses. A departure from the normal type is found in Japan, where the art of Bunraku, the showing of the unique 'three-man puppet', has been cultivated for centuries. This puppet is two-thirds life-size, with an abnormally small head, and is presented on an open stage in full view of the audience. Its name is derived from the fact that three manipulators are required for its animation, two of whom, the assistants, are swathed in black from head to foot, suggesting to the Japanese mind invisibility; and the third, the chief manipulator, garbed in gorgeous ceremonial robes. The chief manipulator works the head and right arm of the puppet, one assistant the left arm and the other the feet. The gestures are perfectly timed, the three manipulators working as one man, and thirty years of training is considered necessary for the achievement of perfection in manipulation.

Neither in the East Indies does the puppet showman conceal himself from view to work his 'Wayangs', as the puppets are called, but squats behind a horizontal banana-tree trunk which forms his stage and into which soft wood he sticks the pointed supporting rods of his puppets. 'Wayangs' have been claimed to be the most elegant puppets in the world, and certainly they have an air of aristocratic aloofness and are incapable of an inartistic movement. Monsters, demons and heroes alike gesticulate with refinement and delicacy. The plays performed, and consequently the characters involved, are traditional, and so ancient is the art of puppetry in Java that it has influenced other arts, 'wayangs' being a prominent feature of 'batik' design, and the dance having adopted many of the stylized movements and gestures of the puppets. The illustration (Plate 173B) of a puppet hero shows clearly how such figures are the embodiment of the natural beauty and innate artistry of the Javanese and Balinese people.

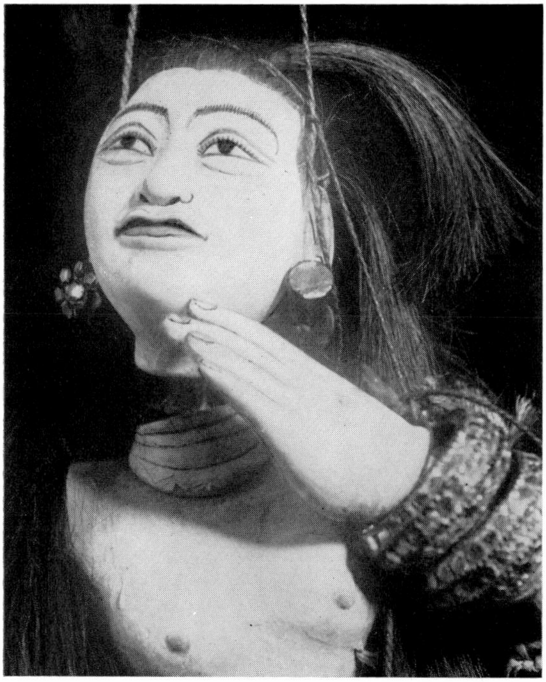

(A) Burmese puppet-dancer. *Author's Collection.*

(B) Head of a Javanese Wayang. *Author's Collection.*

(C) Chinese shadow-puppets. A scene from *Pilgrimage to the West*, a play adapted from a classical opera: Hsuan Tsang and one of his disciples on their journey to the West to fetch the Buddhist scriptures. *China Pictorial.*

PLATE 173

(A) Gypsy Violinist, made by the Author.

(B) Archangel, made by the Author.

(C) Puppets for Shakespeare's *The Tempest*, by the Roel Puppets. *By courtesy of Olive Blackham.*

(A) Ophelia, a hand-puppet by Mary Saunders and now in the Victoria & Albert Museum. *By courtesy of Mary Saunders.*

(B) Head of Pantaloon, a nineteenth-century English puppet of the Barnard Troupe. *By courtesy of Waldo S. Lanchester.*

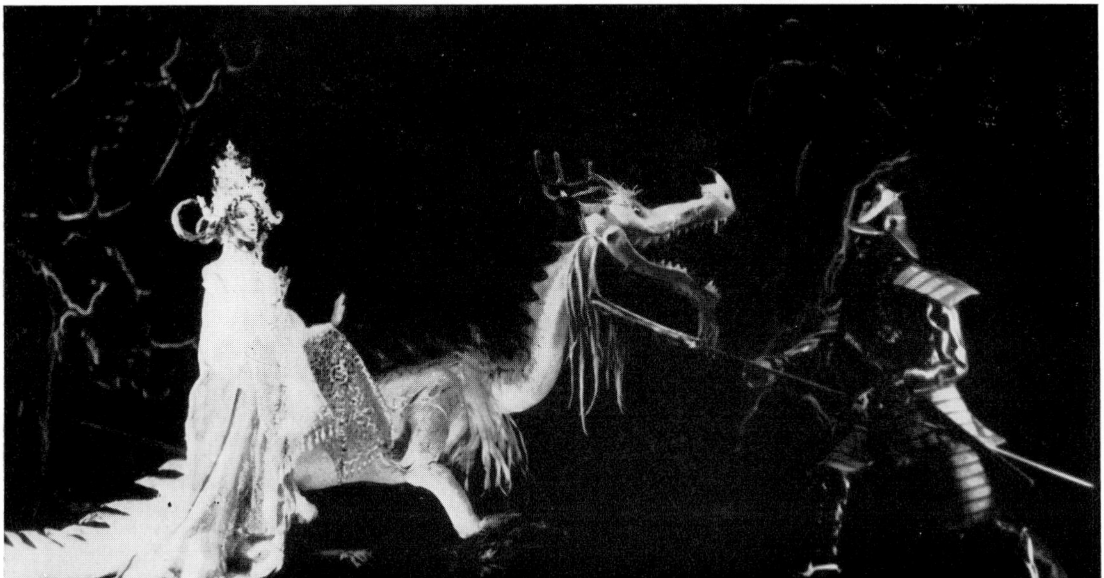

(C) Puppets made by the late Prof. Richard Teschner of Vienna.

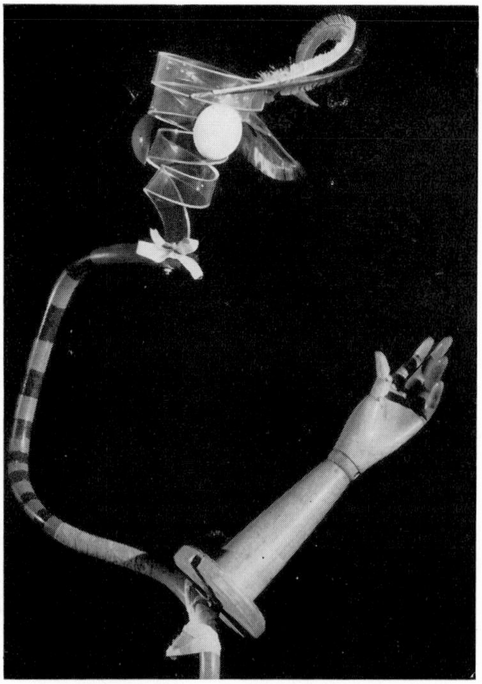

(A) A puppet by Fred Schneckenburger of Switzerland. *F. Schneckenburger.* (Photo by M. Wolgensinger.)

(B) Orlando, a Sicilian string and rod puppet. *Miss L. M. Forrest.*

(C) Puppets for G. B. Shaw's *Shakes v. Shav*, by the Lanchester Marionettes. *Waldo S. Lanchester.*

PLATE 176

Burmese puppet plays are borrowed mainly from the Ramayana, poetic legends hailing from India, and some of the puppets are almost exact miniature replicas of the temple performers who enact the dance-drama. Again the carving of the puppets is superb and even the controls of the string-puppets are sometimes carved in representation of birds or animals. The control is that instrument to which the strings of the puppet are attached, and is held in the manipulator's hand. To this type of puppet, i.e. one worked by strings, the name 'marionette' is given, irrespective of the part of the world from which it comes, and it is usual to refer to string-puppets by this name. Sometimes Burmese puppets have heads of papier-mâché, but whatever the material the craftsmanship is superb and the colouring exquisite. Minute pieces of mirror-glass in their thousands are inset in the fantastic head-dresses and jewellery which adorn the puppets, and these alone are masterpieces of ingenuity and object lessons in patience.

The rod-puppets of the East have inspired many puppeteers in the West, and the splendid rod-puppets of Russia, too, doubtless owe their origin to this source; but their influence has never been seen more strongly than in the puppets of the late Richard Teschner of Vienna. Teschner, a great artist, carver of precious stones, painter and rare musical instrument maker, created a species of puppet delicate to the point of extreme fragility, exotic to the point of unhealthiness. Magnificently costumed and bejewelled, animated by slender rods from below, these ethereal creatures performed their rhythmic movements within a shadowy stage, fronted by a circular convex glass and surrounded by the signs of the zodiac. The accompaniment was a slow musical-box tinkle, for Teschner eschewed the use of the human voice as being disproportionate to his dream-like creations. Amongst many characters, each a perfect work of art, he produced some which were completely nude, and showed these occasionally to selected audiences. On his death a few years ago, his priceless collection passed into the safe keeping of the Austrian nation.

Austria is rich in puppet masterpieces, for in the eighteenth century, in the full blossoming of the rococo, puppets enjoyed a vogue probably unsurpassed in its artistry before or since. The aristocracy caused puppet theatres to be built in their palaces, and the rarest talent was employed in the creation of the puppets and the material they played. Famous artists designed the theatres and the stage sets, famous composers wrote music especially for puppet productions, and though few of these exclusive theatres and puppets remain, the influence of the rococo is still to be seen in the productions of the Salzburg Marionettentheater, where three generations of the Aicher family have created a magnificent collection of marionettes, beautiful both in appearance and performance. Catering to a large extent for audiences which arrive in Salzburg thirsting for Mozartiana, several plays centring around the child prodigy have been produced which epitomize all that the Salzburg Festival stands for, and have in their production every ingredient necessary to the exudation of sheer, delightful rococo frivolity.

Untouched by the Italian Renaissance, which so gently invaded Austria, is the art of the German puppet-makers. Here a strong Gothic influence is still to be seen, and for 'carrying power' to large audiences, the rugged and angular-faced characters created by the German wood-carvers cannot be bettered, and their comparison with the puppets of France or Italy reveals at a glance how different racial characteristics are reflected in puppets. The German puppet has the intensity of a Gothic saint, the French that indefinable doll-like quality which somehow seems to have lingered over from the monarchy – a legacy of artificiality which to a greater or lesser extent permeates so much of French art; and in the Italian is the benign chubbiness of a Renaissance madonna. In Sicily, however, is to be found a direct link with the twelfth century. Here is shown the play which lasts a year, one episode given each day, in the legends of 'Orlando Furioso'. Great puppets, 4 feet in height, requiring all the strength of a man to lift and manipulate them, are resplendent in metal armour. Battle is the order of the day, and to the cheers of the audience, Christian and Saracen knights engage in mortal combat, and often enough, at the stroke of a sword, a head is severed and rolls into the audience, trailing from its wounds a few red ribbons to simulate blood! Such a display is far removed from the gentleness of a Teschner production, but the huge puppets in their flashing armour typify the romantic wildness of a less gentle people, and the exploits of Orlando stir primitive instincts which would scarcely be aroused by Teschner's aestheticism. Psychologically the Orlando Furioso performance is probably much healthier from the point of view of its effect upon the audience; the spontaneous release of nervous and physical energy which it incites from its beholders leaves them doubtlessly more satisfied than would the cloying sweetness of Teschner's efforts, shown as they were in the atmosphere of a studio mysteriously temple-like, and almost sickly in their preciousness.

The outstanding figure in Swiss puppetry is Fred Schneckenburger, who has evolved a form of puppet almost entirely divorced from tradition, and one eminently suitable for biting, even savage satire. Throughout the centuries puppetry has been an excellent vehicle for satire, for not only is the puppet, by virtue of its limitations, at once a caricature of flesh-and-blood life, but through it human eccentricities in mannerisms and physical weaknesses can be lampooned to a fine degree of wickedness and almost in complete defiance of the law of libel. Schneckenburger's genius lies not in the craftsmanship of his creations, which are often crudely constructed, but in his masterly interpretation of character through puppets quite unlike anything the world has previously seen. Sophistication and an acid cynicism are manifest in his work, almost as if he sees human folly in every endeavour, and human frailty in every character, and these he exposes to the merciless glare of the stage spotlights. Some of his puppets are hurriedly hacked – one cannot say carved – from rough wood, but he is ready to use any material, however unorthodox – pieces of newsprint, bent metal tubing, the hand of a shop-window dummy, animal tusks, feathers, often with complete disregard for natural human form, in his art which shows clearly the influence of both abstract and surrealist painting and sculpture. Schneckenburger's brilliance can best be seen in performance, and on the only occasion he visited London he presented a short play, *Mr Irresolute*, in which the principal character, unable to make up his mind which way to turn, towards good or evil, conveniently splits into two halves, one going one way and the other the opposite way, providing an unexpected and essentially puppetesque climax. Since *Mr Irresolute*, Schneckenburger has become more and more abstract. His extreme sophistication, brilliance of wit and startling creations have made his work popular in exclusive Parisian cabarets, though he insists that the more adult his audiences, the more they ask, 'What is it? What does it mean?'; whereas, children, though he rarely plays for them, on seeing his puppets know instinctively what they mean and accept their strange forms without question.

In England during the last thirty years, a puppet renaissance has been taking place. Rescued from near oblivion by a small number of enthusiasts in the nineteen-twenties, the interest in puppetry, helped to some degree by television, has grown to the proportions of the proverbial bull-frog, and like the bull-frog will deflate very rapidly once the maximum has been reached. The phenomenal rise to popularity of the puppet has drawn a great many charlatans into the realm of British puppeteers to help reap the harvest while it lasts, but though there are more puppets and puppeteers than ever before, it is to be regretted that for the most part, true art has been temporarily obscured by commercialism. Puppets relying solely on novelty and appeal to the very young quickly become tiresome, and with few exceptions television has presented only this type of performance, thereby furthering the popular fallacy that puppets are principally children's fare. The older-established puppet companies, however, offer adult entertainment of a high order of artistry, and such productions as Marlowe's *Dr. Faustus*, Purcell's *Dido and Aeneas*, Shakespeare's *Macbeth* and *A Midsummer Night's Dream*, Tchekov's *The Bear* and *Shelter*, Dickens' *A Christmas Carol*, Haydn's *Philemon and Baucis*, Kneymborg's *People Who Die*, and many others, have been beautifully presented.

A good number of Old English marionettes are still in existence, though mostly of the nineteenth century, and a few of these are true works of art. Some present-day puppet-makers are interested in creating works which will be treasured by future generations. Among British wood-carvers who turn their skill to puppet-making John Bickerdike and Jack Whitehead are outstanding, and in the sphere of glove-puppet-making, the work of Mary Saunders, some of whose creations have been bought for the nation, is of the highest order of artistry. Mary Saunders is almost the British counterpart of Richard Teschner, producing as she does exotic puppets with superbly modelled features; puppets which, though for the most part naturalistic, seem to belong to another world, a world of eternal mystery and unearthly beauty. The finest materials are employed in their rich costumes, and the final touch which characterizes a Mary Saunders creation is the rare perfume which each character exudes, a fragrance selected to suit the character with the same painstaking care as goes into every detail of the puppet's making.

The fascination of dolls is universal, and it is perhaps an inborn instinct which makes people eager, even avid, collectors of puppets both ancient and modern. Those who aim to collect a number of puppets are few and are restricted mainly to puppeteers themselves, but puppets are at the outset so intriguing that the appearance of one in a room, be it period or contemporary, is a sure means of provoking curiosity and comment. Just as a T'ang horse or a Ming roof-finial fits so comfortably in a contemporary scheme of decoration, so a Burmese marionette-dancer or Javanese shadow-puppet becomes at once an harmonious and intriguing focal-point, and for this reason is snapped up almost immediately it makes its appearance in an antique shop. Often enough the people who buy these things – and indeed the people who sell them – have little or no idea of what they are. A marionette without strings is described as a 'doll', albeit a loosely jointed one; and I have heard of a Javanese shadow-puppet described as a 'fan' by an ignorant dealer. Yet even in their unenlightenment people buy them, realizing their decorative possibilities.

The simplest kind of puppet is the flat, cut-out figure used in 'The Juvenile Drama' of the last century, printed on a sheet measuring roughly $8\frac{1}{2}$ inches by $6\frac{3}{4}$ inches, ready to be cut out and used on the stage of a toy theatre. These sheets came in two varieties, plain and hand-coloured, selling respectively at a penny and twopence and giving rise to the expression 'Penny Plain, Tuppence Coloured'. These charmingly naïve prints are still to be found, and suitably mounted and framed make delightful wall decorations. Read Robert Louis Stevenson's essay, *A Penny Plain and Twopence Coloured*, and you will certainly want to possess a few sheets of your own. For five pounds it is still possible to have a collection of minor works of art! It is certain that they are fast disappearing, they will never be produced again, and they will certainly increase in historical and monetary value as the years go by.

Shadow-puppets of the Far East can be used as effective wall decorations; unframed or, in the case of Chinese paper-shadows, mounted in a lampshade where their brilliant colouring is seen to advantage. Not so easy to find, these, but worth searching for. Price? Chinese shadows can be bought for a few shillings, but the shadow-puppets of Java are upwards of five pounds, unless you are very lucky.

Puppets carved directly from wood, unembellished and unhampered by clothes, can be wax-polished and mounted on a simple supporting stand. Burmese animal puppets can be displayed thus and certain European and English rod-and-string puppets. When costumed, a marionette divested of its strings can be made to recline gracefully in the corner of a settee, or will curl-up lovingly on a bookshelf, but if in period costume, which asks for care and preservation, it is best to have the puppet in a glass cabinet of some description. A puppet displayed under a glass shade, Victorian fashion, can look captivating, and is particularly happy as an isolated piece of decoration in a contemporary setting. Again, a wide picture frame can be fitted with a shallow box-backing, and puppets arranged against a painted or fabric background and, protected by a glass-front, make a three-dimensional wall decoration of unusual and striking appearance.

Puppets ranking as true works of art are not easy to find. If one wants a Chelsea candlestick or even a Fabergé egg, one can, if one has the money, go right away and buy it. But although a masterpiece of the puppet-maker's art would cost much, much less, the hunt for it would be more hazardous. An antique shop with a puppet for sale is rare. Neither is it essential to scour the Oriental dealers for a Javanese 'Wayang'. One is just as likely to encounter one in a junk-shop. Puppets of the last century are the easiest to find, but often enough are poor specimens artistically. Heads were frequently made in papier-mâché, and have become battered by time and hard work. Magnificent heads, like the one in Plate 175B, are rare, but when found often cost only a pound or two. Lovely eighteenth-century examples are more easily found on the Continent than in Britain, though England's supply is by no means exhausted, and they are often in better condition than nineteenth-century puppets. Perhaps the exquisite carving and sumptuous costumes earned for them a respect from their earliest days, and generations have treasured them.

There are today artists and craftsmen in the sphere of puppetry as great as any who have lived in the past, and the collector with one eye on his own pleasure and the other on posterity will perhaps be anxious to secure a modern puppet. In this field lies the greatest sport of the puppet hunter, for present-day puppet-makers of the highest repute are loath to part with their creations which have been made, usually, to play a specific part on the puppet stage, and are too busy earning their master's living to be shut up in a glass case. The quest is not hopeless, however. Puppeteers, like any creative artists, are flattered when people genuinely want examples of their work, and although they may be more disposed to offer to make a puppet specially for the collector than to part with an existing one, they will be on their mettle and will make a wonderful job of it.

Perhaps though, after all, it is better to insist upon a puppet which has been used in performance. Perhaps, after all, much of the puppet's charm lies in its associations; in the fascinating and faintly macabre soullessness with which it turns and surveys with unseeing eyes the others of its race, amid the painted landscapes and tinselled hangings of the puppet theatre. For as Anatole France has said: 'They do not live like ourselves, and yet they do live. They live as do the immortal gods.'

LIST OF MUSEUMS AND GALLERIES

This list covers only the major museums and galleries where subjects mentioned in the three volumes of *The Concise Encyclopaedia of Antiques* may be seen in Great Britain, Europe and the United States of America. It does not seek to be exhaustive and contains only those provincial museums and collections where a certain number of good examples can be seen; most provincial galleries can show one or two good specimens and are worth calling at.

The list is arranged under main subject headings—e.g. Furniture, Textiles, Ceramics, etc., and thereafter under the title of each article as it appears in the three volumes concerned.

FURNITURE

Furniture

GREAT BRITAIN

Castle Museum, York
Collection of Wooden Bygones, Oxley Wood House, Northwood, Mddx
Museum of English Rural Life, University of Reading
Townend, Troutbeck, nr Windermere
State apartments, Hampton Court Palace, London
State apartments, Kensington Palace, London
Museum of Welsh Antiquities, Bangor. (Welsh Furniture)
Bowes Museum, Barnard Castle
Holburne of Menstrie Museum, Bath
Cecil Higgins Museum, Bedford
Aston Hall, Birmingham
Art Gallery & Museum, Brighton
Thomas-Stanford Museum, Brighton
Georgian House, Bristol
The Red Lodge, Bristol
Towneley Hall Museum, Burnley
Astley Hall, Chorley
Valence House Museum, Dagenham, Essex
Burrell Collection, Glasgow
West Yorkshire Folk Museum, Halifax
The Old House, Hereford
Wilberforce Museum, Hull
Christchurch Mansion, Ipswich
Broghton House, Kirkcudbright
Temple Newsam House, Leeds
Anne of Cleves House, Southover, Lewes
Victoria & Albert Museum, London
Courtauld Institute of Art, London
Binning Collection, Fenton House, London
Geffrye Museum, Shoreditch, London
St John's Gate, Clerkenwell, London
Wallace Collection, London
City Art Gallery, Manchester
Heaton Hall, Manchester
Wythenshawe Hall, Manchester
The Lady Lever Art Gallery, Port Sunlight
Ford Green Hall, Stoke-on-Trent
Hall's Croft, Old Town, Stratford
Torre Abbey Art Gallery, Torquay
Oak House, West Bromwich
The Priest House, West Hoathly, Sussex

Victorian Furniture

GREAT BRITAIN

Victoria & Albert Museum, London
London Museum, London
William Morris Gallery, Walthamstow, London
Shipley Art Gallery, Gateshead

French Furniture

GREAT BRITAIN

Bowes Museum, Barnard Castle
Victoria & Albert Museum, London
Wallace Collection, London

EUROPE

Louvre, Paris
Musée des Arts Decoratifs, Paris

Musée Nissim de Camondo, Paris
Musée Marmottan, Paris
Rijksmuseum, Amsterdam
Residenzmuseum, Munich
Nationalmuseum, Stockholm

U.S.A.

Metropolitan Museum of Art, New York
Frick Collection, New York
Philadelphia Museum of Art
Cleveland Museum of Art, Cleveland, Ohio

American Furniture

U.S.A.

M. H. de Young Memorial Museum, San Francisco, California
Wadsworte Atheneum, Hartford, Conn.
Winterthur Museum, Winterthur, Delaware
Colonial Williamsburg, Virginia
Freer Gallery of Art, Washington
Art Institute of Chicago, Chicago, Illinois
Museum of Fine Arts, Boston, Mass.
Detroit Institute of Arts, Detroit, Michigan
Brooklyn Museum, Brooklyn, New York
Metropolitan Museum of Art, New York
Cleveland Institute of Art, Cleveland, Ohio
Philadelphia Museum of Art, Philadelphia, Pennsylvania
Seattle Art Museum, Seattle, Washington
Shelburne Museum, Vermont

Viennese Furniture of the Eighteenth Century

EUROPE

Hofburg, Vienna
Österreichischesmuseum für Angewandtekunst, Vienna
Palais Czernin, Vienna
Palais Harrach, Vienna
Palais Schonberg, Vienna
Palais Schwarzenberg, Vienna
Österreichisches Barockmuseum, Vienna
Historischesmuseum der Stadt, Vienna
Niederösterreichisches Landesmuseum, Vienna
Bundesmobiliendepot, Vienna

Chest Furniture

GREAT BRITAIN

Bowes Museum, Barnard Castle
Malmesbury Old Hall, Blackburn
Aston Hall, Birmingham
Hall i'th'wood Museum, Bolton
Thomas-Stanford Museum, Brighton
Georgian House, Bristol
Blaise Castle Folk Museum, Bristol
St Fagan's Folk Museum, Cardiff
West Yorkshire Folk Museum, Halifax
Temple Newsam House, Leeds
Bethnal Green Museum, London
Victoria & Albert Museum, London
Fenton House, Hampstead, London
Geffrye Museum, London
City Art Gallery, Manchester
Lady Lever Art Gallery, Port Sunlight
Museum & Art Gallery, Tunbridge Wells
Oak House, West Bromwich

Chimneypieces

REAT BRITAIN

Victoria & Albert Museum, London

Games Tables and Boards

GREAT BRITAIN

Victoria & Albert Museum, London

English Wall-mirrors

GREAT BRITAIN

Victoria & Albert Museum, London
Temple Newsam House, Leeds

POTTERY and PORCELAIN

Porcelain

GREAT BRITAIN

Bowes Museum, Barnard Castle

Cecil Higgins Museum, Bedford
Museum & Art Gallery, Derby
Usher Art Gallery, Lincoln
Victoria & Albert Museum, London
British Museum, London
Rapallo House Museum & Art Gallery, Llandudno
Public Library, Museum & Art Gallery, Blackburn
Royal Museum & Slater Art Gallery, Canterbury
Art Gallery & Museum, Cheltenham
Art Gallery & Museum, Glasgow
Bethnal Green Museum, London
Fenton House, London
Fletcher Moss Museum, Manchester
Museum & Art Gallery, Rotherham. (Rockingham)
Public Library, Museum & Art Gallery, Stoke-on-Trent
Bantock House, Wolverhampton

Pottery

GREAT BRITAIN

Aldbrough Roman Museum, Aldbrough, Yorks (Roman)
The Glaisher Collection, Fitzwilliam Museum, Cambridge
Willett Collection, Art Gallery & Museum, Brighton
City Art Gallery, Leeds
The Schreiber Collection, Victoria & Albert Museum, London
Museum & Art Gallery, Nottingham
Williamson Art Gallery, Birkenhead
Public Library, Museum & Art Gallery, Blackburn
Museum & Art Gallery, Bootle
Library & Museum, Buxton
Segontium Museum, Caernarvon
Royal Museum & Slater Art Gallery, Canterbury
Art Gallery & Museum, Cheltenham
Astley Hall, Chorley
Colchester & Essex Museum, Colchester
Royal Albert Memorial Museum & Art Gallery, Exeter
Public Museum & Art Gallery, Hastings
Heaton Hall & Wythenshawe Hall, Manchester
Municipal Art Gallery & Museum, Oldham
Ypres Tower Museum, Rye

Cottage Pottery and Popular Art

GREAT BRITAIN

Royal Albert Memorial Museum, Exeter
Yorkshire Museum, York
Bideford Museum, Bideford
Fitzwilliam Museum, Cambridge
Library & Museum, Castleford
Art Gallery & Museum, Brighton
Stoke-on-Trent Public Museum & Art Gallery, Hanley
Art Gallery & Museum, Hastings
Sussex Archaeological Museum, Lewes
Christchurch Mansion Museum, Ipswich
Bethnal Green Museum, London
Temple Newsam House, Leeds
Somerset County Museum, Taunton
Poole Museum, Poole
Royal Institution of South Wales Museum, Swansea

Wedgwood China

GREAT BRITAIN

Stoke-on-Trent Public Museum & Art Gallery, Hanley
Victoria & Albert Museum, London
Castle Museum, Nottingham
Lady Lever Art Gallery, Port Sunlight
Wedgwood Collection, Barlaston, Stoke-on-Trent & Wigmore Street, London

Toby Jugs

GREAT BRITAIN

Victoria & Albert Museum, London
British Museum, London
Stoke-on-Trent Public Museum & Art Gallery, Hanley

U.S.A.

Metropolitan Museum, New York

Armorial China and Glass

GREAT BRITAIN

City Museum, Bristol
British Museum, London
Victoria & Albert Museum, London

Chinese Lowestoft and Export Porcelain

GREAT BRITAIN

Victoria & Albert Museum, London

Pharmacy Jars

GREAT BRITAIN

British Museum, London
Victoria & Albert Museum, London
London Museum, London
Guildhall Museum, London
Museum of the Pharmaceutical Society, London
Wellcome Historical Medical Museum, London
Fitzwilliam Museum, Cambridge
Ashmolean Museum, Oxford
Hall's Croft, Stratford-on-Avon

EUROPE

Louvre, Paris
Musée Céramique, Sèvres, Paris
Musée de la Pharmacie Centrale des Hôpitaux de Paris
Musées des Cinquantenaire, Brussels
Medisch Pharmaceutisch Museum, Amsterdam
Museum Boymans, Rotterdam
Med.-Hist. Museum, Copenhagen
Historischesmuseum, Basle

U.S.A.

Smithsonian Institution, Washington

English Painted Enamels

GREAT BRITAIN

Public Library, Museum & Art Gallery, Bilston
Victoria & Albert Museum, London
Museum & Art Gallery, Wolverhampton
Castle Museum, York

Chinese Ceramics

GREAT BRITAIN

Victoria & Albert Museum, London
British Museum, London
Sir Percival David Foundation, London University
Museum of Eastern Art, Oxford
Fitzwilliam Museum, Cambridge
City Art Gallery, Bristol
Royal Scottish Museum, Edinburgh
The Burrell Collection, Glasgow
City Art Gallery, Birmingham
City Art Gallery, Manchester
Temple Newsam House, Leeds
Lady Lever Art Gallery, Port Sunlight

EUROPE

Musée Guimet, Paris
Musée des Art Decoratifs, Paris
Musée Céramique, Sèvres, Paris
Musées Royaux d'Art et d'Histoire, Brussels
Rijksmuseum, Amsterdam
Museum für Ostasiatische Kunst, Cologne
Museum für Kunst und Gewerbe, Hamburg
Kunstindustrimuseum, Copenhagen
National Museum, Copenhagen
National Museum, Stockholm
Ostasiatiska Samlingarna, Stockholm
Hellner Museum, Stockholm

Jade

GREAT BRITAIN

Towneley Hall Art Gallery & Museum, Burnley, Lancs

Fitzwilliam Museum, Cambridge
G. Eumorfopoulos Collection, British Museum, London
Victoria & Albert Museum, London
City Art Gallery, Manchester
Museum of Eastern Art, Oxford

EUROPE

Musée Cernuschi, Paris
National Museum, Stockholm
Museum of Far Eastern Antiquities, Stockholm

Chinese Mortuary Figures

GREAT BRITAIN

G. Eumorfopoulos Collection, British Museum, London
Victoria & Albert Museum, London
And in all the major museums of Europe and America

PLATE and METALWORK

Silver

GREAT BRITAIN

Holburne of Menstrie Museum, Bath
Cecil Higgins Museum, Bedford
Museum & Art Gallery, Belfast
British Museum, London
Victoria & Albert Museum, London
Laing Art Gallery & Museum, Newcastle-upon-Tyne
Ashmolean Museum, Oxford
City Museum & Art Gallery, Birmingham
Thomas-Stanford Museum, Brighton
Art Gallery & Museum, Burrell Collection, Glasgow
Ormonde Collection, Bankfield Museum, Halifax
Bethnal Green Museum, London
Heaton Hall, Wythenshawe Hall & Fletcher Moss Museum, Manchester
Museum & Art Gallery, Sunderland

Continental Silver

GREAT BRITAIN

British Museum, London
Victoria & Albert Museum, London
Wallace Collection, London
Fitzwilliam Museum, Cambridge
Ashmolean Museum, Oxford

EUROPE

Louvre, Paris
Musée Carnavalet, Paris
Museu de Arte Antigua, Lisbon
Bayerisches Nationalmuseum, Munich
Stadtische Kunstsammlungen, Augsburg
Kunsthistorischesmuseum, Vienna
Palazzo Madama, Turin
Palazzo Pitti, Florence
Museo dell' Opera del Duomo, Florence
Museo Nazionale, Messina

American Silver

U.S.A.

Los Angeles County Museum, Los Angeles, California
Wadsworte Atheneum, Hartford, Conn.
Yale University Art Gallery, New Haven, Conn.
Art Institute of Chicago, Chicago, Illinois
Baltimore Museum of Art, Baltimore, Maryland
Museum of Fine Arts, Boston, Mass.
Fogg Museum of Art, Cambridge, Mass.
Detroit Institute of Arts, Detroit, Michigan
Art Museum, Princeton, New Jersey
Metropolitan Museum of Art, New York
Cincinnati Art Museum, Cincinnati, Ohio
Toledo Museum of Art, Toledo, Ohio
Philadelphia Museum of Art, Philadelphia, Pennsylvania

Sheffield Plate

GREAT BRITAIN

Sheffield City Museum, Sheffield
City Museum & Art Gallery, Birmingham
Laing Art Gallery & Museum, Newcastle-upon-Tyne
City Museum & Art Gallery, Birmingham

Pewter

GREAT BRITAIN

Victoria & Albert Museum, London
British Museum, London
London Museum, London
Guildhall, London
Castle Museum, Norwich
City Museum & Art Gallery, Bristol
Fitzwilliam Museum, Cambridge
City Museum & Art Gallery, Birmingham
Yorkshire Museum, York

Arms and Armour

GREAT BRITAIN

City Museum & Art Gallery, Birmingham
Blair Castle & Atholl Museum, Perth
Admiral Blake Museum, Bridgwater
City Museum, Bristol
The West Gate, Canterbury
Chiddingstone Castle, Edenbridge
Royal Scottish Museum, Edinburgh
Farleigh Castle Museum, Hungerford
The Scott Collection, Glasgow Art Gallery & Museum, Glasgow
The Whitelaw Collection of Scottish Arms, Glasgow Art Gallery & Museum, Glasgow
Ilfracombe Museum, Ilfracombe
Inverness Museum, Inverness
Dick Institute Museum, Kilmarnock
Abbey House Museum, Leeds
Lichfield Museum, Lichfield
Lincoln Municipal Museum, Lincoln
Rapallo House Museum & Art Gallery, Llandudno
The Royal Artillery Museum, Woolwich
Imperial War Museum, London
Tower of London
Victoria & Albert Museum, London
British Museum, London
Wallace Collection, London
Ludlow Museum, Ludlow
Laing Museum, Newcastle-upon-Tyne
Padiham Memorial Park Museum, Padiham
Thorpe Prebend House & Museum, Ripon
Preston Hall Museum & Art Gallery, Stockton-on-Tees
St Edward's Hall Museum, Stow-on-the-Wold
Henry Stilby Fire-arm Collection, Wyndham Museum, Yeovil

EUROPE

Musée des Arts Decoratifs, Paris
Louvre, Paris
Musée de l'Armée, Paris
Museum fur deutsche Geschichte, Berlin
Deutsches Klingenmuseum, Solingen
Bayerisches Nationalmuseum, Munich
Deutsches Museum, Nuremberg
Veste Coburg, Coburg
Schweizerisches Landesmuseum, Zurich
Historisches Museum, Basle
Landeshaus, Graz
Kunsthistorischesmuseum, Vienna
Tajhusmuseum, Copenhagen
Kunzl Livinstkammarenm, Stockholm
Musée de la Porte de Hal, Brussels
Het Legersche museum, Leiden
Real Armeria, Madrid
Museo Stibbert, Florence
Bargello, Florence
Castello Sant Angelo, Rome
Palazzo Venezia, Rome
Armeria Reale, Turin
Palazzo di Capodimonte, Naples
Museo Poldi Pezzoli, Milan
Palazzo Ducale, Venice

Metalwork

GREAT BRITAIN

Bowes Museum, Barnard Castle

The Old Merchants House, Great Yarmouth
Public Museum & Art Gallery, Hastings
John Every Collection, Anne of Cleves House, Lewes
Victoria & Albert Museum, London
British Museum, London
Laing Art Gallery & Museum, Newcastle-upon-Tyne
City Museum & Art Gallery, Nottingham
Municipal Art Gallery & Museum, Wolverhampton

Firebacks and Dogs

GREAT BRITAIN

John Every Collection, Anne of Cleves House, Lewes
Victoria & Albert Museum, London

PAINTING, PRINTS and BOOKS

Painting and Sculpture

GREAT BRITAIN

National Gallery, London
British Museum, London
Victoria & Albert Museum, London
Sir John Sloane Museum, London
Wallace Collection, London
National Maritime Museum, London
National Portrait Gallery, London
Dulwich College Gallery, London
The Foundling Hospital, London
Guildhall Art Gallery, London
Ham House, London
Hampton Court, London
Iveagh Bequest, London
Ken Wood, London
South London Art Gallery, London
Leighton House, Holland Park, London
William Morris Gallery, Walthamstow, London
Wellington Museum, Apsley House, London
Whitechapel Art Gallery, London
Arts Council Gallery, London
Imperial Institute, London
Royal Academy, London
Art Gallery & Museum, Birmingham
Art Gallery & Museum, Manchester
Art Gallery & Museum, Liverpool
Art Gallery & Museum, York
Art Gallery & Museum, Port Sunlight
Fitzwilliam Museum, Cambridge
Ashmolean Museum, Oxford
Art Gallery & Museum, Norwich
Art Gallery & Museum, Bournemouth
Art Gallery & Museum, Bristol
Art Gallery & Museum, Southampton
Art Gallery & Museum, Plymouth
Art Gallery & Museum, Preston
Art Gallery & Museum, Canterbury
Art Gallery & Museum, Leeds
Art Gallery & Museum, Truro
Art Gallery & Museum, Wakefield
The National Museum of Wales, Cardiff
The National Gallery of Scotland, Edinburgh
The National Portrait Gallery of Scotland, Edinburgh
The Glasgow Art Gallery, Glasgow
Aberdeen Art Gallery, Aberdeen
Belfast Art Gallery and Museum, Belfast

EIRE

The National Gallery of Ireland, Dublin
The Gallery of Modern Art, Dublin

FRANCE

Louvre, Paris
Musée de L'Art Moderne, Paris
L'Orangerie, Paris
Petit Palais, Paris
Musée Cognacq, Paris

Collections at:

Aix, Ajaccio, Amiens, Angers, Avignon, Caen, Bordeaux, Dijon, Douai, Grenoble, Le Mans, Le Puy, Lille, Lyon, Montauban, Monaco, Nice, Nancy, Nantes, Nimes, Orléans, Strasbourg, Tours, Toulouse

BELGIUM

Brussels

HOLLAND

The Hague, Amsterdam, Rotterdam

GERMANY

Berlin, Dresden, Munich, Hamburg, Bremen, Dusseldorf

AUSTRIA

The Albertina, Vienna

SWITZERLAND

Zurich, Basle, Geneva

ITALY (*a selection*)

Accademia, Venice
Palazzo Ducale, Venice
Museo Correro, Venice
Ca' Rezzonico, Venice
Museo Capitolino, Rome
Museo Vaticano, Rome
Galleria Corsini, Rome
Galleria nazionale dell'Arte moderna, Rome
Galleria Borghese, Rome
Bargello, Florence
Biblioteca Laurentiano, Florence
Galleria Riccardiano, Florence
Galleria Uffizi, Florence
Palazzo Pitti, Florence
Galleria dell'Arte moderna, Florence
Accademia Carraria, Bergamo
Galleria Martinengo, Brescia
Galleria Brera, Milan
Museo Poldi Pezzoli, Milan
Castello Sforzesco, Milan
Galleria Reale, Naples

Museums of:

San Martino, Padua, Parma, Pisa, Verona, Siena, Turin

also Museums of:

Copenhagen, Stockholm, Budapest, Warsaw, Madrid, Toledo, Lisbon

Italian Painting

GREAT BRITAIN

National Gallery, London
Barber Institute, Birmingham University
Fitzwilliam Museum, Cambridge
Ashmolean Museum, Oxford

EUROPE

Louvre, Paris
Uffizi, Florence
Brera, Milan
Accademia, Venice
Museo Vaticano, Rome
Palazzo Pitti, Florence
Prado, Madrid
Kunsthistorischesmuseum, Vienna

U.S.A.

Metropolitan Museum, New York
National Gallery of Art, Washington

Old English Watercolours

GREAT BRITAIN

Haworth Art Gallery, Haworth Park, Accrington, Lancs
Cecil Higgins Museum, Bedford
Museum & Art Gallery, Belfast
Victoria Art Gallery, Bath
Museum & Art Gallery, Bolton
City Museum & Art Gallery, Birmingham
Art Gallery & Museum, Brighton
Fitzwilliam Museum, Cambridge
Usher Art Gallery, Lincoln
British Museum, London
Victoria & Albert Museum, London
City Art Gallery, Leeds
Fletcher Moss Museum, Manchester
Werneth Park Branch, Oldham, Lancs
Public Museum & Art Gallery, Stoke-on-Trent
Literary & Philosophical Society Museum, Whitby
Municipal Art Gallery & Museum, Wolverhampton

Old English Drawings and Prints

GREAT BRITAIN

Museum & Art Gallery, Birmingham
Victoria & Albert Museum, London
Philpot Museum, Lyme Regis
Harris Museum & Art Gallery, Preston
Thorpe Prebend House & Museum, Ripon

GREAT BRITAIN

Holburne of Menstrie Museum of Art, Bath
Courtauld Institute of Art, London
Tate Gallery, London

Portrait Miniatures

GREAT BRITAIN

Victoria & Albert Museum, London
Wallace Collection, London
National Portrait Gallery, London
National Maritime Museum, Greenwich
Fitzwilliam Museum, Cambridge
Ashmolean Museum, Oxford
Holburne of Menstrie Museum, Bath
Glynn Vivian Art Gallery, Swansea
Art Gallery, Bristol
Ham House, Ham, Surrey

EUROPE

Nationalmuseum, Stockholm
Rosenborg Castle, Copenhagen

U.S.A.

Metropolitan Museum, New York
Cleveland Museum, Cleveland, Ohio

Silhouettes and Glass Pictures

GREAT BRITAIN

Victoria & Albert Museum, London

Bird Prints

GREAT BRITAIN

Natural History Museum, London

EUROPE

Zoological Museum, Amsterdam
Taylor Museum, Haarlem
University Library, Copenhagen

American Prints

U.S.A.

New York Public Library
New-York Historical Society
Mariners' Museum, Newport Mews, Virginia
Philadelphia Museum of Art, Philadelphia
Metropolitan Museum of Art, New York
Boston Museum of Fine Arts, Boston
American Antiquarian Society, Worcester, Massachusetts
Library of Congress, Washington, D.C.
Museum of the City of New York, New York

Japanese Prints

GREAT BRITAIN

British Museum, London
Victoria & Albert Museum, London
Museum of Eastern Art, Oxford
Fitzwilliam Museum, Cambridge
Whitworth Gallery, Manchester
Maidstone Museum, Maidstone

EUROPE

Chester Beatty Library, Dublin, Eire
Bibliothèque Nationale, Paris
Musée Guimet, Paris
Prentenkabinet, Amsterdam
Rijksmuseum, Leiden
Musées Royaux d'Art et d'Histoire, Brussels

Books

GREAT BRITAIN

British Museum, London
Bodleian Library, Oxford
University Library, Cambridge
National Library of Scotland, Edinburgh
National Library of Wales, Aberystwyth
John Rylands Library, Manchester
The College Libraries of Oxford and Cambridge and collections at the other universities, such as the Brotherton Library, Leeds
The Libraries of Eton College and Winchester College
The Cathedral Libraries throughout the country

Colour Plate Books

GREAT BRITAIN

Harris Museum and Art Gallery, Preston
British Museum, London
Victoria & Albert Museum, London

SCULPTURE and CARVING

Antique Statuary and Wax Modelling

GREAT BRITAIN

National Portrait Gallery, London
Victoria & Albert Museum, London
British Museum, London

Antique Bronzes

GREAT BRITAIN

Wallace Collection, London
Victoria & Albert Museum, London
Fitzwilliam Museum, Cambridge
Ashmolean Museum, Oxford

EUROPE

Kunsthistorischesmuseum, Vienna
Staatlischesmuseum, Berlin
Louvre, Paris
Bargello, Florence

U.S.A.

Metropolitan Museum of Art, New York

Carved Wooden Figures

GREAT BRITAIN

Wallace Collection, London
Victoria & Albert Museum, London
British Museum, London
Fitzwilliam Museum, Cambridge

EUROPE

Louvre, Paris
Musée de Dijon
Bayerisches Nationalmuseum, Munich
Stadtische Kunstsammlungen, Augsburg
Nationalmuseum, Nuremberg
Museo di Castello, Milan
Palazza Madama, Turin
Museo Nazionale, Florence
Museo Nazionale, Pisa
Kunsthistorischesmuseum, Vienna
Palazzo Venezia, Rome

Nottingham Alabaster Carving

GREAT BRITAIN

Victoria & Albert Museum, London
Glasgow Museum, Glasgow
British Museum, London
Nottingham City Museum & Art Gallery, Nottingham
Ashmolean Museum, Oxford
Fitzwilliam Museum, Cambridge
Also isolated plaques in other provincial museums, and sometimes in churches

Greek and Roman Statuary

GREAT BRITAIN

British Museum, London
Ashmolean Museum, Oxford

EUROPE

Acropolis Museum, Athens
National Museum, Athens
Staatlischesmuseum, Berlin
Ny Carlsberg Olyptatek, Copenhagen
Delphi Museum, Delphi
Galleria Uffizi, Florence
The Museum, Istanbul
Hermitage Museum, Leningrad
Prado, Madrid
Glyptothek, Munich
Museo nazionale, Naples
Olympia Museum, Olympia
Louvre, Paris
Villa Albani, Rome
Museo Capitolino, Rome
Museo Conservatori, Rome
Museo Terme, Rome
Museo Vaticano, Rome
Kunsthistorischesmuseum, Vienna

U.S.A.

Museum of Fine Art, Boston
Metropolitan Museum, New York

Netsuke and Inro

GREAT BRITAIN

Victoria & Albert Museum, London
British Museum, London

EUROPE

Musée Guimet, Paris
Musée d'Ennery, Paris

U.S.A.

Metropolitan Museum of Art, New York
Museum of Fine Arts, Boston
Carnegie Museum, Pittsburg

Chessmen

GREAT BRITAIN

British Museum, London
Victoria & Albert Museum, London
London Museum, London

Garden Statuary and Furniture

GREAT BRITAIN

Victoria & Albert Museum, London

GLASS

Glass

GREAT BRITAIN

Bowes Museum, Barnard Castle
Holburne of Menstrie Museum, Bath
Cecil Higgins Museum, Bedford
Haworth Art Gallery, Accrington
City Museum & Art Gallery, Birmingham
Public Library Museum, Brierley Hill, Staffs
Museum & Art Gallery, Belfast
Astley Hall, Chorley, Lancs
Museum & Art Gallery, King's Lynn
The Wernher Collection, Luton Hoo
British Museum, London
London Museum, London
Victoria & Albert Museum, London
Art Gallery & Museum, Rawtenstall
Yorkshire Museum, York
Public Library, Museum & Art Gallery, Blackburn
Art Gallery & Museum, Brighton
Towneley Hall Art Gallery and Museum, Burnley
Library & Museum, Buxton
Public Library & Museum, Castleford
Art Gallery & Museum, Glasgow
Museum of Art, Hove
Bethnal Green Museum, London
Heaton Hall, Manchester
Laing Art Gallery & Museum, Newcastle-upon-Tyne
Municipal Art Gallery & Museum, Oldham
Harris Museum & Art Gallery, Preston
Saffron Walden Museum, Saffron Walden
Spalding Museum, Spalding
Wollescote Hall, Stourbridge

EUROPE

Rijksmuseum, Amsterdam

Irish Glass

GREAT BRITAIN

Victoria & Albert Museum, London
Museum & Art Gallery, Belfast

EIRE

National Museum, Dublin

U.S.A.

Corning Museum of Glass, New York, U.S.A.

Glass Candelabras and Lustres

GREAT BRITAIN

Victoria & Albert Museum, London

French Glass Paperweights

EUROPE

Musée des Beaux Arts, Paris
Baccanar Glassworks Museum, France

TEXTILES

European Carpets and Tapestries

GREAT BRITAIN

Victoria & Albert Museum, London. (general)
Ham House, nr Richmond, Surrey. (English)
Osterley Park, Osterley. (Gobelins and Beauvais)
Hampton Court Palace, London. (late Mediaeval)
City Museum & Art Gallery, Birmingham
Burrell Collection, Glasgow
Bowes Museum, Barnard Castle
Wernher Collection, Luton Hoo
Knole, near Sevenoaks, Kent
Hatfield House, Hatfield

EUROPE

Louvre, Paris. (general)
Musée de Cluny, Paris. (Mediaeval)
Musée des Arts Decoratifs, Paris. (Mediaeval and later)
The Castle, Angers. (15th–16th century)
The Cathedral & Museum, Rheims. (late Mediaeval)
Rijksmuseum, Amsterdam
Musée du Cinquantenaire, Brussels. (general)
Historischesmuseum, Basle. (15th century)
Historischesmuseum, Berne. (15th century Tournai)
Landesmuseum, Zurich. (15th–16th century)
Palaces & Galleries, Florence. (esp. 16th century)
Museo Vaticano, Rome. (Sistine Chapel)
Palaces & Galleries, Rome. (16th–18th century)
Palazzo Real, Madrid. (Flemish 16th century and Spanish 18th century)
La Seo Catedral Museo, Saragoza. (Mediaeval)
La Catedral Museo, Zamora. (Mediaeval)
Kunsthistorischesmuseum, Vienna. (general)
Hofburg, Vienna. (general)
Österreichischesmuseum für Angewandtekunst, Vienna
Germanischesmuseum, Nuremberg. (15th–16th century)
Bayerisches Nationalmuseum, Munich. (general)
Schloss Nymphenburg, Munich. (18th century)

Oriental Carpets and Rugs

GREAT BRITAIN

British Museum, London
Victoria & Albert Museum, London

Needlework and Embroidery

GREAT BRITAIN

Burrell Collection, Art Gallery & Museum, Glasgow
Victoria & Albert Museum, London
City Art Gallery, Manchester
Whitworth Art Gallery, Manchester
Galleries of the Regional College of Art, Manchester
Thorpe Prebend House & Museum, Ripon
The Priest House, West Hoathly, Sussex
Museum & Muniment Room, Guildford
City Museum & Art Gallery, Hereford
Museum of Art, Hove
Ferens Art Gallery, Hull
Fitzwilliam Museum, Cambridge
Bankfield Museum, Halifax
National Museum of Wales, Cardiff
Gallery of English Costume, Platt Hall, Manchester
Hardwick Hall, nr. Chesterfield

CLOCKS and WATCHES and BAROMETERS

Clocks and Watches

GREAT BRITAIN

British Museum, London
Science Museum, London
Victoria & Albert Museum, London
Clockmakers Company, Guildhall, London
Wallace Collection, London

EUROPE

Bayerisches Nationalmuseum, Munich
Germanischesmuseum, Munich
Germanischesmuseum, Nuremberg
Hessisches Landesmuseum, Cassel
Herzog Anton-Ulrich Museum, Brunswick
Kunsthistorischesmuseum, Vienna
Conservatoire des Arts et Métiers, Paris
Louvre, Paris

Barometers

GREAT BRITAIN

Science Museum, London
Wallace Collection, London
Victoria & Albert Museum, London
Royal Scottish Museum, Edinburgh
Museum for the History of Science, Oxford

EUROPE

Conservatoire des Arts et Métiers, Paris
Deutschesmuseum, Munich
Zeylers Museum, Haarlem
Rijksmuseum for the History of Science, Leiden

MUSIC

Musical Instruments

GREAT BRITAIN

Victoria & Albert Museum, London
Royal College of Music Collection, London
Horniman Museum, London
Benton Fletcher Collection, London
Central Library, Manchester
Royal Manchester College of Music, Manchester
Ashmolean Museum, Oxford
Pitt-Rivers Museum, Oxford
Art Gallery and Museum, Glasgow

EUROPE

National Museum of Ireland, Dublin
Rijksmuseum, Amsterdam
Gemeente-Museum, The Hague
Conservatoire Royal de Musique, Brussels
Musikhistorisk Museum, Copenhagen
Musik-historiska Museum, Stockholm
Kunsthistorischesmuseum, Vienna
Conservatoire de Musique, Paris
Berliner Musikinstrumenten-Sammlung, Schloss Charlottenberg, Berlin
Bayerisches Nationalmuseum, Munich
Deutchesmuseum, Munich
Institute for Scientific Research on the Theatre and Music, Leningrad

U.S.A.

Museum of Fine Arts, Boston, Mass.

Musical Boxes

GREAT BRITAIN

Victoria & Albert Museum, London

MISCELLANEOUS

Ship Models

GREAT BRITAIN

National Maritime Museum, Greenwich
Science Museum, South Kensington
Imperial War Museum, London
Royal United Service Museum, London
Parker Gallery, London
Public Library & Museum, Bideford
City Museum, Queen's Road, Bristol
Public Museum & Art Gallery, Hastings
Museum of Fisheries & Shipping, Hull
Ilfracombe Museum, Ilfracombe, Devon
Anne of Cleves House, Southover, Lewes
Public Museums, Liverpool
Museum & Art Gallery, Maidstone, Kent
Dorman Memorial Museum, Middlesbrough
Municipal Museum of Science & Industry, Newcastle-upon-Tyne
Bridewell Museum of Local Industries, Norwich
City Museum & Art Gallery, Plymouth
"Victory" Museum, Portsmouth
Eastgate House Museum, Rochester
Marlipins Museum, Shoreham-by-Sea
Tudor House Museum, Southampton
Public Museum, Sunderland
Whitby Museum, Whitby
Peterborough Museum, Peterborough
Public Libraries, Museum & Art Room, South Shields
National Museum of Wales, Cardiff
Public Libraries, Museums & Fine Art Galleries, Dundee
Royal Scottish Museum, Edinburgh
Art Galleries & Museum, Glasgow
Trinity House of Leith, Leith
Public Library & Arbuthnot Museum, Peterhead
Orkney Natural History Society Museum, Stromness, Orkney
Lukis & Island Museum, St. Peter Port, Guernsey

Model Soldiers

GREAT BRITAIN

British Museum, London
Bethnal Green, London
Blenheim Palace, Woodstock
Canterbury Museum, Canterbury
Tunbridge Wells Museum, Tunbridge Wells
Royal United Service Museum, London
London Museum, London
Edinburgh Castle Museum, Edinburgh
Anne of Cleves House, Southover, Lewes
Castle Museum, York

EUROPE

Musée de Cluny, Paris
Musée de la Ville de Compiegne, nr Paris
Musée de l'Armeé, Paris
Musée de Strasbourg, Strasbourg
Bayerisches Nationalmuseum, Munich
Germanischesmuseum, Nuremberg
Stadtischesmuseum, Weimar
Plassenburg, Kulmbach
Landesmuseum, Zurich

Dolls and Doll's Houses

GREAT BRITAIN

Bowes Museum, Barnard Castle
Saltwell Museum, Gateshead
Toll Cross, Glasgow
Abbey House, Leeds
The Toy Museum,
1957 Leicester & Hove
1958 Glasgow
Bethnal Green Museum, London
London Museum, London

Kensington Palace, London
Harris Museum, Preston
Somerset County Museum, Taunton
Museum and Art Gallery, Tunbridge Wells
West House, Sussex
Horniman Museum, London
Horsfall Art Museum, Ancoats
Bolling Hall Museum, Bradford
Cambridge & County Folk Museum, Cambridge
National Museum of Wales, Cardiff
Colchester & Essex Museum, Colchester
Castle Museum, Guildford
Gunnersbury Museum, London
Kirkstall Abbey Museum, Leeds
Nottingham Castle Museum, Nottingham
Peterborough Museum, Peterborough
Castle Museum, York

EUROPE

Kunstgewerbe Museum, Vienna
Museum of Toys, Zagorsk
Landesmuseum, Zurich
Rijksmuseum, Amsterdam
Openlucht Museum, Arnheim
Maximiliansmuseum, Augsburg
Danskfolkesmuseum, Copenhagen
Stadthistorisches Museum, Frankfurt
Oskar s'Eyffert Museum, Dresden
Gemcente Museum, The Hague
Koustarny Museum, Moscow
Bayerisches Nationalmuseum, Munich
Germanischesmuseum, Nuremberg
Norskefolkemuseum, Oslo
Camaralet, Paris
Cluny, Paris
Spielzeugmuseum, Sonneberg
Nordiska museet, Stockholm
Landesgewerbemuseum, Stuttgart
Centraal Museum, Utrecht

Puppets

GREAT BRITAIN

British Museum, London
Geffrye Museum, Shoreditch, London
Victoria & Albert Museum, London
Indian Museum, London

Automata

GREAT BRITAIN

Victoria & Albert Museum, London
Bowes Museum, Barnard Castle, Co. Durham

EUROPE

Neuchatel Museum, Switzerland

Charters, Seals and Parchments

GREAT BRITAIN

British Museum, London
Public Record Office, London
and many provincial museums

Coins and Medals

GREAT BRITAIN

Ashwell Village Museum, Ashwell, Herts
The Holburne of Menstrie Museum of Art, Bath
Victoria Art Gallery, Bath
Modern School Museum, Bedford
Public Library, Museum and Art Gallery, Blackburn
Fitzwilliam Museum, Cambridge
National Museum of Wales, Cardiff
Victoria Jubilee Museum, Cawthorne
Gorey Castle Museum, Jersey
Chelmsford & Essex Museum, Chelmsford
Colchester & Essex Museum, Colchester
National Museum of Antiquities, Edinburgh
The Hunterian Museum, Glasgow
Gloucester City Museum, Gloucester
Charterhouse School Museum, Godalming
King's Lynn Museum and Art Gallery, King's Lynn
Library of the Thoresby Society, Leeds
Lichfield Museum, Lichfield
Lincoln Municipal Museum, Lincoln
British Museum, London
Lord Wandsworth College Museum, Long Sutton, Hants
Philpot Museum, Lyme Regis

Athelstan Museum, Malmesbury
Manchester Museum, Manchester
Art Gallery & Museum, Merthyr Tydfil
Castle Museum, Norwich
Library & Museum, Oswestry
Ashmolean Museum, Oxford
Arbuthnot Museum, Peterhead
Poole Museum, Poole
Public Museum, Rochester
City Museum, Sheffield
Marlipins Museum, Shoreham, Sussex
Spalding Museum, Spalding
Swindon Museum, Swindon
Somerset County Museum, Taunton
Ancient House Museum, Thetford, Norfolk
Museum & Art Gallery, Tunbridge Wells
Wells Museum, Wells
Public Library & Museum, Whitehaven
Church Porch Folk Museum, Winchcombe
Yorkshire Museum, York

EUROPE

Cabinet des Médailles, Bibliothèque Nationale, Paris
Cabinet des Médailles, Bibliothèque Royale, Brussels
Koningklijk Kabinet van Munten, The Hague
Koorgelige Montsamling, Copenhagen
Statens Historiska Museum, Stockholm
Universitets Museum, Oslo
Museum für Hamburgische Geschichte, Hamburg
Staatliche Münzsammlung, Munich
Musée d'Archeologie, Geneva
Historischesmuseum, Basle
Castello Sforzesco, Milan
Museo Nazionale, Rome
Museo Nazionale, Naples
National Museum, Athens
National Museum, Zagreb
National Museum, Budapest
National Museum, Prague
Bundessammlung von Münzen, Vienna
Hermitage Museum, Leningrad

U.S.A.

American Numismatic Society, New York

Jewellery

GREAT BRITAIN

Bowes Museum, Barnard Castle
City Museum & Art Gallery, Birmingham
Tower of London, London
The Waddeston Bequest, British Museum, London
The Cheapside Hoard, London Museum, London
Victoria & Albert Museum, London
Wallace Collection, London
Peter Jones Collection, Walker Art Gallery, Liverpool
Wernher Collection, Luton Hoo
Museum & Art Gallery, Rotherham
Museum & Art Gallery, Worthing

Postage Stamps

GREAT BRITAIN

The Tapling Collection, British Museum, London
The Routledge Collection, Tullie House Museum, Carlisle

EUROPE

Postmuseum, Berne
Haus der Philatelie, Munich
Postmuseum, Vaduz
Le Musée Postal, Paris
Dutch Postal Museum, The Hague
Belgian Postal Museum, Brussels

Objets de Vertu

GREAT BRITAIN

Wallace Collection, London
Wernher Collection, Luton Hoo

EUROPE

Louvre, Paris

U.S.A.

Metropolitan Museum, New York

Playing Cards

GREAT BRITAIN

Victoria & Albert Museum, London
British Museum, London
London Museum, London

Wine, Spirit and Sauce Labels

GREAT BRITAIN

Hon. Mrs Ionides Collection and the Cropper Collection, Victoria & Albert Museum, London

Wallpapers

GREAT BRITAIN

Victoria & Albert Museum, London

EUROPE

Deutsches Tapetenmuseum, Cassel

U.S.A.

Cooper Union Museum, New York

Victoriana

GREAT BRITAIN

Victoria & Albert Museum, London

INDEX
OF NAMES AND PLACES

INDEX

OF NAMES AND PLACES

INDEX